THE TECHNIQUE AND PRACTICE OF PSYCHOANALYSIS

Volume I

THE TECHNIQUE AND PRACTICE OF PSYCHOANALYSIS

Volume I

Ralph R. Greenson

INTERNATIONAL UNIVERSITIES PRESS, INC.

Madison   Connecticut

DEDICATED

TO

MY TEACHERS
MY STUDENTS
AND
MY PATIENTS

Acknowledgments

IT is impossible to thank individually all those who have contributed to this book. I consider all the authors listed in the bibliography among my official teachers; here I only want to express my gratitude more personally.

My father, Joel O. Greenschpoon, M.D., a general practitioner, is responsible for transmitting to me his concern and devotion to his patients and the profession of medicine. Otto Fenichel, my training analyst, inspired me by his unwavering dedication to the teaching of psychoanalysis and by his incorruptible honesty.

There is one unofficial group who must remain anonymous for reasons of discretion, but to them I owe perhaps the greatest debt of all. I refer to my patients, who managed to teach me a great deal about technique while I was attempting to treat them. I also learned much from the many candidates in training in the Los Angeles Institute for Psychoanalysis whom I have taught in seminars on psychoanalytic technique for more than twenty years. The psychiatric residents at the UCLA Medical Center at Los Angeles, California, also stimulated my teaching and learning of psychoanalysis.

There are some whom I can thank individually. I want to acknowledge my gratitude to Drs. Hanna Fenichel, Milton Wexler, Lawrence Friedman, Rudolf Ekstein, and Alfred Goldberg for the many fruitful discussions we have had over the years on technical problems. I benefited in particular from exchanging ideas with a number of my colleagues in Los Angeles, who participated in a post-

graduate seminar on special technical problems which continued
for one and a half years, from the fall of 1959 to the summer of
1960. They included Drs. Richard Evans, Gerald Aronson, Arthur
Ourieff, William Horowitz, Jack Vatz, Samuel Futterman, Marvin
Berenson, Neal Peterson, Norman Atkins, and Seymour Bird. I also
am grateful to Dr. Richard Newman, who read the manuscript in
its entirety.

Nathan Leites was very helpful in formulating some of the definitions and in emphasizing the importance of ample clinical examples. I owe a special vote of thanks to Bernard Brodie for his
painstaking work in correcting my grammatical lapses and in refin-
ing and clarifying my literary style. Bess Kaufman also assisted in
this task. My secretary of twenty years, Susan Alexander, devoted
many long hours beyond the call of duty to this book, beginning
with the first draft in 1953. Lottie M. Newman encouraged me to
continue with the book when diverse allurements threatened to
sidetrack me. She has also served as an experienced guide and helpful editor of the many drafts of this book. Finally, and above all, I
must thank my wife, Hildi, my daughter Joan, and my son, Dr.
Daniel Greenson, for listening to, reading, and correcting the endless variations and changes in the different versions of the manuscript.

Contents

Acknowledgments   vii

Introduction   1

Chapter 1
Survey of Basic Concepts

1.1 THE HISTORICAL DEVELOPMENT OF
     PSYCHOANALYTIC THERAPY   7
     1.11 *Changes in Technical Procedures*   8
     1.12 *Changes in the Theory of the Therapeutic Process*   10

1.2 THEORETICAL CONCEPTS ESSENTIAL
     FOR TECHNIQUE   15
     1.21 *The Relation between Theory and Practice*   15
     1.22 *The Psychoanalytic Theory of Neurosis*   17
     1.23 *The Metapsychology of Psychoanalysis*   20
     1.24 *The Theory of Psychoanalytic Technique*   26

1.3 THE COMPONENTS OF CLASSICAL PSYCHO-
     ANALYTIC TECHNIQUE   32
     1.31 *The Production of Material*   32
           1.311 FREE ASSOCIATION   32
           1.312 THE TRANSFERENCE REACTIONS   33
           1.313 THE RESISTANCES   35
     1.32 *Analyzing the Patient's Material*   37
     1.33 *The Working Alliance*   45
     1.34 *The Nonanalytic Therapeutic Procedures and
           Processes*   48

ix

1.4 INDICATIONS AND CONTRAINDICATIONS FOR
     PSYCHOANALYTIC THERAPY:
     A PRELIMINARY VIEW   51

     Additional Reading List   56

Chapter 2
Resistance

2.1 WORKING DEFINITION   59

2.2 THE CLINICAL APPEARANCE OF RESISTANCE   60
     2.21 *The Patient Is Silent*   61
     2.22 *The Patient "Does Not Feel Like Talking"*   62
     2.23 *Affects Indicating Resistance*   62
     2.24 *The Posture of the Patient*   63
     2.25 *Fixation in Time*   63
     2.26 *Trivia or External Events*   64
     2.27 *Avoidance of Topics*   64
     2.28 *Rigidities*   65
     2.29 *The Language of Avoidance*   65
           2.210 LATENESS, MISSING HOURS, FORGETTING TO PAY   67
           2.211 THE ABSENCE OF DREAMS   67
           2.212 THE PATIENT IS BORED   68
           2.213 THE PATIENT HAS A SECRET   68
           2.214 ACTING OUT   68
           2.215 FREQUENT CHEERFUL HOURS   69
           2.216 THE PATIENT DOES NOT CHANGE   69
           2.217 SILENT RESISTANCES   70

2.3 HISTORICAL SURVEY   71

2.4 THE THEORY OF RESISTANCE   76
     2.41 *Resistance and Defense*   76
     2.42 *Resistance and Regression*   82

2.5 CLASSIFICATION OF RESISTANCES   85
     2.51 *According to the Source of Resistance*   85
     2.52 *According to Fixation Points*   88
     2.53 *According to Types of Defense*   90
     2.54 *According to Diagnostic Category*   93
     2.55 *A Practical Classification*   94

2.6 TECHNIQUE OF ANALYZING RESISTANCES   96
    2.61 *Preliminary Considerations*   96
        2.611 DYNAMICS OF THE TREATMENT SITUATION   98
        2.612 HOW THE ANALYST LISTENS   100
    2.62 *The Recognition of Resistance*   101
    2.63 *Confrontation: The Demonstration of Resistance*   104
    2.64 *The Clarification of Resistance*   107
    2.65 *The Interpretation of Resistance*   111
        2.651 INTERPRETING THE MOTIVE FOR RESISTANCE   111
        2.652 INTERPRETING THE MODE OF RESISTANCE   118
        2.653 RECAPITULATION   121
    2.66 *Special Problems in Analyzing Resistance*   124
        2.661 RESISTANCES IN THE FIRST HOURS   124
        2.662 RESISTANCE TO RESISTANCE   126
        2.663 THE SECRET   128
    2.67 *Deviations in Technique*   133

2.7 RULES OF TECHNIQUE CONCERNING RESISTANCE   136
    2.71 *Analyze Resistance before Content, Ego before Id,
        Begin with the Surface*   137
    2.72 *The Patient Determines the Subject of the Hour*   145
    2.73 *Exceptions to the Rules*   146
        2.731 MINOR RESISTANCES   146
        2.732 LOSS OF EGO FUNCTIONS   147

Additional Reading List   149

Chapter 3

Transference

3.1 WORKING DEFINITION   151

3.2 CLINICAL PICTURE: GENERAL CHARACTERISTICS   155
    3.21 *Inappropriateness*   155
    3.22 *Intensity*   157
    3.23 *Ambivalence*   159
    3.24 *Capriciousness*   160
    3.25 *Tenacity*   161

3.3 HISTORICAL SURVEY   162

3.4 THEORETICAL CONSIDERATIONS   171
   3.41 *The Origin and Nature of Transference Reactions*   171
      3.411 TRANSFERENCE AND OBJECT RELATIONS   172
      3.412 TRANSFERENCE AND EGO FUNCTIONS   174
      3.413 TRANSFERENCE AND REPETITION   177
      3.414 TRANSFERENCE AND REGRESSION   180
      3.415 TRANSFERENCE AND RESISTANCE   182
   3.42 *The Transference Neurosis*   183

3.5 THE WORKING ALLIANCE   190
   3.51 *Working Definition*   192
   3.52 *Survey of the Literature*   194
   3.53 *Development of the Working Alliance*   195
      3.531 ABERRATIONS IN THE WORKING ALLIANCE   195
      3.532 THE WORKING ALLIANCE IN THE CLASSICAL
           ANALYTIC PATIENT   203
   3.54 *The Origins of the Working Alliance*   206
      3.541 THE CONTRIBUTIONS OF THE PATIENT   206
      3.542 THE CONTRIBUTION OF THE ANALYTIC SITUATION 208
      3.543 THE CONTRIBUTIONS OF THE ANALYST   209

3.6 THE REAL RELATIONSHIP BETWEEN PATIENT
    AND ANALYST   216

3.7 CLINICAL CLASSIFICATION OF TRANSFERENCE
    REACTIONS   224
   3.71 *The Positive and Negative Transference*   225
      3.711 THE POSITIVE TRANSFERENCE   225
      3.712 THE NEGATIVE TRANSFERENCE   233
   3.72 *Transference Reactions in Terms of Object Relations* 238
   3.73 *Transference Reactions in Terms of Libidinal Phases* 240
   3.74 *Transference Reactions in Terms of Structure*   241
   3.75 *Identification as a Transference Reaction*   244

3.8 TRANSFERENCE RESISTANCES   247
   3.81 *The Search for Transference Gratification*   248
   3.82 *Defensive Transference Reactions*   252
   3.83 *Generalized Transference Reactions*   256
   3.84 *Acting Out of Transference Reactions*   258
      3.841 ACTING OUT WITHIN THE ANALYTIC SETTING   263
      3.842 ACTING OUT OUTSIDE OF THE ANALYSIS   266

3.9 THE TECHNIQUE OF ANALYZING THE
     TRANSFERENCE   268

   3.91 *General Considerations*   268
   3.92 *The Safeguarding of the Transference*   271
      3.921 THE PSYCHOANALYST AS A MIRROR   271
      3.922 THE RULE OF ABSTINENCE   275
   3.93 *When Do We Analyze the Transference?*   281
      3.931 WHEN IT IS A RESISTANCE   281
      3.932 WHEN AN OPTIMAL LEVEL OF INTENSITY HAS
            BEEN REACHED   284
      3.933 SOME MODIFICATIONS AND ELABORATIONS   287
      3.934 WHEN OUR INTERVENTION WILL ADD NEW INSIGHT   289
         3.9341 Strong Affects   291
         3.9342 Contradictions   292
         3.9343 Repetitions   292
         3.9344 Similarities   293
         3.9345 Symbolism   293
         3.9346 Key Associations   294
   3.94 *Technical Steps in Analyzing the Transference*   295
      3.941 DEMONSTRATING THE TRANSFERENCE   296
         3.9411 Silence and Patience   296
         3.9412 Confrontation   297
         3.9413 The Use of Evidence   298
      3.942 CLARIFICATION OF THE TRANSFERENCE   301
         3.9421 Pursuit of the Intimate Details   301
         3.9422 Pursuit of the Transference Trigger   305
      3.943 INTERPRETATION OF THE TRANSFERENCE   308
         3.9431 The Pursuit of the Affects, Impulses,
              and Attitudes   310
         3.9432 Tracing the Antecedents of the
              Transference Figure   312
         3.9433 Exploring the Transference Fantasies   314
      3.944 WORKING THROUGH OF TRANSFERENCE
         INTERPRETATIONS   315
         3.9441 Theoretical Considerations   316
         3.9442 Clinical Material   316
         3.9443 Technical Procedures: Pursuit
              and Reconstruction   319
      3.945 ADDENDA   324

3.10 SPECIAL PROBLEMS IN ANALYZING TRANSFERENCE
REACTIONS   325

3.10.1   *Acute Emotional Storms and Dangerous
          Re-enactments*   327
3.10.2   *The Monday Hour*   330
          3.10.21   THE WEEKEND IS A HOLIDAY   330
          3.10.22   THE WEEKEND IS A DESERTION   332
          3.10.23   THE WEEKEND AND EGO FUNCTIONS   333
          3.10.24   OTHER CLINICAL FINDINGS   334
          3.10.25   THE TECHNICAL PROBLEMS   335
3.10.3   *Intractable Transference Reactions*   337
          3.10.31   ERRORS IN APPRAISAL OF TRANSFERENCE
                    CAPACITY   337
                    3.10.311   Erotized Transference   338
                    3.10.312   Masked Perversion-Psychosis   341
                    3.10.313   Other Types of Intractable
                               Transference Reactions   343
          3.10.32   ERRORS IN TECHNIQUE   345
                    3.10.321   Occasional Errors   346
                    3.10.322   Errors Due to Prolonged
                               Countertransference Interference   348
                    3.10.323   Other Protracted Errors in
                               Technique   350
3.10.4   *The Question of Changing Analysts*   353
3.10.5   *Candidates in Training*   355

Additional Reading List   356

Chapter 4

The Psychoanalytic Situation

4.1 WHAT PSYCHOANALYSIS REQUIRES OF
    THE PATIENT   358
    4.11   *Motivation*   358
    4.12   *Capacities*   361
    4.13   *Traits of Personality and Character*   363

4.2 WHAT PSYCHOANALYSIS REQUIRES OF
    THE PSYCHOANALYST   364
    4.21   *The Skills Required of the Psychoanalyst*   365
           4.211   UNDERSTANDING THE UNCONSCIOUS   365

4.212   COMMUNICATING TO THE PATIENT   372
4.213   FACILITATING THE DEVELOPMENT OF THE
        TRANSFERENCE NEUROSIS AND THE
        WORKING ALLIANCE   376
4.22   *Traits of Personality and Character of the Psychoanalyst*   380
4.221   TRAITS RELATED TO UNDERSTANDING THE
        UNCONSCIOUS   380
4.222   TRAITS RELATED TO COMMUNICATING WITH
        THE PATIENT   384
4.223   TRAITS RELATED TO FACILITATING THE
        DEVELOPMENT OF THE TRANSFERENCE
        NEUROSIS AND THE WORKING ALLIANCE   388
4.23   *Motivations of the Psychoanalyst Required by the
       Analytic Situation*   396

4.3   WHAT PSYCHOANALYSIS REQUIRES OF THE
      ANALYTIC SETTING   408

Additional Reading List   411

Bibliography   413

Author Index   433

Subject Index   437

Introduction

IT IS my opinion that despite the many difficulties involved, it is time for a textbook on psychoanalytic technique. I have the impression that there is a great danger in allowing ambiguities, divergencies, and deviations to be transmitted by word of mouth from training analyst to analysand, from supervising analyst to candidate, and from colleague to colleague, in private discussions without their being duly noted and recognized for what they are.

The standard works on technique written by Freud, Glover (1955), Sharpe (1930), and Fenichel (1941), excellent as they are, are only outlines. They do not describe in sufficient detail what the psychoanalyst actually does when he analyzes a patient. As a result, for example, analyzing a resistance can mean one thing to one analyst and something astonishingly different to another, yet each may believe he is analyzing a resistance according to classical psychoanalytic principles.

The panel on "Variations in Classical Psycho-Analytic Technique" held at the 20th Congress of the International Psycho-Analytical Association in Paris in 1957 illustrated the diversity of the points of view (see Greenson, et al., 1958). Glover's questionnaire on common technical practices, which he distributed to the members of the British Psycho-Analytical Society in 1938, revealed an unexpected amount of disagreement among the members as well as a high degree of hesitancy, timidity, and indecision in revealing their techniques (Glover, 1955, p. 348). Helen Tartakoff's excellent

1

review (1956) of recent books on psychoanalytic technique stressed the finding that the term "psychoanalysis" in the titles of each of the new publications was loosely applied to very different therapeutic methods based on the author's personal and special theoretical postulates.

This confusion and uncertainty is borne out by the startling fact that the Committee on Evaluation of Psychoanalytic Therapy of the American Psychoanalytic Association disbanded in 1953 after six and a half years of fruitless debate attempting to find an acceptable definition of psychoanalytic therapy (Rangell, 1954). See Fromm-Reichmann (1954), and Eissler (1956) as examples of widely divergent views of the meaning of dynamic psychiatry and psychoanalysis. A textbook on psychoanalytic technique would not eliminate differences of opinion or controversies about technical matters, but it might serve usefully as a common reference point by setting forth in detail and systematically how one psychoanalyst works when he claims to be analyzing certain psychic phenomena in a patient.

It should be pointed out that although there is little public communication about details of technique, there is a great deal of private talk between analysts within small closed groups. As a consequence there exist numerous isolated factions—a fact which makes for esoteric aloofness and retards scientific progress (Glover, 1955, p. 261).

Those who wish to suggest innovations or modifications of technique do not usually confer with others who are more traditional in their viewpoint. They tend to form cliques and to work underground, or at least segregated from the mainstream of analytic thought. As a consequence the innovators are apt to lose contact with those groups in psychoanalysis that might help validate, clarify, or amend their new ideas. The secluded innovators are prone to become "wild analysts," while the conservatives, due to their own insularity, tend to become rigid with orthodoxy. Instead of influencing one another constructively they each go their separate ways as adversaries, blind to whatever benefits each might have gained from an open and continuing discussion.

The single most important reason for maintaining an open forum on psychoanalytic technique is the need to expose the serious student to other techniques besides those of his personal analyst and his supervisory analysts. A big disadvantage in learning technique from only a handful of sources is that it increases the likelihood that the candidate in training will retain certain neurotic transference feelings and attitudes toward his teachers which will block his opportunity to discover the technique best suited to his own personality and theoretical orientation. It is not rare to find young psychoanalysts who bear the unmistakable stamp of their personal analyst to a degree that resembles the slavish imitation seen in adolescents. On the other hand, the recent graduate who conspicuously opposes his training analyst may be equally enmeshed in an unresolved transference neurosis. Glover (1955, p. 262) called such reactions "training transferences" and emphasized their stultifying effects in the inexperienced psychoanalyst.

It is an impressive fact that the fundamentals of psychoanalytic technique that Freud laid down in five short papers some fifty years ago still serve as the basis of psychoanalytic practice (Freud, 1912a, 1912b, 1913b, 1914c, 1915a). No acknowledged major changes or advances have taken hold in standard psychoanalytic technique.

In part this is a tribute to Freud's genius for having recognized so early and clearly what is essential in psychoanalytic therapy. There are other reasons, however, for the lack of progress. One decisive factor seems to be the complicated emotional relationship between the student of psychoanalysis and his teachers, a relationship which is an inevitable consequence of the methods used for teaching psychoanalysis (Kairys, 1964; Greenacre, 1966a).

The training analysis carried out as part of a professional training program usually leaves a considerable residue of unresolved transference reactions which restrict and warp the student's development in the field of psychoanalysis. When an analyst attempts to carry out psychoanalytic therapy for the purpose of training, he complicates his relationship to his patient by inadvertently assuming responsibility for the student's professional progress. He inevitably loses some of his customary incognito, splits the patient's motivations, and increases the candidate's tendencies to dependency, identifications, submissiveness, and pseudonormal behavior. In addition, the analyst himself becomes a partisan, usually unknowingly and unwillingly, in a triangle situation, consisting of the student, the psychoanalytic training institute, and the training analyst.

One of the secondary consequences of the unresolved transference-countertransference problems is the reluctance psychoanalysts display in revealing openly to one another how they actually work. This state of affairs may have influenced Freud himself who, according to Jones (1955, pp. 230-231), often spoke of his intention to write a systematic exposition of psychoanalytic technique but never did. Strachey (1958) suggests that the absence of any full discussion of countertransference in Freud's writings may confirm this supposition.

The reluctance of psychoanalysts to expose their methods of practice stems partly from another but related source. The work of the psychoanalyst depends on many intimate and personal processes within himself (Greenson, 1966). As a result there is a feeling of exposure and vulnerability in revealing how one analyzes. Since much of the patient's material is highly instinctualized and evocative, and since the analytic understanding of a patient depends on a special empathic intimacy with him, shame, hostility, or fear reactions may arise when exposure of this situation is called for. As a consequence it is not rare to find among psychoanalysts some variety of stage fright, exhibitionism, or combinations of both. The fact that so many analysts are inhibited in discussing openly what they do in their practice makes the psychoanalyst particularly prone to slip into one of two extreme positions: orthodoxy or sectarianism.

Psychoanalysis is a lonely profession and one feels comfort in belonging to a group, but this blocks and impedes scientific progress by encouraging conformity. There is an additional vocational hazard in the loneliness of psychoanalytic practice—the absence, as a rule, of another analytically trained observer of the analytic situation as it progresses.

The analyst's own view of what he does is unreliable and apt to be distorted in some idealized direction. I am not suggesting that it would be preferable to have observers or auditors, because I believe that their presence, even if unobserved, would distort the analytic situation. (Other writers, particularly Merton M. Gill, have expressed different views.) What I do suggest is that the psychoanalyst, working alone with his patient and thus shielded from the scrutiny of his peers, is predisposed to a biased and uncritical attitude toward his own technique.

When one describes in any detail what one does in psychoanalytic work, one reveals not only a great deal of one's intimate involvement with the patient, but also a great deal of one's personal life in general. The psychoanalyst's unique and most important working tool is the workings of his own preconscious and unconscious mind. It is inevitable that if he is going to recount how and why he approached a situation in the analysis, he will be forced to reveal much of his fantasy life, ideas, traits of character, etc. Ordinary humility and self-protection will make him tend to avoid any undue exposure of his intimate self.

Perhaps a book which depicts the practice of classical psychoanalytic therapy will help stimulate a full, open, and continuing discussion of psychoanalytic technique. In this way, variations, innovations, modifications, and deviations might be clarified and tested, thus establishing their scientific value for psychoanalysis and giving impetus to the progress of psychoanalytic technique.

I had intended to write these volumes by approaching the technical problems in chronological order as they arise in the course of psychoanalytic therapy. I had planned to begin with the Initial Interviews, Transition to the Couch, the First Analytic Hours, etc. I soon discovered that it was impossible to talk intelligibly in depth and in detail about any technical problem without a thorough understanding of Resistance and Transference. I also realized that the student would benefit from a concise outline of some basic concepts of psychoanalytic theory and technique to serve as a preliminary orientation. Therefore, these volumes are organized so that after an introductory survey the first volume begins with the chapters on Resistance and Transference, which are the foundations of psychoanalytic technique. The last chapter of Volume I is devoted to The Psychoanalytic Situation. It is included at that point because it offers an overall view of the complex interrelationship between the different procedures and processes which go on in the patient and in the psychoanalyst. (See the table of contents for details.) The second volume will be organized along more chronological lines.

The text is arranged so that each technical chapter begins with a preliminary definition which is illustrated by simple clinical examples. This is followed by a brief survey of the literature and theory before going on to the practical and technical considerations. Throughout the volumes there are bibliographical references to the major works on the subject matter under discussion. Whenever there are numerous bibliographic references to a selected topic, I have noted them at the end of the given chapter under the specific heading in an Additional Reading List. I have done so in order to avoid interfering with the flow of reading the material which long bibliographical lists cause. At the end of the book there is a comprehensive bibliography.

1

Survey of Basic Concepts

1.1 The Historical Development of Psychoanalytic Therapy

ONE way of ascertaining what is essential in psychoanalytic therapy is to take a bird's-eye view of its historical development and to note the major changes in the technical procedures and in the therapeutic processes. What follows is a selective summary of the highlights of Freud's writings on these matters. A more detailed investigation of each subject, including the contributions of others, will be found in the appropriate place in the text that follows.

Let me clarify the terminology. I am using the term *technical procedure* to refer to a measure, a tool, a course of action, an instrumentality, undertaken by the therapist or the patient, with the purpose of furthering the therapeutic processes. Hypnosis, suggestion, free association, and interpretation are examples of technical procedures. A *therapeutic process* refers to an interrelated series of psychic events within the patient, a continuity of psychic forces and acts which have a remedial aim or effect. They are usually instigated by the technical procedures. Abreaction, recapturing memories, and insight are therapeutic processes. (See E. Bibring [1954] for a similar but more comprehensive methodological approach.)

Psychoanalytic technique was not suddenly discovered or

7

invented. It evolved gradually as Freud struggled to find a way of effectively helping his neurotic patients. Although he later disclaimed any enthusiasm for therapy, it was his therapeutic intent which led to the discovery of psychoanalysis.

Freud was an astute clinician and could discern what was meaningful in the complicated sequences of clinical events that followed the various technical procedures he employed. He also had a gift for theoretical and imaginative thinking which he blended together to construct hypotheses relating technique to clinical findings and to therapeutic processes. Fortunately, Freud possessed that complex combination of temperament and character traits that enabled him to be a conquistador, an "adventurer" of the mind and a careful scientific investigator (Jones, 1953, p. 348; 1955, Chapt. 16). He had the boldness and inventiveness to explore new regions of thought vigorously and creatively. When proved wrong, he had the humility to change his technique and theory.

A careful reading of Freud's technical and clinical papers reveals that the changes in technique were neither abrupt nor complete. One can observe a shift in emphasis or a change in the order of importance assigned to a given procedure or a therapeutic process. Nevertheless, it is possible to delineate different phases in the development of technical procedures and in the theory of the therapeutic process. Freud himself briefly described three phases, but that was before he had arrived at a structural point of view (1914c).

1.11 CHANGES IN TECHNICAL PROCEDURES

Although Freud had heard the case of Anna O. from Breuer in 1882 and had studied hypnosis with Charcot from October, 1885 to February, 1886, he confined himself to using the conventional therapeutic methods of the time when he first began to practice. For some twenty months he employed electrical stimulation, hydrotherapy, massage, etc. (Jones, 1953, Chapt. 12). Dissatisfied with the results, he began to use hypnosis in December of 1887, apparently attempting to suppress the patient's symptoms.

The case of Emmy von N., treated in 1889, is significant because here for the first time Freud used hypnosis for the purpose of catharsis. His therapeutic approach consisted of hypnotizing the patient and commanding her to talk about the origin of each of her symptoms. He would ask what had frightened her, made her vomit, or upset her, when the event had occurred, etc. The patient responded by producing a series of memories, accompanied often by great affect. At the end of certain sessions Freud would suggest that the patient forget the disturbing memories which had arisen.

By 1892 Freud realized that his ability to hypnotize patients was severely limited, and he had to face the choice of abandoning the cathartic treatment or of attempting it without achieving a somnambulistic state (Breuer and Freud, 1893-95, p. 108). To justify this approach, he recalled that Bernheim had demonstrated that patients could be made to recall forgotten events by waking suggestion (p. 109). Freud therefore went on the assumption that his patients knew everything that was of pathogenic significance and that it was only a question of obliging them to communicate it. He ordered his patients to lie down, shut their eyes, and concentrate. He would apply pressure to the forehead at given moments and insist that memories would appear (p. 270).

Elisabeth von R. (1892) was the first patient Freud treated completely with waking suggestion. By 1896 he had abandoned hypnosis altogether.[1] It is less certain when he gave up using suggestion as his primary therapeutic tool. However, by 1896 Freud had already completed the essential work on *The Interpretation of Dreams,* although it was not published until 1900. It seems plausible to assume that the ability to comprehend the structure and meaning of the dream had increased his skill in interpretation. As a consequence Freud was enabled to rely more and more on the patient's spontaneous production of material. He could use interpretations and constructions to arrive at the repressed memories.

There is no exact date for the discovery of the procedure of free association. Apparently it gradually developed between 1892 and 1896, becoming steadily refined from the hypnosis, suggestion, pressing and questioning that accompanied it at its inception (Jones, 1953, pp. 242-244). Hints of it are already mentioned in 1889 in the case of Emmy von N. (Breuer and Freud, 1893-95, p. 56). Jones describes a historic occasion when Freud was pressing and questioning Elisabeth von R. and she reproached him for interrupting her flow of thoughts. Freud had the humility to accept this sug-

[1] See Strachey's note, *Standard Edition,* 2:111.

gestion and the method of free association had taken a giant step forward.

Freud explained that by giving up hypnosis and suggestion, the widening of consciousness, which had supplied the analyst with the pathogenic memories and fantasies, was now missing. Free association was a completely satisfactory substitute in that it permitted the involuntary thoughts of the patient to enter the treatment situation. This is Freud's description of this method: "Without exerting any other kind of influence, he invites them to lie down in a comfortable attitude on a sofa, while he himself sits on a chair behind them outside their field of vision. He does not even ask them to close their eyes, and avoids touching them in any way, as well as any other procedure which might be reminiscent of hypnosis. The session thus proceeds like a conversation between two people equally awake, but one of whom is spared every muscular exertion and every distracting sensory impression which might divert his attention from his own mental activity. . . . In order to secure these ideas and associations he asks the patient to 'let himself go' in what he says, "as you would do in a conversation in which you were rambling on quite disconnectedly and at random" (1904, pp. 250-251). The procedure of free association became known as the fundamental or basic rule of psychoanalysis (Freud, 1912a, p. 107).

Free association has remained the basic and unique method of communication for patients in psychoanalytic treatment. Interpretation is still the decisive and ultimate instrument of the psychoanalyst. These two technical procedures give psychoanalytic therapy its distinctive stamp. Other means of communication occur during the course of psychoanalytic therapy, but they are affiliated, preparatory, or secondary, and not typical of psychoanalysis. This point will be discussed in Section 1.34.

1.12 CHANGES IN THE THEORY OF THE THERAPEUTIC PROCESS

The *Studies on Hysteria* (1893-95) can be regarded as the beginning of psychoanalysis. In it one can discern how Freud struggled to discover what is essential in the therapeutic process in the treatment of hysterics. It is impressive to note that some of the phenomena that Freud described at that time have become the foundation of the psychoanalytic theory of therapy. It is characteristic of

Freud that he began by struggling to overcome certain obstacles to his therapeutic approach only to realize later that these obstacles were crucial for understanding the patient's neurosis and the therapeutic process. It was Freud's perseverance and flexibility that enabled him to cope successfully with a variety of obstacles that led to the discovery of psychoanalysis.

In the Preliminary Communication [1893] Breuer and Freud (1893-95) maintained that *"each individual hysterical symptom immediately and permanently disappeared when we had succeeded in bringing clearly to light the memory of the event by which it was provoked and in arousing its accompanying affect, and when the patient had described that event in the greatest possible detail and had put the affect into words"* (p. 6). They believed that only by abreacting could a patient achieve a completely "cathartic" effect and thus be freed from the hysterical symptom. These experiences, they claimed, were absent from the patient's memory under normal conditions and could be reached only by hypnosis.

The pathogenic ideas had persisted with such freshness and affective strength because they had been denied the normal wearing-away process. Thus they were dealing with affects in a "strangulated" state (p. 17). The discharge of strangulated affects would deprive the pathogenic memory of its force and the symptoms would disappear.

At this point in the history of psychoanalysis, the therapeutic processes were considered to be abreaction and remembering, with the emphasis on the abreaction. One hypnotized the patient and tried to get him to remember the traumatic event because he would then have a curative cathartic experience. Anna O., whom Breuer treated in 1882, had spontaneous hypnotic trances in which she spontaneously relived traumatic past events. After she recovered from a somnambulistic state she felt relieved. The experiences of Anna O. thus paved the way for the method of cathartic therapy. She herself called it a "talking cure" or "chimney-sweeping" (p. 30).

Freud became increasingly aware of a force within the patient opposing the treatment. It crystallized in the case of Elisabeth von R., whom he could not hypnotize and who refused to communicate certain of her thoughts despite his urgings (p. 154). He came to the conclusion that this force, which was a resistance to the treatment, was the same force which kept the pathogenic ideas from becoming conscious (p. 268). The purpose was one of defense. "The hysterical patient's 'not knowing' was in fact a 'not wanting to know'" (p. 269-270). The task of the therapist, Freud believed, was to overcome this resistance, and he did this by "insisting," pressing, pressure on the forehead, questioning, etc.

Freud recognized that the personal influence of the physician could be of great value and suggested that the therapist act as an elucidator, a teacher, and a father confessor (p. 282). However, he also became aware that under certain conditions the patient's relation to the physician can become "disturbed," a factor which turns the patient-physician relationship into the "worst obstacle we can come across" (p. 301). This may occur if the patient feels neglected, if the patient becomes sexually dependent, or if the patient transfers onto the figure of the physician the distressing ideas from the content of the analysis (p. 302). One dealt with this by making it conscious and tracing it back to the moment in treatment when it had arisen. Then one attempted to persuade the patient to communicate despite these feelings (p. 304).

Thus, Freud had discovered the phenomena of resistance and transference, but essentially they were considered to be obstacles to the work. The main objective was to achieve affective abreaction and to recover traumatic memories. Transference reactions and resistances were to be circumvented or overcome.

In the *Studies on Hysteria*, Freud attempted to focus his therapeutic efforts on the patient's individual symptoms. He realized that this form of therapy was a symptomatic one and not causal (p. 262). In the Dora case, which was published in 1905 but written in 1901, Freud stated that psychoanalytic technique had been completely revolutionized (1905a, p. 12). He no longer tried to clear up each symptom, one after the other. He found this method totally inadequate for dealing with the complex structure of a neurosis. He now allowed the patient to choose the subject matter of the hour and he started his work on whatever surface of the unconscious the patient presented at the moment.

Apparently Freud realized that a therapeutic process could not be effected in a single operation because neurotic symptoms had multiple causes. Although he already had recognized the principle of overdetermination in the *Studies on Hysteria* (pp. 173-174), he made this point explicit only in his paper on "Freud's Psycho-Analytic Procedure" published in 1904. In that essay he stated that the change in technique from hypnosis and suggestion to free association led to new findings and "finally necessitated a different though not contradictory conception of the therapeutic process" (p. 250). Hypnosis and suggestion conceal the resistances and obstruct the physician's view of the psychic forces. By evading resistances one can only get incomplete information and transitory therapeutic success. The therapeutic task is to overcome resistances, to undo repressions—then the gaps in the memory will be filled in.

I believe we see here a shift in the theory of the therapeutic process from the dominant importance of abreaction of affects to the overcoming of amnesia. This does not contradict the fact that abreaction has a therapeutic effect. By permitting the discharge of emotional tensions, the patient usually experiences a temporary sense of relief. Furthermore, catharsis is valuable because the emotional discharge reduces the quantity of affect and smaller quantities of affect are easier to handle. More important is the fact that the verbalization which accompanies the discharge of emotions and impulses makes it possible to study them more clearly. But catharsis is no longer an ultimate aim of therapy. I believe this is what Freud alluded to in his "different though not contradictory" statement above.

The new emphasis was now on making the unconscious conscious, the removal of amnesia, the recovery of repressed memories. Resistance became a cornerstone of psychoanalytic theory and was related to those forces which had brought about the repression. The analyst used the art of interpretation to overcome the resistances.

In the Dora case (1905a) Freud first emphasized the crucial role of the transference. "Transference, which seems ordained to be the greatest obstacle to psycho-analysis, becomes its most powerful ally, if its presence can be detected each time and explained to the patient" (p. 117). In the postscript to that case, Freud described how the patient had broken off treatment because he had failed to analyze the multiple transference elements which interfered with the treatment situation.

In the paper on "The Dynamics of Transference" (1912a), he described the relationship between transference and resistance, the positive and the negative transference and the ambivalence of transference reactions. Part of one paragraph deserves to be quoted because it states Freud's new therapeutic orientation very distinctly. "This struggle between the doctor and the patient, between intellect and instinctual life, between understanding and seeking to act, is played out almost exclusively in the phenomena of transference. It is on that field that the victory must be won—the victory whose expression is the permanent cure of the neurosis. It cannot be disputed that controlling the phenomena of transference presents the psycho-analyst with the greatest difficulties. But it should not be forgotten that it is precisely they that do us the inestimable service of making the patient's hidden and forgotten erotic impulses immediate and manifest. For when all is said and done, it is impossible to destroy anyone *in absentia* or *in effigie*" (p. 108).

From 1912 on, the consistent analysis of transference and resistance became the central element of the therapeutic processes. Later that same year Freud warned against transference gratifications and suggested that the psychoanalyst be opaque as a mirror to his patients and maintain his anonymity (1912b, p. 118). In his paper on "Remembering, Repeating and Working-Through (1914c), Freud described the special problem of acting out in relation to transference and resistance and connected it to a compulsion to repeat. He also used the term "transference neurosis" to signify that during psychoanalysis the patient replaces his ordinary neurosis by his involvement with his analyst. This is amplified in Chapter XXVIII in the *Introductory Lectures* (1916-17, pp. 454-455).

Something new was added to the discussion of therapeutic processes in that chapter when Freud mentioned that an alteration of the ego is made possible by analyzing the transference (p. 455). He stated that the work of interpretation, which transforms what is unconscious into what is conscious, enlarges the ego at the cost of the unconscious. In *The Ego and the Id* (1923b), Freud expressed this idea quite succinctly: "Psycho-analysis is an instrument to enable the ego to achieve a progressive conquest of the id" (p. 56). In 1933 Freud wrote that the therapeutic efforts of psychoanalysis are intended "to strengthen the ego, to make it more independent of the super-ego, to widen its field of perception and enlarge its organization, so that it can appropriate fresh portions of the id. Where id was, there ego shall be" (p. 80). Again in "Analysis Terminable and Interminable" (1937a) Freud stated: "The business of the analysis is to secure the best possible psychological conditions for the functions of the ego; with that it has discharged its task" (p. 250).

If one reviews the historical developments in the major procedures and processes of psychoanalytic therapy, one can observe that hypnosis has been abandoned, but all the other elements have been retained, albeit with a very different role in the therapeutic hierarchy (Loewald, 1955). Suggestion is not used for obtaining memories and is no longer a major therapeutic device in psychoanalysis. It may be utilized as a temporary supportive measure, the need for which will ultimately have to be analyzed. (This will be discussed in Section 1.34.)

Abreaction is no longer considered a therapeutic goal but is valuable in other ways. The analyst still attempts to get beyond the barrier of consciousness, but he uses free association, dream analysis, and interpretation. The major field for analytic work is the area of transference and resistance. We hope to make the unconscious conscious, recover warded-off memories, and overcome the infantile amnesia. But even this is no longer conceptualized as an ultimate aim. The ultimate aim of psychoanalysis is to increase the relative strength of the ego in relation to the superego, the id, and the external world.

1.2 Theoretical Concepts Essential for Technique

1.21. The Relation between Theory and Practice

Before we can proceed to a more thorough and systematic examination of therapeutic procedures and processes, it would be well to review briefly some of the basic theoretical concepts of the psychoanalytic point of view. There is a reciprocal relationship between theory and practice. Clinical findings can lead to new theoretical formulations, which in turn can sharpen one's perceptiveness and technique so that new clinical insights may be obtained. The reverse is also true. Faulty technique can lead to distortions in the clinical findings, which in turn can lead to faulty theoretical concepts. Whenever there is a lack of integration between theory and technique, both aspects are likely to suffer (Hartmann, 1951, p. 143). For example, one can deal with a resistance more effectively if one is aware of the multiple functions of resistance, its relationship to defenses in general, as well as its purpose in a particular instance.

There are analysts who tend to isolate their practical from their theoretical knowledge. Some do it by drifting along with the patient until some fragment of the patient's material becomes understandable and is then unselectively communicated to the patient. They misuse the notion that it is the analyst's unconscious mind and empathy which are his most important tools for therapy, and they ignore the need to do some intellectual work with the data they may have obtained. As a consequence there is no overall view of the patient, no reconstructions of larger segments of the patient's life, there are just collections of insights. Errors in the other direction are equally serious; there are analysts who too quickly formulate theories on the basis of skimpy clinical data. For them, the experience of analysis becomes a thinking contest or an intellectual exercise. Such analysts avoid instinctual or emotional involvement with their patients, they forego intuition and empathy and become data collectors or interpretation dispensers.

Psychoanalytic therapy makes strenuous contradictory demands on the analyst. He must listen to the material of his patient, permitting his own associative fantasies and memories to have free play as he does so; yet he must scrutinize and expose to his intellectual capacities the insights so obtained before they can be safely transmitted to the patient (Ferenczi, 1919a, p. 189). The ability to let oneself associate freely is acquired from the analyst's experience of having been successfully analyzed. To use one's theoretical knowledge effectively in practice, it must have been mastered intellectually; it must also be accessible when needed without dominating one's clinical skills. If the psychoanalyst's work is to remain a scientific discipline, it is imperative that he maintain the capacity to oscillate between the use of empathy and intuition on the one hand and his theoretical knowledge on the other (Fenichel, 1941, pp. 1-5; Kohut, 1959).

In the early years of psychoanalysis most of the advances came from clinical discoveries. In recent years, however, there seems to be a lag on the side of technique. When Freud discovered the crucial importance of systematically analyzing the resistances of his patients, he was some twenty years ahead of discovering the ego implications of this procedure. Today we seem to know a great deal more about ego functions than we are able to use directly in our technique (Hartmann, 1951). But I believe that our greatest hope for progress in technique lies in a better integration of clinical, technical, and theoretical knowledge.

1.22 THE PSYCHOANALYTIC THEORY OF NEUROSIS

The theory and technique of psychoanalysis are based essentially on clinical data derived from the study of neuroses. Although in recent years there has been a tendency to enlarge the scope of psychoanalytic investigation to include normal psychology, the psychoses, sociological and historical problems, our knowledge of these areas has not progressed as far as our comprehension of the psychoneuroses (A. Freud, 1954a; Stone, 1954b). The clinical findings of the neuroses still provide us with the most reliable source material for formulating psychoanalytic theory. To grasp the theory of psychoanalytic technique it is necessary for the reader to have a working knowledge of the psychoanalytic theory of neurosis. Freud's *Introductory Lectures* (1916-17) and the texts of Nunberg (1932), Fenichel (1945a), and Waelder (1960) are excellent condensed source books. Here I can only outline what I have found to be the most important theoretical concepts required for the understanding of technique.

Psychoanalysis maintains that psychoneuroses are based on the neurotic conflict. The conflict leads to an obstruction in the discharge of instinctual drives eventuating in a state of being dammed up. The ego becomes progressively less able to cope with the mounting tensions and is ultimately overwhelmed. The involuntary discharges manifest themselves clinically as the symptoms of psychoneurosis. The term "neurotic conflict" is used in the singular, although there is always more than one important conflict. Custom and convenience make us refer to the single conflict (Colby, 1951, p. 6).

A neurotic conflict is an *unconscious* conflict between an id impulse seeking discharge and an ego defense warding off the impulse's direct discharge or access to consciousness. At times clinical material may reveal a conflict between two instinctual demands, for example, heterosexual activity may be used to ward off homosexual desires. Analysis will reveal that in such an instance the heterosexual activity is being used for purposes of defense to avoid the painful feelings of guilt and shame. Heterosexuality, in this example, is fulfilling an ego demand and opposing a more forbidden instinctual impulse, homosexuality. Therefore, the formulation that a neurotic conflict is a conflict between the id and the ego is still valid.

The external world also plays an important role in the formation of neuroses, but here too the conflict must be experienced as an internal conflict between the ego and the id for a neurotic conflict to arise. The external world may mobilize instinctual temptations, and situations may have to be avoided because they bring the danger of some type of punishment. We will then be dealing with a neurotic conflict if the instinctual temptation or the danger has to be blocked off from consciousness. A conflict with external reality has become a conflict between the id and the ego.

The superego plays a more complicated role in the neurotic conflict. It may enter the conflict on the side of the ego or the side of the id or both. The superego is the agency that makes the instinctual impulse seem forbidden to the ego. It is the superego that makes the ego feel guilty even for the symbolic and distorted discharges, so that they are felt consciously as essentially painful. The superego may also enter the neurotic conflict by becoming regressively reinstinctualized, so that the self-reproaches take on a drivelike quality. The guilt-laden patient may then be driven into situations which again and again result in pain. All parts of the psychic apparatus participate in neurotic symptom formation (see Fenichel, 1941, Chapt. II; 1945a, Chapt. VII, VIII; Waelder, 1960, pp. 35-47; and Additional Reading List).

The id never stops seeking discharge, and its impulses will attempt to gain some partial satisfaction by utilizing some derivative and regressive outlets. The ego in order to appease the demands of the superego has to distort even these instinctual derivatives so that they appear in some disguised form, hardly recognizable as instinctual. The superego causes the ego to feel guilty nevertheless, and the distorted instinctual activity causes pain in a variety of ways. It is felt as a punishment and not as a satisfaction.

The key factor in understanding the pathogenic outcome of the neurotic conflict is the ego's need constantly to expend its energies in attempting to keep the dangerous drives from gaining access to consciousness and motility. Ultimately this leads to a relative insufficiency of the ego, and derivatives of the original neurotic conflict will overwhelm the depleted ego and break through into consciousness and behavior. From this point of view the psychoneuroses can be understood as relative traumatic neuroses (Fenichel, 1945a; Chapt. VII, VIII). A relatively innocuous stimulus may stir up some id impulse, which may be linked to the dammed-up instinctual reservoir. The impoverished ego is unable to keep up its defensive work and is flooded to the extent that it has to allow some instinctual discharge, although even this is disguised and distorted. These disguised and distorted involuntary discharges manifest themselves clinically as the symptoms of the psychoneurosis.

Let me illustrate this with a relatively simple clinical example. Some years ago a young woman, Mrs. A., came for treatment accompanied by her husband. She complained that she was unable to leave her house alone and felt safe only with her husband. In addition, she complained of a fear of fainting, a fear of dizziness, and a fear of becoming incontinent. Mrs. A.'s symptoms had begun quite suddenly some six months earlier while she was in a beauty parlor.

The analysis, which lasted several years, revealed that the actual trigger for the outbreak of the patient's phobias was the event of having her hair combed by a male beautician. We were able eventually to uncover the fact that at that moment she was reminded of her father combing her hair when she was a little girl. The reason she had gone to the beauty parlor that day was her pleasurable expectation of seeing her father, who was to visit the young married couple for the first time since their marriage. He was to stay in their home and she was filled with great delight, consciously. However, unconsciously, she was full of guilt feelings for loving her father and for her predominantly unconscious hostility toward her husband.

The apparently innocuous event of having her hair combed stirred up old incestuous longings, hostilities, guilt, and anxiety. To put it briefly, Mrs. A. had to be accompanied by her husband in order to be sure he had not been killed by her death wishes. Also his presence protected her from acting out sexually. The fears of fainting, of dizziness, and of incontinence were symbolic representations of losing her moral balance, losing her self-control, soiling her good character, humiliating herself, and falling from her high position. The young woman's symptoms had links to the pleasurable body sensations of childhood as well as to infantile punishment fantasies.

I believe one can formulate the events as follows: the combing of her hair stirred up repressed id impulses which brought her into conflict with her ego and superego. Despite the absence of obvious neurotic symptoms prior to the outbreak of the phobias, there were indications that her ego already was relatively depleted and her id lacked adequate discharge possibilities. Mrs. A. had had difficulty in sleeping for years, nightmares, and inhibitions in her sexual life. As a consequence the fantasies mobilized by the hair combing increased the id tensions to a point where they flooded the infantile defenses of the ego and involuntary discharges took place, eventuating in acute symptom formation.

Two additional points should be noted, although further clarification will have to be postponed at this time. The ego attempts to cope with the forbidden or dangerous id impulses by resorting to the various defense mechanisms it has at its disposal. The defenses may be successful if they provide for periodic discharge of instinctual tensions. They become pathogenic when many varieties of libidinal and aggressive impulses are excluded from contact with the rest of the total personality (A. Freud, 1965, Chapt. V). Eventually the repressed returns in the form of symptoms.

An adult neurosis is always built around a nucleus from childhood. The case of Mrs. A. demonstrates that her sexual feelings were still fixated to her childhood image of her father, and sexuality was just as forbidden as it had been in her childhood years. Although she had overcome her childhood neurosis sufficiently so that she could function effectively in many areas of her life, Mrs. A. remained neurotically regressed in regard to all matters concerning genital sexuality. The childhood phobias and body anxieties returned with her adult neurosis. (The only neuroses without a childhood basis are the pure traumatic neuroses, which are extremely rare and rarely pure. They often become linked up to the psychoneuroses [Fenichel, 1945a; Chapt. VII].)

1.23 The Metapsychology of Psychoanalysis

Psychoanalytic metapsychology refers to the minimum number of assumptions upon which the system of psychoanalytic theory is based (Rapaport and Gill, 1959). Freud's metapsychological writings are neither complete nor systematic and are scattered throughout his writings. The seventh chapter of *The Interpretation of Dreams* (1900), the "Papers on Metapsychology" (Freud, 1915b,

1915c, 1915d, 1917b), and the addenda to *Inhibitions, Symptoms and Anxiety* (1926a) are the main reference sources. Actually, Freud formulated only three metapsychological points of view explicitly —the topographic, the dynamic, and the economic. The genetic point of view he seemed to take for granted. Although he did not define the structural point of view, Freud did suggest that it might replace the topographic (1923b, p. 17). (See Rapaport and Gill [1959] and Arlow and Brenner [1964] on this point.) The adaptive point of view is also implicit and essential to psychoanalytic thinking (Hartmann, 1939).

The clinical implications of metapsychology intimate that in order to comprehend a psychic event thoroughly, it is necessary to analyze it from six different points of view—the topographic, dynamic, economic, genetic, structural, and adaptive. In clinical practice we analyze our patients' productions only partially and in fragments, in a given interval of time. Nevertheless, experience teaches us that we do use all these points of view when we try to work through our initial insights. I shall attempt to sketch an outline of these concepts. For a more comprehensive survey the reader is referred to Fenichel (1945a, Chapt. II), Rapaport and Gill (1959), and Arlow and Brenner (1964).

The earliest point of view Freud postulated was the *topographical* one. In the seventh chapter of *The Interpretation of Dreams* (1900) he described the different modes of functioning that govern conscious and unconscious phenomena. The "primary process" holds sway over unconscious material and the "secondary process" directs conscious phenomena. Unconscious material has only one aim—discharge. There is no sense of time, order or logic, and contradictions may coexist without nullifying one another. Condensation and displacement are other characteristics of the primary process. Designating a psychic event as conscious or unconscious implies more than merely a difference in quality. Archaic and primitive modes of functioning are characteristic of unconscious phenomena.

Let me illustrate. A male patient tells me the following dream: "I am building an addition to the front of my house. I am suddenly interrupted by my son's crying. I look for him full of fearful expectation and I see him in the distance, but he keeps running away from me. I begin to get angry and I finally catch up with him. I start to reprimand him for running away when I notice that he has a triangular cut in the corner of his mouth. I tell him not to talk because the cut will become bigger. I can see the pink flesh underneath the skin and I feel queasy. Then I realize it isn't my son at all but my older brother. He smiles at me condescendingly as though he had made a fool of me. I turn away from him but am embarrassed because I feel that now I am sweaty and hot and he might notice that I smell bad."

The patient's associations may be condensed to the following: My older brother used to bully me when I was younger, but he had a nervous breakdown and then I became the stronger of the two. My brother copies me in everything. When I bought a stationwagon, he bought one. "When my wife and I got pregnant, he became pregnant." My brother seems to have a problem with his masculinity. His son is still in curls at four and doesn't speak. I tried to tell him that it was wrong to keep a boy in curls.

At this point I intervened and indicated that the patient had said: "When my wife and I got pregnant, he became pregnant." The patient replied defensively that this was merely a manner of speech. Then he laughed and said that perhaps he had thought he could have a baby when he was a child. His mother had regretted that he was born a boy, had curled his hair and kept him in dresses. In fact he remembers playing with dolls until he was six years old. The triangular wound reminds him of a bad gash he saw on a playmate as a child. Gash makes him think of vagina. His wife had an operation on her vagina once and it makes him sick to think of it.

Again I intervene and point out to the patient that the dream contains the idea it is better to keep quiet if you want to hide your gash; if you talk, your gash will become more exposed. The patient is pensive and then says that he guesses he is afraid to uncover some of his own worries about being masculine. Maybe some activity of a homosexual nature did occur with his brother as we had previously hypothesized.

The dream and the associations clearly demonstrate some characteristics of the primary and secondary processes. "I am building an addition to the front of my house" seems to symbolize a pregnancy fantasy in my male patient's unconscious. This also comes out later in the patient's associations when he said, "My wife and I got pregnant and my brother became pregnant." The triangular gash symbolizes the patient's view of a vagina. It also hints at his castration anxiety as indicated by feeling queasy in the dream and feeling sick at the idea of an operation on the vagina which came up in his associations. The son changes into his brother, but this does not cause any amazement in the dream since logic and time are of no consequence. However, this change expresses in a condensed form that on the surface the patient may seem to be in command, but in the past and in the analytic situation the patient had and still has some passive, anal, and feminine attitudes and fantasies. The triangular gash is a displacement from below to above as well as a condensation. The little boy who runs away· is also a condensation of the patient's son about whom he has homosexual desires and anxieties, the patient's older brother, and the patient himself. The analysis is represented by the building of an addition, by the fearful expectations, by the running away, and by the admonition to keep quiet. The analyst is represented as running after the little boy, as getting angry at him for running away, as smiling condescendingly, and as being the embarrasser who might notice the bad smell.

I believe this dream and the associations demonstrate many qualities of the primary and secondary processes as they occur in a fragment of clinical work.

The *dynamic point of view* assumes that mental phenomena are the result of the interaction of forces. Freud (1916-17, p. 67) used the analysis of errors to demonstrate dynamics: "I would ask you to bear in mind as a model the manner in which we have treated these phenomena. From this example you can learn the aims of our psychology. We seek not merely to describe and to classify phenomena, but to understand them as signs of an interplay of forces in the mind, as a manifestation of purposeful intentions working concurrently or in mutual opposition. We are concerned with a *dynamic view* of mental phenomena." This assumption is the basis for all hypotheses concerning instinctual drives, defenses, ego interests, and conflicts. Symptom formation, ambivalence, and overdetermination are examples of dynamics.

A patient who suffered from premature ejaculation had an unconscious fear of and hatred for the vagina. It represented to him a dreadful, gigantic cavity which would devour him. It was a dirty, slimy, sickness-spreading sewer. At the same time the vagina was a luscious, juicy, milk-giving breast which he longed to take into his mouth. During intercourse he would oscillate between fantasies that the huge vagina would engulf him and that his erect penis might tear and rip those delicate and fragile walls until they bled. His premature ejaculation was a means of expressing impulses to soil and degrade that hateful organ and also to run away from that dangerous and fragile genital. It was also a symbolic plea to the bearer of the vagina: "I am only a little boy who just urinates in a vagina, be nice to me." The premature ejaculation was a compromise between varieties of destructive sensuality and oral supplication. As his analysis progressed and his wife remained his wife during intercourse, he could express aggressive sensuality in forceful phallic activity and his orality in the foreplay.

The *economic point of view* concerns the distribution, transformations, and expenditures of psychic energy. Such concepts as binding, neutralization, sexualization, aggressivization, and sublimation are based on this hypothesis.

An example of economics may be seen in the case of Mrs. A. whom I described in Section 1.22. Before the outbreak of the patient's phobias, she was in a state of dammed-up instinctual tensions, but her ego functions were still able to carry out their defensive functions adequately enough so that Mrs. A. could function without obvious symptoms. She was able to maintain her mental equilibrium by avoiding sexual relations with her husband, and if she had to participate, she would not allow herself to become sexually aroused. This required a great deal of her ego's defensive energies, but she was able to keep matters under control until the hair-combing incident. At that point the father's visit and the hair combing brought back sexual and romantic memories from the past. In addition, it increased her hostility to her husband. Mrs. A.'s ego could not cope with this new influx of id strivings seeking discharge. The instinctual impulses broke through in feelings of fainting, dizziness, and incontinence. This led to a phobia about leaving her house unaccompanied by her husband. In order fully to understand the breakdown of Mrs. A.'s defensive capacities, it must be approached in terms of changes in the distribution of her psychic energies.

The *genetic point of view* concerns the origin and development of psychic phenomena. It deals not only with how the past is contained in the present, but with why, in certain conflicts, a specific solution was adopted. It brings into focus the biological-constitutional factors as well as the experiential.

Example: A patient of mine, Mr. N., claimed he was the favorite child of both his mother and father. For proof he cited how he was allowed to go to summer camp as a boy and later to college. His two younger brothers received neither of these benefits. He also claimed to be happily married, although he rarely had sexual relations with his wife and was often unfaithful to her. He felt he was basically a fortunate person, although he suffered from periodic depressions and from impulsive bouts of gambling.

One of this patient's major defensive maneuvers was to collect screen memories. The memories he recalled were true, but they were retained to ward off the memory of unhappy experiences. At times he actually had been treated as the favorite child, but that was rare and not typical. His parents were inconsistent and hypocritical, which was a decisive factor in shaping his particular symptomatology. The parents would often reject and deprive him and when he complained, they would point out some special pleasure they had given him some time in the past. What his parents did to him consciously, my patient did unconsciously by using screen memories. He denied the past and present unhappiness by screen formations which proclaimed the opposite. His periods of depression revealed the underlying sadness. The gambling was an attempt to prove he was lucky, the favorite child of "Lady Luck."

The *structural point of view* assumes that the psychic apparatus can be divided into several persisting functional units. This was Freud's last major theoretical contribution (1923b). The concept of the psychic apparatus as consisting of an ego, id and superego is derived from the structural hypothesis. It is implied whenever we talk of interstructural conflicts like symptom formation or intrastructural processes like the synthetic function of the ego.

A clinical illustration is the patient described earlier with the premature ejaculation. When he began treatment he would lose the ego function of discrimination in sexual situations. All women became his mother, all vaginas were charged with oral-sadistic and anal-sadistic fantasies. As he progressed he no longer regressed in that way in sexual situations. His ego could differentiate between his mother and his wife; his id strivings were then able to progress from oral and anal to phallic.

Finally, today we also formulate an *adaptive point of view* although Freud only implied this. "The concept of *adaptedness* is implicit, for instance, in Freud's propositions concerning the co-ordination between drive and object, and in Hartmann's and Erikson's propositions concerning inborn preparedness for an evolving series of average expectable environments" (Rapaport and Gill, 1959, pp. 159-160).

All propositions concerning the relationship to the environment, objects of love and hate, relations to society, etc., are based on this hypothesis. Every clinical example I have used previously is also an example of attempts at adaptation.

1.24 THE THEORY OF PSYCHOANALYTIC TECHNIQUE

Psychoanalytic therapy is a causal therapy; it attempts to undo the causes of neurosis. Its aim is to resolve the patient's neurotic conflicts, including the infantile neurosis which serves as the core of the adult neurosis. Resolving the neurotic conflicts means reuniting with the conscious ego those portions of the id, superego, and unconscious ego which had been excluded from the maturational processes of the healthy remainder of the total personality.

The psychoanalyst approaches the unconscious elements through their derivatives. All warded-off components of the id and ego produce derivatives—"half-breeds," which are not conscious and are yet highly organized in accordance with the secondary process and accessible to the conscious ego (Freud, 1915b, pp. 190-192; Fenichel, 1941, p. 18).

The procedure that psychoanalysis requires the patient to use to facilitate the communication of derivatives is free association, the fundamental method of psychoanalysis, the so-called "basic rule" (Freud, 1913b, pp. 134-136; 1915b, pp. 149-150). These derivatives appear in the patient's free associations, dreams, symptoms, slips, and acting out.

The patient is asked to try, to the best of his ability, to let things come up and to say them without regard for logic or order; he is to report things even if they seem trivial, shameful, or impolite, etc. By *letting* things come to mind, a regression in the service of the ego takes place, and derivatives of the unconscious ego, id, and superego tend to come to the surface. The patient moves from strict secondary-process thinking in the direction of the primary process. It is the analyst's task to analyze these derivatives for the patient. (The meaning of the term "to analyze" and other technical and clinical terms will be discussed in Section 1.3.)

Although the patient suffering from a neurosis enters psychoanalytic treatment with the conscious motive of wanting to change, there are unconscious forces within him which oppose change, which defend the neurosis and the *status quo*. These forces oppose the procedures and processes of treatment and are called the *resist-*

ances. Resistances stem from those same defensive forces of the ego which form part of the neurotic conflict. In the course of treatment the patient will repeat all the different forms and varieties of defensive maneuvers that he used in his past life. The analysis of the resistances is one of the cornerstones of psychoanalytic technique. Since resistance is a manifestation of the defensive and distorting function of the ego, it is resistance which psychoanalytic technique attempts to analyze first. Insight can be effective only if the patient is able to establish and maintain a reasonable ego. Resistances interfere with the reasonable ego and have to be analyzed before any other analytic work can be done with success.

For example, a young man seems to be hesitant to tell me anything derogatory about his wife. Whenever he finds fault with her he is quick to excuse her or justify her shortcomings. When I point out this defensive attitude to him, the patient at first denies it and then tearfully admits that I am right. He acknowledges that he tries to cover up his wife's deficiencies because he is sure I would expect him to get a divorce if I "really" knew how inadequate she is. When I pursue this point about divorce, the patient recalls that in his childhood his father repeatedly threatened to divorce his mother whenever he found fault with her. Thus, it seemed clear that the patient's hesitancy indicated that he was afraid I would act like his father. He tried to protect his wife from me as he had wanted to protect his mother from his father.

Only after the patient recognized this source of resistance could he go on to realize that it was he, not I, who had such a strong, "fatherly" resentment against his wife. It took a great deal more analysis for him to become aware that although he wanted to defend his mother against his father, he himself had had an enormous resentment against his mother. Unconsciously he wanted me to urge him to divorce his wife as he once had wanted his father to do to his mother.

In this clinical example, it was necessary to analyze each aspect of the resistance step by step to enable the patient to face the reality of the situation. First, he had to recognize that he feared I would want him to divorce his wife and consequently he was hiding certain things about her from me. Then he had to realize that he had confused me with his father and his wife with his mother. Finally, the patient was able to detect that underlying his protective feelings toward his mother, there was also great hostility. Each step in the analysis of resistances implies that the reasonable ego of the patient has to be enabled to face some irrational, distorted aspect of its own activity.

This clinical example leads to another basic concept in the theory of psychoanalytic technique. Neurotic patients are prone to *transference reactions*. The transference is one of the most valuable sources of material for the analysis, one of the most important motivations, and also the greatest obstacle to success. The instinctual frustration of the neurotic tends to make him unconsciously seek objects upon whom he displaces his libidinal and aggressive impulses. The patient tends to repeat his past, in terms of human relations, in order to obtain satisfactions he had not experienced or belatedly to master some anxiety or guilt. Transference is a reliving of the past, a misunderstanding of the present in terms of the past. The central importance of the transference reactions in the theory of technique stems from the fact that, if the transference reactions are properly handled, the patient will experience, in the treatment situation and in regard to the psychoanalyst, all the significant human relations of his past which are not consciously accessible to him (Freud, 1912a).

The psychoanalytic situation is so structured as to facilitate the maximal development of the transference reactions. The psychoanalyst's deprivational attitude and his relative incognito help bring out the full range of transference feelings and fantasies. However, it is the consistent analysis of the transference, both in and outside the analytic situation, which enables the patient to endure the different varieties and intensities of transference.

Transference is also the source of the greatest resistances during the analysis. A patient may work hard in the beginning of an analysis in order to gain favor with the analyst. It is inevitable that the patient will feel some form of rejection because all our patients have experienced rejection in their past lives and the analyst's attitude is essentially nongratifying. The hostile feelings of the repressed past or the forbidden sexual longings of childhood or adolescence will evoke strong tendencies in the patient to fight against the analytic work unconsciously. The quality and quantity of the "transference resistances" will be determined by the patient's past history. The duration of these reactions will also be influenced by how effectively the psychoanalyst analyzes the transference problems which stirred up the resistances.

A word should be added at this point about the relatively non-neurotic, rational, and realistic attitudes of the patient toward the analyst: the *working alliance* (Greenson, 1965a). It is this part of the patient-analyst relationship that enables the patient to identify with the analyst's point of view and to work with the analyst despite the neurotic transference reactions.

Psychoanalytic technique is aimed directly at the ego since only the ego has direct access to the id, to the superego, and to the outside world. Our aim is to get the ego to renounce its pathogenic defenses or find more suitable ones (A. Freud, 1936, pp. 45-70). The old defensive maneuvers proved to be inadequate; new, different, or no defense might permit some instinctual outlet without guilt or anxiety. The id discharge would lessen the instinctual pressure, and the ego would then be in a relatively stronger position.

The psychoanalyst hopes to induce the relatively mature aspects of the patient's ego to contend with what it once banished from consciousness as too dangerous. It is the analyst's expectation that under the protection of the working alliance and nonsexual positive transference the patient will look afresh at what he once considered too threatening, will be able to re-evaluate the situation, and eventually will dare to attempt new ways of dealing with the old danger. Slowly the patient will realize that the instinctual impulses of childhood which were overwhelming for a child's ego resources and were distorted by a child's superego can be looked at differently in adult life.

The psychological work which occurs after an insight has been given and which leads to a stable change in behavior or attitude is called *working through* (Greenson, 1965b). It consists of such processes as the utilization and the assimilation of insight and reorientation (E. Bibring, 1954). It will be discussed in the next section.

Psychoanalysis tries in this way to reverse, to roll back, the process of neurosis and symptom formation (Waelder, 1960, p. 46). The only reliable solution is to achieve structural changes in the ego which will allow it to renounce its defense or to find one which permits adequate instinctual discharge (Fenichel, 1941, p. 16).

Let me try to illustrate a typical sequence of events with a clinical example. A twenty-seven-year-old woman, Mrs. K., seeks analysis for a variety of reasons. For several years she has had episodes of feeling out of things, numb, "gone," "like a zombie." In addition, she has periods of depression, an inability to have an orgasm in sexual relations, and most recently, an impulsive-obsessive idea to have a sexual affair with a Negro. This last symptom was most torturous for her and impelled her to come for treatment. I shall use this single symptom as the focal point to illustrate the theoretical description I have given of the aims and goals of psychoanalytic technique. (See Altman's [1964] report of a panel on this subject, particularly Ross's contribution.)

All psychotherapies would attempt to relieve the patient from her symptoms, but only psychoanalysis attempts to do this by resolving the neurotic conflicts which are at the bottom of the symptoms. Other therapies might try to help the patient by strengthening her defenses, or by using the transference and suggestion to subdue or displace her sexual impulses for Negro men. Or they might try to help the defense-instinct conflict by suggesting some instinctual outlet that might be possible under the protection of a superegolike transference to the psychotherapist. Some therapists might use drugs to tranquilize the libidinal drives and in that way help out the patient's beleaguered ego. Some others might suggest drugs like alcohol or phenobarbital, which might temporarily dull the demands of the patient's superego. All these methods can be helpful, but they are temporary since they do not effect a permanent change in the psychic structures involved in the causative unconscious conflicts.

Psychoanalytic therapy would try to make the patient aware of all the different unconscious impulses, fantasies, desires, fears, guilts, and punishments that are expressed in a condensed way in her symptom. The patient I am using as an example was slowly given insight into the fact that the Negro was a disguise for her powerful, sexually attractive, and frightening red-headed stepfather from her puberty years. The impulsive-obsessive idea of having sexual relations with Negroes was demonstrated as being partly derived from disguised incestuous desires for the stepfather. It was also a screen for sadistic-masochistic impulses and concealed a "toiletization" of sexuality. The Negro also represented a condensation of an anal-phallic man from age three. The painful quality of the symptom was uncovered as a self-punishment out of guilt for the forbidden impulses.

As the patient was able gradually to face these insights her ego no longer had to expend so much of its energies in attempting to repress the forbidden impulses and fantasies. Her reasonable ego could now accept the notion that incestuous fantasies are not the same as actions and are part of growing up in our society. Mrs. K. could now recognize that her superego had been too severe and sadistic. She realized that she had been reproaching herself cruelly, in a manner resembling her masochistic sexual fantasies. Being beaten and beating and soiling were exposed as regressive attempts to obtain substitutes for a sexual satisfaction.

As the patient permitted all these hitherto unconscious phenomena to become conscious, a change was noticeable in the three psychic structures. The ego did not have to use repression, reaction formations, and isolation against the impulses that were uncovered. This was possible because her severe superego had become less sadistic toward the ego. Once the anal sadomasochistic impulses could be exposed to consciousness, they lost their intensity, and her id strivings changed in the direction of seeking pleasures genitally. The change in her instinctual urges made it possible for Mrs. K. to experience some sexual gratification with her husband, and she lost the impulsive obsession in regard to Negro men.

The analysis of transference reactions and resistances played an important role in all these developments. For example, the sexual feelings Mrs. K. had toward her stepfather came to light when she became aware that she felt I was sexually attractive "even though you are old enough to be my father." Her fantasies of being beaten came up in the analysis as a fear that I would beat her and then as a wish that I would do so. Mrs. K. had enormous resistances to talk about certain of her sexual fantasies because she felt as though I was watching her on the toilet. This led to our uncovering her "toiletization" of sexuality.

Mrs. K. worked hard in her analysis and after some six months developed a relatively reliable working alliance with me. Despite painful transference reactions and resistances, she could eventually identify with my analytic point of view and try to understand her neurotic reactions.

The temporary and partial improvement impelled the patient to go further in her treatment. She was now able to allow herself to regress more deeply in the analytic situation and permitted herself to experience still earlier forms of her neurotic conflicts. The sexual desires for Negro men also served an important defensive function against strong homosexual impulses to women. These in turn were shown to be derived from deeply repressed oral sucking impulses toward the mother, which the patient had felt as a threat to her separate identity. Alongside of this conflict was an enormous primitive rage toward the mother, which was perceived as dangerous to the mother's existence and was also felt as a threat to Mrs. K.'s own existence. Insight into the various levels of the neurotic defense-instinct conflict made for gradual changes in the structure of the patient's ego, id, and superego. Some old defenses were discarded as unnecessary, some new ones were found which made instinctual gratification possible without guilt. The entire relationship among the psychic structures was changed, and with that a new and more gratifying and effective relationship to the outside world emerged.

1.3 The Components of Classical Psychoanalytic Technique

Now that the reader has an overall view of psychoanalytic therapy from the historical development and the theoretical framework, the present section will outline a general introduction to technique as it is currently practiced. It will consist of working definitions or descriptions of the therapeutic procedures and processes which are utilized in classical psychoanalysis. The purpose is to provide a glossary of technical terms and concepts and to demonstrate how some of them are used in the partial and diluted analytic therapies as compared to psychoanalytic therapy (E. Bibring, 1954; Greenacre, 1954; Gill, 1954; and the Additional Reading List).

1.31 THE PRODUCTION OF MATERIAL

1.311 Free Association

In classical psychoanalysis the predominant means of communicating clinical material is for the patient to attempt free association. Usually this is begun after the preliminary interviews have been concluded. In the preliminary interviews the analyst had arrived at an assessment of the patient's capacity to work in the psychoanalytic situation. Part of that evaluation consisted of determining whether the patient had the resilience in his ego functions to oscillate between the more regressive ego functions as they are needed in free association and the more advanced ego functions required for understanding the analytic interventions, answering direct questions, and resuming everyday life at the end of the hour.

The patient usually associates freely most of the hour but he may also report dreams and other events of his daily life or past history. It is characteristic for psychoanalysis that the patient is asked to include his associations as he recounts his dreams or other experiences. *Free association has priority over all other means of producing material in the analytic situation.*

However, free association may be misused in the service of resistance. It is then the task of the analyst to analyze such resistances in order to re-establish the proper use of free association. It may also occur that a patient cannot stop free-associating because of a breakdown of ego functions. This is an example of an emergency situation arising in the course of an analysis. The analyst's task then would be to attempt to re-establish the ego's logical, secondary-process thinking. He may have to employ suggestion and direct commands in order to do so. This is an unanalytic maneuver, but it is indicated in the above instance because we may be dealing with an incipient psychotic reaction.

Free association is the major method of producing material in psychoanalysis. It is used on selective occasions in those forms of psychotherapy which attempt some amount of uncovering, the so-called "psychoanalytically oriented psychotherapies." It is not used in the anti-analytic therapies, the covering-up or supportive therapies.

There will be a further discussion of free association in the chapter dealing with what psychoanalysis demands of the patient (Section 4.12). The introduction of free association in connection with the transition to the couch will be described in Volume II.

1.312 The Transference Reactions

Ever since treating Dora, Freud recognized that the patient's transference reactions and resistances produced the essential material for the analytic work (1905a, pp. 112-122). From then on the analytic situation was arranged so that it would facilitate the maximal development of the patient's transference reactions. The resistances are aimed at preventing this development or at obstructing the analysis of the transference. Both resistance and transference are the bearers of vital information about the patient's past, repressed history. Chapters 2 and 3 of this volume are devoted to a systematic and thorough discussion of these topics. Here I shall attempt only a preliminary orientation.

Transference is the experiencing of feelings, drives, attitudes, fantasies, and defenses toward a person in the present which are inappropriate to that person and are a repetition, a displacement of reactions originating in regard to significant persons of early childhood. A patient's susceptibility to transference reactions stems from his state of instinctual dissatisfaction and his resultant need for discharge opportunities (Freud, 1912a).

It is important to focus on the fact that the patient tends to repeat *instead* of to remember; the repetition is always a resistance in regard to the function of memory. However, by repeating, by re-enacting the past, the patient does make it possible for the past to enter into the treatment situation. Transference repetitions bring into the analysis material which is otherwise inaccessible. If properly handled, the analysis of transference will lead to memories, reconstructions, and insight, and an eventual cessation of the repetition.

There are many ways of classifying the various clinical forms of transference reactions. The most commonly used designations are the *positive* and the *negative transference*. The positive transference refers to the different forms of sexual longing as well as liking, loving, and respecting the analyst. The negative transference implies some variety of aggression in the shape of anger, dislike, hate or contempt toward the analyst. It should be borne in mind that all transference reactions are essentially ambivalent. What appears clinically is only the surface.

For transference reactions to take place in the analytic situation, the patient must be willing and able to risk some temporary regression in terms of ego functions and object relations. The patient must have an ego capable of temporarily regressing to transference reactions, but this regression must be partial and reversible so that the patient can be treated analytically and still live in the real world. People who do not dare regress from reality and those who cannot return readily to reality are poor risks for psychoanalysis. Freud divided the neuroses into two groups on the basis of whether or not a patient could develop and maintain a relatively cohesive set of transference reactions and still function in the analysis and in the external world. Patients with a "transference neurosis" could do this, while patients suffering from a "narcissistic neurosis" could not (Freud, 1916-17, pp. 341, 414-415, 420-423).

Freud also used the term *transference neurosis* to describe that constellation of transference reactions in which the analyst and the analysis have become the center of the patient's emotional life and the patient's neurotic conflicts are relived in the analytic situation (Freud, 1914c, p. 154). All the important features of the patient's illness will be relived or re-enacted in the analytic situation (Freud,

1905a, pp. 118-119; 1914c, pp. 150-154; 1916-17, Chapter XXVII).

Psychoanalytic technique is so geared as to insure the maximal development of the transference neurosis. The relative anonymity of the analyst, his nonintrusiveness, the so-called "rule of abstinence," and the "mirrorlike" behavior of the analyst all have the purpose of preserving a relatively uncontaminated field for the budding transference neurosis (Fenichel, 1941, p. 72; Greenacre, 1954; Gill, 1954). The transference neurosis is an artifact of the analytic situation; it can be undone only by the analytic work. It serves as a transition from illness to health.

On the one hand, the transference neurosis is the most important vehicle for success in psychoanalysis; on the other, it is the most frequent cause of therapeutic failure (Freud, 1912a, 1914c; Glover, 1955, Chapt. VII, VIII). The transference neurosis can be resolved only by analysis; other procedures may change its form, but will only perpetuate it (Gill, 1954).

Psychoanalysis is the only form of psychotherapy which attempts to resolve the transference reactions by systematically and thoroughly analyzing them. In some briefer or diluted versions of psychoanalysis one does so only partially and selectively. Thus, one might analyze only the negative transference when it threatens to disrupt the treatment or one analyzes only as deeply as required for the patient to be able to work in the therapeutic situation. In such cases there is always a residual of unresolved transference reactions after the treatment is completed. This implies that there is some unanalyzed neurosis left unchanged.

In the anti-analytic forms of psychotherapy the transference reactions are not analyzed but gratified and manipulated. The therapist assumes the role of some past figure, real or fantasied, and gratifies some infantile wish of the patient's. The therapist might act like a loving or encouraging parent, or like a punishing moralist, and the patient might feel some temporary improvement or even "cured." But these "transference cures" are fleeting and last only as long as the idealized transference to the therapist is untouched (Fenichel, 1945a, pp. 559-561; Nunberg, 1932, pp. 335-340).

1.313 The Resistances

Resistance refers to all the forces within the patient which oppose the procedures and processes of psychoanalytic work. To a greater or lesser degree it is present from the beginning to the end of treatment (Freud, 1912a). The resistances defend the *status quo* of the patient's neurosis. The resistances oppose the analyst, the analytic work, and the patient's reasonable ego. Resistance is an operational concept, it is not newly created by the analysis. The analytic situation becomes the arena where the resistances reveal themselves.

The resistances are repetitions of all the defensive operations that the patient has used in his past life. All varieties of psychic phenomena may be used for the purpose of resistance, but no matter what its source, the resistance operates through the patient's ego. Although some aspects of a resistance may be conscious, an essential part is carried out by the unconscious ego.

Psychoanalytic therapy is characterized by the thorough and systematic analysis of resistances. It is the task of the psychoanalyst to uncover how the patient resists, what he is resisting, and why he does so. The immediate cause of a resistance is always the avoidance of some painful affect like anxiety, guilt or shame. Behind this motive will be found an instinctual impulse which has triggered the painful affect. Ultimately one will find that it is the fear of a traumatic state which the resistance is attempting to ward off (A. Freud, 1936, pp. 45-70; Fenichel, 1945a, pp. 128-167).

There are many ways of classifying resistances. The most important practical distinction is to differentiate the *ego-syntonic* resistances from the *ego-alien* ones. If a patient feels a resistance is alien to him, he is ready to work on it analytically. If it is ego syntonic, he may deny its existence, belittle its importance, or rationalize it away. One of the crucial early steps in analyzing a resistance is to convert it into an ego-alien resistance for the patient. Once this has been accomplished, the patient will form a working alliance with the analyst. He will have temporarily and partially identified himself with the analyst in his willingness to work analytically on his resistances.

Other forms of psychotherapy attempt to evade or overcome resistances by means of suggestions or by using drugs or exploiting the transference relationship. In the covering-up or supportive therapies the therapist attempts to strengthen the resistances. This may well be necessary in patients who may be slipping into a psychotic state. It is only in psychoanalysis that the therapist seeks to uncover the cause, purpose, mode, and history of the resistances (Knight, 1952).

1.32 ANALYZING THE PATIENT'S MATERIAL

In classical psychoanalysis, a great number of therapeutic procedures are employed in varying degrees. It is characteristic of all techniques that are considered analytic that they have the direct aim of increasing the patient's insight about himself. Some procedures do not add insight per se, but strengthen those ego functions which are required for gaining understanding. For example, abreaction may permit a sufficient discharge of instinctual tension so that a beleaguered ego will no longer feel imminently endangered. The more secure ego is then enabled to observe, think, remember, and judge, functions it had lost in the acute anxiety state. Insight now becomes possible. Abreaction is one of the *nonanalytic* procedures that is frequently used in psychoanalytic treatment. It is often an indispensable prerequisite for insight.

The *anti-analytic* procedures are those which block or lessen the capacity for insight and understanding. The use of any measure or course of action which diminishes the ego functions of observing, thinking, remembering, and judging belongs in this category. Some obvious examples are the administering of certain drugs and intoxicants, quick and easy reassurances, certain kinds of transference gratifications, diversions, etc.

The most important analytic procedure is *interpretation*; all others are subordinated to it both theoretically and practically. All analytic procedures are either steps which lead to an interpretation or make an interpretation effective (E. Bibring, 1954; Gill, 1954; Menninger, 1958).

The term "analyzing" is a shorthand expression which refers to those insight-furthering techniques. It usually includes four distinct procedures: *confrontation, clarification, interpretation,* and *working through*. In the ensuing chapters there will be ample discussion and clinical examples of how each of these procedures are employed. Here I shall limit myself to working definitions and simple illustrations.

The first step in analyzing a psychic phenomenon is *confrontation*. The phenomenon in question has to be made evident, has to be made explicit to the patient's conscious ego. For example, before I can interpret the reason a patient may have for avoiding a certain subject in the hour, I first have to get him to face that he is avoiding something. Sometimes the patient himself will recognize this fact and it will be unnecessary for me to do so. However, before any further analytic steps are taken, it must be certain that the patient discerns within himself the psychic phenomenon we are attempting to analyze.

Confrontation leads to the next step, *clarification*. Usually these two procedures blend together, but I find it valuable to separate them because there are instances where each of them cause distinct problems. Clarification refers to those activities that aim at placing the psychic phenomenon being analyzed in sharp focus. The significant details have to be dug out and carefully separated from extraneous matter. The particular variety or pattern of the phenomenon in question has to be singled out and isolated.

Let us take a simple example. I confront a patient, Mr. N., with the fact that he is resisting and he recognizes that it is indeed so, he does seem to be running away from something. The patient's further associations may then lead in the direction of revealing why he is resisting or what he is resisting. Let us take the former instance. The resistant patient's associations lead him to talk of various events of the past weekend. Mr. N. went to a P.T.A. meeting at his daughter's school and felt abashed by the presence of so many wealthy-appearing parents. This reminds him of his childhood and how he hated to see his father attempt to ingratiate himself with his wealthy clients. His father was a tyrant in his dealings with his employees and an "ass-kisser" with the rich. He was afraid of his father until he left home to go to college. Then he developed a contempt for him. He still has a feeling of contempt for him, but he doesn't show it. After all, it would serve no purpose, his father is too old to change. His father must be getting close to sixty, his hair is almost all white, "whatever is left of it." The patient becomes silent.

I had the impression that Mr. N.'s associations were pointing to certain feelings he had about me and it was those feelings which had caused him to be resistant in the early part of the hour. I also felt that this probably had to do with contempt and, more precisely, the patient's fear of expressing his contempt for me directly. When the patient became silent, I said that I wondered if he didn't feel some contempt for another white-haired man. The patient's face flushed and his first response was to say: "I suppose you think I was talking about you. Well, it's just not true. I don't feel any contempt for you—why should I? You treat me very well—most of the time. I have no idea how you treat your family or your friends. But, that's none of my business. Who knows, maybe you are one of those men who steps on the little guy and makes up to the 'big shots.' I don't know and I don't care."

At that moment I pursued the point. I replied that I felt he was relieved not to know how I really behaved outside the hour. If he knew he might feel contempt and he would be afraid to express it to me directly. Mr. N. was silent for a few seconds and answered that if he imagined me doing something contemptible, he wouldn't know what to do with the information. This reminded him of an occasion a few weeks back. He had been in a restaurant and heard a man's angry voice belaboring a waiter. For a fleeting instant the voice sounded like mine and the back of the man's head resembled mine. He was relieved a few moments later to see that it wasn't true.

It was now possible to point out to the patient that he was trying to avoid feeling contempt for me because if he were to do so, he would be afraid of expressing it, just as he had with his father. It was this specific complex pattern of emotional responses that had to be singled out for clarification before one could go on with the further analysis of his resistances.

The third step in analyzing is *interpretation*. This is the procedure which distinguishes psychoanalysis from all other psychotherapies because in psychoanalysis interpretation is the ultimate and decisive instrument. Every other procedure prepares for interpretation or amplifies an interpretation and may itself have to be interpreted. To interpret means to make an unconscious phenomenon conscious. More precisely, it means to make conscious the unconscious meaning, source, history, mode, or cause of a given psychic event. This usually requires more than a single intervention. The analyst uses his own unconscious, his empathy and intuition, as well as his theoretical knowledge, for arriving at an interpretation. By interpreting we go beyond what is readily observable and we assign meaning and causality to a psychological phenomenon. We need the patient's responses to determine the validity of our interpretation (E. Bibring, 1954; Fenichel, 1945a; and Additional Reading List).

The procedures of clarification and interpretation are intimately interwoven. Very often clarification leads to an interpretation which leads back to a further clarification (Kris, 1951). The clinical case cited above indicates this. Let me illustrate an example of interpretation and validation from the same patient.

In an hour, some two weeks after the session reported above, Mr. N. reports a fragment of a dream. All he can remember is that he is waiting for a red traffic light to change when he feels that someone has bumped into him from behind. He rushes out in fury and finds out, with relief, it was only a boy on a bicycle. There was no damage to his car. The associations led to Mr. N.'s love of cars, especially sport cars. He loved the sensation, in particular, of whizzing by those fat old expensive cars. The expensive cars seem so sturdy, but they fall apart in a few years. The little sports car of his can outrun, outclimb, outlast the Cadillacs, the Lincolns, and the Rolls Royces. He knows this is an exaggeration, but he likes to think so. It tickles him. This must be a carry-over from his athletic days when he loved to be the underdog who defeated the favorite. His father was a sports fan who always belittled my patient's achievements. His father always hinted that he had been a great athlete, but he never substantiated it. He was an exhibitionist, but Mr. N. doubted whether his father really could perform. His father would flirt with a waitress in a café or make sexual remarks about women passing by, but he seemed to be showing off. If he were really sexual, he wouldn't resort to that.

It is clear that the patient's material concerns comparing himself with his father in terms of sexual ability. It also deals with people who pretend to be what they are not. The strongest affect in his associations was the moment when he said he was "tickled" by the fantasy of beating out the big cars. He knew this was a distortion, but he liked imagining it. In the dream his fury changes to relief when he discovers he has been bumped by "only a boy on a bicycle." It seemed to me that these two affect-laden elements must contain the key to the meaning of the dream and the analytic hour.

I interpreted to *myself* that the boy on the bicycle means a boy masturbating. The red light probably refers to prostitution since "red-light district" is a common term for those areas where prostitutes congregate. I knew my patient claimed to love his wife but preferred sex with prostitutes. Up until this point in the analysis the patient had no memories concerning the sexual life of his parents. However, he often mentioned his father's flirtations with waitresses, which I took to be screen memories. I therefore felt that I would point my interpretation in the direction of his adult attitude of superiority versus his childhood concern with the sexual life of his father. (I deliberately neglected, for the time being, all the references to bumping, behind, anger, etc.)

I said to Mr. N. toward the end of the hour that I felt he was struggling with his feelings about his father's sexual life. He seemed to be saying his father was sexually not a very potent man, but I wondered if he had always thought so. The patient responded rather quickly, in fact, a bit too quickly. In essence he was in haste to agree that his father always seemed to him to be arrogant, boastful, and pretentious. He didn't know what his sex life was like with his mother, but he is quite sure it couldn't have been very satisfactory. His mother was sickly and unhappy. She spent most of her life complaining to him about his father. Mr. N. was quite sure his mother disliked sex, although he couldn't prove it.

I intervened at this point and said that I supposed the idea that his mother rejected sex with his father tickled him. The patient said that it didn't tickle him, but he had to admit it gave him a sense of satisfaction, a sense of triumph over the "old boy." In fact, he now recalls finding some "girlie magazines" (magazines with photos of nude women) hidden in his father's bedroom. He also recalls that he once found a packet of condoms under his father's pillow when he was an adolescent and he thought, "My father must be going to prostitutes."

I then intervened and pointed out that the condoms under the father's pillow seemed to indicate more obviously that his father used the condoms with his mother, who slept in the same bed. However, Mr. N. *wanted* to believe his wish-fulfilling fantasy: mother doesn't want sex with father and father is not very potent. The patient was silent and the hour ended.

The next day he began by telling me that he was furious with me as he left my office. As he drove away he drove wildly, trying to pass all the cars on the freeway, especially the expensive ones. Then he got the sudden impulse to race against a Rolls Royce if he could only find one. A fleeting thought crossed his mind. On the front of the Rolls Royce are the initials R. R. Those are Dr. Greenson's initials, he suddenly realized. With that he began to laugh, all by himself in the car. "The old boy is probably right," he thought, "it does tickle me to imagine that my mother preferred me and I could beat out my father. Later I wondered whether this had something to do with my own screwed-up sex life with my wife."

I suggest that this clinical vignette illustrates the complicated steps that are involved in making even a simple interpretation and also how one has to wait for the patient's clinical responses to determine whether one is on the right track. The patient's affective response to my first intervention, his haste in responding, indicated I had touched something quite alive. The new memories of the "girlie magazines" and the condoms confirmed that I was essentially correct. His reactions after the hour, the anger, the association to Rolls Royce, the laughter and connecting it up to his own sex life seemed to indicate that the dosage and timing were in order. (In Volume II more will be said about interpretation.)

The fourth step in "analyzing" is *working through*. Working through refers to a complex set of procedures and processes which occur after an insight has been given. The analytic work which makes it possible for an insight to lead to change is the work of working through (Greenson, 1965b). It refers in the main to the repetitive, progressive and elaborate explorations of the resistances which prevent an insight from leading to change. In addition to the broadening and deepening of the analysis of resistances, reconstructions are also of particular importance. A variety of circular processes are set in motion by working through in which insight, memory, and behavior change influence each other (Kris, 1956a, 1956b.)

In order to illustrate the concept of working through let us return to the case of Mr. N. In the first hour I reported how I had interpreted his wishful fantasy that his mother didn't like sex, and rejected his father sexually, and his father was sexually impotent. He did not like this interpretation, but later that day realized it seemed to be correct. By the time he came for his next hour he had amplified this insight and connected it to the fact that his own sex life with his wife was disturbed. What was most difficult for him was to look at his wife the day after sexual relations. He felt she must abhor him for having behaved sensually. When I questioned this, he connected his reactions to a childhood memory of his mother humiliating him for masturbating.

In the course of the next several weeks, however, Mr. N. became increasingly aware of the fact that alongside of his wish that his wife enjoy herself sensually with him, *he* had contempt for *her* when she became sexually excited. The feeling that she abhorred him after intercourse was a projection of his own feelings. Shortly thereafter Mr. N. recalled a memory of his mother winking slyly at his father when they saw two dogs copulating on the street. At first there was little affect connected to this memory. However, the patient behaved strangely toward his wife at this time. He found her utterly unappealing, avoided her altogether sexually, and sought out prostitutes. I interpreted to him that he seemed to be acting as he imagined his father had.

The patient replied to this that he didn't blame his father for avoiding his mother sexually. Although his mother had been an attractive woman, he recalled some memories when she was in bed and she was "not exactly a sex pot." Her face seemed flushed and sweaty, her hair was matted down, and there was a repulsive odor. These memories were associated to sickness and to menstruation. I interpreted that menstruating was related to bitches being in heat. Later, I reconstructed for Mr. N. the likelihood that the picture of his mother with the flushed, sweaty face, and the repulsive odor was connected to seeing his mother in sexual intercourse with his father. I suggested the possibility that the notion of his mother not liking sex and the many memories of his father's flirtations with other women were attempts to contradict the unconscious memory of having seen his mother sexually excited by his father. I pointed out that the memory of his mother winking at his father while watching two dogs mating was also a screen memory of this kind.

Mr. N. agreed that my reconstruction seemed plausible, but "it left him cold." In a following hour I told him that his neglect of his wife sexually and his pursuit of prostitutes were further attempts "to prove" that good women, married women, women who are the mothers of children, don't care for sex and husbands of such women don't have sex with them. The weekend following this interpretation the patient reported having the most satisfying sexual experience of his life thus far, with his wife. This was followed by several weeks of resistance to analysis and to sex based on the idea all grownups are hypocrites and liars except for a few rebels and mavericks.

Once again Mr. N. was struggling with his childhood conflicts about the sexual life of his parents. If he had to give up the denial of the existence of their sexuality, he hated them and despised them for their hypocrisy. His mother winking at his father epitomized this. His wife was also a "phoney" and so was I and my wife. The only honest people were those who shunned society and convention. It was more honest to pay for sex in cash than to buy it with expensive homes, clothes, furs, cars, etc. I interpreted to him that this seemed to be an attempt to degrade his mother and father and other married people because of his rage and envy of his mother's winking. Underneath his contempt was envy. He would have reacted quite differently if his mother had winked at him and not his father.

Mr. N. reacted to this interpretation and further reconstruction with sullen anger and resistance. Then slowly over a period of weeks, he began to mull over the relationship between contempt and envy. He realized there might be some merit to my formulation. He begrudgingly admitted I was right and he hated to give up the idea that mother didn't want sex with father and preferred no sex at all. If she had sex, she did it submissively and then he made his father impotent in his fantasy. The picture of his mother sexually excited by father enraged him or made him indignant. He felt like a little boy or like a superior adult. Maybe he ought to let them have their own sex life and he ought to concentrate on his own bedroom.

I believe this clinical material illustrates some of the work that goes on in working through. What I have described covers a period of some six months. It begins with the dream of the patient in his sports car at a red light being bumped by a boy on a bicycle. On and off since then we worked on the problem of his emotional reactions to the sex life of his parents and how that determined his own sexual difficulties. On the surface there was superiority toward the father and sympathy toward the mother. Father was an impotent braggart and mother a reluctant nonvirgin. Then, against great resistances we found flashes of anger toward mother and father. Then mother became repulsive and he had contempt for both parents. Toward the end of this period we uncovered envy of the parental sex life. Finally, Mr. N. got the notion that perhaps they are entitled to the privacy of their bedroom and he ought to do likewise.

This was not the end of Mr. N.'s sexual problem, but it does demonstrate the achievement of a significant amount of valuable insight. There were many back-and-forth movements, but progress continued. For instance, the theme of homosexuality was not pursued during this period, but was taken up at later times. There were intrusions of other problems, and for shorter or longer periods of time sexual problems receded into the background or were complicated by admixtures of aggression. There were also regressive phases when the libido was involved on other levels. My aim, however, was to offer an example of working through as it occurs in psychoanalysis.

It should be noted that some of the work of working through is done by the patient outside of the analytic hour. Working through is the most time-consuming element in psychoanalytic therapy. Only rarely does insight lead very quickly to a change in behavior; and then it is usually transitory or remains isolated and unintegrated. Ordinarily it requires a great deal of time to overcome the powerful forces which resist change and to establish lasting structural changes. The interesting relationship between the work of mourning and working through, the importance of the repetition compulsion and the death instinct will be discussed in Volume II (see also Freud, 1914c, 1926a, 1937a; Fenichel, 1941, Chapt. VI; Greenacre, 1956; Kris, 1956a, 1956b; Greenson, 1965b).

The four steps that I have outlined represent a schematized version of what is implied by the concept of analyzing a psychic event. All these steps are necessary, but some may be done spontaneously by the patient, particularly the confrontation or part of the clarification. These steps do not follow in the exact order described, since each procedure can produce new resistances which will have to be taken up first. Or, an interpretation can precede a clarification and can facilitate a clarification of a given phenomenon.

An additional variable is the fact that the imponderables of everyday life can intrude into the patient's life and take precedence for psychoeconomic reasons over everything else that is going on in the analysis. Nevertheless, confrontation, clarification, interpretation, and working through are the four basic procedures that the analyst performs when he analyzes.

1.33 THE WORKING ALLIANCE

The psychoanalytic patient enters analysis because his neurotic suffering impels him to embark on this difficult therapeutic journey. His problem is severe enough to induce him to undertake this long-term, painful, costly program. His ego functions and his capacity for object relations[2] are, despite his neurosis, considered healthy enough to endure the rigors of psychoanalytic therapy. Only a relatively healthy neurotic can be psychoanalyzed, without major modifications or deviations.

The psychoanalytic patient produces the material for the treatment via free association, transference reactions, and resistances. The analyst uses the procedures of confrontation, clarification, interpretation, and working through. But all of this does not fully explain

---

[2] I find the term "object relations" and similar terms, such as "love objects" and "lost objects," unsatisfactory. They seem to cast an impersonal and detached quality upon concepts which are fraught with intense personal meaning. Nevertheless, I have continued to use them throughout because they have gained wide acceptance in psychoanalytic circles and I find no better replacement that would meet all the requirements implied by these terms. The term "object" goes back to the notion that the id needs objects to satisfy the drives. In this sense, the original need-satisfying objects had little distinction or uniqueness other than they were need-satisfying.

what happens or fails to happen in the course of therapy. There is one other major therapeutic ingredient which is vital for the success or failure of psychoanalytic treatment. I am referring to the "working alliance," which is not precisely a technical procedure or a therapeutic process but is necessary for both (Greenson, 1965a). Here I shall only present an outline of the subject. For a full discussion of the working alliance see Section 3.5.

The working alliance is the relatively nonneurotic, rational relationship between patient and analyst which makes it possible for the patient to work purposefully in the analytic situation. Freud (1913b, p. 139) wrote of an "effective transference," a rapport, which must be established before an interpretation should be given to the patient. Fenichel (1941, p. 27) described a "rational" transference, Stone (1961, p. 104) a "mature" transference, Zetzel (1956) a "therapeutic alliance," and Nacht (1958a), the analyst's "presence," all of which refer to a similar concept.

The clinical manifestations of this working alliance are the patient's willingness to carry out the various procedures of psychoanalysis and his ability to work analytically with the regressive and painful insights which arise. The alliance is formed between the patient's reasonable ego and the analyst's analyzing ego (Sterba, 1934). The significant occurrence is a partial and temporary identification that the patient makes with the analyst's attitude and method of work which the patient experiences firsthand in the regular analytic sessions.

The patient, the analyst, and the analytic setting contribute to the formation of the working alliance. The awareness of neurotic suffering and of the possibility of help from the analyst impels the patient to seek out and work in the analytic situation. The patient's ability to form a relatively rational, desexualized, and de-aggressified relationship to the analyst stems from his capacity to have formed such neutralized relationships in his past life. The patient's ego functions play a decisive role, since the capacity to establish a multiple relationship with the analyst is possible only with a resilient ego.

The analyst contributes to the working alliance by his consistent emphasis on understanding and insight, by his continual analysis of the resistances, and by his compassionate, empathic, straightforward, and nonjudgmental attitudes (Freud, 1912a, p. 105;

1913b, p. 123; Fenichel, 1941, p. 85; Sterba, 1929, pp. 371-372). The analytic setting facilitates the development of the working alliance by the frequency of the visits, long duration of the treatment, use of the couch, silence, etc. This promotes not only regression and neurotic transference reactions but also the working alliance (Greenacre, 1954).

The analyst's way of working, his therapeutic style, and the analytic setting produce an "analytic atmosphere," which is an important means of inducing the patient to accept on trial something hitherto repelled. This atmosphere promotes the working alliance and entices the patient temporarily and partially to identify with the analyst's analytic point of view. The analytic atmosphere can also become a resistance when it casts an aura of make-believe and "not real life" over the analytic work.

The working alliance is that part of the relationship to the analyst which makes it possible for the patient to cooperate in the analytic hour. Under this benign influence the patient tries to understand the analyst's instructions and insights, reviews and mulls over the interpretations and reconstructions, which aids in the integration and assimilation of the insights. The working alliance along with the neurotic suffering provide the incentive for doing the analytic work; the bulk of the raw material is provided by the patient's neurotic transference reactions.

In order to analyze the transference neurosis successfully, it is necessary for the patient to have developed a reliable working alliance with the analyst. The transference neurosis is the vehicle that enables the patient to bring the warded-off, inaccessible material into the analytic situation. The patient's ability to oscillate between the working alliance and the neurotic transference reactions is a prerequisite for doing the psychoanalytic work. This ability is parallel to the split in the patient's ego between a reasonable, observing, analyzing ego, and an experiencing, subjective, irrational ego.

This split can be seen in free association. When the patient permits himself to be carried away by a painful memory or fantasy, the experiencing ego is in the foreground, and there is no awareness of the meaning or appropriateness of the emotions at the time. If the analyst were to intervene at this point, the patient's reasonable ego would come back into the fore and the patient would now be able to recognize that the affects in question came from the past;

there would be less anxiety, and perhaps eventually less distorted derivatives would come up. This splitting off of ego functions can be seen most clearly when one analyzes transference resistances (Sterba, 1929, p. 379). The capacity to split off ego functions also makes it possible for the patient to separate the working alliance from the neurotic transference. To summarize: the working alliance provides the day-to-day motivation as well as the capacity to perform the analytic work. The essential warded-off, inaccessible raw material is provided by the neurotic transference reactions, primarily by the *transference neurosis*.

1.34 THE NONANALYTIC THERAPEUTIC PROCEDURES
AND PROCESSES

In classical psychoanalysis other varieties of therapeutic procedures and processes are utilized to some degree, but they serve the purpose of preparing for insight or of making it effective. All nonanalytic measures eventually have to become the subject of analysis themselves (E. Bibring, 1954). This brief discussion will be limited to the three major nonanalytic therapeutic agents.

Abreaction or catharsis refers to the discharge of warded-off emotions and impulses. Breuer and Freud (1893-95), once considered it a curative method of treatment. Today abreaction is considered valuable in giving the patient a sense of conviction about the reality of his unconscious processes. Emotional intensity may vivify the details of an experience which might otherwise remain vague and unreal. The expression of affects and impulses may bring a temporary sense of subjective relief, but this is not an end in itself and, in fact, may become a source of resistance.

For example, a patient may confess some guilt-evoking event to the analyst. Then, feeling relieved, he may avoid the subject instead of analyzing its cause, history, meaning, etc. However, it is important to help a patient relive the emotions of a traumatic experience in order to recapture important details that might otherwise be overlooked.

When dealing with experiences of traumatic or near-traumatic proportions, the patient should be encouraged to re-experience as much of the intensity as he can bear. The main purpose is to enable the patient to discharge a sufficient quantity of tension so that he can better cope with the remainder. For example, a patient in a chronic depression should be allowed to experience enough acute grief to allow him to work effectively analytically. In the analysis of a patient of mine with such a problem, for several months it was necessary for him to spend part of each hour sobbing uncontrollably before he was able to work analytically on his depression. The same principle holds true for anxiety states.

Abreaction in itself is nonanalytic, since it does not directly bring insight. In the clinical case material throughout this book, there will be many illustrations of how abreaction may be used in strictly psychoanalytic therapy.

Suggestion refers to the induction of ideas, emotions, and impulses in a patient, independent of, or to the exclusion of, the patient's realistic thinking (E. Bibring, 1954). It is present in all forms of psychotherapy because it is derived from the parent-child relationship, and people in distress readily assume the emotional position of a child toward the therapist-parent.

Suggestion is valuable in psychoanalysis as long as it helps the patient enter and work in the analytic situation. Although the psychoanalyst does not guarantee great results from his treatment, the patient will have an unrealistic degree of confidence and trust in him because of the suggestive influences stemming from his psychoanalyst's attitudes. My patients sense an underlying feeling of optimism in me, despite my verbal utterances or my conscious opinions.

During the course of an analysis, there are occasions when it is advisable to encourage a patient to try to endure some pain or frustration. It is better if the reason for this attitude can be explained. Sometimes one can only say something like, "You might feel better if you face it." Usually such suggestions or reassurances are successful. Or one may say such things as: "You will remember your dreams when you are no longer afraid," and the patient will begin to recall his dreams.

There are two main dangers in using suggestion. One is using it unnecessarily and seducing the patient to become habituated to this regressive means of support. The other danger is using it without realizing it. Then the suggestive influence of the analyst will not be analyzed and the patient will acquire, in effect, a new neurotic symptom from the unanalyzed suggestions of his analyst. This will happen when interpretations are given as dogma. Patients will then cling to the interpretation as they do to an obsessive idea. Glover's paper [1931] on inexact interpretations and suggestion is a classic on this subject (1955, pp. 353-366).

The crux of the matter is that suggestion and reassurance eventually have to be openly acknowledged, brought into the analytic situation, and their effects analyzed.

Manipulation refers to an evocative activity undertaken by the therapist without the knowledge of the patient. The term has acquired an unsavory connotation in psychoanalytic circles because it has been misused by the so-called "wild analysts." However, it is just as much a part of analytic therapy as suggestion and abreaction. It is often used to further various processes which arise during a classical therapeutic analysis. (See Gill [1954] for the classical view of this point and Alexander [1954a, 1954b] for an opposing view.)

It is a manipulation to remain quiet in an hour in order to allow an affect to grow in strength so that it becomes more demonstrable. It is a manipulation not to analyze the transference in order to allow it to reach a certain intensity or to allow it to regress. It is a manipulation to bring up your impending departure when your patient does not mention it. However, all these manipulations have an indirect analytic purpose—an insight-furthering purpose. They are to be acknowledged if questioned and the reactions to them analyzed. Other manipulations are more subtle. For example, tone of voice and intonation have evocative effects which can bring reactions and memories into the analysis and thereby further the analytic processes. What is crucial is being aware of a manipulation, or at least of the possibility of having used it unknowingly. Ultimately it must be allowed into the analytic arena and as thoroughly analyzed as any other intervention of the analyst, real or imagined (Gill, 1954).

The *deliberate and conscious* assumption of roles or attitudes is' anti-analytic since it creates an unanalyzable situation. There is an element of deception and trickery which eventuates in a realistic mistrust of the therapist. I do not question the fact that it may be necessary in certain psychotherapeutic situations; but it makes analysis impossible. Eissler's contribution on this problem is both thorough and systematic (1950b). (For a divergent point of view see Alexander, French, et al., 1946, and the Additional Reading List.)

A final word on this introduction to psychoanalytic technique.

The terms "handling" and "management" of transference, etc., refer to the addition of nonanalytic measures to analytic procedures used within the framework of psychoanalytic therapy. Clinical examples throughout the volumes will illustrate this point. The "art" of psychoanalytic technique as it is used in classical psychoanalysis is based on the blending of the analytic with the nonanalytic procedures. It is hard to teach. The principles of psychoanalytic techniques are more readily teachable. In these volumes I intend to focus primarily on the basic components of so-called classical psychoanalytic technique.

1.4 Indications and Contraindications for Psychoanalytic Therapy: A Preliminary View

The problem of determining the indications and contraindications for psychoanalytic treatment hinges on two separate but related issues. The first and most important question we have to answer is: Is the patient analyzable? The second and contingent question is: Will psychoanalytic treatment *best* serve the patient's needs? I would like to amplify this latter issue by a clinical example.

Let us assume you have a patient who desires psychotherapy and you believe he is able to work effectively and well in the analytic situation. Would you advise him to undertake psychoanalysis if you discover that he is about to be drafted into the armed forces? Psychoanalysis is a long-term treatment, ordinarily requiring three to five years of time. The total life situation must be considered in evaluating whether or not you would recommend this form of psychotherapy.

The problem of analyzability is a complex one because it depends on many different qualities and traits of the patient, both healthy and pathological. Furthermore, it is also necessary to be thoroughly familiar with the many exacting demands that the psychoanalytic process and procedure make on the patient. The brief summary of theory and technique thus far presented permits us only a preliminary view. We shall have to postpone a more definitive discussion until the later chapters.

Freud (1905a) recognized quite early that single criteria, no matter how important or clear-cut, do not permit an accurate prediction of a patient's analyzability. One has to try to assess the total personality, and that is extremely difficult to evaluate after a few preliminary interviews (Knight, 1952). Yet it is precisely then that the therapist has to make his recommendations as to the choice of treatment. Prolonged preliminary interviews and psychological testing may help with certain patients; in the present state of our knowledge, however, even this combination of approaches does not offer reliable predictions in many cases. In addition, prolonged interviewing as well as psychological tests can produce disturbing side effects.

The traditional, medical approach for determining the form of treatment is first to arrive at a diagnosis. Freud (1916-17, p. 428) seemed to have this in mind when he differentiated the transference neuroses from the narcissistic neuroses. He believed that since psychotic patients are essentially narcissistic, they could not be treated by psychoanalysis since they could not develop a transference neurosis. This distinction remains essentially valid, but today many patients seek treatment who cannot be categorized that precisely because they have features of both neurosis and psychosis. Furthermore, in recent times some analysts believe it is possible to do classical analysis with psychotic cases and to achieve good therapeutic results (Rosenfeld, 1952). Most psychoanalysts, however, are of the opinion that narcissistically fixated patients require deviations from the standard psychoanalytic procedure (Frank, 1956; M. Wexler, 1960). Knapp and his co-workers (1960) reviewed 100 applicants for psychoanalytic treatment and found that the judges rejected those considered schizoid, borderline or psychotic. This is in accordance with Freud's views about the treatability of the transference neurosis as compared to the narcissistic neuroses. I believe most analysts would still agree with this point of view (Fenichel, 1945a; Glover, 1958; and Waldhorn, 1960).

In line with this thinking, psychoanalytic therapy would be indicated for anxiety hysteria, conversion hysteria, obsessional and compulsion neurosis, psychoneurotic depressions, and many of the character neuroses and so-called "psychosomatic" illnesses. It would be contraindicated for the various forms of schizophrenia and manic-depressive psychosis. Other character disorders such as impulse neuroses, perversions, addictions, delinquencies, and borderline cases would be of questionable analyzability and would have to be determined by special features of the individual case (Fenichel, 1945a; Glover, 1955, 1958).

There is no doubt that the clinical diagnosis can be of value in determining a patient's suitability for analysis, but unfortunately it often takes a great deal of time to arrive at a definitive diagnosis. Sometimes the presenting psychopathology is merely a superficial screen for more malignant pathology which is hidden and latent. The presence of hysterical symptoms does not mean the patient is essentially a hysteric; or, vice versa, bizarre symptomatology may still have the structure of hysteria. Symptoms are not as bound to specific diagnostic syndromes as we used to believe (Greenson, 1959a; Rangell, 1959; and Aarons, 1962). Sometimes one can arrive at a reliable diagnosis only at the end of a long analysis.

It used to be assumed that the presence of a phobia indicated anxiety hysteria, but today we know that phobias may be present in hysterics, obsessionals, depressive and schizoid patients. The same is true for conversion symptoms, psychosomatic symptoms, sexual inhibitions, etc. The presence of a specific symptom reveals something about some aspects of the patient's pathology. It does not tell us whether this pathological formation is central or peripheral, whether it is a predominant or minor factor in the patient's personality structure.

Although the diagnosis tells us a great deal about the pathology, it may indicate relatively little about the healthy resources of the patient in question (Knight, 1952; Waldhorn, 1960). Some obsessional cases make excellent patients and others are unanalyzable. The questionable categories of patients, e.g., perversions and borderline cases, have varying degrees of healthy resources. Yet, it is their supply of assets, not the pathology, which may be the decisive factor. The assessment of the total patient, rather than the clinical diagnosis or the pathology, has to be the center of focus. Knight (1952) has stressed this in the past and Anna Freud's (1965) new book makes this its major thesis in regard to children. (See also Anna Freud, et al., 1965.)

A valuable method of approach to the problem of analyzability is to explore the patient's endowment in regard to the specific demands of psychoanalytic therapy. As stated previously, psychoanalytic treatment is a time-consuming, long-range, costly therapy that is by its very nature frequently painful. Therefore, only patients who are strongly motivated will work wholeheartedly in the analytic situation. The patient's symptoms or discordant traits of character must cause him sufficient suffering to enable him to endure the rigors of the treatment. The neurotic misery must interfere with important aspects of the patient's life, and the awareness of his plight must be sustained if the patient is to remain motivated. Trivial problems and the wishes of relatives, lovers or employers do not justify undertaking psychoanalytic treatment. Scientific curiosity or the wish for professional advancement will not motivate an analysand to undergo a deep analytic experience, unless it is also combined with an adequate therapeutic need. Patients who demand quick results or who have a large secondary gain from their illness will also not have the necessary motivation. Masochists who need their neurotic suffering may enter analysis and later become attached to the pain of the treatment. They present a difficult problem for appraisal in terms of motivation to get well. Children are quite differently motivated than adults and also need to be assessed from a different point of view (A. Freud, 1965, Chapt. 6).

Psychoanalysis requires the patient to have the capacity to carry out, more or less consistently and repeatedly, ego functions which are in contradiction to one another. For example, in order to approximate free association the patient must be able to regress in his thinking, to let things come up passively, to give up control of his thoughts and feelings, and to partially renounce his reality testing. Yet we also expect the patient to understand us when we communicate to him, to do some analytic work on his own, to control his actions and feelings after the hour, and to be in contact with reality. Despite his neurosis, the analyzable patient is expected to have resilient and flexible ego functions (Knight, 1952; Loewenstein, 1963).

We also require the patient to possess the capacity to regress and rebound from it in his relationship to his psychoanalyst. He is expected to develop a variety of regressive transference reactions, sustain them, and also work on them as a co-worker of the analyst (Stone, 1961; Greenson, 1965a). Narcissistically oriented and psychotic patients are generally not suitable for psychoanalysis (Freud, 1916-17; Knapp, et al., 1960). The ability to empathize is essential for psychological-mindedness and is dependent on the capacity for temporary and partial identification with others (Greenson, 1960).

It is necessary for effective communication between patient and analyst and must be present in both. Withdrawn, emotionally uninvolved people are not good subjects for psychoanalytic therapy.

Free association eventually leads to the exposure of painful, intimate details of one's personal life. It follows, therefore, that a suitable patient must possess a high degree of honesty and integrity of character. It also requires the ability to communicate intelligibly about subtle combinations of emotions. People with severe thinking problems and speech disorders are also poor risks (Fenichel, 1945a; Knapp, et al., 1960). Impulse-ridden characters, people who cannot endure waiting, frustration, or painful affects are also poor candidates for psychoanalysis.

Another set of factors that has to be taken into account is the external life situation of the patient. Severe physical illness or incapacity may drain a patient's motivation or deplete his energies for psychological work. Sometimes a neurosis may be a lesser evil when compared to some devastating illness or to some miserable life situations. Patients who are in the midst of an exciting love affair are usually not able to work in analysis. The presence of an angry, combative, intrusive husband, wife or parent may make psychoanalysis temporarily unfeasible. One cannot do analytic work on a battlefield. There must be some opportunity for contemplation and introspection away from the analytic hour. Then there are the practical elements of time and money, both of which are usually essential. Psychoanalytic clinics may alleviate the financial stress, but nothing thus far known can substitute for the long time required by psychoanalytic treatment. The shortage of available psychoanalysts is a real problem and, in some geographic locations, a decisive one.

All the foregoing considerations are helpful in determining whether psychoanalysis is indicated or contraindicated for a particular patient. Years of clinical work have taught us, however, that only the actual experience of a period of analysis can safely determine whether a patient is suitable for psychoanalysis. Apparently there are too many variables and unknowns for any other method to yield reliable predictions. Freud (1913b) seemed to be aware of this problem and stated that only a "trial analysis" of several weeks could give an accurate "sounding" of the situation. Fenichel (1945a) agreed with this point of view, but Glover found that two thirds of the British analysts did not (1955, pp. 261-350).

I believe that the difference of opinion is based more on tactics than on substance (Ekstein, 1950). It stems from the clinical finding that announcing a definite time interval as a probationary period complicates the analytic situation. Most analysts, therefore, solve this dilemma by not setting a specific time limit for a trial analysis, but intimate the provisional element in different ways. I have found it useful to indicate my viewpoint to my patients along the following general lines: First I tell the patient that I think psychoanalysis is the best treatment for him, listen to his reactions, and wait for his decision. Once he agrees to undertake psychoanalysis, I explain the role of free association and suggest he try it, implying that in due time we shall both become clearer about the choice of psychoanalysis after we have worked together for a while.

I am deliberately vague about the length of time it will take me to be certain because experience has taught me this can vary enormously. Once a patient begins analysis it takes me months and sometimes years to come to a definite decision, and the time span becomes longer the longer I practice. It is also far easier to rule out those who are unsuitable for psychoanalysis, and for working with me in particular, than to be sure of a good therapeutic result. These issues will be discussed in greater detail in Volume II, in the sections on the first analytic hours and termination.

Additional Reading List

The Historical Development of Psychoanalytic Therapy

Freud (1914b, 1925a), A. Freud (1950b), Kubie (1950), Loewald (1955), Menninger (1958, Chapt. 1).

The Psychoanalytic Theory of Neurosis

Arlow (1963), Brenner (1955, Chapt. VIII), Fenichel (1945a), Freud (1894, 1896, 1898), Glover (1939, Section II), Hendrick (1934), Lampl-de Groot (1963), Nagera (1966), Nunberg (1932, Chapt. V, VIII, IX), Waelder (1960).

The Metapsychology of Psychoanalysis

Hartmann (1939, 1964), Hartmann and Kris (1945), Hartmann, Kris, and Loewenstein (1946), Zetzel (1963).

The Theory of Psychoanalytic Technique

Altman (1964), E. Bibring (1954), Gill (1954), Hartmann (1951), Kris (1956a, 1956b), Loewald (1960), Loewenstein (1954), Menninger (1958), Sharpe (1930, 1947).

Variations in Psychoanalytic Technique

Alexander (1954a, 1954b), E. Bibring (1954), Bouvet (1958), Eissler (1958), Fromm-Reichmann (1954), Gill (1954), Greenacre (1954), Greenson (1958b), Loewenstein (1958a, 1958b), Nacht (1958a), Rangell (1954), A. Reich (1958), Rosenfeld (1958).

Free Association

Kanzer (1961), Kris (1952), Loewenstein (1956).

The Transference Reactions

Glover (1955, Chapt. VII, VIII), Greenacre (1954, 1959, 1966b), Hoffer (1956), Orr (1954), Sharpe (1930), Spitz (1956b), Waelder (1956), Winnicott (1956a), Zetzel (1956).

The Resistances

Fenichel (1941, Chapt. I, II), Glover (1955, Chapt. IV, V, VI), Kohut (1957), Kris (1950), Menninger (1958, Chapt. V), W. Reich (1928, 1929), Sharpe (1930).

Interpretation

Fenichel (1941, Chapt. IV, V), Kris (1951), Loewenstein (1951).

Working Through

Loewald (1960), Novey (1962), Stewart (1963).

The Working Alliance

Frank (1956), Spitz (1956a), Stone (1961), Tarachow (1963, Chapt. 2), Zetzel (1956).

The Use of Nonanalytic Procedures

E. Bibring (1954), Gill (1954), Gitelson (1951), Knight (1952, 1953b), Stone (1951).

Indications and Contraindications for Psychoanalytic Therapy

Guttman (1960; see particularly Karush), Nunberg (1932, Chapt. XII), Waelder (1960, Chapt. XI).

2

Resistance

I HAVE selected the subject of resistance as the first technical chapter of this book because it was Freud's discovery of the importance of *analyzing* resistances that ushered in the beginning of psychoanalysis and psychoanalytic technique (Breuer and Freud, 1893-95, pp. 268-270; Freud, 1914c, p. 147; Jones, 1953, p. 284). The handling of resistances has remained one of the two cornerstones of psychoanalytic technique.

Psychoanalysis can be differentiated from all other forms of psychotherapy in the way in which it deals with resistances. Some methods of treatment aim at strengthening the resistances; they are designated as the "covering-up" or "supportive" therapies (Knight, 1952). Other varieties of psychotherapy may attempt to overcome resistances, or evade resistances in different ways; for example, by suggestion or exhortation, or by exploiting the transference relationship, or by using drugs. It is only in psychoanalytic therapy that we attempt to overcome resistances by analyzing them, by uncovering and interpreting their causes, purposes, modes, and histories.

2.1 Working Definition

Resistance means opposition. All those forces within the patient which oppose the procedures and processes of analysis, i.e., which hinder the patient's free association, which interfere with the

59

patient's attempts to remember and to gain and assimilate insight, which operate against the patient's reasonable ego and his wish to change; all of these forces are to be considered resistance (Freud, 1900, p. 517). Resistance may be conscious, preconscious, or unconscious, and may be expressed by means of emotions, attitudes, ideas, impulses, thoughts, fantasies, or actions. Resistance is in essence a counterforce in the patient, operating against the progress of the analysis, the analyst, and the analytic procedures and processes. Freud had already recognized the importance of resistance in 1912 when he stated: "The resistance accompanies the treatment step by step. Every single association, every act of the person under treatment must reckon with the resistance and represents a compromise between the forces that are striving towards recovery and the opposing ones" (Freud, 1912a, p. 103).

In terms of the patient's neurosis, the resistances serve a defensive function. The resistances oppose the effectiveness of the analytic procedures and defend the *status quo* of the patient. The resistances defend the neurosis and oppose the patient's reasonable ego and the analytic situation. Since all aspects of mental life can serve a defensive function, all of them can serve the purposes of resistance.

2.2 The Clinical Appearance of Resistance

Before we can analyze a resistance we have to be able to recognize it. I therefore propose at this point to describe briefly some of the most typical manifestations of resistance which appear during the course of analysis. The examples that I shall cite are simple and obvious for the purpose of being clearly informative for instructing beginners. It should be remembered that resistances occur in a variety of subtle and complex ways, in combinations or in mixed forms, and the single, isolated examples are not the rule. It is also to be stressed that all kinds of behavior can serve a resistance function. The fact that a patient's material may clearly reveal unconscious content, instinctual impulses, or repressed memories does not preclude the possibility that an important resistance may be at work at the same time. For example, a patient may vividly describe some aggressive activity during the course of an hour in order to ward off recounting an experience which might reveal that he was facing a sexual temptation. There is no activity which cannot be misused for purposes of resistance. Furthermore, all behavior has both impulse and defense aspects (Fenichel, 1941, p. 57). However, the clinical examples which follow will be limited to the simple, typical, and most obvious manifestations of resistance.

2.21 THE PATIENT IS SILENT

This is the most transparent and frequent form of resistance met with in psychoanalytic practice. Generally, it means that the patient is either consciously or unconsciously unwilling to communicate his thoughts or feelings to the analyst. The patient may be aware of his unwillingness, or he may perceive only that there seems to be nothing on his mind. In either case our task is to analyze the reasons for the silence. We want to uncover the motives for the opposition to the analytic procedure of free association and we would say something like: "What might be making you run away from the analysis at this time?" Or we would pursue the feeling of "nothing on his mind." "What might be creating the nothing in your mind?" Or: "You seem to have turned something into a nothing, what might it be?" Our approach is based on the assumption that the only blanks in the mind occur in deepest sleep, otherwise the "nothing" is caused by resistance (Freud, 1913b, pp. 137-138; Ferenczi, 1916-17c).

Sometimes despite the silence, the patient may unwittingly reveal the motive or even the content of his silence by his posture, movements, or facial expression. Turning the head away from view, covering the eyes with the hands, squirming on the couch, and flushing may indicate embarrassment. If simultaneously the patient absentmindedly then removes her wedding ring from her finger and then pokes her little finger through it repeatedly, it would seem that despite her silence she is revealing to me that she is embarrassed by her thoughts of sexuality or marital infidelity. Her silence indicates that she is not yet conscious of those impulses and a struggle is going on between an urge to uncover and an opposing impulse to bury those feelings.

Silence, however, can also have other meanings. For example, silence may be a repetition of a past event in which silence played an important role (Greenson, 1961; Khan, 1963b). The patient's silence may portray his reaction to the primal scene. In such a situation, silence is not only a resistance, but also the content of a piece of reliving. There are many complex problems of silence which will be discussed in Sections 2.217, 3.9411, and in Volume II. By and large and for most practical purposes, silence is a resistance to the analysis and has to be handled as such.

2.22 THE PATIENT "DOES NOT FEEL LIKE TALKING"

This is a variation of the preceding situation. In this instance the patient is not literally silent but is aware that he does not feel like talking, or he does not have anything to say. Very often this statement will be followed by silence. Our task is the same: to explore why or what it is the patient does not feel like talking about. The state of "not feeling like talking" has a cause or causes, and our job is to get the patient to work on the causes. It is essentially the same task as exploring the unconscious "something" which brings about the conscious "nothing" in the silent patient's mind.

2.23 AFFECTS INDICATING RESISTANCE

The most typical indication of resistance from the standpoint of the patient's emotions is to be observed when the patient communicates verbally, but there is an *absence* of affect. His remarks are dry, flat, monotonous, and apathetic. One has the impression that the patient is uninvolved and detached from what he is reporting. This is particularly important when the absence of affect concerns events which ought to be highly charged with emotion. In general, the *inappropriateness* of affect is a very striking sign of resistance. There is a bizarre quality to the patient's utterances when the ideation and the emotion are not in accord.

Recently, a patient began his hour stating that the night before he had experienced "a great sexual thrill—in fact, the greatest sexual pleasure" of his life with his new bride. He went on to describe the experience, but I was struck and puzzled by his slow, hesitant speech and his frequent sighing. Despite the apparent importance of the verbal content, I could sense that the words and the feelings did not fit; some resistance was at work. I eventually interrupted the patient and asked: "It was a great thrill, but yet it was also sad." At first he denied this, but then he drifted on in his associations to tell me the wonderful sexual experience signified the end of something; it was a kind of good-bye. Slowly it became apparent that he had been pushing away the awareness that a good sex life with his wife meant good-bye to his wild infantile sexual fantasies which had lived on unchanged and unfulfilled in his unconscious mind (see Schafer, 1964).

2.24 THE POSTURE OF THE PATIENT

Very often patients will reveal the presence of resistance by the posture they assume on the couch. Rigidity, stiffness, or curled-up protectedness can indicate defensiveness. Above all, any unchanging position, which is maintained a whole hour and hour after hour, is always a sign of resistance. If one is relatively free of resistance, one's posture changes somewhat in the course of the hour. Excessive movement also indicates something is being discharged in movements instead of words. Discrepancy between posture and verbal content is also a sign of resistance. The patient who talks blandly about some event, but who squirms and wriggles, is telling only a fragment of a story. His movements seem to be recounting another part of the narrative. Clenched hands, the arms crossed tightly over the chest, ankles locked together, are indications of holding back. Furthermore, a patient's sitting up during the hour, or keeping one foot off the couch, are indications of wishes to escape from the analytic situation. Yawning in the hour indicates resistance. The way a patient enters the office, avoiding the eye of the analyst, or making some small talk which is not continued on the couch, or leaving at the end of the hour without looking at the analyst—all these are indications of resistance (F. Deutsch, 1952).

2.25 FIXATION IN TIME

Ordinarily when a patient is talking relatively freely, there will be oscillations between the past and the present in his verbal productions. When a patient talks consistently and unchangingly about the past without interspersing anything about the present, or conversely if a patient talks continuously about the present without occasionally dipping back into the past, some resistance is at work. Clinging to a given time period is an avoidance, analogous to rigidities and fixedness in emotional tone, posture, etc.

2.26 TRIVIA OR EXTERNAL EVENTS

When the patient talks about superficial, insignificant, relatively meaningless events for any prolonged period of time, he is avoiding something that is subjectively meaningful. When there is repetitiousness of content without amplification or affect, or without deepening of insight, we have to presume resistance must be in operation. If the talk of trivia does not strike the patient himself as being odd, we are dealing with some running-away activity. A lack of introspection and thoughtfulness is an indication of resistance (Kohut, 1959). In general, verbalization which may be profuse but which does not lead to new memories, or new insights, or greater emotional awareness, is an indication of defensiveness (Martin, 1964).

The same is true of talking about external events—even events of great political magnitude. If the external situation does not lead to a personal, internal situation, a resistance is at work. (It is striking how rarely patients do talk of political events. I recall being impressed that not one of my patients mentioned the assassination of Gandhi when it occurred. Parenthetically, every single patient spoke of President Kennedy's death (see also Wolfenstein and Kliman [1965].)

2.27 AVOIDANCE OF TOPICS

It is very typical for patients to avoid areas which are painful. This may be done consciously or unconsciously. This is particularly true for certain aspects of sexuality, aggression, and the transference. It is striking how many patients are able to talk rather profusely and still manage scrupulously to avoid bringing in particular facets of their sexual or aggressive impulses or certain of their feelings toward the analyst. As far as sexuality is concerned, the most painful aspects seem to have to do with bodily sensations and with bodily zones. Patients may talk about sexual desires or excitement in a general way but are reluctant to mention the particular kind of bodily sensation or urge that excited them. Patients may recount a sexual event but are loath to mention simply and directly what part or parts of the body were involved. Phrases such as "We made oral love last night" or "My husband kissed me sexually" are typical examples of this kind of resistance.

In a similar vein, patients will talk in general terms of feeling annoyed or aggravated when they actually mean they were furious and felt like killing somebody.

Sexual or hostile fantasies in regard to the person of the analyst are also among the most fastidiously avoided subjects early in the analysis. Patients may show great curiosity about their analyst but will talk about him in the most conventional terms and are reluctant to face their sexual or aggressive feelings. "I wonder if you are married" or "'You seem pale and tired today" are veiled expressions of such fantasies. Any important subject which does not enter the analytic hour occasionally is a sign of resistance and has to be pursued as such.

2.28 RIGIDITIES

All recurrent routines which the patient carries out without change in the analytic hours have to be considered a resistance. In behavior which is free of resistance there is always some amount of variation. It is true that we are all creatures of habit; but if these habits do not serve a significant defensive purpose, they are subject to a certain degree of change.

Some typical examples are the following: beginning every hour with the recital of a dream or announcing no dream; beginning every hour by reporting on one's symptoms or complaints, or by talking about the previous day's events. Just the fact that one begins every hour in a stereotyped way indicates resistance. There are patients who collect "interesting" information in order to be prepared for the analytic hour. They search for "material" in order to fill up the hour or to avoid silences or to be a "good" patient, all indications of resistance. In general, be it coming consistently late, or consistently punctual, just the fact of rigidity indicates something else is being held in check, something is being warded off. The particular form of the rigidity may also indicate what is being defended against. For example, habitually coming early to the hour may indicate a fear of being too late, a typical "toilet" anxiety regarding fear of loss of sphincter control.

2.29 THE LANGUAGE OF AVOIDANCE

The use of clichés, technical terms, or sterile language is one of the most frequent indications of resistance. It usually indicates an avoidance of the vivid, evocative imagery of one's personal language. Its aim is to withhold personally revealing communication. (See Stein [1958] for a more thorough study of this subject.) The patient who says "genital organs" when he really means penis is avoiding the imagery that would come to mind with the word penis. The patient who says, "I was hostile" when he means "I was furious" is also avoiding the imagery and sensations of fury as compared to the sterility of "hostility." Here it should be noted that it is important for the analyst to use personal, vivid language in speaking to his patients.

A physician in analysis with me for several years begins to speak medical jargon in the middle of an analytic hour. In stilted tones he reports that his wife developed a "painful protruding hemorrhoid" just prior to a mountain trip they were planning. He said the news caused him "unmixed displeasure" and he wondered whether the hemorrhoid could be "surgically excised" or whether they would have to postpone their holiday. I could sense the latent anger he was withholding and could not refrain from saying: "I think you really mean that your wife's hemorrhoids are giving you a pain in the ass." He replied angrily: "That's right, you son of a bitch, I wish they would cut it out of her, I can't stand these women and their swellings that interfere with my pleasures." This last detail, incidentally, referred to his mother's pregnancy which precipitated his infantile neurosis at the age of five.

The use of the cliché isolates affects and evades emotional involvement. For example, the frequent use of such phrases as "really and truly," or "I guess," and "you know," "etc., etc.," are always indications of avoidance (see also Feldman, 1959). From my clinical experiences with patients in such situations, I have found that "really and truly" and "honestly" usually mean that the patient senses his ambivalence, is aware of the opposites in his feelings. He *wishes* that what he is saying were the whole truth. "I really mean it" means, I wish I really meant it. "I'm truly sorry" means I wish I were truly sorry, but I am aware of the opposite feeling as well. "I guess I was angry" means I'm sure I was angry, but I am reluctant to admit it. "I don't know where to begin" means I know where to begin, but am hesitant to begin there. The patient who says to the analyst repeatedly: "You know, you do remember my sister Tilly" usually means, I'm not at all sure, you dolt, whether you do remember, so I remind you in this way. All these are rather subtle, but usually repetitive indications of resistances and have to be recognized as such. The most recurrent clichés are indications of character resistances and cannot be handled until the analysis is well under way. Isolated ones can be approached early in the analysis.

2.210 Lateness, Missing Hours, Forgetting to Pay

Obviously the patient's coming late, missing hours, and forgetting to pay are indications of a reluctance to come or to pay for the analytic hour. Again this can be conscious and therefore relatively easily accessible, or it may be unconscious in the sense that the patient can rationalize the occurrence. In the latter event it cannot be analyzed until there is enough supporting evidence to confront the patient with the likelihood that he is actively but unconsciously doing something to avoid the issue. Only if this point is reached can one approach the underlying source of the resistance. The patient who "forgets" to pay is not merely reluctant to part with his money but also is unconsciously attempting to deny that his relationship to the analyst is "only" a professional one.

2.211 The Absence of Dreams

Patients who know they dream and forget the dream are obviously resisting the remembering of their dreams. Patients who report dreams but whose dreams indicate running away from analysis, like finding the wrong office, or coming to a different analyst, etc., are also obviously struggling with some form of avoidance of the analytic situation. Patients who do not recall dreaming at all have, I believe, the strongest resistances, because here the resistance has succeeded in attacking not only the content of the dream but also the memory of having dreamed.

Dreams are the single most important means of access to the unconscious, to the repressed, and to the instinctual life of the patient. Forgetting dreams is an indication of the patient's struggle against revealing his unconscious, and in particular, his instinctual life, to the analyst (Freud, 1900, pp. 517-521). If one has succeeded in overcoming a resistance in a given hour, the patient may respond by suddenly being able to recall a hitherto forgotten dream, or a new fragment of a dream may come to mind. Flooding the hour with many dreams is another variety of resistance and may indicate the patient's unconscious wish to continue his sleep in the presence of the analyst (Lewin, 1953).

2.212 The Patient Is Bored

Boredom in the patient indicates that he is avoiding becoming aware of his instinctual urges and his fantasies. If the patient is bored, it means he has managed to ward off conscious awareness of his impulses and in their place he has the peculiar empty tension of boredom (Fenichel, 1934; Greenson, 1953). When a patient in analysis is working well with the analyst, he is eager to search out his fantasies. Boredom, no matter what else it may mean, is a defense against fantasies. Parenthetically, it should be stated that boredom in the analyst may indicate that the analyst is blocking out his fantasies regarding the patient, a countertransference reaction. It may also mean that the patient is resisting and that the analyst has not yet detected it consciously, but his unconscious perception of it has made him discontent, restless, and bored.

2.213 The Patient Has a Secret

Obviously the patient with a conscious secret is stating that there is something he is avoiding. This is a special form of resistance, the handling of which requires particular technical considerations. The secret may be an event that the patient wants to keep quiet or even a word he is unable, i.e., unwilling, to say. At this point all that can be said is that it is a form of resistance; it has to be designated as such, but it is something to be respected and not crushed, coerced, or begged out of the patient. It will be discussed in greater detail in Section 2.663.

2.214 Acting Out

Acting out is a very frequent and important occurrence during psychoanalysis. No matter what else it may mean, it always serves a resistance function. It is a resistance insofar as acting out is a repetition in action instead of words, memories, and affects. Furthermore, there is always some distortion involved in acting out. Acting out serves multiple functions, but its resistance function eventually has to be analyzed since failure to do so can imperil the entire analysis.

One simple kind of acting out that frequently occurs early in the course of analysis is the patient's talking about the material from the analytic session outside of the analytic hour to someone other than the analyst. This is obviously a form of avoidance in which the patient displaces a transference reaction onto somebody else in order to avoid and dilute some aspect of his transference feelings. It must be pointed out as a resistance and its motives explored. This practice will be discussed in greater detail when I describe acting out of transference reactions (Section 3.84) and also in Volume II.

2.215 Frequent Cheerful Hours

By and large, analytic work is serious. It may not always be grim or miserable, and not every hour is depressing or painful, but generally it is, to say the least, hard work. The patient may have some gratification in the sense of accomplishment and even an occasional feeling of triumph. Sometimes a correct interpretation brings spontaneous laughter to the patient and the analyst. But frequent cheerful hours, great enthusiasm, and prolonged elation indicate that something is being warded off—usually something of the opposite nature, some form of depression (Lewin, 1950; Greenson, 1962). The flight into health, the premature loss of symptoms without insight, are signs of similar kinds of resistance and have to be handled as such.

2.216 The Patient Does Not Change

Sometimes one works apparently well and successfully with a patient and yet there is no apparent change in the patient's symptomatology or behavior. If this persists over a long period of time and there is no manifest resistance, one must look for some hidden, subtle resistance. One can expect changes in the patient's behavior or in his symptomatology if the analysis is making impact and therefore having influence upon the patient. If other signs of resistance are absent, we are probably dealing with a subtle form of acting out and transference resistance (Glover, 1955, Chapt. IV; see also Volume II).

2.217 Silent Resistances

Here I refer to the subtle resistances which are difficult to pin down and which often come to mind when one is thinking about the patient away from the analytic situation. The analyst often becomes aware of these kinds of resistances when he is describing the patient spontaneously to someone else. These resistances are not detectable in a single hour or even in many hours, but only when one has a certain distance from the analysis. We are dealing here with subtle character resistances in the patient which the analyst has difficulty contending with—or, for that matter, recognizing.

There is obviously a countertransference component in the analyst as well as character resistance on the part of the patient (Glover, 1955, pp. 54, 185-186; Fenichel, 1941, pp. 67-69).

Let me illustrate: I have been working for many years with a patient and in my considered judgment things are going slowly but well. I would have stated that I like the patient and am satisfied with our work. Yet, one day when I meet the analyst who referred her to me, in response to his question about how she was doing, I found myself saying, "Well, you know she is a *Qvetsch*." (*Qvetsch* is a Yiddish word meaning a chronic "groaner" or complainer.) I am surprised at my remark, but later realize: (a) it was accurate; (b) I had not consciously realized it before; (c) I was unconsciously protecting the patient from my discontent with her. After this conversation I began to work on this problem both with her and within myself.

This list is a most incomplete one. The most serious omission from this list of resistances is of course the resistances due to the transference. However, this omission is deliberate because I shall discuss transference and resistances due to the transference situation in Chapter 3. There are many other typical resistances which I might have added to this outline, but they resemble others which I have discussed. Let us take as an example the patient who reads books and articles on psychoanalysis in an attempt to discover things for himself and thus avoid the surprise of coming upon the material unprepared. This is similar to the resistance of gathering material for the hour to avoid blank spaces or silence. Another patient makes a point of becoming socially friendly with other analysts as a means of diluting his own personal reactions to his analyst, which is like talking about the analytic work outside the hour. Smoking in the hour resembles other actions which replace putting feelings and urges into words, etc.

2.3 Historical Survey

Before going on to a discussion of the theory of resistance, I shall briefly outline the historical development of the psychoanalytic point of view on this subject. Rather than attempt a systematic digest of each paper mentioned, these papers being readily available to the reader, I shall limit myself to those aspects of the contribution which indicate a significant change.

The *Studies on Hysteria* (1893-95) which Freud wrote with Breuer constitute a remarkable document, because one can observe how Freud came upon such monumental discoveries as resistance and transference. It was a characteristic of Freud's genius that when he met an obstacle in his path, he was not content to evade it or simply overcome it, he had the happy facility of turning it to advantage. This is particularly true of his work with resistance and transference. In describing the case of Elisabeth von R., whom Freud treated in 1892, he mentioned the term resistance for the first time and made some preliminary formulations. He believed the patient "fended off" some incompatible ideas, and that the strength of the resistance corresponded to the amount of energy with which the ideas had been forced out of her associations. In this chapter, he hypothesized that the idea was cut off from the rest of her ideational life and from her free associations, like a foreign body (p. 157). Freud also introduced the terms defense, motive for defense, and mechanisms of defense in his discussion of the problem (p. 166).

In the chapter on the "Psychotherapy of Hysteria" in that same volume, Freud asserted that the patient's inability to be hypnotized really meant the unwillingness to be hypnotized (p. 268). One had to overcome in a patient a psychical force that was opposed to pathogenic ideas becoming conscious. This force must have played a part in creating the hysterical symptom. Because the ideas were painful, the patient's ego evoked for defense a repelling force that drove the pathogenic idea out of consciousness and opposed its return in memory. The patient's not knowing is really a not *wanting* to know (pp. 268-270).

The analyst's task is to overcome this resistance. He does this, according to Freud, by "insisting"; i.e., by pressure on the forehead, by insisting that a recollection will occur, and by other means. The patient is told to tell all, even if it is trivial or embarrassing. This method works by disassociating the patient's will from the search for memories. What emerges is an intermediate link, not always a recollection (pp. 270-271). (This is an important contribution to the concept of free association.)

Resistances are stubborn and return repeatedly. They take many forms, and Freud discussed the patient's rationalizations about his resistance, or the concept of resistance to resistance (p. 279).

Let me quote Freud directly on the technique of handling resistances: "What means have we at our disposal for overcoming this continual resistance? Few, but they include almost all those by which one man can ordinarily exert a psychical influence on another. In the first place, we must reflect that a psychical resistance, especially one that has been in force for a long time, can only be resolved slowly and by degrees, and we must wait patiently. In the next place, we may reckon on the intellectual interest which the patient begins to feel after working for a short time. . . . But lastly —and this remains the strongest lever—we must endeavour, after we have discovered the motives for his defence, to deprive them of their value or even to replace them by more powerful ones. . . . One works to the best of one's power, as an elucidator (where ignorance has given rise to fear), as a teacher, as the representative of a freer or superior view of the world, as a father confessor who gives absolution, as it were, by a continuance of his sympathy and respect after the confession has been made" (p. 282).

Freud then raised the questions: Should one not use hypnosis, and would not the use of hypnosis reduce the work? He answered both questions in the negative. Emmy von R. was easy to hypnotize and had little resistance until sexual matters were brought up; then she could not be hypnotized, then she was unable to recall. In all hysteria, the defense is the root of the matter. Remove the resistances, and the material is there in proper order. The closer one gets to the nucleus of the hysteria, the greater the degree of resistance (pp. 284-289).

At this point Freud changed one of his previous ideas by stating that the repressed is not a foreign body, but more like an infiltrate. If we remove the resistance and can get circulation back into this hitherto isolated area, it can become once again integrated. It is hopeless to try to get to the nucleus immediately, one has to start with the periphery (pp. 290-292). (Here we have an indication of the technical rule that interpretation must start from the surface.)

In *The Interpretation of Dreams* (1900) Freud made many references to the concept of resistance. At different places he spoke of censorship as being due to resistance, or of censorship imposed by resistance (pp. 308, 321, 530, 563). It is clear that the concepts of resistance and censorship are very closely related to each other. Censorship is to dreams what resistance is to free association (p. 520). He noted the clinical finding that in attempting to have the patient recall the forgotten fragment of a dream the analyst meets the greatest resistance. If one can succeed in overcoming a resistance, one can often recall a hitherto forgotten dream. It was in his considerations regarding the forgetting of dreams that Freud made the statement that *"whatever interrupts the progress of analytic work is a resistance"* (p. 517).

"Freud's Psycho-Analytic Procedure" contains Freud's earliest unequivocal statement that the factor of resistance has become one of the cornerstones of his theory (1904, p. 251). Hypnosis, suggestion, and abreaction have been completely abandoned in favor of free association and the analysis of resistance and transference (p. 252).

In the Dora Case (1905a), Freud described how the transference relationship became the most important source of resistance and also how this transference resistance was acted out by the patient. Eventually this led to the breaking off of the analysis, because Freud was not fully aware of its importance when he treated the patient in 1900 (pp. 116-120).

In the paper on "The Dynamics of Transference" (1912a) Freud went beyond merely stating that transference causes the most powerful resistances and is the most frequent cause of resistance. He explored the dynamic forces which cause the libido to regress and rise up against the analytic work in the form of resistance (p. 102). Freud described how resistance accompanies the psychotherapy step by step. Every single association, every act of the patient under treatment must reckon with resistance (p. 103).

The patient's associations are also a compromise between the forces of resistance and those striving for recovery. So too is the transference. Here Freud has an important footnote that the battles in the sphere of transference resistance are often selected for the most bitter conflicts in the analysis. He compares the situation to the following combat situation. "If in the course of the battle there is a particularly embittered struggle over the possession of some little church or some individual farm, there is no need to suppose that the church is a national shrine, perhaps, or that the house shelters the army's pay-chest. The value of the object may be a purely tactical one and may perhaps emerge only in this one battle" (p. 104).

In the paper "Remembering, Repeating and Working-Through" (1914c), Freud for the first time mentions the repetition compulsion, a special aspect of resistance, namely, the tendency of the patient to repeat a past experience in action instead of remembering. These resistances are particularly tenacious and require working through (pp. 150-151). Furthermore, he states in this essay that it is necessary to do more than name the resistance in order to overcome it. The patient needs time to get to know the resistance better, and to discover the repressed instinctual impulses which feed it (p. 155). (This is one of the few technical remarks Freud makes about how one attempts to analyze resistance.)

In the *Introductory Lectures* (1916-17) Freud introduced the term "adhesiveness of the libido," a special variety of resistance (p. 348). Here, too, he asserts that the narcissistic neuroses present an unconquerable barrier which is not accessible to psychoanalytic technique (p. 423).

In *Inhibitions, Symptoms and Anxiety* (1926a) Freud discusses resistances in terms of their sources. He describes five different types and three sources of resistance. He distinguishes three kinds of resistance stemming from the ego, and in addition a superego and an id source of resistance (p. 160). (This subject will be pursued in Section 2.5.)

The paper "Analysis Terminable and Interminable" (1937a) contains some new theoretical contributions to the nature of resistance. Freud suggests that there are three factors which are decisive for the success of our therapeutic efforts: the influence of traumas, the constitutional strength of the instincts, and alterations of the ego (p. 224). These alterations are those already present in the patient due to the effects of the defensive process. Freud also amplifies on his speculations concerning why the analytic process is so slow in certain patients. He describes patients with a lack of mobility of their libido and ascribes this to adhesiveness of the libido and psychical inertia, which he designates "perhaps not quite correctly" as "resistance from the id" (p. 242). These patients are in the throes of a "negative therapeutic reaction" due to an unconscious sense of guilt which is derived from the death instinct (p. 243).

Freud also states in this paper that resistance may be caused by the analyst's errors, some of which stem from the enormous emotional hazards of the profession (pp. 247-249). He closes this essay with some clinical remarks about the greatest resistances in men and women. In women the greatest source of resistance seems to be connected to their penis envy, while in men the greatest resistance stems from their fear of passive feminine wishes in relation to other men (pp. 250-253).

In this historical survey of Freud's ideas about the resistance one can see how he began by regarding resistance essentially as an obstacle to the therapeutic work, and later how it has become something much more. Whereas his original technique was focused on abreaction and the obtaining of memories, later the resistances themselves become the source of very important knowledge about the life history of the patient, and particularly about his symptomatology. These ideas are developed, reaching their culmination in the paper "Analysis Terminable and Interminable," where the concept of resistance also involves the id and superego.

One must also add a few words about contributions other than Freud's. The single most important advance was the book by Anna Freud, *The Ego and the Mechanisms of Defense* (1936). This was the first attempt to systematize our understanding of the various mechanisms of defense and to relate them to the problems of resistances in the course of psychoanalytic treatment. In this work she demonstrated that resistances are not only obstacles to the treatment but are also important sources of information about ego functions in general. The defenses which come to light as resistances during treatment carry out important functions for the patient in his outside life as well. The defenses are also repeated in the transference reactions (pp. 30-44).

Two papers by Wilhelm Reich (1928, 1929) on character formation and character analysis were also important additions to the psychoanalytic understanding of resistance. The neurotic character refers to the generally ego-syntonic, habitual attitudes and modes of behavior of the patient which serve as an armor against external stimuli and against instinctual uprisings from within (1928, pp. 132-135). These character traits have to be made the subject of analysis, but how and when are matters of controversy (A. Freud, 1936, p. 35; Fenichel, 1941, pp. 67-68).

Hartmann's (1964) ideas about adaptation, relative autonomy, conflict-free spheres, intrasystemic conflicts, and neutralization have important implications for problems of technique. Ernst Kris's concept of regression under the control of the ego, or in the service of the ego, is another outstanding contribution (1950, p. 312). These concepts illuminated and specified what until then had been subsumed under the basket heading of "the art" of psychoanalysis. Finally, some of the newer ideas about the differences in defenses, resistances, and regressions in neuroses and psychoses also seem to me to be of promise (Winnicott, 1955; Freeman, 1959; Wexler, 1960).

2.4 The Theory of Resistance

2.41 RESISTANCE AND DEFENSE

The concept of resistance is of basic significance for psychoanalytic technique and because of its central position, its ramifications touch upon every important technical issue. Resistance has to be approached from multiple points of view in order to be properly comprehended. The present theoretical discussion will touch only on a few fundamental considerations which are of general importance for understanding the clinical and technical problems. More specific theoretical questions will be dealt with in relation to particular problems. For a more comprehensive metapsychological approach, the reader is referred to the classical psychoanalytic literature (Freud, 1912a, 1914c, 1926a, 1937a; A. Freud, 1936; Fenichel, 1945a, Chapt. VIII, IX; Gill, 1963, Chapt. 5, 6).

Resistance opposes the analytic procedure, the analyst, and the patient's reasonable ego. Resistance defends the neurosis, the old, the familiar, and the infantile from exposure and change. It may be adaptive. The term resistance refers to all the *defensive operations* of the mental apparatus as they are evoked in the analytic situation.

Defense refers to processes which safeguard against danger and pain and is to be contrasted to instinctual activities which seek pleasure and discharge. In the psychoanalytic situation, the defenses manifest themselves as resistances. Freud used the terms synonymously throughout most of his writings. The function of defense is originally and basically an ego function, although every kind of psychic phenomenon may be used for defensive purposes. This touches upon the question raised by Anna Freud when she stated that the many strange modes of representation which occur in the dream work are instigated at the behest of the ego, but are not carried out completely by it. Analogously, the various measures of defense are not entirely the work of the ego; the properties of instinct may also be made use of (A. Freud, 1936, p. 192). This idea seems related to the notions of the prestages of defense and the special problem of defenses in the psychotic patient as contrasted to the psychoneurotic (Freeman, 1959, pp. 208, 211).

I believe it is safe to state that no matter what its origin may be, for a psychic phenomenon to be used for defensive purposes, it must operate through the ego. This is the rationale for the technical rule that the analysis of resistance should begin with the ego. Resistance is an operational concept; it is nothing new that is created by the analysis; the analytic situation only becomes the arena for these forces of resistance to show themselves.

It is to be remembered that during the course of analysis the forces of resistance will utilize all the mechanisms, modes, measures, methods, and constellations of defense which the ego has used in the patient's outside life. They may consist of the elementary psychodynamisms which the unconscious ego uses to preserve its synthetic function, such as the mechanisms of repression, projection, introjection, isolation, etc. Or the resistances may consist of more recent complicated acquisitions, such as rationalization or intellectualization which are used for defensive purposes (Sperling, 1958, pp. 36-37).

The resistances operate within the patient, essentially in his unconscious ego, although certain aspects of his resistance may be accessible to his observing, judging ego. We have to distinguish between the fact *that* the patient is resisting, *how* he does it, *what* he is warding off, and *why* he does so (Fenichel, 1941, p. 18; Gill, 1963, p. 96). The defense mechanism itself is by definition always unconscious, but the patient may be aware of one or another secondary manifestation of the defensive process. The resistances come to light during the process of analysis as some form of opposition to the procedures or processes of being analyzed. In the beginning of the analysis the patient will usually feel this as some contrariety in regard to the analyst's requests or interventions rather than as an intrapsychic phenomenon. As the working alliance develops, as the patient identifies with the analyst's working attitudes, the resistance will be perceived as an ego-alien defensive operation within the patient's experiencing ego. This shifts during the course of the analysis in accordance with the fluctuations of the working alliance. It should be stressed, however, that throughout the course of the analysis, along every step of the way, there will be some contention with resistances. It may be felt intrapsychically or in terms of the relationship to the analyst; it may be conscious, preconscious, or unconscious; it may be negligible or monumental in its effects, but resistance is omnipresent.

The concept of defense entails two constituents: a danger and a protecting agency. The concept of resistance consists of three agencies: a danger, a force impelling to protect the (irrational) ego, and a force pushing toward taking a risk, the preadaptive ego.

Another parallel in the relation between defense and resistance is the recognition of the existence of hierarchies of resistance just as we postulate hierarchies of defense. The conception of defense refers to a variety of unconscious activities of the ego, but we can distinguish between the deep, unconscious, automatic defense mechanisms and those closer to the conscious ego. The more primitive the place in this hierarchy occupied by a particular defense, the more closely it is connected to repressed material, the less likely it is to become conscious. Those defenses higher up on the scale operate more in accordance with the secondary process and regulate more neutralized discharges (see Gero, 1951, p. 578; Gill, 1963, p. 115). This reasoning can be carried over to our understanding of resistances. The resistances too include a wide range of processes both in terms of whether they make use of primary or secondary process in their functioning and also in regard to whether they are attempting to regulate an instinctual or neutralized discharge. I believe I can illustrate this point by a description of the goings-on in a patient who stated that he was afraid to "let me enter into him" because then he would be devoured, he would be destroyed, gone. How different is this resistance from that of a patient who revealed to me that he always quietly hummed a tune when I began to speak in order to lessen the impact of what I might say.

Defense and resistance are relative terms; the defense and what is defended against form a unit. Defensive behavior will provide some discharge for that which is defended against. All behavior has impulse and defense aspects (Fenichel, 1941, p. 57). The cruel self-reproach of the obsessional clearly betrays the underlying sadistic impulses he is attempting to ward off. All defense is "relative defense" (p. 62). A given fragment of behavior may be a defense in regard to a drive more primitive than itself, and this same behavior may be reacted to as a drive in relation to a defense more advanced than itself (Gill, 1963, p. 122).

I can illustrate this in terms of resistance-impulse units as they emerge in the course of an analysis. A middle-aged man, a psychiatrist, tells me that he thoroughly enjoys sex with his wife "even her moist, smelly vagina." Then he adds that "strangely enough" after intercourse he usually awakens from a deep sleep to find himself washing his genitals in the bathroom. In light of the previous discussion I will try to explain his resistance activities as follows: the patient's telling me he thoroughly enjoys sex is clearly instinctual in content; but on the other hand it is an attempt to please me, to show me how healthy he is, and to obscure any doubts I might have about his potency. One can readily observe impulse manifestation and then resistance in this. All of this, however, is defensive in regard to the next phrase, "even her moist, smelly vagina." The defensive aspect is betrayed by the word "even." But this description too obviously contains an impulse-gratifying exhibitionistic element. It is also a resistance against facing the meaning of the next piece of behavior, the washing in the bathroom. This last activity was reacted to like an ego-alien resistance in view of the previous statement of how he enjoyed her vagina and by the fact that he found the washing strange. But it was also a defensive action against a feeling of dirtiness that had awakened him and that he felt impelled to overcome by washing.

I believe this brief analysis exemplifies and confirms the concept of the relativity of resistance or defense. The concepts of "resistance to resistance" and "defenses against defense" are analogous approaches to this theme (see Freud, 1937a, p. 239; Fenichel, 1941, p. 61).

The hierarchy and layering of resistances and impulses should not lead one to expect to find an orderly stratification of these components in the minds of people undergoing psychoanalysis. This was carried to an extreme by Wilhelm Reich (1928, 1929), who advocated analyzing resistance-impulse units in reverse chronological order. Fenichel (1941, pp. 47-48) and Hartmann (1951, p. 147) stressed the many factors which may disrupt this historical stratification and which cause "faulting" and other more chaotic conditions.

I would like to summarize this part of the theoretical discussion about resistances and defense by quoting a paragraph from Merton Gill (1963, p. 123): "We cannot draw a hard-and-fast line between the various levels of defense. If the defenses exist in a hierarchy, the lower levels must be unconscious and automatic, and may be pathogenic. The defenses high in the hierarchy must be conscious and voluntary, and may be adaptive. And, of course, specific defensive behaviors may include both kinds of characteristics. The idea that defenses can disappear after an analysis could be held only by someone who maintained a very restricted view of defense, since in a hierarchical conception the defenses are as much the woof of personality functioning as the drives and drive derivatives are its warp."

Let us now turn to the question of relating the motives and mechanisms of defense to the motives and mechanisms of resistance (A. Freud, 1936, pp. 45-70; Fenichel, 1945a, pp. 128-167). By motive of defense we are referring to what *caused* a defense to be brought into action. The immediate cause is always the avoidance of some painful affect like anxiety, guilt, or shame. The more distal cause is the underlying instinctual impulse which stirred up the anxiety, guilt, or shame. The ultimate cause is the traumatic situation, a state in which the ego is overwhelmed and helpless because it is flooded with anxiety it cannot control, master, or bind—a state of panic. It is this state which the patient tries to avoid by instituting the defenses upon any sign of danger. (For a compact, lucid discussion of the ego in anxiety, see Schur, 1953.)

Let me illustrate with a simple clinical example. An ordinarily good-natured male patient begins to talk evasively in an analytic hour when he describes seeing me at a concert the night before. It is clear that he is embarrassed and anxious. After this point is acknowledged by the patient, we explore the underlying reasons and we discover that he felt jealous and resentful that I seemed to be enjoying the company of a young man. In subsequent hours we uncover the fact that this rivalry situation mobilized in him a tendency to a terrible rage outburst. He had suffered from frightening temper tantrums as a child when his younger brother seemed to be favored over him. Part of his later neurotic character deformation was an unreasonably rigid good-naturedness. I believe this example demonstrates the immediate, distal, and ultimate causes of resistance. The embarrassment was the immediate motive. The jealous resentment was the distal cause of resistance. The ultimate basis for the resistance was the fear of the violent rage.

The danger situations, which may evoke a traumatic state, go through a sequence of development and change with the different phases of maturation (Freud, 1926a, pp. 134-143). They can be characterized roughly as the fear of abandonment, the fear of bodily annihilation, feeling unloved, the fear of castration, and the fear of loss of self-esteem. In the course of analysis every thought, feeling, or fantasy which stirs up a painful emotion, be it from free association, a dream or from the analyst's intervention, will evoke some degree of resistance. If one probes what lies behind the painful affect, one will discover some dangerous instinctual impulse and eventually some link to a relatively traumatic event in the patient's history.

The problem of working through has a particular relevance to the theory of resistance since it was in his discussion of this matter that Freud introduced the terms "compulsion to repeat," "adhesiveness of the libido," and "psychical inertia" (1914c, p. 150; 1937a, pp. 241-242). These phenomena were linked together by what Freud designated "perhaps not quite correctly" as "resistance from the id," a manifestation of the death instinct (1937a, p. 242). Without intending to dismiss these ideas summarily, I must say that the concept of a resistance stemming from the id seems either imprecise or a contradiction. According to our working definition of resistance: all resistances operate through the ego, no matter where the danger or mode originates. The clinging to old gratifications as implied in the terms adhesiveness of the libido and psychical inertia may have some special instinctual basis, but my clinical experiences indicate that in such instances it is an underlying fear of the new or mature satisfactions which makes the old gratification intractable.

In my opinion, the role of the death instinct in regard to resistances seems too complex and too remote to warrant a thorough discussion in a book on technique. I am referring to the concept of a death instinct as distinct from the concept of aggressive instinctual drives. Interpreting clinical material to a patient in terms of a death instinct tends too readily to be facile and mechanistic.

From a technical point of view, the compulsion to repeat can best be handled therapeutically by recognizing it as an attempt at belated mastery of an old traumatic situation. Or the repetition may represent the hope for a happier end to a past frustration. Masochism, self-destructiveness, and the need for suffering can be best approached clinically as manifestations of aggression turned upon the self. In my experience, the interpretation of resistances as an expression of a death instinct leads only to intellectualization, passivity, and resignation. It has seemed clinically valid to me that in the final analysis we find the same basic motive true for resistance as well as for defense: the main motive for resistance and for defense is to avoid pain.

2.42 RESISTANCE AND REGRESSION

Regression is a descriptive concept and refers to a return to an earlier, more primitive form of mental activity (Freud, 1916-17, p. 342). One tends to return to those stopping places which had been points of fixation in earlier times. Fixation and regression form a complementary series (1916-17, p. 362; Fenichel, 1945a, p. 65). One can best understand this relationship by using the analogy of an army attempting to advance through enemy territory. It will leave the greatest number of occupation troops at those places where it has had the greatest difficulties or the greatest security and satisfaction. However, in so doing, the advancing army is weakened and, should it meet difficulties in its path, it will return to those points where it left the strongest occupation troops.

Fixations are caused by innate disposition, constitutional factors, and experience which form a complementary series. We know little about the hereditary, congenital factors, but we do know that excessive satisfactions at a given point in development will make for fixation. There is a reluctance to give up great satisfactions, particularly if they are combined with a sense of security. A child who is given a great deal of anal-erotic stimulation by his mother's inordinate concern for his anal activities not only is getting a great deal of sensual gratification but he has the security of obtaining his mother's approval. Fenichel was of the opinion that excessive frustrations may also cause fixations (1945a, p. 65). He maintained a fixation may arise because (a) there is the lingering hope that one will eventually get the longed-for satisfaction, and (b) the frustration makes for a repression of the drives involved which keep them from progressing. Combinations of excessive gratification and excessive frustration and particularly abrupt changes from one to the other will make for fixation.

Regression and fixation are interdependent (A. Freud, 1965, p. 96). Nevertheless, it should be borne in mind that fixation is a developmental concept and regression is a defensive process. My own clinical experience is not in accord with Fenichel's formulations about the causes of fixation and regression. I have found that fixations are caused primarily by excessive gratifications and regression is set in motion by excessive pain or danger. One does not cling to some absent satisfaction unless there is a memory of excessive pleasure connected to it. This may be true only in a relative sense. The more advanced gratification is too dangerous and the more regressed one is too unrewarding. Thus, the fixation point is the most satisfying. It offers the best combination of gratification and security.

The regression is motivated by a flight from pain and danger. This seems to be true whenever we are dealing with a pathological regression. The patient who renounces his oedipal love and rivalry, his masturbation, and his phallic, exhibitionistic pride and once again becomes clingingly defiant, spitefully submissive, toilet-oriented and obsessive, is a case in point. If gratification plays a role in the regression, it does so only if it produced traumatic anxiety. If the gratification does not become traumatic, it will cause a fixation at the oedipal level, not a regression.

Regression may take place in terms of object relations and in regard to sexual organization (Freud, 1916-17, p. 341). It may also be understood in terms of topography, like the shift from secondary process to primary process. Gill (1963, p. 93) believes this also implies a structural regression, a regression in the ego's perceptual function, expressed in transforming thoughts into visual images. Winnicott (1955, pp. 283, 286) maintains that the most important aspect of regression is the regression of ego functions and object relations, particularly in the direction of primary narcissism.

Anna Freud's (1965, pp. 93-107) discussion of regression is the most thorough and systematic. She states that regression can occur in all three psychic structures; it can concern psychic content as well as functioning; and it may influence the instinctual aim, the object representations, and the fantasy content. (I would add the erogenous zone and the self-image to this list). Id regressions are more stubborn and adhesive, while regressions in terms of ego functions are often more transitory. Temporary regression in ego functions is part of the normal development of the child. In the process of maturation, regression and progression alternate and interact with each other.

Regression occupies a special position among the defenses, and there seems to be some doubt whether it really belongs among them (A. Freud, 1936; Fenichel, 1945a; Gill, 1963). However, there is no doubt that the ego does use regression in a variety of forms for purposes of defense and resistance. The role of the ego is somewhat different in regard to regression. In general it seems that the ego is more passive than it is in other defensive operations. Very often regression is set in motion by an instinctual frustration on a given level which impels the drives to seek outlets in a backward direction (Fenichel, 1945a, p. 160). Yet under certain conditions the ego does have the ability to regulate regression as it does in sleep, wit, and in some creative activities (Kris, 1950, pp. 312-313). Actually, for mental health and above all for psychological-mindedness, primitive functions are needed to supplement the more highly differentiated ones (Hartmann, 1947; Khan, 1960; Greenson, 1960). As with all defenses, it is important to discriminate between the relatively more pathogenic and adaptive regressions.

It is also important to keep in mind that regression is not a total, all-encompassing phenomenon. Usually we see selective regressions. A patient may regress in certain ego functions and not in others. Or there may be a great deal of regression in terms of instinctual aims and relatively little regression in terms of object relations. The "unevenness" of regression is a very important concept in clinical practice (A. Freud, 1965).

This discussion has important implications in terms of therapeutic processes. For psychoanalytic therapy, regression is needed—indeed our setting and attitude facilitate this development (see Chapter 4; also Menninger, 1958, p. 52). However, most analysts have in mind an *optimal* amount of regression. We select patients who, for the most part, can regress only temporarily and partially. Yet there is some difference of opinion on this matter. For example, Wexler (1960, pp. 41-42) cautions against using procedures like free association, which will lead certain borderline patients to object detachment, whereas Winnicott (1955, p. 287) feels it is the analyst's task to encourage a full regression even in a psychotic patient.

2.5 Classification of Resistances

2.51 ACCORDING TO THE SOURCE OF RESISTANCE

During the course of his many writings on problems of defense and resistance, Freud at various times attempted to distinguish between different types of resistance. In *Inhibitions, Symptoms and Anxiety* he distinguished five kinds of resistance and classified them according to their source (1926a, p. 160). (1) The resistance of repression, by which he meant the resistance of the ego's defenses. (2) Resistance of the transference. Since transference is a substitute for memory and is based on a displacement from past objects onto present objects, Freud classified this resistance too as derived from the ego. (3) The gain from illness, or secondary gain, he also placed under the ego resistances. (4) The fourth variety he considered those which required working through, namely, the repetition compulsion and the adhesiveness of the libido, which he considered to be resistances from the id. (5) The last resistances Freud designated were those which arose from unconscious guilt and the need for punishment. He believed that these resistances originated in the superego.

Glover (1955), in the two chapters devoted to defense resistance in his book on technique, classifies resistances in many different ways, but goes along with Freud's classification according to sources of resistance. Fenichel (1941) considered this method of differentiation unsystematic, and pointed out that Freud himself had the same impression (pp. 33-34).

Before pursuing our discussion of the sources of resistance, I believe it would be wise to state the truism that all psychic structures participate in all psychic events, although to varying degrees. If this is kept in mind, we will be less prone to oversimplify or overgeneralize our formulations. In accordance with our discussion of resistance and defense, I believe that the function of defense, the activity of avoiding pain, no matter what the evocative stimulus is, is initiated by the ego. The ego is that psychic structure which mobilizes warding-off, avoidance functions. It may do so by employing the unconscious primary mechanisms of defense, such as repression, projection, introjection, etc. However, it may also do so by utilizing any other conscious and unconscious psychic function. For example, heterosexual activity may be used as a defense, and, in the analysis, as a resistance against facing homosexual impulses. Pregenital sexual pleasures may not only be expressing infantile id components, but, if they become a source of resistance, they may also be serving a defensive, resistive function against the oedipal situation (Friedman, 1953). Freud, Glover, and Anna Freud described id resistances as those resistances which require working through and which stem from the repetition compulsion and the adhesiveness of the libido. In my opinion, these resistances too operate via the ego. A particular instinctual activity is repeated and remains intractable to insight only if it has enlisted the aid of the ego's defensive functions. Working through operates not directly upon the id but only upon the ego. For working through to succeed, the ego has to be induced to give up its pathological defensive function. Thus the id may participate in the resistance maneuvers, but it seems to me only by allowing itself to be used by the ego for defensive purposes. It should be stressed that this formulation holds true for the transference neuroses; the problem may be a different one in the psychoses (Winnicott, 1955; Freeman, 1959; Wexler, 1960).

A similar situation exists in terms of the superego. Guilt feelings may prompt the ego to institute various mechanisms of defense. But we can also see situations where the sense of guilt demands satisfaction, demands punishment, and takes on an idlike quality. The ego may defend itself against this by utilizing a variety of reaction formations which have a supermoral quality. We see this quite typically in the obsessional neurosis, for example. However, in severe masochistic characters, we can see a situation when the need for suffering is pleasurable, and where the patient gives vent to his superego demands, indulging in behavior which openly brings him pain. When this happens we have a resistance in the analysis because this sought-for pain is relatively pleasurable and simultaneously is warding off some other anxiety (Fenichel, 1945a, p. 166). It is serving both a gratifying and defensive, resistive function. Our therapeutic task will be to get the patient's reasonable ego to recognize the resistance function and to persuade it to dare to face the greater, underlying painful anxiety so that it can be analyzed.

Thus I have the impression that no matter what the original source of an activity may be, its resistance function is always derived from the ego. The other psychic structures have to be understood as operating through the ego. The motive for defense and resistance always is to avoid pain. The mode or measures of resistance can be any type of psychic activity, from the defense mechanisms to instinctual activities. The evocative stimulus which triggers the resistance maneuver may *originate* in any of the psychic structures—ego, id, or superego. But the *perception* of danger is an ego function.

Freud's ideas on signal anxiety are of basic importance in approaching these complicated interrelationships. I would like to use the ego's role in anxiety to exemplify some of the vital issues. In *Inhibitions, Symptoms and Anxiety* he described (a) the ego as the seat of anxiety, (b) anxiety as a response of the ego, and (c) the ego's role in *producing* anxiety and its role in defense and symptom formation (1926a, pp. 132-142, pp. 157-168). These problems were meticulously reviewed and clarified by Max Schur (1953) in his paper on "The Ego in Anxiety." He modifies Freud's concept that the ego produces anxiety to signal danger and to induce defenses and formulates instead: ". . . the ego evaluates the danger and experiences some shade of anxiety. Both evaluation and experience act as a signal to induce defenses. Not only in anticipation of danger, but also in its very presence, and even if the situation has some elements of a traumatic situation, and if the anxiety reaction of the ego is a regressive one, with resomatization, this experience may still serve as signal for the rest of the ego to call for the reserves to take necessary measures. This formulation in no way alters the concept of the function of an anxiety as stimulus of adaptation, defense and symptom formation. . . . The ego is able to *produce danger* and not anxiety. It can do so by manipulating situations and by engaging in fantasies. . . . The concept of 'automatic' anxiety originating in the id (e.g., in sexual frustration) is substituted by the concept of the ego evaluating certain changes in the id as danger and reacting with anxiety. This formulation stresses the fact that anxiety is always an ego response" (pp. 92-93).

2.52 ACCORDING TO FIXATION POINTS

All attempts to classify resistances will necessarily overlap. Nevertheless, it is of help to the psychoanalyst to have ready at his fingertips various kinds of classifications since it can alert him to the typical id material, ego functions, object relations, or superego reaction he may be dealing with. Let me give the following example of an anal resistance which came up during the third year of analysis of a young man, Mr. Z., who was essentially an oral-depressive neurotic character. The recognition of the anal quality of a particular resistance was helpful in eliciting and understanding the underlying unconscious material.

The patient lies on the couch, tense and taut. His fists are clenched, his jaw is tight, one can see the muscles in his cheeks taut, his ankles are crossed tightly, his face is somewhat flushed, his eyes stare straight ahead, he is silent. After a few moments he says, "I'm depressed. Even more than before. I hate myself. I beat myself unmercifully last night . . . [pause]. But it is justifiable. I just don't produce . . . [pause]. I'm not getting anywhere . . . [pause]. I'm stuck. I don't want to work. I refuse to work when I feel like this . . . [silence]. I don't want to talk . . . [long silence]."

The words are spoken in short, clipped phrases and syllables. They are spat out. I can feel in the tone, in the manner, in the posture, that he is angry, but more than that: he is spitefully and defiantly angry. Even though he talks only about hating himself, I feel he is angry and spiteful toward me. Moreover, I am alerted by the kinds of things he says: "I can't produce, I'm stuck." All of this, the content and the attitude, bespeak a kind of anal spite reaction. I keep quiet and then after a considerable silence say to him, "You not only seem to hate yourself but you also seem angry and spiteful toward me." The patient answers, "I'm angry with myself. I woke up at 12:15 and I couldn't sleep after that. I just dozed on and off [silence]. I don't want to work. I would rather give up analysis than work on this. And you know I could almost do it. It's a strange thing to say, but I could almost do it. I could quit right now and go on this way the rest of my life. I don't want to understand it. I don't want to work."

Again I wait and then after a while say, "But this kind of anger is telling us something. It is more than just hating yourself." The patient answered, "I don't want to dissipate the anger. I can sense I am angry, but I don't want to let go of it, I want to hold on to it. I go on all day, all day like this. All of this hatred and anger. I loathe myself. I know you are going to say that loathing is tied up with the toilet, but I don't mean loathing, I mean I hate myself, although I used the word loathing. I keep thinking of murder, of being hanged, or being hanged on a gallows, and I can see myself with a rope around my neck over a trapdoor and it opens and I fall, and I wait for the trapdoor to open and wait for the fall and for my neck to be broken. I can feel myself, I imagine myself dying. Or else I imagine myself being shot by a firing squad. I'm always being executed by some kind of authority, by the state, by some kind of agency. I seem to have a morbid curiosity about hanging and being hanged, and I am always involved with the trapdoors. I am much more involved with hanging than with the firing squad. There is much more variation in the hanging, it is much more frequent, and all through it I hate myself."

Again there follows a period of silence and then I say, "It's not just hate and it's not just myself." To this the patient answers, "I won't give in to it. I'm not going to give in to you. You are trying to push something off on me. I don't want to acknowledge there is any pleasure in it. I have a feeling you hate the idea of my pleasure, and I hate it. I'm just furious about this whole thing. I think you really hate my having pleasures of any kind. You're accusing me, you're a vicious, evil-minded person, you're attacking me. I have to sustain myself, I have to fight you. You seem to be alert to my dirty-mindedness and I have to deny it and have to say it is not there. I have to agree it is terrible if it were there."

At this point I say, "Yes, and you seem to beat yourself in order to prevent me from saying anything." To this the patient answers, "Yes, and I wonder why hanging and why this trapdoor, there's something about the trapdoor and a toilet flushing. I just don't want you to say it. I still resent you, and I feel that the self-flagellation is a protection . . . [pause]. You know, it's a funny thing, I now have the feeling that I'm just beginning my analysis, that I am essentially unanalyzed, and I wonder how long it will take—but it doesn't matter."

I use this case to illustrate that the way the patient was angry, the mode of the resistance, the spiteful, anal anger, was the starting point for a very important piece of analysis. We went from the spiteful anger to the hanging fantasy, which then led to the toilet fantasies and back to the projection of anal hostility onto me. Subsequent months of analysis revealed many important historical determinants. The key to it all, however, was the anal quality of his resistance, the way in which he was angry in that particular hour. Recognizing that spite and defiance are typical of the anal phase of libidinal development, the feeling stuck, the not wanting to produce, the tightness of the jaws, the sadistic and masochistic beating fantasies, the shame, are also all understandable as elements of the anal phase. This was crucial in working with the resistance of that particular hour.

Just as it was possible to classify the above resistance as pertaining to the anal phase, it is similarly possible to decribe oral, phallic, latency, and adolescent resistances. The clue may be given in the instinctual quality of a resistance, or the object relations, or the character trait which is in the foreground, or by a particular form of anxiety or attitude, or by the intrusion of a certain symptom. Thus in the case cited above, we can list the spite, defiance, stubbornness, shame, sadomasochism, retentiveness, and withholding, the marked ambivalence and the obsessive recriminations, all of which are typical of the anal phase. This statement is not intended to deny the existence of "uneven" or heterogenous resistances.

It should be stressed that the form and type of resistance change in a patient during the course of the analysis. There are regressions and progressions which occur, so that every patient manifests a plethora of resistances. In the case cited above, for example, there were long periods of analysis devoted to a working through of phallic drives and anxieties, where masturbation guilt, incestuous fantasies, and castration anxiety were in the foreground. There was a prolonged period of depression and oral resistances manifested by passivity, introjection and identifications, suicidal fantasies, fleeting addictions, anorexia and bulimia, tearfulness, fantasies of being rescued, etc.

2.53 ACCORDING TO TYPES OF DEFENSE

Another fruitful approach to the resistances is to ascertain the type of defense the resistance makes use of. For example, we might distinguish the nine types of defense mechanisms which Anna Freud (1936) described, and note how the resistances employ them in opposing the analytic procedure. *Repression* enters the analytic situation when the patient "forgets" his dream, or his time for the hour, or his mind is blank about crucial experiences, or key people in his past are blotted out, etc.

The resistance of *isolation* enters the clinical picture when patients split off the affects stirred up by an experience from its ideational content. They may describe an event in great verbal detail, but they are prone neither to mention nor to show any emotion. Such patients often isolate the analytic work from the rest of their life. Insights gained in the analysis do not carry over into their everyday lives. Patients who use the mechanism of isolation in their resistance to analysis, often retain the memory of traumatic events, but the emotional connection is lost or displaced. In analysis they will misuse their thinking processes in order to avoid their emotions.

One could go on and list all the various mechanisms of defense against instinctual impulses and affects and describe how the forces of resistance seize upon one or another and utilize them against the analytic procedure. The reader is referred to the basic works on this subject (A. Freud, 1936, pp. 45-58; Fenichel, 1945a, Chapt. IX). For our present purpose it is sufficient to point out that all the ego's mechanisms of defense can be used for purposes of resistance.

However, not only do we see the simple and basic defenses utilized as resistance, but we also see more complex phenomena made use of by the forces of resistance. By far the most important types of resistance met with in analysis are the *transference resistances*. Transference resistances, which are very complex phenomena, will be dealt with in detail in the next chapter. Here I only want to point out that transference resistance refers to two different sets of resistances: (1) those developed by patients because they have transference reactions; (2) those developed by patients to avoid transference reactions. The entire concept of transference is related to resistance, and yet transference reactions are not to be understood only as resistances. I shall therefore postpone a discussion of transference resistance until we have clarified our understanding of the nature of transference.

Acting out is another special resistance maneuver which deserves separate consideration. Here again we are dealing with a phenomenon which always serves a resistance function in the analysis and is quite complicated in its meaning. Acting out contains important id and superego elements as well as ego functions. We define acting out as the enactment of a past event in the present, which is a slightly distorted version of the past, but which seems cohesive, rational, and ego syntonic to the patient. All patients engage in some acting out during analysis, and in inhibited patients this may be a welcome sign. Some patients, however, are prone to repeated and protracted acting out, which makes them difficult if not impossible to analyze. Analyzability depends, in part, on the ego's capacity to bind stimuli sufficiently so that the patient can express his impulses in words and feelings. Patients who tend to discharge their neurotic impulses in action pose a special problem for analysis. The problem of recognizing and handling acting out will be discussed in Section 3.84 and again in Volume II. The reader may familiarize himself with the subject by referring to some of the basic work on the subject (Freud, 1905c, 1914c; Fenichel, 1945b; Greenacre, 1950).

Character resistances are another complex and extremely important type of defense which deserve special mention (W. Reich, 1928, 1929). The question of what is meant by character is not easy to answer. For our present purposes I would simplify the answer and state that by character we refer to the organism's habitual mode of dealing with the internal and external world. It is the ego's constant organized and integrated position and posture in regard to the demands made upon it. The character consists essentially of habits and attitudes. Some of them are predominantly defensive, others are essentially instinctual. Some are compromises. The character trait of cleanliness may well be understood as a defense, a reaction formation, against pleasurable soiling. But we can also see sloppiness as a character trait which is not a reaction formation but an expression of pleasurable soiling.

The character resistances are derived from the character defenses. They pose a special problem in analytic technique because they are habitual, rigidly fixed, and usually ego syntonic. Glover (1955) calls them the silent resistances. By and large the patient is at peace and even approves of his character defenses, since they often appear to conventional society as virtues. The special technical measures which character resistances require will be described later in Section 3.8. W. Reich (1928, 1929), A. Freud (1936), and

Fenichel (1941) should be referred to for a more complete discussion of the nature of character and character resistances.

Screen defenses have also been described which can be used by patients for purposes of resistance. Some patients tend to make extensive use of screen memories, screen affects, and screen identity to ward off an underlying more painful memory, affect, or identity. This defensive formation is also a complicated psychic event and contains important gratifications as well as defenses (Greenson, 1958a).

2.54 ACCORDING TO DIAGNOSTIC CATEGORY

Clinical experience has taught us that certain diagnostic entities make use of special types of defense and therefore that particular resistances will predominate during the course of the analysis. However, many different forms of resistance come to light in all analyses. The clinical entities we describe are rarely seen in pure form; most patients have some admixture of different pathology along with the central diagnosis we give them. Further, during the course of analysis, we see temporary regressions and progressions which complicate the clinical picture and the type of resistances.

An example of this is Mr. Z., the case illustration I used to demonstrate and anal resistance (Section 2.52). The patient had an oral-depressive, neurotic character disorder. However, he had gone through some anal traumata in childhood and he therefore did relive a period of anal spite, hatred, and rage in the particular phase of analysis I described. Just prior to that period his hatred was carefully isolated and confined to special female love objects in his outside life. During the peak of his anal spite he displaced and projected his rage and hatred onto me.

If we briefly survey the typical transference neuroses we treat analytically, I believe we will find the following resistances predominant:

The hysterias: Repression and isolated reaction formations. Regression to phallic characteristics. Emotionality, somatizations, conversions, and genitalizations. Identifications with lost love objects and guilt-producing objects.

The obsessional neuroses: Isolation, undoing, projections, and massive reaction formations. Regression to anality with reaction formation of the character traits: orderliness, cleanliness, and stinginess becoming important resistances. Intellectualization as a resistance to feelings. Magical thinking, omnipotence of thought, rumination. Internalization of hostility and sadistic superego reactions.

The neurotic depressions: Introjections, identifications, acting out, impulsivity, and screen defenses. Oral and phallic instinctuality regressively distorted. Emotionality, counterphobic behavior and attitudes, addictiveness and masochism.

The character neuroses: Depending on whether it is basically a hysterical, obsessional, or depressive character, we would expect to find what is generally described as rigid, ego-syntonic, "silent," habits, traits and attitudes (Freud, 1908; Abraham, 1924; W. Reich, 1928, 1929; A. Freud, 1936, Chapt. VIII; Fenichel, 1945a, Chapt. XX).

2.55 A PRACTICAL CLASSIFICATION

All the classifications described above have their advantages and their limitations. Clinical experience, however, dictates that I mention still another approach which is essentially a practical one. I have found it advantageous to distinguish the ego-alien resistances from the ego-syntonic ones. Ego-alien resistances appear foreign, extraneous, and strange to the patient's reasonable ego. As a consequence, such resistances are relatively easy to recognize and work with. The patient will readily form a working alliance with the analyst in his attempt to analyze the particular resistance.

The following is a typical example. A woman patient was talking quickly, almost breathlessly, and I detected a tremor in her voice. She appeared to be trying desperately to fill up every moment of the analytic hour. There were no pauses, no moments of reflection, just an outpouring of disconnected fragments of memories. In the preliminary interviews I felt quite certain the young woman was essentially a neurotically depressed person. There was no evidence of a psychotic or borderline condition. I also knew she had been "in analysis" with a reputable analyst in another city who considered her an analyzable patient.

I interrupted the patient and told her she seemed to be frightened, she seemed to be trying to fill up every second of the hour, as though she were afraid of being silent for a moment. The patient replied quite timorously that she was afraid I would criticize her for having a resistance, if she were to keep still. I answered quizzically: "Criticize you for having a resistance?" The young woman then responded by telling me that she felt her previous analyst acted as if it was a failing of hers to have a resistance. He seemed very strict and disapproving and she felt he considered her basically unworthy of psychoanalysis. This reminded her of her father who had a violent temper and often shouted at her as a child that she was "no damned good."

I believe the above illustration demonstrates an ego-alien resistance. It also depicts the ease of forming a working alliance with the patient in analyzing the resistance.

Let us contrast this state of affairs with the ego-syntonic resistances. They are characterized by being felt as familiar, rational, and purposeful. The patient does not sense the resistance function of the activity under scrutiny. Such resistances are therefore harder to recognize for the analyst and the patient, and it is more difficult to establish a working alliance in regard to them. These resistances are usually well-established, habitual patterns of behavior of the patient, character traits, sometimes of social value. Reaction formations, acting out, characterological resistances, counterphobic attitudes, and screen defenses belong in this category.

The following is a simple example. A male patient has come to his analytic hour, over a course of two years, from two to five minutes early. At different times I have tried to bring this rigidity to his attention, but he has never felt it to be a problem or worthy of analysis. He admits he is punctual, but he considers this a virtue, a sign of self-discipline, and character. I have not pursued the analysis of this trait but have worked on other aspects of his neurosis which seemed less intractable.

At the end of an hour I tell the patient that I would be about ten minutes late for his next appointment because I would be coming from the university. The patient makes no comment. In the session I want to report, the patient seems quite agitated. He tells me that he was furious with me for being late although he knows I had warned him of this. He accuses me of torturing him deliberately since I must know how much he hates lateness. (He had never acknowledged this before.) He had wanted to come late himself but felt driven by an irresistible force to come his "usual" three minutes early. In the waiting room he couldn't sit quietly. He was tempted to leave the office but was seized by the idea that if he "bumped" into me in the hall I might think he was going to the toilet. That was an intolerable idea. He had no intention of going to the toilet anyway. Even if he had had an urge to go, he would not give in to it because he dreaded the possibility of meeting me there, "face to face." In fact, the thought occurs to him now that he comes early so that he might use the toilet without the risk of an "encounter" with me. He would rather be dead than "caught with his pants down."

The patient becomes silent after this outburst. I say nothing. He resumes in a sad tone of voice: "I suddenly realize I have a new phobia, a fear of meeting you in a toilet." I add gently that the discovery was new, the fear had been there all the time, hidden by his punctuality.

I believe this clinical vignette illustrates the special problems of analyzing ego-syntonic resistances. They require additional work compared to the ego-alien resistances. Actually they have to be made ego alien for the patient before effective analysis can be accomplished. In other words, our task will be first to help the patient establish a reasonable ego in regard to the particular resistance. Only if this is accomplished will the resistance emerge as an ego-alien resistance. Then one can hope to obtain a history of the particular resistance and to analyze it. When the patient can understand the historical reasons for the origin of the resistance defense, he will be able to differentiate his past needs for that defense and the present inappropriateness of that defense.

Ordinarily in the beginning of analysis one works with the ego-alien resistances. Only after the patient has been able to form a reliable working alliance is it possible to start looking for and working on the ego-syntonic resistances. These latter resistances are present from the beginning, but it is pointless to attack them since the patient will either deny their significance or will only give lip service to analyzing them. One must have accomplished some previous work with ego-alien resistance *and* also achieved a reliable working alliance before one can effectively analyze the ego-syntonic resistances.

This subject will be brought up again in Section 2.6. The reader is advised to compare W. Reich (1928, 1929), A. Freud (1936), Fenichel (1941), and Sterba (1951) on this matter.

2.6 Technique of Analyzing Resistances

2.61 PRELIMINARY CONSIDERATIONS

Before launching into a detailed discussion of technical problems it is well to review some fundamental points. Psychoanalysis as a technique came into existence only when resistances were analyzed and not avoided or overcome by other means. One cannot define psychoanalytic technique without including the concept of the consistent and thorough analysis of resistance. It is important to remind ourselves again of the intimate relationship between resistance, defense, ego functions, and object relations.

Resistance is not only to be understood as opposition to the course of analysis, although that is its most direct and obvious clinical manifestation. The study of a patient's resistances will shed light on many basic ego functions as well as on his problems in relating to objects. For example, the absence of resistances may indicate that we are dealing with a psychotic process. A sudden burst of obscene and abusive language and behavior in a hitherto prim and proper housewife may be such a manifestation. Furthermore, resistance analysis also illuminates the way the various ego functions are influenced intrastructurally by the id, the superego, and the external world. In addition, resistances to the therapeutic procedures repeat the neurotic conflicts among the different psychic structures. As a result the analytic situation gives the analyst an opportunity to observe firsthand, on his analytic couch, compromise formations which are analogous to symptom formations. The ever-changing relationship between the forces of the resistances on the one hand, and the urge to communicate on the other, may be seen at its clearest in the patient's attempts at free association. This is one of the reasons free association is considered the primary instrument of communication in psychoanalytic procedure.

The term "analyzing" is a condensed expression for many technical procedures all of which further the patient's insight (see Section 1.32). At least four distinct procedures are included or subsumed under the heading of "analyzing": *confrontation, clarification, interpretation,* and *working through.*

Interpretation is the single most important instrument of psychoanalytic technique. Every other analytic procedure prepares for an interpretation, amplifies an interpretation, or makes an interpretation effective. To interpret means to make an unconscious or preconscious psychic event conscious. It means making the reasonable and conscious ego aware of something it had been oblivious to. We assign meaning and causality to a psychological phenomenon. By interpretation, we make the patient conscious of the history, source, mode, cause or meaning of a given psychic event. This usually requires more than a single intervention. The analyst uses his own conscious mind, his empathy, intuition, and fantasy life, as well as his intellect and theoretical knowledge, in arriving at an interpretation. By interpreting we go beyond what is readily understandable and observable by ordinary conscious, logical thinking. The patient's responses are necessary in order to determine whether the interpretation is valid or not (E. Bibring, 1954; Fenichel, 1941; Kris, 1951).

In order to engage the patient's ego effectively in this psychological work, it is a prerequisite that what is to be interpreted must first be demonstrated and clarified. In order to analyze a resistance, for example, the patient must first be cognizant that a resistance is at work. The resistance must be demonstrable and the patient must be confronted with it. Then the particular variety or precise detail of the resistance has to be placed into sharp focus. *Confrontation* and *clarification* are necessary adjuncts to interpretation and have been recognized as such ever since our knowledge of ego functions has increased (E. Bibring, 1954, p. 763). Sometimes the patient requires no confrontation, clarification or interpretation by the analyst because the patient is able to do this on his own. Sometimes the three procedures occur almost simultaneously or a flash of insight may precede confrontation and clarification.

Working through refers essentially to the repetition and elaboration of interpretations which lead the patient from an initial insight into a particular phenomenon to a lasting change in reaction or behavior (Greenson, 1965b).

Working through makes an interpretation effective. Thus, confrontation and clarification prepare for an interpretation and working through completes the analytic task. But it is interpretation that is the central and major therapeutic instrument in psychoanalysis.

2.611 Dynamics of the Treatment Situation

The treatment situation mobilizes conflicting tendencies within the patient. Before we attempt to analyze the patient's resistances, it would be helpful to survey the alignment of the forces within the patient (see Freud, 1913b, pp. 142-144). I shall begin by enumerating those *forces which are on the side of the psychoanalyst*, the psychoanalytic processes and procedures.

(1) The patient's neurotic misery, which impels him to work in the analysis, no matter how painful. (2) The patient's conscious

rational ego, which keeps the long-range goals in view and comprehends the rationale of the therapy. (3) The id, the repressed, and their derivatives; all those forces within the patient seeking discharge and tending to appear in the patient's productions. (4) The working alliance, which enables the patient to cooperate with the psychoanalyst despite the coexistence of opposing transference feelings. (5) the deinstinctualized positive transference, which permits the patient to overvalue the competence of the analyst. On the basis of little evidence the patient will accept the analyst as an expert. The instinctual positive transference may also induce the patient to work temporarily, but that is far more unreliable and prone to turn into its opposite. (6) The rational superego, which impels the patient to fulfill his duties and obligations. Menninger's "contract" and Gitelson's "compact" express similar ideas (Menninger, 1958, p. 14). (7) Curiosity and the desire for self-knowledge, which motivate the patient to explore and reveal himself. (8) The wish for professional advancement and other varieties of ambition. (9) Irrational factors, such as competitive feelings toward other patients, getting one's money's worth, the need for atonement and confession, all of which are temporary and unreliable allies of the psychoanalyst.

All the forces listed above influence the patient to work in the analytic situation. They differ in value and effectiveness and change during the course of treatment. This will become clearer as we discuss different clinical problems in subsequent chapters.

The forces within the patient *opposing the analytic processes and procedures* may be broken down as follows:

(1) The unconscious ego's defensive maneuvers, which provide the models for the resistance operations. (2) The fear of change and the search for security, which impel the infantile ego to cling to the familiar neurotic patterns. (3) The irrational superego, which demands suffering in order to atone for unconscious guilt. (4) The hostile transference, which motivates the patient to defeat the psychoanalyst. (5) The sexual and romantic transference, which leads to jealousy and frustration and ultimately to a hostile transference. (6) Masochistic and sadistic impulses, which drive the patient to provoke a variety of painful pleasures. (7) Impulsivity and acting-out tendencies, which impel the patient in the direction of quick gratifications and against insight. (8) The secondary gains from the neurotic illness, which tempt the patient to cling to his neurosis.

These are the forces which the analytic situation mobilizes in the patient. As one listens to the patient, it is helpful to have this rather simplified division of forces in the back of one's mind. Many of the items listed above will be discussed in greater detail in the later sections of this book.

2.612 How the Analyst Listens

It might seem unnecessarily pedantic to set down in writing how a psychoanalyst should listen. Yet clinical experience has taught us that the way a psychoanalyst listens is just as unique and complex a procedure as doing free association is for the patient. This matter will be pursued in greater depth in Sections 4.211, 4.212, 4.221, and 4.222. Here only an outline will be sketched as a preliminary briefing.

The analyst listens with three aims in mind: (1) To translate the productions of the patient into their unconscious antecedents. The patient's thoughts, fantasies, feelings, behavior, and impulses have to be traced to their unconscious predecessors. (2) The unconscious elements must be synthesized into meaningful insights. Fragments of past and present history, conscious and unconscious, must be connected so as to give a sense of continuity and coherence in terms of the patient's life. (3) The insights so obtained must be communicable to the patient. As one listens, one must ascertain what uncovered material will be constructively utilizable by the patient.

Clinical experience has suggested a few basic guidelines in order to accomplish these divergent aims (Freud, 1912b, pp. 111-117). (1) One listens with evenly suspended, evenly hovering, free-floating attention. One does not make a conscious attempt to remember. The analyst will remember the significant data if he pays attention and if the patient is not stirring up the analyst's own transference reactions. Nonselective, nondirected attention will tend to rule out one's own special biases and will allow the analyst to follow the patient's lead. From the evenly suspended, free-floating position, the analyst can oscillate and make blendings from among his free associations, empathy, intuition, introspection, problem-solving thinking, theoretical knowledge, etc. (Ferenczi, 1928b; Sharpe, 1930, Chapt. II).

All activities which interfere with the capacity to make the oscillations described above are to be avoided. An analyst should not take any notes if this interferes with his free-floating listening. Word for word notes are obviously contraindicated since that would distort his main purpose. The analyst is primarily an understander and a conveyor of insight. He is not essentially a recorder or a collector of research data (Berezin, 1957). In order to listen effectively one must also pay attention to one's own emotional responses since these responses often lead to important clues. Above all, the analyst must be alert to his own transference and resistance reactions since they can impede or help his understanding of the patient's productions.

The analytic situation is essentially a therapeutic one. The analyst is to administer insight and understanding for therapeutic purposes. He listens to gain insight and he listens from a position of free-floating attention, with restrained emotional responses, with compassion, and with patience. All other scientific pursuits have to be put aside if he is to perform his complicated tasks effectively.

2.62 THE RECOGNITION OF RESISTANCE

The analyst's first task is to recognize that a resistance is present. This may be simple when the resistance is obvious, as they are in the clinical examples cited in Section 2.2. It is more difficult when the resistance is subtle, complex, vague, or ego syntonic to the patient. In the latter instances, the patient may complicate our task by attempting to cover up the fact that he is running away from something. Or the situation may be difficult to ascertain because the patient's material contains a mixture of some meaningful unconscious id content as well as resistance. Observing the patient intellectually may have to be supplemented by the analyst's empathy in order to detect these subtle resistances. Clinical experience and psychoanalytic work under the supervision of an experienced analyst are the best ways of learning to recognize these complex manifestations of resistance. Nevertheless, I would like to illustrate the problem of detecting resistances with a clinical example in order to make some technical points.

A thirty-two-year-old professional man who has been in analysis some six months begins his Monday hour by telling me he is tired, has a headache, and feels somewhat irritable, but he can't pin it down. The weekend had been boring and even a bit depressing. His daughter had wet her bed for the first time in months and his son had a recurrence of an ear infection. The patient, too, had been a bed wetter as a boy and he recalls how his mother had humiliated him for this. His daughter would not suffer what he had had to suffer. His wife is a far more considerate nurse than his mother had been. Of course, this kind of responsibility is a drag and he can't blame his wife for being tired. Nevertheless, she was quite willing to have sex and even went out of her way to do the things he liked. She volunteered to suck his penis and she did, but she is not very good at it. Maybe his preference for being sucked is a sign of homosexuality. That had come up in the Friday hour, he believes. Yes, we had talked about his interest in comparing penis sizes with other men. This idea had tormented him when he had dated other women. Did they prefer men whose penes were larger than his? His son seems to be "well hung," maybe he won't have the sexual problems the patient had to endure. Somebody once said, "Anatomy is fate." But he had never been a believer in axioms and he had always despised religion.

The above is an excerpt of the highlights of about forty minutes of the hour. As I listened I heard a depressive and angry undertone and the material seemed to be in accord with this mood. The weekend was boring, the daughter had wet, the son was ill, the wife was only passably pleasing sexually, other men had larger penises, and fate had been unkind to him. As I went along with him in his associations I expected a breakthrough of some underlying angry or depressive impulse at different points in the hour and I did not intervene. But this failed to materialize. It seemed to me that the patient was struggling with some latent strong emotions, but his material seemed to point to too many different significant possibilities.

Was he angry at his mother, fate, his wife, or was all of this related to me? Did he feel more angry than aggrieved or depressed? I was not certain what was the most important underlying content seeking discharge, and whether it would eventually emerge on its own or whether the resistances would be sustained. I therefore allowed him to go on until almost the end of the hour. At this point I decided to intervene because despite the presence of some unconscious derivatives, there seemed to be a goodly amount of resistance and yet his reasonable ego seemed accessible to an interpretation.

I said to him: "You feel you have been mistreated by your mother, your wife, your kids, and by fate. You sound slightly depressed and angry, but you seem to be holding back your feelings." The patient could hardly wait for me to finish and blurted out: "Yes, there is more. As you were talking, I felt disgusted and enraged at your saccharine tone. Then I remembered that before Friday's hour I was furious with you for keeping me waiting while you gave that pretty woman patient some of my time. I guess I didn't mention it in that hour, but I know I thought of it after I left. As I was driving home I made a wrong turn and almost drove into another car. That night as I was falling asleep I had a peculiar sensation in my hands, they felt paralyzed. I had the thought that maybe I will have to kill someone if I want to get well. Maybe I'll have to have a temper tantrum right in your presence. Sometimes I get the feeling I'd love to wring the necks of all you good, kind people. You're even more hypocritical than I am. At least I have the honesty to have symptoms."

I believe the patient's response indicates that I was correct in recognizing the presence of resistance and in pointing it out. I might have intervened at earlier points in the hour and tried to pursue one or another of the themes he presented. For example, I could have tried to get him to explore how his mother had humiliated him or his fear of homosexuality that had already been present in Friday's hour, or his resentment at having been cheated by fate. But it was my feeling that he was hovering over some emotions and impulses that were struggling to break through; I therefore decided to focus on the struggle, i.e., the battle between the unconscious impulses seeking discharge and the resistances opposing them. This struggle is what came most clearly to the surface in his free association. Our task is a simpler one when one or the other prevails in a clear-cut fashion as they do in the clinical examples in Section 2.2 or in those so-called "good hours" when derivatives become less and less distorted. In listening to a patient our first duty is to determine whether unconscious derivatives, i.e., "content," predominate or forces of resistance, or whether we are dealing with a stalemate.

This leads to the next question: how does one recognize resistance when the material is not obvious. The answer is based on our understanding of free association and the opportunity it affords the patient in analysis. By asking the patient to let things come to mind and to report them without the usual social censorship, we try to rule out the conscious resistances. The result exposes the struggle between the more unconscious resistances and the unconscious id derivatives trying to gain discharge. Fenichel (1941, p. 34) used the analogy of releasing a compass needle and watching it swing back and forth. There are two signs of possible disturbance: the needle does not come to rest but it keeps on swinging, or else it comes to rest too quickly, too directly. In the first instance of the needle swinging constantly the patient is talking about heterogeneous material which does not localize around some unconscious impulse or some common denominator seeking expression. Localization would take place if there were no significant resistances at work. When the needle sets itself too exactly and directly, then we can assume that the patient has a conscious program and is omitting the stray thoughts that must arise if his associating is done relatively freely.

I have found it useful to ask myself as I listen to the patient: is he going toward or away from something unconsciously meaningful? Is the material deepening or flattening out? Is the patient adding something significant or is he padding the hour? If he seems to be going toward something, I remain quiet until that something becomes clear. If he seems to be going away from something, I wait until that is sufficiently clear, then I recognize this as resistance and proceed to work with it. Sometimes I remain uncertain. I usually say to the patient at the end of such an hour that I am not clear about what is going on.

2.63 CONFRONTATION: THE DEMONSTRATION OF RESISTANCE

The first step of the general procedure in analyzing resistance was devoted to a description of what the analyst must perform by himself before he can work with his patient on resistances. The succeeding points are all steps the analyst attempts to carry out conjointly with his patient. To put it briefly, our task is to get the patient to understand *that* he is resisting, *why* he is resisting, *what* he is resisting, and *how* he is resisting.

Demonstrating the resistance may be relatively simple or even an unnecessary step if the resistance is obvious to the patient. If this is not the case, if the patient is unaware of the resistance, then it is essential to confront the patient with the fact that a resistance is present before we attempt anything further. The patient's ability to recognize a resistance will depend on two things: the state of his reasonable ego and the vividness of the resistance. A highly reasonable ego will take cognizance of the slightest resistance and a barely reasonable one will demand overwhelming evidence of resistance. Our task is to assess, via observation and empathy, the status of the patient's reasonable ego in order to determine how clear must the evidence of the resistance be in order for the patient to recognize it as such. Confronting the patient ought to be undertaken only when there is a likelihood that the confrontation will be meaningful to him, and when he will not succeed in his attempt to deny or minimize its validity. Premature demonstration of resistance is not only a waste of time but it dissipates material that might be effective at some later point. No matter how clear the evidence of resistance may seem to be, the decisive factor is—will this confrontation have meaning for the patient? Let me illustrate with a simple example:

A patient, early in analysis, comes a few minutes late and breathlessly explains that she had difficulty finding a parking place for her car. To point this out to the patient right then and there as a resistance would be an error. First of all, you might be wrong and your intervention would have distracted the patient from the real content she was ready to communicate. But furthermore, you will have wasted a potentially valuable opportunity by using a questionable instance that the patient might successfully deny. If you had waited silently, and if your idea were correct, this little resistance would be followed by others. The patient I am describing fell silent at different intervals of the session. She then reported that she had forgotten her dream of the preceding night. Again silence. My silence had permitted her resistance to grow which increased the likelihood that she would not be able to deny my later confrontation.

In order to increase the demonstrability of a resistance, it is advisable to let the resistance develop. For this your silence is the best method of approach. But at times one can use another technique to increase the resistance and the demonstrability. Again I can illustrate this best with a clinical example:

A young man, Mr. S., early in his analysis, comes to his hour and begins by saying: "Well, I had a rather successful marital experience last night with my wife. It was very satisfactory for both parties concerned." He then goes on to talk in a very restrained way about how he enjoys "making love" to his wife, and then proceeds to talk about rather innocuous goings-on. I intervene at this point and say, "You mentioned earlier that you enjoyed a 'marital experience' last night. Please explain to me what you mean by a 'marital experience.'" The patient hesitates, flushes, and then haltingly begins to explain, pauses, and says, "I guess you want me to be more specific . . ." and pauses again. Now I answer: "You seem bashful when it comes to talking about sexual matters." The patient then spends the rest of the hour describing his difficulties in talking about sex. He has now begun to work on his resistances.

It was obvious to me that the patient had considerable reluctance to talk about his "marital experience" and yet he was attempting to glide over it by going on to speak of trivia. I highlighted his reluctance by asking for elaboration of precisely that part of his material. Then the existence of resistance was inescapable. We then proceeded to work on his resistance about talking of sex, which was the vital subject matter of that hour.

The two illustrations exemplify two methods of facilitating the demonstration of resistances by increasing the resistance: the analyst's silence and asking for elaboration about a resistant point. These methods will vivify the resistance and make it recognizable by the patient's reluctant reasonable ego. By asking the patient to notice that he seems reluctant to talk about sexual matters the analyst has shifted the conflict situation for the patient by saying in effect: "Don't talk about sex but tell me about your trouble in talking about sex." We first have to analyze his resistance to talking on sexual matters before we can effectively analyze his sexual problems. Furthermore, he will not be able to present a clear picture of his sexual problems until he is able to communicate effectively on this subject.

Another technique for helping the patient recognize the presence of resistance forces is to point out all the clinical evidence. In the case of the lady who came a few minutes late to her hour because she could find no parking place, I waited until there were at least two other signs of resistance. Then I intervened by saying, "You seem to be avoiding something. You came a bit late, then you became silent, and now you tell me you forgot your dream." The patient herself is now persuaded that she is running away. If I had intervened at the first small sign, she might have dismissed it with a rationalization. It should be noted that I merely point out what brought me to the conclusion she was resisting. I did not insist she was resisting. I suggested this as a possibility to her. If she were to deny this, I would not try to convince her on the basis of the clinical evidence. I would become silent and observe whether she now tries to cover up the resistances or if they intrude even more pronouncedly. One can only prove something to a reasonable ego—one will have to wait until a reasonable ego appears or until the evidence is so overwhelming that even the puniest reasonable ego will have to acknowledge it.

2.64 THE CLARIFICATION OF RESISTANCE

Let us continue with the procedure for analyzing a resistance. We have made the patient aware that he has a resistance. What do we do next? There are three possibilities that we may now pursue: (1) Why is the patient avoiding? (2) What is the patient avoiding? (3) How is the patient avoiding? The first two questions: why and what is the patient avoiding; can be considered together as the motive for the resistance. The question how is the patient avoiding, refers to the mode or means of resistance. It does not matter which of the two we pursue, the motive or the mode of resistance. In either case, the analysis would proceed by *clarifying* the matter under scrutiny. We would attempt to sharpen our focus on the psychic process we are trying to analyze. We would carefully single out and isolate the particular motive or mode of resistance we are attempting to explore. The significant details would have to be dug out and carefully separated from the extraneous matter.

I shall start with the clarification of the motive for resistance because, all things being equal, it takes precedence over the mode of resistance, since it is more productive. Only when we feel that the means of resistance is striking or unusual would we pursue that question first. Or if we have already guessed from the material why and what the patient is running from, would we explore the method the patient is using.

The question, "Why is the patient resisting?" can be reduced to: what painful affect is he trying to avoid. The answer to this question is closer to consciousness usually than the answer to the question "What instinctual impulses or traumatic memories make for the painful affect." As stated earlier, the immediate motive for defense and resistance is to avoid pain, i.e., painful affects. The resistant patient is trying to ward off some painful emotion like anxiety, guilt, shame, or depression, or some combination of them. Sometimes, despite the resistance, the painful affect is obvious because the patient behaves in a way which is characteristic of that specific affect. For example, a patient talking hesitantly or in clichés or rambling around in trivia may betray his sense of shame by blushing or by covering his face with his hands, turning his head away so that one cannot see any part of his face, covering his genital area with his hands or suddenly crossing his thighs tightly together, etc. Hiding behavior indicates shame. Tremor, sweating, dryness of tongue and mouth, muscular tension, quivering or rigidity may be signs of fear. In a patient who has been talking in a slow, mournful tone, the clenched jaw, sighing, silence, painful swallowing, and tight fists may indicate the struggle against tears and depression.

In all these instances, I am trying to detect the nonverbal, bodily reactions that are taking place. They may offer us clues as to what particular painful affect the patient is struggling with. If I think I can detect the specific affect, I confront the patient with, "You seem to be embarrassed, or afraid, or sad, or afraid of crying." I say "You seem," not "You are." Why? Because, first of all, I might be wrong, and secondly I want to give him a chance to run if he needs to. Later on, I may become more assertive if I am more certain of my correctness or if his running from working with the resistances ought to become the subject of discussion.

If I cannot detect the particular painful affect, then I would simply ask, "What feelings are you trying to push away?" or "How did you feel when you were trying to describe to me your sexual experience of last night?" or "What are you feeling as you lie there silently?"

Some technical points of importance have to be mentioned here. My language is simple, clear, concrete, and direct. I use words that cannot be misunderstood, that are not vague or evasive. When I am trying to pin down the particular affect the patient might be struggling with, I try to be as specific and as exact as possible. I select the word which seems to portray what is going on in the patient, the word which reflects the patient's situation of the moment. If the patient seems to be experiencing an affect as though he were a child, for example, if the patient seems anxious like a child, I would say: "You seem scared," because that is the childhood word. I would never say, "You seem apprehensive" because that would not fit, that is a grown-up word. Furthermore, "scared" is evocative, it stirs up pictures and associations, while "apprehensive" is drab. I will use words like bashful, shy, or ashamed, if the patient seems to be struggling with feelings of shame from the past. I would not say humiliation or abasement or meekness.

In addition, I also try to gauge the intensity of the affect as accurately as possible. If the patient is very angry, I don't say, "You seem annoyed," but I would say, "You seem furious." I use the ordinary and vivid word to express the quantity and quality of affect I think is going on. I will say things like: You seem irritable, or edgy, or grouchy, or sulky, or grim, or quarrelsome, or furious, to describe different kinds of hostility. How different are the associations to "grouchy" as compared to "hostile." In trying to uncover and clarify the painful affect and the memories associated to that specific affect, the word one uses should be right in time, quality, quantity, and tone. More will be said about this when I discuss transference interpretations and tact in Section 3.943 and Volume II.

Just as we attempt to clarify the affect causing the resistance, so would we try to clarify the impulse causing the affect, if that were to present itself in the analysis.

Let me illustrate. A patient who has been in analysis for over three years and who ordinarily has little difficulty talking about sexual matters suddenly sounds evasive when he describes sexual intercourse with his wife that occurred early that morning. He is obviously embarrassed about something that happened. I decide to give him a chance to clarify this himself. He finally says: "I guess it's hard to tell you that we had some anal play this morning." Pause, silence. Since I had a good working alliance with him in general, I pursued the point directly. I merely repeat: "Anal play?" but I add the question mark. The patient gulps and sighs and replies: "Yes, I somehow wanted to poke my finger into her anus, her ass hole, I guess I mean, and I'll be damned if I understand that since she seemed to dislike it, but I persisted. I wanted to force something into her against her will, I wanted to burst into her, tear her in some way. Maybe I was angry with her unbeknownst to myself or maybe it wasn't my wife at all. I just know I wanted to hurt her down there."

This is an example of partially clarifying an instinctual impulse, in particular, clarifying the instinctual aim. In this instance the aim was to inflict intrusive, tearing pain on a woman "down there." During the rest of the hour and in the next hour we were able to clarify this further. The woman he was hurting in his fantasy was his mother and he was trying to tear into her "cloaca," where he imagined his baby brother had been born from, when he was age three. The other meanings of this activity, particularly those connected to me, his "anal-ist," would lead us too far afield.

Just as we have clarified the painful affect or forbidden impulse which motivates a resistance, so might it become necessary to clarify the mode of a resistance, *how* a patient is resisting. Before we can explore the unconscious history of the means the patient uses to resist, we first have to be sure that the issue under discussion is sharply defined for the patient and extraneous or ambiguous material is dissected away.

For example, one of my patients, Professor X., who is an extremely intelligent and articulate biologist, has a strange way of reporting a dream. He begins the hour by stating he had an interesting dream last night and "you were in it and there was something sexual going on." Then he reflects a moment silently and says, "I'm not sure it was last night, it may have been this morning. I went into a large schoolroom and there was no seat for me. I felt embarrassed at being late just as I often do now when I come late to a meeting. The last time this happened I had to go to a small office nearby and drag in a small chair and I felt very foolish. That's the way I used to feel when I would visit one of my father's classes when he taught summer school. He had large classes and the students were a good deal older than I was. He was an excellent teacher, but I think he himself was awed by the students or maybe I was projecting. Now I get the thought that maybe he also had homosexual tendencies that made him ill at ease, or is that also one of my projections? Anyway I was in this large classroom which turned into a moving picture theater. Something went wrong with the film and I was furious with the movie operator. As I went to scold him I saw he was tearful. He had soft big eyes like a Greek, that's where you come in. At least that's what occurred to me when I awoke this morning. Those big droopy eyelids overflowing with tears remind me of you and if I think of a man crying, it makes me feel soft and loving and I suppose that's connected to homosexuality and my father, although I can't recall my father crying. He was always so absorbed in his work or his hobbies, and the only emotions he showed were toward my sister and older brother. My sister was in the dream, that part when I was in the movie theater. When the movie got dark and there was nothing on the screen she said to me that we shouldn't have come. That's when I got angry with you. My sister wanted to be an actress at one time; in fact, we often acted in plays together and she would play the boy's role and I the girl's. Now that I think of it, there were all boys in the classroom and in the movie there were mostly girls, etc., etc."

This is a sample of a particular mode of resistance this patient demonstrated when he reported dreams or told of an incident from his present or past life. He never told the incident precisely as it occurred but often started in the middle, jumped to the beginning, then to the end, interspersed his report with associations and some interpretations, and then filled in some details from the beginning, middle, or end that he had omitted. I was loath to interrupt him because I did not want to disturb the flow of his associations. However, I was never sure of the manifest content of what he was reporting and what his associations were. I was never certain if I had heard the complete dream or incident he was recounting and if I inquired, his responses also contained mixtures of fact, fantasy, and associations.

I finally asked him whether he was aware of the fact that he could not simply tell a dream or incident from his life from beginning to end, but would start in the middle and I described in detail how he communicated. At first he protested weakly that he thought he was supposed to say things as they came into his mind, but he smiled and sighed after a bit and said that he knew he had this tendency to "scramble" his assignments or duties. He then spontaneously reported that he never read a book from the beginning but usually started from the middle and read piecemeal toward the end and then toward the beginning. In school, and he had many years of postgraduate study in which he excelled, he never started homework assignments from the beginning but either from the middle or the end. He did the same in other spheres as well. While he was in elementary school he started writing a book on advanced mathematics, and while he was a beginner in his profession he started teaching men many years his senior.

I shall describe some of the unconscious determinants and meanings of this mode of resistance in Section 2.652 on the interpretation of the mode of resistance. Here let me state that the crux of the matter had to do with the fact that his father was a well-known teacher and academician, and his entire family were renowned for their studiousness. At the moment, the point I want to stress is how the clarification of the mode of resistance was the starting point for many important insights into the unconscious factors.

2.65 THE INTERPRETATION OF RESISTANCE

2.651 Interpreting the Motive for Resistance

Here I must interpolate that sometimes it is not necessary for the analyst to demonstrate and clarify the resistance because the patient does this for himself spontaneously. These steps do not necessarily go in the sequence described since both events may occur more or less simultaneously. After the resistance is demonstrable and clear, we are ready to attempt to interpret the unconscious determinants. That means we try to uncover the hidden instinctual impulses, fantasies or memories which are responsible for the resistance. (It is customary in psychoanalytic discussions to designate as "content" the repressed or warded-off unconscious impulses, fantasies or memories which determine a given psychic event.) In analyzing the motive for a resistance we would attempt to explore the content which caused the painful affect that brought about the resistance.

Let us return to the patient, Mr. S., in Section 2.63, who became bashful when he tried to talk of his "marital experience." In order to understand his embarrassment we would now try to uncover what impulses, fantasies, or historical events were associated to his talking about sexual matters. The exploration of the content might lead us to feelings, impulses, and fantasies that occurred as he was speaking in the hour, to transference reactions, or to his past history, or from one to the other. Ordinarily we let the patient decide which avenue to pursue and ask an open-ended question such as: "What occurs to you when you imagine talking about sex?"

The shy Mr. S., with the "marital experience," responded to my question and began to recount that sex was considered a dirty and forbidden subject at home, that he was scolded for asking about how babies are born and told this was not a fit subject for a decent boy, etc. He later overcame this shyness with his school companions, but he still reacts with embarrassment when sexual matters come up with a stranger or authority. This then led to his feelings about me as a stranger and authority. Though he intellectually knew I must be familiar with all kinds of sexual experiences, nevertheless he found himself reacting as though I would be very prudish and would reprimand him. I interpreted to him that the moment he mentioned sex I had become a father figure and he became a little boy. If the patient had not spontaneously let his thoughts drift back to me and had only talked about his embarrassment at home, I would have said to him before the end of the hour: "And now you react to me as though I were your parent and you become embarrassed." The analysis of resistances must always include the analysis of the transference resistance, a subject that will be elucidated in Chapter 3.

The further analysis of Mr. S.'s embarrassment in talking about sex took place over a period of several years. In the process of working through we discovered that he felt he had to hide his sexual interest because he was afraid of being considered oversexed. This was connected to childhood memories of sexual games with his sisters and sexual fantasies concerning his mother. His masturbation fantasies concerned watching "grownups" in intercourse and then watching them being beaten. He also had deeply repressed masochistic wishes of being beaten as well as a tendency to identify with the woman's role. Mr. S. had great anxiety in his relationship with men since it was still full of instinctual impulses, both hostile and sexual. He was also uncertain about his gender identity, his feeling of being male. This is a condensed report on the analysis of the motives for his resistance to talking about sex.

But let us return to our analysis of the motive for resistance. The patient avoids because he wants to escape some painful feeling. But *what* content, what material is evoking the painful affect? The man with the "marital experience" revealed the content by trying to talk about sex despite his timidity. In this instance, it was clear that sexual material was the immediate cause of the embarrassment and the resistance. But there are instances when it is not clear either why or what the patient is resisting. A patient may keep silent more or less for an entire hour and not betray any clue of what is going on by his bodily reactions or facial expressions. In my experience this is a rare occurrence. The absolute silence and the lack of body and facial expression would seem to be clues to fantasies about death, coma or deep sleep. On the two occasions it has happened in my practice it means a combination of murderous rage and suicide (Greenson, 1961).

Let us assume that we have first worked on the why, and we have ascertained the specific painful affect, but still have no clue as to what evoked it.

Again an example: a young woman patient, Mrs. K., who was mentioned earlier (Section 1.24), in her third year of analysis, has been working quite productively of late and then has an hour in which she shows considerable resistance. She begins the hour by saying she didn't feel like coming to the session, she has nothing on her mind, why don't I give her a hint as to what to talk about, her life is going along quite smoothly, her baby is wonderful, her new apartment is comfortable, maybe she ought to let well enough alone, she has improved, and does she really need to go on in her analysis, she went to an interesting art gallery and didn't buy anything, she had a date with an "egghead," the men she meets are either "slobs" or "eggheads"—and on and on, interspersed by short silences. I was aware her tone had a quality of irritability and annoyance. So after some ten minutes of this, I intervene and say: "You seem annoyed." She answers: "I guess I am, but I don't know about what." I say: "Something is irritating you. Lets try to find it. Just let your thoughts drift with the idea, 'something is annoying me.'"

The patient is silent for a moment and then says suddenly: "Oh, I forgot to tell you my mother phoned me last night from New York." The patient then goes on to recount the phone conversation and her reactions to it in a steely, cold tone, in a stilted, jerky rhythm. The mother had reproached her for not writing, and the patient was furious but controlled herself and acted only aloof and disdainful. Bitterly, she says that she would send her mother her regular check, but she'd be damned if she would write. Pause, silence. "I don't intend to get involved with her again . . . even though I know you want me to. . . . You say it will help my analysis and maybe you're right, but I can't, and I won't, and I don't want to get involved with you either."

I keep silent. I recollect that in the hour before she had told me of a date she had had with an artistic young man. She had felt he was interesting, even fascinating, but there was something about him which had repelled her. In that hour we did not discover what that repulsive feeling was due to. The patient then goes on to tell me about her two-year-old daughter, how she loves to play with her, and how beautiful the baby's body is, not ugly like a grown woman's, and how she loves to bathe her. She stops and suddenly recalls a dream: She was a member of the frog women—she was supposed to go into the harbor of Moscow and to memorize what she saw under water. The water was cold and dark but she was protected by her rubber suit. There was the danger that something would explode and she had to hurry and get out. There was some idea that she had to finish by 4 o'clock.

The patient's associations lead to a story she had heard that people who die in their sleep die at 4 A.M. Maybe she is afraid I might die; she had heard I had some heart condition. When she awoke, the roof of her mouth was sore, she must have been rubbing it with her tongue in her sleep. That's a problem we have never gotten to the bottom of. Her stomach aches. She feels tight. She ought to work on this, but she feels weary and depressed. Silence. I say at this point: "You are afraid of what you are going to find under water, in your unconscious mind. You are scared, so you put on your rubber suit, so you won't feel things, so you won't get involved—in what?"

The patient thinks a moment and says: "I'm tempted to run, to go back to how I was before analysis, being bored and empty. I'm tired of fighting and searching, I want to relax and take it easy. You're pushing me and I want you to do the work. I had a fantasy yesterday that I developed cancer of the larynx and couldn't talk and then you'd have to do all the work." Pause.

I reply: "You're annoyed at me because I won't feed you; I won't be your good mommy." The patient literally shouts at me. "Don't say that word, I can't stand it. I hate it and you, too. Yes, I want you to help me but not just work for me; I want you to be warm and kind. All you do is work, work, work [pause]. . . . I guess you're right. I want you to take care of me like I take care of my baby. You know, yesterday when I was bathing her, I looked at her genitals, her vulva, and it looked so beautiful, like a flower, like a luscious piece of fruit, an apricot. I could have kissed it, only I know it wouldn't be good for her." I say simply: "For her?" The patient goes on: "Well, not just for her, I suppose, but also for me. Which reminds me, you know that artist I dated a few days ago. We went to the beach and I noticed his thighs were very fleshy, and his behind, too, like a woman's. Maybe that is what repulsed me." I answer: "And fascinated you, too. That's the dangerous harbor you are afraid to find under water. That's what you're running from." The patient: "I bought a bikini bathing suit for my daughter, she looks just adorable in it—its bright red—I could eat her up in it—and I mean literally—eat her up."

This is an unusually productive hour for one that began with considerable resistance. However, the patient was a hard worker in her analysis and had established a good working alliance. I think it is a clear example of how I like to pursue the question what are the motives for defense. If we review the hour, one can see the patient was aware of her resistance, she didn't feel like coming, she didn't want to get involved. The early material of the hour gave no definitive clue, only some hostility to men, but not enough to go on. Then I confronted her with her resistance and asked her to associate to feeling annoyed. This led to her recalling her angry, cold talk with her mother, and her anger with me. Then she remembered her dream, a sign that the resistance interpretation was on the right track. The manifest content of the anxiety dreams shows beautifully her fear of discovering some unconscious impulses. The harbor symbolizes mother as does the water. The frog-woman idea hints at homosexuality. Then, too, she recalled the dream while she was talking of bathing her baby. Her first associations led to her fear and wish I would die. She needs me and fears me. She rubbed the roof of her mouth, a repetition of infantile sucking impulses. Then

more resistance and not wanting to work and her fury at my interpretation that she wants me to be her "mommy."

Thus, in the resistance we see the repressed impulses returning
—the dread of her infantile longings for her mother. Then her associations to her baby and the frank oral-incorporative and sexual
desires toward the baby's vulva. Again an attempt to displace her
anxiety onto her baby and again getting her to see she is running
from her own fears. Then the confirmation by her association to the
thighs and behind of her artist friend. And the final confirmation
going back to her baby's red (red=Moscow) bathing suit and the
urge to eat her up.

The answer to the question, what is the patient avoiding, what
caused the painful affect which made her angry at me and the analysis, is: She was trying to avoid her oral active and passive homosexual, sadistic strivings toward her mother, her child, and me.
These were the motives for her resistance.

I stated earlier that in attempting to analyze the motive for
resistance, one ordinarily begins with trying to uncover the painful
affect because the painful affect is usually more accessible to the
conscious ego than the content evoking the painful affect. That is
not always true and sometimes the content may reveal itself in the
analytic hour before we are clear about the affect. Our task then
is to pursue the content of the resistance which will, if we are successful, illuminate the affect. We start with the material on hand
and then proceed to search for what is missing—we go from the
known to the unknown. The following example illustrates how the
content of a resistance became known before the affect:

A male patient comes to an hour after I had been out of town for a
week. He reports that he had a wonderful vacation while I was gone.
He speaks glowingly of how he had gone on a short trip to the country,
how very rested he felt, how well he got along with his wife and children,
how he was able to do a lot of physical exercise and reading. And then,
after five minutes of describing how he enjoyed himself while I was on
vacation, he suddenly runs out of things to say and becomes silent. I keep
silent. He wonders what we had been talking about before I had gone
on vacation. Pause. He wonders if *I* remembered what he had been talking about before I had gone. Do analysts remember what their patients
tell them? Another pause. He wonders where I had gone and what I
had done. He wonders, did I go alone or did I go with my wife. He

thought that I seemed somewhat drawn and pale the last hour before my absence. He recalls now having some concern about my health. He even recalls a thought that maybe I would die. He wonders, had I left somebody's name for him to go to in case I should become sick or die.

All this he says with much hesitation and much pausing. It is obvious that he is resisting. It is also quite obvious that what he is avoiding is talking in greater detail and with more feeling about his reactions to my absence. I therefore confront him by saying, "You seem reluctant to really talk about the different feelings you had about me when I went away, when I left you behind." To this he promptly brings up how he resented being left behind, and how often this happened to him in his past. His father often went away alone on vacations, leaving him and his mother home alone. Then he goes on to other memories when he and his mother went away alone, leaving his father behind, which then led to all kinds of death wishes about his father. At the end of the hour, it is clear that the painful feelings he was trying to avoid were his angry death wishes and disappointment in me for having left him behind.

I submit this illustration as an example of how the event that is the motive for the resistance becomes clear despite the resistance and thus becomes the starting point for the analysis of the resistance. This then leads to the affects, impulses, fantasies, and memories.

Again it should be stressed that by uncovering the specific event or affect which triggered the resistance, in this case the event, one goes from the resistance to the history of that particular event or affect or fantasy in the patient's life. Whether one begins with the affect or the event, or the fantasy, one eventually arrives at the history of the affects or events or fantasy. If this succeeds, the analyst can then come back to the current resistance in the analysis and point out to the patient: "Yes . . . and my going away seems to have stirred up a similar reaction in you which you are afraid to tell me." Once more the patient becomes aware that the resistances which occur in the analysis are a repetition of events that happened before in the patient's life. To repeat: resistances are not an artifact of analysis, they are not new creations, but repetitions, new editions of past events.

A clinical note of importance that should be reiterated at this point is that the most frequent source of resistance is the transference situation. Every clinical example I have cited bears this out, although I have not always stressed it. All other things being equal or being obscure or unknown, one has to look for the transference reactions as the source of resistance. I shall go into this in detail in Chapter 3.

2.652 *Interpreting the Mode of Resistance*

Sometimes, in attempting to analyze a resistance, it is not the affect, the impulse, or the causative event which is the most promising avenue for exploration. It may be that the mode of resistance, the method or means of resistance, offers the most fruitful avenue for investigation. This is apt to be the case if the mode of resistance is often repeated, in which case we are probably dealing with a trait of character. Although the analysis of the mode may not often be the first approach to the analysis of resistance, the typical and habitual methods of resistance eventually have to become the subject of analysis, since this procedure is the gateway to analyzing the so-called character defenses. If the mode of resistance is bizarre and "out of character" for the patient, it is usually a symptomatic act and usually more easily accessible to the patient's reasonable ego.

The steps in analyzing the mode of resistance are the same as outlined for other aspects of resistance. First of all we have to get the patient to recognize that a given piece of behavior is a resistance. This may be simple or quite difficult, depending on whether the activity is ego syntonic or ego alien. If the resistance behavior is an ego-syntonic character trait, the question then is, how difficult is it to make the behavior ego dystonic; in other words, can one enlist the aid of the patient's reasonable ego and get it to join with the analyst in regarding this activity as resistance (Fenichel, 1941, pp. 66-68). Can one succeed in splitting off a reasonable ego from the patient's experiencing ego, and so get the patient to explore the activity in question?

The demonstrability will depend on two factors: first, on the ego's relationship to the activity, i.e., how ego syntonic it is; and second, on the working alliance, i.e., how willing the patient is to take an analytic attitude. The more coherent, adaptive, and successful an activity appears to the patient, the more difficult it will be to persuade him this activity is a resistance. In our society, for example, it is not easy to get a woman patient to regard her habitual neatness in her free associations and in her outside life as something to be analyzed. Neatness is a virtue in American society, one is praised and highly esteemed for this trait in the family. The bombardment of the advertising community helps make neatness an ego ideal for many people even in later life.

How different this is from attempting to analyze a more ego-alien activity. For example, a patient in a very strong hostile transference falls asleep momentarily during an hour. Despite the aggressive attitude toward me the patient could recognize that falling asleep during the hour was a resistance.

The situation is more difficult when reality factors are intermingled with the patient's unconscious resistances.

For example, a patient spends a good portion of her hour talking about the dangers of a nuclear bomb attack and the advisability of moving away to the Midwest where she would be safer. When I suggest that perhaps she would feel safer moving away from me and psychoanalysis, she is obviously angry and falls silent. Then she truculently reminds me that people are building bomb shelters. After a pause I acknowledge that there is some possibility of a nuclear attack, but I believe her reactions are inappropriately intense. Most experts are of the opinion that shelters are not sufficient protection and moving away also would not guarantee her safety. Then the patient begins to talk. She admits her fears might be out of proportion, but the merest thought of an atomic explosion terrifies her. I tell her that every reasonable person fears an atomic war, but there must be something else going on in her that makes her fear so strong that she would contemplate uprooting her life. Slowly the patient begins to associate, her thoughts leading to her unhappy marriage, her years of frustration and inhibition, and her desire to get it "out of her system," to start a new life. I am now able to show her that it is the accumulated rage inside her which threatens to explode. That is what makes the nuclear bomb explosion seem so imminent. This is why her fear intensifies to terror. The patient seems to understand and the next several hours we work productively on this theme.

I want to pause at this point to underscore a small but important technical point. Whenever reality factors compound a resistance, the reality factors have to be adequately acknowledged (Marmor, 1958). If one does not do so, the patient will cling all the more vociferously to the reality element of the resistance and will spend his time trying to convince the analyst of the logic of his argument.

Note how my patient brought up bomb shelters when I tried to interpret her flight to the Midwest as a flight from the analysis. Only after I admitted there was some reality to her fear could she begin to work with me, could she form a working alliance. Until then her anxiety about the nuclear bomb was ego syntonic. My acknowledgment of the reality factor promoted the establishment of a working alliance and then the fear of the nuclear explosion, at least in its intensity, became ego alien to her. She was able to work on this as an internal problem and eventually did recognize the flight to the Midwest as a transference resistance.

Once the patient has recognized the resistance aspect of his behavior, our next task is *clarification*. We now seek out the pattern of behavior outside of analysis and then pursue the history and purpose of this activity. What happened in the patient's life to cause him to adopt this way of resisting? Let me return to Professor X., the man who reported his dreams in a "scrambled" fashion (see Section 2.64).

Professor X. recounted how he read books in this "scrambled" manner and did his homework in this way. He could not study sitting at a desk but only lying down or walking! This became understandable when I realized his father had been a well-known teacher and had groomed his son to follow in his footsteps. The boy wanted to rebel because he had deep-seated hostile, jealous, rivalrous feelings toward his father, and his way of working was an expression of spite and defiance. But there was also a deep love for his father, which had a strong pregenital anal and oral cast. He was afraid to get too close to his father since that would mean anal and oral penetration and swallowing up. His history revealed that his father loved to assume the role of doctor when the patient was ill. There was much rectal temperature taking by the father, enemata, throat swabbings, etc. The "scrambled" behavior was also a manifestation of his struggle against identification with the father since identification was tantamount to being devoured and annihilated. It represented the return of the repressed longings for fusion and loss of ego boundaries (see Greenson, 1954, 1958a; Khan, 1960).

Another scientist patient used to describe all his experiences in a very matter-of-fact tone and in technical terms. He would even go into great detail about intimate sexual events, but he never betrayed any emotion. He was never hesitant or eager, but mechanical and thorough in his reporting. I tried to get him to see that he was omitting all his emotional reactions by using technical terms, by describing these events as though he were reporting an impersonal experiment. He was a cold, detached observer reporting to a fellow scientist instead of a patient recounting an intimate experience to his therapist.

For a long time the patient justified himself by stating that the facts were the important thing, not the emotions. Then I was able to show him that emotions are also "facts" but that he had an aversion to acknowledge those "facts" about himself. The patient then realized he left out emotions in reporting to me because he felt it was shameful for an adult scientist to have feelings. Furthermore, he also recognized he hid his emotions from others as well, even from his wife in his sexual relations. This behavior he then traced to his childhood, when his engineer father showed contempt for emotional people, considering them weak and unreliable. Eventually, the patient recognized that he considered showing emotions as equivalent to becoming incontinent and uncontrolled. He equated coldness with cleanliness, and emotional warmth with dirtiness and loss of control.

The analysis of the mode of resistance, in cases such as this, became possible only when the patient was no longer able to justify his use of the method in question. It had to become ego dystonic before he would willingly pursue the analysis of this old, habitual way of behavior. It took over a year for the last patient described above to change his attitude about his detached way of speaking. Even when we were able to trace this mode of behavior back to his childhood conflicts concerning toilet training and anal-sadistic impulses, he was not able to sustain a reliable working alliance. His underlying anxieties eventually took on a paranoid quality and robbed him of genuine motivation to continue the analysis. He was willing to be analyzed only if he could remain essentially unchanged and unmoved emotionally. We finally agreed to discontinue the analysis.

2.653 Recapitulation

If we now recapitulate the general procedures in the analysis of resistance, they can be outlined as follows:

(1) Recognize the resistance.
(2) Demonstrate the resistance to the patient.
  (a) Allow the resistance to become demonstrable by waiting for several instances.
  (b) Intervene in such a way so as to increase the resistance; help it become demonstrable.

(3) Clarify the motives and modes of resistance.
   (a) What specific painful affect is making this patient resistant?
   (b) What particular instinctual impulse is causing the painful affect at this moment?
   (c) What precise mode and method does the patient use to express his resistance?
(4) Interpret the resistance.
   (a) What fantasies or memories are causing the affects and impulses behind the resistance?
   (b) Pursue the history and unconscious purposes of these affects, impulses, or events in and outside the analysis, and in the past.
(5) Interpret the mode of resistance.
   (a) Pursue this and similar modes of activity in and outside of the analysis.
   (b) Trace the history and unconscious purposes of this activity in the patient's present and past.
(6) Working through.
   Repetitions and elaborations of steps (4) (a) (b) and (5) (a) (b).

It is important to realize that only a small fragment of the work can be accomplished in a given hour. Many hours end up with only the dim awareness that there is some resistance at work, and all one can do toward the end of such an hour is to point out to the patient that he seems to be avoiding something. Sometimes one can clarify only the affect, and even that incompletely; sometimes only the historical antecedent, sometimes only the mode. Whenever possible and as much as possible one tries to explore avoidances with the patient, assaying how much of this probing the patient can meaningfully and usefully do in a given hour. The analyst's own zeal for exploration and uncovering of unconscious phenomena must play a secondary role to how much the patient is able to endure and to utilize. The patient should be neither traumatized nor allowed to enter into some playful, gamelike exploration of resistance.

It is important not to make interpretations of resistance prematurely, since that only leads the patient to rationalize or intellectualize, or it makes an intellectual contest of the interpretation of resistance. In either case it deprives the experience of emotional impact. Thus it adds to the resistances instead of diminishing them. The patient must be given the opportunity to feel his resistances, to become aware of their strength and tenacity. It is important to know when to be passive and when to be active in the analytic work. Too much patience can permit the patient to waste valuable time when he might be working effectively. Too much activity may either interfere with the patient's ability for being active and gratify his passive wishes; or it may remobilize events for which the patient is not ready and thereby stir up a traumatic situation. Above all, too much activity can serve to evade the emotional impact and turn the analysis of resistance into a guessing game (see Freud, 1914c, p. 155; Fenichel, 1941, pp. 36-43).

It is important, furthermore, not to play into the resistance of the patient by using the same kind of resistance he does. If he is silent, you must be alert that your silence is not a counterresistance. Or if he uses stilted language, obscenities, or clichés, you must avoid going along with this resistance or doing the opposite. It is important to be direct and to the point without being crude, playfully provocative, or reproachful.

The steps and the order of the various steps vary from hour to hour and from patient to patient. One can pursue only what seems to be the most promising avenue of exploration at a given time. One has to keep an open and alert mind and be willing to alter one's approach or be willing to stick to it if it seems correct.

The analyst's indispensable ally in this work is the patient's reasonable ego. It must be present or it must be evoked by the analyst's interventions; otherwise one has to wait for the emotional storms to subside and for the reasonable ego to return. This can be expressed in terms of the relationship to the analyst. A working alliance must be present or evocable before one embarks on the deep analysis of resistance. It is a prerequisite for interpretation (Greenson, 1965a). This will be illustrated in detail in Chapter 3.

Finally, it is important to realize that no matter how skillfully and how correctly one works with resistances, the resistances will return. One should remember Freud's remark that resistance will be present at every step, in every aspect, in every hour of the analysis, until the analysis has been completed. Working through is necessary for a given resistance to lose its pathogenesis. Resistance analysis is not a detour of the analysis but a necessary and vital part of every analysis.

2.66 SPECIAL PROBLEMS IN ANALYZING RESISTANCE

2.661 Resistances in the First Hours

Early in analysis, in the first hours, when a resistance has been recognized by the analyst and has been demonstrated to the patient, before one proceeds to the exploration of the motive or mode of resistance, one should consider interpolating the following steps.

1. The patient should be told that resistance is an activity of the patient. It is an action he is bringing about either unconsciously, preconsciously, or consciously (Fenichel, 1941, p. 35). It is not something which is happening to the patient passively, although he may feel it as such. This is important because many patients feel resistance just happens to them, it befalls them, and they tend to feel helpless or resigned. I have found it helpful to educate them on this point.

For example, a patient will tell me that his mind is a blank. After waiting a suitable length of time, I have found it useful to inform my patients that the mind seems to be blank only when one is trying to avoid something. I ask them then to let their thoughts drift with the notion, "I am avoiding something," and to report what comes up. Inevitably some associations will come into focus. I may accentuate this point by reminding them that their minds are not blank if they are lying undisturbed on a couch at home, or if they are just letting their thoughts wander while driving a car. It must be so here, unless something is interfering and either keeping things from going on in their minds or keeping them from detecting what is going on.

2. The patient should be told at an appropriate time that the detection of resistance and the analysis of resistance are important, worthy, and respectable parts of psychoanalysis. Resistance is not an error or a fault or a weakness of the patient. He is not to feel criticized or rejected for having resistances. Here of course it is of crucial importance to be aware of one's tone of voice in demonstrating resistance to the patient. The analyst's words may say to the patient that it is perfectly all right to have resistances, but if his tone is reproachful, the words are meaningless. The patient should

be made aware that the analysis of resistance is a necessary, inevitable, and productive part of the psychoanalytic procedure.

After I have succeeded in analyzing some aspect of a resistance
early in the analysis, I try to demonstrate the validity of the point
that the analysis of resistance is fruitful and worthwhile.

I think these interventions are important early in analysis because they help to establish a certain atmosphere in the analytic
situation. I want my patient to feel that he is entitled to know certain things about what goes on in analysis, in order to feel that he
is my co-worker in the analytic situation. I want to facilitate the
development of a working alliance. I don't want him to feel that he
is a child, to be kept in the dark, or that I am the expert far beyond
and above him. I do not want to create an authoritarian atmosphere,
a mysterious atmosphere, or a parental atmosphere. I want this to
be a situation between two hardworking, serious adults, one in need
of help, and one an expert, but both equally serious and responsible
in their work together. And I want to give him whatever educational
means he needs in order to help him become an analytic patient; to
help him work in the analysis. I do not want to make him an analyst, but I want him to be familiar with certain aspects of the process
of being analyzed after he has experienced them, so that he can cooperate with me to the best of his conscious ability. This point will
be amplified in Section 3.5 and in Volume II.

When a patient detects on his own not only that he is resisting,
but why he might be resisting, or what he might be resisting, then
I feel he has made an important step in the analysis. One often hears
the expression that a patient is "in analysis." I think this refers to
the above situation. It means that a part of the patient's ego, the
observing, reasonable ego, has the capacity, now on its own, from
time to time to look at the experiencing part of his ego and to work
as an ally of the analyst, i.e., in temporary identification with the
analyst's way of working. A working alliance has been temporarily
and partially established. By no means does this mean he can completely analyze his own resistances, but at least he is aware of the
importance of analyzing resistances and has an analytic attitude
toward resistances, instead of trying to avoid, hide or cover up his
resistances.

Very early in the analysis I am careful not to use the term resistance but to use such phrases as, you are avoiding, you are running

away, you seem to be ducking, skimming the surface, hiding, etc. Although the word resistance is an ordinary English word, it is also a technical term and I try to avoid using it.

3. In the first hours I make a point of asking the patient how he felt while he was describing some event in the hour. I do this to accustom him to bringing his emotions and bodily reactions into his associations. Similarly I ask him what he was imagining while a certain activity was going on, in order to make him aware of the importance of his fantasy life.

The three procedures described above all have in common the aim of promoting the development of a working alliance between the patient's reasonable ego and the analyst's analyzing ego. This will be described in greater detail and from different points of view in Chapters 3 and 4 and in Volume II.

2.662 *Resistance to Resistance*

In clinical practice, one frequently finds that "the" resistance does not consist of a single force opposing some content. Actually, the resistance may be made up of more than one oppositional force, arranged in different layers. Furthermore, what is resistance in one instance may be that which is being warded off in another, since resistance is a relative concept (see Section 2.41). For example, a patient is talking trivia because he is ashamed to become silent and reveal that he has nothing to say. We then have two avoidances at work: he is running away from something which makes him silent, and he is covering up the silence by talking trivia. In this example he treats the silence as though it were a forbidden impulse. We call this situation resistance to resistance (Breuer and Freud, 1893-95, p. 279; Fenichel, 1941, p. 62).

The patient's use of trivia is the more superficial resistance and has to be handled first. Then our first task would be to ascertain why the patient is ashamed to be silent. Only after that could we proceed to the analysis of the reasons for the underlying silence. One of the typical causes of this kind of resistance to resistance is the patient's wish to be a "good" patient, i.e., the favorite. The patient is under the mistaken impression that "good" patients have no resistance. Thus the silence he had been protecting did have an instinctual association. It happens frequently early in analysis. Other patients are ashamed to be angry or afraid to be angry or sexual, etc., and they attempt to cover up the silence which might indicate the underlying emotions.

Another frequent cause of resistance to resistance is the reaction to a new and painful insight. The patient might try to cover up his anger or anxiety about a new discovery by eagerly finding confirmatory evidence in order to silence further interpretations.

For example, early in an analysis, I pointed out to a patient, for the first time, his competitive sibling-rivalry feelings in regard to his colleagues at work. He reacted by promptly agreeing with me and quickly found several further examples in his everyday life and in his past. The next hour, however, after a quick burst of confirmatory information continuing the last hour, he fell silent. He seemed agitated about his silence and in exploring the agitation I discovered he was desperately trying to find more material in order to hide the fact that he resented and feared my interpretation. He resented my interpretation because he felt that my knowing this would cause him to lose his fantasy of being my favorite patient. He tried to hide the wish to be my favorite by quickly plunging into painful material as though he didn't care about my reactions.

If we review the resistance situation in the patient, it is structured as follows: a new insight causes pain, resentment, and anxiety in regard to me. The patient fears revealing his anger to me will lose him his favorite position. He tries to push aside his hostility and searches for material in a reactive, counterphobic way, as though saying, "I don't care what you discover about me—only good work matters." However, the new material peters out because the hidden resentment is seeking discharge and demands to be heard. The patient also feels guilty for trying to deceive me and the silence is also a form of self-punishment.

By and large, I have found patients will hide their resistances for two main reasons. (1) They are ashamed or afraid to reveal a state of resistance. Resistance means defect and will lead to loss of love or punishment. (2) They are afraid to expose a resistance-producing situation—usually in order to avoid material which they sense might lead to a hostile transference reaction. These are patients who are afraid to become angry. They often try to cover up their anger by the opposite—ingratiation and submissiveness. Good examples are candidates in training who will avoid mentioning a meeting in which I have said something incorrect or will only talk about what they agreed with and will skip the rest.

There can be even more complicated constellations of resistance to resistances and various contents. Let me give the following clinical example from a single analytic hour.

A patient begins an hour by repeating rather flippantly that his three-year-old daughter was ill, but he does not want to talk about it because he does not want to get depressed. He then keeps up a stream of chatter touching on innocuous everyday events. When he shows no indication of getting back to the child's illness, I intervene by saying: "Why do you have to avoid your little girl's sickness?" He responds angrily with: "Why won't you leave me alone—why do you keep pushing me?" and so on. I keep quiet. Slowly he begins to talk about his daughter's illness, how they called a consultant who said she might need surgery, how he dreaded this possibility, how he is afraid she might die. He writhes on the couch, as though in pain. Tears stream silently down his cheeks, which he doesn't even bother to mop. I keep quiet. The patient pauses momentarily and shouts: "I wish I were dead. I would rather kill myself." Silence. At this point I intervene and say, "I can understand your worry about your child, but why do you hate yourself so?" The patient then brings out how guilty he feels toward the little girl; she frustrates him by loving her mother more; she disappoints him by not being a boy; he neglects her; this was all his doing; he deserves to die . . . pause . . . "besides no one gives a goddamn about me anyway."

If we review this hour, we can see how complicated the resistances are: the flippant avoidance of the depressing subject, the anger against me for pushing him, his fears concerning the child covering his guilt toward the child, covering his resentment toward the child, covering his identification with the unwanted child, which ended in a reproach to me. This hour illustrates how a variety of resistances are used against different contents, and how one content may be used to ward off still deeper underlying content. The concept of working through concerns itself not only with uncovering the same resistances in different situations and in other times and places, but also in uncovering the great variety of resistances that are used to ward off a given impulse or memory or experience, etc. This will be taken up in greater detail, however, in Volume II.

2.663 The Secret

Our usual task in analysis is to uncover the patient's unconscious secrets; the patient is not aware of the memories he has kept hidden;

they are secret to his conscious ego, too. Although he may have unconscious and preconscious resistances to our explorations, he is ordinarily on the side of the analytic work, at least consciously. But it does happen occasionally that a patient will try consciously to withhold certain material from the analyst. In most instances, this conscious, deliberate, withholding is fleeting and usually overcome by the patient himself—who then confesses his secret. Very often it happens within a single analytic hour. But there are patients who maintain a secret for long periods of time and who cannot overcome this conscious resistance without our help. It is worthwhile discussing some of the special problems that the analysis of the secret requires, because if the secret does not yield to analysis, or if it is not correctly handled, it can endanger the entire analysis. The paper by Alfred Gross (1951) on this subject is required reading for the student.

There are a few basic principles which have to be especially stressed in regard to the analytic method of handling secrets. First of all, there can be no question of any concession in regard to our attitude that we are determined to analyze all the significant psychic events going on in the patient. The secret, by its very nature of being a secret, is a significant psychic event and has to be analyzed. There can be no compromise upon this point. Freud (1913b, pp. 135-136) expressed this view very clearly when he explained that if the psychoanalyst were to permit any secret of any kind, all the taboo memories, thoughts, and impulses would hide behind this refuge and evade analysis. He compared it to what would happen in a village if the police allowed one spot to become a haven in which they did not exercise their power. All the riff-raff of the village would eventually congregate there and thus escape detection. Freud recounted his personal experience of trying to analyze a high government official whom he permitted to keep certain secrets of state out of the analysis. It was impossible to complete the analysis under those conditions. Many patients try to find a pretext for keeping things secret. They will claim, for example, that they cannot mention names because it is not discreet, it is wrong to involve innocent people, etc. The slightest concession to secrecy, for whatever reason, is incompatible with the analytic situation. One permissible secret means the end of effective analysis.

I can confirm Freud's findings and conclusions by some experiences I had during World War II. I was in charge of a Combat Fatigue Section in an Air Force Hospital where it was my duty to treat, among others, a group of officers and men who had escaped from enemy prisoner-of-war camps. These men, however, were instructed by Washington not to disclose to anyone how they were helped to escape by the underground. This was done to protect the members of the underground whose valuable work was continuing. These escapees suffered from a variety of anxiety states and traumatic neuroses and were in desperate need of therapy. Yet it was impossible to do effective psychotherapy with these men as long as they felt obligated to keep certain data secret. The names of the underground were of no consequence in the history of the men, yet the fact that they felt justified in withholding this information vitiated the treatment. Fortunately, I had recourse to a psychoanalyst who was Chief of the Psychiatric Service, Col. John Murray, who arranged with Washington to have certain psychiatrists on every post cleared for working with top-secret material. The patients were so informed and only then did it become possible to do effective psychotherapy.

Our basic attitude is that there shall be no concession about secrets, they have to be analyzed. However, it is also important to realize that it is an error to use coercion, threats, or pleadings to get the patient to tell his secret. It is just as incorrect to force patients to give up their secrets as it is to allow secrets. The analytic attitude is that we shall attempt to analyze secrets as we would any other form of resistance. We are just as determined and just as patient. We may be aware that a patient has a conscious secret, but we know that it is the unconscious factors that have to be analyzed before the patient can reveal the secret. The patient knows the content of the secret, but he is unconscious of the important reasons which make it necessary to maintain the secrecy. Our method of approach is to attack the motive for the secret.

Let me put this in concrete terms. A patient tells me that there is something he cannot and will not tell me. My response is in effect: Don't tell me *what* your secret is, but tell me *why* you can't tell me about it. In other words, I am pursuing the motive for the secret, not the content. The method is similar to the techniques I outlined for pursuing the analysis of the motives for resistance. I would ask the patient what kind of feeling he would have if he were to tell me. If he could imagine that he had told me, how would he be feeling. I would go on to ask him: "How do you imagine I would react if you had told me?" In other words, I would pursue the painful affects and fantasies that the secret material arouses in the patient, including the painful transference fantasy. Then I would pursue the history of this painful transference situation in his past life, i.e., when did this happen to you before?

I would like to cite a simple clinical example of the points mentioned above: A female patient, in the first six months of analysis, tells me there is a certain word she just cannot get herself to say. This patient is ordinarily a cooperative patient and I can see her struggling with herself to say the word. I remain silent for a while and then, when I see she seems defeated in her attempts to communicate, I ask her: "How would you feel if you had said the word?" She answers that she would feel devastated, crushed. She would feel like crawling under a rock, she would feel like an insect, a dirty, little ugly insect. I do not have to pursue the question about her transference fantasy because she spontaneously takes it up. "You would be disgusted with me, you would detest me, you would be shocked and repelled and ask me to leave." I remain quiet. The patient goes on: "This is ridiculous. You wouldn't do that at all . . . but that is how I feel. I am reacting as though the word is upsetting to you." I say nothing. The patient goes on telling me about the first time she recalled saying the word at home. She was having lunch with her mother and she said the word playfully, teasingly. Her mother was shocked and disgusted. She ordered the nine-year-old girl to leave the table and told her she ought to wash out her mouth with soap. The patient had sensed the word was "dirty" but was startled at her mother's reaction. At this point the patient is able to tell me the secret word; it is the obscene word "fuck."

Although the patient was able to use the word "fuck" in the analysis from this point on, the above clinical description did not end the analysis of her secret. The fact that this word was said playfully and teasingly to her mother also had important connotations. The word "fuck" was also associated to many other oral and anal sexual and sadistic fantasies (Stone, 1954a). However, from this time forward, the word "fuck" was not a conscious secret; we searched for the unconscious factors that had made it so abhorrent.

This sequence of events is fairly typical. When one has analyzed the motive for the secret, including the transference fantasies and the painful affects, the patient usually will be able to confess the secret. But this does not end the technical problems in analyzing secrets. The secret is something intimate and important to the patient, no matter how trivial it may seem when exposed to the light of day. For the patient, telling the analyst a secret is to reveal something extremely personal and valuable. The information has to be treated with respect and delicacy, but one has to pursue the analysis of it.

After a secret has been exposed there are then two possible paths to pursue. It depends on the patient's reactions which course we would follow. We can either explore the patient's reaction to having exposed the secret or we can investigate the content of the secret. Very often these two paths cross.

Let me go back to the woman who could not say the word "fuck." She finally was able, as I described above, to express this word to me after we did some work on her feeling of embarrassment. After she said the word she became silent, and I picked up her silence and asked her about it. She was now reacting to her having said the "dirty" word. She felt as though she had gone to the toilet in my presence; I had seen her in the act of moving her bowels. In other words, to confess this secret meant to defecate in front of me.

To her, the struggle with the secret was equivalent to her struggles with hiding her toilet activities. She was not prudish about discussing her sexual activities, but she was extremely shy about talking about the toilet, particularly about anal goingson. Her mother had been very strict about toilet training, and the child had had the impression that all elimination functions were ugly and had to be kept secret—otherwise one would be found disgusting and repulsive. This was particularly true of toilet sounds, which were the most offensive to her. For her to tell me the secret was to expel gas noisily in front of me, a most painful situation for the patient.

The further analysis of her secret occurred a few days later and actually was referred to many times over the next several years. I refer here to the analysis of the content—in this case the analysis of what the word "fuck" meant to her. "Fuck" was her infantile conception of sex— it was oedipal sex, anal sex, and oral sex. It was the sounds and smells of parental intercourse, of parental toilet activities, and it was the sensual sucking of a child at the mother's breast. It also contained a primitive aggressive component on all these levels (See Stone, 1954a; Ferenczi, 1911).

The analysis of a secret is a very rewarding, although difficult subject for analysis. In general, secrets are related to secretions. They always have some anal or urethral connotation, and are considered shameful and loathsome or its opposite, that is, very valuable and to be hoarded and protected. Secrets also are connected to the parents' secret sexual activities, which now the patient repeats via identification and which the patient does in revenge in the transference situation. In addition to all of this, secrecy and confession are always involved with problems of exhibitionism, scoptophilia, and teasing. The secret is inevitably involved in the transference situation as a special form of resistance.

The section on special resistances will have to be interrupted at this point for several reasons. Some special problems of technique are too complex to be profitably discussed so early in this book, and will be handled later. I refer here to acting out, character resistances, and the silent patient—also those resistances which are complicated by an activity containing an important id satisfaction, i.e., certain masochistic resistances, screen resistances, and so-called "adhesiveness of the libido" resistance.

Other special forms of resistance will be discussed in Section 3.8 on the transference resistances, because the transference element is of decisive importance. In connection with interpretation I shall discuss resistances following incorrect dosage, timing, or tact of interpretation, as well as resistances preceding and following vacations and after social contact of analyst and patient, etc. (see Volume II).

2.67 DEVIATIONS IN TECHNIQUE

Having discussed the general procedure as well as some special problems in the technique of analyzing resistance, we will find it helpful to contrast the point of view presented here with two deviant approaches. Melanie Klein and Franz Alexander are the leaders of two separate schools of psychoanalysis which differ quite sharply in some ways from the classical position, both in theory and technique. Although this book is devoted primarily to an exposition of the so-called classical psychoanalytic technique, a brief description of these two divergent, but important, approaches can serve to highlight some of the essential points I have made. Both schools of thought have been responsible for some valuable contributions to psychoanalysis, although they have also been the source of great controversy. For these reasons, the student should be familiar with their basic works (see Klein, 1932; Klein, et al., 1952, 1955; Alexander, et al., 1946). Here I can offer only a highly condensed version of their views concerning the analysis of resistance.

First of all, it is striking that the term "resistance" is completely absent in the index of the first two books by Klein mentioned above and occurs only twice in the third. If one reads the various clinical examples, however, one can deduce that Klein and her followers do recognize that at times their patients are in opposition to the analytic procedure. But this clinical finding is not worked with as I have described in the preceding pages. No attempt is made to form a working or therapeutic alliance with the reasonable ego of the patient in order to get him to recognize and understand the motive, or mode, or history of his resistance (Zetzel, 1956). All resistances are *immediately* interpreted in terms of the underlying instinctual impulses which the analyst translates into specific and detailed fantasies, even if they concern preverbal times. The clinical evidence for their analytic interpretations is, in my view, remarkably slim; they rarely present any detailed case material; and the interpretations are strikingly similar in patient after patient. One gets the impression that the individual history of the patient has had little influence on the personality development and on the neurosis.

I shall cite as an example some clinical material from a paper by Thorner (1957, pp. 286-287) in a recent compilation of Kleinian writings. He describes a patient with examination anxiety and other symptoms who reports a dream—red spiders crawling in and out of his anus, and the doctor who examined him told the patient that he was unable to see anything wrong with him, to which the patient replied: "Doctor, you may not see anything, but they are there all the same." The Kleinian analyst handles this dream by interpreting that the patient feels he is being persecuted by bad internal objects. The analyst then reports that the patient accepted the interpretation with great relief, following which he gave his analyst "fresh infantile memories," which stood for "good and helpful objects."

It is dangerous to interpret material of a patient one does not know, but one obvious resistance element in the dream seems clear, i.e., there is a doctor who is unable to see anything wrong with his patient and the patient complains about this. This aspect of the dream is ignored. Perhaps it would be more correct to say that this resistance is avoided by plunging into the depths. The analyst handles the situation by the Kleinian cliché of interpreting "persecution" by "bad internal objects." There is no attempt to get to the patient's present relationship to the analyst or his personal, historical experiences with anal examinations, incompetent doctors, red spiders, etc. The patient's individual experiences are neglected. Furthermore, the analyst does not seem to be concerned with the evaluation of the patient's readiness to face the instinctual contents; there seem to be no concessions to problems of dosage or timing. Interpretations of the most primitive infantile instinctual components or introjects are made from the very beginning of the analysis. The Kleinians seem to work with their patients in a way which caricatures the technical rule of making the unconscious conscious. They do not seem to be concerned with the problem of the presence or absence of the patient's reasonable ego. They make one content interpretation after another, directed, so it seems, at some computer-like intellect, with a stereotyped id.

I participated in a workshop on Melanie Klein's contributions in December, 1962, under the chairmanship of Elizabeth Zetzel, as part of the Midwinter Meeting of the American Psychoanalytic Association. There were some twenty analysts there from all over the United States with diverse backgrounds, interests, and experience. Everyone agreed that Melanie Klein and her followers had made valuable contributions to our understanding of early object relations, the earliest varieties of hate and aggression, and the special vicissitudes of primitive hostility. There was also general agreement that the Kleinians ignored working with resistances as such, neglected the working alliance, underestimated the personal history of the patient, and universalized detailed, complicated fantasies of preverbal times.

Alexander and his followers seem to go to the opposite extreme. Whereas the Kleinians interpret the most infantile instinctual strivings behind the resistances from the beginning of the analysis, Alexander's school tries to handle resistances by a variety of manipulations. Their aim seems to be to help their patients *avoid* resistances, above all, regression, which they consider essentially wasteful. Alexander advocates the manipulation of the frequency of interviews in order to prevent the patient from becoming too regressively dependent. He would reduce the frequency of the interviews to two or even one per week. One has to prevent the patient's tendency "to sink himself into a safe, comfortable transference neurosis" (Alexander, et al., 1946, p. 33). He suggests that when a patient repeats material he has brought up many times before, it is a good idea to interrupt the treatment, so that the patient "learns which of his previous difficulties he still retains . . ." (p. 36). Furthermore, Alexander believes that the analyst "should encourage the patient (or even require him) to do those things which he avoided in the past, to experiment in that activity in which he had failed before" (p. 41).

French, a co-worker of Alexander's, clearly indicates his views on the handling of resistances by warning against placing too much faith in insight. I quote now from a paragraph on dealing with hostile impulses: "By digging in behind hostile impulses to the problem that gave rise to them, therefore, it is often possible to eliminate the hostile impulses without at any time focusing the patient's attention directly upon them, merely by helping the patient to find a solution to the underyling problem" (Alexander, et al., 1946, p. 131).

It is obvious that the methods of dealing with resistance advocated by Alexander and his followers cannot be considered psychoanalytic. They are essentially manipulative and anti-analytic. The patient does not learn to recognize and understand his resistances, there is no premium on insight as a means of overcoming resistances, there is no attempt to change the ego structure. The omnipotent therapist decides which resistances the patient can deal with and which he must forever avoid. This may be effective symptomatic psychotherapy, but it is surely not psychoanalysis.

2.7 Rules of Technique Concerning Resistance

At this point I believe we can set down certain general principles for guidance in determining our technical procedure. These rules are meant to be not commands or laws but rather guideposts which indicate the general direction. All rules have to be used elastically; they have to suit the patient, the analyst, and the situation. A technical measure is valuable only if one comprehends the clinical problem, the patient's capacities, and the aims one is attempting to achieve. One can reach the same goal by taking bypaths and detours, but on a long journey it is of practical importance to keep in mind a road map which indicates the terrain, the topography, the obstacles, etc. The rules that follow are such guidelines. They are particularly valuable when one feels lost or uncertain. Freud called the rules he set down "recommendations," and he did not claim any unconditional acceptance for them. He felt that there was such diversity of psychical constellations and such a wealth of determining factors that any mechanization of technique would prove to be ineffective at times. Nevertheless, he did believe that certain procedures were useful for the average situation (Freud, 1913b, p. 123).

2.71 ANALYZE RESISTANCE BEFORE CONTENT, EGO BEFORE ID, BEGIN WITH THE SURFACE

In the early days of psychoanalysis, the technique was focused on trying to obtain the repressed memories, the task was simply to make the unconscious conscious. Resistances could be evaded by making interpretations from the patient's free associations. Freud soon realized that the emphasis was wrong, that what was effective therapeutically was not getting the forgotten memory, but overcoming the resistance. Memories obtained with the resistances still intact would be powerless to bring about a change because they would succumb in the old way to the forces of resistance (1913b, p. 141). In 1914 Freud stated that it was the analyst's job to analyze and interpret the patient's resistances. If we succeed in this, the patient will often discover the forgotten memories and make the right connections (1914c, p. 147).

With the recognition of the central role of the forces of resistance, the old topographical formulation of making the unconscious conscious was replaced by a dynamic formulation; we analyze resistances before content (Fenichel, 1941, p. 45). This formulation does not contradict the old one, it merely qualifies it. Making the unconscious conscious is helpful only if doing so alters the dynamics of a neurotic conflict. There is no point in uncovering the repressed if it will meet the same defensive forces which caused it to be repressed in the first place. A change must first be made in the resisting agency. The various procedures for analyzing resistances (see Section 2.6) are aimed at making favorable alterations in the resisting forces.

At this point it is helpful to bring in the structural point of view, because it clarifies our therapeutic task even more sharply. Our ultimate aim is to enable the ego to cope better with the id, superego, and external world (Freud, 1923b, pp. 56-57). In the process of analysis the patient's ego may be regarded as having two different aspects and functions. The unconscious, irrational ego is the initiator of the pathogenic defenses and is seen as the experiencing ego during treatment. The conscious, reasonable ego is the ally of the analyst and appears clinically as the patient's observing ego during the analysis (Sterba, 1934). The technical rule that one should analyze resistance before content can be expressed structurally: one should analyze the ego before the id (Freud, 1933, p. 80; Fenichel, 1941, p. 56). More precisely, the analyst's interventions should aim at making the patient's reasonable ego better able to cope with the old danger situations.

In the past the patient felt these dangers to be too threatening and his irrational ego instituted the pathogenic defenses that resulted in the neurotic symptoms. In the analytic situation, with the help of the working alliance and with the proper sequence of interpretation, we expect the patient's reasonable ego to expand its powers as it becomes more familiar with how it can operate in the present as contrasted to the past, how it once evaluated danger and how it might now re-evaluate such dangers, etc. Working with the patient's observing ego and demonstrating the unreasonableness of the experiencing ego's operations makes it possible for the reasonable ego to extend its sovereignty. We analyze resistance before content or ego before id so that when we interpret the warded-off content to the patient, he will deal with it more appropriately and not merely repeat his past neurotic patterns.

In order to illuminate the reasoning behind these formulations, let me give a clinical example:

A patient, Mr. Z.,[1] a young man who has been in analysis approximately a year and a half, begins the hour by telling the following dream: "I dreamed that I was lying on a huge bed. I was completely nude. A large woman entered and said she had to bathe me and proceeded to bathe my genital organ. I became furious and ashamed because my genital did not become erect."

---

[1] Mr. Z. was previously referred to in Sections 2.52 and 2.54.

I remain silent and the patient begins to speak. Here is the gist of his associations: "The woman in the dream resembled a friend of the family. Actually, she looked like the mother of my good friend John. She is also a friend of my family's and in particular a friend of my mother's, but she is not like my mother. She is not spoiled. She is not a spoiled brat like my mother was. I liked this woman. I often wished I had a mother like that [pause]. . . . I had a date over the weekend and we indulged in some sexual play [pause]. . . . She is a married woman. And she was quite willing; in fact, she was the aggressor. Women who behave this way are like prostitutes. They don't have any feeling for love, they're just interested in sex. They want to be serviced. All of this talk makes me rather uncomfortable . . . [pause]."

At this point I think it is clear, first of all, that we are dealing with a situation in which Mr. Z. is struggling to express and to hide certain infantile sexual wishes and fears. If one looks at the manifest content of the dream, and also the associations, it is not too hard to recognize that this material concerns the patient's being a little boy, lying on a big bed, and having the childish wish to have his mother fondle his penis. But there is also some anger and shame because his penis is not as impressive as his father's. He resents these women who prefer large penises, but he also wants to have them play with his penis. Now all of this content is rather clear, but it would be wrong to proceed to interpret any of this to the patient because it is also obvious that there are strong tendencies in Mr. Z. to run away from all of this, to hide it, to cover it all up. Notice the language, how stilted, how evasive, how sterile it is. "I was completely nude." A woman proceeds to bathe my "genital organ." "My genital organ did not become erect." "We indulged in some 'sexual play.'" Then the frank admission, "I am uncomfortable talking about all this."

In such a situation, when there is some repressed content coming to the fore, but when there is also considerable resistance, I feel it would be pointless to proceed to the warded-off content until I had first analyzed and partially worked through some of the patient's resistances. If I attempted to point out to the embarrassed Mr. Z. that he seemed to want some motherly person to fondle his penis, he would angrily accuse me of being a lewd old man, or he would become completely frozen in silence. I am fairly certain of this because on other occasions he had such reactions even after I had attempted to work on his resistances.

Therefore, I decide to work first upon the resistances and only after I see indications of some change in them would I attempt to confront him with the content. I say to him when he becomes silent: "You seem to be embarrassed today when you try to tell me about your sexual experiences. Even your language seems stilted." (I say "today" because there were occasions when he was able to be more direct about sexual matters and in this way I am reminding him of that.) To this Mr. Z. replies: "Well, there is no use in being crude [pause]. . . . I don't know what kind of language to use here. I often wonder how you would react to vulgar language. How would you react if I were to say the first words that came to my mind. I realized just after I said this, that that is probably just what you want [pause]. . . . Yes, It's not you who would disapprove, it's me; I don't approve of this kind of vulgar language . . . [pause]. The dream was so vivid, the feelings in the dream were so strong . . . I felt so childish."

At this point I feel that for the time being the patient has managed to work successfully with some aspect of his transference resistance; he understands that he was projecting his feelings of disapproval onto me and that those feelings of disapproval were inappropriate. We could have pursued this resistance further, but at this time he seems ready to pursue the content of the dream, because he spontaneously goes back to the feelings in the dream. I therefore make the next intervention. "You became angry and ashamed, but how did you feel in the dream when the woman began to fondle your penis?"

Here one should notice that I am going a step beyond the patient. I do not use his stilted language, but I use everyday language, and I speak in a straightforward tone. I talk about a woman fondling his penis, not bathing it. The patient responds at first with silence. Then he says, "Yes, at first I liked it [pause]." Then he continues that when he was on the date, the woman did "this" . . . she did play with his penis. But he wants to assure me that she was the aggressor and not he. However, he has to admit he liked it; in fact, he liked it enormously; in fact, if he has to admit it, he preferred this kind of sexual pleasure to all other. But somehow or other he feels it is wrong [pause]. . . . The woman was a married woman. Her husband was a big wheel. He was delighted to be deceiving her husband, but really it wasn't much of a deception since they were separated. "It wasn't a real victory, only a hollow victory. It's like in my job; I look as though I am working hard, but it's not a real job and I'm not really working hard. It is like everything else; I don't want to do anything, I want to be given something. I pretend all the time to be active and hardworking, but really I want somebody to give me something."

The patient seems to be working well, his resistance has disappeared for the moment. So, at this point I make another interpretation. I say that it seems to me that he enjoyed the feeling of being given some sexual pleasure by a big woman, and although he enjoyed it, he also was ashamed of it because he felt like a little boy. To this the patient answers, yes, in the dream the bed was so big, it was huge, he must have been very little by comparison. Then he pauses and says, "You must think this has to do with my mother? Pfui. It is true, the girl I had the date with sort of had the same sort of heavy thighs which I found so repulsive in my mother."

This clinical example illustrates that by starting with the resistance it was possible to accomplish a genuine piece of analytic work with this patient. I believe if I had avoided the resistance and gone directly to the content, there would have been either angry denial or else an intellectual discussion or submissiveness, with no real emotion and no real insight. Using this clinical fragment as an illustration, let us try to re-examine the rationale behind the technical rule: analyze resistance before content.

In order for an interpretation or confrontation to be effective we must be sure that the patient can perceive, can understand, can apprehend the interpretation or confrontation. Therefore, we must be sure that a reasonable ego is available to the patient. We analyze the resistances first, because the resistances will interfere with the formation of a reasonable ego. To be more precise: the embarrassed patient has a limited reasonable ego. If I confront him with embarrassing content, he will lose even his limited reasonableness. I have to work in the area in which he can use his limited reasonable ego. I point out that he is feeling embarrassed; that is obvious, that is accessible to his reasonable ego, that will not make him run, he can bear facing that. I wonder along with him what made him embarrassed today, reminding him indirectly that he is not always embarrassed. At first he defends himself unreasonably, saying it's no use being crude, and wondering how I would react to that. His reasonable ego, not feeling isolated and alone, takes a big step forward, expands its reasonableness, and he dares to recognize that it is not I who would disapprove, but it is he who does. He then realizes his reaction is inappropriate, he looks at this behavior analytically, he has formed a temporary and partial identification with me, a working alliance, in regard to his resistance. I had pointed out something about his behavior which he could follow and understand along with me. As he formed this alliance with me, his reasonable ego became stronger and he now dared to look analytically at what he had been experiencing. I had succeeded in bringing about a split in his ego, which now had an experiencing and an observing function. Then he was able to increase the reasonable, observing ego. Sterba's excellent paper (1934) on this subject is essential reading.

My embarrassed patient would have become angry or remote and would not have worked with me if I had begun with the disturbing contents of his dream and associations. I began with something accessible to his conscious ego, something he was more willing to acknowledge as his own feeling. To quote another topographical formulation: I began with the surface (Freud, 1905a, p. 12; Fenichel, 1941, p. 44). I appealed to his reason and he could be reasonable about admitting that he had been embarrassed. A working alliance with me was then achieved and he himself could then analyze his inappropriate transference reaction to me. If he had not, I would have interpreted this for him. Then we had a strong reasonable ego to work with and I could now dare to approach the painful warded-off material.

I decided to work on his *wish* to be fondled by a big woman, because his masturbation fantasies were still a great source of guilt to him and he had made several halting attempts to work on this before. I felt that if I could get him to recognize the infantile nature of his sexual wishes, he could better understand his guilt, his impotence, and his shame. I asked him how he felt when the woman began to fondle his penis, because he obviously omitted that point in his recital of the dream, and he did not reveal his sexual reactions when his lady friend did this to him. The intervention was quite productive as he struggled against his resistances again and finally realized he preferred this passive sexual pleasure to all others.

I then felt he might be ready to be confronted with the fact that this was infantile, i.e., incestuous—so I led him in that direction by pointing out this activity made him ashamed because it made him feel like a little boy being given some sexual pleasure by a big woman. He picked this up and struggled with it. He recognized he liked deceiving husbands, realized this was a hollow victory, and then dared to think it could be his mother, by first saying, "You must think this. . . ." Then finally he accepted it and confirmed it. How his little reasonable ego expanded and was able to struggle successfully with all kinds of resistances as the hour progressed! Throughout the hour one could observe his battle with the resistances. If they had increased in force and had stunted the reasonable ego, it would have been necessary to work further on the resistances and forego working with the content.

These rules of technique are basic: analyze resistance before content, ego before id, and start with the surface. Working with content may be more interesting, more scintillating; working with resistances is more plodding. But if the ego's resistances are not analyzed, the analytic work will come to a standstill. The patient will terminate, will regress destructively, or the analysis becomes an intellectual game or a hidden transference gratification.

The rule that we analyze resistance before content must *not* be understood to mean that we analyze the resistance alone or approach it first and that we avoid the content completely until the resistance is resolved. Actually, there is not always a sharp dichotomy between resistance and content. In the different examples I have given there are many illustrations of how resistance becomes the content and then a given content comes to be used as a resistance. Furthermore, the analysis of every resistance leads to its history, which is content. Finally, we may have to use some of the content to help expose the resistance. The basic technical rule means that content interpretation will not become effective until the significant resistances have been analyzed sufficiently. The last example of the embarrassed patient illustrates that clearly. He could not work with the material until he overcame his transference resistance to some appreciable extent. Let me now give an example of using content in helping to analyze resistance.

A woman patient, Mrs. K.,[2] in her fourth year of analysis begins an hour by telling me the following dreams: (1) "I am being photographed in the nude, lying on my back in different positions; legs closed, legs apart." (2) "I see a man with a curved yardstick in his hand; it had writing on it which was supposed to be erotic. A red, spiny backed little monster was biting this man with sharp, tiny teeth. The man was ringing a bell for help, but no one heard it but me and I didn't seem to care."

Let me add here that this patient had been working in the last several hours on the problem of her fear of her homosexual impulses, which she connected to her clitoris sexuality as opposed to her vaginal sexuality. Now that she had achieved the ability to have a vaginal orgasm, she was more daring in exploring these areas. Furthermore, she had never really

[2] I have referred to Mrs. K. previously in Sections 1.24 and 2.651.

felt her penis envy and had only recently realized that her attitude—I'm glad I am a girl, I would have failed as a man—was a defense against a deep-seated and as yet untouched hostility to the man's penis. If we know all this, it is obvious that the manifest content of the dream is a continuation of these themes. Being photographed in the nude refers to problems of exposure as penisless. The man with the yardstick whom she ignores apparently represents her analyst. The red monster he is struggling with could represent a projection of or a revenge for her feelings about the male genital.

The patient begins to talk in a somewhat sad, empty tone of voice. She recounts plans for a party she is giving for her two-and-a-half-year-old child. She hopes the child will enjoy it, not dread parties as she used to when she was a child. She has been out with her fiancé and she found herself biting at him, reproaching him for his decadent past, he had been a philanderer, a wastrel. Pause. Her menstrual period is one day late and she thinks she is pregnant, but she doesn't seem to care about it. Pause. She has the feeling something is wrong inside, something repulsive is inside her, which reminds her of the feelings the man had in *The Immoralist*, who felt repelled by his wife's tuberculosis. Pause. "I went to a boring party and hated it [silence]. I wish you would say something, I feel empty. I got mad at my baby and hit her, then the baby became very loving [silence]. I feel remote and far away."

At this point I intervene and say: "You feel remote and empty because you seem to be afraid to look at that hateful monster inside you." The patient answers: "That monster was red, actually dark red-brown, like old menstrual blood. It was a medieval fiend, like one sees in the paintings of Hieronymus Bosch. I am like that; if I were a painting, that's what I would be, full of all kinds of demons of sex, bowel movement, homosexuality, and hate. I suppose I don't want to face my hate for myself, for Bill, for my baby, and for you. I haven't really changed and I had thought I had made much progress [silence]."

I intervene: "We recently uncovered a new monster: your anger at men's penises and your disgust with your vagina. And you are running away from it by trying to escape into emptiness." The patient replied: "You sound so sure of yourself, as though you have it all solved. Maybe I am running. I read a book about a man giving his wife cognac to get her drunk so she would be a better sexual partner and she pretended to be drunk so she could let out her real feelings. Maybe I'm like that. I'd really show you men what I could do sexually. I sometimes get the feeling that underneath this meek slave-girl exterior I present, I have a streak of grandiosity. I'd show you poor 'fuckers' how to really use a penis if I had one. Yes, when Bill was trying his damndest to satisfy me the other night, I looked at him and it flashed through my mind, who's the 'slavey' now. And that yardstick, I recall asking you once, what yardstick do you use to measure neurosis with? I hate to feel stupid and sometimes you and this analysis make me so. I could be as sharp as you, if I dared. But then I become afraid I would lose you or I'd become repulsive to you and you would desert me. I suppose I have to develop more trust in you. I can't expect Bill to take all this—but you ought to be able to. . . ."

I submit this fragment of an hour to demonstrate how I worked with the patient's resistance by bringing in the content to help me. I interpreted to her she was running away into emptiness to avoid the monster of her penis envy, her hateful, internal penis and the masculine identification. This formulation helped her recognize how she tried to deny and then to project this hateful introject onto me and onto her fiancé. She could see its resistance-producing effect and was able to begin to explore it inside herself. The clarification of the content helped her to work with her hostile-depressive transference resistance.

2.72 THE PATIENT DETERMINES THE SUBJECT OF THE HOUR

This rule of technique is an extension of the old rule: begin every interpretation from the surface. We revised this topographical formulation and expressed it structurally to read: we begin our interpretations with what is accessible to the conscious, reasonable ego of the patient. The rule that we analyze resistance before content is an application of this rule. Since resistances are a product of ego functioning, they are more accessible to the reasonable ego than id material. This reasoning is also valid for the parallel formulations: analyze defense before the repressed; analyze ego before id.

Freud (1905a, p. 12) made the technical recommendation in the Dora Case: let the patient choose the subject matter of the hour. At that time he related it to his advice that we start our analytic work at the surface of the patient's mind. We do not impose our interests or theoretical concerns upon the patient. The method of free association is based on our wish to let the patient choose the subject matter of the hour. By his associations we have access to what is living psychic reality for the patient at the moment. His associations reveal to us what he is concerned with, what is trying to emerge into consciousness, what matters to him. The associations or lack of them also indicate to us what he is trying to avoid. It is for this reason that I am including this rule under technical rules concerning resistance. The patient very often determines the subject matter of the hour by what he is silent about, by what he avoids, by how he avoids, etc.

This does not mean that the patient can deliberately determine what *we* will talk about. For example: a patient begins an hour and says, "I want to talk to you about my wife." He then proceeds to spend a good portion of the session describing his wife's puzzling reactions to him. I remain silent because it seems to me he is talking about something emotionally meaningful to him and I do not detect anything evasive in his productions. However, he makes a slip at one point and says: "My mother is very demanding sexually . . . I mean my wife is." At this point I change the focus of his talk by asking him to tell me how his mother compares with his wife. Actually, I do not change the subject; he had unconsciously changed it: I merely followed his lead.

Let the patient "choose" the subject matter of the hour means (1) let the patient *begin* every hour with the manifest material which concerns him, and (2) do not intrude your interests upon him. If the material of yesterday's hour seemed very important to you, you must forego your interest and follow him as long as he is working productively. Candidates will often intrude the material of their supervisory session into their work with their patients when it is not really relevant. Some analysts will pursue the interpretation of a dream when it is not the most meaningful part of an hour, because the analyst enjoys working with dreams. (3) The patient chooses the material of the hour to begin with, but we select from his material what we believe to be or ought to be his actual concern. For example: the patient talks to us about his sexual pleasures, but we select his *embarrassment* in talking about sex. We select what we feel he really is concerned with, even though he may be consciously unaware of it. One can make an analogy to the dream and say the patient chooses the manifest content and we pick out the latent significant material.

2.73 EXCEPTIONS TO THE RULES

2.731 *Minor Resistances*

Although psychoanalytic technique is distinguished from all other methods by the fact that we analyze resistances, we do not analyze each and every resistance. Small and temporary resistances can be handled merely by keeping quiet and letting the patient overcome his own resistance. Or else one can make some facilitating remark. For example: the patient is silent or hesitant, and you say, "Yes?" or "What?" and the patient then begins talking. One does not necessarily have to go back and analyze the meaning, the purpose or the content of every resistance. This holds true as long as the patient seems to overcome the resistance himself and can communicate meaningfully. If the resistance, however, persists or grows, then one would have to analyze it. In other words, the general rule is that small and temporary resistances do not have to be analyzed; they can be merely overcome.

Pursuing small resistances is not only unnecessary but can lead away from the important material. Furthermore, the patient should be permitted to take some active role in overcoming his resistances. Finally, the pursuit of every small resistance turns the analyst into a nag and the analysis into a harassment. Part of the tact of doing analytic work is knowing how to discriminate between resistances requiring analysis and those which do not.

2.732 Loss of Ego Functions

Situations sometimes arise in analyses when there is loss of resistance due to a loss of ego functions. Then our task is to permit and even encourage the development of a certain degree of resistance. This can occur in analytic work with psychotic or borderline cases, but it can also occur in neurotic patients at the height of reliving their infantile neurosis. The necessary interventions in such situations may well be unanalytic, but the situation does not call for insight; it calls for emergency measures. Since such occurrences do arise during the course of analysis, it is worthwhile to spend a few moments discussing the technical problems.

Emotional storms occur in all analyses which succeed in penetrating to the core of the infantile neurosis. During the height of the emotional outpouring there is a greater or lesser degree of loss of ego functions, depending on the intensity and the quality of the affect being discharged. If such an occurrence takes place early enough in the hour, our therapeutic task may be a simple one. Patience and supportive silence will suffice to give the patient ample opportunity to discharge his pent-up emotion. As the panic, rage, or depression diminish, one can detect the return of some reasonable ego and one can resume trying to work analytically. But if the emotional storm does not subside or if it occurs at the end of the hour, it becomes necessary to intervene. Although ideally we would want the patient to have full discharge of his feelings, expediency makes it necessary to interfere. It would be dangerous to permit a patient to leave at the height of an emotional storm, without a functioning reasonable ego. Our task then is to re-awaken one and yet not cause unanalyzable complications.

It has been my experience that the following kinds of steps seem to be effective with a minimum of complications. Let us assume the patient is in the throes of an intense grief reaction, is sobbing violently, and the hour is over. I would wait until almost the last moment before interrupting. Then I would say: "I am sorry to interrupt you when you are feeling so miserable, but I'm afraid our time is up." If the patient responds to this, and they usually do, I would then say, "Let's take a few extra moments, until you feel more composed." I would then give the patient an opportunity to say something if he so desires, but in any event, I give him a chance to see that I am neither anxious nor upset, nor impatient. My demeanor indicates that I have compassion for his plight, but reality has to be faced. I help bring about some controls by bringing the reality of the end of the hour to him, but I indicate that I am sorry to interrupt his outpouring of emotion—which I am. Finally, it is important that the analyst show that he is not afraid of the patient's outburst and offer himself as a model for the patient to identify with. At the end of such an hour, I usually say something like: "This emotional outpouring of yours is painful for you, but it is important for our work. We have to understand it and analyze it and master it."

Other situations arise during an analysis in which the patient loses, or fears he is losing, some or many ego functions. For example, a patient may begin to talk incomprehensibly in a word salad, or babble like a baby. Here too one has to be patient, unafraid, and firm. One has to interrupt finally and say to the patient: "Now let us look at what has happened—you were talking like a little child." By intervening in this way, the analyst serves as a reminder and model to the patient for his temporarily lost reasonable ego. By his firm tone he indicates he is not afraid, which reassures the patient.

A patient may slip into a state of great panic and become terrified and helpless on the couch. One of my patients complained that words were slipping from her, she was afraid she would wet the couch. I let her bear as much of this as I thought she was able to and then I said: "All right, let's come back to the analysis. Now let us try to look at all of this, let us now go back to the beginning and study this."

In some situations some patients have become terrified that they would lose all the controls and are frightened that they would become violently aggressive or sexual. When I have felt this fear was genuine and when there was some reason to validate their fears, I have said or behaved in a manner which indicated: "Don't worry, I won't let you hurt yourself or me."

As I said before: These interventions are not analytic, but I believe these situations are at the time nonanalytic. I use unanalytic procedures, but I try to avoid anti-analytic ones, i.e., acts that will disturb the later analysis. Only after the acute crisis has passed can one resume analysis. It has been my experience, however, that interventions made with a therapeutic intent and later thoroughly analyzed do not cause irrevocable damage to the analytic situation. On the other hand, the strictly passive and silent analytic role can be a greater danger by allowing the patient to regress to a traumatic level. The analyst's silence and passivity will be correctly perceived by the patient as indications of lack of concern, anxiety, and confusion in the analyst. This can be far more harmful. When such occurrences take place, the analyst needs to do some self-analysis of his countertransference behavior.

In closing this chapter on the technique of analyzing resistance, I once again feel impelled to repeat that the most important resistances are the transference resistances. I have not stressed this in the clinical examples cited above, since I first wanted to discuss the concept of resistance in general.

Additional Reading List

The Patient Is Silent

Arlow (1961), Glover (1955), Loewenstein (1961), Loomie (1961), Van der Heide (1961), Zeligs (1961).

Resistance and Defense

Freeman (1959), Freud (1916-17, Chapt. XIX; 1923b, Chapt. V; 1926a; 1933), Gero (1951), Hartmann (1951), Hoffer (1954), Kohut (1957), Lampl-de Groot (1957), Loewenstein (1954), Sperling (1958), Winnicott (1955).

Acting Out and Resistance

Altman (1957), Bird (1957), Ekstein and Friedman (1957), Kanzer (1957), Spiegel (1954), Zeligs (1957).

Character Disorders and Resistance

Gillespie (1958), Gitelson (1958), Glover (1958), Katan (1958), Nacht (1958b), Waelder (1958).

Ego-alien and Ego-syntonic Resistances

Glover (1955), Menninger (1958), Sharpe (1930).

3

Transference

T HE development of the technique of psychoanalysis has been determined essentially by the evolution of our knowledge about the nature of transference. The greatest advances in psychoanalytic technique were derived from Freud's (1905c) major discoveries about the twofold power of transference; it is an instrument of irreplaceable value, and it is the source of the greatest dangers. Transference reactions offer the analyst an invaluable opportunity to explore the inaccessible past and the unconscious (Freud, 1912a, p. 108). Transference also stirs up resistances that become the most serious obstacle to our work (p. 101). Every definition of psychoanalytic technique must include as a central element the *analysis* of the transference. Every deviant school of psychoanalysis can be described by some aberration in the way the transference situation is handled. Transference reactions occur in all patients undergoing psychotherapy. Psychoanalysis is distinguished from all other therapies by the way it promotes the development of the transference reactions and how it attempts systematically to analyze transference phenomena.

3.1 Working Definition

By transference we refer to a special kind of relationship toward a person; it is a distinctive type of object relationship. The main characteristic is the experience of feelings to a person which do not

151

befit that person and which actually apply to another. Essentially, a person in the present is reacted to as though he were a person in the past. Transference is a repetition, a new edition of an old object relationship (Freud, 1905c, p. 116). It is an anachronism, an error in time. A displacement has taken place; impulses, feelings, and defenses pertaining to a person in the past have been shifted onto a person in the present. It is primarily an unconscious phenomenon, and the person reacting with transference feelings is in the main unaware of the distortion.

Transference may consist of any of the components of an object relationship, i.e., it may be experienced as feelings, drives, wishes, fears, fantasies, attitudes, and ideas or defenses against them. The people who are the original sources of transference reactions are the meaningful and significant people of early childhood (Freud, 1912a, p. 104; A. Freud, 1936, p. 18). Transference occurs in analysis and outside of analysis, in neurotics, psychotics, and in healthy people. All human relations contain a mixture of realistic and transference reactions (Fenichel, 1941, p. 72).

Before we proceed to amplify the elements outlined above, it is necessary to clarify the terminology. The heading of this chapter is "Transference" and that is the old and familiar term which Freud introduced and which most analysts continue to use. In recent years there has been a movement to modify this because it was felt that the term "transference" might be misleading. "Transference" is singular and transference phenomena are plural, multiple and diversified; the term "transferences" is grammatically more correct. Unfortunately "transferences" sounds artificial and strange to me, and I have had to resort to a compromise between correctness and familiarity. I prefer to use the term "transference reactions" to refer to the entire class of transference phenomena. When I use the term "transference," I shall use it as a collective noun, shorthand for transference reactions.

Transference reactions are always inappropriate. They may be so in the quality, quantity, or duration of the reaction. One may overreact or underreact, or one may have a bizarre reaction to the transference object. The transference reaction is unsuitable in its current context; but it was once an appropriate reaction to a past situation. Just as ill-fitting as transference reactions are to a person in the present, they fit snugly to someone in the past.

For example, a young woman patient reacts to my keeping her waiting for two or three minutes by becoming tearful and angry, fantasying that I must be giving extra time to my favorite woman patient. This is an inappropriate reaction in a thirty-five-year-old intelligent and cultured woman, but her associations lead to a past situation where this set of feelings and fantasies fit. She recalls her reactions as a child of five waiting for her father to come to her room to kiss her good night. She always had to wait a few minutes because he made it a rule to kiss her younger sister good night first. Then she reacted by tears, anger, and jealousy fantasies—precisely what she is now experiencing with me. Her reactions are appropriate for a five-year-old girl, but obviously not fitting for a thirty-five-year-old woman. The key to understanding this behavior is recognizing that it is a repetition of the past, i.e., a transference reaction.

Transference reactions are essentially repetitions of a past object relationship. The repetition has been understood in a variety of ways and apparently serves multiple functions. Instinctual frustration and inhibition cause the neurotic to seek belated opportunities for satisfaction (Freud, 1912a, p. 100; Ferenczi, 1909). But the repetition has also been understood as a means of avoiding memory, a defense against memory, as well as a manifestation of the compulsion to repeat (Freud, 1912a, 1914c; A. Freud, 1936; Fenichel, 1945b).

It is this fact, that a piece of behavior repeats something in the past, that makes it likely to be inappropriate to the present. The repetition may be an exact duplication of the past, a replica, a reliving, or it may be a new edition, a modified version, a distorted representation of the past. If a modification of the past transpires in the transference behavior, then it is usually in the direction of wish fulfillment. Very often fantasies of childhood are experienced as having actually taken place (Freud, 1914b, pp. 17-18; Jones, 1953, pp. 265-267). Patients will experience feelings toward the analyst that can be construed as a sexual seduction by the father, which are later revealed to be a repetition of a wish that occurred originally as a childhood fantasy. Transference feelings that are acted out usually turn out to be such attempts at wish fulfillment (Freud, 1914c; Fenichel, 1945b; Greenacre, 1950; Bird, 1957). An extension of this idea is to be seen in patients who attempt to complete unfulfilled tasks in their acting out (Lagache, 1953).

The objects who were the original sources of the transference reaction are the important people of a child's early years. They usually are the parents and other upbringers, the dispensers of love, comfort, and punishment, the siblings and other rivals. However, transference reactions may be derived from later figures and even current figures, but analysis will reveal that these later objects are secondary and were themselves evolved from the primary, early childhood figures. Finally, it should be added that parts of the self may be displaced onto others, that is, projection may take place. These will also appear like transference reactions, but I question whether this type of response correctly belongs in the realm of transference reactions. This will be discussed in greater detail in Section 3.41.

Transference reactions are more apt to occur in later life toward people who perform a special function which originally was carried out by the parents. Thus, lovers, leaders, authorities, physicians, teachers, performers, and celebrities are particularly prone to activate transference responses. Furthermore, transference reactions can also occur to animals, to inanimate objects, and to institutions, but here, too, analysis will demonstrate that they are derived from the important people of early childhood (Reider, 1953a).

Any and all elements of an object relationship may be contained in a transference reaction; any emotion, drive, wish, attitude, fantasy, and the defenses against them. For example, a patient's inability to feel anger toward his analyst may stem from his childhood defense against expressing anger. As a boy he learned that the best way to prevent terrible quarrels with his explosive father was to remain unaware of anger in himself. In the analysis he was unaware of the anger that lay behind his persistent blandness.

Identifications may arise during analysis, which may be transference reactions. One of my patients would take on one or another of my character traits from time to time during the analysis. This was apt to occur when he felt left behind by a more successful competitor. It was as though he had to become like me when he could not possess me as a love object. His history indicated that he employed this mechanism when he competed with his older brothers for the love of his father.

Transference reactions are essentially unconscious, although some aspect of the reaction may be conscious. The person experiencing a transference reaction may be aware that he is reacting excessively or strangely, but he is unknowing of its true meaning. He may even be intellectually aware of the source of the reaction, but he remains unconscious of some important emotional or instinctual component or purpose.

All people have transference reactions; the analytic situation only facilitates their development and utilizes them for interpretation and reconstruction (Freud, 1905c, 1912a). Neurotics are particularly prone to transference reactions, as are frustrated and unhappy people in general. The analyst is a prime target for transference reactions, but so are all the important people in the life of an individual.

To summarize: Transference is the experiencing of feelings, drives, attitudes, fantasies, and defenses toward a person in the present which do not befit that person but are a repetition of reactions originating in regard to significant persons of early childhood, unconsciously displaced onto figures in the present. The two outstanding characteristics of a transference reaction are: it is a repetition and it is inappropriate. (For an amplification of this definition see Section 3.41.)

3.2 Clinical Picture: General Characteristics

In this section I would like to familiarize the student with some of the most typical manifestations of transference phenomena as they are apt to occur during the course of analysis. I believe this can best be done by focusing on those characteristics of the patient's reactions to the analyst which indicate the likelihood of a transference reaction. It should be borne in mind that the presence of the qualities I am highlighting is not absolute evidence of transference. The quality under scrutiny must also be a repetition and inappropriate.

3.21 INAPPROPRIATENESS

A basic question immediately arises as we attempt to illustrate the clinical picture of transference reactions. Could we not classify all reactions to the analyst as transference? According to our definition, the answer is no. Let us take a simple example: A patient becomes angry with his analyst. One cannot determine from this fact alone whether one is dealing with a transference reaction. One first has to ascertain whether the analyst's behavior justifies the anger. If the patient became annoyed because the analyst interrupted the patient's associations by answering the telephone, then I would not consider the patient's annoyance a transference reaction. His response seems realistic, in accordance with the circumstances, and appropriate to a mature level of functioning. This does not imply that the patient's reaction is to be ignored, but we handle such occurrences differently than we do transference phenomena. We might explore the patient's history and fantasies in regard to anger reactions, but, despite our findings, we would remind the patient and ourselves that his overt reaction to the frustration was realistic. If the patient had become furious and not just annoyed, or if he had remained completely indifferent, then the inappropriate intensity of the reaction would indicate that we are probably dealing with a repetition or a reaction from childhood. The same would hold true if his annoyance lasted for hours or if he reacted to the interruption with laughter.

Let me cite a typical example of an inappropriate reaction. My telephone rings repeatedly during an analytic hour and I answer, thinking it is an emergency. To my dismay it turns out to be a wrong number and I indicate my annoyance by inadvertently mumbling "Goddamn it" under my breath. Then I am silent. The patient resumes talking where he left off. After a few minutes I interrupt him and ask him how he felt about the phone call. He replies: "How am I supposed to feel? It was not your fault." Silence. He tries to return to the earlier conversation, but it seems strained and artificial. I then point out how he seems to be trying to cover up certain of his emotional reactions by acting as he imagines he "is supposed to." This leads the patient to recall a momentary flash of anger as he heard me answer the phone. This was followed by a picture of me shouting at him angrily. The patient then recalls a host of memories of how he was forced to submit to his father's ideas about how he was "supposed" to behave. I interpreted to him how he had reacted to me as though I were his father.

The inappropriateness of a reaction to a current situation is the prime sign that the person who triggers the reaction is not the decisive or true object. It indicates that the reaction probably belongs to and fits an object in the past.

3.22 INTENSITY

By and large, *intense emotional reactions* to the analyst are indicative of transference. This is true for the various forms of love as well as hate and fear. The usual restrained, nonintrusive, consistent behavior and attitudes of the analyst do not realistically call for intense reactions. Here again appropriateness has to be kept in mind. It is important to acknowledge that a patient may be justified in reacting with great intensity if the analysts's behavior and the analytic situation warrant this. For example: An analyst falls asleep while listening to his patient. The patient becomes aware of this and finally manages to awaken the analyst by calling to him. The patient becomes furious when the analyst does not concede his error but instead interprets that the patient unconsciously wanted to put him to sleep by being boring.

In such a situation, I would not consider the patient's fury a transference reaction, but essentially justifiable and appropriate. In fact, any other reaction would have been a more likely sign of a transfer from the past. This does not mean that the patient's reaction is not to be analyzed, but the ultimate analytic aim is different if we are dealing with a transference reaction rather than with a realistic one. Furthermore, there is always the possibility in all intense reactions, no matter how justifiable they seem, that in addition to the realistic superstructure, there is also a transference core. In the ordinary course of analysis, however, intense reactions to the analyst are a reliable indication of a transference reaction.

The converse of intense reactions to the analyst, the absence of reactions, is just as surely a sign of transference. The patient may be having reactions but is withholding them because he is embarrassed or afraid. This is an obvious manifestation of transference resistance. The situation is more complicated when the patient is not consciously aware of any but the blandest and most innocuous of feelings. It may be that there are strong feelings within the patient, but they are repressed, isolated or displaced. Sometimes it requires persistent analysis of the fear of reacting emotionally to the analyst before a patient will dare to allow himself some spontaneous reactions. Such resistances to the transference were described in Chapter 2. At this point I want to mention briefly the frequent clinical experience that my patients will react quite reasonably to my idiosyncrasies but tend to become distraught by any sign of peculiarity in another analyst. This is a clear-cut example of a displacement of a transference reaction and has to be recognized as a defense against transference feelings toward the patient's own analyst. A similar resistance is manifested by patients who react blandly in the hour and who have unexplained intense emotional reactions toward strangers after the hour.

It may happen that a patient will not be particularly concerned with his analyst for a short period of time, because important events are going on in his life apart from the analysis. However, prolonged absence of feelings, thoughts, or fantasies about the analyst is a transference phenomenon, a transference resistance. The analyst is too important a person in the life of the analysand to be absent from his thoughts and feelings for any considerable period of time. If the analyst is really not important, then the patient is not "in analysis." The patient may be going through the motions of analysis to please someone else or coming for some purpose other than for treatment.

It may also occur that some other person in the patient's life may absorb the patient's intense emotions and that the absence of intense feelings for the analyst may not be due primarily to a transference resistance. For example: a patient during the first part of his analysis is freed from his fear of emotional involvement and in the later course of his analysis falls in love. The love affair will in all likelihood contain important elements from the patient's past, but the contribution from the analytic situation may or may not be of decisive significance. One would have to explore such a situation very carefully and repeatedly before coming to any reliable conclusions. Is the patient falling in love to please you? Is he falling in love to spite you because you do not give him sufficient love? Is he falling in love out of identification with you? Has the patient fallen in love with someone who resembles you? Is the falling in love a sign of maturity? Does there seem to be some realistic hope for a sustained happy relationship?

These questions are not easy to answer; there are no clear-cut answers and only prolonged exploration and time can offer a reasonably reliable answer. This is the basis for the practical rule suggested by Freud that the analyst should ask the patient to promise not to make any major changes in his life situation during the analysis

(1914c, p. 153). This piece of advice can also be misconstrued by the patient because of the transference distortions and has to be given at the proper time and in the proper context (Fenichel, 1941, p. 29). The fact that the duration of analytic treatment has increased in recent years has prompted a further modification of this rule. Today I believe we would tell the patient that it would be better not to make important changes in his life situation until the change in question has been sufficiently analyzed. This problem will be pursued further in Volume II.

3.23 AMBIVALENCE

All transference reactions are characterized by ambivalence, the coexistence of opposite feelings. It is customary in psychoanalysis to assume that by ambivalence we mean that one aspect of the feelings is unconscious. There is no love for the analyst without hate hidden somewhere, no sexual longings without some covert repulsion, etc. The ambivalence may be easily detectable when the feelings involved are capricious and change unexpectedly. Or one aspect of the ambivalence may be tenaciously maintained in consciousness for long periods, while its opposite is stubbornly defended. It can also happen that the ambivalence is handled by the patient displacing one component onto some other person, often another analyst. This is frequently seen in the analysis of candidates in training. They will maintain a positive relationship to their personal analyst and displace their unconscious hostility onto a supervisor or seminar leader—or vice versa.

It should not be forgotten that preambivalent reactions also may take place in the transference. The figure of the analyst is split into a good and a bad object, each of which leads a separate existence in the patient's mind. When patients reacting in this way—and they are always the more regressed patients—become able to feel ambivalence to the same whole object it denotes quite an achievement.

Let me cite a clinical example. For several years a borderline patient of mine would give bizarre responses to my interventions whenever he felt anxious. I was slowly able to piece together the following explanations. When he felt angry and hateful toward me, he became afraid and therefore never listened to my words because he felt those were like poisoned darts, and his defense was to become impervious to them. At such times he concentrated only on my tone of voice, paying meticulous attention to the changes in pitch and rhythm. Low tones and regular rhythm made him feel I was feeding him good food like mother used to make and serve when they ate alone. High tones and irregular rhythm meant mother was serving him bad food because father was there and made her nervous and spoiled the food. It took many years of analysis for him to allow me to become a whole person and to remain so whether he loved, hated, or feared me.

3.24 CAPRICIOUSNESS

Another outstanding quality of transference reactions is capriciousness. Transference feelings are often inconstant, erratic, and whimsical. This is particularly true early in analysis. Glover (1955) has designated these reactions very aptly as "floating" transference reactions.

A typical example of the sudden and unexpected changes which can take place in the transference situation is the following sequence of events which occurred during a single week in the analysis of a young hysterical-depressive woman patient in her second month of treatment. She had been working well despite the fear that I would find her unrewarding and ordinary. Her feelings toward me were of awe and admiration with the underlying hope that I would like her.

Suddenly in one hour, after considerable difficulty, she admits a feeling that she is in love with me. She attributes the beginning of this feeling to the end of the last hour when she noticed my trousers were wrinkled and my tie askew. She was convinced this meant I was not a materialist, not a greedy capitalist, but a dreamer, an idealist, even an artist. All day and night she fantasied about me in this way; her feelings grew in intensity and she enjoyed this state of affairs. Even when we begin to analyze this reaction and trace it back to the past, her feelings persist.

The next day she is overwhelmed with guilt. Her child has developed an earache during the night and the patient feels this was the result of her negligence; she has spent too much time daydreaming about her new love instead of caring for her child. She is convinced I must have contempt for such a frivolous woman. When I attempt to pursue the history of this reaction, she feels I am punishing her, as she well deserves.

On the next, the third day, she feels my greeting is cold, almost a smirk, and my silence is disdain. She now feels that I am not an idealist or a dreamer careless about appearance, I am arrogant and contemptuous of my patients, who are "poor rich neurotics." She defends herself and her group by attacking me as one of those evil-minded psychoanalysts who lives off the rich but who despises them. She finds the odor of my cigar repulsive, even nauseating.

The following hour she finds my attempts to analyze her hostile feelings clumsy but endearing. I am probably well intentioned and warm-hearted, only moody. I must have changed my brand of cigar and bought a more expensive one because of her criticism, and she was grateful for my consideration. She hopes I will some day become her guide and mentor because she has heard I am brilliant. When I keep silent she feels I am being "stuffy," conventional, and a killjoy. I probably am a grind and a hack who only loves his work. She leaves the hour feeling that I may be a good analyst, but she pities anyone married to me.

This is a rather extreme example of capriciousness, but it highlights the erratic and whimsical character of transference reactions early in the analysis of some hysterical and neurotically depressed patients.

3.25 TENACITY

It is a striking characteristic of transference reactions that they possess a contradictory nature. I have just described how capricious and transitory transference can be, and now I must add that transference phenomena are often distinguished by their tenacity. Whereas sporadic reactions are most apt to occur early in analysis, prolonged and rigid reactions are more likely to appear in the later phases, although there is no absolute rule about this.

Patients will take on a chronic set of feelings and attitudes toward the analyst which will not readily yield to interpretation. These tenacious reactions require a long period of analysis, sometimes years. This long duration does not mean that the analytic work is stalemated, because during such periods other behavioral characteristics of the patient may change and new insights and memories may appear. The patient is compelled to hold on to this fixed position because the feelings involved are overdetermined and serve important instinctual and defensive needs. These tenacious reactions may be relatively intense or subtle.

A patient of mine, Mrs. K., maintained a positive sexual and erotic transference reaction to me for almost three years. These feelings sur-

vived and were not measurably influenced by my persistent interpretations of their resistive function, my prolonged silences, my occasional errors and lapses. Only after she had improved sufficiently to be able to achieve a partial vaginal orgasm which helped abate her fear of homosexuality, did this chronic positive transference change. Only then did she dare to let herself consciously feel her hatred and revulsion toward me and toward men in general.[1]

Tenacity and lack of spontaneity are signs of transference reactions. Even in the best conducted analyses, the human frailties of the analyst would give rise to occasional hostility if a defensive positive transference were not at work. Analytic work is often painful, and that too would occasion some resentment. Above all, transference reactions stem from the patient's warded-off past and that must include a great deal of unconscious aggression which is seeking discharge. Conversely, the compassionate neutrality of the analytic attitude does not call for the prolonged hostility of some patients. The tenacity and rigidity of transference reactions are due to a combination of unconscious defense and instinctual satisfaction.

The five qualities noted above are the most typical characteristics denoting a transference reaction. The outstanding trait, which overrides all others and is included in all the others, is inappropriateness. It is inappropriateness in terms of intensity, ambivalence, capriciousness, or tenacity which signals that transference is at work. This holds true not only when such responses occur in regard to the analyst, but also when they arise in regard to other people. Reactions which are out of character or out of place are transference phenomena.

3.3 Historical Survey

I would like briefly to sketch the major contributions Freud and others have made to our understanding of the theoretical and technical problems concerning transference. I shall take them up in chronological order covering the years 1895 to 1960. I shall stress only those points which I consider to be significant advances and shall omit many valuable papers which are essentially summaries or repetitions. The student is advised to read the original papers.

---

[1] Mrs. K. was previously referred to in Sections 1.24 and 2.651. See Section 2.71 for a more detailed clinical account of this patient's change.

My version of the meaningful contents is not only extremely condensed but also a subjective selection. This subject has already been touched upon in Section 1.1.

Freud's first description and discussion of the role of transference is to be found in Chapter IV on psychotherapy in the *Studies on Hysteria* (1893-95). At first he considered it a disadvantage that the patient unduly forced his personal relations to the physician into the foreground, although he recognized that the personal influence alone can remove certain resistances (p. 301). Some patients tended to feel neglected, others feared becoming dependent, even sexually dependent. Later he described some patients who tended to transfer onto the figure of the physician distressing ideas which arose from the content of their analysis. These patients, said Freud, had made a "false connection" onto the analyst (pp. 302-303). In some cases this seemed to be a regular occurrence. He then went on to describe the technique of handling this situation. (1) It should be made conscious. (2) One should demonstrate how it is an obstacle. (3) One should attempt to trace its origin in the hour. At first Freud was "greatly annoyed" at this increase in work, but he soon realized its value (p. 304).

The Dora case is a landmark in psychoanalytic technique (Freud, 1905a). Here, in all humility and with great clarity, Freud described how he learned about the decisive importance of transference by his failure to recognize and handle it in one of his patients. This led to a premature interruption of treatment and a therapeutic failure. In this paper, Freud described how his patient experienced feelings in regard to his person during the analysis that were new editions, facsimiles, reprints, and revised editions of feelings which originally belonged to persons of significance in the past (p. 116). Such feelings seem to be a new creation, but actually are a revival of old emotional reactions. Freud called this phenomenon transference, and declared it to be a necessary part of psychoanalytic therapy. It produces the greatest obstacles, but it is also a most important ally in the treatment. He realized too late that the patient's transference feelings to him had changed and that she was acting out with him a fragment of her past. She broke off with Freud as she had not dared to do with her lover (pp. 118-119). Freud then recognized that the analysis of the hostile transference is necessary for a successful therapeutic result (p. 120).

A paper by Ferenczi in 1909, "Introjection and Transference," is the next step forward. Here Ferenczi touched on certain new ideas about transference, some of which we are still struggling with today. He pointed out that transference reactions occur in neurotics not only in the analytic situation, but elsewhere. He considered transference reactions a special form of displacement and remarked that physicians are particularly likely to be made objects of transference reactions, not only analysts. However, he believed that this predisposition existed in the patient and that the analyst is only the catalyst. Usually these reactions occur in a positive and negative form. Furthermore, Ferenczi believed that all neurotic patients have a hunger for transference. These frustrated people have a tendency to introjection and a hunger for identifications (pp. 47-49). They tend to take in the person of the analyst into their private world. He contrasted this to the paranoiacs and other psychotics, who do not introject the analyst but tend to create a distance between themselves and the analyst. He thought that this hunger of the patient for the analyst comes from a stimulus hunger (p. 51). Furthermore, he theorized that the origins of transference reactions go back to certain projections of infancy. The analyst is a "cover person," is a screen for the important objects in the infantile past of the patient (p. 62). The transference reaction is an attempt at cure.

Ferenczi went on further and discussed how in hypnosis and suggestion we are also dealing with transference reactions which have a sexual basis and which originate from both of the parental figures. The patient's readiness to transfer onto the hypnotist is derived either from parental love or from parental fear (pp. 62-63, 67). The patients then become blindly believing and obedient. Similar reactions occur in psychoanalytic therapy without hypnosis. One can discern the difference between father and mother transference in hypnosis, and one can see changes, namely, the patient's vacillations between love reactions which are mother reactions and fear reactions which are reactions to the father.

Freud's paper, "The Dynamics of the Transference" (1912a), adds some further valuable insight into transference. The patient's readiness for transference reactions comes from his dissatisfactions (p. 100). They are so strong in the neurotic patient because of his neurosis and do not arise from the analytic procedure (p. 101). Transference reactions are indications of a regression in libido. Both transference and resistances are compromise formations (pp. 102-103). Every conflict of the patient has to be fought out in the transference situation (p. 104). It is of crucial importance in the analysis, since it makes it possible for the patient to struggle in the present with his unresolved conflicts concerning important object relations in his past. One cannot slay the enemy *in absentia* or in effigy (p. 108). It is necessary to work these problems out in the ongoing transference situation occurring during analysis.

In this paper Freud discussed some of the relationships between transference and resistance, particularly the differences between the positive (i.e., sexual and erotic) transference and the negative transference, and how they influence resistance formations (pp. 105-106). He distinguished between the sexual, erotic transference and the negative transference, on the one hand, and, on the other, "rapport," which is the nonsexual, positive transference reaction. In Freud's opinion all transference reactions are essentially ambivalent (p. 106). It is interesting to note, said Freud, that patients not only have transference reactions to the analyst and to physicians but also to institutions (p. 106).

The paper "Recommendations to Physicians Practising Psycho-Analysis" (1912b) is noteworthy because in it Freud for the first time described countertransference, and the analyst's need for "psychoanalytic purification." Here Freud states for the first time the famous "mirror" simile. In order to resolve the transference it is necessary for the analyst to maintain his anonymity. "The doctor should be opaque to his patients and, like a mirror, should show them nothing but what is shown to him" (p. 118).

The essay "On Beginning the Treatment" (1913b) contains the recommendation by Freud that the theme of transference should be left untouched as long as there is no appreciable sign of resistance. He also suggested that one make no interpretations to the patient until a rapport has been developed between analyst and patient. Rapport will come about if we show a serious interest in the patient, work on his resistances, and indicate an attitude of sympathetic understanding (pp. 139-140). (I would be tempted to say this is the first description of the working alliance.)

In the paper "Remembering, Repeating and Working-Through" (1914c), Freud discussed in some detail the patient's tendency to act out in the transference situation. He also introduced a new hypothesis in explaining transference reactions, namely, the concept of a repetition compulsion, but that is not yet tied up with the death instinct. Furthermore, in this paper there is the first mention of the concept of the transference neurosis (p. 154). The transference neurosis is an artifact of the treatment and replaces the patient's ordinary neurosis. It is curable by the analytic work.

"Observations on Transference-Love" (1915a) is noteworthy for two main reasons. In it for the first time Freud mentioned the "rule of abstinence." It is a fundamental principle, said Freud, that the patient's needs and longings be allowed to persist in order that they may impel him to do the analytic work (p. 165). It is also an outstanding paper because of Freud's sensitive, personal, and literary presentation of the problem of properly dealing with a patient's romantic love for the analyst.

The chapters on "Transference" and "Analytic Therapy" in the *Introductory Lectures* (1916-17) are essentially a rather systematic and thorough review of Freud's basic ideas about transference up to that time. Furthermore, there is a discussion of the term transference neuroses as a category of neurosis to be contrasted to the narcissistic neuroses as well as a brief discussion of the transference problems in the psychoses (pp. 445, 423-430).

A major change in Freud's theoretical ideas about the nature of transference phenomena was put forth in *Beyond the Pleasure Principle* (1920). Certain childhood reactions are repeated in the transference not because there is the hope of pleasure but because there is a compulsion to repeat which is even more primitive than the pleasure principle and overrides it (pp. 20-23). The repetition compulsion is a manifestation of the death instinct (p. 36). For the first time, transference reactions were regarded as manifestations of both the libidinal and death instincts.

After these papers there were no major new developments until Glover's series of technical papers published in 1928. They were the first systematic clinical description of some of the typical problems in the development and resolution of the transference neurosis and transference resistances. Glover distinguished different phases of transference development, and the typical problems in handling the various transference reactions.

Ella Freeman Sharpe's (1930) technical papers illuminated the importance of analyzing the fantasies of the patient in regard to the analyst. In her literate and sensitive presentation she emphasized how the representations of the superego, ego, and id are played out in fantasies regarding the analyst. Transference reactions are not only displacements but may be projections. In keeping with the Kleinian point of view, Ella Sharpe was of the opinion that analyzing the transference is not a separate task but is the task from the beginning to the end of the analysis, that the transference situation has to be constantly sought out. Of particular clinical value is her description of some of the complicated problems in the subtle transference resistances to be found in the compliant, submissive patient.

Freud's "Analysis Terminable and Interminable" (1937a) is notable because in it Freud continued the discussion of controversial hypotheses about transference and transference resistances. He emphasized the problem of protracted negative transference and acting out, which he attributed to the compulsion to repeat, a manifestation of the death instinct. He drew attention to physiological and biological factors (pp. 224-226). Freud also discussed the poor prognosis and limitations of psychoanalytic therapy and the special problems inherent in patients with a so-called negative therapeutic reaction (pp. 241-243). In this paper he touched upon the question of whether or not it is right for the analyst to stir up latent problems in the patient. Freud was adamant that the analyst should not manipulate the transference; his task is to analyze and not to manipulate (pp. 232-234).

Richard Sterba's two papers on transference (1929, 1934) make an important contribution to our understanding of the therapeutic process. He described the split in the patient's ego which occurs when he is able to identify partially with the analyst's observing function. In this way the patient is able to become an active participant in the analysis. He not only produces the material, but on the basis of the identification he can work with it analytically. This idea is a central element in what later became known as the "therapeutic" or "working alliance."

Fenichel's (1941) slim volume on technique is essentially a highly condensed, systematic, and thorough review of the theoretical basis of psychoanalytic technique. It also offers an outline of the technical steps to be considered in approaching the typical problems of technique.

The most outstanding contribution in Macalpine's paper "The Development of the Transference" (1950) is her careful dissection of how the analytic situation itself converts the patient's transference readiness into transference reactions. She isolated some fifteen different factors which play a role in inducing the necessary regression in the patient undergoing psychoanalysis.

Phyllis Greenacre's "The Role of Transference" (1954) added some important insights into the origins of transference, the "matrix" of transference reactions. She also carefully explained the importance of safeguarding the transference, the avoidance of "contamination." Her notion of the "tilted" relationship in the analytic situation, the unevenness between patient and analyst, is another helpful idea (p. 674). Greenacre realizes that the transference relationship is an inordinately complex one and suggests we ought to pay more attention to the splitting of the transference relationship (Greenacre, 1959).

The Discussion of Problems of Transference (held at the 19th International Psycho-Analytical Congress in 1955) is an excellent summary of the current psychoanalytic point of view (see Waelder, et al., 1956). Elizabeth Zetzel's (1956) analysis of the importance of the "therapeutic alliance" is an outstanding contribution. In that paper, she stresses how differently it is regarded by the classical analysts and the followers of Melanie Klein. This distinction is, in my opinion, the basis for some important differences in theory and technique. Spitz's (1956b) paper deepens our understanding of how the analytic setting revives some of the earliest aspects of the mother-child relationship. Winnicott's (1956a) essay stresses the modifications in technique required by patients who did not experience adequate mothering in the early months of life. It is his opinion that only when a patient has been able to develop a transference neurosis can we depend essentially on interpretive work.

In a very sensitive and penetrating study on the "Therapeutic Action of Psycho-Analysis," Loewald (1960) focuses on certain nonverbal elements in the transference relationship. He describes a type of mutuality that resembles the mother's nonverbal and growth-promoting interactions with the child. This hinges partly on the mother's selective, mediating, and organizing functions which aid the child in forming an ego structure. The mother's picture of the child's potentials becomes part of the child's image of himself. A similar process occurs unnoticed in psychoanalytic therapy.

Leo Stone's (1961) book on *The Psychoanalytic Situation* is, in my opinion, an important step forward in clarifying some of the problems of transference phenomena. The concept of necessary gratifications, the therapeutic intent of the analyst, and his emphasis on different, coexisting, relationships between analyst and patient, represent a significant advance in our theory and technique. I believe it was Zetzel's paper on the therapeutic alliance and Stone's book on the psychoanalytic situation which led me to formulate the working alliance (Greenson, 1965a). The separation of the relatively nonneurotic relationship to the analyst from the more neurotic transference reactions has important theoretical and technical implications. A patient must be able to develop both types of relationships in order to be analyzable.

One cannot conclude a historical survey of such a basic topic without including a brief description of some controversial developments. I have selected what seem to me to be the two most important current deviations among psychoanalysts, the schools of Melanie Klein and Franz Alexander.

The followers of the Kleinian school consider the interpretation of the unconscious meaning of transference phenomena to be the crux of the therapeutic process. However, they believe that the patient's relationship to his analyst is almost entirely one of unconscious fantasy (Isaacs, 1948, p. 79). Transference phenomena are regarded essentially as projections and introjections of the most infantile good and bad objects. Although these early introjects arise in a preverbal phase, the Kleinians expect their patients to comprehend the meaning of these primitive goings-on from the beginning of the analysis (Klein, 1961; Segal, 1964). They do not analyze resistance as such, but instead make interpretations about the complex, hostile and idealized projections and introjections of the patient in regard to the analyst. It seems as though they expect to influence the internal good and bad objects in the patient's ego by interpreting what they sense is going on. They do not communicate with a cohesive, integrated ego; they do not attempt to establish a working alliance, but seem instead to establish direct contact with the various introjects (Heimann, 1956).

Kleinians hold the view that *only* transference interpretations are effective. No other interpretations are considered important. Their approach is equally valid, they claim, for working with children, psychotics, and neurotics (Rosenfeld, 1952, 1958). One cannot do justice to these views with so short a description; it is necessary to be familiar with the entire school of thought. The student should read the three most recent books published by Melanie Klein and her followers (1952, 1955; Segal, 1964). For a lucid and temperate discussion of this subject, the student is referred to the chapter on Melanie Klein's work by Brierley (1951).

Although one may find much to disagree with in the Kleinian approach, nevertheless the Kleinians use the psychoanalytic approach insofar as they *interpret* the transference. Alexander and his followers (1946) challenge this basic attitude of analyzing and interpreting the transference. On the contrary, they advocate that the transference should be regulated, controlled, and manipulated. It should not be allowed to flower in accordance with the patient's neurotic needs. One should not permit the patient to get into deep regressions since these regressions will lead to dependent transference reactions which are essentially resistances and not productive. It is best to avoid the patient's distrust and antipathy; a hostile and aggressive transference is a needless complication. Analysts may avoid all mention of the infantile conflicts and avoid thereby the dependent transference reactions. A transference neurosis of moderate intensity is permissible, but intense transference neuroses are to be avoided. One ought to focus much more on the present and less on the past.

This is but a small sample of the views expressed by Alexander and French in their book *Psychoanalytic Therapy*. This volume created quite a stir in psychoanalytic circles in America (it seems to have been ignored in Europe), since many of the contributors were psychoanalysts of prominence and the views expressed contradicted many accepted basic principles of psychoanalytic theory and technique. The reverberations of this attempt to alter psychoanalysis led, in my opinion, to the setting up of fixed training standards in the American Psychoanalytic Association. It was believed that candidates trained according to the methods advocated by Alexander and his followers would not have undergone a deep psychoanalytic experience.

As I stated in the beginning of this chapter, every aberration in psychoanalysis can be demonstrated in the deviant way that transference phenomena are regarded.

3.4 Theoretical Considerations

3.41 THE ORIGIN AND NATURE OF TRANSFERENCE REACTIONS

Before we explore some of the theoretical issues concerning transference phenomena, it is imperative to be more precise about the meaning of the term. There are many different theories about what constitutes a transference reaction and I have the impression that some of the divergencies stem from a failure to define one's terms in sufficient detail. Let me repeat at this point the definition of transference I employed in Section 3.1. *Transference is the experiencing of feeling, drives, attitudes, fantasies, and defenses toward a person in the present which do not befit that person but are a repetition of reactions originating in regard to significant persons of early childhood, unconsciously displaced onto figures in the present.*

This definition rests on four basic propositions: (1) Transference is a variety of object relationship. (2) Transference phenomena repeat a past relationship to an object. (3) The mechanism of displacement is the essential process in transference reactions. (4) Transference is a regressive phenomenon. For a psychic phenomenon to be considered transference, all four of these elements must be present. Each of the four components has important theoretical and clinical connotations.

Psychoanalytic treatment does not create transference reactions; it merely brings them to light by facilitating their development. Transference phenomena in neurotics are a specialized class of relationship to another person. They represent a kind of intermediary realm between illness and real life (Freud, 1914c). Other modes of relating to the analyst occur during psychoanalytic treatment. A working alliance and a real relationship also take place and play an important role in the psychoanalytic therapy of neurotic patients. They differ from transference phenomena and will be considered separately.

More primitive ways of relating to the analyst may occur as well. Reactions of a delusional or psychotic character take place but it is not certain whether they may be rightfully called transference reactions (Freud, 1915b). In order to avoid any ambiguity, if the term transference or transference reaction is employed without further specification in these writings, it shall refer to neurotic transference phenomena. In a variety of severely regressed patients, we may see transient psychotic reactions to the therapist. These manifestations are quite different from neurotic transference reactions. The main distinctions stem from the fact that the psychotic has lost his object representations and as a consequence can no longer differentiate between the self and object world (Freud, 1915b; M. Wexler, 1960; Jacobson, 1964). It should not be forgotten, however, that psychotic patients may have neurotic and healthy components and the converse is equally true (M. Katan, 1954). One does see patients who manifest both neurotic and psychotic transference reactions.

The multiform ways of relating to the analyst during psychoanalysis have to be distinguished from one another because they imply important clinical, theoretical, and technical differences. Simply lumping them all together as transference phenomena does not do justice to the complexities of human relationships and to the intricacies of the therapeutic processes involved in psychoanalytic treatment.

3.411 Transference and Object Relations

A transference reaction in neurotics is a relationship involving three whole people—a subject, a past object, and a present object (Searles, 1965). In the analytic situation it usually comprises the patient, some significant person from the past, and the analyst. A patient who becomes afraid of his analyst in the same way he once feared his father is misunderstanding the present in terms of his past as long as he is in the grip of the transference reaction (Fenichel, 1945a). However, the neurotic patient knows the analyst is his analyst and not his father, and he also knows that he, the patient, is not the analyst and also not his father. In other words, the neurotic may react temporarily and partially *as if* the analyst were identical to his father, but intellectually he can clearly distinguish the analyst from his father and his self. In clinical terms, the neurotic patient is able to split off his experiencing ego from his observing ego. He may do this spontaneously or he may need the help of the analyst's interpretations.

Neurotic transference phenomena are based on two achievements: (1) the individual's capacity to differentiate between the self and the object world; (2) the ability to displace reactions from a past object representation to an object in the present (Jacobson, 1964; Hartmann, 1950). This means that the neurotic has an organized, differentiated self, an entity separate and distinct from his environment, which has the capacity to remain the same in the midst of change (Jacobson, 1964; Lichtenstein, 1961; Mahler, 1957 [see Rubinfine, 1958]; and Greenacre, 1958).

Very young children have not yet achieved their separation, their individuation, from the mother. Older children have a hunger for new objects. In the treatment situation they do not merely repeat the past, they try new ways of relating (A. Freud, 1965). Psychotics have lost their internal object representations and strive to fill up the feeling of a terrible void by creating new objects (Freud, 1915b). They are prone to fuse and confuse remnants of their self and object representations. Furthermore, their world is full of part objects which they introject and project in their attempts to build or rebuild their lost object relationships (M. Wexler, 1960; Searles, 1963).

One of my schizophrenic patients was convinced for years that she was made of soap and blamed me for this. These ideas were based in part on her literal and concrete acceptance of the axioms, "Silence is golden" and "Cleanliness is next to Godliness." She felt my attempts to get her to talk resulted in the loss of her "pure" silent state. I had used "dirty words" and this had turned *her* into soap. (Note the confusion of self and analyst.) The basic problem, however, was her sense of emptiness, her awareness of having lost her world of objects. The feeling of being made of soap was an acknowledgment of this as well as an attempt at restitution.

This kind of relatedness to the analyst is very different from neurotic transference reactions. The reader is referred to the works of Freud (1915b, 1911a), Searles (1963), Little (1958), and Rosenfeld (1952, 1954) for further clinical and theoretical material on transference phenomena in psychotics.

The foregoing deliberations merely hint at some of the problems that lie behind the differences in the therapeutic approach to the child, the adult neurotic, and the psychotic (A. Freud, 1965). Freud's (1916-17) separation of the transference neuroses from the narcissistic neuroses seems to be based on similar grounds. People who are essentially narcissistic will not be able to maintain a consistently analyzable transference relationship. Their relationship to the therapist will abound with fusions of self and object images, primitive forerunners of identification (Jacobson, 1964). There are transitions between narcissistic relations and object relations, as Winnicott (1953) has demonstrated with the concept of transitional objects. The serious student is advised to read Jacobson (1964), Fenichel (1945a), Spitz (1957, 1965), and Mahler (1965) for a more thorough view of the beginnings of self and object representations. I agree with Greenacre's (1954) formulation that the matrix of the transference relationship is the early mother-infant union. Man is not able to endure aloneness very well for any considerable period of time. The analytic situation mobilizes two antithetical sets of reactions. The sensory isolation of the patient on the couch stirs up the feeling of aloneness, frustration, and a hunger for object relations. On the other hand, the high frequency of visits, the long duration of the treatment, and the devotion to the patient's needs stir up memories of the early closeness between mother and child.

3.412 Transference and Ego Functions

Transference reactions demonstrate the neurotic patient's strengths and weaknesses in terms of his ego functions. As previously stated, neurotic transference phenomena indicate that the patient has a stable self representation which is sharply differentiated from his object representations. This implies his early ego development has been essentially successful, he has had "good-enough" mothering, and he can relate to whole people (Winnicott, 1955, 1956b). When he "misunderstands the present in terms of his past," the misunderstanding is only partial and temporary. The regression in ego functions is a circumscribed one and limited to certain aspects of his relationship to the transference figure. Furthermore, it is reversible.

For example, a patient of mine is in the throes of an intense, hostile transference reaction. He spends most of several hours complaining vociferously that I am incompetent, unscrupulous, and callous. Yet, he comes punctually to his appointments, listens attentively to my interventions, and functions adequately in his outside life. Even though he thinks of quitting the analysis, he does not seriously contemplate such a move.

A patient in such a state of mind is allowing himself to be carried away by his feelings and fantasies. He is letting himself regress in terms of his object relations and ego functions. He renounces certain of his reality-testing functions partially and temporarily. (This is to be differentiated from role playing or pretending.) In the case cited above, the transference reaction was mobilized when I did not answer one of his questions. This action of mine overrode momentarily all my qualities which were in contradiction to his charge that I was incompetent, unscrupulous, and callous. The patient's ego function of discrimination was impaired during this phase of treatment. I became his harsh and punitive father when I remained silent. The patient was able to work with this reaction, began to understand it, when his observing ego and the working alliance were re-established.

Other mechanisms indicative of a regression in ego functions occur in transference reactions, but they are a *supplement* to the mechanism of displacement. Projection and introjection may take place, but they are not the basic process in neurotic transference. They may operate in addition to the displacement. I want to stress this point because it is in conflict with the views of the Kleinian school whose followers interpret all transference phenomena on the basis of projection and introjection (Klein, 1952; Racker, 1954; Segal, 1964). They neglect the displacement from a past object relationship and therefore relatively ignore the historical experiences of the patient. I believe this is due in part to their failure to differentiate projection and introjection from displacement as well as to an inexact usage of the terms projection and introjection.

At the risk of seeming pedantic I shall define these terms briefly, as they are used in the classical psychoanalytic literature. Displacement refers to the shift of feelings, fantasies, etc., from an *object* or *object representation* in the past to an object or object representation in the present. When a person projects, he is ejecting something from within his *self representation* into or onto another person. Introjection is the incorporation of something from an external object into the *self representation*. Projection and introjection may occur during analysis, but they occur *in addition to the displacement*. They are *repetitions* of projective and introjective mechanisms which once took place in regard to past objects of historical importance (Jacobson, 1964).

Let me give an example of projection as a neurotic transference reaction. Professor X.[2] who suffered from stage fright complained frequently during his analysis that he felt I was mocking him, laughing at him behind his back, or deriding him whenever I made an interpretation. There were many determinants for this reaction in the patient's history. His father had been known to be a tease who delighted in sadistically embarrassing the patient, especially before company. The patient had developed a very strict superego and flagellated himself severely for a variety of activities he considered shameful. In the course of the analysis his sense of shame was changed to a feeling that I would shame him if I knew what he had done. The patient had projected parts of his superego onto me. His fantasy of being humiliated by me not only was painful but also contained masochistic and exhibitionistic pleasure. This was a carry-over from his childhood relationship to his father which was replete with sexual and aggressive fantasies. However, one important aspect of his humiliation fantasies was based on projection.

In one hour he shamefacedly reported that he got drunk over the weekend and had entertained a gathering of his friends by doing an imitation of "Gruesome Greenson, the great psychoanalyst." He was amazed at how long a period of time he was able to keep his audience laughing at his analyst. In the analytic hour he realized he did this occasionally at home by imitating certain expressions or gestures of mine whenever there were people present who knew me. The patient became quite apprehensive when he spoke of this; he felt certain "the roof would fall in." This phrase led him to recall a hitherto forgotten memory of being caught by his father doing a burlesque of his father's manner of speech. His father beat him unmercifully and then tormented him for crying. This episode ended the patient's attempt to imitate his father and led eventually to the stage fright.

It seemed clear to me that, in part, the patient had projected his impulses to be a humiliator onto me. This was a defense against his hostility, a means of avoiding anxiety, as well as other things. But this projection was a supplement to the basic determinant of his feeling of humiliation—the history of a father who humiliated him and whom he longed to humiliate in retaliation.

[2] See also Sections 2.64 and 2.652.

The acting out or enactment of transference reactions is indicative of other regressive features in the ego functions in transference. The relationship of transference to memory will be discussed in some detail in the following sections on repetition and regression.

3.413 Transference and Repetition

One of the outstanding characteristics of transference reactions is their repetitiousness, their resistance to change, their tenacity. There are many factors which play a role in this phenomenon and there are diverse theoretical explanations. Here only some of the major issues will be briefly touched upon.

Transference is a reliving of the repressed past—to be more exact, of the warded-off past. The repetitiousness and rigidity of transference reactions, as contrasted to more realistic object relations, stem from the fact that the id impulses which seek discharge in the transference behavior are opposed by one or another unconscious ego counterforce. Transference satisfactions are never wholly satisfying because they are only substitutes for real satisfaction, regressive derivatives, and compromise formations (Fenichel, 1941). They are the product of a constant countercathexis. Only if the countercathexis, the defense, is resolved can adequate discharge take place.

Instinctual frustration and the search for gratification are the basic motives for transference phenomena. Satisfied people and people in a state of apathy have far fewer transference reactions. Satisfied people can modulate their behavior in accordance with the opportunities and demands of the external world. Apathetic people have withdrawn into a more narcissistic orientation. The neurotic who suffers from a variety of unresolved neurotic conflicts is in a constant state of instinctual dissatisfaction and, as a result, is in a state of transference readiness (Freud, 1912a). A person in such a condition will meet every new person with conscious and unconscious libidinal and aggressive anticipatory ideas. These are already present before the patient meets the analyst, and the neurotic's history is replete with transference behavior long before he comes for treatment (Frosch, 1959).

The warded-off impulses which are blocked from direct discharge seek regressive and distorted channels in their attempts to gain access to consciousness and motility. Transference behavior is an example of the return of the repressed. The person of the ana-

lyst becomes a prime target for the dammed-up impulses because
the patient uses him as an opportunity to express the short-circuited
impulses instead of facing the original objects (Fenichel, 1941).
The transference is a resistance in this sense, but it is a necessary
detour on the road to insight and memory. The analyst's nonintrusive, nongratifying behavior makes the patient's transference reactions demonstrable. Freud's (1915a) so-called rules of the "mirror"
and of abstinence are founded on this basis. If the psychoanalyst
will not gratify the patient's neurotic instinctual wishes, these impulses will become demonstrable as transference distortions and
will become the vehicle for valuable insights. These issues will be
discussed more thoroughly in Sections 3.92, 4.213, 4.223.

The repetition of a psychic event may also be a means of achieving belated mastery over it (Freud, 1920; Fenichel, 1945a). The
active repetition of a traumatic experience is a case in point. The
infantile ego learns to overcome the feeling of helplessness by actively repeating the situation that once induced the original sense
of panic. Games, dreams, and thoughts concerning the painful event
make it possible to discharge some of the excessive excitation which
had flooded the ego. The ego which was passive in the original
traumatic situation actively reproduces the event at a time it
chooses, in circumstances favorable to it, and thus slowly learns to
cope with it.

Repetition of a situation may lead from coping and mastery to
pleasure. In part this may be due to the sense of triumph over a
once-feared event. This is usually transitory unless there still is a
counterphobic element at work (Fenichel, 1939). This means that
the event is repeated *because* it is feared, the repetition is an attempt to deny that the anxiety still persists. For example, excessive
sexual activity may mean that the person in question is trying to
deny his anxiety. His actions indicate that he is attempting to persuade himself he is no longer afraid. His counterphobic sexuality
is also an attempt to get witnesses who will confirm this. The excessive repetitiveness indicates that a neurotic conflict is involved. The
unconscious ego prevents full instinctual discharge and the activity
has to be performed again and again.

Transference reactions may well be approached from the points
of view sketched above. A frightening relationship to a person in the
past is repeated as an attempt to achieve belated mastery over the

anxiety which was contained in the original experience. For example, a woman seeks out harsh, cruel men as love objects. In the transference she reacts repeatedly as though the analyst were cruel and punitive. In addition to its other meanings, this type of reaction can be profitably understood as a belated attempt to master the original anxiety. As a child she was helplesss before her harsh father. As a patient she unconsciously selects the aggressive components of her psychoanalyst to react to, as a means of achieving control over her anxiety. She enacts the painful situation *instead* of remembering the original experience. The repetition in action is a prelude, a preparation for memory (Freud, 1914c; Ekstein and Friedman, 1957).

Lagache (1953) added a valuable point to our understanding of the repeated acting out of transference phenomena. He demonstrated that the acting out may be an attempt to complete unfulfilled tasks. This is related to Anna Freud's (1965) ideas concerning the transference problems in children due to their hunger for new experiences. Some of these points will be elaborated upon in Section 3.84 on the acting out of transference reactions.

This discussion of the meaning of the repetition of transference phenomena leads us to Freud's (1920, 1923b, 1937a) concept of the repetition compulsion. Freud speculated that the compulsion to repeat is ultimately derived from a primal death instinct. He believed there is a self-destructive drive in living creatures which impels them to return to the Nirvana of the original inanimate state. This theoretical issue has been hotly debated in psychoanalytic circles and is beyond the scope of this volume. The reader is urged to read Kubie (1939, 1941), E. Bibring (1943), Fenichel (1945a), the recent excellent panel on the subject reported by Gifford (1964), and Schur (1966). I can only state at this point that, in my experience, I have never found it necessary to understand or interpret the compulsion to repeat as a manifestation of a death instinct. Clinically it has always seemed possible to explain repetitiousness within the bounds of the pleasure-pain principle (Schur, 1960, 1966).

Another theoretical problem which is raised by the repetitiveness of transference reactions is the question of an instinct to master (Hendrick, 1942; Stern, 1957). There can be no doubt that the human being is impelled in this direction. However, it would seem that the urge to master is a general tendency, a general principle, and not limited to a specific instinct (Fenichel, 1945a). The concepts of adaptation and fixation are also relevant issues but would lead us too far afield. The writings of Hartmann (1939, 1951), Waelder (1936, 1956), and E. Bibring (1937, 1943) are particularly illuminating.

3.414 Transference and Regression

The analytic situation offers the neurotic patient the opportunity to repeat, by means of regression, all his past stages of object relations. Transference phenomena are so valuable because they highlight, in addition to the object relations, the developmental phases of the different psychic structures. One can observe in the transference behavior and fantasies early forms of ego, id, and superego functioning. There are two general points which must be kept in mind concerning the regression in transference. In the neurotic patient in the treatment situation, we see temporary regressions as well as progressions. The analyzable patient can regress and rebound from it. The regressive phenomena are usually circumscribed and not generalized. For example, we may see a regression in the id manifested by anal-sadistic impulses toward figures of authority. At the same time instinctual impulses for a love object may be operating on a higher level and certain ego functions may be quite advanced. This leads to the second generalization. Regressive phenomena are uneven and therefore each clinical fragment of transference behavior has to be studied with great care. Anna Freud's (1965) discussion of regression illuminates and clarifies many of the problems (see also Menninger, 1958; and Altman's panel report [1964]).

In terms of object relations, the transference situation gives the patient an opportunity to re-experience all varieties and mixtures of love and hate, oedipal and preoedipal. Ambivalent and preambivalent feelings to objects come to the surface. We can see transitions between abject helplessness with the craving for symbiotic closeness and stubborn defiance. Dependency may alternate with spite and rebellion. What looks like self-sufficiency may turn out to be a resistance against revealing an underlying dependency. The wish to be loved may lead to superficial therapeutic benefits but can cover a deep-seated fear of object loss. In general, the regressive nature of transference relations is manifested by the inappropriateness, the ambivalence, and the relative preponderance of aggressive strivings.

The regression in ego functions which takes place in transference reactions can be demonstrated in various ways. The very definition of transference indicates this. The displacement from the past indicates that an object in the present is being confused, in part, with an object from the past. The ego's reality-testing, discriminating function is temporarily lost. Primitive mental mechanisms like projection, introjection, splitting, and denials will occur. The loss of a sense of time in regard to object relations also resembles the regressive features we observe in dreaming (Lewin, 1955). The tendency to act out transference reactions indicates a loss in the impulse-control balance. The increased tendency to somatization reactions as a transference manifestation also speaks for a regression in ego functions (Schur, 1955). The externalization of parts of the self, i.e., ego, id, and superego, is another sign of regression.

The id also participates in the regression in many ways. The libidinal aims and zones of the past will become involved with the person of the psychoanalyst and will color the transference picture. The more regressive the transference becomes, the greater will be the preponderance of the hostile, aggressive strivings. Melanie Klein (1952) was among the first to stress this clinical point. Edith Jacobson (1964, p. 16) explains this on the basis of an energic regression and speculates about an intermediary phase with an undifferentiated, primordial drive energy.

The regressive features of transference also influence the superego. The most common finding is the increased strictness in the patient's superego reactions which are displaced onto the psychoanalyst. In the beginning there is usually a prevalence of shame reactions. We also see regressions to a time when superego functions were carried out externally. The patient no longer feels guilt, instead he is only afraid to be found out. The more the patient regresses the more likely will the analyst be felt to possess hostile, sadistic, critical attitudes toward the patient. This is due to displacements from past objects supplemented by the projection of the patient's own hostility onto the psychoanalyst.

Before leaving this brief discussion of regression it should be pointed out once again that the analytic setting and procedures play an important role in maximizing the emergence of the regressive features of transference phenomena. This will be discussed in some detail in Chapter 4.

3.415 Transference and Resistance

Transference and resistance are related to each other in many ways. The phrase "transference resistance" is commonly used in the psychoanalytic literature as a shorthand expression for the close and complex relationship between transference phenomena and resistance functions. However, transference resistance can.mean different things, and I believe it would be wise to clarify this term before going on to the clinical material.

I have already discussed Freud's (1905c, 1912a, 1914c) basic formulation that transference phenomena are the source of the greatest resistances as well as the most powerful instrument for psychoanalytic therapy. Transference reactions are a repetition of the past, a reliving without memory. In this sense, all transference phenomena have a resistance value. On the other hand, the reactions to the analyst provide the most important bridges to the patient's inaccessible past. Transference is a detour on the road to memory and to insight, but it is a pathway where hardly any other exists. Not only does the transference offer clues to what is warded off, it also may supply the motive and incentive for work in the analysis. This is an unreliable ally because it is capricious and also produces superficial "transference improvements" which are deceptive (Fenichel, 1945a; Nunberg, 1951).

Certain varieties of transference reactions *cause* resistances because they contain painful and frightening libidinal and aggressive impulses. Sexual and hostile transference responses are particularly prone to be the source of important resistances. Very often the erotic and aggressive components appear together. For example, a patient develops sexual feelings for her analyst and then becomes furious at his lack of reciprocity, which she perceives as a rejection. Or the patient is unable to work in the analytic situation because of the fear of humiliation in exposing infantile or primitive fantasies.

It may occur that the transference reaction itself makes the patient unable to work. For example, a patient may regress to an extremely passive, dependent stage of object relationship. The patient may not be aware of this but will act it out in the analytic hours. It may appear as a pseudostupidity or a blissful inertia. The patient may be re-experiencing some early aspect of the mother-child relationship. In such a state the patient cannot perform the analytic work unless the analyst succeeds in re-establishing a reasonable ego and a working alliance.

The situation becomes more complicated when certain transference reactions are clung to tenaciously in order to hide other types of transference feelings. There are patients who stubbornly maintain a façade of realistic cooperation with the analyst for the purpose of concealing their irrational fantasies. Sometimes a patient will split off certain feelings and displace them onto others in order to remain unaware of his ambivalence toward the analyst. It often happens that my patients will express great hostility toward other psychoanalysts while they profess great admiration for me. Analysis will reveal that both sets of feelings actually pertain to me.

The most difficult resistances to overcome are the so-called "character transference" reactions. In such situations, general traits of character and attitudes which have a defensive function are manifested toward the analyst as well as toward people in everyday life. These are so deeply rooted in the patient's character structure and so well rationalized that they are difficult to make the subject of analysis. These problems will be described in greater detail in Sections 3.82 and 3.83.

To summarize: Transference and resistance are related to each other in many ways. The term transference resistance condenses this clinical fact. Transference phenomena in general are a resistance to memory despite the fact that they indirectly lead in this direction. Transference reactions may cause a patient to become unable to work analytically because of the nature of the reaction. Some transference reactions may be used as a resistance against revealing other transference reactions. The analysis of transference resistances is the "daily bread," the regular work of pychoanalytic therapy. More time is spent in analyzing the transference resistances than in any other aspect of therapeutic work.

3.42 THE TRANSFERENCE NEUROSIS

Freud used the term transference neurosis in two different ways. On the one hand, he used the term to designate a group of neuroses characterized by the patient's ability to form and maintain a relatively cohesive, multiform, and accessible set of transference reactions (Freud, 1916-17). The hysterics, phobics, and obsessive compulsives were thus differentiated from the narcissistic neuroses, the psychoses. In the latter group, the patients were able to develop only fragmentary and sporadic transference reactions and therefore were not treatable by classical psychoanalysis. Freud also used the term transference neurosis to describe a regular occurrence in the transference reactions of a patient undergoing psychoanalytic treatment (Freud, 1905c, 1914c, 1916-17, Chapt. XXVII).

During the course of an analysis, it can be observed that the patient's interests become increasingly more focused on the person of the analyst. Freud (1914c, p. 154) pointed out how the neurotic patient's compulsion to repeat is rendered not only harmless but useful by admitting it "into the transference as a playground in which it is allowed to expand in almost complete freedom and in which it is expected to display to us everything in the way of pathogenic instincts that is hidden in the patient's mind." If the transference situation is handled properly, "we regularly succeed in giving all the symptoms of the illness a new transference meaning and in replacing his ordinary neurosis by a 'transference-neurosis' of which he can be cured by the therapeutic work." The transference neurosis takes over all the features of the patient's illness, but it is an artificial illness and is accessible at every point to our interventions. It is a new edition of the old disease.

In the early phases of psychoanalytic treatment we usually see sporadic transient reactions, designated as "floating" transference reactions by Glover (1955, p. 37). If these early transference reactions are properly handled, the patient will develop more enduring transference reactions. Clinically, the development of the transference neurosis is indicated by an increase in the intensity and duration of the patient's preoccupation with the person of the analyst and the analytic processes and procedures. The analyst and the analysis become the central concern in the patient's life. Not only do the patient's symptoms and instinctual demands revolve around the analyst, but all the old neurotic conflicts are remobilized and focus on the analytic situation. The patient will feel this interest as some variety and mixture of love and hate as well as defenses against these emotions. If the defenses predominate, some form of anxiety or guilt will be in the foreground. These reactions may be intense, explosive, subtle, or chronic. In any event, once the transference neurosis has set in, such constellations of feelings are omnipresent.

In the transference neurosis the patient repeats with his analyst his past *neuroses*. By proper handling and interpretation it is our hope to help the patient relive and eventually remember or reconstruct his infantile neurosis. The concept of transference neurosis includes more than the infantile neurosis because the patient will also relive the later editions and variations of his childhood neurosis as well. Let me try to illustrate this with a clinical example.

I shall use the case of Mrs. K.[3] This young woman came for psychoanalytic treatment because she had recently become tormented by obsessive ideas and impulses to become sexually promiscuous with a Negro. This alternated with feelings of being a "zombie" or else she felt empty, bored, worthless, and depressed. She had recently married an outstanding man in the community some twenty years her senior whom she had loved prior to the marriage but toward whom she now felt resentment and fear. The outstanding feature in her past history was the fact of her having been brought up by a warmhearted, erratic, alcoholic mother, who alternately worshipped and adored her, indulged her, and at times abandoned her. The father deserted the family when the patient was one and a half years old and the mother's later three marriages each lasted about one year. There were two brothers, three and two years younger, whom the mother ignored and who were looked after by the patient. They were her companions, her responsibility, and her rivals. There was great poverty, much changing of home locations, and little education. When the girl was fifteen her mother insisted she was able to shift for herself; and although shy, frightened, and untrained, the patient did make a successful career for herself as a fashion model. At twenty Mrs. K. met and fell in love with her future husband who taught her the niceties of life and who married her five years later. She had been married some two years when she came for analysis. I shall now try to sketch the main transference developments of a successful analysis lasting some four and a half years.

The early transference reactions consisted of her urgency to be accepted as a patient by me, whom she fantasied as the "top" analyst of the community and thus a guarantor of a successful analysis. At the same time she dreaded that I would find her boring, unworthy, unattractive,

[3] See also Sections 1.24, 2.651, 2.71, 3.25.

or untreatable. She was torn, on the one hand, by her desire to be a good patient and reveal all her weaknesses, and, on the other hand, by her wish to be loved by me, to be found sexually and mentally attractive, and therefore to hide her defects. I was to make restitution for her lack of a father by making her my favorite patient and by doing for her what I would not do for any of my other patients. I would be the ideal, incorruptible father of whom she would be proud and also the delinquent father who would satisfy her incestuous wishes. Very early Mrs. K.'s symptom of promiscuity impulses shifted to me, as an oedipal figure. This alternated with an image of me as the stern, disapproving, and puritanical, idealized father.

While this was going on the analysis was concerned with attempting to understand the patient's great shame about masturbation, which she "discovered" only at age twenty-one, and which seemed to occur without fantasies and with little orgastic relief. The analysis of her shame led us to recognize that I was not only the puritanical father but also the fanatically clean mother of her toilet-training days. Mrs. K.'s boredom and her feeling of emptiness were revealed to be defenses against sexual fantasies, and became resistances in the analysis. She was afraid to fantasy, because to fantasy meant to become excited, and to become excited meant to lose control and to wet. This was manifested in the analysis by her reluctance to continue talking when she became emotional or excited. If I were to see her weep, or flushed, I would find her unattractive. She removed the Kleenex tissue from the pillow after each hour because she did not want me to see her "soiled" tissue. How could I love her if I knew she was dirty and performed toilet functions. I was either the idealized, desexualized, de-toiletized father who deserted her dirty mother, or I was the compulsively clean mother who loathed dirty children. She then recalled many memories of seeing her drunken mother naked and being repelled by her ugly genitals. Now she dreaded being like her mother, or having her dirty mother inside her, and was terrified that I would abandon her like father had deserted mother. She would rather be empty than full of dirty mother. But empty meant silence and resistance in the analysis and that was equivalent to being a bad patient. Here the working alliance and her longing to be loved by her father analyst won out and she was able to work on what was hidden behind the emptiness.

Behind the emptiness came a flood of sexual fantasies concerning a great variety of oral, sucking, scoptophilic actions performed both actively and passively with a forbidden man. That man was the analyst or a Negro or Arab who was both sadistic and masochistic. She and her partner alternated roles. At this time I was not only her accomplice in her sexual adventures, but I also permitted her to hate her mother, which she did with gusto. In this period of analysis she longed for each analytic hour, dreaded weekends and even the end of each hour, for I had become the main content of her fantasies, and absence from me meant emptiness and boredom. She felt "hooked up" to me and charged with feelings in my presence and felt drab and flat away from the hour.

As Mrs. K. slowly realized that I was determined to analyze her and was neither afraid of her impulses nor revolted by them, she slowly dared to permit more regressive impulses to come up. With me as her father protector, she dared to recall occasional dreams and fantasies of oral sucking and sadistic impulses toward feminine men and finally to women. As she trusted me more she also dared to feel some primitive hatred and rage toward me. Earlier she could feel mild hostility to me as the critical father or the disapproving mother. Later she could hate me as the robber of her capital, her secret, and the valuable lump she felt she had inside her which gave her security. She could also love me as her good investment, her security for the future, her guarantee against emptiness, the man who gave her substance. At this time I was also her defense against penis envy by being the penis-man she possessed.

At this stage of analysis, Mrs. K. was able for the first time to experience an orgasm during intercourse. This gave her the courage to become aware of strong homosexual feelings toward her baby daughter, which she could recognize as being a repetition with reversal of roles of her childhood impulses toward her mother. The fact that these impulses could be experienced without interfering with her capacity to obtain heterosexual orgasms if she so desired, enabled her finally to go through a violent phase of penis envy. She could hate me furiously as a possessor of a penis, who "only wanted a hole to stick his filthy thing in," who didn't give a damn for women, who impregnated them and deserted them. When the patient was able to express these feelings and find that I was neither destroyed nor antagonized she began to feel that I loved her and accepted her unconditionally and permanently—even when I did not agree with her. I had become a fixture inside her, reliable and permanent—a loving, parental, internal object. Now she could allow herself to become a full-fledged mother and wife and could work out her hate and love for her mother without feeling that this would overwhelm her. The case of Mrs. K. will be described in greater detail in Volume II.

This brief sketch, as complex as it may seem to read, by no means does justice to all the transference reactions of the patient. It does indicate, I hope, how the patient's symptoms, conflicts, impulses, and defenses become focused on the analyst and on the analytic procedure and to a great extent replaced her original neurosis. The transference neuroses enabled me to observe and work on the patient's conflicts in the living present. Transference experiences are vivid, alive, and real and bring a sense of conviction unparalleled in psychoanalytic work.

In his description of the transference neurosis, Freud (1914c) indicated that the patient's ordinary neurosis is "replaced" by the transference neurosis. Anna Freud (1928) concurs with this and insists that only a structure of this kind deserves the name of transference neurosis.

In the clinical material cited above, one can observe how during different intervals Mrs. K.'s involvement with me supplanted the original neurosis. For a period of time the patient's promiscuity impulses focused on me and were absent elsewhere. Her conflicts about losing control were intense during the analytic hour and concerned her fear of letting out dirty material, and hiding the "soiled" Kleenex. During this period her anal anxieties outside the analysis did not disappear, but they receded into the background. In my experience, that particular aspect of the patient's neurosis which becomes active and vivid in the transference situation will diminish in the patient's outside life. However, often it merely pales and becomes relatively insignificant compared to the transference neurosis—only to reappear in the patient's outside life when another constellation dominates the transference picture. For example, Mrs. K.'s promiscuity fantasies shifted to me exclusively for a period of time. However, when the analysis became focused on her toilet anxieties and shame, her obsessive-impulsive ideas about dark-skinned men returned.

Another question should be raised concerning the extent to which the transference neurosis totally replaces the patient's neurosis. I have had the experience that some aspects of the patient's neurosis become displaced onto a figure in the patient's outside life who then appears to function as a supplementary transference figure. For example, many of my male patients fall in love romantically with a woman during the course of their analysis. This is a transference manifestation but occurs outside of the analysis. This will be discussed in Section 3.84.

This question of the transference neurosis replacing the patient's ordinary neurosis touches upon the problem of what happens in the analysis of young children. Anna Freud (1928), Fraiberg (1951), and Kut (1953) used to maintain that young children manifest a variety of isolated transference reactions but do not develop a transference neurosis. Only after the resolution of the oedipus complex, in latency, does one see evidence of a transference neurosis developing in the analytic treatment of children. Anna Freud (1965) and Fraiberg (1966) have recently modified their points of view on this matter. Older children do develop intense, enduring, distorted reactions to the analyst which resemble the transference neurosis in adults. These reactions do not replace the old neurosis to the same degree that they do in adult analysis (see Nagera, 1966). The Kleinian child analysts do not differentiate between transference reactions and transference neurosis and claim that transference phenomena in young children are identical to those in adults (Isaacs, 1948).

Glover (1955), Nacht (1957), and Haak (1957) have described how certain forms of the transference neurosis can become an obstacle to uncovering the infantile neurosis and can lead to a stalemated situation. One of the most frequent causes of this is the analyst's countertransference, which unwittingly prevents the full sweep of the patient's transference reactions. For example, undue warmth on the part of the analyst can prevent the hostile transference from developing fully. Above all, the incomplete interpretation of some aspects of the transference reactions will produce a protracted stalemated situation. This subject will be discussed more fully in subsequent sections.

The question might be raised: what does one do to insure that a transference neurosis will occur? The answer is as follows: if the analytic atmosphere is essentially that of compassion and acceptance and if the analyst consistently searches for insight and interprets the patient's resistances, a transference neurosis will develop. This will be covered more fully and demonstrated in Sections 3.7 and 3.9.

The classical psychoanalytic attitude toward the transference neurosis is to facilitate its maximal development. It is recognized that the transference neurosis offers the patient the most important instrumentality for gaining access to the warded-off past pathogenic experiences. The reliving of the repressed past with the analyst and in the analytic situation is the most effective opportunity for overcoming the neurotic defenses and resistances. Thus, the psychoanalyst will take pains to safeguard the transference situation and prevent any contamination which might curtail its full flowering (Greenacre, 1954). All intrusions of the analyst's personal characteristics and values will be recognized as factors which might limit the scope of the patient's transference neurosis. Interpretation is the only method of dealing with the transference that will permit it to run its entire course. In combination with an effective working alliance it will ultimately lead to its resolution (Gill, 1954; Greenson, 1965a).

The deviant schools of psychoanalysis have a different approach to the transference neurosis. Alexander, French, et al. (1946) over-emphasize the dangers of the regressive elements and therefore advocate various manipulations of the transference situation in order to avoid or curtail the transference neurosis. The Kleinian school goes to the opposite extreme and relies almost entirely on transference interpretations to the exclusion of everything else (Klein, 1932; Klein, et al., 1952; Strachey, 1934; Isaacs, 1948). Furthermore, they see the most infantile and primitive impulses occurring in the transference from the very beginning of analysis and interpret these immediately (Klein, 1961). Finally, the patient's individual history seems to be of little importance since the transference developments seem to be alike in all patients.

Before leaving the theoretical discussion of transference, it should be mentioned that the analytic situation and the personality of the analyst contribute to the patient's transference reactions. This will be discussed in some detail in Chapter 4.

3.5 The Working Alliance

At this point in our discussion of transference phenomena, it is necessary to make a digression. We have stressed the outstanding importance of the transference reactions for the psychoanalytic treatment of the neurotic patient. I can epitomize the psychoanalytic point of view by stating that the psychoanalyst takes great pains to provide an analytic situation that will maximize the unfolding of the various transference reactions. This is our prime method for reaching the pathogenic material which is otherwise inaccessible. However, collecting the historical data is only part of the therapeutic process. Another major component is the giving of insight by means of interpretation.

As important as these two factors are, they are not sufficient for producing lasting changes in the patient. In order for a neurotic patient to enter into and to work effectively in the analytic situation it is imperative that he establish and maintain another kind of relationship to the psychoanalyst, besides his transference reactions. I am referring here to the working alliance. It is my contention that the working alliance deserves to be considered a full and equal partner to the transference neurosis in the patient-therapist relationship (Greenson, 1965a).

My own clinical experiences in regard to the working alliance were enhanced and clarified by Elizabeth Zetzel's paper on "Current Concepts of Transference" (1956). In that essay she introduced the term "therapeutic alliance" and indicated how important she considered it to be by demonstrating that one could differentiate between the classical psychoanalysts and the so-called "British School" by whether they handled or ignored this aspect of the transference. Leo Stone's book on *The Psychoanalytic Situation* (1961) gave me fresh impetus to clarify and formulate the problem of the working alliance between patient and therapist.

The clinical material on which this section is based is derived from a number of patients who developed unexpected difficulties in the course of their psychoanalytic therapy. Some of these patients had undergone one or more analyses with other analysts; others were patients of mine who returned for further analysis. In this group there were patients who in some ways were unable to get beyond the preliminary phases of analysis. Even after several years of analysis they were not really "in analysis." Others seemed interminable; there was a marked discrepancy between the copiousness of insight and the paucity of change. The clinical syndromes these cases manifested were heterogeneous from the standpoint of diagnostic category, ego functions, and dynamics. The key to understanding the essential pathology as well as the therapeutic stalemate was to be found in the failure of the patient to develop a reliable working relationship with the analyst. In each of the cases I shall describe, the patient was either unable to establish or maintain a durable working alliance with the analyst and the analyst neglected this fact, pursuing instead the analysis of other transference phenomena. I found this error in technique in psychoanalysts with a wide range of clinical experience, and I recognized this same shortcoming in myself when I resumed analysis with patients I had previously treated.

It was in working with these seemingly unanalyzable or interminable patients that I became impressed with the importance of separating the patient's reactions to the analyst into two distinct categories: the transference neurosis and the working alliance. Actually this classification is neither complete nor precise, points which I shall attempt to clarify later on. However, this differentiation helps make it possible to give equal scrutiny and attention to two essentially different types of reactions to the psychoanalyst.

3.51 WORKING DEFINITION

The notion of a working alliance is an old one in both psychiatric and psychoanalytic literature. It has been described under a variety of different labels, but, with the exception of Zetzel and Stone, it has either been considered of secondary importance or it has not been clearly separated from other transference reactions.

The term working alliance will be used in preference to the diverse terms others have employed for designating the relatively nonneurotic, rational rapport which the patient has with his analyst. It is this reasonable and purposeful part of the feelings the patient has for the analyst which makes for the *working alliance*. The label working alliance was selected because the term emphasizes its outstanding function: it centers on the patient's ability to work in the analytic situation. Terms like the "therapeutic alliance," of Zetzel (1956), the "rational transference" of Fenichel (1941) and the "mature transference" of Stone (1961) refer to similar concepts. The designation working alliance, however, has the advantage of stressing the vital elements: the patient's capacity to work purposefully in the treatment situation. It can be seen at its clearest when a patient is in the throes of an intense transference neurosis and yet can still maintain an effective working relationship with the analyst.

The reliable core of the working alliance is formed by the patient's motivation to overcome his illness, his sense of helplessness, his conscious and rational willingness to cooperate, and his ability to follow the instructions and insights of the analyst. The actual alliance is formed essentially between the patient's reasonable ego and the analyst's analyzing ego (Sterba, 1934). The medium which makes this possible is the patient's partial identification with the analyst's analytic approach as he attempts to understand the patient's behavior (Sterba, 1929).

The working alliance comes to the fore in the analytic situation in the same way as the patient's reasonable ego, the observing, analyzing ego is separated from his experiencing ego. The analyst's interventions disengage the working attitudes from the neurotic transference phenomena just as his interventions separate the reasonable ego from the irrational ego. These two sets of phenomena are parallel to each other and express analogous psychic events from different points of reference. Patients who cannot set apart a reasonable, observing ego will not be able to maintain a working relationship and vice versa.

However, this differentiation between transference reactions and working alliance is not an absolute one since the working alliance may contain elements of the infantile neurosis which will eventually require analysis. For example, the patient may work well temporarily in order to gain the analyst's love, and this ultimately will lead to strong resistances; or the overevaluation of the analyst's character and ability can also serve the working alliance well in the beginning of the analysis, only to become a source of strong resistance later on. Not only can the transference neurosis invade the working alliance, but the working alliance itself can be misused defensively to ward off the more regressive transference phenomena.

A clinical illustration of this point occurred in a patient of mine who maintained a persistent reasonableness toward me and the analytic situation. Although she knew little about psychoanalysis, she accepted the frustrations and restrictions goodnaturedly and with no trace of conscious annoyance or anger. However, the occasional dreams she could remember were full of unmistakable evidence of fury and rage. When this was pointed out to her, the patient reacted as though that was "only" a dream and she was not "responsible" for her dreams. Even when she forgot her analytic hour she considered it a "natural" mistake, and took my interpretation of her fear of her underlying hostility as the musings of an eccentric which she tolerated with good grace. Only after her superficial associations and rationalizations petered out and silence reigned, did her more regressive hostile and sexual impulses become unmistakably clear to her. Then she recognized how she had clung to the working alliance as a defensive façade.

Despite the intermixtures, the separation of the patient's reactions to the analyst into these two groupings, neurotic transference and working alliance, seems to have clinical and technical value. Before going on to additional case material, I would like to sketch briefly some of the psychoanalytic literature on this subject.

3.52 SURVEY OF THE LITERATURE

Freud (1912a, p. 105) spoke of the friendly and affectionate aspects of the transference which are admissible to consciousness and which are "the vehicle of success in psycho-analysis. . . ." He wrote of rapport as follows: "It remains the first aim of the treatment to attach him [the patient] to it and to the person of the doctor. To ensure this, nothing need be done but to give him time. If one exhibits a serious interest in him, carefully clears away the resistances that crop up at the beginning and avoids making certain mistakes, he will of himself form such an attachment. . . . It is certainly possible to forfeit this first success if from the start one takes up any standpoint other than one of sympathetic understanding" (Freud, 1913b, pp. 139-140).

Sterba (1929) wrote about the patient's identification with the analyst which leads to the patients' concern with the work they have to accomplish in common—but he gave this aspect of the transference no special designation. Fenichel (1941, p. 27) described the "rational transference," an aim-inhibited positive transference which is necessary for analysis. Elizabeth Zetzel's emphasis on the importance of the "therapeutic alliance" was discussed above. Loewald's (1960) paper on the therapeutic action of psychoanalysis is a penetrating and sensitive study of the different kinds of relationships the patient develops toward the analyst during psychoanalysis. Some of his ideas are directly concerned with what I call the working alliance. Leo Stone's book is devoted to the complexities in the relationship between analyst and patient. In it he referred to the "mature transference" which he believed to be: (a) in opposition to the "primordial transference" reactions and (b) essential for a successful analysis (p. 106).

The Symposium on "The Curative Factors in Psycho-Analysis" presented before the 22nd Congress of the International Psycho-Analytical Association (see Gitelson, et al., 1962) contained many references to the special transference reactions which make for a therapeutic alliance and also some discussion of the analyst's contribution to the "good" analytic situation. Gitelson talked of the *rapport* on which we depend in the beginning of analysis and which eventuates in transference. He stressed the necessity for the analyst to present himself as a good object and as an auxiliary ego. Myerson (see Gitelson, p. 202 n.), Nacht, Segal, Kuiper, Garma, King, and Heimann took issue with him on one or another aspect of his approach. In some measure the disagreement seems to be due to the failure to distinguish clearly between the working alliance and the more regressive transference phenomena.

This brief and incomplete survey reveals that many analysts, including Freud, recognized that in psychoanalytic treatment another kind of relationship to the analyst was necessary besides the more regressive transference reactions.

3.53 DEVELOPMENT OF THE WORKING ALLIANCE

3.531 *Aberrations in the Working Alliance*

I shall begin by describing some clinical examples in which the course of development of the working alliance deviated markedly from that of the usual psychoanalytic patient. My reason for beginning this way stems from the fact that in the classical analytic patient the working alliance develops almost imperceptibly, relatively silently, and seemingly independently of any special activity on my part. The irregular cases highlight different processes and procedures which take place almost invisibly in the usual analytic patient.

A few years ago an analyst from another city sent me an intelligent middle-aged man who had had over six years of previous analysis. Certain general conditions had improved in the patient's life, but his first analyst felt the patient needed some additional analysis because he was still unable to get married and he was very lonely. From the very beginning of the therapy I was struck by the fact that he was absolutely passive about recognizing and working with his own resistances. It turned out that he expected me to point them out as his previous analyst had continued to do throughout that analysis.

Then I was impressed by the fact that the moment I made some intervention he had an immediate response, although often an incomprehensible one. I discovered that he felt it was his duty to reply immediately to every intervention since he believed it would be a sign of resistance, and therefore bad, to keep silent for a moment or so and to mull over what I had said. Apparently his previous analyst had never recognized his fear of being silent as a resistance. In free association the patient searched actively for things to talk about, and if more than one thing occurred to him he chose what seemed to be the item he thought I was looking for without mentioning the multiple choices he had. When I would request some information from him, he often answered by doing free association so that the result was often bizarre. For example, when I asked him what his middle name was he answered: "Raskolnikov," the first name that occurred to him. When I recovered my composure and questioned this, he defended himself by saying that he thought he was supposed to associate freely.

I soon gained the distinct impression that this man had never really established a working relationship with his first analyst. He did not know what he was supposed to do in the analytic situation. He had been lying down in front of an analyst for many years, meekly submitting to what he imagined the previous analyst had demanded, namely, constant and instant free association. Patient and analyst had been indulging in a caricature of psychoanalysis. True, the patient had developed some regressive transference reactions, some of which had been interpreted, but the lack of a constant working alliance left the whole procedure amorphous, confused, and ineffectual.

Although I recognized that the magnitude of the patient's problems could not be due solely or even mainly to the first analyst's technical shortcomings, I felt the patient ought to be given a fair opportunity to see whether he might be able to work in an analytic situation. Besides, this clarification would also expose the patient's pathology more vividly. Therefore, in the very first months of our working together, I carefully explained to the patient, whenever it seemed appropriate, the different tasks that psychoanalytic therapy requires of the patient. The patient reacted to this information as though it were all new to him and he seemed eager to try to work in the way I described. However, it soon became clear that he could not just say what came to his mind, he felt compelled to find out what I was looking for. He could not keep silent and mull over what I said; he was afraid of the blank spaces, they signified some awful danger. If he were silent he might think, and if he thought he might disagree with me, and to disagree was tantamount to killing me. His striking passivity and compliance were revealed as a form of ingratiation, covering up an inner emptiness, an insatiable infantile hunger, and a terrible rage. In a period of six months it became abundantly clear that this man was a schizoid "as if" character who could not bear the deprivations of classical psychoanalysis (H. Deutsch, 1942; Weiss, 1966). I therefore helped him obtain supportive psychotherapy with a woman therapist.

A woman I had analyzed for some four years resumed analysis with me after an interval of six years. We both knew when she had interrupted that there was a great deal of unfinished analysis, but we agreed that an analysis-free interval might clarify the unusual obscurities and difficulties we encountered in trying to achieve a better resolution of her highly ambivalent, complaining, clinging, sadomasochistic transference to me. I had suggested her going to another analyst since, in general, I have found a change in analyst is more productive than a return to the former analyst. It usually offers new insights into the old transference reactions and adds new transference possibilities as well. However, for external reasons this was not feasible, and I undertook the resumption of her analysis, albeit with some reservations.

In her very first hours on the couch I was struck by the strange way the patient worked in the analysis. Then I quickly recalled this had often happened in the past, only now it struck me more strongly because I was no longer accustomed to it; it seemed almost bizarre. After a certain moment in the hour the patient would speak almost incessantly, there would be disconnected sentences, a part of a recital of a recent event, an occasional obscene phrase with no mention of its strangeness, or that it was an obsessive thought, and then back to the recital of a past event. The patient seemed to be completely oblivious to her strange way of speaking and never spontaneously mentioned this. When I confronted her on this matter, she seemed at first unknowing and then felt attacked.

I realized that in the old analysis there were many such hours or parts of hours whenever the patient was very anxious and trying to ward off her awareness of the anxiety as well as the analysis of the anxiety. I even recalled that we had uncovered some of the meanings and historical determinants of such behavior. For example, her mother had been a great chatterer, had talked to the child as a grownup before she could understand. Her incomprehensible talking to me was an identification with her mother and an acting out in the analytic situation. Furthermore, the mother had used a stream of talk to express both anxiety and hostility to her husband, who was essentially a quiet man. The patient took over this pattern from the mother and re-enacted it with me in the analytic hour whenever she was anxious and hostile and when she was torn between hurting me and holding on to me.

In addition, we came to understand that this mode of behavior also denoted a regression in ego functions from secondary process toward primary process, a kind of "sleep-talking" with me, a re-enactment of sleeping with the parents. This strange way of talking had recurred many times during the first analysis and although different determinants had been analyzed, it still persisted to some degree up to the interruption of that analysis. Whenever I tried to confront the patient with a misuse of one of the procedures of the analysis, we would get sidetracked by her reactions to my confrontation or by some new material coming up. She might recall some past historical event which seemed relevant, or in the next hours some dreams or new memories would appear and we never really got back to the subject of how she was not able to do some part of the psychoanalytic work.

In her second analysis, I was not to be put off. Whenever the merest trace of the same disconnected way of talking appeared, or whenever it seemed relevant, I would confront her with this particular problem and keep her to this subject until she at least acknowledged what was under discussion. The patient attempted to use all her old methods of defense against my confrontations of her resistances. I would listen for only a short time to her protestations and evasions and repeatedly point out its resistive function. I did not work with any new material unless I was convinced the patient was in a good working alliance with me.

Slowly the patient began to face her misuse of the basic rule. She herself became aware of how she at times consciously, at times preconsciously, and at still other times unconsciously, blurred the real purpose of free association. It became clear that when the patient felt anxious in her relationship to me, she would let herself slip into this regressive "sleep-talking" manner of speech. It was a kind of "spiteful obedience." It was spiteful insofar as she knew it was an evasion of true free association. It was obedience inasmuch as she submitted to this regressive, i.e., incontinent, way of talking. This would arise whenever she felt a certain kind of hostility to me. She felt this as an urge to pour out a stream of poison upon me. This led her to feel I would be destroyed and lost to her and she would feel alone and frightened. Then she would quickly dive down into her sleep-talking which was like saying to me: "I am a little child who is partly asleep and is not responsible for what is coming out of her. Don't leave me; let me sleep on with you; it is just harmless urine that is coming out of me." (Other determinants will not be discussed since that would lead us too far afield.)

It was a fascinating experience to see how differently this analysis proceeded from the previous one. I do not mean to imply that this patient's tendency to misuse her ability to regress in ego functioning completely disappeared. However, my vigorous pursuit of the analysis of the defective working alliance, my constant attention to the maintenance of a good working relationship, my refusal to be misled into analyzing other aspects of her transference neurosis had its effects. The second analysis had a completely different flavor and atmosphere. In the first analysis I had an interesting and whimsical patient who was very frustrating because I was so often lost by her capricious wanderings. In the second analysis I still had a whimsical patient, but I also had an ally who not only helped me when I was lost but who also pointed out I was being led astray even before I realized it.

A young man, Mr. Z.,[4] came to me for analysis after having spent two and a half years with an analyst in another city in an analysis which had left him almost completely untouched. He had obtained certain insights, but he had the distinct impression that his former analyst really disapproved of infantile sexuality, even though the young man realized that analysts were not supposed to be contemptuous of it. In the preliminary interviews the young man told me that he had the greatest difficulty in talking about masturbation and often consciously withheld this information from his previous analyst. He had informed the latter about the existence of many conscious secrets, but nevertheless stubbornly refused to divulge them. He never wholeheartedly gave himself up to free association, and there were many hours of long silence in which he and his analyst both remained mute. The patient's manner of relating to me, however, his history, and my general clinical impression led me to believe that he was analyzable, despite the fact that he had not been able to form a working alliance with his first analyst.

I undertook to analyze Mr. Z. and learned a great deal about his negative reactions to his previous analyst, some of which stemmed from his way of conducting the analysis. For example, in one of the first hours on the couch the patient took out a cigarette and lit it. I asked him what he was feeling when he decided to light the cigarette. He answered petulantly that he knew he was not supposed to smoke in his previous analysis and how he supposed that I too would forbid this. I told Mr. Z. that I wanted to know what feelings, ideas, and sensations were going on in him at the moment that he decided to light the cigarette. He then revealed that he had become somewhat frightened in the hour and to shield this anxiety from my view he decided to light the cigarette.

I replied that it was preferable for such feelings and ideas to be expressed in words instead of actions because then I would understand more precisely what was going on in him. He realized then that I was not forbidding him to smoke but only pointing out that it was more helpful to the process of being analyzed if he expressed himself in words and

4 See Sections 2.52, 2.54, and 2.71.

feelings. He contrasted this with his first analyst who told him before he went to the couch that it was customary not to smoke on the couch. There was no explanation for this and the patient felt that his first analyst was being arbitrary.

In a later hour Mr. Z. asked me whether I was married. I countered by asking him what did he imagine about that. He hesitantly revealed that he was torn between two sets of fantasies, one that I was a bachelor who loved his work and lived only for his patients; the other fantasy was that I was a happily married man with many children. He then went on spontaneously to tell me that he hoped I was happily married because then I would be in a better position to help him with his sexual problems. Then Mr. Z. corrected himself and said it was painful to think of me as having sexual relations with my wife because that was embarrassing and none of his business. I then pointed out to him how, by not answering his question and by asking him instead to tell his fantasies about the answer, he revealed to us what his curiosity was about. I told him I would not answer questions when I felt that more was to be gained by my keeping silent and letting him associate to his own question.

At this point Mr. Z. became somewhat tearful and after a short pause told me that in the beginning of his previous analysis he had asked many questions. His former analyst never answered, nor did he ever explain why he was silent. He felt his analyst's silence as a degradation and humiliation and now realized that his own later silences were a retaliation for this imagined injustice. Somewhat later he realized that he had identified with his first analyst's supposed contempt. Mr. Z. felt disdain for his analyst's prudishness and at the same time was full of severe self-reproach for his own sexual practices which he then projected back onto the analyst.

It was very instructive to me to see how an identification with the previous analyst based on fear and hostility led to a distortion of the working relationship instead of an effective working alliance. The whole atmosphere of the first analysis was contaminated by hostile, mistrustful, retaliative feelings and attitudes. This turned out to be a repetition of the patient's behavior toward his father, a point the first analyst had recognized and interpreted. The analysis of this transference resistance, however, was ineffectual due in part to the fact that the former analyst worked in such a way as to constantly justify the patient's infantile neurotic behavior and so furthered the invasion of the working alliance by the transference neurosis.

I worked with Mr. Z. for approximately four years and almost from the very beginning a relatively effective working alliance was established. However, my manner of conducting analysis, which seemed to him to indicate some genuine human concern for his welfare and respect for his position as a patient also mobilized important transference resistances in a later phase of the analysis. In the third year of his analysis with me I began to realize that despite what seemed to be a good working alliance and a strong transference neurosis, there were many areas of the patient's outside life which did not seem to change commensurate with the analytic work. Eventually I was able to discover that the patient had developed a subtle but specific inhibition in doing analytic work outside of the analytic hour. When Mr. Z. became upset outside the hour, he would ask himself what upset him. Usually he would succeed in recalling the situation in question. Sometimes he even might recall the meaning of that event which I had given him at some previous point, but this insight would be relatively meaningless to him; it felt foreign, artificial, and remembered by rote. It was not his insight; it was mine, and therefore had no living significance for him. He was therefore relatively blank about the meaning of the events which upset him.

Apparently, although he seemed to have established a working alliance with me in the analytic situation, this did not remain outside of the hour. Analysis revealed that the patient did not allow himself to assume any attitude, approach, or point of view that was like mine outside of the analytic hour. He felt that to permit himself to do so would be tantamount to admitting that I had entered into him. This was intolerable because Mr. Z. felt this to be a homosexual assault, a repetition of several childhood and adolescent traumata. Slowly we were able to uncover how the patient had sexualized and aggressified the process of introjection.

This new insight was the starting point for the patient to begin to learn to discriminate among the different varieties of "taking in." Gradually the patient was able to re-establish a homosexual-free identification with me in terms of adopting an analytic point of view. Thus, a working relationship which had been invaded by the transference neurosis was once again relatively free of infantile neurotic features. The previous insights which had remained ineffectual eventually led to a significant and lasting change. The case of Mr. Z. will be described in greater detail in Volume II.

Finally I want to return to those patients who cling tenaciously to the working alliance because they are terrified of the regressive features of the transference neurosis. These patients develop a reasonable relationship to the analyst and do not allow themselves to feel anything irrational, be it sexual, or aggressive, or both. Prolonged reasonableness in analysis is a pseudo reasonableness, the patient is unconsciously holding on to the reasonableness for a variety of unconscious neurotic motives. Let me illustrate.

For about two years a young professional man, who had an intellectual knowledge of psychoanalysis, maintained a positive and reasonable attitude to me, his analyst. If his dreams indicated hostility or homosexuality, he acknowledged it but claimed that he knew he was supposed to feel such things to his analyst, but he "really" didn't. If he came late or forgot to pay his bill, he again admitted that it might seem that he did not want to come or pay his bill, but "actually" it was not so. He had violent anger reactions to other psychiatrists he knew, but insisted they deserved it and I was different. He became infatuated with another male analyst for a period of time and he "guessed" he must remind him of me, but this was said playfully.

All my attempts to get the patient to recognize his persistent reasonableness as a means of avoiding or belittling his deeper feelings and impulses failed. Even my attempts to trace the historical origins of this mode of behavior were unproductive. He had adopted the role of "odd ball," clown, harmless nonconformist, in his high school years and was repeating this in the analysis. Since I could not get the patient to work further or consistently with this material, I finally told the patient that we had to face the fact that we were getting nowhere and we ought to consider some other alternative besides continuing psychoanalysis with me. The patient was silent for a few moments and said "frankly" he was disappointed. He sighed and then went on to make a free-associationlike remark. I stopped him and asked him what in the world he was doing. He replied that he "guessed" I sounded somewhat annoyed. I assured him it was no guess. Then slowly he looked at me and asked if he could sit up. I nodded and he did. He was quite shaken, sober, pale, and in obvious distress.

After some moments of silence he said that maybe he would be able to work better if he could look at me. He had to be sure I was not laughing at him, or angry, or getting sexually excited. The last point seemed striking and I asked him about it. He told me that he often fantasied that perhaps I was being sexually excited by his material and hid it from him. This he never brought up before, it was just a fleeting idea. But this "fleeting idea" led quickly to many memories of his father repeatedly and unnecessarily taking his temperature rectally. This then led to a host of fantasies of a homosexual and sadomasochistic nature. The persistent reasonableness was a defense against these as well as a playful attempt to tease me into acting out with him. My behavior, in the hour described above, was not well controlled, but it led to a realization that the patient's working alliance was being used to ward off the transference neurosis.

The working alliance had become the façade for the transference neurosis. It was his neurotic character structure hiding as well as expressing his underlying neurosis. Only when the patient's acting out was interrupted and he realized he was about to lose the transference object did his rigidly reasonable behavior become ego alien and accessible to therapy. He needed several weeks of being able to look at me, to test out whether my reactions could be trusted. Then he became able to distinguish between genuine reasonableness and the teasing, spiteful reasonableness of his character neurosis and the analysis began to move.

3.532 The Working Alliance in the Classical Analytic Patient

The term classical in this connection refers to a heterogeneous group of patients who are analyzable by the classical psychoanalytic technique without major modifications. They suffer from some form of transference neurosis, a symptom or character neurosis, without any appreciable defect in ego functions. In such psychoanalytic patients the working alliance develops almost imperceptibly, relatively silently, and seemingly independently of any special activity or intervention on the part of the analyst. Usually I can see the first signs of the working alliance in about the third to sixth month of analysis. Most frequently the first indications of this development are: the patient becomes silent and then instead of waiting for me to intervene, he himself ventures the opinion that he seems to be avoiding something. Or he interrupts a rather desultory report of some event and comments that he must be running away from something. If I remain silent, he will then spontaneously ask himself what it can be that is making him so evasive and he will let his thoughts drift into free association which he will say aloud.

It is obvious that the patient has made a partial and temporary identification with me and now is working with himself in the same way that I had been working on his resistances day by day. If I review the situation, I will usually find that prior to this development the patient will have experienced some sporadic sexual or hostile transference reaction which had temporarily caused a strong resistance. Patiently and tactfully I have to demonstrate this resistance, then clarify how it operated, what its purpose was, and eventually interpret and reconstruct its probable historical source. Only after some effective piece of transference-resistance analysis does it seem that the patient is able to develop a partial working alliance. However, it is necessary to go back to the very beginning of the analysis in order to get a more detailed view of its development.

There is great variety in the manner in which a patient enters into the preliminary interviews. This is in part determined by his past history in regard to psychoanalysts, physicians, authority figures, and strangers as well as by his reactions to being sick, needing and asking for help, etc. (Gill, Newman, and Redlich, 1954). Furthermore, his knowledge or lack of knowledge about the procedures of psychoanalysis and the reputation of the psychoanalyst will also influence his initial responses. Thus the patient comes to the initial interview with a preformed relationship to me, partly transference and partly realistic, depending on how much he fills in the unknowns with his inappropriate past.

The preliminary interviews heavily color the patient's reactions to the analyst. This is determined mainly by the patient's feelings about exposing himself as well as by his responses to my method of approach and my personality. Here too I believe we see a mixture of transference and realistic reactions. Exposure of one's self is apt to stir up reverberations of past undressings in front of parents or doctors, etc., and is therefore prone to produce transference reactions. My technique of conducting the interviews will do the same the more it seems strange, painful, or incomprehensible to the patient. Only those methods of approach which seem understandable to the patient may lead to realistic reactions in the patient. My "analyst" personality as it is manifested in the first interviews may also stir up both transference and realistic reactions. It is my impression that those qualities which seem strange or threatening or nonprofessional will evoke strong transference reactions along with anxiety. Those traits which the patient believes indicate a therapeutic intent, compassion, and expertness may produce realistic responses as well as positive transference reactions. The clinical material from the case of Mr. Z. indicates how the manner, attitude, and technique of the analyst in the beginning of both analyses decisively colored the analytic situation.

By the time I have decided that psychoanalysis is the treatment of choice, I will have gained the impression that the patient in question seems to have the potential for forming a working alliance with me along with his transference neurosis. My discussion with the patient of why I believe psychoanalysis is the best method of therapy for him, the explanations of the frequency of visits, duration, fee, etc., and the patient's own appraisal of his capacity to meet these requirements will be of additional value in revealing the patient's ability to form a working alliance.

The first few months of analysis proper with the patient lying on the couch attempting free association can best be epitomized as a combination of testing and confessing. The patient tests out his ability to do free association and to expose his guilt- and anxiety-producing experience. Simultaneously he is probing his analyst's reactions to these productions (Freud, 1915a; Gitelson, 1962). There is a good deal of history telling and reporting of everyday events. My interventions are aimed at pointing out and exploring fairly obvious resistances and inappropriate affects. When the material is quite clear, I try to make connections between past and present behavior patterns. As a consequence, the patient will usually begin to feel that perhaps I understand him. Then the patient dares to regress, to let himself experience some transient aspect of his neurosis in the transference, in regard to my person. When I succeed in analyzing this effectively, then I have at least temporarily succeeded in establishing a reasonable ego and a working alliance alongside of the experiencing ego and the transference neurosis. Once the patient has experienced this oscillation between transference neurosis and working alliance in regard to one area, the patient becomes more willing to risk future regressions in that same area of the transference neurosis. However, every new aspect of the transference neurosis may bring about an impairment or a temporary loss of the working alliance.

A middle-aged, unsophisticated housewife was entering the second year of analysis. In the first year she had experienced great difficulty in acknowledging that at times she experienced romantic and sexual feelings toward me, although there was unmistakable evidence of this in her behavior and in her undisguised dreams. She considered herself happily married and felt that erotic fantasies about the analyst would indicate she was dissatisfied with her marriage. This frightened her because she was extremely dependent on her husband, unconsciously hostile to him, and terrified of losing him. My attempts to get the patient to face her sexual transference and her fear of it would turn this usually good-natured, cooperative woman into a stubborn, spiteful grumbler. In such a state she would respond to my interventions by saying: "Wouldn't anybody, wouldn't everybody react this way? Isn't it natural? Wouldn't you react this way if you were in my place?"

As we worked out some of the fears which made her resist the insights I was trying to convey, the patient gradually became able to face up to her positive feelings for me and did not have to resort to her defense of "wouldn't everyone" and "wouldn't you." At the same time the patient was able to admit to herself and to me that there were shortcomings in her marriage without feeling this heralded the end of her security. She also began to understand and accept my interpretations of some of the origins of the sexual feelings she was feeling for her analyst. The patient was able to cope with the idea that some of her feelings to me stemmed from her childhood sexual love for her father and her older brother. The patient had developed a fairly stable working alliance with me in regard to heterosexual matters.

However, the situation reverted to the early days of her analysis when aggression began to intrude itself significantly into the analytic hour. For example, the patient became unusually silent when I interpreted that her feeling of rejection by me was related to her forgetting to pay her fee at the end of the month. She developed severe gastrointestinal colic with explosive diarrhea and a fear that she was deadly ill with cancer. When I pointed out that this was an expression of her repressed rage to me, she at first denied it. When I told her that her feeling of dependency on me was shaken by my attempts to interpret instead of gratifying her or reassuring her, she responded by "Wouldn't everybody, wouldn't anybody react this way? Isn't this natural? Wouldn't you react this way if you were in my place?" Then she added, "I think I better go to the Mayo Clinic and have myself examined." The working alliance which she had established with regard to heterosexual matters had vanished when the subject of hostility came into the clinical picture. It took weeks of patient, painstaking interpretation of resistances to re-establish a utilizable working alliance. The same sequence of events occurred when homosexuality came into the analytic situation.

3.54 THE ORIGINS OF THE WORKING ALLIANCE

3.541 The Contributions of the Patient

For a working alliance to take place, the patient must have the capacity to form a special variety of object relationship. People who are essentially narcissistic will not be able to do so. The working alliance is a relatively rational, desexualized, and de-aggressified transference phenomenon. Patients must have been able to have formed such sublimated, aim-inhibited relationships in their outside lives. In the course of analysis the patient is expected to be able to regress to the more primitive and irrational transference reactions which are under the influence of the primary process. To achieve a working alliance, however, the patient has to be able to re-establish the secondary process, to split off a relatively reasonable object relationship to the analyst from the more regressive transference reactions. People who suffer from a severe lack of or impairment in ego functions may well be able to experience regressive transference reactions but will have difficulty in maintaining a working alliance. On the other hand, those who dare not give up their reality testing even temporarily and partially and those who must cling to a fixed form of object relationship are also poor subjects for psychoanalysis. This is confirmed by the clinical finding that psychotics, borderline cases, impulse-ridden characters, and young children usually require modifications in psychoanalytic technique (Glover, 1955; Gill, 1954; Garma [see Gitelson, et al., 1962]). Freud had this in mind when he distinguished the transference neuroses which are readily analyzable from the narcissistic neuroses which are not.

As stated previously, the patient's susceptibility to transference reactions stems from his state of instinctual dissatisfaction and his resultant need for discharge opportunities (Ferenczi, 1909). The awareness of neurotic suffering also compels the patient to establish a relationship to the analyst. On a conscious and rational level the therapist offers a realistic hope of alleviating the neurotic misery. However, the patient's helplessness in regard to his suffering mobilizes early longings for an omnipotent parent. The working alliance has both a rational and an irrational component. All the above indicates that the analyzable patient must have the need for transference reactions, must have the capacity to regress and permit neurotic transference reactions, and then have the ego strength or that particular form of ego resilience which enables him to interrupt his regression in order to reinstitute the reasonable and purposeful working alliance (Loewald, 1960).

The patient's ego functions play an important part in the implementation of the working alliance in addition to its role in object relationships. In order to do the analytic work the patient has to be able to communicate in a variety of ways, in words, with feelings, and yet with restraint in regard to his actions. He must be able to express himself in words, intelligibly with order and logic, give information when indicated, and also be able to partially regress and do some amount of free association. He has to be able to listen to the analyst, comprehend, reflect, mull over, and introspect. To some degree he must also be able to remember, to observe himself, to fantasy, and to report this. This is only a partial list of ego functions that play a role in the patient's capacity to establish and maintain a working alliance; we also expect the patient simultaneously to develop a transference neurosis. Thus the patient's contribution to the working alliance depends on two antithetical properties; his capacity to maintain contact with the reality of the analytic situation and his willingness to risk regressing into his fantasy world. It is the oscillation between these two positions that is essential for the analytic work.

3.542   The Contribution of the Analytic Situation

Greenacre (1954), Macalpine (1950), and Spitz (1956b) have pointed out how different elements of the analytic setting and procedures promote regression and the transference neurosis. Some of these same elements also aid in the formation of the working alliance. The high frequency of visits and long duration of the treatment not only encourage regression but also indicate the long-range objectives and the importance of detailed intimate communication. The couch and the silence give opportunity for introspection and reflection as well as fantasy production. The fact that the patient is troubled and unknowing and is being looked after by someone relatively untroubled and expert stirs up in the patient the wish to learn and to emulate. Above all the analyst's constant emphasis on attempting to gain understanding of all that goes on in the patient, the fact that nothing is too small or obscure, ugly or beautiful to escape the analyst's search for comprehension; all of this tends to evoke in the patient the wish to know, to find answers, to find causes. This does not deny that the analyst's probing stirs up resistances; it merely asserts that it also stirs up the patient's curiosity and his search for causality.

In addition, I would add that the constant scrutiny of how the patient and the analyst seem to be working together, the mutual concern with the working alliance, are themselves factors that serve to enhance the working alliance. It encourages self-scrutiny and trust in the analyst.

3.543 The Contributions of the Analyst

I have already suggested that the personality and theoretical orientation of the analyst contribute to the working alliance. It is interesting to observe how some analysts take theoretical positions which are apparently in accord with their manifest personality and how others subscribe to theories which seem to contradict their character traits. Some use technique to project, others to protect, their personality. This finding is not meant as a criticism of either group, since I have seen happy and unhappy unions in both. I have seen rigid analysts who advocate the strictest adherence to the "rule of abstinence" and who at the same time attempt to practice the most crass kind of manipulative, gratifying, "corrective emotional experience" type of psychotherapy. I have seen many apparently carefree and easygoing analysts practicing a strict "rule of abstinence" brand of therapy, and also some of similar character who provoke their patients to act out or indulge their patients in some kind of mutual-gratification therapy. Some analysts practice analysis which suits their personality; some use their patients to discharge their repressed desires. Be that as it may, these considerations are relevant to the problems inherent in the establishment of the working alliance. At this point, however, only a brief outline of the problems can be attempted. The basic issue revolves around the question: What theoretical orientation in the analyst and what characteristics of our analytic personality will insure the development of a working alliance as well as the development of a full-blown transference neurosis?

I have already briefly indicated how certain aspects of the analytic situation facilitate the production of a transference neurosis. This can be condensed down to the following: we induce the patient to regress and to develop a transference neurosis by providing a situation which consists of a mixture of deprivation, a sleeplike condition, and constancy. I have seen patients develop a transference neurosis in their work with a variety of different analysts as long as the analytic situation provided a goodly amount of deprivation administered in a predictable manner over a suitable length of time. For a good therapeutic result, however, one must also achieve a good working relationship.

Now to the question: what kind of attitudes in the analyst is most likely to produce a good working alliance? The case of Mr. Z. indicated how the patient identified with his previous analyst on the basis of identification with the aggressor, on a hostile basis (see Section 3.531). This identification did not produce a therapeutic alliance; it produced a combination of spite and defiance and interfered with the psychoanalytic work. The reason for this was that the personality of the first analyst seemed cold and aloof, traits which resembled the patient's father, and Mr. Z. was not able to differentiate his first analyst from his regressive transference feelings. How differently he reacted to me in the beginning. He was clearly able to differentiate me from his parent and therefore he was able to make a temporary and partial identification with me and thus to do the analytic work.

The most important contribution that the psychoanalyst makes to a good working relationship comes from his daily work with the patient. The analyst's consistent and unwavering pursuit of insight in dealing with any and all of the patient's material and behavior is the crucial factor. Regular and orderly work routines help the patient adjust to some of the strangeness of the psychoanalytic procedures and processes (Gill, 1954; Stone, 1961). This does not mean that the analyst should carry out his various daily analytic tasks with compulsive exactitude or monotonous ritualism. Such rigidity makes for predictability but not for a feeling of trust toward a human being. Other inconsistencies may cause the patient pain, but they do not interfere significantly with the establishment of a working alliance. The importance the analyst gives to each hour and the rarity of his absences stress the significance of the single hour as well as of the continuity of hours, thus helping to impress the patient with the need for serious cooperation. The analyst's willingness to devote years of work to the patient's welfare aids in a similar way. All the work characteristics described above are of basic importance. I do not believe it possible to do therapeutic psychoanalysis if they are lacking. But there are additional requirements for an effective working alliance.

Some analysts work consistently and seriously and still have difficulty in inducing their patients to develop a working alliance. Their patients develop an attitude of submissiveness and compliance instead of a feeling of alliance and participation. The atmosphere of the analysis is pervaded by a subtle but constant undercurrent of anxiety and awe in regard to the analyst and the working relationship. The patient may be aware of this state of affairs only fleetingly and sporadically because it expresses itself in subtle nuances rather than in overt, ego-alien fantasies and actions. This compliant attitude may also be ego syntonic to the analyst, who thus often fails to recognize it and bring it up for analytic scrutiny.

I have often had the opportunity to see such instances clinically, when I have been the second or third analyst of a given patient.

For example, a middle-aged male patient, a university professor, who had over five years of previous analysis, did not dare to look at his watch during the analytic hour. He told me early in the session that he would have to leave five minutes earlier than usual. During the hour I saw him trying to catch a glimpse at his watch out of the corner of his eye. He even rubbed his forehead while surreptitiously stealing a glance at the time. When I pointed out the obvious evasiveness, the patient was startled. On the one hand, he was frightened by the confrontation. On the other hand, he himself was dismayed at his own timidity. Then he realized that this anxiety had remained undetected and unanalyzed throughout his previous analysis.

There is no doubt that the above illustration indicates some countertransference reactions in the analyst, but this may be complicated by the analyst's too literal acceptance of two technical suggestions made by Freud. I am referring here to the concept of the analyst as a mirror and the so-called rule of abstinence, which will be discussed more fully in Sections 3.921 and 3.922 (Freud, 1912b, 1915a, 1919a). These two rules of thumb by Freud have led many analysts to adopt an austere, aloof, and even authoritarian attitude toward their patients. I believe this to be a misunderstanding of Freud's intention, at best, an attitude incompatible with the formation of an effective working alliance.

The references to the mirror and the rule of abstinence were suggested to help the analyst safeguard the transference from excessive contamination, a point Greenacre (1954) has amplified. The mirror refers to the notion that the analyst should be "opaque" to the patient, nonintrusive in terms of imposing his values and standards upon the patient. It does not mean that the analyst shall be inanimate, cold, and unresponsive. The rule of abstinence refers to the importance of not gratifying the patient's infantile and neurotic wishes. It does not mean that all the patient's wishes are to be frustrated. Sometimes one may have to gratify a neurotic wish temporarily. Even the frustration of the neurotic wishes has to be carried on in a way so as not to demean or traumatize the patient.

While it is true that Freud stressed the deprivational aspects of the analytic situation in his writings, I believe he did so because at that time (1912-1919) the big danger was that analysts would permit themselves to overreact and to act out with their patients. Incidentally, if one reads Freud's case histories, one does not get the impression that the analytic atmosphere of his analyses was one of coldness or austerity. In the original record of the case of the Rat Man, for example, appended to the published paper Freud (1909) has a note about the patient dated December 28, "He was hungry and was fed" (p. 303). Then on January 2: "Besides this he apparently only had trivialities to report and I was able to say a great deal to him to-day" (p. 308).

I think it is obvious that if we want the patient to develop a relatively realistic and reasonable working alliance, we have to work in a manner that is both realistic and reasonable, keeping in mind the fact that the procedures and processes of psychoanalysis are strange, unique, and even artificial. Neither smugness, ritualism, timidity, authoritarianism, aloofness, nor indulgence have a place in the analytic situation.

The patient will be influenced not only by the content of our work but by how we work, the attitude, the manner, the mood, the atmosphere in which we work. He will react to and identify particularly with those aspects which are not necessarily conscious to us. Freud (1913b) stated that in order to establish a rapport one needs time and an attitude of sympathetic understanding. Sterba (1929) stressed the identificatory processes. The fact that the analyst continuously observes and interprets reality to the patient leads the patient partially to identify with this aspect of the analyst. The invitation to this identification comes from the analyst. From the beginning of the treatment, the analyst comments about the work they will have to accomplish in common. The use of phrases such as "let us look at this," or "we can see," etc., promotes this tendency.

Glover (1955) emphasized the need of the analyst to be natural and straightforward, decrying the pretense, for example, that all arrangements about time and fee are made exclusively for the patient's benefit. Fenichel (1941) stressed that above all the analyst should be human and was appalled that so many of his patients were surprised at his naturalness and freedom. He believed it is the analytic atmosphere which is the most important factor in persuading the patient to accept on trial something formerly rejected. Loewald (1960) pointed out how the analyst's concern for the patient's potentials stimulates growth and new developments. Stone (1961) goes even further in emphasizing the legitimate gratifications and also the therapeutic attitude and intention of the psychoanalyst which are necessary for the patient.

All analysts recognize the need for deprivations in the procedure of psychoanalysis; they would agree in principle about the analyst's need to be human. The problem arises, however, in determining what is meant by the term humanness in the analytic situation and how one reconciles this with the principle of deprivation. This subject will be discussed further in Sections 3.9, 3.10, 4.22, and 4.23. Here I shall sketch only what I consider to be the main points.

Essentially the humanness of the analyst is expressed in his compassion, his concern, and his therapeutic intent toward his patient. It matters to him how the patient fares, he is neither just an observer nor a research worker. He is a physician and a therapist, a treater of the sick and suffering, and his aim is to help the patient get well. However, the "medicine" he prescribes is insight, carefully regulating the dosage, keeping his eye on the long-range goal, sacrificing temporary and quick results for later and lasting changes. The humanness is also expressed in the attitude that the patient has rights and is to be respected as an individual. He is to be treated with ordinary courtesy; rudeness has no place in psychoanalytic therapy. If we want the patient to work with us as a co-worker on the regressive material that he produces, we must take care that the mature aspects of the patient are consistently nurtured in the course of our analytic work.

We must not forget that for the patient the procedures and processes of psychoanalysis are odd, irrational, and artificial. No matter how much he may know about it intellectually, the actual experience is strange and new and will produce anxiety. He is motivated, however, by his neurotic troubles, and he considers us expert; so he submits and attempts to comply with the analyst's instructions and requests, at least consciously.

The patient coming for treatment is at least temporarily and partially overwhelmed by his neurotic pathology, and in this state of relative helplessness he is inclined to accept uncritically whatever promises to be of benefit to him. The helplessness has forced the patient to a rather indiscriminate reaching out for help. This is the "tilted" or "uneven" relationship Greenacre (1954) and Stone (1961) have described. In order to counteract the patient's tendency to submit out of anxiety or masochism, it is necessary that the analyst concern himself with the patient's need for self-esteem, self-respect, and dignity in the course of being psychoanalyzed. The compliant patient will often bury his feelings of humiliation and anger out of fear of losing love or incurring hostility. This the analyst may not always be able to prevent, but he should be alert to the possibility of it.

We cannot repeatedly demean a patient by imposing rules and regulations upon him without explanation and then expect him to work with us as an adult. If we treat him as a child by behaving with imperious and arbitrary attitudes and expectations, he will remain fixated to some form of infantile neurotic transference reaction. For a working alliance it is imperative that the analyst show consistent concern for the rights of the patient throughout the course of the analysis. This means that we indicate our concern not only for the neurotic misery the patient brought into the analysis and suffers outside of the analysis, but also for the pain that the analytic situation imposes on him. Aloofness, authoritarianism, coldness, extravagance, complacency, and rigidity do not belong in the analytic situation. Let me illustrate with some typical examples.

All new or strange procedures are explained to the patient. I always explain to the patient why we ask him to try to associate freely and why we prefer to use the couch. I wait for the patient's questions or responses before I suggest that he try the couch. All my utterances to the patient are spoken with a tone of voice which indicates my awareness and my respect for the patient's predicament. I do not talk down to the patient, but I make sure he understands my ideas and my intention. I use ordinary language, avoiding technical terms and intellectualized modes of speech. I treat him as an adult whose cooperation I need and who will soon be experiencing serious difficulties in working with the psychoanalytic material.

I explain to the patient that I will charge him for canceled hours which I cannot use for other patients. I tell him that in order not to interfere with his productions I shall be relatively silent. The first time he asks a question I explain why I do not answer it; I am silent the next time. If I do not understand the meaning of an hour, I tell him precisely that; I do not dismiss a patient without a word. If he has great feelings of embarrassment in talking about a particular subject for the first time, I acknowledge that it is painful for him but that it is necessary for the treatment that he try to be as open as possible. When he rails against me for not reacting to some of his feelings, I may tell him that I do my job better by showing him what I understand than by showing him my emotions.

I reply to his requests for reassurance by telling him that I know he feels miserable but that reassurance is only a temporary and deceptive aid. The next time he requests it I will most likely keep silent. I am ready to admit the possibility that I may be wrong in interpretation and will modify it if the clinical material indicates I should. I admit the possibility that he may be right if he thinks my words are tinged with annoyance or sharpness, but I insist that we work analytically on the incident and his reaction to it.

I do not break off an hour when he is in the middle of an anecdote or an intense emotional reaction; I allow the hour to go beyond the usual 50 minutes. If I am late, I try to make up the time in that hour or in the succeeding hours. I inform him of my vacation plans well in advance, and ask him to try to arrange his to coincide. (Similar problems will be discussed at greater length in Volume II.) If he tells a joke, I allow myself to show some pleasure or mirth, but I will nevertheless try to analyze why he told the story and I will feel free to analyze how he felt about my laughter. I will do the same if I react with sadness or annoyance to something he recounts. I do not answer the phone during the hour. If there is an exception, I apologize and ask for his reactions. From time to time I ask him how he thinks he is working with me and how he feels the work is progressing. I usually tell him my general impressions after he is finished, and then analyze his reactions to them.

I believe this is a fairly typical sample of how I safeguard the patient's rights, a factor which is a basic element in the working alliance. I want to stress that the safeguarding of the patient's rights does not do away with or nullify the necessary deprivations. Although the working alliance is an essential part of the process of psychoanalysis, there must be a predominance of deprivations if we expect the patient to be able to regress to the infantile transference neurosis.

The analyst must be able to oscillate between imposing deprivation and showing concern. Sometimes he must compromise between these two positions by inflicting pain with an interpretation but indicating compassion by his tone of voice thus making the pain bearable. The oscillation between deprivational incognito and concern for the patient's rights is another of the several dialectical requirements made of the psychoanalyst.

Though I let my patient see that I am involved with him and concerned, my reactions have to be nonintrusive. I try not to take sides in any of his conflicts except that I am working against his resistances, against his damaging neurotic behavior, and against his self-destructiveness. Basically, however, I am the bearer of understanding and insight conveyed in an atmosphere of serious work, straightforwardness, compassion, and restraint (Greenson, 1958b).

This outline is my personal view of how I attempt to resolve the conflict between the maintenance of distance and the closeness necessary for the analytic work. I realize this is a highly personal matter and I do not offer this as an exact prescription for all analysts. However, I do maintain that despite the great variations in the analyst's personality, these two antithetical elements have to be adequately taken into account and handled if we expect to obtain good analytic results. The transference neurosis and the working alliance are parallel antithetical forces in transference phenomena. Each of these elements is of equal importance for the optimal analytic situation. This problem will be pursued in Chapter 4.

3.6 The Real Relationship between Patient and Analyst

The transference reactions and the working alliance are clinically the two most important varieties of object relations that take place in the analytic situation. More archaic types of human interaction also occur, antecedents of transference as well as transitions to transference phenomena. Such primitive responses are prone to arise in severely regressive states and require more "management" than insight therapy (Winnicott, 1955, 1956b; James, 1964). They will, therefore, not be discussed here. On the other hand, a "real relationship" also comes about in the course of analysis. Before returning to the subject of transference phenomena it is necessary to discuss and clarify the concept of the "real relationship" between patient and analyst. This is not as simple as it might appear at first glance, because the term "real" has essentially two different meanings and usages, each of which may have a dissimilar connotation in the patient and in the psychoanalyst. This topic has been touched upon by many authors, but their astute clinical findings suffer from the lack of a clear definition (Stone, 1954b, 1961; A. Freud, 1954a, 1965).

The term "real" in the phrase "real relationship" may mean realistic, reality oriented, or undistorted as contrasted to the term "transference" which connotes unrealistic, distorted, and inappropriate. The word real may also refer to genuine, authentic, and true in contrast to artificial, synthetic or assumed. At this point, I intend to use the term real to refer to the realistic *and* genuine relationship between analyst and patient. This distinction is of importance because it enables us to compare what is real in the patient's relationship to what is real in the analyst's. In both the patient and analyst, transference reactions are unrealistic and inappropriate, but they are genuine, truly felt. In both, the working alliance is realistic and appropriate, but it is an artifact of the treatment situation. In both, the real relationship is genuine *and* real. The patient utilizes the working alliance in order to comprehend the analyst's point of view, but his transference responses take precedence if they intrude. In the analyst, the working alliance has to take precedence over all his other overt responses to the patient. I shall try to clarify these points by clinical illustrations from patients and analysts.

A young man, in the terminal phase of his five-year analysis, hesitates after I have made an interpretation and then tells me that he has something to say which is very difficult for him. He was about to skip over it when he realized he had been doing just that for years. He takes a deep breath and says: "You always talk a little bit too much. You tend to exaggerate. It would be much easier for me to get mad at you and say you're cockeyed or wrong or off the point or just not answer. It's terribly hard to say what I mean because I know it will hurt your feelings."

I believe the patient has correctly perceived some traits of mine and it was somewhat painful for me to have them pointed out. I told him he was right, but I wanted to know why it was harder for him to tell it to me simply and directly as he had just done than to become enraged. He answered that he knew from experience that I would not get upset by his temper, that was obviously his neurosis and I wouldn't be touched by it. Telling me about my talking too much and exaggerating was a personal criticism and that would be hurtful. He knew I took pride in my skill as a therapist. In the past he would have been worried that I might retaliate, but he now knew it was not likely. Besides, it wouldn't kill him.

I submit this clinical example as a realistic reaction to the analyst. The patient had made some accurate perceptions and had also been able to predict my reactions without distortions. In the past his perceptions had been correct, but his fantasies about my reactions were fantastic, i.e., transference distortions. He had felt I would retaliate and it might kill him. In the past he had developed a good working alliance in regard to temper outbursts at me, but the alliance did not maintain itself as far as realistic criticism of me. That was acquired only in the terminal phase. Thus we can see the value of distinguishing between realism in regard to perceptions and to reactions. Either or both may be realistic or inappropriate.

As I stated in the previous subsection, the patient's capacity to form a working alliance stems from his realistic motive of wanting to obtain help by cooperating with the analyst who is an expert in the field. In addition, the patient must have had, to some extent, the ability to form realistic and deinstinctualized object relations in his past life. The psychoanalyst's devotion and skill contribute realistically to the formation of the working alliance. The analyst's consistent attitude of acceptance and tolerance, his constant search for insight, his straightforwardness, therapeutic intent, and restraint serve as the nucleus upon which the patient builds a realistic object relationship. These trustworthy traits in the analyst induce the patient to form the various identifications which become the core of the working alliance. The analyst's objectionable traits usually lead to realistic reactions as well as transference. In either case they interfere with the formation of a working alliance. The clinical vignette I cited above demonstrates how my talkativeness and exaggerations led to his realistic appraisal that I took narcissistic pride in my interpretive skill. It also led to transference phenomena. After years of analysis these traits of mine no longer produced transference in the patient but were perceived as faults which the patient was able to accept realistically. He could form a working alliance with me despite my weakness.

In adults, all relationships to people consist of a varying mixture of transference and reality. There is no transference reaction, no matter how fantastic, without a germ of truth, and there is no realistic relationship without some trace of a transference fantasy. All patients in psychoanalytic treatment have realistic and objective perceptions and reactions to their analyst alongside of their transference reactions and their working alliance. These three modes of relating to the analyst are interrelated. They influence one another, blend into each other, and can cover one another. Despite the overlapping, it is clinically and practically valuable to separate these three reactions. The patient has realistic perceptions and reactions from the beginning of treatment, but usually finds it hard to express the negative ones. These quickly become the trigger for transference reactions, but they are not analyzable until some degree of a working alliance is established despite the patient's misgivings. This may not be possible if the objectionable traits of the analyst concern an area which is realistically of great importance to the patient.

A young analyst I was supervising told me that one of his patients, a young mother, had spent most of her hour describing her terrible anxieties about the sudden illness of her infant son in the preceding night. The baby had a high fever with convulsions and the mother was frantic until she was able to reach the pediatrician. As she recounted the events to my student she wept several times. After she finished her story the analyst remained silent. When she became silent, he told her, after a few minutes of more silence on both their parts, that she must be resisting. The patient said nothing. Shortly thereafter the hour ended. With this remark, the young analyst concluded his description of the hour in question.

I then asked him whether in retrospect he was satisfied with his work in the hour; was there anything further he might have done. He replied that he thought her long silence might have meant she felt guilty for her repressed death wishes toward her son, but he thought he would wait before bringing that up. I told him that there might have been some deeply buried death wishes in the patient toward the boy, but I felt that her anxiety and sadness were far more obvious and merited some response from him in the course of the hour. The student primly reminded me that Freud had said we are not supposed to gratify our patient's instinctual and narcissistic wishes.

I restrained myself from further comment at this point and asked him what had happened in the next hour. The student replied that the patient had come to the hour, had said absolutely nothing, and had silently mopped the tears that were streaming down her face. From time to time he had asked her what was she thinking. The hour ended with no other words being exchanged. Again I asked the young analyst whether he had any second thoughts about what else he might have done. He shrugged. I asked him whether he had found out what had happened to the baby. He told me the patient had said nothing and he had not asked. The last hour he had reported was the patient's last hour of the week and he was not to see her again until after his supervisory session.

I shook my head in disbelief. I asked the student whether he himself had no concern or curiosity about the baby's welfare. I added that perhaps the young woman's silent tears indicated the baby's condition had worsened. Or perhaps it indicated that she felt the analyst's behavior as a cold and hostile emotional uninvolvement with her. The student retorted that I might be right, but he felt I was overly emotional. I ended the session by telling the young man I felt his emotional unresponsiveness would prevent the formation of a working alliance. Unless he could feel some compassion for his patient and indicate this to her, within limits, he would not be able to analyze her. I predicted that even were she to return, I feared the treatment would not work out. When a patient is in such a state of misery, it is not only natural, but imperative to indicate some compassion.

The next week the young analyst reported his patient had come in on Monday morning and had announced she was quitting. When he asked why, she had replied that he was sicker than she was. She had paid her bill and left. After a while I asked him what had happened to her baby. The young man flushed and shamefacedly admitted he had "forgotten" to ask her. I utilized his forgetting and his flushing as an opportunity to demonstrate to him that he must have some problems in this area. I then suggested that he might benefit from some further analysis. The young man agreed.

These clinical data demonstrate the fact that an objectionable trait in the analyst can produce realistic reactions in the patient which preclude successful psychoanalytic treatment. (See Volume II for a fuller discussion of this and related problems.) In my opinion, the behavior of the young woman patient was realistic and appropriate. This is not to deny that the analyst's behavior also stirred up transference reactions, but they are of secondary importance in this situation. I submit that the analyst's behavior was detrimental to the formation of a working alliance because the patient could sense that this behavior indicated a hostile withdrawal or a fear of a countertransference involvement. I contend that it should be possible for the analyst to indicate some sympathy for the patient's misery without it becoming an overly pleasing transference gratification. For example, he might have simply asked the patient: How's the baby? What did the doctor say? Only later would it be feasible to analyze the patient's reactions, and then in dosages that would be compatible with the patient's capacity to bear additional pain. Many analysts have stressed the dangers of excessive or superfluous frustrations and deprivations (Glover, 1955; G. Bibring, 1935; Menninger, 1958).

Another illustration of this problem is to be seen in how the analyst handles his minor errors in technique which are detected by the patient. I have known analysts who believe it is wrong to admit to a patient that they have made a mistake. They hide behind the impervious cloak of the "analytic silence." I have known others who not only acknowledge their blunders but burden the patient by confessing the unconscious motives for their error. It seems to me that it is authoritarian, unfair, and demeaning to hide the making of an error from a patient who is aware of it. Such behavior by the analyst will provoke justifiable mistrust which can become unanalyzable and can lead to intractable submissiveness or the breaking off of treatment. The outpouring of the analyst's unconscious motivations for an error is a caricature of honesty. The analyst is taking advantage of the patient's predicament for his own personal instinctual gratification or his need for punishment. How different these reactions are from the straightforward and frank admission of error followed by asking the patient to describe his feelings and associations to your mistake as well as to your admission of the error. The analytic situation is an unequal one in the sense that one party is the sick and helpless one and the other is the therapist and expert. But it should be equal in the sense that both the patient and analyst have human rights that should be safeguarded.

If a patient were to ask me why I made an error, I would first ask for his fantasies and then tell him that my reasons for the error do not belong in his analysis but in mine. I would answer in the same way all questions about my intimate life. I ask for associations and then I give my reasons for not answering.

For the analyst to work effectively and happily in the field of psychoanalysis it is important that his analytic and physicianly attitudes be derived essentially from his real relationship to the patient. As I stated in Sections 1.33 and 3.5 and will discuss further in Chapter 4, one cannot work analytically unless one can oscillate between the relatively detached analytic position and the more involved physicianly one. The analyst must be a person who can empathize and feel compassion sincerely and yet use restraint. It is necessary at times to inflict pain, to allow the patient to endure suffering. Yet psychoanalytic treatment cannot be accomplished in an atmosphere of unabated grimness, icy detachment, or prolonged cheeriness. The analyst must be able to blend and oscillate between his bipolar functions of analyzer of data and treater of the sick and suffering.

The analyst's genuine feelings for the patient must be subservient to his working alliance. It is his task to restrain those responses that will be detrimental to the therapeutic process. This does not mean that he is consciously to assume a role that is foreign to him. It means that if he keeps in focus the picture of the patient as the producer of analytic material as well as a suffering neurotic, the analyst will be able to reciprocate by reaching the patient as the analyzer or as the therapist or as a mixture of both. Countertransference reactions have to be detected and restrained. Realistic and strong reactions also have to be restrained, but their nature may indicate the possibility of having selected a patient one cannot work with. Artificial reactions should be necessary only as temporary measures until one can mobilize one's genuine analytic and physicianly attitudes. If this is accomplished, the patient will have the opportunity to experience and gain insight from a unique kind of object relationship in which many varieties of love and hate become constructive instrumentalities and not merely opportunities for pleasure and pain (Winnicott, 1949; Stone, 1961; Greenson, 1966).

Although the patient and the analyst develop transference reactions, a working alliance, and a real relationship to each other, the proportions and sequence differ. In the patient, the transference reactions predominate in the long middle phase of analysis. The real relationship is in the foreground early and gains prominence again in the terminal phase (A. Freud, 1954a, 1965). The working alliance develops toward the end of the introductory phase but recedes periodically until the patient approaches the terminal phase.

In the psychoanalyst, the working alliance should predominate from the beginning to the end. The countertransference should always be in the background. The real relationship should be permitted more leeway only in the terminal phase. There are times, however, when special considerations require that the analyst permit his real feelings to be expressed earlier. The situation of the young analyst quoted above is one where I would have openly indicated my concern about the patient's baby. I do not see how anyone could allow himself to be deeply analyzed by an analyst who would maintain an icy detachment in such a situation. Such humane reactions in the psychoanalyst are a prerequisite for the formation of a working alliance in the patient. Some patients may want a computer-like analyst, but they are really trying to evade a genuine psychoanalytic experience.

There are patients who try to isolate the psychoanalyst from real life and imagine he only exists in his office and his emotional responses are always well tempered and controlled. In such cases I have found it useful to allow myself to show the patient otherwise. Saying it in words is often not sufficient. I have permitted the patient at times to feel my disappointment in his lack of progress or to see that world events do concern me. I try to restrict the intensity of my reactions, but I do not open the door every day with the same expression on my face or close the session in the same way. I don't plan these variations. I allow myself to be flexible in such matters. I am of the opinion that it is of importance to demonstrate in certain actions and behavior that the analyst is truly a human being. This includes permitting some of his human frailties to be visible at times. Stone's (1961) book contains many interesting comments on this and related matters.

There is still one other area which requires an unusual amount of outspokenness on the analyst's part. I am referring to the situation which arises when the analyst detects that he and his patient are in basic disagreement on a political or social issue which is important to each of them. For example, I know from experience that I cannot work effectively with some patients who are very reactionary in their political or social point of view. In such instances, I have found it advisable to tell such a patient of my feelings quite openly and as early in the treatment as possible. I suggest that he should feel free to seek another analyst if he finds my point of view too disturbing. If my own feelings on the matter are very intense and the patient's other qualities do not suffice to make him likable, I tell the patient that I am not able to work with him and insist that he find another analyst. I also admit that it is a shortcoming in me, so as not to traumatize the patient.

There is a great deal more to be said about the real relationship that goes on between the patient and the analyst. Chapter 4 will touch on additional problems and there will be further illustrations throughout the book.

3.7 Clinical Classification of Transference Reactions

There is no way of classifying transference phenomena that would do justice to all the different varieties. No matter how one tries to separate the many clinical forms of transference, one ends up either with an unsystematic classification with a great many important clinical types omitted, or else one may cover the clinically significant varieties but there is a great deal of overlapping. The lesser evil is to sacrifice the systematic in favor of completeness. I shall attempt to describe the most important forms of transference reactions and classify or label them in accordance with what seems to be the most useful approach clinically.

It should be borne in mind that one method of classification does not rule out another. For example, one might describe a situation as representing a positive transference, and with equal validity label the same phenomenon as a mother transference, etc. Another point: these transference reactions will not be differentiated from the standpoint of whether they are sporadic, transient transference reactions or whether they are manifestations of the transference neurosis. Such a differentiation has already been described in the theoretical section and all categories of transference reactions should be understood as existing in both forms. Finally, one should realize that a great number of transference feelings occur simultaneously, just as they do in object relations in general. Theoretically one could describe different layerings or hierarchies of emotions and defense coexisting in any given relationship between people. In the ensuing description of types of transference reactions, I shall limit myself to a discussion of what is predominant, what is clinically significant for a given period of time in an analysis.

3.71 THE POSITIVE AND NEGATIVE TRANSFERENCE

Although Freud (1912a) recognized very early that all transference phenomena are ambivalent in nature, the label of positive and negative transference remained his favorite means of designation. Despite all the ambiguities and shortcomings this mode of classification entails, it has remained the most frequently used designation among practicing psychoanalysts.

3.711 The Positive Transference

The term positive transference is shorthand for describing transference reactions which are composed predominantly of love in any of its forms or any of its forerunners and derivatives. We consider a positive transference to exist when the patient feels toward his analyst any of the following: Love, fondness, trust, amorousness, liking, concern, devotion, admiration, infatuation, passion, hunger, yearning, tenderness, or respect. The nonsexual, nonromantic, mild forms of love make for the working alliance. I am referring here to feelings akin to liking, trust, and respect in particular.

Another important form of positive transference takes place when the patient falls in love with the analyst. This is a regular occurrence in working with patients of the opposite sex, but I have never seen it happen with patients of the same sex with the exception of patients who were overtly homosexual. This falling in love in analysis bears a remarkable resemblance to falling in love in real life. It happens so regularly in analysis because our patients have had painful experiences in this regard in their past life. It is repressed and emerges as transference love during the analysis. It is perhaps, in degree, more irrational and infantile in its manifestations than real love. Freud's (1915a) penetrating and sensitive study of this subject is required reading for the serious student.

The patient in love with her analyst presents a variety of difficult technical problems. First of all, the patient's main aim becomes the wish to gain some satisfaction for her desires, and she resists working on these emotions analytically. During the intense phases of her love, it is difficult if not impossible to gain access to her reasonable ego and to establish a working alliance. One has to be patient and wait for the violent emotions to subside in intensity. Secondly, the ardent love of a woman patient may stir up countertransference feelings in the analyst. This is particularly apt to occur in the young, inexperienced analyst or in the analyst with an unhappy personal life. The unconscious temptation then is to respond in some way to the lady's love, either to gratify her in some form or other or to become harsh and angry with her for the temptation that her love presents. Freud was unmistakably clear in his advice on this situation (1915a, pp. 163-171). There can be no compromise. One cannot permit even the most innocent and partial of erotic gratifications. Any such gratification makes the patient's love relatively unanalyzable. This does not mean that one is to behave in an unfeeling and callous manner. One can be considerate and thoughtful of the patient in her plight and still pursue one's task of analyzing. Perhaps at no other time is the analytic attitude of compassionate, restrained humanness and firmness so absolutely necessary. Let me illustrate this.

A young woman, shy and timid, begins in the third month of her analysis to evince unmistakable signs of believing that she had fallen in love with me. Finally, after some days of struggling with her feelings, she tearfully confesses her love. Then she begs me not to treat this state of affairs in the same cold, analytic way I had treated her other emotions. She pleads with me not to remain silent and aloof. I should please say something, anything—it is so humiliating for her to be in such a position. She weeps and sobs and becomes silent. After a while I say, "I know this is very hard for you, but it is important for us that you try to express exactly how you feel." The patient is silent a moment and then says pleadingly and angrily: "It's not fair, you can hide behind the analytic couch, and I have to expose all. I know you don't love me, but at least tell me if you like me; admit you care a little, tell me I'm not just a number to you—the eleven o'clock patient." She weeps and sobs and is silent again. I too keep silent for a time and then say: "It's true, it is not fair; the analytic situation is not an equal one; it is your task to let your feelings come out and it is my job to understand you, to analyze what comes up. Yes, it's not fair."

This remark of mine seemed to help the patient. She could then express more of her anger and sense of outrage. The succeeding hours had mixtures of hatred and love in them, but she became able to work on these reactions. I think she could hear in my tone and in my words that I was aware of her painful predicament and although I had compassion for her, I was determined to go on with my analytic work. However, first her disappointment and sense of rejection at my nongratifying, working attitude entered the clinical picture and had to be dealt with. The important point was to avoid the twin dangers of either encouraging the patient falsely or of inflicting unnecessary pain which would force her to suppress her feelings and to run away in some form.

The patient's transference love always becomes a source of resistance. It may oppose the work of analysis by the patient's urgent demands and longings for immediate satisfaction. The analytic hour then becomes an opportunity for gratifying the patient's desire for proximity and closeness and the patient loses interest in insight and understanding. A further complication is that the patient will usually react to the analyst's interventions or lack of intervention by feeling hurt and rejected and for these reasons will consciously refuse to work. The patient mentioned above is an example of such a development. The technical task is to encourage the fullest expression of every development of the patient's transference love and at the right moment to start to work on the patient's resistances to the analytic work.

Let me return to the patient mentioned above. After I admitted to her that the analytic situation was not fair in the sense that she had to expose herself and I had the job of analyzing her, she tried to resume expressing her feelings of love for me. But now a note of anger was added to her sad, pleading, urgent tone; I could hear an undertone of bitterness; "I know you are right, I should let myself go, no matter how you feel about it. It is so hard though to cry out for love, to beg, and only to get silence as a response. But after all you must be used to this, I suppose this happens with all your patients. I wonder how you can stand it . . . but after all you get paid for listening."

The patient became silent and I kept silent for a while. Now she was dry-eyed, her eyes open, her mouth tight, her hands clasped firmly across her body. After a while I said: "Now you resent me for having answered you the way I did—please describe that in words." She did; first a torrent of angry feelings; then again a flood of love and this was repeated several times. In a few hours the intensity of these feelings slowly quieted down and she was ready to work. Now I could say to her: "Let's try to understand what has been happening, let's try to understand why you love and how you love. What do you find lovable about me?" By asking this last question I offer myself to the patient as a model for how she might look at her feelings of love. This seemed to help at this point and the patient's reasonable ego became more consistently available. We were then able to re-establish a working alliance and we could explore together what had transpired in the previous hours. The details of the procedure of the next steps will be described in Section 3.9.

Another special technical problem is presented by the partially sophisticated patient who asks, usually early in her analysis, "Doctor, am I supposed to fall in love with you?" This question, like all other questions in analysis, has to be first traced to its source and not immediately answered. But eventually it does become advisable to answer the question, since, in my opinion, the patient is entitled to some knowledge about what they are "supposed to" feel. The best answer I have found to such a question is that all a patient is "supposed" to do is follow the rule of free association, to let one's thoughts and feelings drift freely without censorship, and to report as accurately as one can the thoughts and feelings. There is no single pattern of what a patient is to feel inasmuch as every individual is different. There is no way of knowing what feelings any particular patient is going to experience at any given time in her reactions toward her analyst.

I said earlier that in my experience the romantic, falling-in-love transference occurs only when patient and analyst are of the opposite sex (except for overt homosexuals). This statement should be modified, however. My male patients will often during their analysis fall in love with women who they fantasy are connected to me—my wife, daughter, colleague, patients, etc. Often their love will indicate that it is the link to me which is the important aspect. My male patients also experience sexual feelings toward me—but usually without love. Or they will experience some aspect of love but not simultaneously with sex. The only exception to this is in dreams where my male patients can experience both sensual and love feelings toward me, particularly if I am somewhat disguised.

Idealization is another variety of positive transference that occurs in patients of both sexes (Greenacre, 1966b). Sometimes it turns out to be a return of the hero worship of the latency phase. Idealization is particularly frequent in patients who have lost a parent by divorce or death. My experience has been that the idealization is an attempt to preserve the analyst from primitive destructive impulses. It is so with all fixed and unchanging transference reactions; the rigidity indicates that emotions and impulses of the opposite nature are being held in check. The worshipful attitude hides a repressed loathing which covers a primitive hatred. The superficial envy is a screen against contempt which hides a more regressive envy.

All transference phenomena are ambivalent because the nature of the object relationship which is transferred is more or less infantile and all infantile object relations are ambivalent. However, the ambivalence is handled differently by each person and there are different kinds of ambivalence within the same patient. For example, one can observe that a certain patient manifests predominantly loving and admiring feelings toward her analyst and yet interspersed among her positive remarks will be found occasional flashes of sarcasm or anger. Or this same patient will go through a period of several weeks in which her feelings are almost exclusively warm and loving and then go through a subsequent period of marked hostility and anger.

More difficult to recognize is a situation in which the patient splits off one aspect of the ambivalence onto another object, frequently another analyst or physician (Greenacre, 1966a). Then the patient usually reserves the positive feelings for her own analyst and displaces the negative feelings onto the other analysts. The reverse also occurs. This kind of splitting up of the transference is very prevalent in neurotic depressives and also among candidates in training. The analytic task is first to recognize that the ambivalence is handled by splitting and to demonstrate this to the patient. Sometimes this insight is enough to bring about a change. Often, however, despite recognition, the transference situation is not influenced. This means that the split is serving important defensive needs, and the resistance functions of the split have to become the object of our analytic work.

A good example of this situation was portrayed by a candidate I analyzed for many years. For a long period of time his manifest trans- ference to me was of a consistently positive nature. He respected and admired me and despite my occasional lapses he was always unusually understanding and laudatory toward me. On the other hand, he was excessively critical of every shortcoming he observed or thought he observed in any other training analyst. I pointed out to him this extremely biased behavior, but the patient stubbornly justified his reactions. How- ever, I persisted in interpreting this pattern of behavior as resistance to facing his hostility toward me, and for a long period of time made no other interpretation to him. Finally, the candidate could no longer ward off his hostile feelings. He exploded in anger at me and accused me of being just like the rest of the training analysts, dogmatic, overbearing, and unreasonable. He was startled at his own outburst and at the intense feelings which broke through. Only then was he able to realize that for over a year he had been unconsciously protecting me from his aggressive feelings and had been displacing them onto other training analysts. Only then was he able to recognize that he had performed a similar split in his feelings toward his father; he had maintained a con- scious idealization of his father while he was constantly belligerent and pugnacious with other figures of authority in his environment.

The positive transference can be experienced on any and all levels of libidinal development. This will be described in greater detail in Section 3.73. Here I just want to fill out the picture of posi- tive and negative transference reactions. The analyst can become the tender, loving, milk-giving mother, or the cruel, rejecting, spoiled-milk-giving, or no-milk-giving mother. Such reactions occur in patients of both sexes. When this happens interpretations are reacted to as feedings, good or bad, and silence is felt as abandon- ment or as blissful communion. The patient may become passive and dependent or complain fretfully about not getting anything worthwhile. Depressive, hypochondriacal, and paranoidlike reac- tions may occur during such periods.

The analyst can become the benignly indulgent parent of the anal phase and the patient's copious free associations become fecal offerings which are presented profusely as gifts. The negative side of this picture is the analyst becoming the strict, harsh demander of the patient's contents, the one who wants to take away the patient's valuable possessions. Under such conditions the patient can become stubborn, defiant, and withholding. Or this may be projected onto the analyst who is felt as stubborn, hateful, and withholding. The analyst may become the oedipal figure, jealously and incestuously loved, accompanied by guilt and anxiety. One can also observe the hero-worshipful love of latency and the infatuation-like love of adolescence. In each instance the analyst has to be alert to the fact that this love has a dormant negative aspect which must coexist and which must eventually be brought to light.

The sexual components of the positive transference deserve special mention because they are often the source of the most intense and stubborn resistances. Patients are prone to acknowledge their emotional reactions to the analyst but reluctant to recognize the sensual aspects of their feelings. Yet, all positive transference, except for the sublimated, desexualized feelings, will be accompanied by some libidinous striving, and this means that bodily zones, instinctual aims, and bodily sensations are involved. It is the task of the analysis to clarify these different elements and to elicit the fantasies involved with these sensations and activities. Very often a dream will offer the clearest clues to the hidden sexual strivings.

A male patient, Mr. Z.,[5] in his second year of analysis is struggling with his homosexual wishes and fears, and has the following dream: "I am driving down a huge mountainside in a truck. I am sitting in the rear and the truck is being driven by a man who seems to be the leader of a caravan. We make a pause and as he helps me down he sticks his tongue in my ear." The patient's associations to this material, after he overcame some of his resistance, indicated to me that the rear of the truck and the huge mountainside meant the buttocks and anus of a big man. I pointed this out to him, which led to associations concerning seeing his naked father in the bathroom as a little boy. The tongue in the ear reminded him at first of a tickling game he played with a younger brother. Then, however, he realized that a few days before he had angrily accused me of poking him in the ear with my interpretations. Slowly I was able to show the patient that he had fears but also wishes that I should poke him in his "r-ear." This was a derivative of passive and masochistic anal pleasure he had experienced from enemas administered by his father.

[5] See Sections 2.52, 2.54, 2.71, and 3.531.

It is to be remembered that what is relived in the transference is not only the real events but also the fantasies of the past. Very often the sexual transference reactions are repetitions of fantasies the patient experienced in regard to a parent (Freud, 1914b, pp. 17-18). The last clinical example illustrates the repetition of a real experience. Let me give an example of a fantasy being re-experienced by the same patient, Mr. Z.

I had mentioned in Section 2.52 that this patient had obsessive fantasies about being hanged. He could imagine this occurrence in vivid detail, even to the sensation of his neck snapping and the spread of electric sensations and numbness coursing through his body. At one point in the analysis I became the hangman, he could imagine me putting the noose around his neck, and he could see me spring the trapdoor that sent him falling into space only to be jolted to a halt by the crushing rope around his neck. It was I who was responsible for such feelings and sensations as crushing, snapping, jolting, electric, and numbness. The hangman wore a hood and at first looked like me; when he was unmasked, it turned out to be his father. The obsessive fantasy was a return of a childhood fantasy, his masochistic elaboration and distortion of passive and intrusive wishes he had toward his father. It was also a projection of sadistic fantasies he had regarding his father. Being hanged by me, i.e., his father, was in part an identification he made with his father, in which his father did to him what he, the boy, wanted to do to his father, and also what he wanted his father to do to him (Freud, 1919b). The point I want to emphasize here, however, is that the patient relives fantasies of his past life in the transference.

Among different patients one or another aspect of the positive transference feelings may be warded off because it is felt to be a danger. In men, homosexual impulses are usually so regarded and are strongly defended against. Freud (1937a, p. 250) has stated that they belong to the most stubborn resistances met with in analysis. But other feelings may also be considered a danger. Some patients dread romantic and erotic feelings and develop defenses against them. Their analyses may be characterized by the stubborn persistence of a "reasonable" transference, or they may escape into a superficial but chronic hostility or sarcasm as a defense and resistance. The prolonged absence of a positive transference is usually the result of defenses and will be described more fully under the heading of defense transference (Section 3.82). One must not forget that the atmosphere of the analysis can also cause prolonged negative reactions which are not merely transference reactions. Then we have to face two problems: the countertransference of the analyst and the masochistic patient who puts up with it.

The positive transference reactions will produce strong resistance in analysis when they are ego syntonic. The first steps in analyzing this, after the transference reaction has been recognized by the patient, is to make the transference reaction ego alien. The task is to get the reasonable ego of the patient to realize that his transference feelings are unrealistic, are based on a fantasy, and have some ulterior motive. Then the patient will be more willing to work on his feelings, to try to explore them with the aim of tracing them back to his past life.

Ego-dystonic positive transference reactions, however, can also cause resistances. Patients may feel embarrassed or ashamed of their love or sexual feelings. Or they may fear rejection or humiliation and may therefore try to hide their emotions. In all such instances, resistances will come into the foreground which will first have to be uncovered and analyzed before one can analyze the libidinal transference reaction. One first has to analyze the patient's embarrassment or fear of rejection before one can successfully analyze the other aspects of the transference. This will be amplified in Section 3.82.

3.712 The Negative Transference

The term "negative transference" is used to designate transference feelings which are based on hate in any of its various forms, its precursors, and its derivatives. Negative transference may be expressed as hatred, anger, hostility, mistrust, abhorrence, aversion, loathing, resentment, bitterness, envy, dislike, contempt, annoyance, etc. It is always present in the analysis, although it is often much more difficult to uncover than the manifestations of the positive transference. Not only do patients defend themselves against awareness of the transference hate, but the psychoanalyst himself is apt unconsciously to play along with this resistance. In my experience and in the experience of others, the insufficiently analyzed negative transference is the most frequent cause of stalemated analysis (Freud, 1937a, pp. 241-247; Glover, 1955; Nacht, 1954; Haak, 1957).

Much of what has been described in the discussion of the positive transference has parallels in the negative. These points will not be duplicated here. The most important differences center around the different kinds of resistances evoked by the negative transference.

There is an analogy to the working alliance, the nonsexual liking, trust, and respect for the analyst, which makes for the patient's willingness to risk new insights. From the standpoint of the negative transference we find a chronic, underlying mistrust, which may make the entire analytic procedure painful and essentially something to be rid of. If the patient is able to bear this kind of negative transference without giving in to the impulse to interrupt the analysis, we may see a chronic, submissive, masochistic transference reaction arise. The patient endures the rigors of the analytic work in order to get through with it, to be done with it. There is no pleasurable sense of accomplishment or of satisfaction in a mutually felt working alliance. The patient submits to the analysis because he is unable to break off the treatment and coming to the hour avoids that crisis: it is an avoidance, an acting out of a resistance to analysis by coming to the analysis. The entire analysis may become something to be borne because it is a lesser evil compared to really giving up and contending with the neurotic misery.

Such patients may work well and even effectively for long periods of time, but sooner or later this kind of transference relationship has to be recognized for what it is—a resistance. It is either a subtle, latent, paranoidlike defense, or a hidden masochistic enjoyment or a defense against the positive transference or a combination of all three. It may also be a response to some unrecognized negative feelings in the analyst, realistic or countertransference. In analyzable neurotic patients, the masochism and the defense against feelings of love are more predominant, although some small paranoid element may also be present.

I once treated such a patient, a thirty-five-year-old woman, an avid Communist. She worked hard but bitterly in analysis under the influence of a submissive, suspicious working alliance. On the surface I was not to be trusted because I was not a fellow Communist but a member of the middle class. Yet I was her best opportunity to escape from a more intolerable phobic-compulsive neurosis. On a deeper level she enjoyed the masochistic misery she fantasied I put her through. Below that was her still greater fear of feeling love for me, which would really put her at my mercy and make her truly vulnerable. And at the bottom of it all was her fear of her primitive rage and destructiveness which she felt would destroy both of us if she loved and was rejected. This essentially negative submissive transference was nevertheless relatively productive for long periods of time, though far less so than a genuine working alliance would have been. It took some two and a half years to work through some of the masochistic transference, which once accomplished made the analysis proceed more speedily.

Then a complication arose. The patient became extremely resistant again and her old mistrustful attitude returned. This turned out to be caused by the fact that she and her Communist group were contemplating some form of sabotage, and since we now were involved in World War II she could not tell me this. She wondered what I would do if she told me the details. I told her quite simply that I felt I could not analyze her under such conditions since I would be torn by my duty toward her as a patient and my loyalty to my country, etc. She seemed reassured by my answer because she said it seemed to be quite honest and she would have doubted any other answer. But I had the impression her old mistrust never left her, and our work slowed down again. My entrance into military service shortly thereafter made it necessary for me to transfer her, which was probably the best solution for both of us.

The appearance of transient negative transference reactions early in analysis poses more of a problem than early transient transference love. Hostility and anger early in the analysis, before a reliable working alliance is established, tempt the patient to act out and break off the analysis. The early negative transference must therefore be pursued vigorously, in order to forestall such a development. One can afford to be more passive in working on the positive transference.

However, once a working alliance has been established, the emergence of the negative transference can be an important sign of progress. The reliving of hostility and hatred to the early childhood figures in the transference is a most productive phase of the analytic work as long as a good working alliance is present. I believe that such a development is a necessary phase of every successful analysis. The absence of negative transference, or its appearance only in transient and sporadic reactions, is a sign of an incomplete analysis. Our deeper knowledge of early childhood development seems to indicate that intense and prolonged hateful reactions toward the analyst should emerge and be analyzed before one should think of terminating an analysis.

Freud (1937a) in his "Analysis Terminable and Interminable" brought up the question of whether or not an analyst should stir up the latent nonvisible conflicts of a patient. He felt that the psychoanalyst has no right to assume such an intrusive role, no right to manipulate the transference. Although I am in sympathy with Freud's general attitude, I do not agree with his evaluation of the clinical material. I feel that he did not, at that time, sufficiently recognize the importance of the negative transference. The analysis of the transference hate is as important as that of the transference love. I agree it is not within the province of the analyst to intrude or to manipulate; but since Freud's discovery of the importance of the aggressive instincts, most analysts have come to the conclusion that it is imperative to analyze this aspect of the transference before interrupting the analysis. Despite my reservations about Melanie Klein and her followers, I must say it is to their credit that they emphasized this point. The interminable analyses, the negative therapeutic reactions are, in my experience, invariably examples of insufficient analysis of the transference hate.

The negative transference is important in other ways as well. It is often used for defensive purposes—as a resistance against the positive transference. Many patients, particularly patients of the same sex as the analyst, hold on to their hostile feelings because they use them as a defense against their love, i.e., particularly their homosexual feelings. Many of my male patients would rather be angry and resentful with me because they feel more comfortable in their resentment than in loving me. Loathing and disgust in their reactions to me are defenses, reaction formations against oral, introjective impulses.

Absence of the apparent negative transference has to be recognized eventually as a defense and resistance. In a smoothly proceeding analysis, the negative transference eventually has to play a prominent role. One of the complicating factors is the likelihood that the analyst's countertransference is involved in preventing the development or recognition of some form of hatred. Either the analyst is behaving in such a way as to make it very difficult for the patient to express his hostility, or else the analyst and the patient are conspiring to overlook it. Sometimes patients will cover their hostility with humor or teasing or sarcasm, and in this way it escapes notice. But more important is the splitting of the transference.

Patients will find some analyst surrogate, another analyst or physician or parental figure toward whom they express great hostility. It must be recognized that this hatred is displaced from the person of the analyst for defensive purposes.

The use of auxiliary transference objects is a very frequent occurrence in attempting to deal with the negative transference, far more so than with the positive. Despite one's recognition of the defense-resistance function of this maneuver, it may not be possible to get the transference feelings directed onto the person of the analyst. Some patients will stubbornly maintain this split in the transference as though the renunciation of this mechanism poses a great danger. My own clinical experience seems to indicate that this state of affairs is likely to occur when a patient has lost one of the parental figures very early in life. In the transference neurosis such patients seem more prone to split off their hatred onto auxiliary transference objects in order to preserve the analyst from their hatred. Even though I have worked energetically to overcome this resistance, I feel that at times I have been only partially successful. One of my patients, a woman whose father deserted the family when she was two years old, displaced her hatred of men onto several paternal figures outside the analysis and only occasionally felt this hatred directly for me. The same was true of her mother hatred. I have had similar experiences with other patients with this kind of background.

Persistent positive transference always indicates that the negative transference is hidden, not absent. The analyst must uncover it and must try to make it possible for the patient to feel it directly toward the analyst. This means that ideally in every analysis the patient shall have experienced the different varieties of hate from all libidinal levels toward the analyst. Above all, the early primitive rage to the mother has to be experienced in a deep analysis.

One other aspect of the negative transference deserves emphasis. Fear of the analyst, whether it be in the form of fear of his criticism, or deep-seated mistrust, has to be recognized as a derivative of aggression and hostility. Here again, the Kleinians have pointed out that anxiety reactions are essentially derived from aggressive impulses, and although I would not agree with their fantastic and elaborate constructions, my own clinical experience would confirm that they are correct in the essential formulation: fear of the analyst is ultimately derived from projected hostility.

3.72 TRANSFERENCE REACTIONS IN TERMS OF OBJECT RELATIONS

Another practical method for designating a particular type of transference phenomenon is to label it in accordance with the object relationship from early childhood to which it owes its origin. Thus we may speak of a father transference, or mother transference, brother transference, etc. This designation means that the patient's transference reaction is predominantly determined by his unconscious feelings and impulses toward father or mother, etc. During the course of an analysis the object representation determining the transference reaction will undergo changes as the analytic work progresses. For example, a patient may begin analysis with a predominantly father transference which can slowly change to a mother transference.

The nature of the underlying object giving rise to the transference reaction is determined mainly by the life experiences of the patient (Freud, 1912a, p. 100). The patient will transfer in accordance with his repressed needs in relation to the early family objects. As the repressed becomes accessible to consciousness, however, the needs change, and the nature of the transference reaction will change. As we succeed in analyzing the feelings to the father in the transference, for example, a mother transference reaction may now emerge. However, the person of the analyst also influences the nature of the figure coloring the transference reaction. This is particularly true of transference reactions early in the analysis (A. Freud, 1954a, p. 618). Most of my patients, I have found, react to me as a father figure in their early transference reactions and in the first phase of their transference neurosis. Later on my gender and personality appear less decisive. However, the personal qualities of the analyst do play a role with some patients who have difficulty in allowing themselves to regress fully in the transference situation. They find it necessary to seek auxiliary transference objects outside the analysis in order to re-enact some experiences of the repressed, remote past. Eventually in a successful analysis, the analyst should have become both a father and mother figure.

One can modify the designation of father or mother transference, by adding whether it is primarily positive or negative. It is important to remember that different transference reactions exist side by side, some more conscious, some less so, some stronger, some weaker. What matters is what is predominant, what is urgent, what is pressing for discharge, and the knowledge that the opposite must be present to some degree although it is hidden at the moment.

For example, during the course of an analytic hour a patient expresses gratitude for being able to come to the hour, because he had a miserable weekend. Below the gratitude, I can hear a tone of resentment. The patient goes on to tell in some detail of his hostility and fear of his superiors at work. They seem so awesome and he feels so insignificant. Silence. Then he described his disappointment in his younger son, who seems timid and inhibited in his play with other children. He wonders whether the child would do better in another school. Silence. He enjoyed the work we did with a dream in our last hour; it was interesting although it didn't seem to help him any. He heard that some people find being analyzed a form of torture, but he certainly would not say that for himself. He is fortunate in having a fine analyst. He looks forward to the analytic hour . . . pause . . . "most of the time . . . that is."

I think if one looks over the analytic material of this fragment of an hour, one can hear the patient's struggle with the negative father transference. On the surface one can see his positive feelings, his gratitude in being able to come, his enjoyment of the last hour of dream interpretation, his relief that analysis was not all torture, how lucky he is, etc. But there are also unmistakable signs of his negative father transference and his fear of it: his miserable weekend and the implied reproach, his fear and awe of his superiors, his silence, his disappointment in his son, the possibility of changing schools, his lack of improvement, and his evasive manner of speech. Despite the presence of certain signs of the positive father transference, we would say that this analytic fragment indicates the emergence of the negative father transference and particularly the patient's fear of it.

It has been my clinical experience that my men patients have particularly strong resistances in experiencing toward me their early oral-sadistic hatred toward the mother. On the other hand, my women patients seem to have unusual difficulty in resolving their resistances toward experiencing me as the loving, breast-giving mother figure. Freud, in his "Analysis Terminable and Interminable," stated that the most difficult aspect to analyze in men was their fear of a passive homosexual attitude to men, and in women, their penis envy. My own clinical experience leads me to a different conclusion. What is most difficult in men is the primitive hatred of mother; and in women, the primitive love of mother.

At this point I should mention the fact that the working alliance is composed of an admixture of unconscious motherly and fatherly components. The analyst as a physicianly figure is on the one hand a nurse who ministers to the primitive and intimate needs of the relatively helpless patient and on the other hand a father who is not afraid to face the dangers that terrify the patient and the rest of his environment (Stone, 1961, pp. 118-120).

3.73 TRANSFERENCE REACTIONS IN TERMS OF LIBIDINAL PHASES

Sometimes it is useful to describe a transference reaction in reference to the particular libidinal phase from which it is derived (A. Freud, 1936, pp. 18-19). This means that we can categorize a patient's reactions to his analyst in terms of his instinctual aims, instinctual zones, and the anxieties, attitudes, and values in accordance with those instinctual components.

For example, a patient who reacts to every utterance of the analyst as though it were a feeding, and to silence as though it were a desertion, who is greedy to drink in his every word, who is insatiable and who dreads separation, is obviously reacting on an oral, introjective level. The patient's feelings of love or hate, trust or mistrust would determine whether this is felt primarily as a positive or negative oral mother transference.

One of my patients would listen to me talk with eyes closed and a rapturous expression on her face. It became clear to me that she listened not to my words but only to the sound of my voice. When I pursued this point, she finally told me that the sound of my voice reminded her of the smell of coffee cooking in the kitchen in the morning while she was dozing in bed as a little girl.

Analogously, the analysis may be reacted to as a toilet situation and the patient will feel he either has to produce or get out; his associations are precious material to be shared or hoarded, or foul-smelling productions to be splattered in anger or hidden for preservation. In such a phase the patient may react to the analyst's interventions as enemata, painful intrusions or pleasurable proddings. It is clear that the patient is transferring onto the analyst and the analytic situation the experiences of his anal phase. One can expect to see, in addition to the above-mentioned elements, anxieties about control and autonomy, problems about shame, attitudes of spite, stubbornness, submissiveness, orderliness, cleanliness, parsimony, etc. Isolation is apt to be the predominant mechanism of defense at this time.

The phallic phase, when it is re-experienced in regard to the analyst and the analytic situation, leads to the most dramatic transference experiences. It must be borne in mind that this may be strongly defended against in a variety of ways. Once the defense is overcome, then the incestuous love and the castration anxiety, the jealous rivalry and death wishes, the desire for a baby or a penis, the return of oedipal masturbation fantasies, and the associated guilt feelings make for very vivid transference reactions.

This method of categorizing transference reactions can be done for all levels of libidinal development. The reader is referred to the basic works on this subject for a more comprehensive picture of the possibilities (Freud, 1905d; Abraham, 1924; Fenichel, 1945a; Erikson, 1950; A. Freud, 1965).

3.74 TRANSFERENCE REACTIONS IN TERMS OF STRUCTURE

Sometimes one can best describe certain of the patient's reactions to the analyst from the structural point of view—the analyst may become a superego, id, or ego representation for the patient. In Section 3.411 it was questioned whether this is truly a transference reaction according to our definition. Be that as it may, it is useful to consider them so clinically. Early in the analysis one usually can observe situations in which the analyst represents a superego figure for the patient. This can be transient or protracted, mild or intense. When the analyst takes on the function of the superego, he is felt primarily as critical, hostile, rejecting, and negative. This is in keeping with our theoretical ideas about the cathecting of the superego with aggressive drive energies (Hartmann, Kris, and Loewenstein, 1946, pp. 30-35). The Kleinian school believes that the introjection and projection of the analyst into the patient's superego are basic occurrences in all analyses. The core of the superego in their view is the mother's breast, both good and bad (Klein, 1952, p. 434).

The clinical material, however, seems to lend itself to different interpretations depending on the patient's history and on the developmental level being re-experienced in the analytic situation. When the analyst does become a superego representation, he is always imbued with hostile impulses, attitudes, and fantasies. In addition to the critical figures as they existed in the patient's history, the patient's own hostility to that figure is added, projected onto it. Moreover, the patient's hostility to the analyst may also be projected onto this superego image. But this changes during the course of analysis and one must be careful to avoid stereotyped interpretations.

Let me illustrate with a clinical example. A middle-aged male patient came to analysis because of compulsive-obsessive rigid character traits and an underlying neurotic depression. In the early part of his analysis he was constantly aware of feelings that I disapproved of his way of working. He routinely associated this to his strict father of his childhood days. Slowly it became clear that his father had not been nearly as disapproving as the patient felt me to be. I then interpreted to him how his own hostility toward his father was transferred onto me. I received hostility from two sources: from the patient's memory of his disapproving father displaced onto me and from the patient's anger toward himself projected onto me. Still later on we detected a third source of hostility.

He felt contemptuous of me; I was not a pure scientist but a materialist and a sensualist. My way of speech, my manner of dress, the things he heard about me convinced him I was a "wheeler-dealer" who lived high on the hog, the "Tom Jones" of psychoanalysis. Analysis of these feelings revealed first of all that behind the contempt there was envy. He felt envious of me and now he projected the contempt onto me. I had contempt for his middle-class morals, he believed. As the patient began to change, this constellation changed. The patient allowed himself to experience the frustrations in his sexual life and he embarked on a love affair, an acting out. First he felt I was disapproving of this behavior, but he didn't care. He was tired of being the "goody-goody." He wanted his rightful share of pleasure and if I didn't like it, then "fuck you, doctor." "I am tired of this perfectionism of mine; in fact, I hate that as much as I used to hate you men who used to live it up! I am a nicer person as a philanderer than I was as a prig. I'm even nicer to my wife and children. Now I'm afraid you will try to take this away from me, but I'll fight you on this. And I warn you, I am terribly angry, and no goddamn psychoanalyst is going to interfere with my pleasures."

I believe this clinical vignette illustrates the many shifts and changes that can occur in a patient from the standpoint of what kind of superego figure the analyst represents and what is being displaced and projected onto the analyst. At first I am a displacement of the anti-instinctual father. Then I am the projection of the patient's hostility to himself. Then I become the contemptible instinctual father, the "Tom Jones" of psychoanalysis whom, it turns out, he actually envies. At this point, a change takes place in the patient and his superego allows him to become more instinctual. His new superego hates his old self, but the old anti-instinctual component is shifted back onto me; he is afraid I will interfere. However, he now can feel that he would fight me on this issue.

I believe this clinical fragment indicates the need to be alert to all the possible changes that can go on during the analytic process in terms of the relationship between the patient's self, his superego, and the analyst. Stereotyped interpretations or a rigid, narrow point of view about these matters would limit the analyst's appreciation of the intricacies involved.

Sometimes during the analysis, one can observe how the patient reprojects his superego onto the person of the analyst and behaves as though he had none. This can be seen when patients feel closely watched and harassed during the working week and then overindulge in a variety of instinctual activities over the weekend or during other absences from the analyst. They regress to a level where they feel fear in regard to an external figure instead of feeling guilty internally.

Another aspect of this situation obtains when the patient regresses to the early presuperego days, when most of the superego functions were performed by the powerful external parental figures. When this occurs, the superego figure in the transference is omnipotent, omniscient, severely aggressive and destructive. The patient has displaced and projected onto the analyst the hostility, rage, and fear he experienced toward the early parental figures, before they are clearly separated from the self (Jacobson, 1964).

The analyst may also be perceived as an id figure rather than a superego. This occurs when the patient displaces and projects onto the analyst his own id strivings. At such times the patient may feel that the analyst wants him to masturbate, to be aggressive, to be promiscuous, to perform perverse sexual acts, etc. The analyst is felt to be a seducer, provoker, and tempter. This may lead patients to act out as though they were merely submitting to the analyst's will. Or else this can lead to pseudosexual and pseudoaggressive behavior, which is really a hidden attempt to conform and please the analyst. This pattern can be complicated because the behavior can be pseudoinstinctual consciously, and yet hide real instinctual impulses.

For example, a relatively inhibited patient spends a night having a wild sexual affair with a strange woman doing a variety of sexual activities he ordinarily avoids. At first he claims he was somewhat drunk and this led him into the situation. Somewhat later he realizes he did this to please me; in fact, he had the thought that if he does all of these things, the doctor will stop probing. Only much later did he realize that the ability to perform all of these activities indicated some latent desire within himself.

The analyst can also be used as an extension of the patient's ego. He is used for reality testing according to the formula: what would my analyst do now? How would he react in this situation? The process of using the analyst as an auxiliary ego is of great importance in patients who have difficulty with reality testing, in particular the borderline case. It is helpful to all patients during crisis situations. Here we also have a forerunner of identification with the analyst—a form of imitation. This is a valuable transition for the development of a working alliance in that the patient becomes familiar with the analytic approach to problems. It can also be misused for pathological purposes and, if undetected, patients become replicas of their analysts. This will be discussed in more detail in the next section.

3.75 IDENTIFICATION AS A TRANSFERENCE REACTION

Identifications play an important and complicated role in object formation. Early identifications precede object relations and there are identifications which replace relationships to objects (Jacobson, 1964). There seem to be different kinds of identifications: some are partial, some total; some transitory, some permanent; some accessible to consciousness, some inaccessible; some ego syntonic and some ego dystonic. Since any and all aspects of object relations are repeated in the transference, identifications of all types will also occur. This discussion will be limited to the most important clinical forms of transference identifications. For a more comprehensive survey of the classical literature on this subject the reader is referred to the writings of Freud (1921), Fenichel (1945a), Hartmann, Kris, and Loewenstein (1946), Jacobson (1964), and Hendrick (1951).

One form of identification, absolutely necessary for analysis to be effective at all, was described when we talked of the formation of the working alliance. To repeat: when the analyst makes an interpretation or other confrontation to the patient, he asks the patient temporarily to give up his experiencing, free-associating ego and to observe along with his therapist what he has just been experiencing. In other words, he is asked temporarily and partially to identify with the analyst (Sterba, 1929). At first he does so only when the analyst asks him to, and he must consciously initiate this development. Later on it becomes automatic and preconscious. It is most vividly seen in working with resistances. At first it is necessary for the analyst to point out the resistance and to ask why and what the patient is resisting.

Later on, the patient himself recognizes he is resisting and asks himself why and what he is avoiding. This is an indication of the partial and temporary identification with the analyst which makes for the working alliance. When this step has been achieved, we say, "the patient is in analysis." This kind of identification persists even after analysis. People who have been analyzed, when confronted by emotional problems, will do some self-analysis.

During the course of an analysis patients will identify with the analyst as a means of coping with him as an anxiety-producing figure. I have seen such patients undergo sudden and marked changes in their behavior at home and in their work situation.

A moody, impulse-ridden patient of mine suddenly took on a complacent, reasonable, and thoughtful demeanor. His family and friends remarked about this striking metamorphosis. It was also noticeable in his way of working in the analytic hour. His impetuousness and his mood swings seemed to have disappeared. However, his associations seemed stilted and unproductive. Then, when he described an anger outburst of one of his children, I was struck by the patient's detached and unemotional reaction. He merely asked the child what had made him so angry. This was completely out of character for the patient. I finally realized what was going on when he began to use certain words and phrases which had a familiar ring. He had taken over the vocabulary I was accustomed to using and which was foreign to him. He had identified with me on the basis of an identification with the aggressor, a mechanism Anna Freud (1936) described as a means of attempting to cope with a frightening object.

The patient attempted to interpret his own material to pre-empt me. It was a resistance, a method of defense. He had used similar identifications in his past, in trying to overcome his anxiety of authority figures. This type of identification with the analyst is frequently seen in analysis; the patient takes on the role of the analyst with his family and friends and even with the analyst himself.

But patients will identify with the analyst for other reasons; for example, as a means of expressing an urge for closeness. This resembles the kind of transference hunger Ferenczi (1909) has described. Patients under the influence of a positive transference will take on mannerisms, characteristics, traits and habits of the analyst as a manifestation of their love and, even more important, as a primitive means of relating to an object. It has to be borne in mind that identification is the earliest variety of object relationship and plays a decisive role in building the self representation and the ego structure. It is not always possible to separate the various functions of identification from one another (Fenichel, 1945a, pp. 36-39). I have seen men patients who were customarily neat and precise in their dress become careless and rumpled as I seem to be. Patients will change their brand of cigarettes to mine, or start smoking cigars when I do. A patient suddenly began to study music, which I traced back to some psychoanalytic gossip he had heard about chamber music played in my home. These identifications stem basically from an oral-introjective object hunger, an urge to become like the idealized analyst, to be loved by him or, on the deepest level, to become one with him. There is still another possible motive for this kind of identification. Patients will too eagerly and quickly identify with the analyst in order to form a new identity—to hide their real identity. This can be seen in the so-called "screen-identity" patients —a form of "as if" character (Greenson, 1958a).

There are patients who present the reverse of this picture; they seem only able to develop the most meager identification with their analyst. They may form the partial and transitory working-alliance identification, but little else. I have had patients in analysis for many years, who work very hard at it, but who do not develop any identification with me even in areas where it might be of considerable help. Patients who have anxiety in verbal expression do not take over my verbal dexterity. Patients who are generally timid do not identify with me in my outspokenness. They will identify with me in some trivial way; they may buy a pen like mine or start to wear button-down shirts, but they will not identify with me in any of the more important characteristics. These patients suffer from a fear of identifying and are engaging in a constant struggle against identification. To them, to identify means to be overwhelmed, to be taken over, swallowed up, to lose their own identity. These patients struggle against identifying with the analyst as they struggled in adolescence against identifying with their parents (Greenson, 1954).

One sees bizarre, transient, and sudden identification in very sick borderline or psychotic patients. For them, identification is a desperate means of holding on to or establishing some form of relationship to reality and objects.

Some years ago I interviewed a married woman with two young children with a view to analyzing her. Her behavior and her history seemed to present nothing morbid that would contraindicate the use of psychoanalysis. I had offered her a cigarette in the first interview and she had declined, saying she was not a smoker. In the very next hour I was startled to see her take out a package of cigarettes, the same brand as mine, and proceed to smoke several. It was the first indication I had of an incipient psychotic episode which was just beginning to show itself.

3.8 Transference Resistances

Actually, transference resistances might well be discussed as one of the categories of clinical transference reactions. However, this group of transference phenomena is of special clinical importance and deserves a greater emphasis and careful elucidation. As I stated previously, transference resistances are the most important and fre-

quent causes of obstruction to the analytic work (Freud, 1912a).
More time is spent in analyzing transference resistances than in any
other aspect of the analytic work. Insufficiently analyzed transference resistance is the most important cause of interrupted or stalemated analyses. On the other hand, the effective analysis of
resistances leads to the most productive analytic work.

The term transference resistance is a condensation and refers to
many different clinical constellations. In each instance it is the
transference that is causing the resistance, but in varying ways. For
example: the patient may have transference feelings which he may
seek to gratify instead of analyze. Or the patient may oppose the
analytic procedure because he fears developing certain transference reactions. Or the patient may adopt and cling to certain transference feelings because he dreads other forms of transference reactions, and in order to protect himself he opposes free association.

From a clinical and technical point of view, it is worthwhile to
distinguish various types of transference resistance because they
differ greatly in their dynamics and structure and in the difficulty
of the technical task. The form and structure of the transference
resistance change in the patient during the course of psychoanalysis
and every patient is unique in the sequence of the different types
of resistance. There is also considerable variation in what forms of
transference resistance predominate in a particular patient. It should
further be borne in mind that a variety of transference resistances
may be operating simultaneously, and one of our technical problems is to ascertain what constellation of transference resistance we
shall choose for our therapeutic work at a given time. I have selected
for special elaboration those types of transference resistance which
occur with the greatest frequency and which can be isolated with
the greatest clarity.

3.81 THE SEARCH FOR TRANSFERENCE GRATIFICATION

One of the simplest and most frequent sources of transference
resistance occurs when the patient develops strong emotional and
instinctual urges towarrd the analyst and strives to satisfy them
rather than do the analytic work. This may be derived from libidinal
and aggressive instinctual drives or from the emotions of love or
hatred. Further, any and all of the developmental phases of the

instincts and emotions may be involved. For example, the patient may have sexual desires toward the analyst on a phallic-oedipal level and have incestuous wishes and castration anxiety. Or a patient may have passive-anal impulses toward the analyst or oral wishes to be fed and taken care of, etc. Any of these libidinal elements may impel the patient to try to obtain some form of gratification and to renounce the analytic work.

As an illustration, let me cite the case of a patient who at different times was driven by each of the libidinal components just mentioned. In the beginning of her analysis (she was a depressed patient with a problem of overeating), she was frequently sadly silent because she wanted me to talk to her. At that time, my speaking to her meant that I was willing to feed her. If I would talk, then it meant I was truly concerned about her, would take care of her, feed her, and not abandon her. Then, if these wishes were gratified she would be able to work, to produce, otherwise she felt empty and forlorn and unable to communicate. Later on in the analysis she felt strong sexual impulses toward me which were unmistakably of an incestuous nature. She came to her hour in a flirtatious, frivolous mood, determined to provoke me into some kind of sexual play, even if it were only verbal. For a period of time she refused to work with this material; she demanded that I first had to indicate some reciprocity in my feelings. Still later on in her analysis, she went through a phase in which she refused to produce analytic material unless I prodded her. She insisted that I insert even a small comment into her silence and then she would be able to let out all her stored-up communications. All these different urges became a source of resistance, until she was able to relinquish her desire for satisfaction. Only then was she willing to establish a working alliance and attempt to work analytically on her different instinctual impulses toward me.

Allied to the above examples, and extremely frequent as a source of resistance, is the patient's wish or need to be loved. All patients, to a greater or lesser degree and in a variety of ways, go through periods in which their wish to be loved by their analyst supersedes and blocks their desire to accede to the analytic procedures. The fear of loss of love or respect from the therapist is an ever-present and underlying source of resistance. It may operate alone or it may be found to be on the surface or underlying the different forms of transference resistance. The family romance may also be repeated in the transference (Freud, 1905d; Frosch, 1959).

Let me illustrate this problem from the analysis of Mrs. K.[6] I was alerted to the patient's enormous need to be loved by her history of having been brought up by an irresponsible mother and having been deserted by her father at age two. Her first dream exposed this need. I had seen Mrs. K. in the preliminary interviews and we agreed she would begin analysis in about two months, when I would have an opening. She came to the first analytic hour and we talked briefly about the interim events and about the use of the couch. She was eager to begin. As soon as she lay down she reported the following dream: "I come to my first analytic hour, but you seem different, you look like Dr. M. You lead me into a small room and tell me to undress. I am surprised and ask you whether you're supposed to do that as a classical Freudian. You assure me it is alright. I get undressed and you begin to kiss me all over. Then you finally 'went down' on me. I was pleased, but I kept wondering if it was right."

The patient acknowledged her embarrassment about the dream, and began to talk. Dr. M. is the doctor who referred her to me, and she had a crush on him for a while. He seemed to be very competent, but then she saw he had his shortcomings. He seemed to enjoy her flirtatiousness, which proved to her there was something wrong in his home life. She knows I am married and that reassures her. She is so excited to be lying on the couch doing psychoanalysis. She was so afraid I would not accept her as a patient, she heard I have few private patients. Maybe I will throw her out when I find out how "nothing" she is. She felt I was a bit brusque the last time I saw her, not as warm as in the first few hours. But she was determined to get into analysis with me. She would have waited as long as necessary. She was tired of taking rejects and castoffs. "I want the best [pause]. I want the best, but can I hold on to it? What makes me think I deserve it? [Pause.] Everything worthwhile I ever got I got because I was attractive. Maybe that's why you accepted me as a patient. But why should I dream of you 'going down' on me. I don't even know how to say it politely. Maybe you will teach me how to speak proper English. Or are you already fed up with my drivel? [Pause.] I have trouble with sex. I like the idea of it, but I can't have an orgasm with intercourse. The only way I sometimes do is when my husband uses his mouth on me. I suppose that means something—something bad."

This dream posed several difficult problems because it had overt sexual activity in it as well as resistances, and it is the patient's first analytic hour. The manifest dream seemed to be saying that I reminded her of someone she was infatuated with and that I, not she, want to do

[6] See also Sections 1.24, 2.651, 2.71, 3.25, 3.42.

sexual things with my mouth to her. Further, she was concerned about doing the correct thing and I was primarily interested in giving her sexual pleasure. One could see how our roles had been interchanged. Her associations kept going back to the question of will I accept her, keep her as a patient. They also indicated her feeling of being unworthy, empty, and uneducated, whereas I am looked upon as worthy and the "best." There was also the statement that she can have an orgasm only from cunnilingus.

The special technical problem was how to handle the overt sexual element in the dream in this, the fearful patient's first hour? I decided I would point out her need to be loved, her fear of being rejected by me, and somehow tie this in with the sexual element. To ignore the sexual would be to make it seem "bad," to talk about it might obscure the resistance elements and perhaps get us too deep too early in the analysis. However, since the patient was able to dream it and remember it, I decided I had to comment upon the sexual activity. I said to her approximately as follows: "You must have been very worried after the last hour when I seemed brusque and you wondered if I would really take you as a patient. Then you dream that I use my mouth on you sexually as proof that I really do accept you." I had made a reconstruction upward as described by Berta Bornstein (1949) and Loewenstein (1951, p. 10).

The patient listened attentively and replied: "It's funny that you recognized that I always felt that if a man loved you, he should be able to use his mouth on you sexually. Lots of men are great at making speeches about love, but they back down when it comes to 'that.' I am always embarrassed when they do it at first because I wonder how can they stand it, but I guess it does prove a person loves you, at least in a sexual way."

The need to be loved and the terror of being rejected were major factors in Mrs. K.'s transference resistances. She equated being rejected with being abandoned. Abandonment stirred up great rage, which she turned inward, and consequently she felt like a "nothing." In part this was done to preserve, to hold on to, the idealized analyst because she dreaded that her hostility would destroy him and then she would really be alone, i.e., "nothing."

I can give illustrations from the aggressive side of the ledger as well. There are patients who become full of hostile, destructive impulses, who are bent unconsciously upon destroying their analyst and their analysis instead of analyzing their impulses.

A neurotic depressive male patient of mine with ulcerative colitis had a quarrel with his wife who he claimed neglects to prepare the proper food for him. He stormed out of the house to his analytic hour. It seemed clear to me he had displaced his hostility from his mother onto his wife. When he seemed relatively reasonable, I pointed this out to him. All he heard in this interpretation was that I was on his wife's side. That evening, despite following a strict diet for years, he went to a restaurant alone and ate all the forbidden foods he was able to swallow. He topped it off with a great deal of brandy and black coffee. That night he was in acute pain with severe vomiting and diarrhea. The fury he felt toward his wife, his mother, and me he vented on himself as a means of revenge according to the formula: "I will kill myself and then you will all be sorry." In addition to all its other meanings, this behavior was an attempt to wreck the analysis and hurt the analyst.

Patients who suffer from what is called an "eroticized" transference are prone to very destructive acting out (Rappaport, 1956). This is also seen in impulse-ridden characters, perversions, borderline cases, etc. All these patients have transference resistances that stem from underlying impulses of hatred. They seek only to discharge these feelings and oppose the analytic work. The technical task is to find the moment when one can mobilize the reasonable ego. Usually, once the intensity of the feelings has worn off, once the instinctual demands are less urgent, a reasonable ego does become accessible.

The less intense, subtle, and chronic demands for gratification are harder to detect and to demonstrate to the patient. Once they become recognizable by the patient, then they too become accessible to analytic work.

3.82 DEFENSIVE TRANSFERENCE REACTIONS

Another typical form of transference resistance occurs when the patient repeats and relives, in regard to his analyst, his defenses against instinctual and emotional involvement (A. Freud, 1936, pp. 19-25). This may become the outstanding quality and function of the transference reaction. This form of transference may be designed as defensive transference reactions. Such reactions are always transference resistances and serve the purpose of warding off other aspects and forms of transference phenomena. Several typical clinical varieties occur with great frequency and deserve to be singled out for discussion (see Fenichel, 1941, pp. 68-69).

One of the most frequently seen forms of defensive transference reactions is the persistence of reasonable and rational behavior toward the analyst. Such prolonged absence of irrational reactions appears on the surface to be an absence of transference, but it is actually a transference reaction, albeit a defensive transference reaction. The persistent reasonable and rational behavior is the defensive side of a set of reactions, underneath which is hidden the instinctual, the emotional, and the irrational. This kind of defensive transference reaction is often seen at the beginning of an analysis in patients who want to be "good" patients (Gitelson, 1948, 1954).

Let me illustrate this situation by briefly describing a patient of mine, a man in his late thirties who came to analysis because of sexual impotence of some eight years' duration. The impotence was limited to his wife, he was potent with other women, but he felt guilty both for his infidelity and for his impotence. However, he was unable to give up his extramarital affairs despite loving his wife.

He was extremely competent and successful in his professional work, in a field of cut-throat competition and where success required a high degree of aggressivity and even combativeness.

In his analysis he was very conscientious and cooperative. He tried hard to free-associate, he brought in dreams, he tried to follow my interpretations, he spoke with a moderate amount of feeling, he was not cold or overly intellectualized. At times he would fall silent and would wish that I would say something, but he knew analysts were supposed to be silent. He often felt he was making little progress, but he blamed himself since he was satisfied I was a competent analyst. When he had embarrassing material to talk about, he reproached himself for being so childish since he knew that I would not be critical of him; analysts were accustomed to such material. When I made interpretations he could not agree with or follow, he supposed I must be right and he was just a bit thick or slow-witted.

I then began to point out the persistent reasonableness of his reactions to me and wondered whether he ever had any other feelings or fantasies about me. He was unaware of anything but the feeling that I was a competent analyst doing his best. I pointed out that in some of his dreams there were situations where I was depicted as dead, or mutilated, and such pictures must come from within him. He agreed it seemed plausible, but he could not find such feelings within himself. When I tried to find the figure in the past to whom he had similar reactions, it turned out to be his father. For the patient, the father was a decent, conscientious, hardworking man toward whom he also had persistent reasonable, rational, and warmhearted feelings. He was always tolerant and good-natured about any of his father's shortcomings. This was in marked contrast to his hostile and pugnacious behavior toward other men of authority or toward his competitors. He seemed to protect me and his father from his unconscious instinctual impulses—but why?

A dream supplied the key material. He is on a sailboat. The sail is suspended from a totem pole which had three figures on it, two men and a baby. The top figure looks like me, then comes the baby and at the bottom is his father. His associations lead to the following: When he was seven years old, his father had suffered a heart attack and the patient was given to believe that it was his (the patient's) emotional outbursts that had almost killed the father. This material was not new, but it seemed to have new import for the patient. He hesitates for several moments and then quietly tells me he had heard that I had once had a heart attack. He goes on by saying heartily that he is sure I must take very good care of myself, after all I am a physician. I detect a thinness in his attempt to talk reassuringly. I interrupt him and ask: "Something is worrying you, what else are you thinking?" The patient sighs, pretends to laugh, and then says he heard that I was over fifty years old and that came as a shock to him. He thought I was in my forties. I seem to look young and act young.

I intervene: "My being over fifty shocked you. What occurs to you to that idea—over fifty years old?" The patient says quickly: "My father died at fifty-three and I can't bear the possibility of you dying. I have enough on my conscience. I don't think I ever told you this, but the baby on the totem pole made me think back to the death of our first baby. I told you my wife had placenta previa, but I didn't realize until just now that I felt guilty for having caused it by having intercourse with her shortly before she hemorrhaged."

I interpret to him: "And you became impotent with your wife to make sure you would never hurt another baby." He replies: "Yes, I didn't deserve intercourse with a good woman. Only destructive things seem to come out of me when I let go. You ought to be grateful I am so well controlled here." Pause. Silence.

It has now become clear that behind this patient's chronic reasonableness, behind his defensive transference lay tumultuous feelings and impulses. His reasonableness with me was his way of protecting and preserving me from his destructive hostility. Analyzing the history of his defensive reasonableness eventually made it possible for the patient to experience the stormy impulses which lay behind this protective barrier.

The apparent lack of transference reactions turned out to be a defensive transference. The patient repeated with his analyst a set of defensive reactions he had found it necessary to use in relationship to his father and then in regard to his wife. These defensive reactions were a resistance and opposed the uncovering of the instinctual and affective components which lay hidden underneath.

In the above example, the patient transferred an entire set of defenses onto the analyst, but one sees cases where only a single defensive attitude may be transferred. There are patients who always react to an interpretation by seeming to accept it. They may be repeating a submissive attitude from the past in order to ward off aggressive feelings. One of my patients never made an interpretation on his own initiative, no matter how obvious the material was. He always waited for me to give the interpretation. This defensive behavior was derived from the fact that his older brother was fiercely competitive with him and would attack him severely if the patient in any way threatened his supremacy. Thus the patient acted with me the naïve, unknowing one—the same defensive role he had adopted toward his older brother.

Thus far, the examples of defensive transference reactions described are those in which certain defenses are in the foreground of the transference phenomena. However, there are other defensive transference reactions in which certain instinctual and affective reactions are used as a defense against other instinctual and affective phenomena. For example, a woman patient maintains for long periods of time a strong sexual and erotic transference in order to ward off a deeper underlying hostile, aggressive transference. In patients of the same sex as the analyst, a persistent hostile transference may be used to defend against homosexual feelings. A similar situation exists with attitudes. Persistent submissiveness can be a defense against rebelliousness, or rebelliousness may be a defense against submissiveness which may mean passive homosexuality to the patient, etc. The above illustrations are examples of reaction formations occurring in the transference.

Defensive transference reactions always indicate there is a fear of some underlying instinctual and affective component. Defensive transference is usually ego syntonic and therefore presents an additional technical hurdle. It is first necessary to make the defensive transference ego alien and only then can one proceed to analyze it effectively. Defensive transference reactions are frequently found in pseudonormal characters, in candidates undergoing training analysis, in clinic cases treated without fee, and also in neurotic character disorders who need to maintain a normal façade. The additional technical problem such patients present is the need to expose the defensive transference as a resistance, to make it ego dystonic, to make it appear to the patient as a symptom (Reider, 1950; Gitelson, 1954). Only then can one go on to the analysis of the underlying impulses and affects.

3.83 Generalized Transference Reactions

Thus far in our discussion of the different types of transference phenomena and transference resistances, we have described reactions to the analyst which are derived from experience with specific significant persons in the patient's past. The patient loves or hates or dreads the analyst as he once dreaded or loved his father or mother or brother, etc. The patient's transference behavior toward his analyst is usually quite distinct and different from his behavior toward most of the people in his outside life except for those few who are similar transference figures. Transference reactions are ordinarily specific and circumscribed.

However, under the heading of Generalized Transference Reactions, I should like to describe a form of transference phenomenon which differs from all other previous forms precisely in being unspecific and uncircumscribed. Here the patient reacts to the analyst as he reacts to many or most of the people in his life. The transference behavior is not distinctive, it is typical and habitual. This behavior has been designated as "character transference" by Wilhelm Reich (1928, 1929), but others have considered this term misleading and ambiguous (A. Freud, 1936; Sterba, 1951).

What distinguishes this form of transference from others is that the reactions to the analyst are the patient's habitual, representative, and typical responses to people at large; the transference is characteristic of the patient's object relations in general. It is this quality of nonspecificality, of characteristicness, which led to the use of the term "character transference." However, the term "character" has other meanings and I find the term "generalized transference reaction" more precise.

Patients who react to their analyst with generalized transference will have feelings, attitudes, impulses, expectations, desires, fears, and defenses which had been molded into their character and which have become their presenting surface to the world at large. These traits are the relatively fixed results, the residuals, the compromises of various conflicts between instincts and defenses. This aspect of the personality contains both defensive and instinctual components, often condensed. During the course of psychoanalytic therapy, such transference reactions always serve an important resistance function. The student is referred to the standard works on the subject of character formation for a more thorough description of the dynamics (W. Reich, 1928, 1929; Fenichel, 1945a).

Let me give a typical example of a generalized transference reaction. A man in his middle fifties came for analysis because of a sleep disturbance and a fear of becoming addicted to sleeping pills. He was exceptionally successful in his profession and apparently so also in his family and social life. A vital factor in his various successes was his propensity for enthusiasm. He was a hail-fellow-well-met, witty, hearty, joyous, emotionally generous, outspoken, gregarious, the life of the party, etc. In short, he was an enthusiast.

He began his analysis just as he undertook any other project, eagerly, vigorously, and optimistically. He began each hour with a booming hello, interspersed his associations with jokes; his life's experiences were woven into fascinating stories; he found my interpretations brilliant, remarkable, or delightful. If my remarks pained him, he was awed and eager to confirm my findings. He admired me, flattered me, proclaimed my virtues to one and all, and recruited new patients for me. Although he knew the standard procedure of psychoanalysis, he repeatedly invited me to parties, even arranged parties with special celebrities he thought would interest me, and although I constantly declined, he was sure that sooner or later I would give in. He was convinced he was my favorite patient, although he knew I was bound by psychoanalytic convention to withhold this information. This manner of reacting to me was typical and characteristic of the way in which he reacted to most people, with whom it was highly successful. He was considered lovable and charming by people in all walks of life, by his family, his employees, his many mistresses, important executives, and famous artists.

This generalized transference reaction was difficult to handle. First of all, it was necessary for me to constrain my real and countertransference responses. Then I consistently had to point out to him the indiscriminateness of his behavior, the promiscuity of his loves, the constant restlessness which indicated a hidden discontent. Slowly I was able to demonstrate that this chronic enthusiasm, this feeling of being the favorite was a myth, a screen he tried to perpetuate. It failed him only in his sleep and in his dreams, when he had to relinquish his conscious controls. After many months of work, his enthusiasm became ego alien, he no longer approved of it, he realized it was fraudulent, and he dared let himself feel the underlying depression. Then his transference reaction changed, and I became at various times the hateful, hypocritical mother who seduced him and rejected him, the angry father, etc. Outside of the analysis his behavior changed too. Although he could still become enthusiastic and charming, it was controllable. He was eventually able to develop some worthy enemies and even at times to be boring. Then he was also able to sleep and to dream (Greenson, 1962).

The technical problems in generalized transference reactions are similar to those in defensive transference, since the generalized transference always serves an important defensive purpose and is ego syntonic. The first task is to convert the transference into an ego-dystonic, painful one so that the patient will actively work on the transference instead of trying to perpetuate it. Character resistances have to be changed into transference resistances (Fenichel, 1941, p. 68). Then the transference neurosis will evolve and fruitful analytic work can be accomplished. Further technical problems will be discussed in Section 3.10.

Generalized transference reactions occur in patients who suffer predominantly from character disorders. Each special type will produce a typical generalized transference; for example, an obsessive character will develop a generalized transference to the analyst which will be a replica of his isolated, obsessive object relations in general.

3.84 Acting Out of Transference Reactions

Since the case of Dora, whom he treated in 1900, Freud was aware of the great importance of recognizing and analyzing transference, transference resistances, and, in particular, the acting out of transference reactions. Dora broke off her treatment with Freud because he failed to recognize that a particular transference reaction of hers was derived from her lover and not from her father. Furthermore, the patient acted out this aspect of her transference. She acted toward Freud as she had wanted to do toward her lover, Herr K.; she deserted him. In reviewing the history and outcome of this case Freud (1905a) came to recognize the special importance of transference and the acting out of transference phenomena. He returned to the problem of acting out on several later occasions, particularly in reference to his work on the compulsion to repeat (1914c, 1920, 1937a). In recent years several other authors have made significant contributions to our understanding of the acting out of transference reactions (Fenichel, 1945a, 1945b; Greenacre, 1950; Spiegel, 1954; Bird, 1957, and the Additional Reading List).

Acting out occurs under a great variety of circumstances and not only as a transference reaction. The general subject of acting out will be developed further in Volume II. In the present section acting out will be discussed as a transference phenomenon occurring during the course of analysis and as a special variety of transference reaction.

Acting out refers to a well-organized, cohesive set of actions which appear to be purposeful, consciously willed, and ego syntonic, and which turn out to be a re-enactment of a past memory. The action is a slightly disguised repetition of the past, but the patient is not able to recall the past memory or memories. The patient seems intent upon acting instead of remembering; it is a defense against memory. During the course of analysis, patients will act out their transference reactions instead of reporting them in words and feelings. This may be acted out toward the analyst himself or outside the analysis toward others.

Some amount of acting out is inevitable in every analysis. This is due partly to the fact that the analyst attacks the neurotic defenses and thus encourages the discharge of affects and impulses in less distorted ways. This facilitates the breakthrough into actions. Secondly, transference itself is a reliving, a repetition of the past, and so mobilizes impulses from the past which may be expressed in behavior and actions. However, acting out will also be caused by the mishandling of the transference, particularly by the insufficient analysis of the negative transference. Errors in dosage, timing, and tact of interpretation often lead to acting out. Transference reactions of the analyst toward the patient can also set off acting out. However, the tendency to re-enact instead of remember will arise when non-verbal or preverbal material is attempting to gain expression during analysis or when traumatic material is approached.

Acting out is always a resistance even though it may serve some useful function temporarily. It is a defense against remembering, it is a defense against thinking, and it opposes the integration of thinking, memory, and behavior and thus opposes structural changes in the ego. However, some forms of acting out may serve a constructive purpose. I refer here to the transient, sporadic acting out which may occur in the breaking down of rigid, inhibiting defenses. This type should be differentiated from the habitual acting out of the chronic re-enactor. Then, too, acting out may be a form of trial recollection, a first testing out of a daring to remember (Ekstein and Friedman, 1957). In this sense it is a detour on the road to memory. My clinical experience seems to indicate that the memory which is re-enacted is a screen memory (Greenson, 1958a). The distortion inherent in the acting out is always in the direction of wish fulfill-ment. The overt actions are like the manifest content of a dream, an attempted fulfillment of a wish (Lewin, 1955). Finally, acting out is a form of nonverbal communication; despite its resistance func-tions, it is also a reaching out toward an object (Bird, 1957; Green-son, 1959a). It may be a cry for help (Winnicott, 1956b).

Acting out is only one specific form of neurotic re-enactment which may occur in and outside of analysis. It should be differenti-ated from reliving and symptomatic action, although this is not always clinically possible. In reliving there is a simple repetition and duplication of a past event. There is no distortion and it readily leads to memory. Usually this occurs in altered ego states, under the influence of intense emotions or drugs, fugue states, etc. Sympto-matic actions are not well organized and coherent; they are felt as bizarre, ego alien, and represent a failure of ego functioning. The past event has been greatly distorted and only a fragment of the event may be reported in the symptomatic action. Let me illustrate simple examples of acting out, reliving, and symptomatic action.

Mrs. K.[7] ended each hour by standing up and picking up the Kleenex upon which her head had been resting upon the pillow. As she would

[7] See Sections 1.24, 2.651, 2.71, 3.25, 3.42, 3.81.

walk to the door she would crumple the Kleenex in her hand, taking care to keep it from my view. She would then throw it into the waste-basket beneath my desk as she passed or place it in her purse. This was done as deftly as possible and I had the impression the patient hoped these actions would escape my notice. When I pointed out this behavior to Mrs. K., she readily acknowledged this but seemed surprised that I questioned it. Her attitude was: doesn't everybody? She felt her reactions were self-explanatory and indicated ordinary decorum. She continued to act in this way despite my attempts to understand the underlying meaning.

In one hour I was able to make some headway when I asked her to associate to the "soiled napkin" she tried to hide from me. This led to painful memories about her shame concerning menstruation. The behavior with the Kleenex continued. Finally, we began to analyze her terrible shame about her anus, that part of her she had to hide at all costs. She could not move her bowels when strangers were in her home for fear of being overheard or for fear the odors might betray her. After a bowel movement she spent considerable time in the bathroom to make it seem as if nothing had transpired. I pointed out she acted with the Kleenex as though it indicated a toilet activity she had to hide. Then she recalled many memories of her mother's fanaticism about toilet matters and cleanliness in the bathroom. Only then could she leave the Kleenex upon the pillow at the end of the hour.

Mrs. K. acted out at the end of each analytic hour: I am a clean girl who makes sure her toilet activities are not seen by others. Nobody must know I engage in such actions. It is not true that I do such dirty things; there is no evidence of it left behind. It was a cohesive, well-organized, purposeful set of actions, consciously willed and ego syntonic, serving to deny her past pleasurable toilet activities which she could not remember. In short, it was a form of acting out.

During World War II I gave a tail-gunner on a B-17 bomber, just returned from combat, an intravenous injection of sodium pentothal. He had been suffering from insomnia, nightmares, tremor, profuse sweating, and pronounced startle reaction. He had completed fifty combat missions, but was not aware of any troublesome anxiety and was reluctant to talk about combat. He agreed to take the pentothal because he had been told it felt like being drunk, and besides it meant he didn't have to talk to any officer. As soon as he had about 5 cc. in his vein, he jumped on top of the bed, tearing the needle out of his arm and began to scream at the top of his voice: "They're coming in at four o'clock, they're coming in at four o'clock, get 'em, get 'em, get 'em or they'll get us, those sons of bitches, get 'em. Oh Lord, get 'em, get 'em. Here they come again at one o'clock, at one o'clock, get 'em, get 'em, you bastards, get 'em, oh God, I'm hurt, I can't move, get 'em, get 'em, someone help me, I'm hit, I'm hit, I can't move, help me, Oh you bastards, help me, get 'em, get 'em."

The patient shouted and screamed like this for twenty minutes with his eyes full of terror and sweat pouring down his face. His left hand clutched his right arm which dangled limply. He was quivering and taut. I finally said, "Okay, Joe, I got 'em, I got 'em." With that he collapsed on the bed and fell into a deep sleep.

The next morning I saw him and asked if he recalled the pentothal interview. He smiled sheepishly and said he recalled yelling, but it's all hazy. I told him he talked about a mission when his right hand was hurt and he kept yelling "get 'em, get 'em." He interrupted me: "Oh, yes, I remember we were coming back from Schweinfurt and they jumped us and they started coming in at four o'clock and then at one o'clock and we got hit by flak, etc., etc."

The patient could easily recall the past event he had relived under the sodium pentothal. It was undistorted and accessible, which is typical of reliving.

I would now like to cite the following as a symptomatic action. One of my patients, a middle-aged man, cannot sit down in my waiting room. He stands embarrassedly in the corner until I open the door to my treatment room, and then instantly walks toward me. This behavior distresses him, he knows it is strange, yet he is overpowered by a strong fear when he tries to sit down. He has had similar reactions in other waiting rooms which he would conceal by coming late or leaving and re-entering on one pretext or another. It became more transparent when he began coming regularly for his analytic hour and I began to analyze his tendency to come late.

Over a period of about a year we uncovered the following determinants of his fear of sitting down in the waiting room. To be found sitting down signified to be "caught" sitting down, which meant to be discovered masturbating. He had masturbated sitting on the toilet as a boy and would jump up as soon as he heard someone approaching out of fear they would enter. There were no locks on the bathroom door in his home. To be sitting down when I was standing meant he was little and I was big, and he felt I could assault him physically. Furthermore, his father had insisted he jump to his feet when grownups entered a room, and now he was belatedly complying. He had rebelled against his father when he entered adolescence, and he felt guilty when his father died of a stroke. He had discovered his father sitting in a chair as though he were dozing, only to discover to his horror that he was in a coma. Thus standing up meant he was alive and to be found sitting meant to be like father—dead. Finally, to sit meant to take the feminine position while urinating, and he had to stand in my presence to indicate: see, I am a man.

Here we have an example of how an ego-alien, bizarre activity is carried out against the patient's will; he is compelled to enact it, it is a symptomatic act. Analysis reveals the many historical events which are condensed, distorted, and symbolized in this activity. In clear-cut cases, acting out, reliving, and symptomatic actions are easily distinguishable from each other. In clinical practice one does not often see the pure form, and one is often dealing with some admixture of the three varieties of neurotic re-enactments. Let us now return to our study of the acting out of transference reactions.

3.841 Acting Out Within the Analytic Setting

The simplest form of acting out of transference reactions occurs when the patient acts out something within the analytic setting. Freud gave the example of the patient who behaves defiantly and critically toward his analyst and cannot remember this kind of behavior in his past. He not only feels these emotions toward the analyst, but he acts upon them, refusing to talk, forgetting his dreams, etc. He is acting upon his feelings instead of reporting them; he is re-enacting a piece of the past instead of remembering it (Freud, 1914c, p. 150). Furthermore, he is not only unaware of the incongruity of his reactions, but he usually feels justified in his behavior. Acting out, as we have said, is ego syntonic.

Let me illustrate with the following example. A forty-year-old musician came for analysis because he suffered from chronic insomnia, colitis, and a work inhibition. When I was able to give him my first hour in the morning, at eight o'clock, he developed a remarkable pattern of beginning the hour. First of all, I could hear him coming down the hall because he would announce his arrival by loudly blowing his nose like a trumpet, each nostril separately and repeatedly. When he entered the treatment room, he would cheerfully and musically call out a good morning. Then, humming quietly, he would remove his jacket and drape it around one of the office chairs. He would walk over to the couch, sit down, and still humming quietly, he would begin to empty his pockets. First, the wallet and handkerchief from the back pockets would be placed on the side table; then the keys and change from his other pockets, and the ring from his finger. Then, with an audible groan, he would bend over and take off his shoes, placing them neatly side by side. He then would open the top button of his shirt, loosen his tie, and with an audible sigh of relief, he would lie down on the couch, turn over on his side, place his clasped hands between the pillow and his cheek, close his eyes and remain silent. Then, after a few moments he would begin to speak very softly.

At first I watched this performance silently; it seemed incredible that my patient was doing this seriously. Then, when I realized he was unaware of the inappropriateness of his behavior, I decided to try to fathom its meaning as precisely as possible before I confronted him. It was obvious that his acting out was in some way connected with going to sleep. Slowly I began to realize he was re-enacting the going to sleep of his father and mother, in which I was one parent and he was either the other parent or himself as a child. His history was full of memories of the terrible battles between his mother and father in their bedroom, which awakened him from sleep and terrified him. These fights occurred about four hours after he went to sleep as a child, and his present insomnia was characterized by his awakening after some four hours of sleep. He was acting out with me (a) how he wished his parents would have slept peacefully together, and (b) how he fantasied, as a child, he would have slept with either parent.

When I tried to draw his attention to his peculiar way of starting the hour, he was indignant. There was nothing peculiar about it, or strange, or noteworthy. He was only trying to relax and associate freely; after all, I had told him in the beginning of the analysis that all he had to do was relax and try to say whatever came to his mind. So now he was relaxing. It was true that he felt somewhat sleepy, but that was due to the earliness of the hour. Then he reluctantly admitted that when I spoke to him toward the end of the hour, he did feel it as a jarring note, an intrusion. He also realized that although for some strange reason he liked this early hour, he could hardly remember either what he had said or I had said. I then told him that all of this was due to the fact that he was coming to the hour to continue his sleep with me. He undressed as though he was going to bed and he lay on the couch with closed eyes and blissful expression because he felt that we were sleeping together and this is the peaceful sleep he must have wished for between his father and mother or between himself and one of his parents. Up until this point in the analysis, the patient had been able to recall only his hatred toward his parents for their constant battling at night or his jealous rivalry and sexual wishes to replace either his father or his mother in their double bed. My interpretation about the peaceful sleep wishes were the first step in reconstructing the patient's preoedipal wishes toward his father and mother (Lewin, 1955).

In the instances cited, a patient has feelings toward his analyst which he does not describe or report, but acts upon. One surreptitiously disposes of the tissue, one acts defiantly, and one goes to sleep. In all three a piece of the past is being re-enacted, but the patient cannot remember it and is reluctant to analyze the activity.

Finally, it turns out that the activity is a distortion of a past event, the action is an attempt at wish fulfillment. The patient acts out with the analyst what he wishes he had done in his past. It is my clinical experience that acting out is always a re-enactment of a past wish that originally could not be acted upon. The acting out then is the belated attempt at wish fulfillment.

Acting out within the framework of the analytic hour may not be limited to a certain episode or singular event, but may occur throughout long periods of the analysis. I have seen patients, particularly candidates in training, who act out the role of the "good" patient and who try to cast me in the role of the "perfect" analyst. This may go on for months and even years until one realizes there is a certain sterility and restrictedness in the analysis. Then the task is to expose this behavior as resistance and defense and uncover the underlying hostility. I have seen a parallel situation in patients who maintain an attitude and feeling that they are my favorite patient. My eight o'clock sleepy patient was this way. He consciously believed he was my favorite patient and when I interpreted this as his wish and need, he replied that he knew that I was bound by my Freudian oath to keep my true feelings quiet. When I made interpretations which any other patient would have experienced as painful, he would react by admiring my astuteness and enjoying vicariously my supposed triumph. He loved the analysis and, above all, being analyzed by me. He felt we were a wonderful combination, he and I, me with my brains and he with his imagination. Even though his symptoms did not improve and he retained little insight, he was delighted with the analysis. I had to point out to him energetically, again and again, that he did not seem to be coming for analysis, he was coming to re-enact the delightful feeling of being the favorite. Slowly he began to recall and recount being mother's favorite and father's, too, and then these memories were found to be screens against bitter disappointments from both parents.

3.842 Acting Out Outside of the Analysis

A young married woman patient began a sexual affair unexpectedly during her analysis. I became convinced, by the following clinical findings, that it was an acting out of her transference feelings: the patient had hardly known this man, and he was quite different from the men she was ordinarily attracted to. He was artistic, acted like a professor, and looked like an ancient Roman—these qualities attracted her. The affair occurred when I had to miss a few hours to attend a meeting. She had begun the analysis with a positive transference which blossomed into an erotic, sexual one. This had been interpreted and seemed to have been temporarily resolved. I recalled that during the phase of her strong love for me she had described me as a professor and an artist. Also she had once dreamed of me in a Roman toga and in association to that dream claimed I combed my hair like a Roman, and had heard my nickname was "Romi." It seemed clear that the young lady was acting out her sexual and romantic feelings with the young man. She enacted with him what she had wanted to and was unable to enact with me. These wishes were a repetition of deeply repressed feelings she had had to her stepfather.

A male patient in analysis suddenly develops a close relationship to his internist, a man he had never known socially. Now the patient invites him frequently for dinner and engages in intimate conversations with this doctor. Obviously, his wishes for intimacy with me are being acted upon outside of his analysis. When this occurs, the wish for intimacy with me is not being expressed in the analytic hour. It was my interpretation of the acting out which brought these unconscious wishes (unconscious as far as they refer to me) back into the analysis.

It is characteristic, when transference feelings are being acted out outside the analysis, that the impulses and affects which are being acted out do not appear in the analytic situation proper. A student in analysis with me is constantly critical of the stupidity of his teachers, their laziness and ineptness. At the same time, his transference feelings toward me are consistently positive. It was the lack of any hostile transference to me and the constant hostility toward the teachers that made me realize he was acting out his negative transference.

The splitting off of the ambivalent or preambivalent transference, with one aspect being acted out outside of the analysis, is a frequent form of acting out. It is often to be observed in candidates in training. Usually the ego-alien transference is vented upon some outside analyst and only the ego-syntonic feelings are expressed toward the personal analyst. Thus hostile and homosexual feelings will be discharged onto other analysts and the less disturbing emotions and impulses will be reserved for one's own analyst. Or the split will take place on a "good" and "bad" analyst basis, with some outside analyst serving in the auxiliary role.

It should be remembered that the acting out which occurs during analysis is not only connected to the transference situation. Very often it will be found that such acting out has been going on prior to the analysis. The co-actors in such situations will themselves turn out to be transference figures (Bird, 1957). This will be discussed in Volume II.

I would now like to give an illustration of a combination of acting out and symptomatic action involving the transference. For several hours a male patient finds fault with whatever I do in the analysis. He finds my silence oppressive and my interventions irritating and hostile. Actually, he admits that he likes the analytic hour until I begin to talk or until he expects me to talk. He can tell when I am about to intervene because he can hear my chair squeak or my breathing change. A short dream and the associations to it provided some important clues for the understanding of his reactions. In the dream somebody was listening to a radio commentator, Gabriel Heater, who had the voice of doom. The patient associates to this the fact that this broadcaster was his father's favorite and the entire family was forced to listen to this man whenever his father came home for dinner. This brings up the memory how father's homecoming changed the atmosphere; he was a wet blanket. He spoiled the fun for the family, at least for the patient. He could always tell when his father was coming home because he always came home twenty minutes before seven and he always whistled as he approached the house. Whenever the patient noticed the approach of seven o'clock or heard the whistle, he would become irritable and hostile.

I was struck by the many parallels between how the patient behaved toward me in the hour and how he reacted to his father's homecoming. I made the following formulations to him: As long as I kept silent in the hour and let the patient talk and as long as it was early in the hour, the patient enjoyed the analytic situation just as he enjoyed being at home with his doting mother and his sisters. This was peaceful and pleasurable. About twenty minutes before the end of the hour the patient began to anticipate my interrupting his secret fun at home. The squeaking of my chair or the change in my breathing rate reminded him of his father's whistle. My interpretations were like the "voice of doom," the father's return home, the end of the patient's pleasure with his mother and his sisters. The patient confirmed these formulations by adding that "in all honesty" he had to admit that his father's homecoming was painful only to him; the mother and sisters looked forward to it. This example illustrates how in the analytic hour the patient re-enacted with me a piece of his past history with his family. In the beginning of the hour he was the big talker and I represented the quiet and admiring mother and sisters. Toward the end of the hour, when it was my turn to speak, I became the overbearing and disturbing father. Since the situation was ego dystonic and very painful to the patient, he worked very diligently in attempting to reconstruct and remember the past events which lay behind this neurotic re-enactment.

As was stated earlier, all forms of neurotic re-enactments may occur in pure form, but usually one finds admixtures of reliving, symptomatic action, and acting out. The crux of the matter is determined by whether the neurotic re-enactment is ego syntonic or ego alien. It is always an additional resistance when the re-enactment is ego syntonic. It is then always more difficult to enlist the patient's reasonable ego, to establish a working alliance, and to uncover or reconstruct the underlying memories.

3.9 The Technique of Analyzing the Transference

3.91 GENERAL CONSIDERATIONS

It should be noted that the title of this section is "The Technique of Analyzing the Transference" and not "The Interpretation or the Management of the Transference." The reason for this is that, although interpretation is the decisive instrument for dealing with transference phenomena in the psychoanalytic procedure, other technical implements are also necessary. The interpretation of a transference reaction is the ultimate technical step in dealing with transference phenomena; but in order to interpret the transference effectively there are a variety of necessary preliminary steps. Edward Bibring (1954) stressed the fact that with our increased knowledge of ego psychology the psychoanalyst has become more aware of the necessity for carefully clarifying a particular psychic phenomenon before he attempts to interpret it. Fenichel (1941) and Kris (1951) have also emphasized the importance of clearly demonstrating and illuminating the subject under consideration before one attempts to interpret its unconscious meaning. As I have stated before, demonstration, clarification, interpretation, and working through a psychic event can be considered "analyzing" a given phenomenon.

The reason for bringing the concept of the "management" of the transference into the discussion is that the psychoanalyst is called upon to do more than "analyze" in order to handle the transference properly. By no means should this statement obscure the fact that it is the *analysis* of the transference that is essential and characteristic of psychoanalysis. However, in order to make a psychic event analyzable, it may be necessary at times to undertake other procedures (E. Bibring, 1954; Eissler, 1953; Menninger, 1958, Chapt. VI; as well as this volume Section 1.34).

For example, since classical psychoanalytic technique is aimed at facilitating the maximum development of all the varieties and intensities of the transference reactions, and since transference phenomena arise spontaneously in the patient, our technique must include waiting nonintrusively and patiently. The judicious use of waiting in silence is one of the most important tools for facilitating the development of the transference. Yet, strictly speaking, it is a manipulation. Silence in the analyst can help the patient develop and feel a greater intensity of his transference reactions. The eventual emotional abreaction can bring the greatest conviction to the patient of the reality of his feelings. However, silence in the analyst and emotional abreaction in the patient are, strictly speaking, nonanalytic measures. They can also lead to traumatic situations and massive resistances unless the therapist "analyzes" at the proper time. Only by analyzing can one resolve a transference reaction and thus make way for another variety and intensity of transference reaction to come to the fore.

Suggestion too has its place in the management of the transference. We ask our patients to free-associate and to let their feelings develop spontaneously. We suggest in this way that his feelings are permissible and manageable. Our silence may also suggest to him that we expect him to bear certain feelings, painful as they may be, and that it will all lead to a useful end. When we inquire about whether the patient recalls his dreams, we suggest that he does dream and can remember. Particularly in the beginning of analysis, when the patient knows little about us and about the psychoanalytic procedure, it is suggestion which enables him to risk going along with us. Eventually, that transference feeling which made the patient suggestible or manipulatable will have to be analyzed and resolved. See Charles Fisher (1953) for a further study of this and related problems.

The same is true for all the other nonanalytic interventions. All nonautonomous therapeutic influences upon the patient must eventually be brought to consciousness and thoroughly analyzed. However, it is important to recognize that nonanalytic measures are necessary to some degree in every analysis. Suggestion and manipulation have fallen into disrepute in psychoanalytic circles because they have been misused. They do not replace analysis, they prepare for it or are adjunctive procedures. Interpretations alone, "pure" analysis, is a nontherapeutic procedure, a research tool. Although this section focuses on the *analysis* of transference phenomena, the clinical examples will illustrate and clarify the interrelations between the analytic and the nonanalytic techniques. It is the proper blending of these techniques which makes for the art of psychotherapy.

There are several other factors which make the analysis of transference so complicated and so important. First of all, there are the two antithetical properties of transference phenomena. On the other hand, the transference itself may become the source of the greatest resistance to the analytic work. Then, too, the pathological defenses themselves are also transferred and we have combinations of transference productions and transference resistances simultaneously.

One of the ever-present technical questions is to determine when the current transference is furthering the course of the analysis and when it is in opposition; each of these situations requires different interventions. It has been my clinical experience, and I believe also the experience of other analysts, that the most frequent cause of a patient's prematurely breaking off his psychoanalytic therapy is the improper handling of the transference situation (Freud, 1905a). There is the further problem: to produce material the patient needs to develop a transference neurosis. To work analytically on this material, to assimilate it, the patient also has to develop a working alliance. These two developments are in opposition to each other. How do we accomplish both? (See Section 3.5.)

It follows from this discussion that the technique of analyzing the transference phenomena has to concern itself with the following questions: (1) How do we safeguard the natural evolution of the patient's transference? (2) When do we permit the transference to develop spontaneously and under what conditions is it necessary to intervene? (3) When it becomes necessary to intervene, what technical steps are required for the analysis of a transference reaction? (4) How do we facilitate the development of the working alliance?

I shall take up the first three questions in sequence. I shall add the consideration about the working alliance in each section whenever it is indicated. The working alliance must continuously be kept in mind.

3.92 THE SAFEGUARDING OF THE TRANSFERENCE

The concept of safeguarding the transference refers to the principle of protecting the patient's relationship to his analyst so that he can develop the greatest variety and intensity of transference reactions in accordance with his own unique individual history and his own needs. Throughout Freud's technical papers one can find various references to and recommendations about how this can be accomplished (Freud, 1912b, 1915a, 1919a). Greenacre clarified and amplified many of these points in an important paper presented in 1954. Her essay was of particular significance at the time because there was a considerable difference of opinion among prominent American psychoanalysts as to the necessity for observing classical procedures in psychoanalytic technique.

3.921 The Psychoanalyst as a Mirror

Freud (1912b) made the recommendation that the psychoanalyst should be like a mirror to his patient. This has been misunderstood and misconstrued to mean that the psychoanalyst should be cold and unresponsive to his patient. Actually, I believe Freud meant something very different. His reference to the mirror implied that the analyst's behavior and attitude in the patient's neurotic conflicts should be "opaque" so that it should reflect back to the patient nothing but what the patient had manifested. The analyst's personal values and preferences should not intrude into the analysis of those conflicts. It is the consistent neutrality of the analyst in such situations that makes it possible for the patient's distorted and unrealistic reactions to become demonstrable as such. Furthermore, the analyst must try to mute his own responses so that he is relatively anonymous to the patient (Freud, 1912b, pp. 117-118). Only in this way can the patient's transference reactions come into clear focus so that they can be singled out and distinguished from more realistic reactions. Above all, in order to analyze transference phenomena, it is important to keep the field of interaction between patient and analyst relatively free from contamination and artifacts. Any mode of behavior or attitude on the part of the analyst other than that of consistent, humane nonintrusiveness obscures and distorts the development and recognition of transference phenomena. Let me give some examples of contamination.

Some years ago, a patient of mine who suffered from stomach ulcers and depressions went through a long period of unproductive work in the analysis at the same time that his symptoms flared up. We both recognized that a resistance was operative, but we were unable to make any real meaningful headway against the worsening of the symptoms or the persistence of the strong resistance. Over a period of a few months, I slowly began to realize that the patient had changed in some of his attitudes toward me. Previously he had been prone to joke or tease or spite me in little harmless ways. Now he was more compliant, but joyless and sullen. Earlier, his spitefulness was obvious and sporadic. Now he was superficially cooperative, but covertly stubborn. One day he told me he had dreamed of a jackass and then lapsed into a sullen silence. After a period of silence on my part, I asked him what was going on. He answered with a sigh that he had been thinking maybe the two of us are jackasses. After a pause he added, "I won't budge and you won't either. You won't change and I won't change [silence]. I tried to change but it made me sick." I was puzzled, I had no idea what he was referring to. I then asked him how had he *tried* to change. The patient answered that he had tried to change his political beliefs in accordance with mine.

He had been a lifelong Republican (which I had known), and he had tried, in recent months, to adopt a more liberal point of view, because he knew I was so inclined. I asked him how he knew I was a liberal and anti-Republican. He then told me that whenever he said anything favorable about a Republican politician, I always asked for associations. On the other hand, whenever he said anything hostile about a Republican, I remained silent, as though in agreement. Whenever he had a kind word for Roosevelt, I said nothing. Whenever he attacked Roosevelt, I would ask who did Roosevelt remind him of, as though I was out to prove that hating Roosevelt was infantile.

I was taken aback because I had been completely unaware of this pattern. Yet, the moment the patient pointed it out, I had to agree that I had done precisely that, albeit unknowingly. We then went to work on why he felt the need to try to swallow my political views. This turned out to be his way of ingratiating himself with me. This proved to be indigestible and also lowered his self-esteem, leading to the ulcer symptoms and the depressiveness. (The dream of the jackass expressed in a very condensed form his hostility to the Democratic Party which uses a donkey as a symbol, and his resentment of my persistent lack of astuteness about his predicament—the jackass is noted for stupidity and stubbornness. It also depicts his self-image.)

I treated another patient some years ago who had interrupted her treatment with another analyst after a prolonged stalemate. The immediate cause of the unresolved resistance was her discovery that the previous analyst was a devoutly religious man who attended the synagogue regularly. A friend of hers had reported this to the patient and later the patient had verified it herself. The patient confronted the analyst, but he refused to confirm or deny this fact. He did say that he felt they should continue working together. The patient, unfortunately, became increasingly more resentful of the interventions and interpretations the analyst had made in the past which now seemed to her to have been in the direction of persuading her to accept a belief in God. This the previous analyst denied, but the patient maintained her skepticism. She finally concluded that she was unable to work effectively with him any longer.

This same patient asked me whether I was religious and I told her I would not answer her question because I felt any answer would contaminate our relationship. She accepted this point of view. Later in her analysis with me it became clear that she felt she could not respect anyone, let alone be analyzed by anyone who was devoutly religious. Furthermore, the previous analyst's evasiveness, after she had discovered the facts, made him an untrustworthy figure.

In both cases the contamination of the transference interfered with the full development of the transference neurosis and became a source of prolonged resistance. In both cases the trait that was revealed to the patient was extremely painful and anxiety producing. I do believe that it is of decisive importance how such situations are handled. The most serious consequences arise when such contamination is not recognized by the analyst. It is equally destructive when the analyst refuses to acknowledge the reality of what has transpired. Only straightforwardness on the part of the analyst and thorough analysis of the patient's reactions can repair such breaches of the analyst's incognito.

There is no doubt that the less the patient really knows about the psychoanalyst, the more easily he can fill in the blank spaces with his own fantasies. Furthermore, the less the patient actually knows about the analyst, the easier it becomes for the analyst to convince the patient that his reactions are displacements and projections. However, it should be borne in mind that at best the analyst's incognito is only a relative matter since everything in the analytic office and routine does reveal something about the analyst. Even the analyst's determination to remain anonymous is revelatory. Furthermore, frozen, wooden, or extremely passive behavior interferes with the development of a working alliance. How can a patient permit his most intimate fantasies to emerge in regard to an analyst who shows only fixed emotional uninvolvement or a ritualistic adherence to rules and regulations. It is true that knowledge about the analyst may make transference fantasies more difficult to develop, but strict aloofness and excessive passivity make the development of the working alliance almost impossible. They produce a transference neurosis that may be intense but narrow and intractable.

Greenacre goes so far as to suggest that analysts ought to keep out of the public eye and not become associated with any social, political or scientific causes (1954, pp. 681-683; 1966b). However, after one has lived in a community for a long time, it is not always possible to remain unknown or unidentifiable. This same problem is always present when training analysts attempt to analyze candidates in their own institutes, and it is always a complicating circumstance. However, it does not necessarily make for an unanalyzable obstacle. Psychoanalysts who are known in their community also have a contaminated transference to contend with. Their patients often come to the first interviews with a transference reaction already established, based on the analyst's reputation and the patient's fantasies. Analysts who become a subject for public discussion not only interfere with the image of the analyst as a mirror but also offer various transference gratifications to the patient. Yet analysis is not impossible under such circumstances, if the analyst is alert to the problem. The contaminated transference material has to be brought into the analysis early and consistently and the patient's reaction to such information has to be thoroughly analyzed. (The problem in training analysis is more serious; the analyst has real power over the candidate's professional career.)

However, it should also be pointed out that many patients are extremely intuitive and pick up a good deal of knowledge about their analyst just from the everyday analytic work. Some patients do this sooner and some later, but eventually all patients get to know a goodly amount about their analyst in reality. No matter what its source, however, all knowledge about the analyst has to become the subject matter of the analysis as soon as it becomes the vehicle for unconscious fantasies (see Section 3.6).

The "rule of the mirror," however, possesses dangers for the establishment of the working alliance if it is carried to extremes. Freud himself said that the first aim of the treatment it to establish rapport with the patient, and this can be done only by adopting an attitude of "sympathetic understanding" (1913b, pp. 139-140). See Section 3.543 for a further discussion of this point.

3.922 The Rule of Abstinence

Freud (1915a) made the important recommendation that the treatment should be carried out, as far as possible, with the patient in a state of abstinence. He stated very clearly: "*Analytic treatment should be carried through, as far as is possible, under privation—in a state of abstinence*" (Freud, 1919a, p. 162). "Cruel though it may sound," he added, "we must see to it that the patient's suffering, to a degree that is in some way or other effective, does not come to an end prematurely" (p. 163). The patient's symptoms, which drove him into treatment, consist in part of warded-off instincts seeking satisfaction. These instinctual impulses will turn to the analyst and the analytic situation as long as the analyst consistently avoids offering the patient substitute gratifications. The prolonged frustration will induce the patient to regress, so that his entire neurosis will be re-experienced in the transference, the transference neurosis. However, allowing symptom-substitute gratifications of any magnitude, in or outside of the analytic situation, will rob the patient of his neurotic suffering and his motivations to continue treatment (Glover, 1955, p. 167; Fenichel, 1941, pp. 29-30).

The rule of abstinence has been misunderstood and misconstrued to mean that the patient was prohibited from enjoying any instinctual gratification during the analysis. Actually, Freud was trying to prevent the patient from making a premature "flight into health" and effecting a so-called "transference cure."

In order to ensure the maintenance of adequate motivation, (a) it is necessary for the psychoanalyst consistently to point out to the patient the infantile and unrealistic quality of the instinctual satisfaction which the patient is attempting to obtain; and (b) to make sure that the analyst is in no way consciously or unconsciously gratifying the patient's infantile neurotic instinctual needs. It is item (b) which is of particular concern to us in this discussion of safeguarding the transference.

Transference gratifications of any and all kinds which are undetected and unanalyzed can prevent the optimal evolution of the patient's transference neurosis. One of the most frequent consequences is fixating the patient's transference reactions. For example, analysts who behave toward their patients with a constant open warmth and emotional responsiveness will find that their patients tend to react with a prolonged positive and submissive transference. The patients of these analysts will have difficulty in permitting themselves to develop a negative, hostile transference. Such patients may form a quick but thin working alliance and then have anxiety about allowing their transference reactions to deepen and broaden beyond the early positive and submissive phase. The transference gratifications they receive from their warmhearted analysts prolong their dependency on such supplies of satisfaction and make them ward off the negative transference.

On the other hand, analysts whose manner tends to be aloof and harsh will often find that their patients quickly and persistently form a negative and hostile transference reaction. In such situations it may be difficult for the patients to become deeply and broadly involved in other transference reactions. Their mistrust of the analyst keeps the transference neurosis from developing the full spectrum and range of its potential. If the analysis survives long enough, these patients may then develop a sadomasochistic transference relationship which may be intense but which also proves resistant to analysis and to change.

I recently began treating a patient who had more than six years of analysis with an analyst in another city. The young woman's presenting complaints had barely changed despite hard work on the part of the patient and the analyst. I realized something must have gone wrong in the analyst-patient relationship when the patient would frequently try to quote verbatim long interpretations her previous analyst had given her. For example, I once asked if she knew what was making her so evasive in a particular hour. She promptly replied that perhaps it was an attempt to castrate me for having rejected her dependency needs in the last session. I asked her to explain what that actually meant and she became flustered and finally admitted she wasn't sure, but this was something her previous analyst had often said to her. She had been reluctant to ask for clarification because he had teased her and had become sarcastic on earlier occasions. He would say things like: "It's a pity to throw out your money if you come and you don't listen," or, "Maybe you will remember if I don't gratify this dependency need either."

There are other forms of transference gratification and provocations which can arise from the analyst's unconscious wish to be the guide, mentor, or parent of the patient. This usually leads the analyst to give advice, to make small talk, to be excessively reassuring, or to be over-concerned.

A more serious complication arises when the analyst becomes consciously or unconsciously seductive. This not only stirs up the patient's incestuous longings but brings with it enormous guilt and prolonged overidealization of the analyst. When this eventually breaks down, there is great rage and anxiety (Greenacre, 1966b).

I can summarize this part of the discussion by stating that the analyst must be vigilant about not gratifying his patient's infantile instinctual wishes because doing so will prevent the full development of the transference neurosis. As a consequence, the patient will either interrupt treatment or have an interminable, stalemated analytic experience.

The "rule of abstinence," however, if carried to extremes, conflicts with the establishment of a working alliance. Although clinical evidence has proved that a prerequisite for regressive transference reactions is consistent frustration of the patient's infantile wishes, excessive frustration of the patient also produces interminable or interrupted analyses (see Stone, 1961, p. 53; Glover, 1955, pp. 88-107; Fenichel, 1941, p. 74; Menninger, 1958, pp. 53-58). One of our fundamental technical tasks, therefore, is to reconcile these two sets of antithetical requirements (Greenson, 1966). This needs to be spelled out in some detail because these opposing requirements make inordinate demands on the psychoanalyst and the patient.

It is important to realize that the way the classical psychoanalyst handles the relationship between the patient and himself is both unique and artificial and runs counter to the way human beings usually relate to one another. It is a tilted and uneven relationship in that the patient is expected to let himself feel and express all of his innermost emotions, impulses, and fantasies while the analyst remains a relatively anonymous figure (Greenacre, 1954, p. 674; Stone, 1961, p. 80). Early in analysis, and from time to time afterward, patients will protest against the inequities of this situation. (If they do not complain, this should be explored.) The patient's complaints first have to be analyzed, but one does not have to deny the artificiality or the unevenness of the relationship. In my opinion, the patient has a right to an explanation of the reasons for the analyst's maintaining the relationship as he does. I do not believe this should be optional, because the patient has the *need* to have his rights protected. The analytic procedure is inevitably a painful, one-sided, demeaning experience for the patient. If we want him to emerge as an independent human being and to work along with us as a co-worker, we cannot continually demean him by not explaining the instrumentalities we use. We cannot treat him like a child and then expect him to become a mature individual. Just as it is important to safeguard the transference situation, it is equally important to safeguard the rights, the self-esteem of the patient. I have illustrated these points in the different clinical examples cited in Section 3.5.

The most vivid example and perhaps the most illuminating is the case of Mr. Z.[8] He is the young man who had several years of relatively unpro-

---

[8] See Sections 2.52, 2.54, 2.71, 3.531, and 3.711.

ductive analysis in another city. Some of the difficulty had derived from the atmosphere which his first analyst created in his manner of working. When the young man in one of his first hours with me on the couch took out a cigarette and lit it, I asked him how he felt when he decided to light the cigarette. He answered that he knew he was not supposed to smoke in his previous analysis and now he supposed that I, too, would forbid it. I told him immediately that all I wanted at the moment was to know what feelings, ideas, and sensations were going on in him at the moment that he decided to light the cigarette.

In a later hour, the patient asked me whether I was married. I countered by asking him what his fantasies were about that. I later explained and demonstrated the value of my not answering him. The patient then told me that his former analyst had never answered the many questions he asked in the beginning of his previous analysis but did not trouble to explain why he was silent.

He had experienced his analyst's silence as a degradation and humiliation, and he now realized that his own subsequent silences were a retaliation for this imagined injustice. Somewhat later he saw that he had identified himself with his first analyst's supposed contempt. Mr. Z. felt disdain for his analyst's prudishness, but at the same time was full of severe self-reproach for his own sexual practices, which he then projected onto the analyst. Ascertaining when a patient is entitled to an explanation will be discussed more fully in Volume II.

It is necessary for the analyst to feel close enough to the patient to be able to empathize with the most intimate details of his emotional life; yet he must be able to become distant enough for dispassionate understanding. This is one of the most difficult requirements of psychoanalytic work—the alternation between the temporary and partial identification of empathy and the return to the distant position of the observer, the evaluator, etc. For the analyst there is no area of the patient's life from which he may be excluded, but this intimacy must not lead to familiarity. It is a natural tendency to respond emotionally and instinctually to another human being's intimate needs and sufferings, but these responses in the analyst must predominantly serve his understanding of the patient. They may not be allowed to intrude upon the person of the patient. The analyst's sympathy or undue compassion, if revealed to the patient, might be perceived either as a transference reward or punishment. It would mar the anonymous mirrorlike surface which the analyst requires for demonstrating that the patient's reaction is indeed a transference reaction. Yet if one shows no sympathy for the patient, how can one expect him to bare the most intimate, most vulnerable aspects of his mental and emotional life?

The answer is complicated. On the one hand, the analyst's therapeutic commitments to the patient should be in the background of all his undertakings. This does not have to be verbalized; it should be felt by the patient's reasonable ego.

The analyst is a treater of the neurotically sick; he is not primarily a research worker or a detached data collector. The analysis is a treatment situation, and the analysand is a patient. In order to empathize we have to feel to some degree the same quality of emotions or impulses the patient is feeling. However, this should not be flagrantly demonstrated to the patient. We collect our data by empathizing, but our response has to be restrained. Our task is to oscillate and blend the opposing positions: the involved empathizer, the detached sorter and understander of data, and the restrained but compassionate transmitter of insight and interpretations. This is an oversimplified condensation of the art and science of psychoanalytic therapy.

By observing the rules of maintaining one's incognito and of abstaining from transference gratifications, the analyst can safeguard the evolution of the patient's transference reactions. However, competent psychoanalysts are also human beings with frailties and limitations. I doubt whether any analyst is able to maintain a consistent compassion and concern combined with restraint over a period of many years without some occasional lapse. What is essential for psychoanalytic technique, however, is that the analyst be aware of his shortcomings. He must be especially vigilant in situations that he knows are potentially difficult for him. If errors occur, these must be recognized by the analyst and acknowledged to the patient at the proper time. Then the patient's reactions to the analyst's deviation must be thoroughly analyzed.

One danger is the tendency to gloss over the impact of the error on the patient and to confess merely the fact that the error has occurred. Another danger is to overemphasize the magnitude of the error and out of guilt feelings attempt to make reparation to the patient, instead of just thoroughly analyzing the patient's reactions. When errors occur repeatedly, this is an indication that (a) some analysis is needed by the analyst on this score, and (b) perhaps the patient should be sent to another analyst (see Section 3.10.4).

The safeguarding of the patient's transference, while simultaneously promoting the development of the working alliance, entails the most exacting demands in carrying out classical psychoanalysis. Greenacre is right when she says that psychoanalysis is a severe taskmaster (1954, p. 684). The psychoanalyst, in addition to his constant alertness to the happenings in his patients, must have the honesty and humility to scrutinize his own personal reactions.

To summarize: The analyst has two simultaneous tasks which are essentially in opposition to each other. He has to safeguard the development of both the transference neurosis and the working alliance. To safeguard the transference he has to maintain his anonymity and deprivational attitude toward the patient's neurotic wishes for gratification. To safeguard the working alliance he has to protect the patient's rights, show a consistently therapeutic attitude, and behave in a humane way. These requirements are extremely demanding. Errors are prone to occur which have to be recognized and thus made part of the subject matter of the analysis.

3.93 When Do We Analyze the Transference?

3.931 When It Is a Resistance

From our previous discussion of transference and resistance it became clear how closely interwoven these two phenomena can be. Some transference reactions cause resistances, some transference reactions appear as resistances, some serve as resistances against other forms of transference, and some resistances serve to ward off transference reactions. The important technical point is that whenever a transference reaction of any kind opposes the analytic work, when its predominant function is resistance, or when it serves a significant even if not predominant obstructive purpose, then the transference has to be analyzed.

This rule has to be modified, however, in accordance with our knowledge about the working alliance. We analyze transference resistance only when a reasonable ego, a working alliance is present. If the transference resistance is significant but not demonstrable, our first task is to make sure it becomes demonstrable. In other words, before we analyze we must be sure a reasonable ego, a working alliance is present. The technique for doing so is exactly the same as described for dealing with other resistances.

Usually, *silence* on the part of the analyst is enough to bring the transference resistance into sharp relief. If this does not succeed, then often *confrontation* will make the patient aware of the transference resistance, e.g., such interventions as: "You seem to be afraid to talk to me openly about such and such," or "You seem to be avoiding your feelings about me," etc.

If these two methods are not sufficient, one can try to *intensify* the transference resistance by asking questions about that area which the patient is trying to avoid.

Let me give a simple example: After a few months of analysis a young woman patient begins the hour by telling me I look different this particular morning. "I might even say you seem attractive, sort of." After a pause she says she "guesses" she had "positive feelings" toward me. Then she goes on to talk trivia. I point this out and suggest she is running away from something. She has no idea what this could be and halfheartedly pursues the matter. After a time, I bring her back to the point where she began to run and say I have the impression that the avoiding started when she said she "guesses" she has "positive feelings" to me. I ask her to please clarify this for me; what does she really mean by that term, "positive feelings" for me. Now the patient becomes completely silent; she squirms on the couch, she crosses her legs, she clasps her hands tightly together. I can detect a flush on her cheeks. Then she begins to stammer: "You know what I mean, positive feelings, you know, I don't hate you, I guess, I sort of like you, kind of . . . you know. . . ." Now the transference resistance has become demonstrable. I can pursue the question: why is this so hard for you to tell me? Then her fear of being laughed at comes out. Then, feeling reassured by my not laughing, she can describe her feelings of attraction for me in more concrete terms.

The question of demonstrability is not exhausted by this discussion. There is still the element of intensity, which needs to be considered on its own merits and which plays a special role in all questions of "when do we interpret." It is usually easier to demonstrate a psychic event of great strength than a weaker one. Furthermore, the greater the intensity of a given phenomenon, the more conviction will the patient have when he is confronted with it. Therefore, one usually waits for the transference resistance to reach an intensity that will make it undeniable and that will also bring a feeling of conviction with it. The problem of the optimal level of intensity will be pursued further in Section 3.932.

What kinds of transference reactions are most likely to produce resistances? The answer to this is not a simple one, for all qualities and quantities of transference may produce important resistances. However, there are a few generalizations which seem to be valid and helpful. Ego-syntonic transference reactions will produce resistances because the ego syntonicity will tend to prevent the patient from splitting off an observing ego when the analyst tries to get the patient to work on the transference. In short, the patient is not able to develop a working alliance in regard to certain of his feelings toward me. This can lead to the patient defending, justifying, or denying the transference reaction as suitable material for the analysis. It is particularly apt to occur in chronic and subtle transference reactions. An example is Mrs. K., to whom I referred in Sections 1.24, 2.651, 2.71, 3.25, 3.42, 3.81, 3.84.

Mrs. K. maintained for several years an idealized picture of me as a wonderfully humane person. All the pain and deprivations of the psychoanalytic treatment she blamed on psychoanalysis as a science. She felt I was merely the reluctant tool of this harsh and demanding form of therapy. My attempts to identify this splitting of the transference as a resistance she listened to patiently but did not believe. Actually she felt it was further proof of my modesty. My occasional lapses she cherished as more evidence of how honest and straightforward I was. The patient refused to recognize this prolonged and unchanging set of feelings as a resistance, despite dreams and slips obviously indicating latent anger and hatred. At most she paid lip service to this notion and admitted that perhaps, intellectually, she could follow my ideas, but she could not feel any sign within her of hostile feelings toward me. Only much later in the analysis, when her fear of homosexuality decreased and she became able to enjoy some of her sexual life with her husband, did she dare to let herself feel some of her deep-seated hatred for me. Only then did she develop a working alliance in regard to her hostility to me.

Intensely emotional transference reactions may also produce resistances. Patients in the throes of intense love or hatred may wish merely to vent these emotions upon the analyst and have no desire to analyze, to gain any insight. As long as these feelings are overwhelming or ego syntonic, the patient seeks for discharge gratification, abreaction. The quest for understanding comes to the fore only when the transference intensity is diminished or felt as ego dystonic, ego alien. Intense love and hatred can be productive as transference reactions if a working alliance can be mobilized and maintained despite the strong feelings.

By and large, however, all other things being equal: the hostile, aggressive, negative transference is more likely to produce resistance and a disturbance in the working alliance than loving, positive feelings. Sexual and romantic feelings are more prone to stir up resistance than friendliness or other desexualized varieties of love. Pregenital impulses will cause greater resistances than impulses of greater maturity. Masochism is a great source of resistance, as is the fear of passive homosexual strivings and primitive hatred of the mother in men, and penis envy and primitive love of the mother in women.

The return to the technical question: When do we intervene in the transference situation? Our first answer is: we intervene when the transference is producing a resistance; we try first to make sure that a reasonable ego and a working alliance are present and then analyze the resistance. It does not matter what quality or quantity of transference is involved: we intervene when we see signs of significant resistance, when the analytic work is unproductive, stalemated, or emotionally thin. But there are other transference situations which call for our intervention.

3.932 When an Optimal Level of Intensity Has Been Reached

Another useful rule concerning the question of when do we intervene in the transference situation is the following. The analyst will permit the transference reaction to develop until it reaches an optimal level of intensity. Our task now is to define what we mean by this term "optimal level of intensity." This does not refer to a fixed quantity but depends on the state of the patient's ego and what the analyst is trying to achieve at the given moment. Essentially, we want the transference experience to be emotionally meaningful to the patient, but we do not want him to be overwhelmed by it. We want impact, but not trauma.

Ordinarily the analyst prefers to allow the patient's transference feelings to develop spontaneously and to grow in strength, unless some resistance interferes with the analytic work or with the further development of these feelings. If no resistance is present, the analyst will wait before he intervenes until the intensity of the transference feelings has reached a point which makes the transference reaction genuine and alive to the patient. We know that such an experience brings with it a sense of conviction that is without equal in the process of being analyzed. Lesser intensities of transference reactions can lead to denial, isolation, intellectualization, and other defensive resistances. Greater intensities can lead to traumatic states, panic reactions, and subsequent regressions and avoidances. The optimal intensity leads the patient to recognize that his transference reactions are real and meaningful. When this has occurred, the patient is ready to work analytically with the transference reaction as an experience.

An example of this situation is the following. Very early in her analysis a woman patient playfully brings up the question, "When am I supposed to fall in love with you?" The fact that she brought up the question indicates that some mild positive transference is already present, but it is at this time certainly not a living reality to the patient. If I were to point out to her that this very question indicates that such feelings are present, this patient most likely would deny it or would half seriously acknowledge it and then playfully go on associating. This is what usually happens when candidates prematurely interpret the positive transference. In the case I am describing, I did not make such an interpretation. I asked her only where did she get such an idea. After she told me that she had heard about its happening from a friend who had been in analysis, I said to the patient that there is no set rule for any particular feelings to develop toward the analyst; all she should do is allow her feelings to come up as they will and we would then try to understand her unique and individual feelings. Shortly after this hour I could determine that the patient seemed to be experiencing an increase in positive feelings toward me. She seemed more aware of her appearance. She looked at me somewhat coquettishly as she entered and when she left, and there was something slightly flirtatious about some of her remarks. Since the patient was producing some analytic work, however, and since I felt quite sure that these feelings would grow in intensity, I did not attempt to analyze the transference at this point.

In a few days the patient mentioned that she seemed less interested in her work, in her home, and in her husband. She seemed to be thinking about her "analysis" almost all the time; even during intercourse, she would think about her "analysis." At this point I felt that the intensity of the patient's transference feelings was such that they were real to her and vivid and that working on them now would be a meaningful experience and would further the analysis. Therefore at this point I intervened and said to the patient that it seemed to me that her feelings for *me* had intruded into her life; I seemed to dominate the rest of her life, even her sexual life, and I encouraged her to talk to me about this because it was important. Now the patient began to work seriously and with wonder about how strong her loving feelings to me had become. Gone was the flippancy and gamelike quality. Now she was ready to work in earnest.

It is important to realize that the patient's capacity to bear strong transference emotions will vary during the course of the analysis according to the quality of the transference emotion in question, and in accordance with the strength of the working alliance. Very early in the analysis the patient can bear lesser intensities than he can bear later on in the analysis. Generally, the first time a particular emotion has appeared in the transference the patient will be able to bear only a relatively small quantity of that emotion before resistances develop or he regresses. Early in the analysis it is necessary to gauge carefully how much of this emotion the patient can feel for it to be a meaningful experience to him. Premature intervention may deprive the patient of any emotional impact, in which case the transference would only have helped the patient make an intellectual game of the intervention. On the other hand, delayed intervention can permit the patient to feel such intensity of emotion that he will feel overwhelmed and will regress. It is necessary for the analyst to empathize with the patient in order to assess his ego strength at a given moment and to know when to intervene. The first time certain transference reactions come up during the analysis we intervene earlier; the more often a particular emotional constellation has occurred in the transference, the more likely we will permit greater intensities to develop. Of course, the appearance of resistances will indicate that it is necessary to intervene. However, these general considerations must be kept in mind if no resistances appear.

The quality of the transference reaction also may be an indication of what intensity of feelings the patient can bear. Generally speaking, if the transference reaction is infantile, it should be interpreted early. Some hateful and homosexual transference reactions may require earlier intervention than others.

The state of the patient's ego functions and particularly the state of the defenses will also play a role in determining what intensity of transference reactions the patient can bear. The sudden appearance of new transference feelings which are bewildering to the patient and which stir up anxiety and shame will require earlier intervention than previously experienced transference feelings. A patient is more prone to be overwhelmed by intense transference feelings when his ego is relatively depleted by some external event. The illness of a child which mobilizes guilt and unconscious hostility is a case in point.

Another consideration in reference to the optimal intensity of transference reactions is the question: how long will the patient have to contend with these transference feelings before the next hour? In other words, the optimal intensity will also depend on the frequency of the visits and how close the patient is to the next visit. Before a holiday or a weekend one would intervene earlier and forestall a too intense transference reaction as compared to what we would do if the patient has an analytic hour the very next day. This is an important point in favor of five weekly psychoanalytic sessions. If we see our patients on a daily basis, we can permit intense transference reactions to take place which will lead us back to the more important events of the infantile neurosis. If patients are seen, however, with a frequency in which every hour is followed by a gap, let us say three times a week, then such patients eventually learn from bitter experience that intense transference reactions can be traumatic and they will avoid letting themselves develop such intense feelings. As a consequence their transference neurosis never attains the desired intensity and certain aspects of the infantile neurosis will never be reached or resolved.

3.933 Some Modifications and Elaborations

Sometimes it may be a meaningful experience to the patient to point out the merest trace of a transference feeling. This will be the case when alongside of a moderately strong transference reaction one can detect a hint of another transference reaction of an opposite coloring. For example, a patient gives evidence of a fairly intense positive transference and yet one can hear undertones of hostility.

If the loving transference is used as a resistance against recognizing the underlying hostility, one can interpret the resistance function of the positive transference. However, it may not be a resistance situation but the early emergence of some hitherto unknown ambivalence. In such a situation it may be the correct procedure to point out the trace of hostility to the patient. This depends on the state of the working alliance, on the patient's willingness to recognize a small quantity of transference feeling, and his readiness to explore it. If the condition of the working alliance is such that a confrontation would lead only to denial and rejection, it would be better to wait for a greater intensity of the transference reaction or for the resistances to become demonstrable.

There are occasions when one points out to the patient the prolonged absence of particular transference reactions. This too can be an emotionally meaningful experience, if the absence of the feeling is conspicuous and striking to the patient. Then it is clear that a transference resistance is at work, which requires analysis as described earlier. It is important to withhold intervention for a sufficiently prolonged period so that the confrontation will make an impact and be felt as convincing to the patient. Premature interpretation always leads to an increase of resistance and the tendency to turn the analytic work into an intellectual game.

Sometimes the optimal intensity is not a moderately strong quantity of transference feeling but an extremely high quantity. This is likely to occur toward the end of an analysis when the patient has already repeatedly experienced transference reactions of moderate intensity but has not experienced the extreme intensity that is derived from the height of the infantile neurosis. The analyst has to recognize when it is necessary to allow moderately intense transference reactions to grow in intensity even to what seems to be overwhelming proportions, in order to allow the patient to feel the great strength of the childhood feelings. The patient should be encouraged to allow this to happen so that these early infantile emotions can enter into the arena of the analysis. A capacity for regression is necessary in order for this to happen, and regression will occur as a consequence of the overwhelming emotions. But in patients who have a good working alliance it is only a temporary regression and a valuable therapeutic experience.

Let me illustrate: A woman in the fifth year of her analysis began her hour by describing how agitated she had felt upon leaving the previous analytic hour which had ended with my interpretation that she was struggling to hide her penis envy and that she dreaded admitting to me that this subject upset her. She had felt both angry and excited when she got home. She had spent a restless night and had come to the hour with a peculiar mixture of dread and eagerness. She was really afraid to free-associate in the hour; she felt as though she would lose control of herself. She feared she might scream or perhaps even get off the couch and do something to me.

My silence, which ordinarily was reassuring to her, did not calm her. As her agitation increased, I found it necessary to say that she could let herself go. I would not let anything terrible happen to her. The patient was writhing, wringing her hands, and sweating. She began to shout at me: "I hate you, I hate you. It's all your fault. I want your penis, for me, it's mine." Then she stopped. She placed her hands over her pubic area and said: "I have a terrible urge to wet, to wet all over, just to show you that I can do it. . . . Just to show you how I hate you and despise you . . . it's all your fault . . . I want yours, it really belongs to me, it's mine, I'm going to get it, take it away . . . please give it to me, please, please, I beg of you. . . ." Then the patient began to sob hysterically. After a few minutes of quiet, I was able to interpret to her how she relived with me a hitherto repressed fragment of her infantile neurosis, a deeply buried component of her infantile penis envy.

3.934 When Our Intervention Will Add New Insight

Thus far we have considered two indications determining *when* we intervene in the transference situation: (1) when there is a transference resistance at work; (2) when an optimal level of intensity of transference feelings has been reached. These two indications overlap at times, yet they can appear singly. The same is true of the third, which is that we intervene in order to give the patient some new insight about the transference situation. A new insight may come to light while we are attempting to analyze a transference resistance or only after an optimal intensity has been attained. However, there are transference situations which call for an intervention when the questions of resistance or intensity of transference reaction are not the decisive issues. I refer here especially to transference situations which while transparent in their meaning to the analyst are yet obscure to the patient, but in which the meaning would become accessible to the patient if he were presented with the new insight.

The problems of clarifying and interpreting transference phenomena are not essentially different from clarifying and interpreting any other of the patient's productions. This will be systematically discussed in Section 3.943 on interpretation of the transference. For our present purpose, I shall limit this discussion to the question: when do we feel we can add new and meaningful insight to the transference situation? There are two essential considerations: the state of the patient's working alliance and the clarity of the material from which the interpretation or clarification is to be made. The state of the patient's reasonable ego will be determined by the nature and quantity of the resistances—a problem we have already discussed. The clarity of the transference material to be analyzed will depend on a variety of factors. One of the most important elements will be the intensity and complexities of the affects or impulses toward the analyst. This too has already been discussed.

The patient, Mrs. K., whom I have mentioned at different points,[9] illustrates these problems very well. She had a reasonable ego and developed a working alliance early in the analysis. She worked well and effectively on her sexual and romantic transference feeling to me. She did have strong resistances and did act out some of her feelings, but never to a degree that jeopardized her life or her analysis. The primitive hostility to me was much harder to reach and posed a far greater threat to her and to the analysis. At one time during this phase she became accident prone, and came perilously close to having automobile accidents. She never seriously considered breaking off the analysis until the oral-sadistic hostility to me began to emerge in her fifth year of analysis. One of the factors which complicated the analysis and undermined the working alliance in this phase was the fact that at the same time that her deep-seated hostility to me and to all men emerged, she was also still struggling with strong oral-sadistic and homosexual impulses toward her mother.

Fortunately, our past work had made it possible for her to achieve and maintain a relatively consistent and satisfying heterosexual relationship. Furthermore, she had a joyous and rewarding relationship with her baby daughter. These two achievements plus the memory of our past working alliance supported her vacillating working relationship to me and enabled her to work through the negative transference.

[9] See Sections 1.24, 2.651, 2.71, 3.25, 3.42, 3.81, 3.84, and 3.931.

At this point I want to describe briefly other characteristics of the patient's transference material which are indications for bringing up new insights. I refer here to the detection of other strong affects, contradictions, repetitions, similarities, symbolism, and key associations in the patient's productions, all of which can yield important clues to new meanings of the transference. The following simple clinical examples will illustrate:

3.9341 Strong Affects

The time to make the transference the point of the interpretation is when the transference reaction contains the strongest affects compared to the rest of the patient's material. When we listen to a patient's productions we have to decide which object or situation commands the greatest amount of affect. We will always interpret the transference aspect if it seems to contain a goodly amount of affect. Affects in the analytic hour are more reliable indicators than affects in dreams. The absence of affects where one would expect them also indicates that there is some analytic work to be done. The same is true of inappropriate affects.

For example, a patient spent most of the hour talking about his work and of his fear of losing his job; although he is working well, his boss seems cool to him. He doesn't know the reason for it; he is doing his best. He even worries about his marriage; is he a good husband, a good father, does his wife think of other men? Then he goes on to say how fortunate he is to be in psychoanalytic treatment; he will get rid of his inhibitions and his insecurities, and he won't go around worrying unnecessarily all the time. Toward the end of the hour he mentions that he bumped into an old friend at lunch yesterday. They talked of many things. He told his friend he was in analysis with Greenson, and his friend said he had heard Greenson often drops people from analysis if they don't work at it. But he, the patient, knew this couldn't be true; after all, if one couldn't work hard at analysis, that was due to resistances and they had to be analyzed. One doesn't punish patients and kick them out. Silence.

I could detect a change in the patient's tone during the hour. At first he sounded somewhat depressed and whiney—but only slightly so. When he came to talk about his friend and Greenson, his voice became louder, almost jocular, but forced. I could see a fine film of perspiration around his forehead. When he became silent he wiped his hands against his trouser legs, as though they were moist. It was clear to me that what he feared most at this time was not losing his job or his wife but losing me, his analyst, and I said this to him. He then recalled that he was shocked to hear that an analyst could drop a patient. It had never occurred to him. Then he tried to push it out of his mind as preposterous. He stopped and then asked, full of apprehension. "Is it true, do analysts really tell patients to leave?"

I asked him to tell me what he imagined about that. He became silent for a while, then his associations led to a pastoral scene of endless meadows, quiet and peaceful, but in the distance one saw clouds, dark swirling clouds. This brought the English painter Turner to mind, whose paintings seem so peaceful at first glance but become so ominous when one studies them carefully. I intervened at this point and said: "It seemed preposterous at first that Greenson could 'turn out' a patient, but after you study it a while, the idea is frightening."

3.9342 Contradictions

A woman patient had for over a year a strongly positive father trans-ference to me, with oedipal and phallic features. During this period of time there was evidence of great hostility, jealousy, and loathing of the mother. In a series of hours she began to compare her husband unfavor-ably with me. He seemed coarse, insensitive, even brutal to her at this time. I appeared to her to be gentle, sensitive, and attentive. Yet despite this she felt I also was strong and bold and imaginative. She admired and longed for a masculine man who would be tender. There was more to love than sex; there was more to life than having orgasms. She wanted to be loved as a whole, all over, completely enveloped. She wanted a man who would love to just cuddle her, mouth to mouth and breast to breast. He should hold her in his arms and stroke her and she would drink in his warmth. At this point I interpreted to the patient that although she seemed to prefer a manly man, there also seemed to be some longing in her for qualities in me which she felt to be womanly and warm. This intervention was the beginning of her recognition of pregenital striv-ings toward me as her mother.

3.9343 Repetitions

In an analytic hour a patient begins to talk of how his family doctor has become so hard to reach, he seems so busy, he no longer has the same interest in the patient. Then he goes on to talk about the sad state of education in the United States; few people want to become teachers; they are more interested in making money, etc. From there the patient goes on to talk about his father who, although he stayed married to his mother, was quite obviously unfaithful to her but hypocritically posed as a pillar of society. Then the patient becomes silent. I intervene and ask him: "And what are you afraid to find out about me?" After some feeble protests the patient describes how he dreaded hearing my name ever mentioned outside of the hour for fear he would hear something disillusioning.

3.9344 Similarities

A compliant and docile patient describes in an analytic hour how he lost his temper with a friend of his. They were driving in the car together for almost an hour and the patient tried to get his friend to contribute to the conversation, but his friend kept quiet, just grunted, and refused to give. How selfish, how cold, how inconsiderate! He goes on and on venting his fury. When he quiets down I point out that I too spend almost an hour with him and rarely contribute to the "conversation," except for an occasional grunt. The patient responds with a short laugh and becomes silent. After a lengthy pause he smiles and says resignedly: "Well you have me there." He adds, with a chuckle, "together for almost an hour, no conversation, just grunts, refusing to give—yes, you certainly seem to have a point." I then replied: "You were able to express real anger about your friend, but you seem unable to be angry with me for the same thing." The patient then stopped smiling and began to work.

3.9345 Symbolism

A patient dreams of being in a bookstore looking at some old books. He selects one in brown leather binding but can't tell which is front or back. He finally opens the book and a green beetle jumps out. He tries to kill it with a newspaper, but it keeps fluttering about. It frightens him and he awakens. The patient's associations go to Kafka's *Metamorphosis* and he, the patient, could be the beetle, turning into a loathsome creature because of the analysis. Life seemed simpler before treatment; he has so many new fears. When he came to analysis he was only aware of not being able to fall in love with a girl. So first he found out he was fixated to his mother and then to his father as well. Lately he has had little sexual desire, is it a fear of bringing sex into the hour? The leather binding of the book was like the leather pad on my desk. And the color was like my appointment book. He is not afraid of bugs except at night when he can't see them and can only feel them. Sometimes at night he will feel the flutter of a moth's wings against his face as he is reading in bed. It is scary and also pleasant. It gives him a feeling of something throbbing against him suddenly—a surprised feeling, almost like a thrill. Yet, also frightening, because he is not sure from where it is coming. Fluttering is like the moment of ejaculation and orgasm. Not knowing whether the book starts from front or back brings to mind that the Jews read their books from the back, from behind, and also that I am a Jewish analyst, in contrast to his first analyst, who was Gentile.

I believe this fragment of the hour points via the symbols and associations to the patient's struggle toward and away from the homosexual transference. In many previous dreams, green turned out to stand for Greenson. I point out to him that he seems to be trying to kill off his "fluttering" sexual feelings to Greenson because this is a frightening element in his life; it comes from behind. He responds by saying that he often feels a flutter of excitement when I begin to talk from behind the couch.

3.9346 Key Associations

Sometimes the most important clue as to whether we should interpret the transference and what aspect of it we should pursue is given by a single association. Certain associations take precedence over others, even over quantities of others, because they seem to lead to and open up new and important areas of investigation. Such key associations are characterized by seeming to be more spontaneous, impromptu, surprising, than other associations. Sometimes they link up quite startlingly with the analyst's associations, an occurrence which indicates that such an association is potentially significant.

A patient can recall only a fragment of a dream which had to do with having a tumor in her breast. In her associations she talks about several friends who have had tumors, about her dread of cancer, and of the feeling of carrying around the seeds of one's own destruction within oneself, etc. This leads to memories of her mother's and father's mistreatment of her; hatred; longing for a good parent; fear of unreliable people, etc. As I listen, my thoughts center around the question: Who is the tumor in her breast, the hated and hating mother, the father, or me? Then the patient begins to talk of how her breasts get fuller and more tender during her menses. My associations jump to her ambivalent reactions to the idea of pregnancy. At this point the patient begins suddenly to talk of being hungry and of having a yen for something sweet. Jokingly she says that she doesn't suppose I would have some chocolates handy. These last associations of suddenly feeling hungry and wanting something sweet from me connect to the dream of a tumor in her breast, and my associations to pregnancy lead me to ask her: "Have you been thinking about getting pregnant lately?" She answers that her three-year-old daughter had asked her if it is true that ladies carry their babies near their breasts and had then gone on to ask the patient, why don't you have another baby? This had made the patient depressed because her marriage has deteriorated of late and she doubts she will ever get pregnant again. This reminds her of the abortion she had had early in her marriage and what a pity it was, because otherwise her daughter would not be an only child. Then she says half jokingly: "I would have another baby if I could have it with you. But I know all I will ever get from you is words and the yearly handshake when you go on your vacation. It is sad to realize that you will never touch me. That reminds me, the last time I went to my doctor for a physical checkup he examined my breasts for tumors and while he was doing it I thought of you."

I answer that I think the lump in her breast was her unresolved longing for and resentment of me. She laughs and says, "I hope it's curable. You are probably right. I forgot to mention that the tumor was in my left breast, right over the heart." The key association was the patient's sudden yearning for something sweet.

The preceding illustrations of clinical material exemplify situations which call for interventions by the analyst. In all the transference situations described, the material was relatively transparent to the analyst, and the patient's reasonable ego and working alliance seemed ready to contend with the insight. When these two factors are favorable, then it is necessary for the analyst to intervene in order to add some new insight.

3.94 TECHNICAL STEPS IN ANALYZING THE TRANSFERENCE

Thus far in our discussion of the management of transference phenomena we have been considering two important questions: *why* and *when* do we analyze the transference. Now we come to the heart of the technical problem: *how* do we analyze the transference. This section will be devoted to the various technical measures and sequences of procedures which are required for analyzing the patient's transference reactions. All the steps that I shall describe are necessary ones; but some of them the patient will do spontaneously and therefore do not have to be repeated by the analyst.

I shall outline what I consider to be an ideal and simplified order of procedure in a rather schematic way. Each of the steps, however, may stir up fresh resistances which will require handling and so will interrupt the ideal sequence of events. Or the explorations set in motion by each new technical measure may open up so many new areas and occupy so many hours that the transference factor is no longer the predominant element to be pursued. Nevertheless, this outline of technical steps should serve as a model and as a guide, even though the events in clinical practice are never so orderly and well organized.

In order to analyze transference phenomena, we have to carry out the same basic technical measures that are essential in analyzing any psychic phenomenon; the material has to be demonstrated, clarified, interpreted, and worked through. In addition to these basic procedures, certain additional technical steps are required due to the specific peculiarities of transference phenomena. A general outline of the procedure for analyzing transference follows.

3.941 Demonstrating the Transference

Before proceeding with the exploration of the transference feelings, it is necessary for the patient to be aware that it is precisely his reaction to the analyst which is the subject matter under discussion. This may be obvious to the patient; in fact he himself may recognize this to be so without any help from the analyst. On the other hand, situations do arise where it is quite difficult for the patient to detect his transference feelings. It is imperative, as a first step in analyzing the transference, that the patient be confronted and made aware of his transference reactions. If the patient is in any way unknowing of the transference reactions we wish to investigate, then it has to be demonstrated to him. There are several technical measures which can be of help.

3.9411 Silence and Patience

Very often a patient will spontaneously recognize a transference reaction if one waits for the transference feelings to mount in intensity. Such increase will often result merely from permitting the patient to go on with his productions without intervention by the analyst. There are occasions in every analysis when it is necessary for the patient himself to become aware of his transference reactions and when it would be incorrect for the analyst to demonstrate them. This is particularly true when the intensity of the feelings is sufficiently pronounced, when the patient is no longer a beginner, and when there is a danger that the patient is enjoying some passive gratification in refraining from doing any part of the analytic work himself. Furthermore, the analyst's silence and patience will also highlight any significant resistance which might become obscured by too energetic interventions on the part of the analyst.

Analysts differ a great deal in their style of carrying out analysis. This is particularly true of how they use silence and how they use other more active measures. There is room for a great deal of variation within the framework of classical psychoanalysis. However, every analyst must be able to use silence and also active intervention. There are times when only one of these procedures is correct. It is necessary to know when each of these measures is permissible and when it is obligatory. Analysts who overdo silence or who can only pursue active measures are not able to perform classical psychoanalysis effectively. Classical psychoanalysis demands skill with silence and with words. The subject of dosage, timing, and tact of interpretation will be discussed in Volume II.

3.9412 Confrontation

If we have waited sufficiently and the transference reaction becomes accessible to the patient, i.e., it is vivid enough to him and he does not seem to have any appreciable resistance toward it, then the analyst should try to confront him with the transference reaction in question. He would say something like: You seem to be feeling angry or resentful toward me, to feel affectionate or loving toward me, to have sexual feelings toward me, etc. The language should be simple, direct, and open—a point I have stressed several times before.

I prefer to use the most vivid ordinary term. I avoid being evasive or vague. I talk of "anger" or "hate" or "affection" or "love" or "sex." I try to be exact without being narrow; this is only a confrontation at this point. I am direct but try to avoid being crude or blunt. I preface my confrontation with the phrase "You seem" because I am not always certain, and I want the patient to be able to run or contradict me at this point. I do not want to intimidate him or to be dogmatic. Later on I might say, "I am quite sure you are feeling . . ."—but only if I really am quite sure and if the patient should at that time be faced with my definite opinion.

Sometimes the mere confrontation of the patient with his struggle in expressing his transference feelings may serve to overcome the resistance temporarily. Our tolerant attitude and the verbalization help the patient feel that his struggle is inappropriate and unnecessary. At other times the confrontation serves only as a first step in analyzing the resistance. We would then have to go through the phases of clarification and interpretation described in Section 2.6 on the technique of analyzing resistances. The decisive question is whether at a given point in the sequence of events the indicated procedure is to overcome or to analyze a resistance.

If the particular transference reaction that I wish to demonstrate to the patient is a transference resistance, then I confront him with that fact. I either point out to him that he seemed to be avoiding some feeling or attitude toward me or if I knew more precisely what specific feelings he was trying to avoid I would point them out. In other words, I would confront the patient with both the resistance and the feelings causing the resistance, always starting with the resistance aspect. Thus I might say to the patient: "You seem to be struggling with feelings of love (or hate, or sex) toward me," perhaps, "You seem to have difficulty in expressing your love (or hate, or sex) for me," etc. Note again the language and tone. Furthermore, I always add the phrase "to me" or "toward me." I do so because I don't want the patient to avoid the fact that the feelings in question are toward me, the person, not toward "the analysis" or some other more impersonal concept.

If I am uncertain about the nature of the transference feelings but do have the impression that the subject matter of the hour is transference, and if there is no indication for remaining silent, I might confront the patient merely by asking: "I wonder if you are having some feelings or reactions to me which are not coming out into the open" or "I have the impression that I am involved in your thoughts and feelings" or simply "How do you feel about me?" or "What's going on about me at the moment?"

3.9413 The Use of Evidence

I make a point of showing a patient the source of my hypothesis only when I feel it is desirable to engage his intellect in order to persuade him that he is resisting. I would then have to go on to the analysis of his resistance. Evidence to convince a patient that he is having a transference reaction is used only if the patient otherwise would feel that the analyst has mysterious powers. I find that I use this approach mostly at the beginning of an analysis, as a means of indicating to the patient how an analyst works, to overcome his magical ideas about the analyst and to help him develop a working alliance. Thus, I might say to a woman patient: Your lack of sexual feelings toward your husband and your romantic dreams and fantasies about me seem to show that you are involved sexually and romantically with me.

The use of evidence is an appeal to the patient's intelligence. This can be a valuable aid as a step in cultivating a working alliance in the patient. However, there is the danger that it may lead the patient to overestimate the intellectual and to avoid the emotional knowing of transference phenomena. One must be vigilant in recognizing how the patient reacts to this form of confrontation.

At any stage in the attempt to demonstrate to the patient that he is involved in a transference reaction, the patient might develop a resistance or a hitherto unknown resistance may become visible. If that should occur, then the analysis of the resistance should take precedence over anything else. This is particularly apt to occur when the analyst points out the patient's hatred or anger toward himself in the early phases of analysis. The patient may become resistant and refuse to recognize this transference reaction and instead will feel he is being criticized. One then has to pursue this transference feeling of being criticized before one can return to the demonstration of the negative transference. Let me illustrate:

A young man in his first year of analysis begins the hour by talking with great feelings of anger about a professor in one of his postgraduate classes. His productions flow in this vein: "He just talks without thinking of whether the students can follow. He just spouts off into the air, not to us. What a lousy teacher. I'd hate to have him next semester. I'd hate to have him treat—I mean, teach me." Pause. "I suppose you will make something of that."

The patient then goes on, but I bring him back to the slip and ask: "Aren't you trying to run away from your anger to me? Your slip shows the anger—and then you try to run from it." The patient thinks a moment and replies: "I guess you're right. I guess you're right. But I know you are trying your best, but that professor, he is the stupidest son of a bitch. They shouldn't allow him to teach. I felt like leaving in the middle of the class, but I felt sorry for him. I heard his wife committed suicide. He probably has nothing left but teaching. But why should I feel sorry for him? He's a big shot, a full professor and he doesn't give a shit for me or for any of his students." The patient continues along this line.

Again I intervene and bring up the following: "Aren't you angry with me for going on my vacation next week?" The patient blurts out angrily: "No, I'm not angry. You are always accusing me of being angry. You are entitled to a vacation. You work hard, so why shouldn't you go away. So why should I be angry? You sound as though you looked that up in a book. Whenever an analyst goes on vacation, he tells his patient he is angry." This last is said sarcastically. "That gets me mad." Pause. Silence. I reply: "You are even angry when I point out that you are angry, but I feel your real anger is about my leaving you."

The patient replies: "Maybe so. I know I keep thinking that after you leave I will go to a fancy restaurant and pick up a girl. And to hell with all of you." I reply: "Yes, to hell with all of us who desert you. You don't need us, you'll get someone else to be close to." The patient is quiet for a moment and says: "Yes, I don't need you. Go away on your goddamn vacation. I'll do alright."

This is a relatively simple example of how one tries to pursue the demonstration and clarification of a transference reaction. One has to interrupt the sequence, however, and pursue the resistances that crop up. The patient's slip was a clear indication of his anger, but he refuses to accept this consciously. Then he goes on to feeling sorry for the professor. Then back to his anger at being rejected. I try to tie this up to my vacation, but he denies this angrily. I point out this form of resistance and confirmation, and finally he admits to fantasies about my vacation and his anger at being deserted. I believe it is necessary to pursue the resistances until one mobilizes a reasonable ego in the patient.

It is also important to give the patient time to react to the intervention. I try whenever possible to make sure that there is enough time left in the hour for the patient to react to my transference intervention. This is valid for interventions of any kind, but it is above all true for interpretations or interventions concerning transference. I do not immediately react to his first response, since very often patients will respond quickly with an impulsive yes or no and then, slowly, as one listens to them, one will see that their first response was neither thoughtful nor accurate. It usually reflects either submissiveness or defiance.

Many times patients will contradict themselves in their response to the transference confrontation. All of these reactions also have to become the subject matter of the analysis. However, it is important to give the patient time to mull over what one has said and then to react to it. I want to stress here that the patient ought to have time even to be silent in response to one's confrontation. One must pay attention not only to what he says but how he says it. If my interpretation is correct, he will agree with me and accept it not only verbally but also emotionally, and he will add certain details or memories or other embellishments to my confrontations. If my confrontation is correct and accessible to the patient, I can then go on to the next technical procedure in analyzing the transference.

Many times, however, the patient needs time to contemplate, to explore the correctness of my confrontation as well as to associate to it. If my intervention is incorrect, the patient will reveal its incorrectness not merely by verbally denying it but by some form of resistance and avoidance behavior. However, it may be that the confrontation was correct in content but wrong in its timing. One then has to pursue the resistance. In addition, it is also necessary for the analyst to have the time for properly evaluating the patient's response. It is not always easy to determine whether the patient's response indicates acceptance or rejection, thoughtfulness or escapism, or a combination of all of these elements.

3.942 Clarification of the Transference

Once the patient has recognized that he is involved in a transference reaction, we are now ready for the next technical procedure: the clarification of the transference. Now we want the patient to sharpen, illuminate, deepen, and fill out the transference picture. There are two main avenues of approach.

3.9421 Pursuit of the Intimate Details

Our ultimate objective in analyzing the patient's transference reaction is to be able to interpret the historical origins of this phenomenon. One of the most fruitful areas for picking up clues which can lead us back to the unconscious source is the intimate details of the transference reaction. Details lead to affects, impulses, and fantasies in the patient. We ask the patient, to the best of his ability, to refine, embellish, and elaborate his feelings toward us. We also ask him to include the associations which might occur while he is attempting to do this. Let me illustrate.

My patient, Mrs. K.,[10] in the third month of her analysis, tells me after considerable hesitation that she finds herself having sexual thoughts about me. This is embarrassing to her; after all she is a married woman. She knows I too am married, and besides I wouldn't care for her after all that I know about her. Silence. She guesses this is all a rationalization; she is just too embarrassed to talk about her sexual feelings, it is humiliating and degrading. Pause, silence, sigh. As she is driving in her car she will suddenly get a flash of a picture of me holding her in my arms. While she is reading a book or watching a movie she will see me as the hero and lover and she will feel and see herself as my sweetheart. At night in bed she will think of me and feel like calling out. The patient continues to talk in this way, describing the different places and occasions she has felt sexual longing for me; but I realize that although the picture is broadening out, it is not getting deeper or sharper. I also feel there is a good working alliance present despite the embarrassment and reluctance. I therefore say to her at this point: "You seem to be full of sexual longing for me, it comes up again and again; but it seems hard for you to describe exactly what you would like to do with me sexually; please try."

The patient answers: "I would want you to crush me in your arms, hold me tight, so tight that I can hardly breathe, lift me off the ground and carry me to bed. Then we would make love." Long pause. I ask: "What do you mean 'make love'?" "I mean," answers the patient: "tear off my nightgown, kiss my mouth hard, so hard that it hurts and I can hardly breathe. Force my legs apart and ram your penis into me. It will be huge and it will hurt and I will love it. [Pause.] A funny detail came to mind as I was describing all this. Your face was unshaven and your beard scratched my face. That's strange, you always seem to be clean shaven."

In reflecting on the sexual fantasy the patient has described, I observe: there were two references to being hardly able to breathe, then the masochistic wishes, then being lifted off the ground, carried, and I am huge. I recall that she had experienced several episodes of asthma about age six, at a time her mother had been married to a somewhat

[10] See Sections 1.24, 2.651, 2.71, 3.25, 3.42, 3.81, 3.84, 3.931, and 3.934.

sadistic stepfather. The interpretation of the transference fantasy seems clear: I am the sadistic stepfather gratifying her masochistic, guilt-laden, oedipal strivings. I could make the interpretation myself, but instead I want her to discover it for herself, so I ask her: "Who used to scratch you with his beard when you were a little girl?" The patient fairly shouts: "My stepfather, my stepfather, he used to love to torment me by rubbing his face against mine—and he'd grab me up and squeeze me and throw me up in the air—I could hardly catch my breath. But I thought I hated it."

Let us return to the technique of clarification. I feel the patient is not adding to the transference picture and yet I feel she is able to. So I confront her with this. I tell her I know it is hard for her, would she please tell me more precisely what her sexual fantasy is. I am direct, open, not demanding, but firm. When she says "We made love" I ask her in the same way: please explain to me what you mean by "making love." My words and tone are neither crude nor timid.

A patient tells me she had a thought of "kissing" my "genital organ." At the appropriate moment I asked her to please explain what she meant by kissing my penis, I found her statement vague and somewhat evasive. I indicate by my question that I want to know the intimate details and that it is permissible to talk of them in a realistic way. I demonstrate this by the way I talk. I am neither vulgar nor evasive. I help her on her way by translating "genital organ" into "penis." The "kissing" she will have to translate herself.

A male patient tells me he had a "fellatio" fantasy about me. When I feel it is indicated I tell him I do not understand what he means by "fellatio," would he please explain this to me. When he hems and haws, I say that he seems to have difficulty in talking about doing something sexual with his mouth to my penis. By so doing, I not only point out his transference resistance but also indicate how I would like him to be able to talk of such matters in concrete, everyday, living language.

The same approach is equally valid in dealing with the aggressive drives and feelings. A patient tells me he feels hostile toward me. My response is that I don't understand the term hostile, it is sterile, ambiguous, and unclear. What does he really mean? If I sense the impulse or affect, I use the most precise term for it. I tell my patients that they seem to hate me or loathe me today and to please tell me about it, and to let the feelings come out along with the description. I help them to differentiate between anger, rage, hatred, resentment, and annoyance, because each of these feelings has a different history and comes from different parts of the patient's past. I encourage my patients to describe their aggressive fantasies, the aims of their hostile, destructive impulses, because these are also clues to different historical periods of their life. Let me illustrate:

A young man, Mr. Z.,[11] reports that he is annoyed at me for charging him for a missed hour. I pursue this "annoyance," questioning him if he really means annoyed. He "guesses" he was more than annoyed. My silence prods him into expressing rather heatedly how he thought I am a hypocrite for pretending to be a scientist. I am just as much a businessman as his "tight-assed" old man. Some day he hopes he'll have the courage to rub my nose in all this "psychoanalytic crap." This would be a fine revenge, he would do to me what I am doing to him. To my question: "And what am I doing to you?" he answers: "You make me crawl through all the shit, you never let up, more, more, more. You're never satisfied, produce or get out is what you seem to be saying and it's never enough." One can see, behind the innocent annoyance he "guesses" he had, the anal-sadistic fury and humiliation of childhood.

This same patient, later on in his analysis, begins his hour by stating he hated to come, he hates the analysis and me along with it. When I ask him: "And how do you hate me today?" he answers: Today he hates me with a passion, a cold rage. He wouldn't want to kill me, no that was too civilized. He would like to beat me to a pulp, literally grind me up and mash me into a jelly like a mass of bloody, slimy "goo." Then he'd eat me, in one big "slurp" like the goddamned oatmeal his mother made him eat as a kid. Then he'd shit me out as a foul-smelling poisonous shit. And when I ask him: "And what would you do with this foul-smelling, poisonous shit?" he replied: "I'd grind you into the dirt so you could join my dear, dead mother!"

I think it is now clear how the pursuit of the intimate details of the aggressive, destructive impulses leads to the clues that make an interpretation possible. Whenever transference impulses arise in the analysis our task is to help the patient clarify them as to the precise nature of the instinctual impulse, its aim, zone, and object.

[11] See Sections 2.52, 2.54, 2.71, 3.531, 3.7111, and 3.922.

We work similarly with other affects such as anxiety, depression, disgust, envy, etc. We pursue the exact nature of the feelings, trying to sharpen, deepen, illuminate what particular quality and quantity of emotion are involved. There is always the same relentless search for clarity: what exactly is the patient feeling: what is he fantasying. The attitude is open, direct, unafraid, and undaunted, neither crude nor timid. We are explorers, but we must preserve and not destroy what we are exploring. We must serve as a model for the patient, so that he will some day have the ability to ask himself the same kinds of questions.

It is necessary to repeat, resistances may crop up in any and all phases of our attempt to gain clarification. If the resistance is significant and proves to be a stumbling block, the work of clarification must stop and the resistance has to be analyzed. No matter how tempting the content of the material is, significant resistances have to be analyzed first. Otherwise, the insights will be meaningless to the patient and he is our first concern. Our primary task is to perform an effective piece of therapy and not to gather interesting data.

3.9422 Pursuit of the Transference Trigger

Another valuable method for clarifying a given transference reaction is to uncover what characteristic or piece of behavior in the analyst served as the triggering stimulus. Very often the patient will spontaneously recognize that a certain trait or activity of the analyst stirred up a particular reaction. At other times this transference trigger not only will be unknown to the patient but the patient will have strong resistances in recognizing it. Sometimes the behavior of the analyst will call forth a reaction in the patient which is *not* a transference phenomenon, since it may be an appropriate response. Finally, one should realize that sometimes we analysts may be too inhibited to explore with the patient which of our personal idiosyncrasies may have served as a transference stimulus.

I have heard of analysts who insist on tracing *every* transference reaction back to some feature of the analyst's behavior. This smacks of some narcissistic need in the analyst or of an overevaluation of a technical procedure. Our aim is to clarify in order to interpret the unconscious historical source in the patient's past. The transference trigger may be a valuable aid, but it is only a means to an end and not an end in itself. There are many clinical situations where the search for the transference trigger is unnecessary, irrelevant, or not the most productive approach.

A few clinical examples will illustrate some of the points mentioned above. A woman patient begins her hour by lying on the couch silently, quietly, with eyes closed, and seemingly peaceful and content. After several minutes of silence I say: "Yes?" She smiles softly, sighs, and remains quiet. Now many minutes go by and I am impressed by the serene and blissful picture she seems to present. Ordinarily she is quite verbal and productive and is tense and disturbed when she becomes silent. I begin to let my thoughts drift over the last hours, wondering if I could uncover some explanation for this unusual reaction. Her appointment is late in the afternoon this particular day, because of some change in my schedule. Ordinarily she comes in the morning. It is dark outside, and the lights are on in the treatment room.

The patient remains quiet and I am more and more struck by the glow of pleasure she seems silently to reflect. I say to her after some twenty minutes: "This hour seems different. What are you enjoying so silently and all to yourself?" She replies in a soft and dreamy voice: "I am lying here drinking in the peaceful feeling of this office. It is a haven. I am breathing in the fragrance of your cigar, I imagine you sitting in your big chair, puffing away comfortably and thoughtfully. Your voice sounds like coffee and rich cigar smoke, warm and cheering. I feel protected, safe, looked after. It seems like it's after midnight and everyone at home is asleep except my father and me. He is working in his study and I can smell his cigar and I can hear him making himself coffee. I used to wish I could creep into the room and curl up alongside of him. I would try to and would promise to keep as silent as a mouse, but he always brought me back to bed."

The patient herself recognized that the late hour, the lights in the office, the aroma of my cigar, my silence, and my voice have stirred up a memory of childhood; a longing to be alone with her protective, loving father. She lets herself feel on the couch the pleasure she was deprived of, but fantasied about, in childhood.

My patient, Mr. Z.,[12] enters a phase of analysis in which he finds it very difficult to talk to me about his sexual fantasies. He has already been in analysis for several years, and we have worked through many different aspects of his transference resistances. This particular resistance

[12] See Sections 2.52, 2.54, 2.71, 3.531, 3.711, 3.922, and 3.9421.

feels different somehow. There are many hours of superficial talk, an absence of dreams, and much silence. The only outstanding point he seems to make is that I have seemed different to him lately. I press him to try to clarify how I am different. He doesn't know; he cannot describe it; but finally he haltingly blurts out that I seem repulsive to him. I then tell him, directly and openly: "Alright, I am repulsive to you. Now try to visualize me and try to describe what is repulsive about me." The patient slowly begins to talk. "I see your mouth, your lips, they are thick and moist. In the corner of your mouth is some saliva. I hate to say this to you, Dr. Greenson, I'm not sure it's true." I say simply: "Please go on." "Your mouth is open and I imagine it smells. I can see your tongue wetting your lips. When I try to talk to you about sex lately, that is what I see and it stops me and I freeze. Now I'm afraid of your reaction [pause]. I seem to see you as a lewd, lascivious old man [pause]."

I say: "And now let yourself drift along with the picture of a lewd, lascivious old man, with thick, wet lips." The patient talks on for a while and suddenly recalls a memory from early adolescence when he tramped the streets excitedly, looking for a prostitute, but feeling afraid and awkward. In a dark alley someone approached him, obviously with sex in mind. He understood the person wanted to fondle his penis and then to suck it. The boy was powerless to cope with the situation. Torn by excitement and fear he remained passive and allowed the sexual activity to be performed upon him. He was not sure at first if it was a man or woman, it all happened so quickly, it was dark in the alley; he was so flooded with different emotions. But he does recall the person's mouth, the lips were thick and wet and open. The more he speaks of the event the more clear it becomes to him that the person was a man, a homosexual prostitute. (A year earlier the patient had reported this as a fleeting memory without any details.)

It was clear that the patient was reliving in his transference relationship to me the homosexual experience of his adolescence. The trigger which stimulated the return of this event was his awareness of my thick, moist lips. I helped him work with this material by showing him by my manner that I was able to talk of myself as a lewd and lascivious repulsive old man with thick, moist lips. Timidity on my part would have increased his own anxiety. Resentment or even silence on my part would have been perceived as a reproach.

The analyst deals with this material no differently than he deals with anything else. When a patient tells me she finds I am sexually attractive, I ask her what about me does she find sexually attractive. If a patient tells me that she feels she loves me, I ask her what does she find lovable about me. If a patient tells me I am disgusting, I ask what is disgusting about me. I am careful to be neither too silent nor too active, since any change in my technique will indicate to my patient that I am disturbed in some way. I am as patient and as persistent in digging out the intimate details about the patients' reactions to me as I am about anyone else. I try to deal with their love and sexual transference reactions no differently from the way I deal with their hatred and disgust. This is not always an easy task, and I do not claim to be always successful.

The clinical material described above indicates that the analyst's personal qualities and traits and also certain characteristics of his office setting may serve as triggering stimuli for transference reactions. It should be added that patients may respond in a similar way to the tone of voice and the emotional quality they perceive in the analyst's utterances. I have had patients react with a severe angry-depressive reaction when they felt I had been belittling to them in my manner of speech. Patients have reacted to me as sounding reproachful, sarcastic, seductive, sadistic, crude, flippant, etc. In each case it is necessary to single out and clarify what particular trait or activity of mine precipitated the reaction. If there is any truth to the patient's accusations, this has to be acknowledged; but in any event the patient's reaction has to be analyzed, i.e., clarified and interpreted.

In a sense, all transference reactions are triggered by some aspect of the analytic situation. The analytic situation is set up to facilitate regressive misperceptions and evoke the patient's forgotten reactions to objects in the past. There are times when it is neither necessary nor fruitful to single out and clarify what stirred up the transference reaction. It is sufficient merely to analyze the transference phenomenon in question. On other occasions the uncovering and analysis of the triggering characteristics of the analyst or the analytic situation may prove to be of considerable value. I have stressed the importance of this avenue of approach because I have found in my supervisory work that many analysts tend to neglect this technical procedure.

3.943 Interpretation of the Transference

Now we come to that technical procedure which distinguishes the psychoanalytic method from all other forms of psychotherapy.

Interpretation is the ultimate and decisive instrument of psycho-analytic technique. All other technical procedures utilized in psychoanalysis are groundwork for making interpretation possible. More than that, every other technical device must eventually become the subject matter of the analysis, and its effects upon the patient must be interpreted.

In the framework of psychoanalysis, to interpret means to make an unconscious psychic phenomenon conscious. The ultimate aim of all interpretations is to enable the patient to understand the meaning of a given psychic phenomenon. We interpret the transference by uncovering the unconscious history, the antecedents, origins, purposes, and interconnections of a given transference reaction. This is not accomplished in a single step but is a prolonged process. By means of demonstration and clarification we attempt to get the patient's ego to observe a psychological situation which is preconscious and readily accessible. The patient is asked to split his ego so that one part of his ego can observe what the other part is experiencing. In interpretation we ask the patient to go beyond what is readily observable and to assign meaning and causality to a psychological phenomenon (E. Bibring, 1954).

Demonstration and clarification prepare the patient for our interpretation. Interpretations, to be effective, must not go beyond the patient's limits for comprehension, for emotional understanding. An interpretation is a hypothesis which requires the patient's responses for verification (Waelder, 1960, pp. 3-27). Clarifications lead to interpretations, and interpretations also lead back to further clarifications. Often when the analyst is trying to get the patient to clarify a given phenomenon, the patient will stumble upon its interpretation, the unconscious meaning. Analogously, the correctness of an interpretation will often be verified by the patient's adding some new embellishing material. Let me illustrate with a simple example.

A woman patient in her third year of analysis develops a resistance to coming to her analytic hour because she feels there is something ominous about me which frightens her. I persuade the patient to try to clarify this ominous quality she perceives about me. Hesitantly she begins to draw a picture of me as a man who seems kindly on the surface but who is secretly hostile to women. She goes on to depict a man who seems manly and active but who is actually feminine and passive. He is so passive that he would let his women patients slowly bleed to death without lifting a finger. The moment the patient says, "bleed to death" she gasps: "Oh my God! I know what that is—that's my father. I am mixing you up with my father." The patient is referring to an incident in childhood when, at age four, she discovered she was bleeding from the vagina and ran to her father, in a panic. He tried to comfort her by saying, "It's nothing, it will go away, forget about it." For many complicated reasons this was most disturbing to my patient.

This incident had come up many times during her analysis, but never with the quality of sinister intent on her father's part. Only as she began to clarify her feelings toward me did she come upon the feeling of ominousness which led her to the bleeding, which then led her spontaneously to interpret this as derived from her father. Then the patient proceeded to deepen her awareness of the hidden sadistic qualities in her supposedly kindly, passive father.

If demonstration and clarification of the transference reaction do not lead directly to the interpretation, then it is necessary for the analyst to undertake certain technical steps. By and large these steps are directed toward uncovering the history of the particular transference reaction.

The exploration of the history of a transference reaction can best be facilitated by pursuing any of the component parts which go toward the formation of this special object relationship. Ordinarily we will select for exploration that aspect of the transference which seems to be most accessible to the patient's reasonable and conscious ego. Therefore we usually begin with the resistances if they are present to any significant degree. (See Section 2.71 on analyzing resistance before content.) If there are no important resistances operating we can then go on to explore whatever aspect of the transference seems to be the most urgent and pressing for the patient.

Although any number of approaches is possible, there are three methods that are most valuable in attempting to uncover the history of a transference reaction: (1) pursuing the affects and impulses involved; (2) tracing the antecedents of the transference figures; and (3) exploring the transference fantasies. These three techniques are often fused with one another and one approach will blend into another. For the sake of clarity I shall describe each separately.

3.9431 The Pursuit of the Affects, Impulses, and Attitudes

By and large the most rewarding avenue to follow in attempting to uncover the unconscious source of a transference reaction is to explore the affects and impulses involved. The question we ask our patients can be formulated as: "Where did you have this feeling or impulse before?" A similar question would be: "What occurs to you if you let your thoughts drift with these feelings or impulses?" Sometimes we do not explicitly have to ask the patient such questions; we merely ask the questions silently and the patient's spontaneous associations provide us with the answer. Early in analysis we usually have to ask such questions; later on the patient seems to ask them himself, albeit silently.

I should like to illustrate these points with a few simple examples. Early in his analysis, Professor X.[13] admits he is skipping certain associations because he is afraid I would be critical of him. In fact, he can even imagine me mocking him. He cannot bear this idea; he hates to be humiliated. After he has been silent for a while I ask him: "Where did this happen to you before?" The patient answers: "When I was young, my mother used to do this. She was a terrible tease and delighted in tormenting me by laughing at my shortcomings." He goes on and on. Before the hour ends I make the interpretation: "So you skip certain thoughts that occur to you here with me, because you are afraid I might torment you as your mother did." The patient replies after a pause: "Yes, I guess I did, although this now seems silly."

This same patient, a year later, has an hour which can be summarized as follows: He comes to the hour a few minutes late and wonders if it means anything. As he lies on the couch he sighs and says that analysis seems to be a burden to him of late. He came dutifully today but without any feeling or expectation of pleasure. When I was on vacation he enjoyed himself; he seemed to have a much freer sex life with his wife. Since I have returned his anal itching has returned and also an urge to masturbate. He is worried about the health of his father, who had written that he had hemorrhoid trouble. His father was always worried about his rectum. He always liked to take the children's temperature rectally. Recently the patient was tempted to poke his finger into his wife's rectum during foreplay. He didn't do it because he didn't want to have to tell me about it, although he suspected I might like to hear such kind of stuff. Maybe I would get a kick out of this kind of material or maybe he is projecting. I interpret to the patient that he seems to feel I might enjoy his anal activities as his father had. The patient replies that he often thought of me whenever he did anything which gave him anal pleasure. He even suspects that he is reluctant to come to the hour because, since I returned, he seems to have many more thoughts and im-

[13] See Sections 2.64, 2.652, 3.412.

pulses to do things to his anus and he has the impression there is something homosexual stirring around in him.

It should be noted that in the first example I had to pursue the affect by asking the patient a direct question. In the second example the patient spontaneously associated the return of his anal itching and the return of his analyst to his father's anal interests. It was as though he had silently asked himself the kinds of questions I had asked him in the past.

The uncovering of the transference attitude can be pursued in a manner analogous to that I have described for affects and impulses. We might thus try to unravel the hidden history of when and how such attitudes as passivity, submissiveness, contempt, etc., arose in the patient's life. By and large it is more difficult to uncover material about attitudes because they are too often ego syntonic. It is usually necessary first to make the attitude ego alien before we can expect the patient to be able to produce significant information in his associations.

3.9432 Tracing the Antecedents of the Transference Figure

An equally important source of information about the formation of a given transference reaction may be found by determining the different persons who called forth a particular transference reaction. In other words, we try to answer the question: Toward whom did you feel this way in the past? This is merely a shift in emphasis from our earlier question: When did you feel so in the past? Frequently, these two questions lead into one another and are not separable. However, each question may lead in different directions and each may be of different importance at different times. If we are successful in interpreting a transference reaction, we ultimately hope to be able to establish to what past objects and under what circumstances this present reaction was appropriate.

The patient's transference reaction is inappropriate for the analyst, but it fits somebody in the past. We do not always expect to arrive immediately at the original objects, but we do expect to find some intermediate object who will lead us eventually to the source. There is no set chronological order in which the ancestors of the current transference figure appear. On this point, my findings agree with Fenichel (1941, p. 48), who spoke of "faulting." They are in disagreement with W. Reich (1928, 1929), who stressed the reverse chronological order. The patient may shift from the recent to the remote past several times in an hour. Or the patient's emotions may remain fixed to some intermediate object for a long period of time before they may shift to some other object. A given transference reaction usually has multiple antecedents and all have to be analyzed in order to uncover the full intensity and complexity of the transference reaction. One of the technical problems in analyzing transference reactions is to determine when it has changed its source. Sometimes only very subtle changes in some detail of the transference reaction hint at a shift in the transference-producing object.

Thus, in the case of Professor X.[14]—who skipped certain associations because he feared I would humiliate him—my interpretation first brought out he was reacting to me as he had to his teasing mother. This consisted mainly of verbal play and laughter on her part. Then his fear of being teased concerned his fear of someone pointing a finger at him in scorn, which he was able to connect to his older sisters. At another time his fear of being humiliated contained an element of physical fear along with it. This change indicated a shift to his fear of his humiliating father. On still other occasions he had shame reactions toward me which derived from his schoolteachers, his uncles, his aunts, and his school friends.

In short, the analysis of his fear of being humiliated by me led to a vast gallery of humiliators who were the forerunners and creators of his analyst as a humiliator. Each one of the ancestors added or emphasized or changed some aspect of his humiliation fantasies. We not only uncovered the objects who made him feel humiliated but also traced the derivatives and forerunners of each object. Mother teasing him at three for bed wetting was one figure, belittling his small penis at age five was another, laughing at his few pubic hairs at age fourteen still another. One older sister carried on when his mother left off and mocked him for his inadequate sexual development until age seventeen. On the other hand, his father made him feel ashamed because he was too curious about sexual matters at five and then later in adolescence.

The question, "Toward whom did you feel this way in the past?" is one of the most frequently occurring questions in the analysis of transference reactions. It can be asked explicitly, or silently, but

[14] See Sections 2.64, 2.652, 3.412, and 3.9431.

one may never cease to ask this question as long as any transference reaction of significance is taking place. This is not surprising since all transference phenomena are derived from experiences with the key people of early life, as well as their later counterparts and derivatives.

3.9433 Exploring the Transference Fantasies

If one reviews the different examples cited to illustrate how one can approach the interpretation of transference phenomena, it will be seen that we are exploring the patient's fantasies concerning the analyst. This exploration is not always explicit; often it is implicit. One asks the patient, for example, why does he skip certain associations and he answers that he has the fear that I, the analyst, will humiliate him. Actually he is saying he has a feeling of shame which stems from a fantasy of being humiliated by me. The patient spontaneously connects this fantasy to his mother's teasing him for bed wetting and in this way he reveals to me its content without my explicitly asking him for it.

Sometimes, however, it is necessary to get the patient to focus directly on his fantasies, particularly when the transference affects, impulses, or objects seem vague, inaccessible or unproductive.

For example: the young man, Mr. Z.,[15] who has been in analysis for three years, is unable or unwilling to utilize the insight he has gained about his anxieties in social situations. It becomes clear that he is both consciously and unconsciously afraid to identify with me. He agrees to this interpretation, but it brings no change. I then ask him to try to imagine "becoming like me" and to describe the fantasy stimulated in him by this idea. The patient answers: "I don't want to become like you, to become psychologically minded as you put it, introspective; I don't want to take any part of you inside me. It would be like swallowing a part of you, sucking a part of you in, breathing in your words, or having a part of your mind or body inside of me. It has a sexual feel to it, like taking your penis into my mouth or swallowing your sperm. I won't do it, I just won't give in to you." All this is said with ankles tightly crossed, arms pressed against his sides, fists clenched, and the words spat out from between his teeth.

By describing this fantasy the patient revealed to me the homosexual

---

[15] See Sections 2.52, 2.54, 2.71, 3.531, 3.711, 3.922, 3.9421, and 3.9422.

anxiety which lay behind his refusal to identify with me. I could now proceed to work with him on why and how homosexuality had become interwoven with identification. The opening which led to this insight came from the patient's description of his fantasies concerning me.

Very often when one has been working on the analysis of a particular resistance for a period of time, one can approach the resistance in question by asking: "How do I frighten you today?" which actually means, what fantasy do you have about me today?

I have described three important methods of exploring the history of the transference reactions of a patient: the pursuit of the affects, impulses, and attitudes; the tracing of the antecedents of the transference figures; and the exploration of the transference fantasies. There are many other possible avenues for uncovering the history of transference reactions, but in my experience these three approaches have proved to be the most productive.

The clinical examples I have used in analyzing transference phenomena may give the false impression that every intervention succeeds in getting the patient or the analyst to uncover specific affects, impulses, attitudes, objects, or fantasies. Many times one can tell the patient only that one has the impression that he seems to be struggling with certain feelings toward the analyst. He may agree or disagree, and the associative productions may not immediately lead to any clear-cut unconscious material. It may take several hours for a certain specific aspect of the transference to become interpretable.

3.944 Working Through of Transference Interpretations

Clinical experience teaches us that no single transference interpretation, even when it is absolutely correct, remains effective for a long period of time. It has to be repeated many times to achieve effectiveness. Furthermore, no single interpretation can fully explain a patient's transference reaction. At best, a single transference interpretation is only a partial explanation. In order to achieve full understanding and lasting change in the patient's behavior, working through of the individual interpretations is required. Although the general subject of working through will be discussed more fully in Volume II, I should like briefly to describe at this point the working through of transference interpretations. I refer the student to the standard psychoanalytic texts on this subject (Freud, 1914c, 1916-17, 1917b, 1926a, 1937a; Fenichel, 1941; Lewin, 1950; Greenacre, 1956; and Additional Reading List).

3.9441 Theoretical Considerations

The process of working through refers basically to the repetition and elaboration of insights gained through interpretation. The repetition is necessary particularly in attempting to analyze and overcome transference resistances. This is due to the ego's reluctance to give up old defenses and to risk new approaches; the ego needs time to master the old anxieties and to trust its new adaptive abilities. It is a common clinical experience to get little or no change the first time one interprets the meaning of a particular transference resistance. Later on, the identical interpretation may bring about a vivid change in the patient, only to have the old resistive behavior return when some "imponderable" of everyday life changes the ego's balance of power in regard to the id or superego. Resistances are tenacious, and the ego requires time to absorb new experiences in order to change.

In order to gain deep understanding of the meaning of a transference reaction, it is necessary to uncover and trace its many transformations and ramifications. The overdetermination and multiple functions of transference phenomena are responsible for this. Thus, for example, we have to interpret the meaning of the patient's behavior in the current transference situation and then pursue this same reaction in regard to the original and all the intermediate transference figures. Furthermore, we must also uncover how a given piece of transference behavior may serve as an instinctual outlet in one situation and as a resistance and defense in another. Or we must trace a certain transference phenomenon through the various libidinal phases and also determine how it is to be understood from the point of view of the ego, id, and superego. All the work that follows the new insight and that leads to a change in attitude or behavior can be considered the process of working through (Greenson, 1965b).

3.9442 Clinical Material

I should now like to present some clinical data that will illustrate the interpretation and the partial working through of a transference reaction. This material was culled from a period of three weeks of psychoanalytic therapy.

A young man, Mr. Z.,[16] is in his third year of analysis. Until this point his transference reactions might be summarized by the formulation that I am primarily the puritanical and kindly father who likes the patient but who is critical of his sexual and aggressive impulses. The patient feels inferior both morally and sexually. He is little and inadequate and his sexuality is dirty. I am the great, potent, and clean father he once envied and admired and hoped to emulate. In the last several hours there has emerged a stubborn set of resistances. Mr. Z. has either forgotten his dreams or he has had scanty associations. The material he has spoken about has been stale, with little fantasy and no new memories or insights. Then comes an hour in which he reports the following dream: he is in a large house and goes from room to room. He is followed by a waiter who constantly offers him food which he eats. Finally he meets the hostess who tells him she is glad he could come because she knows he runs a good, clean business and is a good risk. She asks him how he likes the furniture in her home. The patient mumbles an answer because he does not want to give a negative opinion.

The associations to the dream are essentially as follows: He hates big parties, he feels so ill at ease. His parents used to have big parties and he would try to avoid them. His father was a genial host and would offer people food and drink; actually he overdid it; he would force food on people and it would embarrass the patient. The waiter in the dream was so persistent. He followed the patient who couldn't get rid of him. Strange, he kept eating in the dream, whereas in reality he eats very little at parties. Lately he has had a poor appetite which he attributes to his difficulties with his analysis. He doesn't seem to be getting anywhere lately. I interpret at this point: "The interpretations I have been offering you of late, you will not swallow. I follow you everywhere, but you won't accept what I offer you."

The patient agrees and says he feels there is something he is afraid of getting into. He seems to be in a rut. He is disappointed in himself because when he began analysis with me he felt it would go better with me than with his first analyst, who was cold and aloof. I ask him about the furniture in the dream. He answers he is very aware of and sensitive to furniture. He pays a great deal of attention to interior decorating. Long pause. He is afraid I will think this is feminine. He has heard that interior decorators are usually homosexual. Pause. Small talk. I interpret

[16] See Sections 2.52, 2.54, 2.71, 3.711, 3.531, 3.922, 3.9421, 3.9422, and 3.9433.

to him: "You seem to be afraid to talk to me about your homosexual feelings; you would rather just be evasive. Why can't you risk it with me?"

The patient's responses now lead to his fear of me because I am warm and not aloof. He would feel safer if I were cold and distant. In a way I am like his father, I give too much. He can't remember expressing warm and affectionate feelings to his father. He liked him, but always from a distance. Later on, in adolescence, the patient seemed to regard the father as coarse and vulgar. "You are warm, but you are not coarse or vulgar." I interpret. "But maybe you are afraid that if you let your thoughts and feelings go in the direction of homosexuality, I might turn out to be different. After all, in the dream I am also the hostess."

The patient answers that he doesn't let men friends become intimate no matter how much he likes them; he never becomes too close or chummy. He is not sure though of exactly what he is afraid of.

The next hour the patient reports that he awoke at 4 A.M. and couldn't sleep. He tried to masturbate with his usual fantasy of a big woman fondling his penis, but it did not arouse him. Then the thought intruded of being in bed with a man and a woman. He found that revolting. The idea of being in bed next to a huge, fat, grey-haired, big-bellied man was disgusting. He felt I was pushing such ideas onto him. Silence. I say: "And you won't swallow them." The patient is resistant the rest of that hour.

In the next hours he continues to be very resistant. Finally, in one hour after a long silence, he says that after the last session he had an urgent need to urinate and went to the toilet in my office building. He had great difficulty in starting his urinary stream. After he pauses, I say: "Maybe you were afraid I would come in." At first the patient is furious with my remark; then he quiets down and admits it was true; he had had such a thought. Silence. I then ask him: "And how was it in the bathroom with your father when you were a little boy?" The patient then goes on to describe how his father paraded around naked in front of him in the bathroom, performing all his excretory functions without any inhibition. However, he could not recall how he felt about this.

The next several hours are taken up by his telling me that he resumed sexual activity with an old girl friend, but it is not satisfying. I point out to him that I think he plunged into the heterosexual affair to avoid the homosexual feelings which had begun to emerge in the analysis. The patient responds by agreeing with me verbally. However, in the next several hours he becomes quite resistant, but in a different way. Finally, he admits that I now seem to be a coarse and repulsive old man to him and we have the hour which I described earlier (Section 3.9422), as an example of how the analyst can serve as a trigger.

The uncovering of the homosexual memory in adolescence left him depressed, but he had overcome some of his transference resistance and become more productive.

Then comes an hour in which he reports a fragment of two dreams. (1) he was riding a motorcycle. (2) He was in an ancient building. He sees a young man trying to put a key into the keyhole of his room. The patient is annoyed but says, let me help you. His associations go to an old hotel in Jamaica where his mother went alone on a long vacation when he was five years old. He visited it later when he was in the Navy. He doesn't like my office building, it is too modern. Lately I just sit behind him and seem to do nothing. Do I expect him to do all the work? He has never ridden a motorcycle, but he heard that my son does. How is it to have a psychoanalyst for a father? Do analysts walk around naked in front of their kids? I reconstruct for him that when he was five years old his mother had left him alone with his father while she went on vacation. Perhaps at that time, seeing his naked father in the bathroom might have stirred up some sexual feelings in him.

The patient responds by saying he couldn't remember. But he does recall being fascinated by seeing young boys' penises at summer camp. He recalled an incident at age nine or ten when he fondled the penis of a younger boy. It was a sudden and impulsive act. He and the boy were alone in the infirmary at camp because they were ill and the others had gone out to play. The younger boy was lonely and tearful and the patient climbed into his bed to comfort him and then suddenly had the urge to fondle his penis. He was shocked at himself and terrified that the boy might talk. Later on he recalled similar impulses when they would undress for swimming in school, but always toward younger boys. I interpret that it seems to me that he had done to the younger boy what he had *wanted* his father to do to him.

The patient is startled. He replies by saying, do you mean to say the picture of my father as a huge, fat, big-bellied, disgusting man was a cover-up? I say: "Yes, it seems so. You used that picture of him to hide an earlier and more attractive one. He became coarse and vulgar to you and you became distant to him as a protection." The patient thinks for a while and says: "Maybe that's why I never become too friendly with warm and intense men even though I like them. I must be afraid to get too close [pause]. That's probably what has happened in this analysis with me and you."

3.9443 Technical Procedures: Pursuit and Reconstruction

I believe the foregoing material is a typical example of how one interprets and (partially) works through the transference reactions of a patient. To repeat: an effective and full interpretation cannot be accomplished by a single intervention but requires repetition and elaboration, i.e., working through. The material I have presented covers a period of three weeks. Let us review the sequence of events with our attention focused on the technical procedures.

My first interpretation is that he refuses to swallow my interpretations because he is afraid of getting into his homosexual feelings. The patient agrees in part by acknowledging he never lets himself get too close to men friends, but he maintains that he isn't sure exactly what he is afraid of. In the next hour he reports a masturbation fantasy in which the picture of a fat, grey-haired, big-bellied man intruded itself. He finds this disgusting and feels I am "pushing such ideas into him." He becomes resistant for several hours, which I point out to him, but nothing changes or evolves.

Then the patient brings in some new material when he had to urinate in my office building. I interpret his difficulty in urinating as being connected to a fantasy of my being in the toilet with him and trace this to childhood experiences with his father. Again the patient accepts this idea intellectually only, but confirms the idea by recalling many experiences in the toilet with his father. However, he resists recapturing any feelings or impulses. He remains resistant and tries to use a heterosexual affair to ward off the homosexual strivings. I interpret this form of resistance to him for several hours until a new form of transference resistance comes up.

The patient now relives with me the experience of being with a coarse and vulgar old man who had homosexual impulses toward him. The patient dares to let himself feel this, and describes it in the analytic session, which leads to the uncovering of a homosexual experience with a male prostitute in adolescence. In the next hour he is able to remember his dreams which lead via the transference to associations and memories concerning nakedness of fathers and sons.

I now make a reconstruction and tell him that from his behavior, dreams, associations, and memories it seems plausible to construct the following: When he was five years old and full of oedipal sexual feelings, his mother left him alone with his father while she went on a long vacation. At that time, his naked father parading in front of him in the bathroom must have become sexually stimulating and attractive to the patient. The patient is not able to recall any such feelings toward his father but confirms my reconstruction by recall-ing a derivative of this event, namely, a fascination for the penises of the young boys at summer camp. Then he recalls doing and fan-tasying sexual activities with the younger boys, which I interpret as an acting out with the younger boys what he had wanted his father to do with him. The patient seems to confirm this interpreta-tion by spontaneously recognizing that he had used the picture of his father as a repulsive man to protect himself from his homosexual feelings. He then realizes he has been doing the same with me in the analysis.

In a period of three weeks the transference picture of me has changed radically. For a long time I had been portrayed and reacted to as the puritanical father. This façade turned out to be a reactive screen behind which I am revealed as a coarse and vulgar man. This picture of me as a coarse and vulgar man stubbornly resists analysis until it too proves to be a further defensive screen which hides the very frightening image of me as a homosexually attrac-tive object.

In the process of working through, every kind of technical device may be utilized, but there are two major technical procedures which are of particular importance. They are the "pursuit" of the transfer-ence interpretation and reconstruction. By pursuit of the transfer-ence I refer to the clinical fact that in every hour following a new transference interpretation, the analyst has to search out what has happened to the transference as a consequence of the new interpre-tation. A fresh transference interpretation must have repercussions and therefore representation in the following hour. The interpreta-tion may be right or wrong, insufficient or excessive; in any case there will be some derivative of the interpretation in the next hour. The only exception to this can occur when some important unfore-seen event of everyday life takes place outside of the analysis and temporarily usurps the overriding dominance of the analytic situa-tion. Otherwise a new or different transference interpretation will stir up some change in the memories, dreams, associations, fantasies or resistances of the patient. The clinical material above illustrates this point.

The analyst must be vigilant about what is going on in the trans-ference situation after he has made a new or different transference interpretation. This does not necessarily mean that he will continue with his interpretation to the patient. He may do so if the patient seems to indicate that he is working along productively with that interpretation. He may pursue another variation of the transference if the patient's material seems to point in that direction. He may ask the patient what he felt about the last interpretation if he sees no tangible connections or derivatives in the patient's material. Or he may wait patiently and silently for the patient to work with the new interpretation in his own way and at his own speed. In any event, the analyst will be particularly alert to all changes and developments, as well as to absence of changes, which follow any new or fresh transference interpretation.

Reconstruction is another technical device of particular importance in the working through of transference material (Freud, 1937b; Kris, 1956a, 1956b). There is a very close relationship between interpretation and reconstruction, and they often cannot be separated from one another. The special sections on interpretation and working through (Volume II) will delve into this matter at greater length. At this time I want to stress only the special relationship of reconstruction to transference reactions. Transference phenomena are always repetitions of the past; the patient repeats with his analyst what he cannot and will not remember. His transference behavior therefore is particularly suitable for making reconstructions of the past and indeed this characteristic of transference gives it its singular importance (Freud, 1914c, 1937b).

In the process of working through, single interpretations are elaborated upon, deepened, and interconnected in order to make some aspect of the patient's behavior more comprehensible. In trying to give meaning to a fragment of the patient's behavior it is often necessary to reconstruct, from the patient's transference reactions, dreams, associations, etc., some piece of the patient's past forgotten life. Reconstruction is a preliminary labor and, if it is correct, will lead to new memories, new behavior, and to changes in the self-image. It is often the starting point for the "circular processes" of memories leading to insight, leading to changes, which lead to new memories, etc. (Kris, 1956a, 1956b).

If one returns to the clinical material I presented on working through, one sees I made two reconstructions. Reconstruction number one: when the patient was five years old he was full of sexual feelings for his mother. At this time she left him alone with his father and went on vacation. As a result of this rejection his sexual impulses were directed to his father, who paraded naked in front of the boy in the bathroom. The reconstruction seemed to be correct because it stimulated the patient to recall homosexual impulses toward young boys. Eventually he recalled actually fondling the penis of a young boy, and many similar impulses and fantasies later on. Then I made the second reconstruction: the patient then did with a younger boy what he had wanted his father to do to him. Later on he turned away from his father by making him seem coarse and vulgar, and still later he conceived of him as puritanical and aloof.

The patient confirmed this reconstruction by realizing that he avoided closeness to male friends and also that he was running away from the same thing in his relationship to me. This led him to a more convincing awareness of his feelings of love and affection toward me, as well as his need for me. At this point his enormous primitive hostility to his mother began to emerge in the analysis, which seemed to confirm the correctness of the two reconstructions.

The aim of interpretation is to make some unconscious psychic event conscious so that we can better understand the meaning of a given piece of behavior. However, interpretations are usually limited to a single element, a single aspect, a single constellation. As we work through a given interpretation of a single element, as we try to re-create the history and vicissitudes of this element, we have to do more than interpret. We have to reconstruct the piece of life that was going on in and around the patient which would explain the fate of that certain element (Freud, 1937b). We even have to try to reconstruct the goings-on in the mother and the father, for example, if that might help explain what happened to that certain element in the patient at that time.

Correct reconstructions are a valuable aid in accelerating the progress of working through. A correct reconstruction leads to new memories or new material in the form of dreams, associations, screen formations, or new forms of resistance or changes in the self-image (Reider, 1953b). Reconstructions have to be made with tact. They may not be too rigid or brittle or else they will not be able to fit into the unknown gaps of the patient's forgotten history. On the other hand, they may not be too formless, because then they would not serve as a bridge strong enough to guide the patient over the unknown empty spaces. Finally, the analyst must always be willing to amend, modify, or abandon any portion of the reconstruction in keeping with the clinical responses of the patient.

3.945 Addenda

Before leaving the routine technique of analyzing transference reactions, I should like to add a few small points which I have found of clinical and technical value. From the moment the patient meets the analyst, the analyst is a person of importance to the patient. Actually, this should be modified to: the moment the patient seriously considers meeting the analyst, even before the actual meeting, the analyst is a person of importance in the life of that patient. Therefore, every analytic hour, as well as the entire analytic hour, has some relevance to this point. I do not mean to imply that every hour and all hour long we find explicit material about the analyst. I mean that by analyzing all the clinical material it is possible for the analyst to fathom what the patient is feeling about him even though the manifest content does not appear to refer to the analyst either literally or symbolically. I do not mean to suggest that interpretations gathered in this way are always utilizable by the patient. They may merely be hints which are stored up for future use. At times this approach may clarify an otherwise obscure hour.

For example, in an hour a patient rambles cheerfully on about many diverse subjects, going from past to present and back again, never resting very long on any single subject. I cannot find a single common denominator or any outstanding affect charge in any of the material. I then take the entire content as alluding to me and see her productions as a flitting happily back and forth to me and away from me. Since I feel the patient is not inaccessible to me, I tell her this. She laughs and replies: "Throughout the hour I had the sensation of being out in the sunshine floating over some peaceful country scene. This was all in the background, however, and I just told you what was in the foreground. When I came in this morning, you looked summery and I guess that started me off. When I was a little girl my mother would sometimes surprise me by suddenly arranging for a picnic in the park just for the two of us. Those were such happy times, just the two of us alone in the warm sunshine."

I believe this is a good example of how the general content of an hour can be explored from the standpoint of: What does all this say about me?

Another technical point is Fenichel's (1941) concept of the reverse transference interpretation. Usually when the patient talks about the analyst we try to deduce about whom in the past is the patient really talking. Sometimes the patient talks about past figures as a resistance to talking about the analyst, as a means of establishing a distance from the analyst. This latter resistance has to be interpreted first, and only then can one go on to trace this resistance into the past.

Finally, Bornstein's (1919) and Loewenstein's (1951) idea about "reconstruction upward" is a helpful technical point. When a patient's productions or dreams seem to be obvious references to very early and primitive impulses, and there is reasonable doubt that the patient can deal with this material, then the analyst reconstructs the material upward. This means he uses the patient's material; he does not completely ignore the material because that might cause anxiety; but he interprets in a less primitive direction. Mrs. K., who began her first hour with a dream of the analyst performing cunnilingus upon her, is an illustration. The reader may recall that I interpreted this as her way of getting me to prove that I had really accepted her (Section 3.81).

3.10 Special Problems in Analyzing Transference Reactions

Thus far I have described the technical procedures which should be followed in analyzing the everyday varieties of transference reactions. However, transference situations do arise occasionally in the analysis of patients from every diagnostic category which may call for some special handling. For example, an acute emotional storm may lead the patient to embark on some dangerous acting out of his transference feelings. In such a situation, the temporary absence of a reasonable ego in the patient will require some technique other than analysis. In general, however, over the last score or more of years there seems to be an increase in special problems which arise from diverse sources.

First of all, there seems to be a change in the type of patient seeking psychoanalytic therapy since World War II. In part this may be due to the increased popularity of psychoanalysis. On the other hand, we are now attempting to treat patients psychoanalytically who would not have been considered suitable for such treatment in the past (Stone, 1954b; A. Freud, 1954a). This extension of the scope of psychoanalytic therapy may be regarded as an experimental attempt to apply therapeutically our increased knowledge and experience in regard to ego psychology and early childhood development. However, some of the special problems we meet may be due to unrecognized deviations in technique and to errors in the appraisal of the patient.

This present discussion of special problems in analyzing the transference will be limited to those patients who at the outset seem suitable for treatment by classical psychoanalysis. Before embarking on a detailed discussion of the problem of analyzability, I would like at this point to refer back to some of Freud's early and basic ideas on this subject. I shall use them as a general guide until we can elaborate these ideas more fully in Volume II.

When Freud (1916-17) differentiated the transference neuroses from the narcissistic neuroses he was stressing the clinical fact that patients who developed a transference neurosis were able to form and sustain a cohesive yet multiform and influenceable set of transference reactions. These patients he believed were suitable for psychoanalytic therapy. On the other hand, those patients who suffered from narcissistic neuroses had only fragmentary and fleeting transference reactions and were therefore relatively inaccessible and unsuitable for psychoanalytic therapy. Although there has been some modification of these views about transference formation in borderline and psychotic patients, I believe it is still a generally accepted clinical finding that the transference phenomena in such patients cannot be adequately dealt with by predominantly analytic means (Fenichel, 1945a, Chapt. XVIII; Glover, 1955, Chapt. XIII, XIV; Zetzel, 1956; Greenacre, 1959).

I shall exclude from this presentation the treatment of problems arising in obvious borderline and psychotic patients and also cases treated by methods distinctly and deliberately deviant from the classical psychoanalytic method. Such problems go beyond the scope of this volume (A. Stern, 1948; Knight, 1953b; Bychowski, 1953; Jacobson, 1954; Orr, 1954).

3.10.1 ACUTE EMOTIONAL STORMS AND
DANGEROUS RE-ENACTMENTS

The patient's transference feelings may reach an intensity which, for a period of time, prevent the patient from using his capacity to separate his reasonable from his experiencing ego. This often occurs during the reliving of the infantile neurosis. Then, our therapeutic task is to help re-establish a reasonable ego. Very often the best technique is to wait, giving the patient an opportunity to discharge his feelings as fully as possible. In this way the ego is given a chance to reassume its command over the situation. Sometimes it may even be necessary or helpful to allow the patient to run over the limit of the session. At other times it may be wise to point out the impending end of the hour, so that the patient can pull himself together in preparation for leaving the session. Although it can be a danger in terms of transference gratification to give the patient extra time, it can be an even greater one to let the patient leave the hour out of control in the throes of intense emotions. One has to use one's clinical judgment in determining the best course to pursue.

Usually these devices will adequately handle such emotional storms. It is important that the analyst's attitude and tone be patient, compassionate, and firm, neither critical nor saccharine. I usually tell patients toward the end of such a session that I am sorry to have to interrupt, but that the time is up. I usually add something to the effect that I hope we will be able to work further on this problem in the next session.

I make no attempt at interpretation as long as no reasonable ego seems present or accessible. Only if I sense that I can call forth a reasonable ego, mobilize one into action, and if I am sure of my ground, would I make any attempt at interpretation. This may take place as the intensity of the emotion recedes, but can also succeed if the reasonable ego is not too deeply immersed in the turbulent emotions and if the interpretation is precise. Under such conditions the correct interpretation can serve as a call to reason, as a rallying point for the return of the reasonable ego. The key to the correct interpretation is the realization that the acute emotional storm is a re-enactment of a past situation, either an exact duplicate or a wish-fulfilling distortion. Let me illustrate:

A woman patient, during the course of an analytic hour, responds to my request that she tell me more about some recent sexual experience by becoming frightened. At first she can report her feelings of fear; she feels I am asking her to undress. Then she becomes carried away by the situation and becomes terrified. She no longer reports her panic, but experiences it, as though it were happening in the hour. She begins to shout at me frantically, "No, I won't, I won't, I won't. Leave me alone or I'll scream. Go away, go away. Help me, oh God, help me. Stop, stop, stop. Please stop, someone help me. . . ." This goes on and on for many minutes. Since the intensity does not seem to be diminishing and since the hour is coming to a close, I say simply: "Mrs. Smith, pause, Mrs. Smith, that was the gardener who scared you, Mrs. Smith, the gardener, and now you are here with me, Dr. Greenson." When I call the patient Mrs. Smith, she does not seem really to hear me, therefore I repeat it several times. When I say the words, "the gardener," she seems to come back into focus; she has heard me, she seems to be trying to comprehend, to orient herself. By the time I say "and now you are here with me, Dr. Greenson," she can smile a little, as though now she understands what had transpired. It takes a few minutes for her to pull herself together, to regain her composure. She can now leave the hour in control of her emotions and ruminate about the return of the traumatic childhood experience.

I was successful in pointing out the meaning of the transference experience because I could sense that her working ego was accessible and I knew from previous material that this experience came from a childhood seduction by the gardener. I knew I could reach her by the words "the gardener" and could bring her back to reality by reminding her where and with whom she was.

A male patient for many years struggled with his fear of expressing his anger and rage at me directly. Toward the end of one hour he begins to describe what he would say to me if he were drunk. He becomes more and more abusive verbally, begins to bang the wall with his fist, pounds the couch with his feet, and finally jumps off the couch. He comes over to my chair and stands over me, shaking his finger at me and saying, "Who the hell do you think you are anyway?" I say nothing, but as he was about to stomp out of the office, I call out to him: "How does it feel to finally tell Pappa he's not so great after all?" The patient stops still in his tracks at the word Pappa. He turns around and looks at me. Slowly his angry features relax; he shakes his head; he walks slowly back to the couch, and sits down. Then he says slowly: "Well, I finally did it, finally,

finally, finally, after all these years; I told you all off, you and my old man, and my big brother, all of you. I finally feel I'm a grown man and not just a little boy masquerading as a man." Then tears streamed down his cheeks.

Parallel to the emotional storms and often as a component or consequence of such storms, patients will relive certain past situations not only in words and feelings but also in actions. I am referring now to actions which can be dangerous if unchecked. This behavior may be a simple reliving, a slightly distorted ego-acceptable acting out, or a severely distorted, ego-alien symptomatic act. The first example cited above of the woman and the gardener is an illustration of simple reliving in the transference. The case of the angry man is an example of a combination of both symptomatic action and acting out. The technical problem is the same in any case: we have to help the patient establish a reasonable ego, or a working alliance, before he leaves the hour, if at all possible.

The procedure is similar to what I described for emotional storms: wait for the activity to spend itself, to calm down. If we understand the meaning of the behavior and a reasonable ego can be mobilized, then we make the interpretation as precisely and compactly as possible. If both methods fail or are not applicable, then we have to interrupt the behavior by confronting the patient with reality and the dangers of his behavior.

For example, in the case of the angry man cited above, what if he had not stopped when I said, "How does it feel to finally tell Pappa he's not so great after all?" Then I would have called out to him something like this: "Mr. Jones, please wait a moment. You can leave any time you want, but I don't think it's a good idea right now. You are too angry and upset with me and we should work on this a little. It's not safe letting you leave here in this state."

In similar situations I have said things like: "I am sorry you feel so badly and I wish I could help, but I don't seem to understand what is going on. Let's work on this a little before you go."

Upon one occasion a woman patient, a borderline psychotic, got up from the couch and threw her arms around me, saying, "Let's stop wasting time and let's have sex." I firmly took hold of her arms, looked squarely at her and said: "Mrs. Jones, I want to help you and I can do that by working. So let's work together and stop wasting time."

All these situations are potentially dangerous for the patient and should be handled somehow in the hour. The least satisfactory method is to use force of any kind to stop the patient from acting in a particular way. Yet sometimes it is the only possible method of preventing something worse. Then the firm, but compassionate tone, the plea to "let's work," while grasping the patient's arms, is the last resort. To put it succinctly, one behaves like a strong and concerned parent with a child who has lost his controls. Related problems of acting out will be covered in Volume II.

3.10.2 THE MONDAY HOUR

Actually, the heading of this section should be the Friday and the Monday hour, or better still, the analytic patient's reactions to the weekend separation from the analyst. For the sake of brevity, and also because Freud spoke of the "Monday crust" as early as 1913, I have condensed the heading to the Monday Hour. We know that our patients will react emotionally to all separations from the analyst. Some respond as though the weekend is a holiday, a carnival, others as though it were an abandonment or a desertion. Ferenczi (1919c) described the "Sunday neuroses" which occurred when his patients lost the distractions and diversions of their everyday work. Freud, in *Totem and Taboo* (1913a) and later in "Mourning and Melancholia" (1917b), described some of the dynamics and structural changes which occurred in festivals. He pursued some of these ideas further in various writings. A good summary of them was published in 1955 by Grinstein. However, none of the authors stressed the central importance of the transference situation as the determinant for the patient's reaction to the weekend. I propose to explore some of the typical ways in which patients in analysis react to the weekend interruption in the analytic work.

3.10.21 The Weekend Is a Holiday

For some patients the weekend separation is an occasion for celebration, it is an intermission, a respite, a rest; it offers the possibility for recuperation from the rigors and demands of the psychoanalytic treatment. Obviously when this occurs it is a sign that the everyday psychoanalytic work is being carried out under a constant resistance. It is very striking how often it can happen that the patient does not indicate openly the presence of this resistance until the Friday hour or the hour before the vacation occurs. Then, to one's surprise, the patient reacts as to an impending celebration and festivity; in this case one must infer the presence of a latent resentment toward the psychoanalytic treatment that has been occurring silently throughout the working interval. This indicates that the analyst must be some kind of critical superego agency for the patient. The patient has been working in the analysis under the stress of feeling obliged, of being under duress, and has submitted to the situation without articulating this submission. The patient may or may not be consciously aware of this, but his reaction to the impending holiday clearly indicates it. Patients who feel this way on Friday hours before weekends and patients who have a sense of relief and pleasure at the end of every psychoanalytic hour belong in this category.

When the analyst represents a critical superego figure for the patient, then the patient's behavior during the weekend will consist of all sorts of instinctual liberties. There will be a plethora of libidinal and aggressive activities, usually with a regressive, infantile cast. It is striking to note how patients will behave with a certain restraint during the week in regard to their sexual life and then indulge in a variety of pregenital activities on weekends. There is often a great increase in forepleasure activities, masturbation, and promiscuity on weekends. There is a parallel upsurge in aggressive actions. Some patients act out on weekends what they free-associate to during the week. These patients behave as though the analyst is the bearer of their superegos. The Monday hour then becomes an hour for confession and atonement. For them, the Monday hour has become the Sunday confessional. On Monday they very often begin the hour with a recital of all their sins, with much guilt and shame, fear of punishment, and much self-abasement. It is striking that when such patients accidentally meet their analyst during a weekend, they are shocked because they had the fantasy the analyst does not exist in the outside world. Or else they fantasy he is locked in the office and has no life outside of the office. There are patients who are staggered when they meet their analyst at a concert, or at a theater. Some will fail to recognize him, will become hysterically blind, and develop a scotoma for him. It is important to recognize this projection of id and superego, as well as the subtle resistances which must be silently at work during the weekday sessions.

3.10.22 The Weekend Is a Desertion

For many patients the weekends or the interval between analytic hours denotes the loss of a love object. To them, the intermission means separation, detachment, disengagement, disconnection, or termination. In some form or other the patient behaves as though he feels he is losing a love object. He often reacts to the weekend as though it meant a rejection by the analyst. The Friday hour is often spent in nonproductive anger, for the weekend means the analyst is taking a holiday and is abandoning and deserting the patient. For such a patient the Monday hour means a confrontation between him, the excluded one, the wronged one, and the analyst who is the rejector and the aggressor. For neurotically depressed patients the Monday hour can also represent a reunion with a lost love object and be felt as a kind of bliss. Some patients feel relieved to discover the analyst has survived their death wishes. It is important to recognize the level on which this is being experienced, or at least the level on which the predominant reactions are occurring. Furthermore, do we see drives or defenses in the foreground? Do we see aggressive behavior or reparation and restitution attempts?

For many patients the weekend revives the oedipal situation. For such a patient the weekend is a primal scene from which he has been excluded. He struggles with his incestuous feelings, or develops guilt, anxiety, or depression, or perhaps he acts out in some form or other some aspect of the oedipal situation. Some patients struggle with unconscious death wishes and are anxious and guilt-laden every Monday upon meeting their analyst. Some feel sad and depressed at the exclusion. Others feel hostile with jealous envy. Some patients feel this as such, and come to the hour with depressed feelings or hostility. Others deny such feelings by their behavior or by indicating: "I couldn't care less" or "Who needs you." Some patients work very hard in the Monday hour to atone for their guilty wishes or guilty behavior and in this way try to make reparation to the analyst. Some become silent on Monday out of their hostility and resentment at having been rejected. Some patients develop somatic reactions on weekends as an attempt to discharge otherwise inaccessible emotions or drives. It is typical for patients to be habitually early or habitually late on Mondays. I had one patient who sang in the waiting room every Monday hour and whistled joyously, which was his attempt to deny the hostility and guilt he felt upon coming back to the analytic situation.

The loss of a love object on weekends can be experienced on an oral or anal level as well. I have seen patients who felt they had nothing to produce on Monday, and others who came with a big pile of material which they had stored up and retained in order to express a huge mass before me for my approval. For some patients the weekend was an oral deprivation and they came back on Monday hungry to be fed by me, to drink in my voice rather than to hear what I had to say. One such patient, Mrs. K., often spent the entire weekend sunbathing as an attempt to replace the warm, loving sun-father, as Ferenczi (1914d) described.

From a technical point of view, the task is to recognize how the weekend reactions relate to the transference situation and to make the patient aware of this. It is striking how patients can resist accepting the transference meaning of their weekend behavior. The Friday hour and the Monday hour are of particular importance in revealing and demonstrating important transference reactions. A depressed patient of mine became constipated every Friday, holding on to her fecal mass as a substitute for me, and could only move her bowels on resuming her analysis on Mondays. This was the first breakthrough in our understanding of her oral-anal relationship to me.

3.10.23 The Weekend and Ego Functions

For some patients who are in a relatively severe regressed state, the absence of the analyst can be perceived as a loss of ego functions. This is apt to occur in a neurotic patient who is in the throes of an intense infantile transference neurosis, or it may occur at any time in borderline patients. Then the analyst has been functioning as an auxiliary ego and separation from him can bring about a loss of reality testing, disorientation, depersonalization, loss of identity, etc. It may be necessary to see such patients during a weekend or to have telephone contact with them. Sometimes just knowing the analyst's whereabouts makes it unnecessary to arrange for some substitute to replace him.

There are other ways in which the patient may be using the

analyst as an ego function in the transference which may come to light during a separation. The analyst may be used by the patient to temper the critical demands of his superego. Then on weekends such patients may return to their hypercritical anti-instinctual state. Such patients cannot bear to waste time during weekends or holidays and have to pursue some gainful task, either a cultural pursuit or a health measure. For some such patients the id temptations of the weekends can mobilize severe guilt and shame reactions. For them, the Friday hour is embarking on a dangerous journey and the Monday hour is a return to safety.

3.10.24 Other Clinical Findings

There are patients who will stop working on Fridays according to the formula, "I will leave you before you leave me." This question of who is leaving whom can be an important technical point with very sick patients. In order to spare such a patient the feeling of acute abandonment I have often found it advisable to allow him to leave for a brief holiday a day or so earlier than I do. It is not rare for such patients to cancel the last hour before the analyst's vacation. I have seen patients who were silent or otherwise unproductive on Fridays in order to display the attitude: "Who needs you?" They waste the last hour to show their contempt for the analytic work.

When the analyst is felt predominantly as a figure of hatred, the Friday hour can mean the gateway to freedom from misery and one can detect a certain euphoria in the patient. However, under such circumstances the patient can become depressed during the weekend from the turning inward of such hostility, or anxiety can arise from the unconscious expectation of some disaster befalling the analyst.

Reactions to the Monday hour will depend on what has transpired during the weekend and, above all, on what transference meaning the analyst has at that time. Is one returning to a critical superego, a lost love object, a rejecting love object, a needed ego, or a tempting id. Is the figure of the analyst loving or hating, benevolent or harsh, supportive or critical?

No matter what else may be going on in the analysis, the Friday hour heralds the weekend, and the impending separation from the analyst has to be taken into account. Similarly, no matter what else transpires during the weekend, the fact that an event occurred during a separation from the analyst will influence the other findings. It is not rare to find patients reacting on Monday with the feeling: "I am worse and it is your fault because you deserted me over the weekend."

Patients' reactions to the Friday and Monday hours will change during the course of analysis.

A male patient of mine, Mr. Z., who hated Monday hours because he could not admit he missed me, since that would imply homosexuality, used to be spitefully unproductive on Mondays. Eventually, he was able to express his regret when the Friday hour approached and became a hard worker on Mondays.

A depressed woman patient, Mrs. K., felt she stopped living when Fridays arrived and became a "Zombie" on weekends because she felt she was no longer "plugged into" me. After she was able to fall in love outside of the analysis, she looked forward impatiently to the Friday hours and her own weekend vacations.

It should not be forgotten that the weekend offers a valuable replica in miniature of what one can expect at termination.

3.10.25 The Technical Problems

One of the technical problems is to re-establish a working alliance so that one can analyze the patient's reaction to the separation. I believe that the "Monday crust" Freud spoke of referred to the day residues, the experiential events of the separation plus the resistances evoked by the separation which interfere with the resumption of the therapeutic alliance. Once these residues and resistances are expressed and clarified, one can proceed with the analytic work.

Another technical problem deals with the timing and dosage of an interpretation. One must take into account that an interpretation given in a Friday hour or preceding a vacation will have to be handled by the patient himself for a period of time. Therefore, the dosage of new and painful insights should be less than if that same interpretation were given on a regular working day. The analyst has to weigh the question of: can the patient bear this insight alone for such and such a period? I recall an error in this regard when I was still a young analyst.

A young woman patient brought in a dream on a Friday which for the first time had clear-cut homosexual imagery. Her associations also touched on this theme. I made what I thought was a careful interpretation of her homosexual feelings toward a schoolteacher friend. The patient's response in the hour seemed appropriate. When she returned on Monday she was completely silent and remained so for over two weeks. Later I discovered that she had become depersonalized during the weekend as she ruminated about my interpretation. This matter of dosage will be discussed in greater detail in Volume II.

Another problem in technique is the complicating circumstance of what the weekend may mean for the analyst. Although this is mainly a problem of countertransference, and will be discussed in Volume II, it merits a few lines at the moment. Some analysts will react to the Friday hour as though they are leaving their children, with a feeling of heavy-heartedness, or concern, or worry, and for others it is an experience of relief and joy. For some analysts the Monday hour is returning with a sense of relief to those about whom one was worried. Other analysts meet Monday with tired resignation, as a chore. There are analysts who cannot wait for Friday hours or who cannot wait for Monday hours. There are some who even seem compelled to work on Sunday; and there are others who are exhausted and depleted by Tuesday. I must say that although analysis is work, it ought to be enjoyable work and not torturesome and exhausting. It is striking how frequently analysts complain about their fatigue. However, I suspect that at times this complaint is not accurate, that it has become a manner of speech; it has become the acceptable mode to talk about one's exhaustion. It is as though some analysts are embarrassed to admit they enjoy their work, as though enjoyment might imply lack of seriousness (Szasz, 1957).

At this point, I would like to add that many psychoanalysts do suffer from overwork; it seems to be an occupational hazard. Some work far more hours than they can handle effectively. I am impressed by the number of analysts who engage in strenuous extracurricular activities in the evenings like committee meetings, scientific meetings, lecturing, seminars, etc., after a full day's work with patients. They have little time or energy left for their families and are depleted when they begin the day's work with their patients.

Psychoanalytic therapy is a demanding profession and overwork makes it an impossible one (Greenson, 1966).

To summarize: There are special clinical and technical problems of the Monday hour. There are innumerable ways for patients to react to the weekend separation from their analyst: it depends on what childhood figure the analyst represents. But patients do react, and this reaction has to be detected and interpreted. It is necessary to re-establish the working alliance which has become interfered with by the separation and the accumulation of external experiences. All of this is complicated by the countertransference meaning of the weekend separation.

3.10.3 INTRACTABLE TRANSFERENCE REACTIONS

I have already stated that the most frequent cause of stalemated psychoanalyses is the intractable transference reaction. By this term I am referring to a special variety of transference resistance which is characterized by being fixed, unyielding, and uninfluenceable despite what seems to be correct handling. Strangely enough, patients with this problem seem willing and even eager to continue their unproductive analyses for years on end. They seem to find some subtle combination of satisfaction and security in the analytic situation which makes them prefer to cling to treatment rather than to seek some other solution for their problems. Although intractable transference reactions may occur in widely diverse diagnostic groups of patients, for the purpose of focusing primarily on the technical problems, I will divide them into two categories. It is possible to single out a large group of patients whose superficial clinical appearance and behavior would make them appear suitable for classical psychoanalysis and who become recognizable as unsuitable only after a period of analysis. The other group of intractable cases are those which have become so because of some subtle but important errors in technique. Most cases of stalemate will turn out to contain a mixture of both errors.

3.10.31 Errors in Appraisal of Transference Capacity

Ordinarily we expect patients who seem to be suffering from psychoneurotic symptoms and who evidence no sign of psychosis or any marked impoverishment of their object relations, and who seem to have reasonably good ego functions, to be able to work effectively in the analytic situation. However, experience indicates there is a considerable number of patients who seem able to fulfill these requirements in the preliminary interviews and yet later turn out to be unsuitable for psychoanalysis—even when these interviews are adequate in number and performed carefully. The special pathology which escapes detection in the preanalytic investigation emerges clearly only in the process of analysis and, specifically, in the development of the transference. Only then does one realize that the patient's pathology, in terms of his capacity to establish object relations, is defective and precludes classical psychoanalysis. The nature of the defect is to be found in the patient's inability to form a working alliance as well as a transference neurosis. This deficiency supersedes all other considerations, including the diagnostic category. I have occasionally seen schizophrenic patients who were analyzable and psychoneurotics who were not. What seems to be decisive for making a patient analyzable is the capacity to form these two types of relationships simultaneously with the analyst (see Section 3.5).

Thus, it is only a trial at analysis which can truly indicate whether or not a patient is suitable for psychoanalytic therapy (Freud, 1913b; Ekstein, 1950). Once this has been undertaken, it may become difficult if not impossible to persuade a patient to interrupt therapy. Some patients may have to be kept in what appears to be a psychoanalytic situation because they need it to maintain their fragile equilibrium. It is only the façade of psychoanalysis which is therapeutic for them, not the essentials of the procedure. Such patients are often kept on a stationary and artificial nonpsychotic level by such therapy (Fenichel, 1945a, p. 551). Other patients require a prolonged period of preparatory therapy before they are ready for psychoanalysis proper. I shall try to illustrate by describing a few intractable cases of patients who were misled into analysis because of an error in appraising the patient's analyzability.

3.10.311 Erotized Transference

Under this heading I would like to describe the kind of patient who may appear on the surface to be a typical psychoneurotic but who develops, early in the analysis, an intractable erotic transference. It is not merely the high intensity involved, but also a qualitative factor which distinguishes such patients. Freud (1915a) described a type of neurotic woman patient who developed a strong erotic transference which did not yield to analytic technique. He ascribed this to their elemental passionateness, an inability to tolerate surrogates and an intractable need for love. Since then Blitzsten (in a personal communication) and Rappaport (1956) have described similar transference problems, the outstanding feature of which is the patient's refractory erotic demands.

In my own experience, I have had two such patients, both women. (All cases of erotized transference that I have heard of have been women patients in analysis with men.) In both instances I had the clinical impression from the preliminary interviews that I was dealing essentially with a mixture of hysterical and neurotic-depressive elements. Both patients seemed to relate to me appropriately in the initial interviews. I could not find any significant defect in their ego functioning; they seemed psychological-minded, imaginative, had a good history of achievements, an adequate social life, etc. In both cases the presenting complaints included sexual difficulties and unsatisfactory love life in their marriages, tendencies to obsessional jealousy fantasies, promiscuity, and sleeping problems.

Both patients developed a strong sexual transference to me in the first hours of lying on the couch. Their feelings were striking in their intensity and primitiveness. In both cases I had great difficulty in getting the patient to work on this material. They recognized their feelings and could describe their impulses and longings which were heavily weighted in oral terms. They wanted and even demanded physical closeness and bodily contact, which meant incorporation, possession, and fusion to them. They were ready for action, and were barely able to restrain themselves from acting upon their impulses; they were frustrated and angered by verbalization and thought. Although they seemed to listen to my interventions and interpretations, they were not touched or influenced by ordinary analytic measures. If they agreed with an interpretation, it was merely lip service and a means to get me to stop talking. They came to the hours eagerly, but not for insight, only to enjoy the physical proximity. My interventions seemed irrelevant to them.

At first I had the impression that these patients had developed an acute, intense, and very regressive erotic transference neurosis. But I was not able to evoke a working alliance in them. Their transference reactions were completely ego syntonic and not subject to self-observation. I became aware of a desperateness in their proclamations of love for me. What seemed to be a kind of sensual passion was more like an urgent, gnawing hunger. Their feelings to me were not merely neurotically distorted but more like a delusion. Such reactions have been designated as transference psychoses (Little, 1958; Reider, 1957). (In Section 3.4 I discussed the differences between neurotic and psychotic transference phenomena.)

The great intensity and intractability came from a terrible anxiety. In both instances, I detected that the patient was on the verge of falling into the abyss of homosexual love for the mother. Their erotic reactions to me represented a last-ditch attempt to clutch desperately onto their sexual identity. In one of them there was an additional element which eventually came to light. Her extravagant reactions were also a massive denial of her growing awareness that she was losing contact with people in general. There was loss of internal object representations.

I realized in a short time that my initial clinical appraisal of these patients had been in error. The loss of visual contact, the sensory deprivation caused by lying on the couch, mobilized an intense libidinal transference hunger and defense. These patients were not suitable for psychoanalysis because they could not bear the deprivations which *classical* psychoanalysis demands (M. Wexler, 1960). Their capacity for object relations was too meager for them to be able to tolerate all the vicissitudes of transference phenomena which occur in analysis. In the usual psychoneuroses, alongside of the transference neurosis there is the more realistic object relationship to the analyst which goes toward the formation of the working alliance (A. Freud, 1954a). It is this relatively realistic object relationship which allows the patient to risk letting himself develop an intense transference neurosis. The patients I am describing lacked the ability to form and maintain such a relationship in that complex combination of intimacy, intensity, and distance of the analytic situation. Diagnostically I belatedly realized they were more like impulse-ridden, addictive characters with psychotic tendencies.

Once I recognized the severity of the restrictions in their capacity to form object relationships, the readiness to explosive acting out, and the closeness to psychosis, I realized these patients should not be exposed to the rigors of classical psychoanalysis. They needed psychotherapy that would not endanger the defense-instinct balance (Knight, 1953b). I attempted to strengthen those defenses which seemed relatively healthy and to strengthen their other ego functions by offering myself as an obvious auxiliary ego and superego. The sessions were carried out in a face-to-face position, with no emphasis on free association. My attitude was firm, direct, friendly, but above all clearly therapeutic. I demonstrated to them their errors in thought and judgment and offered better alternatives. I became their mentor and guide. I was strict in never being seductive or punitive. Slowly, by identification, their ego functions improved, and along with that, their capacity for more mature object relations. Eventually one patient was able to embark on a more classical analysis with another analyst after one and one half years of psychotherapy. The other patient remained in psychotherapy with me for five years, but the therapy became more analytic toward the latter part. The reasons for these decisions will be discussed in Section 3.10.4 on The Question of Changing Analysts.

3.10.312 Masked Perversion-Psychosis

Under this heading I am referring to another group of patients with intractable transference reactions who are very different from the erotized transference cases except in one regard. Both share the characteristic of being extremely restricted and impoverished in their capacity to permit transference reactions to develop. Whereas the erotized patient will manifest his acute transference feelings early in the analysis, these patients' transference manifestations are subtle and chronic. It often takes many months or even years of analysis to realize that the patient's resistant, rigid, and unchanging transference behavior is not due merely to the warding off of the repetition of childhood conflicts, but that we are dealing with a neurotic façade of an underlying psychosis or perversion or a combination of both (Pious, 1950).

Some time ago I was asked by a colleague to consult with him in regard to a patient he had been treating psychoanalytically for more than ten years. The patient had sought treatment because of an inhibition in relating sexually to women and also difficulty in working effectively. The analysis had dragged on without any major change in the symptoms, nor was there any indication from the patient (or the analyst) of a desire to interrupt treatment. The transference situation had settled down to a constant and consistent series of complaints and reproaches by the patient, reported in a whining, groaning tone and interspersed with an occasional outburst of anger or tears. The analyst would patiently listen and eventually interpret this behavior in terms of its being a repetition of some childhood event. This usually quieted the patient who would return and repeat the same pattern in the next hour. The patient's alternating behavior of sadistic reproaches and then masochistic submission to the misery of his plight was also enacted with other people in his outside life. It became clear to me after many hours of consultation that the patient's entire emotional life was limited to such superficial object relationships of a sadomasochistic nature. This was not merely a symptom; it was a way of life which hid a strong latent homosexual perversion and paranoid trends.

A careful reconstruction of the patient's childhood history made it seem plausible that he had suffered an acute psychotic break in early adolescence which had remained undetected. The sadomasochistic way of relating to objects was a restitution attempt; it was the only way he managed to have any contact at all with real people. The analytic situation was a haven for him because it was distant enough to be safe and permissive enough to allow some modicum of instinctual discharge through the verbalization. However, the treatment was analytic only in its superficial structure. The patient was not engaged in insight therapy —actually he was indulging in a form of play therapy (Glover, 1955, Chapt. XIV; Fenichel, 1945a).

Patients of the type described above are obviously not suitable for psychoanalytic therapy. They may need constant psychotherapy to remain stationary and not deteriorate. Some may slowly improve by means of some form of relationship therapy and also with the aid of drugs. Occasionally a patient may progress to a point where some analytic therapy might be undertaken.

I would like to add a few other clinical types of masked perversion-psychosis which are mistakenly treated by psychoanalysis. I have seen patients whose therapy served primarily as an opportunity for acting out scoptophilic and exhibitionistic impulses, or cases in which the relationship to the therapist and the therapy became a form of addiction. All these patients were essentially narcissistic characters who clung tenaciously to the relationship to the therapist because they had few or no other meaningful relationships to objects. These patients had developed a thin facade of social behavior that gave a false impression in the preliminary interviews. There was such an impoverishment of their object relationships that they were unable to permit themselves to regress. To do so would mean to fall into a state of nothingness, of no objects, of catatonia. Their relationship to their therapist was gratifying and ego syntonic. They had no motivation for changing it; on the contrary, they had every reason for holding on, since it was the most meaningful relationship of their lives.

The error lay in the fact that they were led into a form of therapy which by its very nature would threaten to unsettle that which they needed most, a fixed and concrete relationship to another human being. In a sense these patients were correct in resisting psychoanalysis; they were holding on to their analyst because this was imperative for them. It was necessary for the analyst to realize that his appraisal had been in error; these patients needed a much more tangible and visible relationship to a responsive and supportive therapist. Such patients often decompensate into acute psychotic states if they are subjected to the rigors of the analytic situation.

I realize that the point of view I have presented is controversial. Some analysts do not hesitate to analyze such patients in the classical psychoanalytic manner (Rosenfeld, 1952, 1958). Others would agree that such patients need other therapeutic approaches but hold that one should allow them to regress and accompany them and care for them during their regression. Once they have reconstituted themselves they can then be analyzed. I am much more in accord with Winnicott (1955). For still other viewpoints and approaches, see M. Wexler (1960), Freeman (1959), and Searles (1965).

3.10.313 Other Types of Intractable Transference Reactions

Thus far the patients described as being unsuitable for psychoanalysis because of their propensity for intractable transference reactions might be classified as borderline cases, perversions, or latent psychoses. They came into psychoanalytic treatment because the true diagnosis was not discernible until they had become involved in the analytic situation. However, one does see patients who are essentially psychoneurotics and yet they too develop intractable transference reactions. These cases are not as fixed and as uninfluenceable as the types described above, but are for the most part extreme examples of the types of transference resistance described earlier (see Section 3.8).

I am referring here to those defensive transference resistances which might be designated as persistent reasonable transference reactions. One variation of this type is the idealized transference reaction. There are patients who can maintain for years on end a stubborn positive idealized transference to their analyst. This transference reaction is ego syntonic and yields to analysis only with difficulty. In part it is hard to demonstrate the underlying hostility because these patients are skillful in finding auxiliary transference figures onto whom they displace their hatred. Besides, this idealization appears to be a kind of sublimation and appeals to their narcissism. Furthermore, the splitting of the transference figure makes it possible for the patient to preserve the existence of the analyst by keeping him entombed in this idealized state. If one persists in analyzing the idealized transference as a resistance and gives no neurotic transference gratifications, ultimately the idealization breaks down. Then one can see the enormous rage and hatred in the patient as well as the paranoid suspiciousness (Klein, 1952). It is this which the idealization covers and which makes it difficult to uncover.

Among the types of transference resistances which tend to become impervious to analytic interpretation is the highly generalized ego-syntonic transference reaction. It is characteristic of such patients to react habitually to all people the way they react to their analyst; it has become a character trait. A typical variety is the obsessional character who has isolated all his emotions from his everyday life and who lives by thought and ideas alone. Such a patient has such a deep-seated resistance to all emotional reactions that he tends to interact with people only according to an intellectual plan. All spontaneous emotion is felt to be a danger to be combated. Only control and thinking are reliable and virtuous.

In some instances this way of life has reached such proportions that one has the impression of dealing with a thinking machine and not a human being. Fenichel (1945a, Chapt. XIV) describes a type of obsessional character who is so "frozen" that he may require years of "thawing out" before he can become amenable to psychoanalysis. There seem to be rigid and frigid obsessional characters whose neurosis covers an anxiety so terrifying in quality and quantity that they are not influenceable by psychoanalysis. My experience suggests that often there is an underlying paranoid core which the rigid obsessions control. It is also my impression that such patients should not be treated by psychoanalysis, but should have some other form of psychotherapy. The analyst sitting behind the couch making only occasional interventions simply plays along with the patient's tendencies to isolate emotions and to misuse the intellect. Such patients seem to do better in more limited, face-to-face therapies.

The chronic acting-out patient also can develop intractable transference reactions. Here we are once again impinging on that group of patients who are impulse-ridden, addictive, and close to the area of perversion-psychosis described above. The erotized transference cases also might have been described as a special variety of chronic acting out. In a section devoted to problems of acting out in Volume II, I shall attempt to delve into this category more deeply.

All of this does not exhaust all the different kinds of patients with intractable transference reactions who escape detection until analysis has been undertaken. I recall a patient whose fear of homosexuality was so great that he could not let himself identify with me, since he felt that would be equivalent to letting himself be homosexually invaded. For several years his transference resistance was uninfluenceable, until I was able to understand and get him to understand his underlying anxiety.

The several examples already cited illustrate the clinical and technical problems I intended to highlight, namely, cases of intractable transference developments due primarily to the analyst's faulty appraisal of the patient's transference capability. These patients cannot develop a working alliance *and* a transference neurosis. In some instances a working alliance does develop, but it is invaded by the transference neurosis and becomes ineffectual. In other instances, what seems to be a working alliance is a well-disguised defensive transference neurosis. In all these cases, there is a major defect in the capacity to form object relationships and in the ego functions (see Sections 3.4 and 3.5).

3.10.32 Errors in Technique

It is always a delicate matter to talk about errors in technique. There is the ever-present danger of sounding arrogant by discussing the errors of others, or the pitfall of sounding inept or disingenuous by describing one's own mistakes. Nevertheless, it is necessary to talk about errors in techniques because they are not rare. Furthermore, it has been my experience that one can learn more from such errors, particularly one's own, than from any other single source.

3.10.321 Occasional Errors

The errors in technique which are responsible for the intractable transference reactions are the subtle, long-standing, repeated, and unrecognized flaws in technique. Crass errors in technique which occur occasionally may complicate the transference development, but since they are readily recognizable by both the patient and the analyst, the damage they do is usually temporary and reparable. If this is not the case, such mistakes may lead to the decision to change analysts or the type of treatment.

In line with the latter type of error I recall, early in my career, that I failed to recognize the hostile transference feelings of a patient who vented her spleen about her incompetent internist while she was full of sexual desire toward me. I interpreted the situation to mean that she resented her incompetent mother while desiring her attractive father. The patient seemed to accept this interpretation at least intellectually, but in almost every succeeding hour for the next week there was some allusion in her associations to an inept or bumbling helper, teacher, doctor, etc., alongside of the sexual feelings toward me. At that time I did not realize that the repetitious appearance of the material hour after hour indicated an insufficiency or inexactness of interpretation. Finally, the patient became unproductive, there were no dreams and little verbalization. When I tried to get her to work on her resistance, she seemed reluctant; and when I persisted, she suddenly burst forth with fury and scorn at me: "You keep nagging at me for not working, well why don't you get down off your ivory tower and do a little of the work yourself, or do you think it might soil your lily-white hands!"

I realized then that I had been completely unaware of the patient's hostility to me, which had been present alongside of her feelings of love. I also realized at this point that the patient herself was aware of this, all of which increased her anger and added an element of scorn. After a moment's pause, I said to her: "I suppose you're angry with that clumsy doctor, that awkward and bumbling helper who has been showing up in every hour lately. I just never recognized his face until now; but now I see it's me." The patient half laughed and half snorted at this intervention. At first she protested, feeling that her anger and contempt were not meant for me, but then she acknowledged she had been very disturbed at what she felt was my avoidance of her. She had the impression I was either afraid of her or repelled by her and that I disdained coming to grips with her problems.

At a later point in the hour I told the patient that even though I had not realized that she had been angry with me, I hoped she would be willing to explore this anger she felt toward me. I started her off on free association by asking what occurred to her if she thought of a person with "lily-white hands." My remarks and my attitude seemed to be effective and the patient was able to let herself associate freely. In that hour and in later hours, material did come up about a hitherto hidden aspect of her father, the aristocratic, haughty father whom she admired, envied, and despised. My rather crude oversight and misunderstanding of this material made for a slight delay, but otherwise I saw no other repercussions from my error.

At this point I would like to inject a few remarks about the underlying principles involved in attempting to handle a technical error. First of all, the patient must be given a chance to react to the mistake. It is a further error either to squelch the patient's reaction by too quick an apology or to remain silent and unresponsive so long that the patient becomes traumatized or feels threatened. The error has to be acknowledged openly, but this acknowledgment should be used to get further material from the patient, not to appease or neutralize the patient's reaction. I made no formal apology about the mistake of mine described above because it was not one of etiquette, nor did it involve a breach of good conduct. I was technically wrong about something, not guilty; I was sorry I caused undue pain, but these are the hazards of treatment and have to be reckoned with.

I do not attempt to explain the reasons for my error; that is my problem and not the patient's. I see no reason for burdening the patient with my confession; the patient should not have to be my therapist. I try to indicate to the patient, by word, tone, and attitude, that I want to work on his reactions to my error just as I would work on anything else that occurs in the patient's life. I am just as thorough in exploring this as I am in exploring other things, but not excessively so. I believe the brief description of my remarks and behavior which I employed with my patient illustrate the general principles I have just outlined.

3.10.322 Errors Due to Prolonged Countertransference Interference

The most serious flaws in the handling of transference reactions are the subtle, chronic, unrecognized ones that can go on for years without being detected. These may stem from two main sources: (a) countertransference reactions, and (b) incorrect understanding of the patient (on grounds other than countertransference).

Errors due to countertransference arise when the analyst reacts to his patient as though the patient were a significant person in the analyst's early history. Countertransference is a transference reaction of an analyst to a patient, a parallel to transference, a counterpart of transference. The counter in countertransference means analogue, duplicate of, like the counter in counterpart. It is not like the counter in counteract or counterattack, where it means opposed to or contrary, etc. Countertransference reactions can lead to persistent inappropriate behavior toward the patient in the form of constant misunderstanding or some unconscious rewarding, seductive or permissive behavior by the analyst. Again I must say that a more detailed discussion of this subject will have to wait for Volume II. However, I should like to illustrate the point with a condensed clinical example.

I had been supervising the work of a senior candidate in training for many years. He was a man of considerable ability and talent, the psychoanalytic treatment of the case was progressing favorably, and I had the impression we both enjoyed the supervisory sessions. The candidate told me, however, that he was having considerable difficulty with an unsupervised female patient he had been treating for several years. She had developed a persistent, unyielding hostile transference. We then spent several hours discussing the treatment of that patient. The patient was a young, attractive woman showing an obsessional character disorder with a marked tendency to intellectualize, many reactive anal character traits, and a compulsive-impulsive pseudosexual promiscuity. My overall first impression was that the candidate understood the patient and seemed to be coping adequately with the major technical problems the case presented.

Then I slowly became aware of how much more often he had to refer to his notes in telling me about this patient as compared to the other case I was supervising. He volunteered that he had more difficulty in remembering the material of this patient than any other of his cases. Then I noticed a tactic he used with her that I had never seen him use before. *After* the patient had begun to speak following a silence he would interrupt her and say: "Are you sure you are telling me what you are really thinking?" I pointed out the implied accusation in that remark; he seemed to be suggesting that she might be consciously distorting the material. Secondly, he was constantly interrupting her and not allowing her the freedom to ramble on. Perhaps if he waited longer he might know better whether or not she was consciously withholding. The student reacted to this by blushing and then defending himself, stating that he did not know if he actually said this to the patient, perhaps it was a distortion in his reporting. I realized then that my supervision of this case was not the enjoyable situation it had been with the previous case —for either of us.

As the candidate described to me the details of his work with the patient, I detected a tendency on his part to react with a countersilence to her silence, a tendency to be curt and excessively sparse in his verbal interventions, a tendency to be unnecessarily strict in pointing out her slightest tardiness in paying or in his never answering a question. In short, I felt that the atmosphere of this analysis was one of austerity and severity, perhaps even of harshness and grimness. I felt I was correct in this appraisal when I realized that the patient's hostile, suspicious, and spiteful reactions to her analyst seemed to resemble and be a response to the candidate's attitude. I asked myself would I dare to yield, to soften, to be touched by an analyst who would treat me the way the candidate was treating the patient. This was not a treatment situation, not a situation of a doctor trying to help a sick patient; this was a very thinly disguised battle of attrition between two sullen, angry people trying to defeat each other.

As tactfully as I could, I told the candidate that I felt he disliked the patient and that he was fighting rather than treating her. I did not expect or want him to explain his reactions and his behavior; I had hoped he would bring this matter up with his own analyst. But the student could not be restrained, he paled and after a moment's pause blurted out tearfully that he had recently begun to suspect this himself. He realized he was delighted if she canceled an hour and he tended to give her a little less than 50 minutes. Moreover, he had frequent dreams of her in which she was blurred with his older sister who had made his life miserable when he was a child, etc., etc.

The important point for this discussion is that this sensitive and talented man had unknowingly mistreated a patient for several years by unconsciously taking revenge on her for the wrongs he had endured in his childhood. His transference reactions to this patient had transformed him from a compassionate therapist to a strict and punitive opponent. As a consequence she developed a reaction to him that was partly a transference reaction and partly a realistic reaction to a potentially harmful person. The result was an intractable transference reaction. The candidate undertook regular supervision of this case with another supervisor and apparently after working out his problems in his analysis did a creditable job with the case. We did consider the possibility of having the patient change analysts, but many factors ruled this out. In section 3.10.4 this matter is pursued in some depth.

3.10.323 Other Protracted Errors in Technique

Countertransference is not the only source of major errors in the technique of dealing with transference reactions, although it is usually the most frequent one and the most difficult to detect. Lack of clinical knowledge, faulty theoretical knowledge, and cultural unfamiliarity with a type of person may also do the same. Many years ago I recall listening to a colleague describing his long-standing difficulties with a female patient. It became apparent to me that his interpretations were made on an oedipal level and there was no awareness or recognition of the pregenital relationship to the mother despite some obvious clinical material. When I pointed this out to my colleague, he told me that he had never read about any of these "new ideas" and also that it had never come up in his own analysis. Some years later he somewhat shamefacedly told me he had undergone a further piece of analysis and had also done some extensive reading and now realized how ill-equipped he had been for treating that patient.

I have had occasion repeatedly to listen to case presentations by people who, in my opinion, were under the influence of some faulty theoretical system. I heard about a young woman patient who was constantly manipulated by her therapist, who maintained that he was determined to keep her from developing a regressive dependency on him. He believed this not only was necessary but would shorten the treatment time and achieve as good if not better results than "orthodox" psychoanalysis. He considered himself a "progressive" analyst, a "neo-Freudian." For this particular patient his technique was aimed at not allowing any long silences to occur, he gave a great deal of reassurance and encouragement in trying to overcome her resistances, and he kept the atmosphere of the treatment hour lively and cheerful. This was his conscious intention, and in this he seemed to succeed at least on a superficial level in the early weeks of therapy. However, when the patient began to develop sexual feelings toward him, this lively and reassuring manner seemed to me to take on a provocative and flirtatious air.

When the patient became involved in a sexual affair with a much older man and flagrantly exhibited it to her conventional parents, the therapist congratulated her and made no interpretations of the incestuous and destructive aspects of this behavior. The therapist insisted she was engaging in a corrective emotional experience which he considered a great improvement over her previous sexual timidity. He did not see his own manipulations as an expression of his own instinctual needs, as well as a hostility toward psychoanalysis. He also failed to recognize that his patient's new (?) promiscuity was not true independence but a form of submission to him as well as an acting out of her sexual transference. After I expressed these views I no longer had the opportunity to hear about the patient until I read about her escapades several years later in the newspapers.

I have seen other examples of patients treated for years by so-called "psychoanalysts" who were practicing according to theoretical and technical systems far removed from what I am trying to describe here as classical psychoanalysis. Sometimes these patients seemed to have undergone "transference cures" and remained relatively well as long as the positive transference was maintained, only to break down when it changed, as change it must. At other times I have seen the kind of artificial obsessional neurosis Glover (1955, pp. 353-366) describes in his chapter on inexact interpretation. Sometimes these patients become fanatical advocates of some brand of psychotherapy and spend their lives trying to convert others to their new faith. Inadequately analyzed patients tend to act out their positive transference to the school of therapy their analyst or therapist comes from. Their unrequited love is expressed in their clinging to the jargon of psychoanalysis, in the constant exchanging of verbal intimacies, and in the desperate search for new converts who will act as witnesses to prove their brand of faith is the one and only right one. The "true believer" in a form of psychotherapy is just as much a victim of some unresolved transference reaction as is the "brainwashed" follower. Independence of mind and spirit can come only from the thorough analysis of transference phenomena.

As a last heading in discussing causes of intractable transference reactions due to errors in technique, I should like to mention briefly those situations which are due to a lack of understanding in the analyst of a particular culture to which the patient belongs. I recall the many transference problems I encountered when I attempted for the first time to analyze a Southern Negro. As one might imagine, the transference and countertransference reactions were compounded by the great differences in our backgrounds. In addition to transference feelings stemming from the patient's family figures, there were also intense emotions derived from his feelings toward white people in general. This situation was complicated by my own reactions to Southerners and to Negroes. However, a final obstacle was my unfamiliarity with the culture of the Southern Negro. I had great difficulty in assessing the appropriateness of certain of the patient's reactions because I was often ignorant of what was the reality in a given situation.

For example, the patient had fantasies containing a great deal of mistrust and suspiciousness concerning me. For a long time I was unaware of the fact that every time he drove in his car to my office he was literally entering enemy territory. The drivers of other cars, the police in that neighborhood, even the other people in the halls and elevators of my building were all felt as being potentially dangerous. This feeling naturally stirred up fantasies. This was not just a transference reaction to me, or a derivative of early feelings to his parents. These feelings acquired some of their intensity from actual recent experiences which had happened to him and to people close to him. I had great difficulty in empathizing with this reaction at first, because I was oblivious to this particular aspect of his life.

I often made errors in the dosage of my interpretations with him because I was unaware of the special anxieties or hostilities involved. My ability to empathize was hampered because I was ignorant of some of the particular dangers in the life history of a Southern Negro. The first time I interpreted a disguised sexual object in a dream as being my wife, I was not aware of the intense anxiety that I had mobilized. This was not only a taboo figure because it was his analyst's wife, and a mother figure, but it was also a white woman and I was not just a father figure but a powerful white man.

As a consequence of such errors and many more, the patient maintained a mild and submissive set of transference reactions to me which did not change for years. Only after I became familiar enough with his cultural background and my ability to empathize improved did he dare to trust me enough to allow himself to develop genuine and intense transference feelings.

The above illustration is an extreme example of how a lack of understanding of the patient's culture can interfere in the handling of the transference. I had similar problems, of less severity, when I tried to analyze an aristocratic Englishman. I have seen patients who were relatively untouched by years of analysis because they were from a background in America totally dissimilar from that of their European analysts. I believe most analysts are aware of this possibility and when making referrals try to pick an analyst who will not be alien to the patient. Sometimes it is not possible; then one has to be alert to this complication and pay special attention to it. The greatest damage occurs when the analyst is oblivious of this disparity and takes for granted that he can empathize correctly with the most foreign patients.

3.10.4 THE QUESTION OF CHANGING ANALYSTS

The discussion of such problems as intractable transference reactions and errors in technique seems to lead to the question of when it is indicated to consider a change of analyst. This subject is both complex and delicate; it is rarely mentioned in the literature and yet is often discussed privately among analysts. Since difficulties in the development and management of transference reactions are the most frequent cause for changing analysts, at least a brief review of this matter is in order at this point. A more thorough study of this problem will have to wait until we have covered such topics as analyzability, choice of analyst, and the problems of countertransference.

There seems to be a reluctance among analysts to accept the fact that they might be unable successfully to analyze all analyzable patients. In part this might seem to be a remnant of omnipotence fantasies, and it can also be a consequence of the notion that the sex and temperament of the analyst do not influence the transference reactions of the patient. It is true that the traditional definition of transference stresses the fact that transference phenomena originate in the patient. However, our greater knowledge of ego psychology has clarified the importance of the analytic situation in facilitating transference developments. The personality and skill of the analyst are vital parts of the analytic situation and do influence the course of the transference reactions. To put it another way: while it is true that transference phenomena are essentially displacements from the patient's past, nevertheless the analyst is neither a completely blank screen nor a totally passive participant in the therapeutic process. The personality and ability of the analyst will influence the order and intensity of the patient's transference reactions as well as the ease or difficulty in working with them.

It is striking that although most analysts would agree that they work better with some cases than with others, they do not relate this difference to the question of when a change in analysts is indicated. Glover's questionnaire on this subject confirms the great diversity of opinion on this matter (1955, Part II). The situation is different in regard to the training of candidates. According to the bylaws on the training of candidates in the American Psychoanalytic Association, every candidate is permitted the opportunity of working with a second training analyst if his first didactic analysis does not succeed. Perhaps the older analysts with longer experience are more aware of their limitations.

There are several indications for considering a change of analysts. First of all, it must be certain that the patient is analyzable; otherwise it may well be that a change of therapy is indicated, not a change of therapist. If transference reactions do not respond adequately to interpretation over a sufficient period of time, i.e., if we get intractable transference reactions or if important transference reactions fail to develop, then we should consider changing analysts. What constitutes a "sufficient" length of time is not easy to determine, as Glover's questionnaire has also revealed (pp. 328-330). From a purely subjective standpoint, I try to be on guard against giving in to impatience on my part, and yet I do not wish to continue prolonged unproductive struggles unnecessarily because of my stubbornness or pride.

Finally, I believe a change of analyst is required when there are repeated errors on the part of the analyst or when any single error has created an irreversible situation. These different indications are often not separable from one another, i.e., errors in technique cause intractable transference reactions or make a patient unanalyzable by that particular analyst, etc.

My own clinical experience has taught me the following rules about the question of changing analysts. After a period of four years of treatment, I review every one of my cases from the standpoint of the advisability of changing analysts. It is my custom to consider a change of analyst if at that time I do not see clear signs of being ready to terminate. Patients who come back for a second analysis do better to go to a different analyst, if possible to an analyst of a different gender or personality from the first analyst.

For patients who lost a parent in early childhood, the sex of the analyst can be a decisive factor. Such patients need to work with an analyst of the same sex as the missing parent. Patients will otherwise make excessive use of auxiliary figures, outside of the analysis, as supplementary transference figures. Consistent interpretation of this phenomenon may redirect this transference reaction into being experienced with the analyst. However, this is not always so, particularly if there is too great a discrepancy between the personality of the analyst and the original objects which are the source of the transference feelings. For example, many of my patients have difficulty in reacting to me as a hateful mother figure, but most of them eventually do. One patient, however, who had no father, could never react to me as a hateful mother but had to re-enact this with other figures in the environment. The other side of the coin relates to situations which arise when there is too great a similarity between the personality of the analyst and the original source of transference. This makes for intractable and unanalyzable transference reactions and also calls for a change in analysts. Grete Bibring (1935) and Greenacre (1959) have commented on this finding.

3.10.5 CANDIDATES IN TRAINING

The transference development in the analysis of candidates in psychoanalytic training deserves special mention since it is complicated by several factors. First of all, the training analyst is a person of realistic importance and authority for the progress of the candidate's psychoanalytic education. His decisions, tacit or otherwise, on matters concerning the student's training will be perceived either as important gratifications or punishments which will contaminate the transference situation. Furthermore, the training analyst usually serves as an instructor, supervisor, or training analyst for other candidates, and thus becomes actually involved in real sibling situations. In addition, by teaching or reading papers, the training analyst reveals his personality to the candidate, thus losing the relative anonymous position which facilitates transference phenomena. Finally, the institute itself takes on an additional transference meaning (Kairys, 1964).

The entire situation is further complicated by the fact that the main conscious motive for treatment is the candidate's wish for training. Most candidates either will not admit that they have an important therapeutic need or they are unaware of it. In either case they give the appearance of normality and tend to cling to this façade as a defense. In the analysis, the absence of urgent suffering can block the development of a genuine transference neurosis for long periods of time (Reider, 1950; Gitelson, 1948, 1954). An added resistance is the tendency of a candidate to identify with his training analyst as an unconscious means of ingratiation. Above all, the negative transference reactions tend to remain absent or are expressed only meekly or submissively and then via auxiliary transference figures. Since all of these reactions are prone to stir up transference reactions in the analyst himself, there is the grave danger that transference phenomena in training analyses do not develop to the maximum extent and cannot be handled as well as analyses conducted outside of training. This has led many training analysts to suggest a second analysis after training and with a different analyst (Freud, 1937a; A. Freud, 1950a; Windholz, 1955; Greenacre, 1966a; and Additional Reading List).

Additional Reading List

The Historical Development of the Concept of Transference

Hoffer (1956), Krapf (1956), Orr (1954), Servadio (1956), Waelder (1956).

The Nature and Origin of Transference Reactions

Fairbairn (1958), Greenacre (1966b), Guntrip (1961, Chapt. 18), Hartmann, Kris, and Loewenstein (1946), Klein (1952), Nunberg (1932, 1951), Segal (1964, Chapt. 1).

Early Object Relations

A. Freud (1965), Greenacre (1958, 1960), Hoffer (1949, 1952), Mahler (1963), Spitz (1965), Winnicott (1957).

The Real Relationship between Patient and Analyst

Alexander, French, et al. (1946), de Forest (1954), Ferenczi (1930), Weigert (1952, 1954a, 1954b).

Acting Out of Transference Reactions

Altman (1957), Ekstein and Friedman (1957), Kanzer (1957), Rexford (1966), Zeligs (1957).

Working Through of Transference Interpretations

Greenson (1965b), Kris (1956a, 1956b), Novey (1962), Stewart (1963).

Problems of Training Analysis

Balint (1948, 1954), Bernfeld (1962), G. Bibring (1954), Ekstein (1955, 1960a, 1960b), A. Freud (1950a), Gitelson (1954), Glover (1955), Greenacre (1966a), Grotjahn (1954), Heimann (1954), Kairys (1964), Lampl-de Groot (1954), Nacht (1954), Nacht, Lebovici, and Diatkine (1961), Nielsen (1954), Weigert (1955).

4

The Psychoanalytic
Situation

AFTER having discussed the analysis of resistance and transference, it would seem to be in order to take the psychoanalytic situation as our focal point. The analysis of the psychoanalytic situation offers us an opportunity to re-examine many of the procedures and processes we have already described from a different vantage point. By converging on the interrelationship of patient, analyst, and setting, we may gain additional insight into the unique power of the psychoanalytic situation as a therapeutic instrumentality. Furthermore, it may provide us with another occasion to clarify the complicated interactions among the three essential elements: patient, analyst, and setting. Although their relationship is an interconnected and interdependent one, it is advisable to explore separately each of the three components which constitute the psychoanalytic situation. We shall then ask ourselves: what does each contribute and how does each influence the psychoanalytic situation? (Stone's [1961] book on the subject is suggested as the most comprehensive reference source.)

4.1 What Psychoanalysis Requires of the Patient

4.11 MOTIVATION

Only a patient who is strongly motivated will be able to work wholeheartedly and with perseverance in the psychoanalytic situation. The neurotic symptoms or discordant traits of character must cause sufficient suffering to induce the patient to endure the rigors of psychoanalytic treatment. Curiosity and the wish to understand have to be supplemented by neurotic misery if the patient is to have more than a superficial psychoanalytic experience. He must be willing to bear the distress of revealing his anxiety- and guilt-laden intimate experiences; he must be willing to spend a considerable amount of money and time, give up the secondary gains from his illness, and also forego quick and temporary results.

In recent years, the search for quicker results has led many patients to seek brief psychotherapy, including briefer forms of psychoanalysis. This trend has been encouraged by an increasing number of psychoanalysts who utilize an amalgamation of psychoanalysis and psychotherapy. This development produced a great deal of confusion and conflict in psychoanalytic and psychiatric circles following World War II, when the number of psychiatrists seeking psychoanalytic training greatly increased and there were far too few training analysts. Such books as those by Franz Alexander and his followers on *Psychoanalytic Therapy* (1946) and Frieda Fromm-Reichmann (1950) advocated a variety of brief, manipulative therapeutic devices and yet purported to be psychoanalysis. (For a criticism of these attempts, see Eissler, 1950b, 1956.)

In my opinion, all forms of psychotherapy may be valuable provided one carefully studies their advantages, limitations, and therapeutic effects. In many instances, modifications and deviations from psychoanalysis may well be necessary to meet the needs of the patient (Gill, 1954). Freud (1919a) himself predicted that some day we would have to alloy the "pure gold" of psychoanalysis in order to treat a greater number of patients (p. 168). However, when psychoanalysis is modified to mollify the analyzable resistances of the patient or to satisfy the unconscious materialistic aims of the therapist, then both the patient and the therapist are likely to suffer.

It is quite a different matter when a patient needs psychoanalytic therapy but is psychologically not ready for it. For example, some patients may not be consciously aware of how restricted their lives have become as a result of their pathology. Then it may be necessary to do some preparatory psychotherapy in order to lead the patient to the realization that he needs a more radical therapy.

Anna Freud (1928) described this problem at great length in regard to children and I believe it is also valid for an increasing number of adults (Rappaport, 1956).

Let us return to the question of what the patient's motivation should enable him to do. His suffering should be sufficient to induce him to enter the psychoanalytic situation as a *patient*. People who seek psychoanalysis for research purposes, for professional advancement, for training, or for curiosity should be considered as resistant and in need of preparatory psychotherapy. It is my contention that only one who feels himself a patient can be analyzed beyond a superficial depth. Only such a person will be willing *to try* to enter and work in the analytic situation.

This still leaves open the question whether his incentive is strong enough to enable him to endure the deprivations and regressive states that arise in the course of the analytic treatment. Does the patient have enough motivation to bear the inequality, the unevenness of the relationship between patient and analyst which the analytic situation calls for? It should be borne in mind that when we refer to the patient's ability to bear the pain and frustration inherent in the course of psychoanalysis, we do not mean that we expect him to react with equanimity or restraint or good cheer to the painful situations mentioned previously. Quite the contrary, we expect—in fact, we hope—that he will react intensely with rage, anger, spite, etc., so that these feelings and the defenses against them will become part of the analysis.

What we hope is that he can experience such reactions without destroying himself or the analytic situation. Impulse-ridden oral characters with their poor impulse control and their need for quick satisfactions find the analytic situation extremely difficult to sustain. They are prone to break off the treatment by some disruptive acting out. Equally difficult but less obvious will be the pathological submissiveness of patients with masochistic character disorders who will silently enjoy the pain of the analytic situation. These patients may go through many years of what seems to be analysis without change and without complaint. Narcissistic characters will not be able to bear the relative austerity of the relationship to the therapist, and severely withdrawn patients may not be able to endure the sense of distance between patient and analyst. This subject will be pursued more thoroughly in Volume II.

4.12 CAPACITIES

Of all the psychotherapies currently being practiced, psychoanalysis makes greater and more varied demands on the patient than any other. It is not only that psychoanalysis imposes great hardships in terms of the patient having to endure deprivation, frustration, anxiety, and depression in the analytic situation. What makes psychoanalytic therapy so unusually demanding on the patient is that the procedures and processes of psychoanalysis require of him the capacity to carry out more or less consistently and repeatedly several pairs of antithetical ego functions, to oscillate between them, and also to blend them.

The patient is asked: (a) to regress and to progress, (b) to be passive and to be active, (c) to give up control and to maintain control, and (d) to renounce reality testing and to retain reality testing. In order to accomplish this the analytic patient must have resilient and flexible ego functions. This appears to be in contradiction to our earlier description of a neurosis as being the result of an insufficiency in ego functions. But what is characteristic of the analyzable neurotic is that his defective ego functioning is limited to those areas more or less directly linked up to his symptoms and pathological traits of character. Despite his neurosis, the treatable patient does retain the capacity to function effectively in the relatively conflict-free spheres (Hartmann, 1951).

Thus the analyzable patient will be able to perform the antithetical ego functions described above as long as they do not impinge too closely upon his neurotic conflicts. Since the derivatives of the neurotic conflict are always seeking discharge, one or another of these opposing ego functions will eventually become involved in the neurotic conflict, will be impaired, and will manifest itself as a resistance to the analytic process. The outstanding clinical findings then will be the loss of resilience and elasticity in some ego function, some form of rigidity will become manifest, or some ego function will be temporarily lost.

For example, a patient may not be able to regress in the direction of primary-process thinking in free association and will remain logical and orderly in all his productions. Or a patient will not be able to discontinue free association when I ask for some concrete historical data and will not even be aware of this misunderstanding.

Psychoanalytic therapy requires that the neurotic patient have an ego with sufficient resilience to shift between his opposing ego functions and to blend them, taking into account the limitations that his neurotic conflicts impose. As the treatment progresses one expects a parallel increase in the domain of the flexible ego functions. Let us dissect the various procedures the patient performs and the processes he undergoes in order to see what specific capacities the analytic situation requires of him.

In order to approximate free association the patient must be able to give up his contact with reality partially and temporarily. Yet he must be able to give accurate information, to remember, and to be comprehensible. He must be able to oscillate between secondary- and primary-process thinking. We expect him to let himself drift along in his fantasies, to communicate these as best he can in words and feelings that will be understandable to the analyst. He must be sufficiently psychologically minded so that he can empathize to some extent with the scope of the analyst's ability to follow him. We ask of the patient that he be able to listen and try to understand our interventions and also to associate freely to what we have said. He must have enough ego resilience so that he has the mobility to regress and the ability to rebound from it (A. Freud, 1936; Zilboorg, 1952b; Loewenstein, 1956, 1963; Bellak, 1961; Kanzer, 1961; Altman, 1964). He must have some ability to work along with the analyst and also allow himself to regress and develop varieties and intensities of love and hatred for the analyst. To put it succinctly, he must develop the ability to shift between the working alliance and the transference neurosis. This means that in the realm of object relations, the patient must also possess the flexibility to be able to oscillate between regression and progression and to form different mixtures of the two.

The patient must have some capacity to bear the uncertainty, anxiety, and depression, the frustrations and humiliations that arise in the course of psychoanalysis without resorting to destructive actions. We ask the patient to let himself be carried away by his emotions in the analytic hour so that he can feel the experience as genuine. But we do not wish him to become unintelligible or disoriented. At the end of the analytic hour we expect him to drive home without killing anyone, no matter how regressed he was during the hour. Furthermore, we hope that the patient will think and mull over outside the hour the insights he has gained in the analytic sessions and that he will bring in new meaningful insights, connections, memories, and dreams. Yet we do not want him to live his entire life as though it were all one gigantic analytic session.

We ask the patient to make no radical change in his reality situation until it has been thoroughly analyzed. For this he must be able to be patient, to postpone action, and yet not give in to resignation and despair. (This is an especially important problem in the analysis of candidates in training.) Psychoanalysis requires that he relate himself as genuinely and spontaneously as he can to the significant people in his surroundings, and yet we hope he will bring his experiences into the analytic session. Again and again we see the two contradictory sets of ego functions that are required of the patient; he has to be able to be the experiencer as well as the self-observer, the passive and the active one, the relatively uncontrolled and the controlled one.

In order to produce the analytic material the patient has to be able to regress and progress. He encounters and gathers the material in the regressed state; he communicates it in the progressed state. Before he can assimilate the insights given by the analyst, the patient first has to test their validity, introspect, ponder, mull them over, and then digest them. His synthetic and integrative ego functions, in conjunction with his working alliance, make the working through possible. Over a period of time the new insights lead to reorientation and readjustment (E. Bibring, 1954).

4.13 Traits of Personality and Character

The motivations and capacities of the patient which enable him to work in the analysis are closely related to and dependent upon his personality and character traits. In determining whether a patient will be able to meet the demands of the psychoanalytic situation it is easier to be specific about the negative criteria than about the positive findings. Contraindications for psychoanalysis are much more precise than indications (Freud, 1904; Fenichel, 1945a; Knight, 1952; and Additional Reading List).

A survey of the papers cited indicates that most authors believe that except for long-standing overt psychoses the diagnostic category is not a reliable guide. The appraisal of the patient's suitability for analysis must include an assessment of his healthy traits of personality and character as well as the pathological. This impinges on the subject of analyzability which will be gone into extensively in Volume II. Furthermore, in my opinion, the traits required of the suitable patient are qualitatively similar to those required of the psychoanalyst and I would prefer to discuss them first from the standpoint of the analyst.

4.2 What Psychoanalysis Requires of the Psychoanalyst

In order to practice therapeutic psychoanalysis, the psychoanalyst must be able to carry out certain technical procedures upon the patient and upon himself. In order to execute these procedures properly the psychoanalyst must make use of certain psychological processes which occur within himself. For it is the goings-on in his own mind which are the most valuable means the psychoanalyst possesses for gaining insight into the mind of another human being. As a consequence, the skill of a psychoanalyst is inextricably tied up with his own unconscious mind and the degree to which it is accessible for use by his conscious ego.

High intelligence and cultural level are indeed required of the analyst, but an available and comprehensible unconscious mind is even more important. The requirement that all psychoanalysts must have experienced psychoanalytic therapy before they are allowed to treat a patient psychoanalytically is aimed not only at giving the analyst personal conviction of the validity of unconscious factors and at desensitizing him in areas where his own problems might distort his judgment: the analyst's personal analysis has the ultimate aim of making available to his conscious ego the important unconscious drives, defenses, fantasies, and conflicts of his own infantile life and their later derivatives. Some of these conflicts will have been resolved, some will have been modified into more adaptive forms, others will have remained unchanged but approachable. What is crucial for the practicing psychoanalyst is that his unconscious conflicts are controllable and accessible for use in his work with his patients.

The degree of resolution will undoubtedly influence the skill which the psychoanalyst will be able to employ. His ability to achieve instinctual satisfaction without conflict will increase his ego's ability to neutralize certain functions, enhance the autonomous ego functions and adaptiveness. The same is true for the intrasystemic conflicts (Hartmann, 1951, p. 145).

The skill of the psychoanalyst is derived from psychological processes which also form his personality and character. Even his knowledge and intelligence are influenced by the degree of resolution of his neurotic conflicts. I would go still further and state that the motivations that led him into the field of psychoanalysis also play a role in how he works with his patients. Skill, knowledge, character, and motivation are the essential requirements. They are all interrelated and bound up with the conscious and unconscious emotions, drives, fantasies, attitudes, and values of the psychoanalyst. Nevertheless for purposes of clarity I shall artificially separate these factors into three groups—skills, traits, and motivations—in pursuit of the question: What does psychoanalysis require of the psychoanalyst? The reader is urged to read the two beautiful essays by Ella Sharpe (1930, 1947) on this subject, and also Stone (1961) and Greenson (1966).

4.21 THE SKILLS REQUIRED OF THE PSYCHOANALYST

4.211 Understanding the Unconscious

The most important skill which the psychoanalyst must possess is his ability to translate the patient's conscious thoughts, feelings, fantasies, impulses, and behavior into their unconscious antecedents. He must be able to sense what lies behind the various subjects his patient is talking about in the analytic session. He must listen to the obvious melody but also hear the hidden (unconscious) themes in the "left hand," the counterpoint. He must look at the fragmented pictures the patient paints and be able to translate them back into their original and unconscious form. Let me give a typical and simple example:

A young man talks in his hour of his anger and disgust at his older sister's toilet habits. She leaves the door slightly ajar so he can accidentally see her ugly naked breasts. He can even hear the different toilet noises and they are disgusting. When he goes into the bathroom afterwards he tries not to breathe, but he can still smell her body odors and her powder. The sight of some of her hair in the tub makes him feel like vomiting. Despite the loud conscious anger and disgust it is quite easy to hear in the background the young man's sexual interest in his sister's bodily activities. His unconscious fantasies of taking the different parts of her in his mouth make him feel disgust and nausea. He is not angry at her for being ugly; quite the contrary, he is angry at her for being exciting.

How does one arrive at such an interpretation? A person who has overcome the amnesia of his childhood days can recall or easily imagine that the toilet was the scene of childhood sensual pleasures and that peeping was one of boyhood's joys. Sisters or mothers were once sexually attractive before the barrier of aversion was erected as a defense. One does not "accidentally" see behind a door which is slightly ajar unless one wants such accidents to happen. The forbidden or unavailable can be perceived as extremely attractive or ugly; opposites are very close to each other. One does not have to stay and listen to toilet noises unless one enjoys it, as children usually do consciously and adults unconsciously. The sight of hair probably stirs up fantasies of other hairy parts of the body and one feels like vomiting only if something repellant is felt to be in the mouth.

In general, disgust is the reaction to feeling or imagining something repulsive to be in contact with one's body. Children and adults have strong impulses to take pleasurable or lovable or exciting objects into the mouth. All children do this openly and consciously, adults more discreetly or unconsciously. Inappropriate disgust indicates a repressed wish to touch or put something considered consciously "dirty" into the mouth.

If one has worked such problems out within oneself, it is not difficult to listen to the young man, to associate to his material, and to drift back to the related latent memories or fantasies. One does not have to do much intellectual work in this instance. One's own associations to sisters, toilet scenes and noises, one's own disgust reactions in the past to similar situations lead one now very quickly to the concealed impulses and fantasies. In order to determine whether one's associations seem to fit the patients situation, one has to shift from participant to observer, from empathy to introspection, from problem-solving thinking to intuition, from a more involved to a more detached position.

In order to facilitate such transitions and oscillations the analyst should listen to the patient with evenly suspended attention (Freud, 1912b). From this position one is partaking of both detached and involved points of view and one is ready to shift back and forth as a the situation requires. This ability to oscillate between observer and participant has been described by Ferenczi (1928b), Sterba (1929), Sharpe (1930), Reik (1948), and Fliess (1953).

In the case material cited above, I listened to the patient's utterances and followed my own associations until I felt I grasped the unconscious meaning of this material for the patient. I would now like to describe a situation in which a more complicated set of psychological processes has to be utilized.

A woman patient recounts in her hour an unsatisfactory sexual experience with her husband the night before. She had been sexually desirous, but something in the proceedings blocked her ability to have an orgasm. She was not sure what the disturbing event had been; there was nothing unusual in the foreplay, and yet that was where the trouble originated. Her husband had kissed her amorously, caressed her skin with his hands and mouth, fondled her breasts, etc., but her excitement vanished. The patient sounds somewhat annoyed but also sad as she describes her predicament. Her associations drift off to a recent dinner party, but the sadness seems to increase, the associations trail off, and the patient becomes silent.

I do not understand her silence or her sadness, so I ask the patient to go back to the sexual experience and let her thoughts wander. She says sadly that there was nothing new, it was not her husband's fault, he was considerate and passionate and gentle, all the qualities she ordinarily enjoyed. "He was even smoothly shaven," she adds with a smile, sighs, and now she weeps with tears streaming down her face. I am puzzled. I quickly review what she has told me, but my associations bring me no solid clues. I think back to the previous hour, but that also fails to help me. I thought I had been in good contact with her in this hour, but now I feel I have lost her.

At this point I change the way I am listening to her. I shift from listening from the outside to listening from the inside. I have to let a part of me become the patient, and I have to go through her experiences as if I were the patient and to introspect what is going on in me as they occur. What I am trying to describe are the processes that occur when one empathizes with a patient (see Fliess, 1953; Schafer, 1959; Greenson, 1960). I let myself experience the different events the patient has described and I also let myself experience the analytic hour, her associations, and her affects as she seems to have gone through them in the hour. I go back over the patient's utterances and transform her words into pictures and feelings in accordance with her personality. I let myself associate to these pictures with *her* life experiences, *her* memories, *her* fantasies. As I have worked with this patient over the years I have built up a working model of the patient consisting of her physical appearance, her behavior, her ways of moving, her desires, feelings, defenses, values, attitudes, etc. It is this working model of the patient that I shift into the foreground as I try to capture what she was experiencing. The rest of me is de-emphasized and isolated for the time being.

As I review the events the patient has described (but this time with me as the patient), several new ideas come to the surface. Her husband has "showered" her with kisses, the patient has said. This had not brought up any special imagery to me as an observer. When I became the patient, however, a scene from childhood comes to mind—of taking a shower with father. This has been one of the few joyous memories she has had of her ordinarily gruff father. One element of the memory has stood out in the patient's mind: her father was so hairy. This made him seem sensuous but also frightening. When he kissed her, she remembered most vividly his bristly beard. Now the patient's last remark comes back to me as the analyst: "He was even smoothly shaven." At first I had thought it was a reference to her mother. Now I realize that the smoothly shaven, loving, and considerate husband has stirred up the contrasting picture of her repressed sexual longing for her sensuous and sadistic father. As these thoughts come to my mind, the patient has begun to talk of the dinner party again and how her dinner partner chewed his food with his lips open—a characteristic she had loathed in her father. I am now convinced that my empathy has enabled me to uncover the unconscious disturbance in the patient's sexual experience. Her husband had stirred up memories of her unconsciously beloved father, therefore she was not able to reach orgasm and therefore she wept so sadly at his smooth face.

This clinical vignette illustrates a valuable method for grasping the subtle and complicated hidden emotions in another human being. Empathy means to share, to experience the feelings of another human being. One partakes of the quality of the feelings and not the quantity. Its motive, in psychoanalysis, is to gain understanding; it is not used for vicarious pleasure. It is essentially a preconscious phenomenon; it can be consciously instigated or interrupted; and it can occur silently and automatically, oscillating with other forms of relating to people. The essential mechanism is a partial and temporary identification with the patient on the basis of a working model of the patient within the analyst, which he has constructed from his sum of experience with the patient.

By shifting the working model of the patient into the foreground, and pushing all that is peculiarly or uniquely me into the background, I have let the patient's words and feelings enter this part of me. The model reacts with ideas, feelings, memories, or fantasies, etc. In the above example the word "showered" stirred up the key association in the model—the memory of taking a shower with father, which led to associations with his hairiness and beard—an "aha" experience. The "aha" indicates that the working model of my participating ego had alerted my analyzing ego, the observer. Now my analyzing ego has to determine what the meaning is of the unconscious material.

This brings us to the use of intuition which is closely related to empathy. Both empathy and intuition are means of obtaining quick and deep understanding. Empathy is a method of establishing close contact in terms of emotions and impulses. Intuition does the same in the realm of ideas. Empathy leads to feelings and pictures. intuition leads to the "aha" reaction which indicates you have hit it, or to the "oi" reaction which indicates that you have failed.

In the last clinical example, empathy made me feel my loss of contact, empathy led from being showered with kisses to the shower with the father. Intuition told me I was on the right path and quickly connected hairiness to bristly beard and smoothly shaven and her subsequent crying. My empathy for the patient made this feel right to me.

Empathy is a function of the experiencing ego, while intuition seems to be a function of the observing ego. These two phenomena can lead into one another and blend into one another in a variety of ways. But empathy is emotionally more demanding, it consists of an emotional involvement and requires the capacity for controlled and reversible regressions not only in terms of ego functions but also in object relations. It is similar to the creative experience of the artist that Kris (1950) described. Intuition is less demanding emotionally, it is essentially a thinking process, albeit a regressive one.

Empathy and intuition are the fundamentals of the *talent* for grasping the unconscious meanings behind the conscious material; the best therapists have a goodly supply of both. The capacity for empathy is a basic requirement; for without it, it is hardly possible to do any effective uncovering therapy. The ability to be intuitive makes for dexterity, but without empathy it can be misleading and unreliable.

Until now, the skills of the psychoanalyst I have described are all related to the use of preconscious and unconscious processes. The question that now arises is what role does intellectual knowledge of psychoanalytic theory and practice play in the psychoanalytic situation. Although familiarity with and accessibility to one's unconscious mind is the most important facility for doing psychoanalysis, intellectual knowledge of psychoanalysis is certainly also necessary. It is a cliché that no one is completely or perfectly analyzed, which means that everyone has areas where his conscious ego cannot penetrate. Furthermore, there are fluctuations and changes in one's instinct-defense balance, in one's ego functioning, and in one's countertransference-working alliance equilibrium, all of which can diminish temporarily the accessibility or reliability of one's unconscious mind.

At such times it is of particular importance to have on hand one's theoretical knowledge of psychoanalysis. Even under ideal circumstances, clinical and theoretical knowledge may have to be used to explain to oneself the meaning of a given finding that had been perceived by empathy. For example, let us return to the last clinical example of the woman with the sexual frustration and tears. Empathy and intuition picked up the finding that she was blocked in her sexual excitement because thoughts of her father were threatening to become conscious. It takes, in addition, clinical knowledge to realize that incestuous impulses usually stir up strong guilt feelings which will interfere with sexual excitement. A theoretical understanding of symptom formation will help one understand that the patient's tears in the hour, after she said her husband had been smoothly shaven, indicated her sadness at having lost an old love object—the bristly faced man, her father.

In the first example, concerning the young man who was disgusted by his sister's toilet habits, the theory and clinical understanding of reaction formations will tell one that inappropriate intensity of affects indicates that an opposite affect is being held in repression by the conscious one. With this knowledge in mind one can then be alert to any confirmatory evidence. A knowledge of normal and neurotic childhood instinctual life informs one that what is so desired in childhood may in the course of development be turned into revulsion, in order that one may meet the demands of the external world and the superego.

In these illustrations empathy and knowledge supplement each other. Sometimes they can substitute for one another. The most favorable situation is when they are both available and can be used for validating each other. Empathy and intuition may tell me that the young man has repressed sexual desires toward his sister. Clinical and theoretical knowledge verifies this by comparing his productions with the theory of reaction formations. My memory can aid in this if I can recall previous information from the patient on this point, or if I can remember this material later when related data are forthcoming.

A working knowledge of the theory of neurosis has the same relationship to psychoanalytic technique as the study of pathology has to the practice of internal medicine (Fenichel, 1945a). It furnishes the foundation for practical work by determining the regular features of various pathological syndromes. A thorough knowledge of the typical is the best way one can be prepared for understanding what is unique. Working with patients, clinical case seminars, reading case histories provide the raw material from which the theoretical framework is gleaned.

This theoretical knowledge is actually a precipitate and distillate of thousands of clinical facts and must be used for clinical work if one wants to avoid the danger of doing wild psychoanalysis. Empathy and intuition cannot be taught, but a scientific worker has to learn what is teachable. Theoretical knowledge is no barrier to intuitive psychotherapy; on the contrary, it is an indispensable prerequisite (Sharpe, 1930; Fenichel, 1945a).

I believe that the sequence of training in most psychoanalytic institutes supports this view. Before a candidate is permitted to take a patient in psychoanalytic treatment, he must have undergone some effective personal analysis, and he must have completed those seminars dealing with mental development, structure and meaning of the dream, psychoanalytic theory of neurosis, basic metapsychology, and fundamentals of psychoanalytic technique. Only after a candidate has experienced several years of personal analysis and gained a working knowledge of psychoanalytic theory do we feel he is equipped to begin to use psychoanalytic technique (Lewin and Ross, 1960).

4.212 Communicating to the Patient

Let us assume that the analyst has understood the meaning of the patient's material by the use of empathy, intuition, and theoretical knowledge. His next task is to communicate this to the patient. Actually, he must decide *what* he shall tell the patient, *when* he shall tell it, and *how* he shall do it.

Let us go back to the moment in an analytic hour when the analyst feels he has understood the unconscious meaning of the patient's material. He may have comprehended this only impressionistically and vaguely; it has to be formulated in words and ideas before any further step can be taken. Situations do arise in analysis when one imparts vague notions or hunches to a patient, but this is usually done only when the material is relatively innocuous.

Ordinarily it is necessary to formulate the material in words in order to be as clear and precise as possible. The analyst wants to make contact and to have an impact on the patient. He therefore wishes to avoid being misunderstood, especially since the patient's resistances are ever ready to seize upon such an opportunity. Words, language, and tone of voice play a special and basic role in supplying a bridge for spanning the space between the patient and the analyst, just as they once did between mother and child after bodily separation had taken place (Sharpe, 1940; Greenson, 1950; Loewenstein, 1956; Rycroft, 1956; Stone, 1961). Language and speech are relatively autonomous ego functions, but they are susceptible to regression, reinstinctualization, and reinvasion by neurotic conflicts. This is apt to occur in those patients who have had difficulty in maintaining their separate identity or in patients in the throes of a deeply regressive transference neurosis (Loewald, 1960).

The analyst has to formulate in words what he might tell the patient. He must translate his own primary-processlike thinking into secondary process. Then he must decide whether this can be told the patient at this time. Here his clinical judgment and his empathy have to be used, because only through these faculties can he determine, first, if the information is valuable, and second, if the patient can bear this insight without being traumatized. Intellectual knowledge will help him by recalling similar past interpretations or by noting the closeness to holiday separations etc. He has to decide whether it will not be better to wait for further data, or perhaps to wait for the patient himself to arrive at the interpretation.

Once the analyst has decided to communicate the interpretation, he has to consider *how* to formulate the information. I must interpolate here that this detailed description does not imply that each of these procedures will normally occur separately, slowly, and in sequence. Occasionally they will, but usually they will take place quickly, automatically, and largely simultaneously. The method of determining how one conveys an insight to a patient has already been discussed in Sections 2.6, 3.543, and 3.94. At this point it will suffice to say once again that the capacity for empathy is the most valuable instrument for assessing such questions. The choice of words and the tone may well determine whether optimal contact and impact will be made, whether one has played into the resistances, or whether one has been traumatic.

The analyst's vocabulary must be aimed at the patient's reasonable ego. The analyst must ask himself the question: how close to the patient's reasonable ego is this insight that I want to impart. The more inaccessible the material is, the more care must I take with my formulations and my choice of words. Furthermore, the analyst's vocabulary should not be too distant from the patient's because that would lend a quality of unreality to the intervention. It must have impact and yet not be shocking—values which can be determined only by the analyst's empathic identification with each patient in the particular situation. The force and intonation used are often more important than the choice of words. Tone and intonation convey the preverbal and nonverbal feelings, often the unconscious attitudes of the analyst. Furthermore, tone and intonation sensitivity is derived from the earliest object relations, when separation anxiety is a major factor. The tone leads to or away from contact, and is therefore very important for the trust-mistrust balance in the relationship of patient and analyst (Loewald, 1960; Greenson, 1961).

In the analytic situation an important aspect of the art of communicating to the patient is the analyst's skill in the use of silence.

The analyst's silence has many meanings to the patient, depending on the patient's transference situation as well as the analyst's countertransference. Furthermore, silence is one of the greatest stresses that our patients have to bear in the analytic situation, and should therefore be administered thoughtfully in quality and quantity (Stone, 1961, pp. 45-55). Silence is both a passive and an active intervention on the part of the analyst. The patient needs our silence because he may need time for his thoughts, feelings, and fantasies to emerge from within himself. Our silence also exerts a pressure upon him to communicate and to face his utterances and emotions without distraction. He may feel our silence as supportive and warm, or as critical and cold (Nacht, 1964). This may be due to his transference projections, but it may also be derived from his subliminal awareness of our countertransference reactions (Greenson, 1961).

The analyst communicates to the patient not only by making interpretations and by silence but also by other means and for a variety of other purposes. Before one can interpret, one has to demonstrate and clarify the material under scrutiny. For example, before I can uncover the unconscious meaning of a resistance, the reality of the resistance may first have to be demonstrated and clarified for the patient.

Let me illustrate: A young man, a postgraduate student in the social sciences, begins his hour by saying that he is disappointed; he had hoped to have a very "deep" dream that would open up his early childhood experiences and instead his dream seemed superficial. All he remembers of the dream is that he was in a room full of books and he felt pleased that all the books belonged to him. One book stood out in particular and it had to do with an execution. The patient then talks of his horror in imagining how it must feel to be condemned to death. Then he goes on to talk of his money problems, his increasing expenses, and his dwindling bank account. From here he goes on to wondering how long his analysis will continue and to expressing his feelings of frustration about his slow progress. In yesterday's hour he felt he was getting somewhere, but today it all seems so difficult. How he envies people who have all the time in the world to read novels, while he has to spend every free moment studying. Oh, to be finished and free!

The latter is said sadly, and I noticed the patient's stiff posture on the couch and how his head is resting upon his fist which is on the pillow. At this point I intervene and ask him how he is feeling physically at the moment. He answers that he feels tense and tired. He feels a tension around his rectum, not like it is full and wants to explode, but tight. I wonder if it feels as though he is holding something in and he replies, yes. He has the impression that he is not letting go, as though he is afraid of something. He goes on to ask himself what is he holding back and why, but he doesn't seem to be getting anywhere.

I point out that the room full of books in the dream may well be my room, the very room we are working in. How would he feel about having such a study for himself. At first he reacts with pleasure to such a fantasy, but soon goes on to talk of how impossible it will ever be for him to earn so much money. Now a thought occurs to him: as he was on his way home from the hour yesterday, he thought of asking me if he could skip the day after the Thanksgiving holiday without having to pay for it. He imagined asking this of me and my replying no, he would have to pay. Then he fantasied he would say stubbornly and defiantly that he would not.

He dismissed these thoughts yesterday by thinking that Greenson wouldn't be so adamant, and after all he ought to pay—it was only reasonable, and so on. At this point in the hour he pauses and says wistfully: "What would happen if an irresistible force should meet an immovable body?" His father had often talked about physics to him as a boy. "You are the irresistible force and I am the immovable body," he says. Silence. I now say: "And you hold back because you are afraid of this showdown between us—we would both be destroyed if you let go." The patient sighs. "I can fight with my wife, and I can fight with my professors, but you're the killer." "Yes," I add, "I am the executioner."

Let us return to the beginning of the hour. I sense the patient is resisting, but because I am not sure it is convincingly demonstrable to him, I wait until I find some living material—in this instance, his posture. I confront him by asking simply and directly how he feels physically at the moment. This leads to an awareness of a tightness in his rectum which I designate as holding back. He then confirms this by tightening up in his associations and getting nowhere. Then I pick up the detail in the dream which indicates the dream concerns his possessing what I possess and I ask him what occurs to him to this idea. His associations lead to the fantasies after the last hour, which had been inaccessible until then. The battle between the irresistible force and the immovable object is the battle between us. That is why he holds back—he is afraid of his aggressive impulses, which might destroy us both. That is the interpretation, but it would not have become possible to make that interpretation convincingly, with real emotional impact, without first recognizing the body language in that hour (F. Deutsch, 1947, 1952).

The facilitating interventions that lead to clarifications and elaborations are a necessary and important procedure of psychoanalytic technique. In this way we help the patient produce the clinical material we require for interpretation. These interventions have to be timed correctly so as not to disturb the flow of meaningful material. They have to be made simply, directly, and clearly in order for them to lead to greater illumination or elaboration. One must not do all the work or expect the patient to do it all. One must know when one should lead the patient and how far without making him totally passive and dependent. There are situations where it is better for the patient to do most of the work. All these possibilities have to be kept in mind when one is considering when and how to communicate to the patient.

4.213 Facilitating the Development of the Transference Neurosis and the Working Alliance

The psychoanalytic situation demands of the psychoanalyst that he possess the ability to relate to his patient in such a way that the patient will develop a transference neurosis and also a working alliance. This is another instance where the analyst is required to have proficiency in maintaining two antithetical positions, for the attitudes and techniques which further the development of the transference neurosis are in opposition to those which facilitate the working alliance (Stone, 1961; Greenson, 1965a). This subject has been discussed in great detail in Section 3.5; at this point I will only repeat some of the main considerations.

There are two basic requirements which the analyst must fulfill in order to promote the growth of the transference neurosis in the patient. The analyst must consistently frustrate the patient's quest for neurotic gratification and reassurance, and he must also remain relatively anonymous (see Sections 3.921 and 3.922). However, if the analyst remains incognito and also consistently deprives the patient, how is he going to induce the patient to cooperate with him in the working alliance? Part of the answer lies in the fact that there is an optimal amount of deprivation and incognito. Excessive frustration and anonymity will produce interminable or interrupted analyses. This seems to be borne out by the findings of other psychoanalysts, the most outspoken of whom is Leo Stone (1961, p. 53). Ferenczi (1930), Glover (1955), Fenichel (1941), Grete Bibring (1935), and Menninger (1958), also point out the dangers of superfluous frustrations and deprivations. The analyst must not let the deprivations and frustrations of the analytic situation exceed the patient's ability to withstand such stress. If the latter is traumatized by the analytic deprivation and incognito, he may break off treatment, act out destructively, or remain fixed to an intractable regressive transference resistance. The analyst may misuse the notion of the analytic incognito if he has an unconscious dread of exposure and involvement hiding behind this psychoanalytic rule of technique. Similarly, unconscious sadistic impulses in the analyst may unwittingly persuade him to employ superfluous and harsh deprivations, which he may mistakenly believe to be following the "rule of abstinence."

Such errors of technique stemming from the unrecognized countertransference make for unanalyzable situations. The analyst is then truly behaving like a parental figure in his secretive and deprivational ways, and thus he cannot be differentiated by the patient from his past (G. Bibring, 1935). To facilitate the development of a transference neurosis in the patient, the analyst must gauge the patient's ability to bear the specific stress of the analyst's incognito and his deprivational attitudes. The analyst must have the ability to recognize and control his analytic demeanor in terms of the frustration and anxiety it will impose upon the patient. The difference between bearable and unbearable tension may reflect only a nuance in the analyst's behavior (Stone, 1961).

Let us now turn to the other component of the psychoanalyst's relationship to the patient. Not only must the analyst promote the development of the transference neurosis, but he must also comport himself in such a way as to assure the existence of a working alliance. I have already described, in some detail, the analyst's contribution to the working alliance in Section 3.543. Here I shall only outline the essential ideas.

1. The analyst must demonstrate in his daily work with the patient that he considers the patient's every utterance and every manifestation of behavior worthy of being seriously worked with for the

purpose of gaining insight and understanding. Nothing is too trivial, far-fetched, or repugnant. The high frequency of visits, the long duration of the treatment, the willingness to strive for the long-range goals, the reluctance to miss appointments, all attest to the analyst's devotion to the importance of achieving a thorough understanding of the patient.

2. Behind the quest for insight and accompanying it every step of the way, lies the analyst's therapeutic commitment to the patient. The analyst's physicianly dedication to the patient should be apparent in his careful assessment of how much pain the patient can bear, the tact he uses when it is necessary to impart hurtful insight, and the care he takes not to contaminate the personal relationship unnecessarily.

3. The analyst must also serve as a guide in leading the patient into the strange new world of psychoanalytic treatment. At the proper time he must explain the many strange and artificial instrumentalities and rules necessary for conducting psychoanalysis. In a sense he has to teach the patient how to become a psychoanalytic patient. This does not happen all at once but over a long period of time. The need for this varies enormously from patient to patient and is usually greater in the more regressed patients. The patient should be allowed to experience the surprising strangeness before the analyst explains the purpose of a particular measure. The patient's reactions should first be brought under scrutiny, the teaching should follow the patient's spontaneous reactions and the analysis of them.

4. The analyst must safeguard the patient's self-respect and sense of dignity. He must recognize the unevenness of the relationship in certain areas, and although he cannot change this, he should acknowledge this to the patient. The analyst must not assume an attitude of superiority, authoritarianism or mystery. The method of psychoanalysis is based on a complex and unique interpersonal relationship which is not capricious, but follows a logical and purposeful set of rules. The treatment imposes special hardships on the patient which have to be taken into account by the analyst. The patient must be treated along rigorous scientific lines, but with respect and ordinary courtesy.

5. The analytic relationship is a complicated and fragile human predicament for both parties. The expert in the situation must not

permit his responses to intrude upon the patient and thus obscure the patient's individual and unique reactions. The analyst's responses must be restrained, muted, and in the service of the therapeutic commitment, which recognizes insight and understanding as its most potent single instrumentality. The catalytic agent in this setup, the agent which makes all the other elements succeed or fail, is the analytic atmosphere. This should be accepting, tolerant, and human.

I believe this outline indicates how the analyst may solve the conflict between the deprivational, incognito attitudes required for the transference development and the humane treater of the sick necessary for the working alliance. Let me now turn to the ideas on this subject by other workers in the field.

Leo Stone (1961) is most explicit in his description of what he calls the legitimate gratifications of the patient, and I believe I am in essential agreement with him. However, I prefer to think of what we do most of the time as protecting the patient's rights, because I feel we are dealing with essential needs which *have* to be safeguarded and not with wishes about which there is choice. The analyst's therapeutic commitment to the patient is an absolute requirement, in my opinion, and is not optional. The same is true for the general concern for the patient's predicament. Compassion, interest, warmth, all within limits, are vital for the working alliance.

I believe that many writers on psychoanalytic technique have recognized the two opposing relationships between analyst and patient but were unable to conceptualize the working alliance as a necessary counterpart of the transference neurosis. For example, Freud speaks of the friendly aspects of the transference which are "the vehicle of success in psycho-analysis . . ." (1912a, p. 105). In his paper "On Beginning of Treatment" he states: "It is certainly possible to forfeit this first success if from the start one takes up any standpoint other than of sympathetic understanding" (1913b, p. 140). Ferenczi's (1928b) discussion of tact deals with the analyst's show of "good will" to the patient (p. 90). In his paper "The Principles of Relaxation and Neocatharsis" Ferenczi (1930) describes "the *principle of indulgence,* which must often be allowed to operate side by side with that of frustration" (p. 115). Glover's (1955, p. 308) questionnaire to the British psychoanalysts reveals that one third believed in giving their patients some indication of a positive friendly attitude as distinct from "professional interest."

Similar ideas can be found in the technical writings of many others (Sharpe, 1930; Fenichel, 1941; Lorand, 1946; A. Freud, 1954a, and Additional Reading List).

4.22 TRAITS OF PERSONALITY AND CHARACTER OF THE PSYCHOANALYST

The skills which the psychoanalytic situation requires of the psychoanalyst are derived not only from his training and experience but also from his personality and character, i.e., his temperament, sensitivity, attitudes, habits, values, and intelligence. No one is born a psychoanalyst and no one can suddenly become a psychoanalyst, no matter how fortunately endowed. The personal experience of having undergone a therapeutic psychoanalysis (even if combined with a didactic purpose) is an absolute prerequisite. Natural endowment and richness in life's experiences may join to provide special talents for the profession of psychoanalysis. But as valuable as it may be, talent is not enough. The analytic situation makes such arduous emotional demands upon the analyst that unless talent is supported by an analyzed character structure it will not prove to be enduring. Flashes of brilliance and virtuosity cannot illuminate sufficiently the long path of psychoanalytic therapy.

The relationship betwen analytic skills and personality traits is a complex one, and the origin of skills and traits varies from individual to individual. In the next section I shall concentrate on the motivations of the psychoanalyst which are inextricably interwoven with his skills and traits. Here I can only attempt to enumerate what I consider to be the major faculties and outline the most typical antecedents. A single source may be the fountainhead of many traits and skills and, though they share the same origin, these traits and skills may be of unequal strength. On the other hand, a single trait or skill may have multiple derivations. The reader is urged to read Ernest Jones's chapter on Freud's "Character and Personality" as a model of such explorations (1955, pp. 403-434).

4.221 Traits Related to Understanding the Unconscious

The persistent and continuing search for insight and understanding which is so central in psychoanalytic therapy is derived from several different facets of the analyst's personality. First of all, he must possess a lively interest in people, their way of life, emotions, fantasies, and thoughts. He should have an inquiring mind, searching for knowledge, causes, and origins (Jones, 1955, pp. 426, 433). The energy impelling a man in this direction comes from his curiosity, which should be rich in quantity and benevolent in quality. Too little curiosity in the analyst makes him a victim of boredom, too harsh a curiosity makes the patient suffer unnecessary pain. The analyst pursues insight to bring understanding to his patients and not for his own scoptophilic or sadistic pleasures (Sharpe, 1930, 1947). This attitude is possible only when curiosity is no longer under the domination of the instincts.

In order to be able to spend one's day listening without boredom, an analyst's curiosity should include a pleasure in listening (Sharpe, 1947, p. 120). The special sensitivity which enables the psychoanalyst to distinguish the subtle combination of affects in the patient's modulation of tone and rhythm of speech is related to his appreciation of music. Tone-deaf people do not make the best therapists in my experience. An analyst should meet the unknown in his patient, the strange and the bizarre, with an open mind and not with anxiety or aversion.

It is helpful to be free from the restrictions of conventional society and relatively indifferent to the superficialities of everyday life. Freud's personal life demonstrated these qualities to a high degree (Jones, 1955, 1957). The analyst should be familiar enough with his own unconscious processes to accept with humility the notion that he too probably possesses the same strangeness as the patient; the strange so often turns out to be something once familiar and later repressed.

The analyst's initial reactions to the patient's productions should be one of receptivity even if it requires some credulity to do so. Only in this way can one give full consideration to the patient's material. It is better to be deceived going along with the patient's productions than to reject them prematurely as false. The ability to suspend judgment even to the point of gullibility makes it possible to empathize with the patient, which may eventually lead to an understanding of the underlying motives. Along this line it is interesting to note that Freud was a notoriously poor *Menschenkenner* (Jones, 1955, pp. 412, 420). A detectivelike, suspicious attitude makes for an estrangement from the patient, interferes with empathy and the working alliance. (There are some exceptions to this formulation, however. With delinquents, for example, it may be helpful to indicate quickly that one is aware of their shenanigans; see Aichhorn, 1925; Eissler, 1950a; Redl and Wineman, 1951; Geleerd, 1957.) There is some need for skepticism in the analyst, but it must be kindly. He should be able to discriminate between a probable and plausible reality, a possible but fantastic reality, and a delusion and conscious deception, without losing sight of the unconscious meanings of the distortion.

The capacity and willingness to pursue insight even when it is painful, the love of truth, originate in early oral introjective and intrusive as well as phallic aims. People who possess this quality manifest an independence of mind and intellectual courage in the face of the new, the unconventional, and the unknown. In such persons the wish to understand has become a neutralized, autonomous function (Hartmann, 1951, 1955). If the psychoanalyst has not achieved this capacity, he will tend either toward restricted insight or to a misuse of insights resulting in errors in timing, tact, and dosage of interpretations, which cause unnecessary pain and humiliation to the patient.

The ability to understand the unconscious mind of another person stems from a variety of different skills. By far the most important, as I have already indicated, is the capacity for empathy, which is essentially a preconscious phenomenon. Some of the clinical, dynamic, and structural features were described in Section 4.211 as part of the analyst's skills. At this point I should like to speculate about the personality traits which give rise to empathy.

Empathy is a mode of understanding another human being by means of a temporary and partial identification. To accomplish it the analyst must renounce for a time part of his own identity, and for this he must have a loose or flexible self-image. This is not to be confused with role playing, which is a more conscious phenomenon. It is more likely the process of "serious make-believe" which is experienced when one is moved by a work of art, a performance or a piece of fiction (Beres, 1960; Rosen, 1960). It is an intimate, nonverbal form of establishing contact (Greenson, 1960). Empathy is a regressive phenomenon and appears to be related to the more or less controlled regressions seen in creative individuals (Kris, 1952). In order to empathize the analyst must be able to utilize these regressive mechanisms easily for the purpose of regaining a sense of emotional closeness to his patient.

For empathy to be rewarding, the analyst should have a rich store of his own personal experiences in living, which he can draw upon to facilitate his comprehension of the patient. This should include a familiarity with literature, poetry, theater, fairy tales, folklore, and games (Sharpe, 1947). All of these ingredients make for a lively imagination and fantasy life which are invaluable for analytic work. The make-believe world of man, be it theater, music, art, fairy tales or daydreams, touches upon universal experiences and links mankind together. We are closer to one another in these media than in our conscious activities or social institutions.

This kind of emotional closeness, which empathy both requires and brings, develops in the child in the first months of life. It is mobilized by the nonverbal, intonational, skin touching, loving, and caretaking activities of the mother (Olden, 1953, 1958; Schafer, 1959). Since empathy originates in the earliest mother-child relationship, it seems to have a feminine cast (A. Katan, quoted in Greenson, 1960; Loewald, 1960). For an analyst to be empathic without conflict he must have come to peace with his motherly component. Jones (1955) calls this the mental bisexuality of the analyst.

In a sense empathy is a means of establishing contact with a lost love object, the un-understood patient. It may be in part an attempt at restitution for the loss of contact. This seems to be borne out by my experience that the best empathizers seem to be those analysts who have overcome a tendency to depressions. (For a different point of view, see Sharpe, 1930, pp. 17-18.) Empathy makes emotional demands on the analyst and also requires constant self-scrutiny. One must be able to regress in order to empathize and then rebound from it, in order to sort the data so obtained and to check on their validity. This alternation between the intimacy of empathy and the distance of validation is characteristic of much of the psychoanalyst's work. Rigidly obsessional characters will not be able to allow themselves to empathize and the impulse-ridden will tend to slip from empathy into identification, which will lead to acting out with the patient. As a rule such people do not make suitable candidates for psychoanalytic training (Eisendorfer, 1959; Greenacre, 1961; Langer, 1962; Van der Leeuw, 1962).

4.222 Traits Related to Communicating with the Patient

When the analyst has succeeded in understanding the patient, he is then faced with the problem of communicating the insight effectively. The ability to gauge the dosage, timing, and tact of an interpretation depends on a variety of skills, some of which have already been discussed. Empathy with the patient in the given instance, clinical judgment as well as experience in living in analogous situations, and intellectual knowledge of psychoanalytic theory all contribute to a facility in imparting understanding to the patient. At this point, however, I want to limit the discussion to those special traits which are important for communication and which have not yet been touched upon.

The art of talking to a patient is very different from social conversation, cross-examination, or lecturing. Eloquence, erudition, and logic are not of primary importance. The essential element is an underlying attitude of therapeutic intent. This commitment to help the patient should be manifest or latent in all interactions with the patient, from the first interview to the last. I realize this is a controversial issue, but I want to be unmistakably clear in stating my position: I believe only sick people, patients who suffer from neurotic miseries, can be successfully treated by psychoanalysis. Candidates, research workers, investigators cannot undergo a deep analytic experience unless they are able and willing to become patients.

Parallel to this statement about patients, I believe that deep psychoanalysis is first and foremost a method of treatment, and therefore can be carried out only by therapists, people trained and dedicated to helping or curing the neurotically ill. I do not believe that a medical degree automatically makes one a therapist, or the lack of an M.D. degree indicates a nontherapeutic attitude. It is my conviction that the analyst's wish to help the patient, ever present but under control, is an essential ingredient which enables the analyst to develop those subtle and complex skills in communicating necessary for psychoanalytic work. I refer the reader to Leo Stone's (1951) careful discussion of this problem along a similar vein, as well as to Gill, Newman, and Redlich (1954). For a dissimilar point of view see Joan Riviere's description of Freud's way of working quoted by Jones (1955), and also Ella Sharpe (1930).

This subject will be pursued further in Section 4.23 on the analyst's motivation.

Skill in imparting insight to a patient depends on one's ability to put into words the thoughts, fantasies, and feelings which the patient is not fully aware of and to present them in such a way that the patient can accept them as his own. One must translate from one's own vocabulary into the living language of the patient at the moment. Or more precisely, one must use that segment of the patient's language which one wants him to experience at the moment of interpretation.

For example, I have previously referred to Professor X. who suffers from a form of stage fright.[1] Ordinarily this man's everyday vocabulary was on a high educational and cultural level. In a particular hour his dream associations indicated to me that he was struggling with feelings of humiliation that had plagued him when he was a young boy between the ages of four and seven. In the analytic hour his thoughts centered mainly around his sense of shame and embarrassment when he was introduced at a recent party, when he had to give a short speech, and when his wife looked at him as he stood naked in the bathroom. I wanted to make him aware of a specific quality of shame that came over him in all of these situations. I said to him: "When you were introduced at the party, when you made the speech, and when you stood naked before your wife in the bathroom, you were no longer Professor X. or even John X., instead you became a *pischer*. I used the Yiddish word his mother had habitually employed when she expressed her contempt for him for wetting his pants as a little boy. (The English equivalent would be "piddler.")

This insight hit home, he was a bit taken aback at first, but then vividly recalled several incidents when he was made to feel like a *pischer*. This was not an intellectual exercise, or superficial compliance. The patient re-experienced the terrible shame of being a *pischer,* and also his fury at his mother for inflicting this humiliation on him. In that hour he did not feel any hostility to me, due in part to the fact that my tone of voice in making the interpretation was particularly gentle. It was so since I sensed that the word *pischer* was extremely painful to him. In later hours when he recalled my interpretation, he blotted out my careful tone and he did become furious with me.

If we review the events of the hour we can see that I had several ways of making the interpretation. I chose the word *pischer* be-

[1] See Sections 2.64, 2.652, 3.412, 3.9431, and 3.9432.

cause it seemed to be the word that carried the most highly charged fantasies for him at the moment, it was most illuminating, and he seemed ready to face it. It was his word, inherited from his mother but now part of his own private language; it was lively and real (see Ferenczi, 1911; Stone, 1954a). My gentle tone of voice was an attempt to soften the pain I knew I was about to inflict. I was certain it would have quite an impact, but I did not want it to be overwhelmingly hurtful.

Facility in selecting the right word or language is similar to what one observes in storytellers, humorists, and satirists. I am stressing here verbal dexterity rather than literary ability. However, such expertness must be in the service of the intent to help and must not be used in the analytic situation for exhibitionistic entertainment or disguised sadism. My own personal observations seem to indicate that among psychoanalysts, the best therapists do seem to possess a good sense of humor, do have ready wit, and do enjoy the art of storytelling. The ability to use spoken language vividly and economically is a valuable asset to the analyst and is parallel to the importance of manual dexterity for the surgeon. The latter cannot replace clinical judgment or the knowledge of anatomy and pathology, but it makes it possible for a sound clinician to perform proficiently rather than clumsily. Deep psychoanalysis is always painful, but inexpertness makes for unnecessary and prolonged pain. In some cases it can mean the difference between success and failure.

Skill in verbal communication in the psychoanalyst also depends on his competence in the use of silence. Therefore it is imperative that the analyst be able to be patient. It takes time to understand the patient's material, and so often the important meaning is revealed only after one has let the patient paint his word pictures for a goodly period of time in the hour. What seems to be of real significance in the first fifteen minutes may turn out to be a diversionary tactic or a secondary element after thirty minutes.

Let me illustrate. Professor X. with the stage fright, whom I described earlier,[2] was also obsessed, at times, with the notion of engaging in a homosexual act. In part this turned out to be an expression of exhibitionistic and scoptophilic strivings. In addition, his homosexual strivings were a consequence of his enormous fear of and hostility to women.

[2] See Sections 2.64, 2.652, 3.412, 3.9431, 3.9432, and 4.222.

During one hour he began to talk again of his fantasy of doing something homosexual, preferably with a boy just before the age of puberty. For the first thirty minutes of the hour it seemed clear to me that he was indicating his wish to do to a prepuberty boy what he had wanted his father to do to him when he was prepubescent. It seemed to be concerned with passive and active anal impulses. This had come up some time before but was not fully worked through.

I was mulling over in my mind how I would approach this material when I noted a slight shift in the material. The patient was now talking about terrible feelings of shame when all his boyfriends had entered puberty, had pubic hair, large penises, and low voices, and he alone was still hairless, small penised, and high voiced. Then he was ashamed to undress in the same room with them, they would laugh at him as a freak. I now realized that one of the important functions of his homosexual fantasies was to undo the pain of being the little one, to gain revenge for the earlier humiliations and also to prove that he was no freak. It was this last point that the patient picked up and worked with for several productive hours in the following week. Yet this emerged only toward the end of the hour.

Again it has to be stressed that what may ostensibly appear in the analyst as a virtue may actually turn out to be something quite different. Patience may reveal itself as a hidden passive-sadistic attitude toward the patient or as a screen for obsessional indecisiveness. It may also shield boredom and mental sluggishness in the analyst. It is necessary to be patient when waiting may clarify the material or when one is considering some long-range goal. But it must be remembered that our silence is usually experienced as a form of stress by the patient. It is an activity of the analyst and has many different meanings to the patient, depending on the analytic situation and the transference-countertransference situation (Lewin, 1954, 1955; Loewenstein, 1956; Stone, 1961, pp. 45-55, 95-105).

The patient needs our silence in order to follow in detail his own thoughts, fantasies, and feelings. He needs time partially to forget our presence, or more precisely to let our real presence recede into the background so that he can let himself get involved with his transference fantasies and feelings. The patient may feel our silence to be hostile or comforting, demanding or reassuring, depending on his transference reactions. Moreover, the patient may also detect traces of feelings and attitudes in us of which we are unaware. The analyst should be able to endure the silence of his patients without hostility or boredom. I have been startled on several occasions when a patient correctly "guessed" that though silent and unseen behind him I was impatient. I suspect some patients detect our attitudes intuitively from minute changes in the rate and intensity of our breathing and from little bodily movements.

The art of verbal communication to the patient also requires a sense for the proper timing of an interpretation. This will be discussed in detail in Volume II. Here I wish to state that timing refers to several different issues. First there is the question when in a given hour does one make one's intervention. The decision depends on several variables. One waits until a given psychic event is demonstrable to the patient's reasonable ego. Or one waits until an affect or impulse has reached the intensity one feels is optimal at the time. Finally, one waits until it is clear what is going on in the hour, even if that means waiting until it is clear that one is lost.

Timing also refers to when and how one intervenes at different phases of the analysis. Early in the analysis, or the first time a new variety of painful material emerges, one may intervene earlier, when the intensity of the affects is not great. Later on it may be better silently to allow the patient's feelings to increase in intensity so that he can experience the real primitive strength of his emotions and impulses. Timing also implies that the analyst will keep in mind the difference in dosage that one administers before weekends, holidays, anniversaries, etc.

4.223 Traits Related to Facilitating the Development of the Transference Neurosis and the Working Alliance

The attitudes and character traits which further the development of the transference neurosis are, as I pointed out earlier, basically antithetical to those which further the working alliance (Stone, 1961, pp. 33, 106; Greenson, 1965a). In order to facilitate the growth of the transference neurosis the analyst must consistently frustrate the patient's desire for neurotic gratification and reassurance, and he must also remain relatively anonymous. The rationale for this was described in Section 4.213. To carry out this objective with any degree of consistency the analyst must have resolved his major conflicts about inflicting pain and maintaining a distance from the suffering patient. This means that the analyst must have the ability to restrain his therapeutic intentions, must control his urge for closeness, and must "blanket" his usual personality (Stone, 1961, p. 20).

Freud went so far at one point as to suggest that the analyst model himself on the surgeon, put aside his human sympathy, and adopt an attitude of emotional coldness (1912b, p. 115). In that same paper Freud advocated that the analyst should refrain from intruding his personality into the treatment, and he introduced the simile of the "mirror" (p. 118). A few years later he recommended that the treatment must be carried out in abstinence, and "By this I do not mean physical abstinence alone . . ." (1915a, p. 165).

I have deliberately selected these quotations in this way to highlight how it is possible to gain the impression that Freud believed in an austere and severe analytic atmosphere for the development of the transference neurosis. However, I do not believe this to be an accurate picture of what Freud had in mind. In my opinion, he stressed certain of the "unnatural" aspects of psychoanalytic technique because they were so foreign and artificial to the usual doctor-patient relationship and the customary psychotherapy of his day.

For example, in a paper written in the same year as the one where he cites the recommendations for emotional coldness and the mirrorlike attitude, Freud stated: "Thus the solution of the puzzle is that transference to the doctor is suitable for resistance to the treatment only in so far as it is a negative transference or a positive transference of repressed erotic impulses. If we 'remove' the transference by making it conscious, we are detaching only these two components of the emotional act from the person of the doctor; *the other component, which is admissible to consciousness and unobjectionable, persists and is the vehicle of success in psycho-analysis exactly as it is in other methods of treatment*" (Freud, 1912a, p. 105; my italics).

In a technical paper a year following the "emotional coldness" and "mirror" recommendations Freud wrote: "It remains the first aim of the treatment to attach him [the patient] to it and to the person of the doctor. To ensure this, nothing need be done but to give him time. If one exhibits a serious interest in him, carefully clears away the resistances that crop up at the beginning and avoids making certain mistakes, he will of himself form such an attachment and link the doctor up with one of the imagos of the people by whom he was accustomed to be treated with affection. *It is certainly possible to forfeit this first success if from the start one takes up any standpoint other than one of sympathetic understanding,* such as a moralizing one, or if one behaves like a representative or advocate of some contending party—of the other member of a married couple, for instance" (1913b, pp. 139-140; my italics).

Perhaps the most personally revealing of all Freud's papers on technique is his essay "Observations on Transference-Love" (1915a). I shall quote only selected portions which indicate his concern and involvement with the patient. "Anyone who has become saturated in the analytic technique will no longer be able to make use of the lies and pretences which a doctor normally finds unavoidable; and if, with the best intentions, he does attempt to do so, he is very likely to betray himself. . . . Besides, the experiment of letting oneself go a little way in tender feelings for the patient is not altogether without danger. Our control over ourselves is not so complete that we may not suddenly one day go further than we had intended" (p. 164). "The course the analyst must pursue is neither of these; it is one for which there is no model in real life. He must take care not to steer away from the transference-love, or to repulse it or to make it distasteful to the patient; but he must just as resolutely withhold any response to it. He must keep firm hold of the transference-love, but treat it as something unreal, as a situation which has to be gone through in the treatment and traced back to its unconscious origins" (p. 166).

"Again, when a woman sues for love, to reject and refuse is a distressing part for a man to play; and, in spite of neurosis and resistance, there is an incomparable fascination in a woman of high principles who confesses her passion. . . . And yet it is quite out of the question for the analyst to give way. However highly he may prize love he must prize even more highly the opportunity for helping his patient over a decisive stage in her life. She has to learn from him to overcome the pleasure principle, to give up a satisfaction which lies to hand but is socially not acceptable, in favour of a more distant one, which is perhaps altogether uncertain, but which is both psychologically and socially unimpeachable" (p. 170).

I think these quotations from Freud's writings clearly indicate that although he believed that deprivation and incognito were necessary for the growth and development of the transference neurosis, he sensed the analyst had to be able to maintain attitudes of quite another quality if psychoanalytic therapy was to be effective. If one reads the writings of analysts who devoted themselves to problems of technique, it is impressive how almost all of them become involved with this very question. Deprivation and incognito are necessary but not sufficient. In my opinion, some authors, e.g., Ferenczi (1928b); de Forest (1954); Lorand (1946), and Nacht (1962), go too far in the opposite direction, magnifying the importance of gratification while depreciating the value of deprivation. Freud (1913b) talked of the need for flexibility of all rules; Fenichel (1941) described the oscillations of the analyst and the analyst's need to be free and natural, as did Sterba (1934), Loewald (1960), and Menninger (1958) among many others. In my opinion, it was the work of Elizabeth Zetzel (1956) and Stone (1961) which properly stressed and separated the deprivational aspects of technique from the gratificatory.

In order really to understand a patient, more than intellectual or theoretical considerations are involved. For the kind of insight required by psychoanalysis the analyst must be able to become emotionally involved and committed to his patient. He must like the patient; prolonged dislike or disinterest as well as too strong a love will interfere with therapy (Greenacre, 1959; Stone, 1961, pp. 29, 44, 61). He must have a wish to help and cure the patient, and he must be concerned with the patient's welfare without losing sight of his long-range goals.

A certain amount of compassion, friendliness, warmth, and respect for the patient's rights is indispensable. The analyst's office is a treatment room and not a research laboratory. We can feel a reliable kind of love for our patients because they are all in a sense sick, helpless children, no matter what else they may use as a façade. They will never mature unless we nurture their potentials, safeguard their self-esteem and their dignity, and avoid inflicting unnecessary deprivations and humiliation.

This brings us to the heart of the matter. How can the analyst consistently maintain the attitudes of deprivation and incognito and yet equally consistently indicate his compassion and concern? In the previous section on communication to the patient I have already given some examples of how this might be achieved. Further illustrations will be given in Volume II. Here let me stress again that every procedure of psychoanalysis that is strange or artificial to the patient I carefully explain to him at the appropriate time. For example, when he asks a question for the first time in the analysis, I try to get him to explore the reason for the question and then explain that not answering questions has a purpose; it will shed light on his curiosity and I add that in the future I will usually not answer questions. Yet sometimes I will answer a question when I feel the question is realistic and the answer would save a lot of irrelevant explanation.

A patient once told me of a particularly frustrating hour with a former analyst. The patient had dreamed of playing quarterback on a football team; they were using a T formation and to his amazement the center turned out to be Adolf Hitler. (In the T formation the quarterback stands directly behind the center who is bent over holding the football on the ground between his legs. It is the center's job to hand the ball backward between his legs to the quarterback who then can give it to another player or pass it, etc.) This is a standard football formation, and anyone who knows anything about American football knows this very well.

The analyst in question was a forty-year-old American who would have known this if he had been an average football fan in his youth but who might not if he had never been interested. The patient's uncertainty was therefore justified. The patient wanted to go on to his associations to Adolf Hitler and the peculiar position he had in relation to him in the dream. But first he asked the analyst if he knew what the T formation was since this seemed to be crucial for understanding the dream. The analyst was silent. The patient then reluctantly explained and described what a T formation is, what a quarterback is, what a center is, etc. Most of the hour was wasted in this way. What a pity to spend the time on these trivia when the analyst could have told him (as it turned out) at the beginning of the hour that he knew all of this. But even more important, the analyst's behavior indicated that he was following a "rule," the true purpose of which he did not comprehend, and he was willing to allow the patient and himself to endure an unnecessary amount of frustration and a wasted opportunity.

It is often necessary to probe into the intimate details of the patient's sexual life or toilet habits, and many patients feel this to be very embarrassing. When I find it necessary to question the patient extensively about such matters and I sense this humiliation, I

take cognizance of his feeling of degradation and either explore the
embarrassment with him or at least indicate that I realize the uncovering of this subject is painful but necessary. I point out the
patient's sexual or hostile feelings to me straightforwardly; if he
seems unduly upset by my intervention, however, I will try to indicate by my tone or in words at a later point that I am aware and
have compassion for his predicament. I do not baby the patient, but
I try to ascertain how much pain he can bear and still work productively.

I try to protect the patient's self-esteem, but if I feel it necessary
to say something that I know he will feel as demeaning, I will do so
knowingly, though I may express my regrets in some way. For
example, I recently said to a male patient at the end of an hour:
"I know this was an awkward situation for you. You finally were
able to tell me something that was terrifying to you—that you loved
me and wanted me to love you, and all I did was to say, well, we
shall have to explore this some more."

If the patient relapses into some old neurotic behavior pattern,
I attempt to control my feelings of sadness or disappointment, just
as I restrain my pleasure and pride if he makes a giant step forward.
But I do permit some amount of feeling to become manifest, since
affectlessness would seem cold and inhuman. I try to temper the
patient's feelings of failure or triumph by reminding him (and myself) of our long-range objectives.

In order to maintain this ability to oscillate between the two
opposing positions of frustrator and gratifier, of distance and closeness to the patient and to use varying admixtures of these polarities,
it is essential that the analyst possess a high degree of emotional
mobility and flexibility. I do not mean capriciousness or instability.
The analytic situation requires that the analyst be reliable and trustworthy in human terms and not inhumanly rigid. The analyst must
possess the capacity for emotional involvement with his patients,
but he must possess to the same degree the ability to detach himself.
Involvement makes for the possibility of empathic understanding,
detachment makes for the chance to think, evaluate, remember,
anticipate, etc. Compassion, concern, and warmth should be readily
available in the analyst, but he should also be able to shift when
necessary to the cool, aloof position of the observer. There are also
situations which require a blending of the two; the painful insight

is given with the precision of a surgical dissection, and yet the tone of voice may indicate concern.

When I describe the analyst's compassion and concern, I do not imply that these feelings ought to be openly and conspicuously displayed at the first sign of discomfort in the patient. I suggest that their presence ought to be felt in the way the analyst works, in the atmosphere of the analytic situation. Analysis cannot be carried out successfully in a hale and hearty manner; nor can it be done with good cheer or lightheartedness. Yet, neither can it be fruitful when the underlying tone is grim, gloomy or agonizing. The analyst's attitude of genuine acceptance and tolerance of all the patient's material, his careful attention to all details no matter how ugly or primitive, his straightforward approach toward even the most delicate subjects without either cruelty or false chivalry—all of these elements contribute to the analytic atmosphere.

The wish to cure should not be confused with pathological therapeutic zeal. It should be apparent in the analyst's seriousness of purpose, his rigorous pursuit of insight, his respect for the various instrumentalities of the profession without worship or ritual and his willingness to struggle for years toward the long-range goals. The analyst's ability to administer painful insights is as much a sign of his therapeutic intent as is his concern for the patient's dignity. Bearing the hostile and humiliating outbursts of his patients without retaliation is as important as remaining unperturbed by their sexual provocations. This does not mean that the analyst should not have feelings and fantasies in response to his patients, but their quantity ought to be within limits that enables him to control his responses so that what comes into the open is only as much as the patient requires.

The analyst must permit the patient's transference feelings to reach their optimal intensity without intervening. This requires that the analyst possess the ability to endure stress, anxiety or depression quietly and patiently. All of this is possible only if one has undergone a deep psychoanalytic experience and has continued to do some self-analysis. Nevertheless, the vocational hazards are enormous and the best therapeutic results in the analyst leave a good deal to be desired (Freud, 1937a, pp. 248-250; Wheelis, 1956b; Greenson, 1966). At this point I would like to quote Freud directly on this issue.

"Here let us pause for a moment to assure the analyst that he has our sincere sympathy in the very exacting demands he has to fulfil in carrying out his activities. It almost looks as if analysis were the third of those 'impossible' professions in which one can be sure beforehand of achieving unsatisfying results. The other two, which have been known much longer, are education and government. Obviously we cannot demand that the prospective analyst should be a perfect being before he takes up analysis, in other words that only persons of such high and rare perfection should enter the profession. But where and how is the poor wretch to acquire *the ideal quali-fications* which he will need in his profession? The answer is, in an analysis of himself, with which his preparation for his future activity begins. For practical reasons this analysis can only be short and incomplete. . . .

"It would not be surprising if the effect of a constant preoccupation with all the repressed material which struggles for freedom in the human mind were to stir up in the analyst as well all the instinctual demands which he is otherwise able to keep under suppression. These, too, are 'dangers of analysis,' though they threaten, not the passive but the active partner in the analytic situation; and we ought not to neglect to meet them. There can be no doubt how this is to be done. Every analyst should periodically—at intervals of five years or so—submit himself to analysis once more, without feeling ashamed of taking this step. . . .

"Our aim will not be to rub off every peculiarity of human character for the sake of schematic 'normality,' nor yet to demand that the person who has been 'thoroughly analysed' shall feel no passions and develop no internal conflicts. The business of the analysis is to secure the best possible psychological conditions for the functions of the ego; with that it has discharged its task" (Freud, 1937a, pp. 248-250; my italics).

From the foregoing it can be seen that humility is another basic requirement the analytic situation demands of the psychoanalyst (Sharpe, 1947, pp. 110-112).

The analyst is the bearer of insight which is usually painful, conveyed in an atmosphere of straightforwardness, compassion and restraint. What I have described is my personal view of how I try to resolve the conflict between creating an atmosphere of deprivation and concern, maintaining closeness to the patient and also distance.

I realize that this is a highly personal matter and I do not offer this as an exact prescription for all analysts. However, I do maintain that despite individual variations among psychoanalysts, these two sets of antitheses have to be adequately taken into account. The analyst must possess traits which will enable him to facilitate the growth of the transference neurosis as well as of the working alliance, because both are of equal importance for the development of the optimal analytic situation (Greenson, 1965a).

4.23 MOTIVATIONS OF THE PSYCHOANALYST REQUIRED BY THE ANALYTIC SITUATION

It must become increasingly clear as this discussion proceeds that one cannot really separate the analyst's skills from his traits, and that both are related to his motivations. In fact, it was one of Freud's great discoveries that man's behavior and thought are the result of the interaction of instinctual drives, constitution, and experience. I have attempted to isolate the skills, traits, and motivations from one another in order to clarify and emphasize certain prerequisites for the analytic situation.

I began with the skills and traits because they are more accessible to everyday clinical scrutiny. The motivations are more difficult to dissect because they originate in the primitive unconscious instinctual drives and early object relations. These are difficult to verbalize with any precision and almost impossible to verify. Furthermore, later maturational processes in the ego and the id as well as experiential factors seem to be of overriding importance. Finally, there are so many complex hierarchies of instinct and defense which present a similar surface picture that only a careful study of the individual can reveal the specific qualities of instinct and defense involved in a given motivation. Nevertheless, there are some general considerations which are worthwhile highlighting, even though the points made will be impressionistic and simplified.

The instinctual drives impel man to seek discharge and gratification. As the ego develops, the search for security becomes another basic aim. All subsequent motivations are attributable to the quest for gratification or security or combinations of both. I am limiting this discussion of motives to what I consider to be the three major components of the psychoanalyst's work: (1) the analyst as the gatherer and transmitter of insight and understanding; (2) the analyst as the target of the transference neurosis; and (3) the analyst as the treater of the sick and suffering (Fleming, 1961).

One of the unique features of psychoanalytic treatment is the crucial role of interpretation, insight, and understanding in the therapeutic process (E. Bibring, 1954; Gill, 1954; Eissler, 1958). The analyst must understand his patient in order to acquire insight into his behavior, fantasies, and thoughts. Then his task is to impart the hidden meaning, to interpret this to the patient. The wish to understand another human being in so intimate a way, the desire to gain insight, implies a propensity to get into the insides of another person (Sharpe, 1930, p. 17). It is derived from both libidinal and aggressive impulses. It may be traced back to strivings for symbiotic fusion with the mother, or to hostile destructive impulses toward the mother's insides.

Obtaining insight may be a remnant of strivings for omnipotence, or a means of overcoming anxiety about the stranger. Later libidinal and aggressive components also contribute to the urge to gain insight. The anal connotation of such terms as acquiring, gaining, collecting or gathering insight seems quite transparent. The sexual curiosity of the oedipal phase may add its impetus to this activity so that acquiring insight may become a substitute for the frustrated peeping of childhood days as well as belated compensation for having been left out of the parents' sexual life (Sharpe, 1947, p. 121).

I have already emphasized the special importance that empathy enjoys as a means of getting access to the subtleties and complexities of another person (see Sections 4.211 and 4.221). To acquire insight by means of empathy depends on the analyst's ability to identify, to introject, to be in intimate skin-touching, preverbal contact with the patient, all of which is evolved from the early loving and caretaking activities of mothering.

The wish to transmit insight, to be the bearer of understanding may be linked to libidinal or hostile impulses depending on whether the act of interpretation is unconsciously felt to be helpful or hurtful, pleasurable or painful. Delivering understanding to a patient may unconsciously be a mothering activity, a form of feeding, nurturing, protecting or teaching the patient-child. It may also symbolize an act of fertilization or impregnation. From the seed of little insights, great changes may develop. The bringing of insight may also be used unconsciously as a means of re-establishing contact and communication with a hitherto nonunderstanding, i.e., lost, love object. In this way the transmission of understanding can serve as an attempt to overcome a depressive attitude (Greenson, 1960).

The urge to bring insight to another person may become a means of reparation for guilt feelings connected to the fantasy of having done harm to little ones, sick ones, i.e., siblings, rivals, etc. In an analogous way, the pursuit and transmission of insight may serve a counterphobic function as well as an antidepressant one. The analyst may explore the patient's unknowns in order to overcome his own anxieties, in a sense to continue his own analysis (Freud, 1937a, p. 249).

Although this exploration is by no means complete, I believe it does touch upon some of the more important unconscious forces which are influential in motivating a person to choose a career where one of his most important functions is to be the collector and bearer of understanding. In my opinion, the point of origin of a given motivation is not the decisive factor in determining its value or detriment. What is significant is the degree of deinstinctualization and neutralization that has taken place (Hartmann, 1955, pp. 239-240).

The gradations of neutralization will decide to what extent the function of serving as the bearer of understanding can become a relatively conflict-free, autonomous, reliable ego function. For example, I do not believe it matters whether giving a patient insight means feeding, nurturing, protecting, or teaching to the analyst. What is important is that the feeding, nurturing, protecting, or teaching should be free of its sexual or aggressive undertones and is therefore neither unduly exciting or guilt producing.

Similarly, getting inside the patient in order to obtain insight obviously has libidinal and aggressive antecedents, but the real issue is whether this activity is still closely linked to anxiety- or guilt-producing fantasies. It must be borne in mind, however, that such sublimations are never established once and for all, since pressures from the id, superego, and the external world do make for regressions and progressions. Therefore another important consideration is how accessible to the analyst's conscious, reasonable ego are these aggressive and libidinal motives. Awareness of the countertransference may set other adaptive measures in motion in the psychoanalyst which may supplement the safeguarding function which the neutralization has failed to handle. (For different points of view on this subject, see Winnicott, 1956a; Spitz, 1956a; Balint, 1950a; and Khan, 1963b, 1964.)

It does not do justice to the arduous demands of the analytic profession to hope that the obtaining and delivering of insight might be free from conflict, guilt, and anxiety. These activities ought to be pleasurable to the analyst. The daily work of therapeutic psychoanalysis is difficult and often painful for the analyst. He needs a certain amount of positive pleasure in the performance of his duties to enable him to sustain a lively interest and concern for the goings-on in his patients. The pleasure in listening, looking, exploring, imagining, and comprehending is not only permissible but necessary for the optimal efficiency of the analyst (Sharpe, 1947, pp. 120-121; Szasz, 1957, pp. 204-210).

Another characteristic of psychoanalysis which distinguishes it from all other psychotherapies is its special emphasis on structuring the relationship between patient and therapist so as to further the development of the transference neurosis. In order to facilitate the growth of the neurotic transference reactions it is necessary that the analyst conduct himself in a way that is different from all other patient-therapist relationships. I am referring here to what may be expressed in shorthand as the depriving-incognito behavior of the psychoanalyst. This leads us to the question: What motivations might impel a man to seek a career in a field where one of his major tasks is to comport himself as a relatively nonresponsive blank screen to the patient so that the patient can project and displace onto that screen the unresolved and warded-off imagos of the past?

This aspect of psychoanalytic technique seems to come easily to some analysts who indicate a proclivity for isolation, withdrawal, and uninvolvement. Difficulties arise when these analysts are not able to change their attitude and technique when the analytic situation calls for it. It has been impressive to me to find so many analysts who are timorous and uncomfortable during the initial interviews because they have to sit face to face with the patient. They tend to cut down the number of preliminary interviews in order to reach the safety and comfort of their position behind the couch as quickly as possible. Analysis of candidates in training with similar problems reveals they suffer from a form of stage fright which covers repressed exhibitionistic impulses and a generalized aggressivization and sexualization of looking and being seen. The position behind the couch offers them the opportunity to look without being seen.

I am impressed by the high percentage of psychoanalysts who suffer from a marked degree of stage fright. It is so striking that I am forced to assume that one of the motives that makes psychoanalysis attractive as a profession is the analyst's hidden position behind the couch. The important instrumentality of facilitating the transference neurosis by restraining one's emotional responses and keeping oneself relatively anonymous may well be touching on this pathological source. Modesty and a sense of privacy are the analogous healthy traits of character which might impel one to find this aspect of psychoanalytic technique attractive (Jones, 1955, p. 408).

The decisive factor is how fixed, rigid, and intense is the shyness of the analyst. As long as he has some flexibility and can overcome his timidity when it is necessary it may not become a serious hindrance. On the other hand, strong unexpressed exhibitionistic impulses in an analyst can become a problem in the other direction. For them the position behind the couch and the blanketing of their emotional responses may become a chronic frustration, which may lead to eruptions of inconsistent behavior or unconscious provocation of acting out in the patient.

Generalized emotional withdrawal and uninvolvement with the patient are much more ominous signs and make for an inability to perform psychoanalysis except as a caricature of the true procedure. My experience with candidates suffering from such problems indicates that they are persons who are struggling against great hostility, rage, and anxiety. They need to remain remote in order not to explode with anger or panic. These people are not suitable for psychoanalytic work, yet they sought it out because superficially it seemed to offer them a haven from the fearful direct contact with people. Aloofness is the normal variant of this pathological behavior. The capacity to become temporarily and partially detached and aloof is a prerequisite for psychoanalytic work, particularly in regard to promoting the growth of the transference neurosis. The key point lies in the words temporary and partial. When aloofness is controllable, it is valuable; when it is compulsory and fixed, it is a contraindication for doing analytic work.

The capacity to be consistently depriving and frustrating depends on one's ability to inflict pain. Unresolved conflicts around sadism, masochism, and hatred will produce extremes or inconsistencies. The excessively silent analyst, for example, may be hiding a chronic passive aggressive attitude (Stone, 1961). Analysts who practice in an atmosphere of great austerity and severity may be silently venting their hostility and also unconsciously provoking an attack, a hidden form of masochistic satisfaction. The ability consistently to block the patient's search for symptomatic gratifications is crucial for the development of the transference neurosis. In order to do this without being misled by unconscious sadistic or masochistic impulses, the analyst must be able to modulate his aggressiveness and his hatred. Just as the analyst must be able to love his patient, within limits, so must he be able to hate his patient, also within limits. Inflicting pain, be it in the form of aloofness, silence, making interpretations, or charging fees, are ultimately all derived from hatred. It is important that the analyst be able to do this without unconscious anxiety or guilt and for the patient's therapeutic benefit (Winnicott, 1949).

The patient often becomes the bearer of the analyst's fantasies; he may represent the analyst himself in the past or a sibling or parent, etc. In this way the analytic situation offers the analyst an opportunity to live out his more or less unconscious fantasies vicariously via his patient. As a consequence the analyst may unwittingly use the patient as an accomplice for enacting the analyst's repressed wishes. It is not surprising to find that analysts with a tendency to act out have patients who do so. It is more surprising, but not rare, to find that analysts who lead quite restricted and inhibited lives often have patients who act out frequently and flagrantly. Unconsciously the analysts in question applaud and participate in this behavior (Greenacre, 1950, p. 236).

Just as the setting of the analytic situation promotes fantasy formation in the patient, it does so also in the analyst. His sitting behind the couch unseen, his abundant silence, the physical restrictions imposed on him, the emotional restraint, all tend to mobilize the analyst's imagination. Most important, however, is the fact that the patient's neurotic transference reactions cast the analyst in a variety of roles. He may become the dearly beloved or the hated enemy, the frightening father or the seductive mother in the patient's mind. It is the analyst's task to allow these developments to take place and to intervene only when it is helpful to the patient. More than that, it is his job to embellish and refine the character type the patient has displaced onto him, in order to gain a better understanding of its significance for the patient.

In a strange way the analyst becomes a silent actor in a play the patient is creating. The analyst does not act in this drama; he tries to remain the shadowy figure the patient needs for his fantasies. Yet the analyst helps in the creation of the character, working out the details by his insight, empathy, and intuition. In a sense he becomes a kind of stage director in the situation—a vital part of the play, but not an actor. Or he is like the conductor of a symphony orchestra. He does not write the music, but he clarifies and interprets it. By the use of his creative imagination the analyst participates in the patient's fantasies as a clarifier and interpreter, not as an accomplice or provocateur (Kris, 1950; Beres, 1960; Rosen, 1960; Stone, 1961).

Before we can turn to the motivations of the psychoanalyst as a treater of the sick and suffering, some preliminary discussion is called for because this is a controversial issue. Most analysts would probably agree with the selection of the first two basic components of an analyst's work, namely, (1) serving as the gatherer and transmitter of insight, and (2) conducting himself so as to become the relatively blank screen for the patient's transference neurosis. There would be considerable difference of opinion about the validity and importance of the third point, the analyst as a man committed to relieving the neurotic misery of his patient (Stone, 1961, pp. 12-17, 117-120). In order to present properly the point of view that the analyst's therapeutic intent is a vital factor in the practice of psychoanalysis, I would like to outline briefly some of the historical and scientific background for this dispute. I recommend the works of Freud (1926b) and Jones (1953; 1955, Chapt. 4; 1957, Chapt. 9) for a more comprehensive picture.

Beginning with Freud's earliest analytic writings, the medical profession as a whole, and the neurologists and psychiatrists in particular, have been hostile and combative toward psychoanalysis. Those physicians who did join the psychoanalytic movement were not from the conventional conservative majority of doctors. I believe this to be still true today. Since World War II psychoanalysis seems to have become more acceptable to psychiatrists, but not noticeably so to the other branches of medicine.

The few physicians who joined with Freud in isolation to form the psychoanalytic society in Vienna in 1902 and the International Psycho-Analytical Association in 1910 were more or less outside the mainstream of the medical associations. At the same time some of the most brilliant early contributors to psychoanalysis were non-medical people: Hanns Sachs, Hermine Hug-Hellmuth, Rev. Oskar Pfister, Otto Rank, Melanie Klein, Siegfried Bernfeld, Theodor Reik, and Anna Freud. Two of the five members of Freud's "secret committee" were lay analysts: Hanns Sachs and Otto Rank (Jones, 1955, Chapt. 6). Freud's own academic background was far broader than the usual physician's. In the spring of 1926 Theodor Reik was sued under the Austrian law as a quack, and later that year Freud wrote a small book in defense of lay analysis. In this book Freud said: "After forty-one years of medical activity, my self-knowledge tells me that I have never really been a doctor in the proper sense. . . . I have no knowledge of having had any craving in my early childhood to help suffering humanity. . . . I scarcely think, however, that my lack of a genuine medical temperament has done much damage to my patients. For it is not greatly to the advantage of patients if their doctor's therapeutic interest has too marked an emotional emphasis. They are best helped if he carries out his task coolly and keeping as closely as possible to the rules" (1926b, pp. 253-254).

In my opinion, Freud's self-evaluation is not accurate and may have been influenced by his hostility to the medical profession at the moment. I have tried to demonstrate a very clear therapeutic attitude in Freud's way of working with his patients in the quotations in Section 4.223. I do agree with Freud and others that the medical school curriculum is not the ideal preparation for a psychoanalyst, and that some special combination of partial medical training plus some study of social sciences, humanities, and literature would be superior (Freud, 1926b, pp. 230-232, 246; Lewin, 1946; Fliess, 1954). Freud did concede, however, and here too I am in full agreement: "I am bound to admit that, so long as schools such as we desire for the training of analysts are not yet in existence, people who have had a preliminary education in medicine are the best material for future analysts" (1926b, p. 257).

Freud's attitude notwithstanding, I contend that the therapeutic intent in the analyst is a vital element in his makeup if he is to practice psychoanalysis as a method of treatment. I do not maintain that this urge to be a healer of the sick can be obtained only from medical school training, but no matter where it originates, it is an essential ingredient of practicing psychoanalysis as a therapy. In my personal experience, I have never known an effective psychoanalytic therapist who did not feel strongly a desire to relieve the suffering of his patients. I have met M.D. psychoanalysts who were essentially misplaced researchers or data collectors, and their therapeutic results were below expectations. I have known lay analysts who were physicianly in their way of working and their patients did not seem to suffer from their analyst's lack of an M.D. degree. I should like it to be clear that by the urge to help the sick and suffering I am referring to what Stone calls the frank and evident therapeutic, physicianly commitment, the deep and thoughtful wish to help or cure (1961, pp. 119-120). I do not mean frantic therapeutic zeal.

Psychoanalysis is not the treatment of choice for emergency situations, nor is it suitable for psychiatric first aid. When such instances arise during the course of an analysis, it is usually necessary to do some unanalytic psychotherapy. The well-trained psychoanalyst ought to be prepared to do this, keeping in mind the question of how it might be possible to preserve the analytic situation. Psychoanalysis is a long-range treatment; one's therapeutic intent must be low in intensity, but it must endure throughout the years of treatment.

From time to time in the psychoanalytic literature one gets the impression that the wish to relieve a patient's misery is fundamentally antagonistic to analyzing and understanding his problems (Sharpe, 1947, p. 216). At other times it seems that analysts are more concerned with preserving the purity of psychoanalysis than with improving their therapeutic results (Waelder, 1960, p. 116; Ramzy, 1961; Eissler, 1958). Still others tend to emphasize the psychoanalyst's passive role as a catalyst and underestimate the importance of technical skill (Menninger, 1958, pp. 11, 128). Describing the patient-analyst relationship as a "two-party transaction," between "a party of the first part" and "a party of the second part" diminishes and obscures the special importance of the psychoanalyst's physicianly attitudes (Menninger, 1958).

It is my belief that the therapeutic aspect of the analyst is of particular importance in the analytic situation for the patient as well as for the analyst. For the patient, the physicianly analyst is a powerful activator of the transference neurosis and the working alliance (Stone, 1961, pp. 84-87). The image of the doctor stirs up in the patient memories, fantasies, and feelings from childhood of an authoritative, arbitrary, incomprehensible, and magical figure who possessed the power of the omnipotent, omniscient parents. It is the doctor who comes and takes over when the parents are sick and afraid. It is the doctor who has the right to explore the naked body and who has no fear or disgust of blood, mucus, vomit, urine, or feces (Freud, 1926b, p. 206). He is the rescuer from pain and panic, the establisher of order from chaos; emergency functions performed by the mother in the first years of life. In addition, the physician inflicts pain, cuts, and pierces the flesh and intrudes into every opening in the body. He is reminiscent of the mother of bodily intimacy as well as the representative of the sadomasochistic fantasies involving both parents.

For the psychoanalyst, it is my contention that it is mainly the therapeutic commitment to the patient that makes it possible for him to utilize consistently the various "unnatural" instrumentalities that psychoanalysis requires without becoming ritualistic, authoritarian, remote, or bored. I am referring here to such vocational hazards as listening hour after hour to free and unfree associations and paying attention to all details, listening predominantly in silence, manifesting only well-modulated emotional responses, permitting oneself to become the target of intense emotional storms of the patient, and intervening only for the patient's welfare, allowing oneself to be verbally made love to without becoming seductive or being vilified without defending oneself or counterattacking.

It is mainly the underlying dedication to the task of helping and healing the sick one which permits the analyst under such circumstances to maintain emotional concern and compassion for the patient, without becoming overprotective like a mother or unengaged like a research worker. The physicianly attitude implies a constant awareness of the patient's basically painful and helpless condition as well as a respect for those instrumentalities, procedures, and processes which are necessary for therapeutic results. The doctor is far more reliable in assessing the amount of pain his patient can bear than mother, father, or research worker.

Yet the posture of therapist partakes partially of both mother and researcher. (I am leaving the father out of this discussion since it would lead us too far afield.) I believe the ideal analyst is a motherly father figure or fatherly mother, the duality existing in regard to functions and not as a sexual characteristic. The analytic therapist must be in close empathic (motherly) contact with his patients so that he can nurture their potentials, protect their rights and dignity, know the difference between harmful and harmless gratifications, the limits of their deprivation tolerance, and be willing to wait for years for the fruits of his labors. As a therapist he also must be able to maintain distance between himself and the patient so that he can "research" the patient's data, i.e., recall, sort, think, judge, theorize, and speculate about them. Above all, the therapist must be able to have easy access to both mother and researcher positions, and he must be able to intervene in both capacities. Yet he must act overtly as neither, but as a composite: therapist.

We can now turn finally to our original question: What motivates a man to pursue a career in which he will devote his life to the treatment of the sick and suffering neurotic human being. A joke currently in vogue contains more than a germ of truth regarding this question. Riddle: What is a psychoanalyst? Answer: A Jewish doctor who cannot stand the sight of blood! This joke does highlight certain important considerations. Freud addressed himself to the question of what motivates a person to devote himself to the profession of psychoanalysis and, although he personally disavowed them, he did single out two important early sources of the therapeutic attitude: "My innate sadistic disposition was not a very strong one, so that I had no need to develop this one of its derivatives. Nor did I ever play the 'doctor game'; my infantile curiosity evidently chose other paths" (1926b, p. 253).

I believe that the significant role of the pregenital sadistic drives which contribute to one's interest in doctoring has been well documented since the pioneering paper of Simmel on the doctor game (1926). Such impulses can be detected clinically in the overt behavior of sadistic doctors who inflict unnecessary pain and mutilation, as reaction formations in indecisive, inhibited doctors, and as reparation and restitution phenomena in guilt-laden ones who are compulsive rescuers. Relatively well-neutralized aggressive drives are exemplified in the surgeon who is able to make a conflict-free decision to operate, who performs with dexterity and dispatch, and who feels neither undue triumph nor guilt afterward.

The libidinal contributions to the therapeutic commitment are derived from pregenital and oedipal sources. The urge to get inside the body or mind of another can be motivated by the longing for fusion and closeness as well as by destructive aims. Anal-erotic pleasure may be quite obvious in the undue interest in the "dirty" aspects of doctoring as well as in the reaction formation of excessive cleanliness.

One of Simmel's major contributions was his insight into the role of the doctor as an opportunity for re-enacting the sexual, sadomasochistic misunderstanding of the primal scene of childhood (pp. 292-293). The physician may be the sadistic father sexually torturing the victimized mother-patient, he may become the rescuer, or he may identify with the victim. Sometimes one finds that the physician is trying to act out a fantasy in which he does to his patient what he wanted his parent to do to him in childhood; this may be a variety of homosexuality and incest. Treating the sick may also be derived from the "nursing" mother who alleviates pain by suckling the child (p. 303).

Later factors of significance may stem from different defensive maneuvers. Treating the sick may serve as a means of mastering one's fear of disease, a counterphobic activity. One seeks out actively what one dreads occurring when one is passive (Fenichel, 1939). Defensive activities shade into the realm of sublimation and neutralization. The search for knowledge and truth may become a deinstinctualized and anxiety-free derivative of the urge to gain access to the unknown and dangerous body and mind. A feeling of kinship with suffering humanity may also play a role in the wish to fight against the tyranny of unnecessary sickness and pain.

The psychoanalyst differs from all other medical therapists in that he has no bodily contact with the patient despite the high degree of verbal intimacy. He resembles the mother of bodily separation in this way rather than the mother of bodily intimacy (Stone, 1961, p. 105). Furthermore, the analyst shares his knowledge and findings with the patient far more than other physicians, a point which brings him closer to the profession of teacher.

In closing this discussion on motivation it seems worthwhile to repeat the two critical issues. First, the origin of the longing to become a therapist is not the crucial factor; what is decisive is how well deinstinctualized and neutralized the derivative activities have become. Secondly, if the neutralization is not successful or only partially so, the next question is: are these primitive antecedents readily accessible to the therapist's reasonable ego and therefore amenable to influence and restraint? If this is the case, then these impulses may not only be harmless but may also be valuable indicators of the goings-on in the patient.

4.3 What Psychoanalysis Requires of the Analytic Setting

The term "analytic setting" refers to the physical framework and the routine procedures of psychoanalytic practice which form an integral part of the process of being psychoanalyzed. Although it is true that one or another of these elements may be altered without making psychoanalysis impossible, it is also true that the analytic setting does influence the various processes which do occur in psychoanalytic treatment. For example, we know that transference reactions take place spontaneously in neurotic human beings who are not in psychoanalytic therapy. Yet we also know that the analytic setting does facilitate and maximize the appearance of all the different transference reactions.

Although Freud carefully described how he went about establishing the various routines and procedures with his new patients, he did not conceptualize what he expected them to contribute (Freud, 1912b, 1913b). That he had had some expectations in this regard can be seen in his paper on transference love, where he mentioned that the patient's falling in love is "induced" and "provoked" by the analytic situation (Freud, 1915a, pp. 160-161, 168).

Until relatively recently, the psychoanalytic literature stressed the overwhelming importance of the patient's past history and the analyst's attitude of relative neutrality, incognito, and passivity as the factors determining the course of the transference reactions.

Although this is still essentially valid, we do recognize today that certain elements in the analytic setting and procedures may promote or hinder these developments. The papers of Macalpine, (1950) Greenacre (1954), Lewin (1955), Spitz (1956b), and Stone (1961) have been of particular value in illuminating the significance of the analytic setting for the evolution of the various transference reactions.

In keeping with earlier formulations in regard to the patient's relationship to the analyst, we will study the analytic setting from the point of view of the elements that promote the transference neurosis and those that facilitate the working alliance, i.e., what tends to make the patient regress, and what helps him maintain his more adult level of functioning? It is essential that the analytic setting provide both opportunities consistently (Greenson, 1965a).

The circumstance that two people meet together repeatedly and alone for a long period of time makes for an intensity of emotional involvement. The fact that one is troubled and relatively helpless and the other expert and offering help, facilitates an uneven, "tilted" relationship, with the troubled one tending to regress to some form of infantile dependency (Greenacre, 1954). The routine of having the patient lie on the couch also contributes to the regression in a variety of ways. The reclining position is a carry-over from the days of hypnosis and a modification of the attempt to put the patient to sleep (Lewin, 1955; Khan, 1962). The diminution of the external stimuli, the fact that the patient does not see the analyst, that the analyst is relatively silent, and that there is no physical contact between them also further a sleeplike state (Macalpine, 1950; Spitz, 1956b).

Spitz (1956b) also stressed the fact that the patient is lying down and therefore is lower than the analyst sitting upright behind him, that the patient's locomotion and bodily movements are restricted, and that he speaks but he cannot see to whom; all these push the patient in the direction of objectlessness. It is Greenacre's (1954) contention that this combination of elements recapitulates the matrix of the mother-child relationship of the first months of life. Free association itself is an invitation to regress toward the primary process and the dream (Macalpine, 1950; Lewin, 1955). It resembles as well the prattling of a child in that we ask him to say everything without discrimination and without responsibility (Spitz, 1956b).

The analyst's routines also contribute to the regressive pull of the analytic setting. His relative anonymity, muted emotional responses, and generally deprivational attitude regarding the patient's neurotic wishes all expedite the transference neurosis (Macalpine, 1950; Spitz, 1956b). The circumstance that the analyst is a treater of the sick, a therapist, also activates the many infantile antecedents of the doctor in the patient's fantasy life (see Section 4.23).

Many of the routines described above as furthering the regression toward the infantile neurosis also contribute to the formation and maintenance of the working alliance if they are carried out consistently, with a high degree of frequency, and for a long period of time. All procedures which become predictable make for a relative sense of security; and if they are perceived as having a therapeutic intent, they will make for a feeling of trust, which is the core of the working alliance. Security and trust make it possible for the patient to allow himself to regress just as they give him the courage to risk discarding a neurotic defense and trying a new form of adaptation. The analyst's daily work with the patient, his unflagging pursuit of insight and understanding, his respect and protection of the rights, potentials, and dignity of the patient, his concern and compassion, and his frank and thoughtful commitment to relieving the patient's neurotic misery should be part of the analytic atmosphere.

As is characteristic of so many of the processes of psychoanalysis, there is also a dialectic to be encountered here. The insatiable instinctual hunger of the neurotic patient may turn even the analyst's gratificatory attitudes into a frustration; the patient's ambivalence may twist the analyst's therapeutic concern into a form of rejection and the analyst's patience into indifference. The crux of the matter is the relative strength of the patient's reasonable ego in regard to the id, the superego, and the external world at a given moment. The relationship to the analyst is dependent upon these factors.

As an example of this bipolarity, any intervention may be felt either as a lulling to sleep or as a stark awakening. The imponderables of everyday life can play a decisive role. Despite the fact that the analytic setting is of importance in the therapeutic equation, it cannot replace psychoanalytic technique: the art of interpretation, and the skill in relating to a human being. It must also be remembered with all humility that even with the best technique it requires a goodly amount of time to overcome the formidable tyranny of the neurotic patient's past and his compulsion to repeat (Greenson, 1966).

Additional Reading List

General Considerations

Altman (1964), Greenacre (1954), Greenson (1966), Haak (1957), Khan (1960, 1962), Lewin (1955, 1959), Macalpine (1950), Spitz (1956a, 1956b), Stone (1961).

Required Traits of Personality and Character in Patients

Aarons (1962), Guttman (1960), Knapp, Levin, McCarter, Wermer, and Zetzel (1960), Rosenberg [Zetzel] (1949), Waldhorn (1960).

Gratification and Frustration in the Analytic Situation

Glover (1955), Greenacre (1959), Hoffer (1956), Kubie (1950), Menninger (1958), Nacht (1957).

Bibliography

AARONS, Z. A. (1962), Indications for Analysis and Problems of Analyzability. *Psychoanal. Quart.*, 31:514-531.

ABRAHAM, K. (1913), Shall We Have the Patients Write Down Their Dreams? In: *The Psychoanalytic Reader*, ed. R. Fliess. New York: International Universities Press, 1948, 1:326-328.

——— (1919), A Particular Form of Neurotic Resistance against the Psycho-Analytic Method. *Selected Papers on Psycho-Analysis*. London: Hogarth Press, 1948, pp. 303-311.

——— (1924), A Short Study of the Development of the Libido. *Selected Papers on Psycho-Analysis*. London: Hogarth Press, 1948, pp. 418-501.

AICHHORN, A. (1925), *Wayward Youth*. New York: Viking Press, 1945.

ALEXANDER, F. (1925), A Metapsychological Description of the Process of Cure. *Int. J. Psycho-Anal.*, 6:13-34.

——— (1927), *Psychoanalysis of the Total Personality*. New York & Washington: Nervous & Mental Disease Publishing Co., 1930.

——— (1935), The Problem of Psychoanalytic Technique. *Psychoanal. Quart.*, 4:588-611.

——— (1950), Analysis of the Therapeutic Factors in Psychoanalytic Treatment. *Psychoanal. Quart.*, 19:482-500.

——— (1954a), Some Quantitative Aspects of Psychoanalytic Technique. *J. Amer. Psychoanal. Assn.*, 2:685-701.

——— (1954b), Psychoanalysis and Psychotherapy. *J. Amer. Psychoanal. Assn.*, 2:722-733.

——— FRENCH, T. M., ET AL. (1946), *Psychoanalytic Therapy*. New York: Ronald Press.

ALTMAN, L. L. (1957), On the Oral Nature of Acting Out. *J. Amer. Psychoanal. Assn.*, 5:648-662.

——— (1964), Panel report: Theory of Psychoanalytic Therapy. *J. Amer. Psychoanal. Assn.*, 12:620-631.

ARLOW, J. A. (1961), Silence and the Theory of Technique. *J. Amer. Psychoanal. Assn.*, 9:44-55.

———— (1963), Conflict, Regression, and Symptom Formation. *Int. J. Psycho-Anal.*, 44:12-22.

———— & BRENNER, C. (1964), *Psychoanalytic Concepts and the Structural Theory.* New York: International Universities Press.

BALINT, M. (1948), On the Psycho-Analytic Training System. *Int. J. Psycho-Anal.*, 29:163-173.

———— (1950a), Changing Therapeutical Aims and Techniques in Psycho-Analysis. *Int. J. Psycho-Anal.*, 31:117-124.

———— (1950b), On the Termination of Analysis. *Int. J. Psycho-Anal.*, 31:196-199.

———— (1954), Analytic Training and Training Analysis. *Int. J. Psycho-Anal.*, 35:157-162.

BELLAK, L. (1961), Free Association: Conceptual and Clinical Aspects. *Int. J. Psycho-Anal.*, 42:9-20.

BENEDEK, T. (1953), Dynamics of the Countertransference. *Bull. Menninger Clin.*, 17:201-208.

———— (1955), A Contribution to the Problem of Termination of Training Analysis. *J. Amer. Psychoanal. Assn.*, 3:615-629.

BENJAMIN, J. D. (1947), Psychoanalysis and Nonanalytic Psychotherapy. *Psychoanal. Quart.*, 2:169-176.

BERES, D. (1960), Psychoanalytic Psychology of Imagination. *J. Amer. Psychoanal. Assn.*, 8:252-269.

BEREZIN, M. (1957), Note-taking during the Psychoanalytic Session. *Bull. Phila. Assn. Psychoanal.*, 7:96-101.

BERGLER, E. (1949), *The Basic Neurosis.* New York: Grune & Stratton.

BERNFELD, S. (1962 [1952]), On Psychoanalytic Training. *Psychoanal. Quart.*, 31:453-482.

BIBRING, E. (1937), On the Theory of the Results of Psycho-Analysis. *Int. J. Psycho-Anal.*, 18:170-189.

———— (1943), The Conception of the Repetition Compulsion. *Psychoanal. Quart.*, 12:486-519.

———— (1954), Psychoanalysis and the Dynamic Psychotherapies. *J. Amer. Psychoanal. Assn.*, 2:745-770.

BIBRING, G. L. (1935), A Contribution to the Subject of Transference Resistance. *Int. J. Psycho-Anal.*, 17:181, 1936.

———— (1954), The Training Analysis and Its Place in Psycho-Analytic Training. *Int. J. Psycho-Anal.*, 35:169-173.

BIRD, B. (1957), A Specific Peculiarity of Acting Out. *J. Amer. Psychoanal. Assn.*, 5:630-647.

BORNSTEIN, B. (1949), The Analysis of a Phobic Child: Some Problems of Theory and Technique in Child Analysis. *The Psychoanalytic Study of the Child,* 3/4:181-226.°

BOUVET, M. (1958), Technical Variation and the Concept of Distance. *Int. J. Psycho-Anal.*, 39:211-221.

BRAATØY, T. (1954), *Fundamentals of Psychoanalytic Technique.* New York: Wiley.

° *The Psychoanalytic Study of the Child,* currently 21 Volumes, edited by R. S. Eissler, A. Freud, H. Hartmann, & M. Kris. New York: International Universities Press, 1945-1966.

BRENNER, C. (1955), *An Elementary Textbook of Psychoanalysis.* New York: International Universities Press.

BREUER, J. & FREUD, S. (1893-95), Studies on Hysteria. *Standard Edition,* 2. London: Hogarth Press, 1955.

BRIDGER, H. (1950), Criteria for the Termination of Analysis. *Int. J. Psycho-Anal.,* 31:202-203.

BRIERLEY, M. (1951), *Trends in Psycho-Analysis.* London: Hogarth Press.

BYCHOWSKI, G. (1953), The Problem of Latent Psychosis. *J. Amer. Psychoanal. Assn.* 1:484-503.

——— (1954), The Structure of Homosexual Acting Out. *Psychoanal. Quart.,* 23:48-61.

——— (1958), Struggle Against the Introjects. *Int. J. Psycho-Anal.,* 39:182-187.

COLBY, K. M. (1951), *A Primer for Psychotherapists.* New York: Ronald Press.

DE FOREST, I. (1951), Significance of Countertransference in Psychoanalytic Therapy. *Psychoanal. Rev.,* 38:158-171.

———(1954), *The Leaven of Love: A Development of the Psychoanalytic Theory and Technique of Sandor Ferenczi.* New York: Harper.

DEUTSCH, F. (1939), Associative Anamnesis. *Psychoanal. Quart.,* 8:354-381.

———(1947), Analysis of Postural Behavior. *Psychoanal. Quart.,* 16:195-213.

———(1952), Analytic Posturology. *Psychoanal. Quart.,* 21:196-214.

DEUTSCH, H. (1942 [1934]), Some Forms of Emotional Disturbances and Their Relationship to Schizophrenia. In: *Neuroses and Character Types.* New York: International Universities Press, 1965, pp. 262-281.

——— (1944-45), *The Psychology of Women,* 2 Vols. New York: Grune & Stratton.

DEVEREUX, G. (1951), Some Criteria for the Timing of Confrontations and Interpretations. *Int. J. Psycho-Anal.,* 32:19-24.

EISENDORFER, A. (1959), The Selection of Candidates Applying for Psychoanalytic Training. *Psychoanal. Quart.,* 28:374-378.

EISSLER, K. R. (1950a), Ego-Psychological Implications of the Psychoanalytic Treatment of Delinquents. *The Psychoanalytic Study of the Child,* 5:97-121.

——— (1950b), The Chicago Institute of Psychoanalysis and the Sixth Period of the Development of Psychoanalytic Technique. *J. Genet. Psychol.,* 42:103-157.

——— (1953), The Effect of the Structure of the Ego on Psychoanalytic Technique. *J. Amer. Psychoanal. Assn.,* 1:104-143.

——— (1956), Some Comments on Psychoanalysis and Dynamic Psychiatry. *J. Amer. Psychoanal. Assn.,* 4:314-317.

——— (1958), Remarks on Some Variations in Psycho-Analytical Technique. *Int. J. Psycho-Anal.,* 39:222-229.

EKSTEIN, R. (1950), Trial Analysis in the Therapeutic Process. *Psychoanal. Quart.,* 19:52-63.

——— (1955), Termination of the Training Analysis within the Framework of Present-day Institutes. *J. Amer. Psychoanal. Assn.,* 3:600-614.

——— (1956), A Clinical Note on the Therapeutic Use of a Quasi-religious Experience. *J. Amer. Psychoanal. Assn.,* 4:304-313.

—— (1960a), A Historical Survey on the Teaching of Psychoanalytic Technique. *J. Amer. Psychoanal. Assn.*, 8:500-516.

—— (1960b), Panel report: The Teaching of Psychoanalytic Technique. *J. Amer. Psychoanal. Assn.*, 8:167-174.

—— & FRIEDMAN, S. W. (1957), The Function of Acting Out, Play Action and Play Acting in the Psychotherapeutic Process. *J. Amer. Psychoanal. Assn.*, 5:581-629.

—— & WALLERSTEIN, R. S. (1958), *The Teaching and Learning of Psychotherapy*. New York: Basic Books.

ERIKSON, E. H. (1950), *Childhood and Society*. New York: Norton.

EVANS, W. N. (1953), Evasive Speech as a Form of Resistance. *Psychoanal. Quart.*, 22:548-560.

FAIRBAIRN, W. R. D. (1958), On the Nature and Aims of Psycho-Analytical Treatment. *Int. J. Psycho-Anal.*, 39:374-385.

FELDMAN, S. S. (1948), Mannerisms of Speech: A Contribution to the Working Through Process. *Psychoanal. Quart.*, 17:356-367.

—— (1958), Blanket Interpretations. *Psychoanal. Quart.*, 27:205-216.

—— (1959), *Mannerisms of Speech and Gestures in Everyday Life*. New York: International Universities Press.

FENICHEL, O. (1934), On the Psychology of Boredom. *Collected Papers of Otto Fenichel*, 1:292-302. New York: Norton, 1953.

—— (1939), The Counter-Phobic Attitude. *The Collected Papers of Otto Fenichel*, 2:163-173. New York: Norton, 1954.

—— (1941), *Problems of Psychoanalytic Technique*. Albany, N.Y.: The Psychoanalytic Quarterly, Inc.

—— (1945a), *The Psychoanalytic Theory of Neurosis*. New York: Norton.

—— (1945b), Neurotic Acting Out. *Collected Papers of Otto Fenichel*, 2:296-304. New York: Norton, 1954.

FERENCZI, S. (1909), Introjection and Transference. *Sex in Psychoanalysis*. New York: Basic Books, 1950, pp. 35-93.

—— (1911), On Obscene Words. *Sex in Psychoanalysis*. New York: Basic Books, 1950, pp. 132-153.

—— (1912), Transitory Symptom-Construction during the Analysis. *Sex in Psychoanalysis*. New York: Basic Books, 1950, pp. 193-212.

—— (1914a), Discontinuous Analyses. *Further Contributions to the Theory and Technique of Psycho-Analysis*. London: Hogarth Press, 1950, pp. 233-235.

—— (1914b), Sensations of Giddiness at the End of the Psycho-Analytic Session. *Further Contributions to the Theory and Technique of Psycho-Analysis*. London: Hogarth Press, 1950, pp. 239-241.

—— (1914c), On Falling Asleep during Analysis. *Further Contributions to the Theory and Technique of Psycho-Analysis*. London: Hogarth Press, 1950, pp. 249-250.

—— (1914d), The Psychic Effect of the Sunbath. *The Theory and Technique of Psycho-Analysis*. London: Hogarth Press, 1950, p. 365.

—— (1915), Restlessness towards the End of the Hour of Analysis. *Further Contributions to the Theory and Technique of Psycho-Analysis*. London: Hogarth Press, 1950, pp. 238-239.

—— (1916), *Sex in Psychoanalysis*. New York: Basic Books, 1950.

——— (1916-17a), Interchange of Affect in Dreams. *Further Contributions to the Theory and Technique of Psycho-Analysis.* London: Hogarth Press, 1950, p. 345.

——— (1916-17b), Dreams of the Unsuspecting. *Further Contributions to the Theory and Technique of Psycho-Analysis.* London: Hogarth Press, 1950, pp. 346-348.

——— (1916-17c), Silence Is Golden. *Further Contributions to the Theory and Technique of Psycho-Analysis.* London: Hogarth Press, 1950, pp. 250-251.

——— (1919a), On the Technique of Psycho-Analysis. *Further Contributions to the Theory and Technique of Psycho-Analysis.* London: Hogarth Press, 1950, pp. 177-189.

——— (1919b), Technical Difficulties in the Analysis of a Case of Hysteria. *Further Contributions to the Theory and Technique of Psycho-Analysis.* London: Hogarth Press, 1950, pp. 189-197.

——— (1919c), Sunday Neuroses. *Further Contributions to the Theory and Technique of Psycho-Analysis.* London: Hogarth Press, 1950, pp. 174-177.

——— (1921 [1920]), The Further Development of an Active Therapy in Psycho-Analysis. *Further Contributions to the Theory and Technique of Psycho-Analysis.* London: Hogarth Press, 1950, pp. 198-217.

——— (1923), Attention during the Narration of Dreams. *Further Contributions to the Theory and Technique of Psycho-Analysis.* London: Hogarth Press, 1950, p. 238.

——— (1924), On Forced Phantasies. *Further Contributions to the Theory and Technique of Psycho-Analysis.* London: Hogarth Press, 1950, pp. 68-77.

——— (1925), Contra-Indications to the 'Active' Psycho-Analytical Technique. *Further Contributions to the Theory and Technique of Psycho-Analysis.* London: Hogarth Press, 1950, pp. 217-230.

——— (1928a [1927]), The Problem of the Termination of the Analysis. *Final Contributions to the Problems and Methods of Psycho-Analysis.* New York: Basic Books, 1955, pp. 77-86.

——— (1928b [1927]), The Elasticity of Psycho-Analytic Technique. *Final Contributions to the Problems and Methods of Psycho-Analysis.* New York: Basic Books, 1955, pp. 87-101.

——— (1930 [1929]), The Principles of Relaxation and Neocatharsis. *Final Contributions to the Problems and Methods of Psycho-Analysis.* New York: Basic Books, 1955, pp. 108-125.

——— (1939 [c. 1913]), Laughter. *Final Contributions to the Problem and Methods of Psycho-Analysis.* New York: Basic Books, 1955, pp. 177-182.

——— & RANK, O. (1924), *The Development of Psychoanalysis.* New York & Washington: Nervous and Mental Disease Publishing Co., 1925.

FISHER, C. (1953), Studies on the Nature of Suggestion: Part II. The Transference Meaning of Giving Suggestions. *J. Amer. Psychoanal. Assn.*, 1:406-437.

FLEMING, J. (1946), Observations of the Defenses against a Transference Neurosis. *Psychiatry*, 9:365-374.

——— (1961), What Analytic Work Requires of an Analyst: A Job Analysis. *J. Amer. Psychoanal. Assn.*, 9:719-729.

——— & BENEDEK, T. (1964), Supervision: A Method of Teaching Psychoanalysis. *Psychoanal. Quart.*, 33:71-96.

418 BIBLIOGRAPHY

FLIESS, R. (1949), Silence and Verbalization: A Supplement to the Theory of the 'Analytic Rule.' *Int. J. Psycho-Anal.*, 30:21-30.
——— (1953), Countertransference and Counteridentification. *J. Amer. Psychoanal. Assn.*, 1:268-284.
——— (1954), The Autopsic Encumbrance: Some Remarks on an Unconscious Interference with the Management of the Analytic Situation. *Int. J. Psycho-Anal.*, 35:8-12.
FRAIBERG, S. (1951), Clinical Notes on the Nature of Transference in Child Analysis. *The Psychoanalytic Study of the Child*, 6:286-306.
——— (1966), Further Considerations of the Role of Transference in Latency. *The Psychoanalytic Study of the Child*, 21:213-236.
FRANK, J. (1956), Indications and Contraindications for the Application of the "Standard Technique." *J. Amer. Psychoanal. Assn.*, 4:266-284.
FREEMAN, T. (1959), Aspects of Defence in Neurosis and Psychosis. *Int. J. Psycho-Anal.*, 40:199-212.
FRENCH, T. M. (1946), The Transference Phenomena. In: F. Alexander, T. M. French, et al., *Psychoanalytic Therapy*. New York: Ronald Press.
FREUD, A. (1928 [1946]), *The Psycho-Analytical Treatment of Children*. New York: International Universities Press, 1955.
——— (1936), *The Ego and the Mechanisms of Defense*. New York: International Universities Press, 1946.
——— (1950a), Probleme der Lehranalyse. In: *Max Eitingon in Memoriam*. Jerusalem: Israeli Psychoanalytic Society.
——— (1950b), The Significance of the Evolution of Psychoanalytic Child Psychology. *Congrès International de Psychiatrie, Paris 1950*, 5:29-36. Abstr. in: *The Annual Survey of Psychoanalysis*, 1:200-203. New York: International Universities Press, 1952.
——— (1954a), The Widening Scope of Indications for Psychoanalysis: Discussion. *J. Amer. Psychoanal. Assn.*, 2:607-620.
——— (1954b), Problems of Technique in Adult Analysis. *Bull. Phila. Assn. Psychoanal.*, 4:44-69.
——— (1959), The Nature of the Psychotherapeutic Process (unpublished manuscript) quoted by Ekstein (1960a).
——— (1965), *Normality and Pathology in Childhood: Assessments of Development*. New York: International Universities Press.
——— NAGERA, H., & FREUD, W. E. (1965), Metapsychological Assessment of the Adult Personality: The Adult Profile. *The Psychoanalytic Study of the Child*, 20:9-41.
FREUD, S. (1894), The Neuro-Psychoses of Defence. *Standard Edition*, 3:43-68.*
——— (1896), Further Remarks on the Neuro-Psychoses of Defence. *Standard Edition*, 3:159-185.
——— (1898), Sexuality and the Aetiology of the Neuroses. *Standard Edition*, 3:261-285.
——— (1900), The Interpretation of Dreams. *Standard Edition*, 4 & 5.
——— (1904 [1903]), Freud's Psycho-Analytic Procedure. *Standard Edition*, 7:249-254.

* *The Standard Edition of the Complete Psychological Works of Sigmund Freud*, 24 Volumes, translated and edited by James Strachey. London: Hogarth Press and the Institute of Psycho-Analysis, 1953-

———— (1905a [1901]), Fragment of an Analysis of a Case of Hysteria. *Standard Edition*, 7:3-122.

———— (1905b [1904]), On Psychotherapy. *Standard Edition*, 7:257-268.

———— (1905c), Psychical (or Mental) Treatment. *Standard Edition*, 7:283-302.

———— (1905d), Three Essays on the Theory of Sexuality. *Standard Edition*, 7:125-245.

———— (1908), Character and Anal Erotism. *Standard Edition*, 9:169-175.

———— (1909), Notes upon a Case of Obsessional Neurosis. *Standard Edition*, 10:153-318.

———— (1910a), The Future Prospects of Psycho-Analytic Therapy. *Standard Edition*, 11:139-151.

———— (1910b), 'Wild' Psycho-Analysis. *Standard Edition*, 11:219-227.

———— (1911a), Psycho-Analytic Notes on an Autobiographical Account of a Case of Paranoia (Dementia Paranoides). *Standard Edition*, 12:3-82.

———— (1911b), The Handling of Dream-Interpretation in Psycho-Analysis. *Standard Edition*, 12:89-96.

———— (1912a), The Dynamics of Transference. *Standard Edition*, 12:97-108.

———— (1912b), Recommendations to Physicians Practising Psycho-Analysis. *Standard Edition*, 12:109-120.

———— (1913a), [1912-13]), Totem and Taboo. *Standard Edition*, 13:1-161.

———— (1913b), On Beginning the Treatment. *Standard Edition*, 12:121-144.

———— (1914a), Fausse Reconnaissance (*Déjà Raconté*) in Psycho-Analytic Treatment. *Standard Edition*, 13:201-207.

———— (1914b), On the History of the Psycho-Analytic Movement. *Standard Edition*, 14:3-66.

———— (1914c), Remembering, Repeating, and Working-Through. *Standard Edition*, 12:145-156.

———— (1915a [1914]), Observations on Transference-Love. *Standard Edition*, 12:157-171.

———— (1915b), The Unconscious. *Standard Edition*, 14:159-215.

———— (1915c), Repression. *Standard Edition*, 14:141-158.

———— (1915d), Instincts and Their Vicissitudes. *Standard Edition*, 14:109-140.

———— (1916-17 [1915-17]), Introductory Lectures on Psycho-Analysis. *Standard Edition*, 15 & 16.

———— (1917a [1915]), A Metapsychological Supplement to the Theory of Dreams. *Standard Edition*, 14:217-235.

———— (1917b [1915]), Mourning and Melancholia. *Standard Edition*, 14:237-260.

———— (1919a [1918]), Lines of Advance in Psycho-Analytic Therapy. *Standard Edition*, 17:157-168.

———— (1919b), 'A Child Is Being Beaten.' *Standard Edition*, 17:175-204.

———— (1920), Beyond the Pleasure Principle. *Standard Edition*, 18:3-64.

———— (1921), Group Psychology and the Analysis of the Ego. *Standard Edition*, 18:67-143.

———— (1923a [1922]), Two Encyclopedic Articles: Psycho-Analysis. *Standard Edition*, 18:235-254.

———— (1923b), The Ego and the Id. *Standard Edition*, 19:3-66.

———— (1923c [1922]), Remarks on the Theory and Practice of Dream-Interpretation. *Standard Edition,* 19:109-121.

———— (1925a [1924]), An Autobiographical Study. *Standard Edition,* 20: 3-74.

———— (1925b), Negation. *Standard Edition,* 19:235-239.

———— (1925c), Some Additional Notes on Dream-Interpretation as a Whole. *Standard Edition,* 19:125-138.

———— (1926a [1925]), Inhibitions, Symptoms and Anxiety. *Standard Edition,* 20:77-175.

———— (1926b), The Question of Lay Analysis. *Standard Edition,* 20:179-258.

————(1933 [1932]), New Introductory Lectures in Psycho-Analysis. *Standard Edition,* 22:3-182.

———— (1937a), Analysis Terminable and Interminable. *Standard Edition,* 23:209-253.

———— (1937b), Constructions in Analysis. *Standard Edition,* 23:255-269.

———— (1940a [1938]), Splitting of the Ego in the Defensive Process. *Standard Edition,* 23:271-278.

———— (1940b [1938]), An Outline of Psycho-Analysis. *Standard Edition,* 23:141-207.

FRIEDMAN, L. J. (1953), Defensive Aspects of Orality. *Int. J. Psycho-Anal.,* 34:304-312.

———— (1954), Regressive Reaction to the Interpretation of a Dream. *J. Amer. Psychoanal. Assn.,* 2:514-518.

FROMM-REICHMANN, F. (1950), *Principles of Intensive Psychotherapy.* Chicago: University of Chicago Press.

———— (1954), Psychoanalytic and General Dynamic Conceptions of Theory and of Therapy: Differences and Similarities. *J. Amer. Psychoanal. Assn.,* 2:711-721.

———— (1955), Clinical Significances of Intuitive Processes of the Psychoanalyst. *J. Amer. Psychoanal. Assn.,* 3:82-88.

FROSCH, J. (1959), Transference Derivatives of the Family Romance. *J. Amer. Psychoanal. Assn.,* 7:503-522.

GELEERD, E. R. (1957), Some Aspects of Psychoanalytic Technique in Adolescence. *The Psychoanalytic Study of the Child,* 12:263-283.

GERO, G. (1951), The Concept of Defense. *Psychoanal. Quart.,* 20:565-578.

———— (1953), Defenses and Symptom Formation. *J. Amer. Psychoanal. Assn.,* 1:87-103.

GIFFORD, S. (1964), Panel report: Repetition Compulsion. *J. Amer. Psychoanal. Assn.,* 12:632-649.

GILL, M. M. (1951), Ego Psychology and Psychotherapy. *Psychoanal. Quart.,* 20:62-71.

———— (1954), Psychoanalysis and Exploratory Psychotherapy. *J. Amer. Psychoanal. Assn.,* 2:771-797.

———— (1963), *Topography and Systems in Psychoanalytic Theory* [*Psychological Issues,* Monogr. 10]. New York: International Universities Press.

———— NEWMAN, R., & REDLICH, F. C. (1954), *The Initial Interview in Psychiatric Practice.* New York: International Universities Press.

GILLESPIE, W. H. (1958), Neurotic Ego Distortion. *Int. J. Psycho-Anal.,* 39: 258-259.

GITELSON, M. (1948), Problems of Psychoanalytic Training. *Psychoanal. Quart.*, 17:198-211.

—— (1951), Psychoanalysis and Dynamic Psychiatry. *Arch. Neurol. & Psychiat.*, 66:280-288.

—— (1952), The Emotional Position of the Analyst in the Psycho-Analytic Situation. *Int. J. Psycho-Anal.*, 33:1-10.

—— (1954), Therapeutic Problems in the Analysis of the 'Normal' Candidate. *Int. J. Psycho-Anal.*, 35:174-183.

—— (1958), On Ego Distortion. *Int. J. Psycho-Anal.*, 39:245-257.

—— (1964), On the Identity Crisis in American Psychoanalysis. *J. Amer. Psychoanal. Assn.*, 12:451-476.

—— ET AL. (1962), The Curative Factors in Psycho-Analysis. *Int. J. Psycho-Anal.*, 43:194-234.

GLOVER, E. (1939), *Psycho-Analysis: A Handbook for Medical Practitioners and Students of Comparative Psychology.* New York & London: Staples Press.

—— (1955 [1928, 1940]), *The Technique of Psycho-Analysis.* New York: International Universities Press.

—— (1958), Ego Distortion. *Int. J. Psycho-Anal.*, 39:260-264.

GOSTYNSKI, E. (1951), A Clinical Contribution to the Analysis of Gestures. *Int. J. Psycho-Anal.*, 32:310-318.

GREENACRE, P. (1948), Symposium on the Evaluation of Therapeutic Results (C. P. Oberndorf, P. Greenacre, L. Kubie). *Int. J. Psycho-Anal.*, 29:11-14, 32.

—— (1950), General Problems of Acting Out. *Trauma, Growth, and Personality.* New York: Norton, 1952, pp. 224-236.

—— (1954), The Role of Transference: Practical Considerations in Relation to Psychoanalytic Therapy. *J. Amer. Psychoanal. Assn.*, 2:671-684.

—— (1956), Re-evaluation of the Process of Working Through. *Int. J. Psycho-Anal.*, 37:439-444.

—— (1958), Toward an Understanding of the Physical Nucleus of Some Defence Reactions. *Int. J. Psycho-Anal.*, 39:69-76.

—— (1959), Certain Technical Problems in the Transference Relationship. *J. Amer. Psychoanal. Assn.*, 7:484-502.

—— (1960), Considerations Regarding the Parent-Infant Relationship. *Int. J. Psycho-Anal.*, 41:571-584.

—— (1961), A Critical Digest of the Literature on Selection of Candidates for Psychoanalytic Training. *Psychoanal. Quart.*, 30:28-55.

—— (1966a), Problems of Training Analysis. *Psychoanal. Quart.*, 35:540-567.

—— (1966b), Problems of Overidealization of the Analyst and of Analysis: Their Manifestations in the Transference and Countertransference Relationship. *The Psychoanalytic Study of the Child*, 21:193-212.

GREENSON, R. R. (1950), The Mother Tongue and the Mother. *Int. J. Psycho-Anal.*, 31:18-23.

—— (1953), On Boredom. *J. Amer. Psychoanal. Assn.*, 1:7-21.

—— (1954), The Struggle against Identification. *J. Amer. Psychoanal. Assn.*, 2:200-217.

―――― (1958a), On Screen Defenses, Screen Hunger and Screen Identity. *J. Amer. Psychoanal. Assn.*, 6:242-262.

―――― (1958b), Variations in Classical Psycho-Analytic Technique: An Introduction. *Int. J. Psycho-Anal.*, 39:200-201.

―――― (1959a), Phobia, Anxiety and Depression. *J. Amer. Psychoanal. Assn.*, 7:663-674.

―――― (1959b), The Classic Psychoanalytic Approach. *American Handbook of Psychiatry*, ed. S. Arieti. New York: Basic Books, pp. 1399-1416.

―――― (1960), Empathy and Its Vicissitudes. *Int. J. Psycho-Anal.*, 41:418-424.

―――― (1961), On the Silence and Sounds of the Analytic Hour. *J. Amer. Psychoanal. Assn.*, 9:79-84.

―――― (1962), On Enthusiasm. *J. Amer. Psychoanal. Assn.*, 10:3-21.

―――― (1965a), The Working Alliance and the Transference Neurosis. *Psychoanal. Quart.*, 34:155-181.

―――― (1965b), The Problem of Working Through. In: *Drives, Affects, Behavior*, ed. M. Schur. New York: International Universities Press, 2:277-314.

―――― (1966), That "Impossible" Profession. *J. Amer. Psychoanal. Assn.*, 14:9-27.

―――― ET AL. (1958), Variations in Classical Psycho-Analytic Technique. *Int. J. Psycho-Anal.*, 39:200-242.

GRINSTEIN, A. (1955), Vacations: A Psycho-Analytic Study. *Int. J. Psycho-Anal.*, 36:177-186.

GROSS, A. (1951), The Secret. *Bull. Menninger Clin.*, 15:37-44.

GROTJAHN, M. (1950), About the "Third Ear" in Psychoanalysis. *Psychoanal. Rev.*, 37:56-65.

―――― (1954), About the Relation between Psycho-Analytic Training and Psycho-Analytic Therapy. *Int. J. Psycho-Anal.*, 35:254-262.

GUNTRIP, H. (1961), *Personality Structure and Human Interaction*. New York: International Universities Press.

GUTTMAN, S. A. (1960), Panel report: Criteria for Analyzability. *J. Amer. Psychoanal. Assn.*, 8:141-151.

HAAK, N. (1957), Comments on the Analytical Situation. *Int. J. Psycho-Anal.*, 38:183-195.

HARTMANN, H. (1939), *Ego Psychology and the Problem of Adaptation*. New York: International Universities Press, 1958.

―――― (1947), On Rational and Irrational Action. *Essays on Ego Psychology*. New York: International Universities Press, 1964, pp. 37-68.

―――― (1950), Comments on the Psychoanalytic Theory of the Ego. *Essays on Ego Psychology*. New York: International Universities Press, 1964, pp. 113-141.

―――― (1951), Technical Implications of Ego Psychology. *Essays on Ego Psychology*. New York: International Universities Press, 1964, pp. 142-154.

―――― (1955), Notes on the Theory of Sublimation. *Essays on Ego Psychology*. New York: International Universities Press, 1964, pp. 215-240.

―――― (1956), The Development of the Ego Concept in Freud's Work. *Essays on Ego Psychology*. New York: International Universities Press, 1964, pp. 268-296.

———— (1964), *Essays on Ego Psychology: Selected Problems in Psychoanalytic Theory*. New York: International Universities Press.

———— & KRIS, E. (1945), The Genetic Approach in Psychoanalysis. *The Psychoanalytic Study of the Child*, 1:11-30.

———— ———— & LOEWENSTEIN, R. M. (1946), Comments on the Formation of Psychic Structure. *The Psychoanalytic Study of the Child*, 2:11-38.

HEIMANN, P. (1950), On Counter-Transference. *Int. J. Psycho-Anal.*, 31:81-84.

———— (1954), Problems of the Training Analysis. *Int. J. Psycho-Anal.*, 35: 163-168.

———— (1956), Dynamics of Transference Interpretations. *Int. J. Psycho-Anal.*, 37:303-310.

HENDRICK, I. (1934), *Facts and Theories of Psychoanalysis*. New York: Knopf.

———— (1942), Instinct and the Ego during Infancy. *Psychoanal. Quart.*, 11:33-58.

———— (1951), Early Development of the Ego: Identification in Infancy. *Psychoanal. Quart.*, 20:44-61.

HILL, L. B. (1951), Anticipation of Arousing Specific Neurotic Feelings in the Psychoanalyst. *Psychiatry*, 14:1-8.

HOFFER, W. (1949), Mouth, Hand, and Ego-Integration. *The Psychoanalytic Study of the Child*, 3/4:49-56.

———— (1950), Three Psychological Criteria for the Termination of Treatment. *Int. J. Psycho-Anal.*, 31:194-195.

———— (1952), The Mutual Influences in the Development of Ego and Id: Earliest Stages. *The Psychoanalytic Study of the Child*, 7:31-41.

———— (1954), Defensive Process and Defensive Organization. *Int. J. Psycho-Anal.*, 35:194-198.

———— (1956), Transference and Transference Neuroses. *Int. J. Psycho-Anal.*, 37:377-379.

ISAACS, S. (1948), The Nature and Function of Phantasy. In: *Developments in Psycho-Analysis*, by M. Klein et al. London: Hogarth Press, 1952, pp. 67-121.

JACOBSON, E. (1950), Contribution to the Metapsychology of Cyclothymic Depression. In: *Affective Disorders*, ed. P. Greenacre. New York: International Universities Press, pp. 49-83.

———— (1954), Transference Problems in the Psychoanalytic Treatment of Severely Depressive Patients. *J. Amer. Psychoanal. Assn.*, 2:595-606.

———— (1964), *The Self and the Object World*. New York: International Universities Press.

JAMES, M. (1964), Interpretation and Management in the Treatment of Preadolescents. *Int. J. Psycho-Anal.*, 45:499-511.

JOKL, R. H. (1950), Psychic Determinism and Preservation of Sublimation in Classical Psychoanalytic Procedure. *Bull. Menninger Clin.*, 14:207-219.

JONES, E. (1953), *The Life and Work of Sigmund Freud, Volume I*. New York: Basic Books.

———— (1955), *The Life and Work of Sigmund Freud, Volume II*. New York: Basic Books.

———— (1957), *The Life and Work of Sigmund Freud, Volume III*. New York: Basic Books.

424   BIBLIOGRAPHY

KAIRYS, D. (1964), The Training Analysis: A Critical Review of the Literature and a Controversial Proposal. *Psychoanal. Quart.*, 33:485-512.

KANZER, M. (1953), Past and Present in the Transference. *J. Amer. Psychoanal. Assn.*, 1:144-154.

——— (1957), Panel report: Acting Out and Its Relation to Impulse Disorders. *J. Amer. Psychoanal. Assn.*, 5:136-145.

——— (1961), Verbal and Nonverbal Aspects of Free Association. *Psychoanal. Quart.* 30:327-350.

KATAN, M. (1954), The Importance of the Non-psychotic Part of the Personality in Schizophrenia. *Int. J. Psycho-Anal.*, 35:119-128.

——— (1958), Contribution to the Panel on Ego-Distortion ('As-If' and 'Pseudo As-If'). *Int. J. Psycho-Anal.*, 39:265-270.

KEISER, S. (1958), Disturbances in Abstract Thinking and Body-Image Formation. *J. Amer. Psychoanal. Assn.*, 6:628-652.

KHAN, M. M. R. (1960), Regression and Integration in the Analytic Setting. *Int. J. Psycho-Anal.*, 41:130-146.

——— (1962), Dream Psychology and the Evolution of the Psycho-Analytic Situation. *Int. J. Psycho-Anal.*, 43:21-31.

——— (1963a), The Concept of Cumulative Trauma. *The Psychoanalytic Study of the Child*, 18:286-306.

——— (1963b), Silence as Communication. *Bull. Menninger Clin.*, 27:300-317.

——— (1964), Ego Distortion, Cumulative Trauma, and the Role of Reconstruction in the Analytic Situation. *Int. J. Psycho-Anal.*, 45:272-278.

KLEIN, M. (1932), *The Psycho-Analysis of Children*. London: Hogarth Press, 1949.

——— (1950), On the Criteria for the Termination of a Psycho-Analysis. *Int. J. Psycho-Anal.*, 31:78-80.

——— (1952), The Origins of Transference. *Int. J. Psycho-Anal.*, 33:433-438.

——— (1961), *Narrative of a Child Analysis*. London: Hogarth Press.

——— HEIMANN, P., ISAACS, S., & RIVIERE, J. (1952), *Developments in Psycho-Analysis*. London: Hogarth Press.

——— ——— & MONEY-KYRLE, R., eds. (1955), *New Directions in Psycho-Analysis*. New York: Basic Books.

KNAPP, P. H., LEVIN, S., McCARTER, R. H., WERMER, H., & ZETZEL, E. R. (1960), Suitability for Psychoanalysis: A Review of 100 Supervised Analytic Cases. *Psychoanal. Quart.*, 29:459-477.

KNIGHT, R. P. (1949), A Critique of the Present Status of the Psychotherapies. *Psychoanalytic Psychiatry and Psychology*, ed. R. P. Knight & C. R. Friedman. New York: International Universities Press, 1954, pp. 52-64.

——— (1952), An Evaluation of Psychotherapeutic Techniques. *Psychoanalytic Psychiatry and Psychology*, ed. R. P. Knight & C. R. Friedman. New York: International Universities Press, 1954, pp. 65-76.

——— (1953a), The Present Status of Organized Psychoanalysis in the United States. *J. Amer. Psychoanal. Assn.*, 1:197-221.

——— (1953b), Borderline States. *Psychoanalytic Psychiatry and Psychology*, ed. R. P. Knight & C. R. Friedman. New York: International Universities Press, 1954, pp. 97-109.

KOHUT, H. (1957), Panel report: Clinical and Theoretical Aspects of Resistance. *J. Amer. Psychoanal. Assn.*, 5:548-555.

—— (1959), Introspection, Empathy and Psychoanalysis. *J. Amer. Psychoanal. Assn.*, 7:459-483.

KRAPF, E. E. (1955), The Choice of Language in Polyglot Psychoanalysis. *Psychoanal. Quart.*, 24:343-357.

—— (1956), Cold and Warmth in the Transference Experience. *Int. J. Psycho-Anal.*, 37:389-391.

KRIS, E. (1934), The Psychology of Caricature. *Psychoanalytic Explorations in Art.* New York: International Universities Press, 1952, pp. 173-188.

—— (1950), On Preconscious Mental Processes. *Psychoanalytic Explorations in Art.* New York: International Universities Press, 1952, pp. 303-318.

—— (1951), Ego Psychology and Interpretation in Psychoanalytic Therapy. *Psychoanal. Quart.*, 20:15-30.

—— (1952), *Explorations in Art.* New York: International Universities Press.

—— (1956a), On Some Vicissitudes of Insight in Psycho-Analysis. *Int. J. Psycho-Anal.*, 37:445-455.

—— (1956b), The Recovery of Childhood Memories in Psychoanalysis. *The Psychoanalytic Study of the Child*, 11:54-88.

KUBIE, L. S. (1939), A Critical Analysis of the Concept of a Repetition Compulsion. *Int. J. Psycho-Anal.*, 20:390-402.

—— (1941), The Repetitive Core of Neurosis. *Psychoanal. Quart.*, 10: 23-43.

—— (1950), *Practical and Theoretical Aspects of Psychoanalysis.* New York: International Universities Press.

—— (1958), Research into the Process of Supervision in Psychoanalysis. *Psychoanal. Quart.*, 27:226-236.

KUT, S. (1953), The Changing Pattern of Transference in the Analysis of an Eleven-year-old Girl. *The Psychoanalytic Study of the Child*, 8:355-378.

LAGACHE, D. (1953), Some Aspects of Transference. *Int. J. Psycho-Anal.*, 34: 1-10.

LAMPL-DE GROOT, J. (1954), Problems of Psycho-Analytic Training, *Int. J. Psycho-Anal.*, 35:184-187.

—— (1956), The Role of Identification in Psycho-Analytic Procedure. *Int. J. Psycho-Anal.*, 37:456-459.

—— (1957), On Defense and Development: Normal and Pathological. *The Psychoanalytic Study of the Child*, 12:114-126.

—— (1963), Symptom Formation and Character Formation. *Int. J. Psycho-Anal.*, 44:1-11.

LANGER, M. (1962), Selection Criteria for the Training of Psycho-Analytic Students. *Int. J. Psycho-Anal.*, 43:272-276.

LEVY, K. (1958), Silence in the Analytic Session. *Int. J. Psycho-Anal.*, 39:50-58.

LEWIN, B. D. (1946), Training in Psychoanalysis. *Amer. J. Orthopsychiat.*, 16:427-429.

—— (1948), The Nature of Reality, the Meaning of Nothing: With an Addendum on Concentration. *Psychoanal. Quart.*, 17:524-526.

—— (1950), *The Psychoanalysis of Elation.* New York: Norton.

426   BIBLIOGRAPHY

———— (1953), The Forgetting of Dreams. In: *Drives, Affects, Behavior,* ed. R. M. Loewenstein. New York: International Universities Press, 1:191-202.
———— (1954), Sleep, Narcissistic Neurosis, and the Analytic Situation. *Psychoanal. Quart.,* 23:487-510.
———— (1955), Dream Psychology and the Analytic Situation. *Psychoanal. Quart.,* 24:169-199.
———— (1959), The Analytic Situation: Topographic Considerations. *Psychoanal. Quart.,* 28:455-469.
———— & Ross, H. (1960), *Psychoanalytic Education in the United States.* New York: Norton.
LICHTENSTEIN, H. (1961), Identity and Sexuality. *J. Amer. Psychoanal. Assn.,* 9:179-260.
LITTLE, M. (1951), Counter-Transference and the Patient's Response to It. *Int. J. Psycho-Anal.,* 32:32-40.
———— (1958), On Delusional Transference (Transference Psychosis). *Int. J. Psycho-Anal.,* 39:134-138.
LOEWALD, H. W. (1952), The Problem of Defence and the Neurotic Interpretation of Reality. *Int. J. Psycho-Anal.,* 33:444-449.
———— (1955), Hypnoid State, Repression, Abreaction and Recollection. *J. Amer. Psychoanal. Assn.,* 3:201-210.
———— (1960), On the Therapeutic Action of Psycho-Analysis. *Int. J. Psycho-Anal.,* 41:16-33.
LOEWENSTEIN, R. M. (1951), The Problem of Interpretation. *Psychoanal. Quart.,* 20:1-14.
———— (1954), Some Remarks on Defences, Autonomous Ego and Psycho-Analytic Technique. *Int. J. Psycho-Anal.,* 35:188-193.
———— (1956), Some Remarks on the Role of Speech in Psycho-Analytic Technique. *Int. J. Psycho-Anal.,* 37:460-468.
———— (1958a), Remarks on Some Variations in Psycho-Analytic Technique. *Int. J. Psycho-Anal.,* 39:202-210.
———— (1958b), Variations in Classical Technique: Concluding Remarks. *Int. J. Psycho-Anal.,* 39:240-242.
———— (1961), The Silent Patient: Introduction. *J. Amer. Psychoanal. Assn.,* 9:2-6.
———— (1963), Some Considerations on Free Association. *J. Amer. Psychoanal. Assn.,* 11:451-473.
LOOMIE, L. S. (1961), Some Ego Considerations in the Silent Patient. *J. Amer. Psychoanal. Assn.,* 9:56-78.
LORAND, S. (1946), *Technique of Psychoanalytic Therapy.* New York: International Universities Press.
———— & CONSOLE, W. A. (1958), Therapeutic Results in Psycho-Analytic Treatment Without Fee. *Int. J. Psycho-Anal.,* 39:59-64.
MACALPINE, I. (1950), The Development of the Transference. *Psychoanal. Quart.,* 19:501-539.
MAHLER, M. S. (1963), Thoughts about Development and Individuation. *The Psychoanalytic Study of the Child,* 18:307-324.
———— (1965), On the Significance of the Normal Separation-Individuation Phase. In: *Drives, Affects, Behavior,* ed. M. Schur. New York: International Universities Press, 2:161-169.

———— & LA PERRIERE, K. (1965), Mother-Child Interaction during Separation-Individuation. *Psychoanal. Quart.*, 34:483-498.

MARMOR, J. (1958), The Psychodynamics of Realistic Worry. *Psychoanalysis and the Social Sciences*, 5:155-163. New York: International Universities Press.

MARTIN, P. A. (1964), Psychoanalytic Aspects of That Type of Communication Termed "Small Talk." *J. Amer. Psychoanal. Assn.*, 12:392-400.

MEERLOO, J. A. M. & COLEMAN, M. L. (1951), The Transference Function: A Study of Normal and Pathological Transference. *Psychoanal. Rev.*, 38: 205-221.

MENNINGER, K. A. (1958), *Theory of Psychoanalytic Technique*. New York: Basic Books.

MILNER, M. (1950), A Note on the Ending of an Analysis. *Int. J. Psycho-Anal.*, 31:191-193.

MITTELMANN, B. (1948), The Concurrent Analysis of Married Couples. *Psychoanal. Quart.*, 17:182-197.

MONEY-KYRLE, R. (1956), Normal Counter-Transference and Some of Its Deviations. *Int. J. Psycho-Anal.*, 37:360-366.

NACHT, S. (1954), The Difficulties of Didactic Psycho-Analysis in Relation to Therapeutic Psycho-Analysis. *Int. J. Psycho-Anal.*, 35:250-253.

———— (1957), Technical Remarks on the Handling of the Transference Neurosis. *Int. J. Psycho-Anal.*, 38:196-202.

———— (1958a), Variations in Technique. *Int. J. Psycho-Anal.*, 39:235-237.

———— (1958b), Causes and Mechanisms of Ego Distortion. *Int. J. Psycho-Anal.*, 39:271-273.

———— (1962), The Curative Factors in Psycho-Analysis. *Int. J. Psycho-Anal.*, 43:206-211.

———— (1964), Silence as an Integrative Factor. *Int. J. Psycho-Anal.*, 45: 299-303.

———— LEBOVICI, S., & DIATKINE, R. (1961), Training for Psycho-Analysis. *Int. J. Psycho-Anal.*, 42:110-115.

NAGERA, H. (1966), *Early Childhood Disturbances, the Infantile Neurosis, and the Adulthood Disturbances: Problems of a Developmental Psychoanalytic Psychology* [The Psychoanalytic Study of the Child, Monogr. 2]. New York: International Universities Press.

NIELSEN, N. (1954), The Dynamics of Training Analysis. *Int. J. Psycho-Anal.*, 35:247-249.

NOVEY, S. (1962), The Principle of "Working Through" in Psychoanalysis. *J. Amer. Psychoanal. Assn.*, 10:658-676.

NUNBERG, H. (1932), *Principles of Psychoanalysis*. New York: International Universities Press, 1955.

———— (1951), Transference and Reality. *Int. J. Psycho-Anal.*, 32:1-9.

OLDEN, C. (1953), On Adult Empathy with Children. *The Psychoanalytic Study of the Child*, 8:111-126.

———— (1958), Notes on the Development of Empathy. *The Psychoanalytic Study of the Child*, 13:505-518.

OLINICK, S. L. (1954), Some Considerations of the Use of Questioning as a Psychoanalytic Technique. *J. Amer. Psychoanal. Assn.*, 2:57-66.

ORENS, M. H. (1950), Setting a Termination Date: An Impetus to Analysis. *J. Amer. Psychoanal. Assn.*, 3:651-665.

ORR, D. W. (1954), Transference and Countertransference: A Historical Survey. *J. Amer. Psychoanal. Assn.*, 2:621-670.

PAYNE, S. (1950), Short Communication on Criteria for Terminating of Analysis. *Int. J. Psycho-Anal.*, 31:205.

PIOUS, W. L. (1950), Obsessive-compulsive Symptoms in an Incipient Schizophrenic. *Psychoanal. Quart.*, 19:327-351.

RACKER, H. (1953), A Contribution to the Problem of Counter-Transference. *Int. J. Psycho-Anal.*, 34:313-324.

——— (1954), Notes on the Theory of Transference. *Psychoanal. Quart.*, 23: 78-86.

——— (1957), The Meanings and Uses of Countertransference. *Psychoanal. Quart.*, 26:303-357.

RAMZY, I. (1961), The Range and Spirit of Psycho-Analytic Technique. *Int. J. Psycho-Anal.*, 42:497-501.

RANGELL, L. (1954), Similarities and Differences between Psychoanalysis and Dynamic Psychotherapy. *J. Amer. Psychoanal. Assn.*, 2:734-744.

——— (1959), The Nature of Conversion. *J. Amer. Psychoanal. Assn.*, 7:632-662.

RAPAPORT, D. & GILL, M. M. (1959), The Points of View and Assumptions of Metapsychology. *Int. J. Psycho-Anal.*, 40:153-162.

RAPPAPORT, E. A. (1956), The Management of an Eroticized Transference. *Psychoanal. Quart.*, 25:515-529.

REDL, F. & WINEMAN, D. (1951), *Children Who Hate.* Glencoe, Ill.: Free Press.

REICH, A. (1951), On Counter-Transference. *Int. J. Psycho-Anal.*, 32:25-31.

——— (1958), A Special Variation of Technique. *Int. J. Psycho-Anal.*, 39: 230-234.

REICH, W. (1928), On Character Analysis. In: *The Psychoanalytic Reader*, ed. R. Fliess. New York: International Universities Press, 1948, 1:129-147.

——— (1929), The Genital Character and the Neurotic Character. In: *The Psychoanalytic Reader*, ed. R. Fliess. New York: International Universities Press, 1948, 1:148-169.

REIDER, N. (1950), The Concept of Normality. *Psychoanal. Quart.*, 19:43-51.

——— (1953a), A Type of Transference to Institutions. *Bull. Menninger Clin.*, 17:58-63.

——— (1953b), Reconstruction and Screen Function. *J. Amer. Psychoanal. Assn.*, 1:389-405.

——— (1957), Transference Psychosis. *J. Hillside Hosp.*, 6:131-149.

REIK, T. (1937), *Surprise and the Psychoanalyst.* New York: Dutton.

——— (1948), *Listening with the Third Ear.* New York: Farrar, Straus.

REXFORD, E. N., ed. (1966), *A Developmental Approach to Problems of Acting Out: A Symposium.* New York: International Universities Press.

RICKMAN, J. (1950), On the Criteria for the Termination of an Analysis. *Int. J. Psycho-Anal.*, 31:200-201.

ROBBINS, L. L. (1956), Panel report: The Borderline Case. *J. Amer. Psychoanal. Assn.*, 4:550-562.

ROSEN, V. H. (1958), The Initial Psychiatric Interview and the Principles of Psychotherapy. *J. Amer. Psychoanal. Assn.*, 6:154-167.

———— (1960), Some Aspects of the Role of Imagination in the Analytic Process. *J. Amer. Psychoanal. Assn.*, 8:229-251.

ROSENBERG [ZETZEL], E. (1949), Anxiety and the Capacity to Bear It. *Int. J. Psycho-Anal.*, 30:1-12.

ROSENFELD, H. (1952), Transference-Phenomena and Transference-Analysis in an Acute Catatonic Schizophrenic Patient. *Int. J. Psycho-Anal.*, 33:457-464.

———— (1954), Considerations Regarding the Psycho-Analytic Approach to Acute and Chronic Schizophrenia. *Int. J. Psycho-Anal.*, 35:135-140.

———— (1958), Contribution to the Discussion on Variations in Classical Technique. *Int. J. Psycho-Anal.*, 39:238-239.

ROSS, N. (1960), Panel Report: An Examination of Nosology according to Psychoanalytic Concepts. *J. Amer. Psychoanal. Assn.*, 8:535-551.

ROWLEY, J. L. (1951), Rumpelstilzkin in the Analytical Situation. *Int. J. Psycho-Anal.*, 32:190-195.

RUBINFINE, D. L. (1958), Panel report: Problems of Identity. *J. Amer. Psychoanal. Assn.*, 6:131-142.

RYCROFT, C. (1956), The Nature and Function of the Analyst's Communication to the Patient. *Int. J. Psycho-Anal.*, 37:469-472.

———— (1958), An Enquiry into the Function of Words in the Psycho-Analytical Situation. *Int. J. Psycho-Anal.*, 39:408-415.

SACHS, H. (1947), Observations of a Training Analyst. *Psychoanal. Quart.*, 16:157-168.

SAUL, L. (1958), *Technic and Practice of Psychoanalysis*. New York: J. B. Lippincott.

SCHAFER, R. (1959), Generative Empathy in the Treatment Situation. *Psychoanal. Quart.*, 28:342-373.

———— (1964), The Clinical Analysis of Affects. *J. Amer. Psychoanal. Assn.*, 12:275-299.

SCHMIDEBERG, M. (1950), Infant Memories and Constructions. *Psychoanal. Quart.*, 19:468-481.

———— (1953), A Note on Transference. *Int. J. Psycho-Anal.*, 34:199-201.

SCHUR, M. (1953), The Ego in Anxiety. In: *Drives, Affects, Behavior*, ed. R. M. Loewenstein. New York: International Universities Press, 1:67-103.

———— (1955), Comments on the Metapsychology of Somatization. *The Psychoanalytic Study of the Child*, 10:119-164.

———— (1960), Phylogenesis and Ontogenesis of Affect- and Structure-Formation and the Phenomenon of Repetition Compulsion. *Int. J. Psycho-Anal.*, 41:275-287.

———— (1966), *The Id and the Regulatory Principles of Mental Functioning*. New York: International Universities Press.

SCOTT, W. C. M. (1952), Patients Who Sleep or Look at the Psycho-Analyst during Treatment: Technical Considerations. *Int. J. Psycho-Anal.*, 33:465-469.

———— (1958), Noise, Speech and Technique. *Int. J. Psycho-Anal.*, 39:108-111.

SEARLES, H. F. (1960), *The Nonhuman Environment in Normal Development and in Schizophrenia*. New York: International Universities Press.

———— (1965), *Collected Papers on Schizophrenia and Related Subjects*. New York: International Universities Press.

SECHEHAYE, M. A. (1956), The Transference in Symbolic Realization. *Int. J. Psycho-Anal.*, 37:270-277.

SEGAL, H. (1964), *Introduction to the Work of Melanie Klein.* New York: Basic Books.

SERVADIO, E. (1956), Transference and Thought-Transference. *Int. J. Psycho-Anal.*, 37:392-395.

SHARPE, E. F. (1930), The Technique of Psycho-Analysis. *Collected Papers on Psycho-Analysis.* London: Hogarth Press, 1950, pp. 9-106.

——— (1940), Psycho-Physical Problems Revealed in Language: An Examination of Metaphor. *Collected Papers on Psycho-Analysis.* London: Hogarth Press, 1950, pp. 155-169.

——— (1947), The Psycho-Analyst. *Collected Papers on Psycho-Analysis.* London: Hogarth Press, 1950, pp. 109-122.

SILVERBERG, W. V. (1948), The Concept of Transference. *Psychoanal. Quart.*, 17:303-321.

——— (1955), Acting Out versus Insight: A Problem in Psychoanalytic Technique. *Psychoanal. Quart.*, 24:527-544.

SIMMEL, E. (1926), The "Doctor Game," Illness, and the Profession of Medicine. In: *The Psychoanalytic Reader*, ed. R. Fliess. New York: International Universities Press, 1949, 1:291-305.

SPERLING, S. J. (1958), On Denial and the Essential Nature of Defence. *Int. J. Psycho-Anal.*, 39:25-38.

SPIEGEL, L. A. (1954), Acting Out and Defensive Instinctual Gratification. *J. Amer. Psychoanal. Assn.*, 2:107-119.

SPITZ, R. A. (1956a), Countertransference: Comments on Its Varying Role in the Analytic Situation. *J. Amer. Psychoanal. Assn.*, 4:256-265.

——— (1956b), Transference: The Analytical Setting and Its Prototype. *Int. J. Psycho-Anal.*, 37:380-385.

——— (1957), *No and Yes: On the Genesis of Human Communication.* New York: International Universities Press.

——— (1965), *The First Year of Life.* New York: International Universities Press.

STEIN, M. H. (1958), The Cliché. *J. Amer. Psychoanal. Assn.*, 6:263-277.

STERBA, R. F. (1929), The Dynamics of the Dissolution of the Transference Resistance. *Psychoanal. Quart.* 9:363-379, 1940.

——— (1934), The Fate of the Ego in Analytic Therapy. *Int. J. Psycho-Anal.*, 15:117-126.

——— (1951), Character and Resistance. *Psychoanal. Quart.*, 20:72-76.

——— (1953), Clinical and Therapeutic Aspects of Character Resistance. *Psychoanal. Quart.*, 22:1-20.

STERN, A. (1948), Transference in Borderline Neuroses. *Psychoanal. Quart.*, 17:527-528.

STERN, M. M. (1957), The Ego Aspect of Transference. *Int. J. Psycho-Anal.*, 38:146-157.

STEWART, W. A. (1963), An Inquiry into the Concept of Working Through. *J. Amer. Psychoanal. Assn.*, 11:474-499.

STONE, L. (1951), Psychoanalysis and Brief Psychotherapy. *Psychoanal. Quart.*, 20:215-236.

——— (1954a), On the Principal Obscene Word of the English Language. *Int. J. Psycho-Anal.*, 35:30-56.

———— (1954b), The Widening Scope of Indications for Psychoanalysis. *J. Amer. Psychoanal. Assn.*, 2:567-594.

———— (1961), *The Psychoanalytic Situation*. New York: International Universities Press.

STRACHEY, J. (1934), The Nature of the Therapeutic Action of Psycho-Analysis. *Int. J. Psycho-Anal.*, 15:127-159.

———— (1958), Editor's Introduction to Freud's Papers on Technique. *Standard Edition*, 12:85-88.

SZASZ, T. S. (1957), On the Experiences of the Analyst in the Psychoanalytic Situation: A Contribution to the Theory of Psychoanalytic Treatment. *J. Amer. Psychoanal. Assn.*, 4:197-223.

TARACHOW, S. (1963), *An Introduction to Psychotherapy*. New York: International Universities Press.

TARTAKOFF, H. H. (1956), Recent Books on Psychoanalytic Technique: A Comparative Study [Glover: The Technique of Psychoanalysis; Wolstein: Transference; de Forest: The Leaven of Love; Braatøy: Fundamentals of Psychoanalytic Technique]. *J. Amer. Psychoanal. Assn.*, 4:318-343.

THORNER, H. A. (1957), Three Defences against Inner Persecution. In: *New Directions in Psychoanalysis*, ed. M. Klein, P. Heimann, & R. Money-Kyrle. New York: Basic Books, pp. 282-306.

TOWER, L. E. (1956), Countertransference. *J. Amer. Psychoanal. Assn.*, 4: 224-255.

VAN DER HEIDE, C. (1961), Blank Silence and the Dream Screen. *J. Amer. Psychoanal. Assn.*, 9:85-90.

VAN DER LEEUW, P. J. (1962), Selection Criteria for the Training of Psycho-Analytic Students. *Int. J. Psycho-Anal.*, 43:277-282.

WAELDER, R. (1936), The Problem of the Genesis of Psychical Conflicts in Earliest Infancy. *Int. J. Psycho-Anal.*, 18:406-473, 1937.

———— (1956), Introduction to the Discussion on Problems of Transference. *Int. J. Psycho-Anal.*, 37:367-368.

———— (1958), Neurotic Ego Distortion: Opening Remarks to the Panel Discussion. *Int. J. Psycho-Anal.*, 39:243-244.

———— (1960), *Basic Theory of Psychoanalysis*. New York: International Universities Press.

———— ET AL. (1956), Discussion of Problems of Transference. *Int. J. Psycho-Anal.*, 37:367-395.

WALDHORN, H. F. (1960), Assessment of Analyzability: Technical and Theoretical Observations. *Psychoanal. Quart.*, 29:478-506.

WEIGERT, E. (1952), Contribution to the Problem of Terminating Psychoanalyses. *Psychoanal. Quart.*, 21:465-480.

———— (1954a), Counter-Transference and Self-Analysis of the Psycho-Analyst. *Int. J. Psycho-Anal.*, 35:242-246.

———— (1954b), The Importance of Flexibility in Psychoanalytic Technique. *J. Amer. Psychoanal. Assn.*, 2:702-710.

———— (1955), Special Problems in Connection with Termination of Training Analyses. *J. Amer. Psychoanal. Assn.*, 3:630-640.

WEISS, J. (1966), Panel report: Clinical and Theoretical Aspects of "As If" Characters. *J. Amer. Psychoanal. Assn.*, 14:569-590.

WEXLER, M. (1951), The Structural Problem in Schizophrenia. *Int. J. Psycho-Anal.*, 32:157-166.

———— (1960), Hypotheses Concerning Ego Deficiency in Schizophrenia. *The Out-Patient Treatment of Schizophrenia*. New York: Grune & Stratton, pp. 33-43.

WHEELIS, A. (1956a), Will and Psychoanalysis. *J. Amer. Psychoanal. Assn.*, 4:285-303.

———— (1956b), The Vocational Hazards of Psycho-Analysis. *Int. J. Psycho-Anal.*, 37:171-184.

WINDHOLZ, E. (1955), Problems of Termination of the Training Analysis. *J. Amer. Psychoanal. Assn.*, 3:641-650.

WINNICOTT, D. W. (1949), Hate in the Counter-Transference. *Int. J. Psycho-Anal.*, 30:69-74.

———— (1953), Transitional Objects and Transitional Phenomena. *Int. J. Psycho-Anal.*, 34:89-97.

———— (1955), Metapsychological and Clinical Aspects of Regression within the Psycho-Analytical Set-up. *Collected Papers*. New York: Basic Books, 1958, pp. 278-294.

———— (1956a), On Transference. *Int. J. Psycho-Anal.*, 37:386-388.

———— (1956b), The Antisocial Tendency. *Collected Papers*. New York: Basic Books, 1958, pp. 306-315.

———— (1957), *Mother and Child*. New York: Basic Books.

WOLFENSTEIN, M. & KLIMAN, G. (1965), *Children and the Death of the President*. Garden City, N.Y.: Doubleday.

WORDEN, F. G. (1955), A Problem in Psychoanalytic Technique. *J. Amer. Psychoanal. Assn.*, 3:255-279.

ZELIGS, M. A. (1957), Acting In. *J. Amer. Psychoanal. Assn.*, 5:685-706.

———— (1961), The Psychology of Silence: Its Role in Transference, Counter-transference and the Psychoanalytic Process. *J. Amer. Psychoanal. Assn.*, 9:7-43.

ZETZEL, E. R. (1953), Panel report: The Traditional Psychoanalytic Technique and Its Variations. *J. Amer. Psychoanal.*, 1:526-537.

———— (1956), Current Concepts of Transference. *Int. J. Psycho-Anal.*, 37:369-376.

———— (1963), The Significance of the Adaptive Hypothesis for Psychoanalytic Theory and Practice. *J. Amer. Psychoanal. Assn.*, 11:652-660.

———— see also Rosenberg, E.

ZILBOORG, G. (1952a), The Emotional Problem and the Therapeutic Role of Insight. *Psychoanal. Quart.*, 21:1-24.

———— (1952b), Some Sidelights on Free Associations. *Int. J. Psycho-Anal.*, 33:489-495.

Author Index

Aarons, Z. A., 53, 411, 413
Abraham, K., 94, 241, 413
Aichhorn, A., 382, 413
Alexander, F., 50, 57, 133-136, 169-170, 190, 357, 359, 413, 418
Altman, L. L., 30, 57, 150, 180, 357, 362, 411, 413
Arieti, S., 422
Arlow, J. A., 21, 56, 149, 413-414

Balint, M., 357, 399, 414
Bellak, L., 362, 414
Benedek, T., 414, 417
Benjamin, J. D., 414
Beres, D., 382, 402, 414
Berezin, M., 101, 414
Bergler, E., 414
Bernfeld, S., 357, 403, 414
Bernheim, H., 9
Bibring, E., 7, 29, 32, 37, 39, 48-49, 57-58, 98, 179-180, 269, 309, 363, 397, 414
Bibring, G. L., 221, 355, 357, 377, 414
Bird, B., 150, 153, 259-260, 267, 414
Blitzsten, L., 339
Bornstein, B., 251, 325, 414
Bouvet, M., 57, 414
Braatøy, T., 414, 431
Brenner, C., 21, 56, 414-415
Breuer, J., 8-12, 48, 59, 71-73, 126, 163, 415
Bridger, H., 415
Brierley, M., 170, 415
Bychowski, G., 326, 415

Charcot, J.-M., 8
Colby, K. M., 17, 415

Coleman, M. L., 427
Console, W. A., 426

de Forest, I., 357, 391, 415, 431
Deutsch, F., 63, 376, 415
Deutsch, H., 196-197, 415
Devereux, G., 415
Diatkine, R., 357, 427

Eisendorfer, A., 383, 415
Eissler, K. R., 2, 50, 57, 269, 359, 382, 397, 404, 415
Eissler, R. S., 414
Eitingon, M., 418
Ekstein, R., 56, 150, 179, 260, 338, 357, 415-416, 418
Erikson, E. H., 25, 241, 416
Evans, W. N., 416

Fairbairn, W. R. D., 356, 416
Feldman, S. S., 66, 416
Fenichel, O., 1, 16-21, 26, 29, 35-36, 39, 45-47, 52-53, 55-57, 61, 68, 70, 76, 78-80, 82-84, 86-87, 91-94, 96, 98, 103, 118, 123-124, 126, 137-138, 142, 152-153, 159, 167, 172, 174, 177-180, 182, 192, 194, 213, 241, 245-246, 252-253, 257-259, 269, 276, 278, 312, 316, 325-326, 338, 342, 344, 363, 371, 377, 380, 391, 407, 416
Ferenczi, S., 16, 61, 100, 132, 153, 164, 207, 246, 330, 333, 357, 367, 377, 379, 386, 391, 415-417
Fisher, C., 270, 417
Fleming, J., 397, 417
Fliess, R., 367, 403, 413, 418, 428, 430

433

Fraiberg, S., 188-189, 418
Frank, J., 52, 57, 418
Freeman, T., 76-77, 86, 150, 343, 418
French, T. M., 50, 134, 136, 170, 190, 357, 359, 413, 418
Freud, A., 17, 20, 29, 36, 53-54, 56, 75-77, 80, 83-86, 91-92, 94, 96, 152-153, 173-174, 179-180, 188-189, 217, 223, 238, 240-241, 246, 252, 256, 326, 340, 356-357, 359-360, 362, 380, 403, 414, 418
Freud, S., 1, 3-4, 7, 10, 17, 20-21, 23, 25, 26, 28, 45, 48, 67, 76, 82-83, 92, 94, 98, 142, 179, 205, 241, 245, 248, 263, 356, 367, 380, 396, 398, 402-403, 405
  bibliographic references, 56, 415, 418-420
  case histories of, 9, 12-13, 33, 145, 212, 258-259
  characteristics of, 8, 10-11, 380-381, 403
  on aims of therapy, quoted, 14-15, 395
  on analyzability, 51-52, 54, 326, 338-339
  on anxiety, 81, 87
  on countertransference, 165
  on defense, 71, 77
  on limitations of therapy, 167
  on "Monday crust," 330, 335
  on narcissistic and transference neurosis, 34, 52, 54, 74, 166, 184, 207, 326
  on psychoanalyst, 395, 398, 406
  on psychosis, 173
  on reconstruction, 322-323
  on resistance, 13-14, 35-36, 59-61, 71-75, 80, 85-87, 123, 137-138, 151, 165, 167, 182, 194, 239-240, 389
  on secret, 129
  on technique, 10-15, 55, 137-138, 145, 158-159, 211-212, 225-226, 232-233, 236, 238, 271-272, 275-276, 359, 389-390
  on transference and transference neurosis, 13-14, 34-36, 46, 73-74, 151-155, 162-167, 171-172, 177-178, 182-184, 188, 194-195, 322, 339, 379, 389-390
Freud, W. E., 53, 418
Friedman, C. R., 424
Friedman, L. J., 86, 420
Friedman, S. W., 150, 179, 260, 357, 416
Fromm-Reichmann, F., 2, 57, 359, 420
Frosch, J., 177, 249, 420

Gandhi, 64
Garma, A., 195, 207
Geleerd, E. R., 382, 420
Gero, G., 78, 150, 420
Gifford, S., 179, 420
Gill, M. M., 4, 20-21, 25, 32, 35, 37, 50, 57-58, 76, 78-80, 84, 190, 204, 207, 210, 359, 384, 397, 420, 428
Gillespie, W. H., 150, 420
Gitelson, M., 58, 99, 150, 194-195, 205, 207, 253, 256, 356-357, 421
Glover, E., 1-3, 35, 50, 52-53, 55-57, 69-70, 85-86, 92, 149-150, 160, 166, 184, 189, 207, 213, 221, 233, 276, 278, 326, 342, 351, 354, 357, 377, 379, 411, 421, 431
Gostynski, E., 421
Greenacre, P., 3, 32, 45, 47, 57, 92, 153, 168, 173-174, 190, 208, 211, 214, 229, 259, 271, 274, 277-278, 281, 316, 326, 355-357, 383, 391, 401, 409, 411, 421, 423
Greenson, R. R., 1, 4, 29, 35, 42, 45-46, 53-54, 57, 61, 68-69, 84, 93, 98, 113, 120, 123, 169, 190-191, 216, 222, 246-247, 258, 260, 278, 316, 337, 357, 365, 367, 372-374, 376, 382-383, 388, 394, 396, 398, 409, 411, 421-422
Grinstein, A., 330, 422
Gross, A., 129, 422
Grotjahn, M., 357, 422
Guntrip, H., 356, 422
Guttman, S. A., 58, 411, 422

Haak, N., 189, 233, 411, 422
Hartmann, H., 15-17, 21, 25, 56-57, 76, 80, 84, 150, 173, 180, 241, 245, 356, 361, 365, 382, 398, 414, 422-423
Heimann, P., 134, 169-170, 190, 195, 357, 423-424, 431
Hendrick, I., 56, 179, 245, 423
Hill, L. B., 423
Hoffer, W., 57, 150, 356-357, 411, 423
Hug-Hellmuth, H., 403

Isaacs, S., 134, 169-170, 189-190, 423-424

Jacobson, E., 172-174, 176, 181, 243-245, 326, 423
James, M., 217, 423
Jokl, R. H., 423
Jones, E., 4, 8-9, 59, 153, 380-381, 383-384, 400, 402-403, 423

Kairys, D., 3, 356-357, 424
Kanzer, M., 57, 150, 357, 362, 424
Karush, A., 58
Katan, A., 383
Katan, M., 150, 172, 424
Keiser, S., 424
Kennedy, J. F., 64
Khan, M. M. R., 61, 84, 120, 399, 409, 411, 424
King, P., 195
Klein, M., 133-135, 167-170, 175, 181, 189-190, 236-237, 241-242, 344, 356, 403, 423-424, 430-431
Kliman, G., 64, 432
Knapp, P. H., 52, 54-55, 411, 424
Knight, R. P., 36-37, 52-54, 58-59, 326, 341, 363, 424
Kohut, H., 16, 57, 64, 150, 425
Krapf, E. E., 357, 425
Kris, E., 39, 42, 45, 56-57, 76, 84, 98, 241, 245, 269, 322, 356-357, 369, 382, 402, 423, 425
Kris, M., 414
Kubie, L., 56, 179, 411, 421, 425
Kuiper, P., 195
Kut, S., 188-189, 425

Lagache, D., 153, 179, 425
Lampl-de Groot, J., 56, 150, 357, 425
Langer, M., 383, 425
La Perriere, K., 427
Lebovici, S., 357, 427
Levin, S., 52, 54-55, 411, 424
Levy, K., 425
Lewin, B. D., 68-69, 181, 260, 265, 316, 372, 387, 403, 409, 411, 425-426
Lichtenstein, H., 173, 426
Little, M., 173, 340, 426
Loewald, H. W., 15, 56-57, 168-169, 194, 207, 213, 372-373, 383, 391, 426
Loewenstein, R. M., 54, 56-57, 149-150, 241, 245, 251, 325, 356, 362, 372, 387, 423, 426, 429
Loomie, L. S., 149, 426
Lorand, S., 380, 391, 426

Macalpine, I., 168, 208, 409-411, 426
McCarter, R. H., 52, 54-55, 411, 424
Mahler, M. S., 173-174, 357, 426-427
Marmor, J., 119, 427
Martin, P. A., 64, 427
Meerloo, J. A. M., 427
Menninger, K. A., 37, 56-57, 85, 99, 150, 180, 221, 269, 278, 377, 391, 404-405, 411, 427
Milner, M., 427

Mittelmann, B., 427
Money-Kyrle, R., 134, 170, 424, 427, 431
Murray, J., 130
Myerson, P. G., 195

Nacht, S., 46, 57, 150, 189, 195, 233, 357, 374, 391, 411, 427
Nagera, H., 53, 56, 189, 418, 427
Newman, R., 204, 384, 420
Nielsen, N., 357, 427
Novey, S., 57, 357, 427
Nunberg, H., 17, 35, 56, 58, 182, 356, 427

Oberndorf, C. P., 421
Olden, C., 383, 427
Olinick, S. L., 427
Orens, M. H., 428
Orr, D. W., 57, 326, 356, 428

Payne, S., 428
Pfister, O., 403
Pious, W. L., 341, 428

Racker, H., 175, 428
Ramzy, I., 404, 428
Rangell, L., 2, 53, 57, 428
Rank, O., 403, 417
Rapaport, D., 20-21, 25, 428
Rappaport, E. A., 252, 339, 360, 428
Redl, F., 382, 428
Redlich, F. C., 204, 384, 420
Reich, A., 57, 428
Reich, W., 57, 76, 80, 92, 94, 96, 256-257, 312-313, 428
Reider, N., 154, 256, 323, 340, 356, 428
Reik, T., 367, 403, 428
Rexford, E. N., 357, 428
Rickman, J., 428
Riviere, J., 134, 170, 190, 384, 424
Robbins, L. L., 428
Rosen, V. H., 382, 402, 428-429
Rosenberg, E., see Zetzel, E. R.
Rosenfeld, H., 52, 57, 170, 173, 343, 429
Ross, H., 372, 426
Ross, N., 30, 429
Rowley, J. L., 429
Rubinfine, D. L., 173, 429
Rycroft, C., 372, 429

Sachs, H., 403, 429
Saul, L., 429
Schafer, R., 63, 367, 383, 429
Schmideberg, M., 429
Schur, M., 80, 87-88, 98, 179, 181, 316, 422, 426, 429
Scott, W. C. M., 429

Searles, H. F., 172-173, 343, 429
Sechehaye, M. A., 430
Segal, H., 169, 175, 195, 356, 430
Servadio, E., 356, 430
Sharpe, E. F., 1, 57, 100, 150, 166-167, 365, 367, 371-372, 380-381, 383-384, 395, 397, 399, 404, 430
Silverberg, W. V., 430
Simmel, E., 406-407, 430
Sperling, S. J., 77, 150, 430
Spiegel, L. A., 150, 259, 430
Spitz, R. A., 57, 168, 174, 208, 357, 399, 409-411, 430
Stein, M. H., 66, 430
Sterba, R. F., 46-48, 96, 138, 142, 167, 192-194, 212, 245, 256, 367, 391, 430
Stern, A., 326, 430
Stern, M. M., 179, 430
Stewart, W., 57, 357, 430
Stone, L., 17, 46, 54, 57-58, 131-132, 169, 191-192, 194, 210, 213-214, 217, 222-223, 240, 278, 326, 358, 365, 372, 374, 376-377, 379, 384, 386-389, 391, 401-402, 404-405, 407, 409, 411, 430-431
Strachey, J., 4, 9, 190, 418, 431
Szasz, T. S., 336, 399, 431

Tarachow, S., 57, 431
Tartakoff, H. H., 1-2, 431

Thorner, H. A., 134, 431
Tower, L. E., 431

Van der Heide, C., 149, 431
Van der Leeuw, P. J., 383, 431

Waelder, R., 17-18, 29, 56-58, 150, 168, 180, 309, 356, 404, 431
Waldhorn, H. F., 52-53, 411, 431
Wallerstein, R. S., 416
Weigert, E., 357, 431
Weiss, J., 196-197, 431
Wermer, H., 52, 54-55, 411, 424
Wexler, M., 52, 76, 85-86, 172-173, 340, 343, 431-432
Wheelis, A., 394, 432
Windholz, E., 356, 432
Wineman, D., 382, 428
Winnicott, D. W., 57, 76, 84-86, 150, 168, 174, 217, 222, 260, 343, 357, 399, 401, 432
Wolfenstein, M., 64, 432
Wolstein, B., 431
Worden, F. G., 432

Zeligs, M. A., 149-150, 357, 432
Zetzel, E. R., 46, 52, 54-57, 134-135, 168-169, 191-192, 194, 326, 391, 411, 424, 429, 432
Zilboorg, G., 362, 432

Subject Index

Abreaction, 7, 11-15, 37, 48-50, 73, 75, 269, 284
Abstinence, rule of, 35, 166, 178, 209, 211-212, 275-281, 377, 390-391
Accident prone, 290
Acting out, 26, 68-69, 73-74, 212, 290, 360, 377, 383, 400-401, 407
  chronic, 345
  outside of psychoanalysis, 267-268; *see also* Transference reactions
  in psychoanalytic setting, 263-266
  and reliving infantile neurosis, 325-330
  and resistances, 91-92, 94-95, 99, 133, 260
  and transference, 68-69, 153, 165-167, 177, 179, 181-182, 234, 242, 258-268, 351
Activity, 361, 387; *see also* Passivity, Procedures
Adaptation, 25-26, 76, 88, 180, 365, 399, 410
Adaptive point of view, 21, 25-26
Addiction, 52, 94, 340, 345
Adolescence, 90, 201, 231, 247, 262, 307, 313, 319-320, 387
Affect
  absence of, 62, 120-121
  defense against, 252-255
  and ego, 47-48
  inappropriate, 62, 370-371
  indicating resistance, 62-63, 102-103, 108-109, 113-114, 122, 126-128
  indicating transference, 291-292
  and interpretation, 40-41, 310-312, 314, 388
  primitive and intense, 338-340

  reliving of, 48-49
  splitting and displacement of, 183, 188
  strangulated, 11
  strong, and transference, 283-284, 291-292
  see also Avoidance, Transference, Transference reactions, *and sub* specific affects
Aggression
  avoidance, 64-65
  and death instinct, 82
  fear of, 374-376
  preponderance of, in transference, 181-183
  and psychoanalyst's motivation, 396-401, 406-407
  repressed, 206
  turned against self, 82
  see also Anger, Hostility, Transference, Transference reactions
Aggressivization, 24, 201
Ambivalence, 23, 34, 90, 159-160, 162, 180-184, 229, 410; *see also* Transference reactions
Amnesia, infantile, 13, 15, 366
Anal itching, 311-312
Anal phase, drives, 88-90, 93, 109, 120-121, 131-132, 180, 186-188, 230-231, 240-241, 304, 333, 397, 407
Analyzability, 51-56, 92, 180, 207-208, 326, 338-340, 353-354, 364
"Analyzing," 26, 37-45, 59, 97, 269
Anger, 88-90, 154-156, 193, 202, 227-228, 233-237, 240, 299-300, 304, 328, 365-366; *see also* Aggression, Hostility, Rage

437

Annoyance, 113-115, 156, 193, 202, 215, 233, 304
Anorexia, 90
Anxiety, 305, 334
and aggression, 237
anal, 188, 241
belated mastery, 178-179
concerning body, 19-20, 24
capacity to bear, 362, 377, 394
historical determination of, 197-198
motive of defense, 80-82, 86-88, 107, 255
paranoid, 121
pervading analysis, 211, 214
and psychoanalyst's motivation, 396-401, 407
social, 314
see also Castration anxiety, Fear
Anxiety dream, 114-115; see also Nightmares
Anxiety hysteria, 52
Anxiety state, 37, 49, 130
Apathy, 177
Art, 382-383
"As if" character, 196-197, 246
Atonement, need for, 99, 331
Attention, free-floating (suspended), 100-101, 367
Autonomy, 76, 365, 372, 382, 398
Avoidance, 38-39, 63-65, 234, 285
language of, 65-71, 105-107, 124, 126-128
of painful affect, 80-82, 86-88, 91, 107, 113, 116-117, 122, 131
see also Resistance, Transference

Beating fantasy, 31, 88-90, 113
Bed wetting, 314
Bisexuality, 383
Blandness, 157-158
Blushing, 107
Body
anxieties, 19-20, 24
avoidance of talking about, 64-65
language, 107-108, 113, 376
Borderline patient, 52-53, 85, 147, 159, 207, 244, 247, 252, 326, 329, 333
Boredom, 68, 185-186, 381, 387
Bulemia, 90, 249

Cancer, fear of, 206, 294
Capriciousness, 159-162, 182
Case illustrations (of patients mentioned repeatedly)
Mrs. A., 19-20, 24

Mrs. K., 29-32, 113-116, 143-145, 161-162, 185-188, 250-251, 260-261, 283, 290, 302-303, 325, 333, 335
Mr. N., 24-25, 38-44
Mr. S., 105-106, 112-113
Professor X., 110-111, 120, 176-177, 311-313, 385-387
Mr. Z., 88-90, 93, 138-143, 199-201, 204, 210, 231-232, 278-279, 304-308, 314-315, 317-323, 335
Castration anxiety, 81, 90, 241
Catatonia, 343
Catharsis, 9, 11, 13, 48
Censorship, 73
Character
anal, 348
analysis of, 76
deformation, 81
disorders, 52, 93, 256, 360
formation, 76, 371
impulse-ridden, 55, 207, 245, 249, 252, 340, 345, 360, 383
neurosis, 52, 93-94, 203, 371
obsessive-compulsive, 242, 344-345, 383
oral-depressive, 88, 93
resistances, 70, 90, 92-95, 118, 133, 258
traits, 90, 92, 94-95, 118, 183, 359-360, 400
transference, 183, 256-258, 344
Child
assessment of, 53-54
development, 83-84
fantasy of, 366
helplessness of, 179
object relations of, 173
therapy of, 170, 174, 207; see also Child analysis
see also Mother-child relationship
Child analysis, 179, 188-189, 360
Childhood neurosis, 20, 26, 147, 185-190, 287-289, 410
reliving of, 327-329
see also Transference neurosis
Clarification, 37-39, 45, 97-98, 107-111, 120, 122, 145, 204, 269, 290, 298-310, 374-376
Cleanliness, 94, 121, 241, 261, 407
Cliché, 65-67, 107, 123
Cloaca, 109
Communication, nonverbal, 260, 373, 382-383, 397-398; see also Language, Psychoanalyst, Talking, Verbalization
Complementary series, 82
Condensation, 21-23

Conflict
  intrasystemic, 76, 365
  neurotic, 17-20, 23-27, 30-31, 97, 137, 165, 177-178, 184, 361, 364-365, 372
  resolution, 364-365
  stirring up latent, 167, 236
  see also Symptom formation
Confrontation, 37-38, 45, 97-98, 104-106, 108, 115, 141-142, 197-198, 203, 211, 245, 269, 281-282, 288, 296-301, 303
Consciousness, and neurotic conflict, 17-20; see also Ego; Therapy aims of; Unconscious
Constitution, 82-83, 396, 406
Contradictions, 291-292; see also Verbalization
Conversion hysteria, 52
Conversion symptoms, 53, 93
Corrective emotional experience, 209, 351
Couch, 214, 399-400, 409
Counterphobic mechanism, 94-95, 127, 178, 407
Counterresistance, 123
Countertransference, 3-4, 68, 70, 149, 165, 189, 211, 221-223, 226, 233-234, 236, 258, 336-337, 348-350, 352-353, 370, 374, 377, 387, 398-399
Creativity, 84, 382, 402
Cunnilingus, 251, 325
Curiosity, 99, 200, 359, 381, 392, 397, 406

Danger situation, 80-81, 86-88; see also Castration anxiety, Fear
Death, see Event, Fear, Parent
Death instinct, 45, 75, 81-82, 166-167, 179
Death wishes, 19, 117, 220, 241, 332; see also Fantasy
Defense(s)
  breakdown of, 24
  concept, 71
  and conflict, 17-20, 23-25, 29-31, 71-72, 177-178, 184
  against defense, 80
  excessive talking as, 197-199
  against fantasy, 186-187
  hierarchies, 78
  motive of, 80-82, 86-88, 115
  in neurosis and psychosis, 77
  paranoidlike, 234-235
  position of regression among, 84
  prestages, 77
  "relative," 79-80

repeated in transference reaction, 76; see also Transference reactions, defensive
  and resistance, 12, 15-16, 27-29, 35-37, 60, 75-82, 85-88, 90-93, 97
  strengthening of, 341
  and sublimation, 407
  theory of, 76-82
  against transference love, 232, 236
  see also Screen defense, and sub specific mechanisms
Deinstinctualization, see Neutralization, Sublimation
Delinquency, 52, 382
Denial, 178, 181, 285, 288, 301, 332, 340
Dependency, 276-277, 408-409
  avoidance of regressive, 135-136, 170, 351
  and rebellion, 180
Depersonalization, 333, 336
Depression, 101-103, 107-108, 148, 185-186, 272-273, 305, 362
  chronic, 49
  defense against, 128, 383, 394, 398
  and elation, 69
  neurotic, 52-53, 160-161, 229-230, 242, 249, 252, 258, 332, 335
  periodic, 25, 30, 88-90
  psychotic, 52
Deprivation, see Abstinence, Frustration-gratification
Diagnosis, 52-53, 93-94
  errors in, 326
  and transference capacity, 337-341
  see also Personality; Therapy, indications and contraindications
Diarrhea, 206, 252
Disgust, 365-366, 371
Displacement, 21-23, 85, 243, 252
  and transference, 151-158, 164, 171, 173, 175-176, 181, 183, 230, 237, 274, 354
Doctor, image of, 405
Doctor game, 406
Dream, 9, 15, 26, 40, 231, 250-251
  absence of, 65, 67-68
  affect in, 291
  analysis, 254, 374-375
  beginning every hour with, 65
  demonstrating primary and secondary process functioning, 21-23
  in first hour, 250
  flooding hour with, 68
  followed by embarrassment, 138-142
  forgetting of, 73, 91, 263, 317
  in Friday hour, 336

Dream—*Continued*
  indicating sexual conflict, 138-142
  Kleinian analysis of, 134-135
  rage in, and reasonableness in behavior, 193
  regressive features, 181
  and resistance, 272-273
  "scrambled" report of, 110-111, 120
  and suggestion, 270
  and transference, 229, 231, 250-251, 266, 293-294, 317-319
  use of manifest content to analyze resistance, 143-145
Drug therapy, 30, 36, 59
Dynamic point of view, 21, 23-24, 137

Economic point of view, 21, 24
Education, psychoanalytic, 2-3, 383
  selection of candidates, 383, 400
  see also Supervision, Training analysis
Ego
  alteration, 14, 75
  and analyzability, 54-55, 345, 361-363
  antithetical functions required of patient, 361-363
  and conflict, 17-20, 23-25, 29-31, 97, 361
  conflict-free sphere, 76, 361, 398
  conscious, 26, 38, 78, 97-99, 310, 364, 398
  and danger signal, 80-81, 86-88
  defect, 345, 361
  defensive operations of, 77, 84; *see also* Defense
  effect of technical procedures on, 37
  and free association, 32-33, 47-48, 361-362
  functions and transference, 174-177, 180-181, 333-334
  and identification, 246
  loss of boundaries, 120
  loss of functions, 147-149, 333-334, 361-363
  observing vs. experiencing, 47-48, 78, 118, 125-126, 138, 142, 172-173, 175, 192-193, 205, 245, 309-310, 327-329, 361-363, 369
  reasonable, 27, 30-31, 46-47, 60, 77, 87, 94-97, 102, 104, 106, 118, 123-126, 134-135, 138, 141-142, 148, 172, 183, 192-193, 205, 226, 228, 252, 268, 280-281, 284, 290, 300, 310, 325-329, 373, 388, 398, 408, 410
  and resistance, 75-78, 80-82, 85-88, 97-98; *see also* Resistance, of ego

split, 47-48, 141-142, 167, 172, 309
strength, 207, 286, 410
strengthening of, 14-15, 37, 341
and technique, 14-17, 26-32, 207-208
and transference, 167, 177, 241-244, 333-334
and trauma, 178
unconscious, 26, 36, 77-78, 99, 178
and working alliance, 206-208
  see also Psychoanalyst
Ejaculatio praecox, 23-25
Elation, 69
Embarrassment, 81, 108-110, 112-113, 132, 141-142, 146, 233, 250-251, 302, 385, 392-393
Emotional storms, 147-148, 215, 325-330
Empathy, 16, 54, 98, 100, 104, 279-280, 286, 353, 366-373, 381-384, 393, 402
Enema, 120, 231, 241
Enthusiasm, 69, 257-258
Envy, 229, 241, 305, 332
Evasiveness, 81, 139, 198, 211, 273
Events, reaction to, 64
Examination anxiety, 134
Exhibitionism, 133, 386-387, 400

Family romance, 249
Fantasy
  aggressive, 303-304
  anal-sadistic, 131
  of being favorite, 258, 265-266
  of being hanged, 89, 232
  of being humiliated, 176, 314
  about death, 113
  homosexual, 202, 387
  incest, 90
  infantile, 153
  and neurotic conflict, 19-20
  obsessive, 89, 232
  oral, 186-187
  primitive, 182-183
  about psychoanalyst, 65, 166-167, 182-183, 331-332; *see also* Transference fantasy
  of psychoanalyst, 397-402, 407
  repeated in transference, 232
  sadomasochistic, 202
  sexual, 186-187, 302-303, 306-307
  suicidal, 90
  see also Masturbation
Father
  fear of, 311, 313
  fixation, 19-20
  primitive, 175-176, 179
  rivalry with and love for, 120
Father transference, 164, 172, 306, 310

Father-child relationship, and transference, 185-188, 238-240, 406-407
Fear
    of abandonment, 81
    of annihilation, 81
    of dying, 115
    and hostility, 237
    of involvement, 400
    of loss of love, 127, 180, 214, 249
    of loss of self-esteem, 81
    of new (change), 82, 99
    of psychoanalyst, 237
    of rejection, 233, 251
    and repetition, 178-179
    see also Anxiety, Cancer, Object
Fees, 206, 215, 256, 304
Fellatio, 303, 307
Festivals, 330-331
Fixation
    and regression, 82-83
    and resistance, 88-90
    and transference, 180
Flippancy, 128, 286
Forepleasure, 331
Forgetting, 91, 114, 193
    of dreams, see Dream
    to pay, 67, 206
Free association, 7, 15-16, 26, 32-33, 47-48, 59, 71, 214, 228, 409
    and analyzability, 54-55, 85
    capacity, 207-208, 361-362
    concept, 72
    discovery of, 9-10
    key association, 294-295
    misuse of, 196-199
    omitting some, 311-313
    resistance to, 73, 97
    and split in ego, 47-48
    used as resistance, 33
Frigidity, 30-31
Frustration, sexual, 367-368, 370
Frustration-gratification, 35, 37, 83-84, 143, 169, 177, 209, 212-213, 221, 275-281, 327, 362, 376-379, 388-395, 399-401, 406

Gambling, 25
Games, 178, 406
Genetic point of view, 21, 24-25
Gratification, 83-84, 177
    demand for, 248-252
    see also Frustration-gratification; Psychoanalytic situation; Transference, search for gratification
Grief, 49, 148

Guilt, 28, 80, 107, 128, 142, 181, 184, 241, 287, 331-333, 398-399, 401, 407
    unconscious, 19, 85-87, 90, 99

Health
    flight into, 69, 276
    mental, 84, 152, 395, 400
Heredity, 83
Heterosexuality, as defense against homosexuality, 17-18, 86, 318, 320
Holiday, see Vacations
Homosexuality, 17-18, 44, 86, 102-103, 110, 115-116, 143, 187, 202, 206, 255, 335-336, 340, 342, 386-387, 407
    fear of, 345; see also Heterosexuality
    and transference, 255, 267, 283-284, 287, 290, 294, 307, 314-315, 317-321; in men, 225, 228, 231-232, 236, 240
Hostility, 94, 102-103, 114-116, 232-237, 239, 242, 254, 265, 283, 287, 303-304, 332, 334, 344, 346-347, 385, 400-401
    anal, 88-90
    to men, 19, 24, 144-145, 162, 197, 290
    primitive, 31, 135
    to superior, 159
    to women, 386-387
    see also Aggression, Anger, Rage, Transference
Humiliation, 42, 176, 311-314, 362, 385, 391-392
Humor, 236, 386
Hypnosis, 7-11, 13, 15, 71-73, 164, 409
Hysteria, 8-13, 52-53, 71-72, 93, 160-161, 184

Id
    and conflict, 17-20, 23-25
    influence on ego, 97
    resistances, 74-75, 81-82, 85-87, 133
    and technique, 14-15, 26-32
    and transference, 177, 180-181, 241-244, 332, 334
    and transference fantasy, 167
    see also Instinctual drives
Idea, pathogenic; see Memory, pathogenic
Idealization, 35, 229-230, 246, 283, 344
Identification
    with aggressor, 210, 246
    hunger for, 164
    with lost object, 93
    masculine, of women, 145
    of patient with psychoanalyst's work method, 46, 78, 125, 141, 192-194, 203, 210, 245

Identification—*Continued*
  primitive, 174
  of psychoanalyst with working model
    of patient, 369
  in psychotherapy, 341
  struggle against, 247, 314-315
  and transference, 154, 279
  as transference reaction, 244-247
  types and functions of, 244-247, 383,
    397
  with unwanted child, 128
Identity, 93, 113, 246-247, 372, 397-398,
    402
  loss of, 333
  see also Screen identity
Impotence, 142, 253
Impulse disorder, 52; *see also sub* Char-
    acter
Impulsivity, 94, 99
Incontinence, fear of, 19-20, 24, 65
Incorporation, 175
Indecisiveness, obsessive, 387
Infantile neurosis, *see* Childhood neurosis
Inhibition, 100, 244
  sexual, 19-20, 24, 53
  see also Work
Insight, 7, 16, 27, 98, 127, 190, 280, 322,
    335, 363, 373, 378-379, 381-382,
    385, 391-395
  bringing, meaning to psychoanalyst,
    397-399
  interpretation promotes, 289-295
  of psychoanalyst, 100-101
  sequence in gaining, 29-32
  without subsequent change, 191, 201
  and technical procedures, 37-45, 48-51
  and transference, 178, 182, 280, 289
  see also Interpretation
Insomnia, *see* Sleep, disturbances of
Instinct to master, 179-180
Instinctual drives, impulses
  clarification of, 107-113, 122, 304
  and conflict, 17-20, 23-25, 29-32
  constitutional strength of, 75
  damming up of, 24, 177-178
  and interpretation of transference, 310-
    312, 314
  seeking discharge, 99, 207, 275-276,
    396
  see also Aggression, Libido, Sex
Intellectualization, 77, 82, 94, 122, 285
Interpretation, 7, 9, 15, 16, 37, 39-45, 59
  of content, ego before id, 137-145, 305,
    310
  correctness (validation) of, 39-41, 98,
    301, 309-310, 383

dosage, timing, tact, 133, 259, 267-268,
    335-336, 352-353, 372-376, 382, 384-
    388
  ego before id, 137-145
  exclusively in terms of: instincts, 190;
    unconscious transference, 169-170
  experienced as: criticism, 299-300;
    humiliation, 176
  followed by too much confirmatory evi-
    dence, 127
  incomplete, 189
  inexact, 50, 351
  insight-promoting, 289-295, 373, 381-
    387
  and manipulation, 50-51, 190, 269-270
  motive of, 111-118
  premature, 122-123, 285-286, 288
  reaction to, 254-255, 300-301, 309-310,
    315
  and reasonable ego, 325-329
  and reconstruction, 321-325
  of resistance, 97-98, 111-124, 285-286,
    374-376
  start from surface, 73, 137-145
  and suggestion, 49-50, 270
  of transference, 109, 189-190, 245,
    268-271, 281-289, 308-315, 320-325
  use of evidence for, 298-301, 376
  and weekend interruption, 335-337
  and working alliance, 327-329, 335
  and working through, 315-324
  see also Psychoanalyst, language of
Interview
  preliminary, 52, 204, 274-275, 338-339,
    384, 399
  prolonged, 62
Introjection, 77, 86, 90, 94, 164, 169, 173,
    175-176, 181, 201, 240-241
Introspection, 100, 362-363, 366-367
Intuition, 98, 369-371, 406-407; *see also*
    Empathy
Isolation, 31, 77, 91, 93, 157, 223, 241,
    258, 285, 344-345, 399
  sensory, 174

Jealousy, 81, 99, 120, 153, 231, 241, 292,
    339
Joke, 215, 272, 406

Language, 100-101, 372-376, 384-388;
    see also Communication, Psychoana-
    lyst, Talking, Verbalization
Latency, 90, 229
Lateness, 65, 67, 95-96, 105, 262-263,
    311, 333
Lay analysis, 403-404

Libido
  adhesiveness, 74-75, 81-82, 85-86, 133
  phases of, *see sub* specific phases
  and psychoanalyst's motivation, 396-
    401, 407
  regression of, 164, 180-181
  and resistance, 88-90
  and transference, 166
  see also Instinctual drives, Sex
Listening, 100-101, 367, 381, 399, 405
Loneliness, 174
Love
  falling in, during analysis, 225-233,
    266
  fear of, 234-235
  see also Object, Transference love

Magic thinking, 94
Manipulation, 35, 50-51, 135-136, 167,
    170, 190, 236, 269-270, 351, 359
Masochism, 82, 87, 94, 99, 133, 214, 233-
    235, 284, 401
Masturbation, 42, 83, 90, 262, 331
  difficulty in talking about, 199
  fantasy, 113, 142, 241
Memory
  without affect, 91
  and insight, 42-44, 322
  pathogenic, 11-12, 15, 71-72
  recall of, *see* Remembering
  repressed, 8-9, 11
  resistance to, 183
  and transference, 176-178, 182
  see also Acting out, Screen memory
Men
  primitive hatred of mother, 239-240,
    284
  special transference problems of, 225,
    228-229, 236, 239-240
Money, 67; *see also* Fees
Mother
  bodily intimacy with, 397, 405-407
  primitive hatred of, 31, 239-240, 284
  symbolic representation of in dream,
    114-115
  teasing, 311-313
Mother transference, 164, 224, 238-240
Mother-child relationship
  and empathy, 383
  and language, 372-373
  and transference, 168-169, 174, 183,
    185-188, 409
Mothering, 397
  "good enough," 174
  inadequate, 168
Monday hour, 101, 330-337

Mood swings, 245-246
Motility, 177, 409
Mourning, and working through, 44-45

Narcissism, 177, 207, 344, 360
  primary, 84
Narcissistic neurosis, 34, 52, 54, 74, 166,
    174, 184, 207, 326
Neatness, 119
Negative therapeutic reaction, 75, 167,
    236
Negro
  analysis of, 352-353
  fantasy about, 30-31, 185-186
Neurosis, 12, 326, 361
  and defense (resistance), 60, 76
  intractable transference in, 343-345
  nonanalyzable, 338
  and psychosis, 52, 77, 338; *see also*
    Psychosis
  regression in, 76
  theory of, 17-20, 371
  and transference, 152, 164, 170-174,
    183-184
  and transference neurosis, 183-190, 326
  see also Conflict, Symptom formation,
    and sub specific neuroses
Neurotic misery, *see* Suffering
Neutralization, 24, 76, 79, 365, 382, 398-
    399, 407-408; *see also* Sublimation
Nightmares, 20, 261
Normality, *see* Health
Note taking, 101

Object
  auxiliary transference, 237-238, 267,
    344, 356
  fear of loss of, 81, 180
  good and bad, 134-135, 159, 169
  hunger, 173-174, 246
  loss of, 332-334, 398; *see also* Parents
  past and present, 172-173, 175-176,
    312-314, 325, 377
  and self, 172-174, 243
  transitional, 174
Object relations
  and character transference, 256-258
  early, 135, 373, 396-397; *see also*
    Mother
  and identification, 244-247
  impoverished, 337-343
  in psychosis, 173
  repression in, 175, 180-181
  and regression, 83-85
  and resistance, 83-85, 88, 90, 97
  terminology, 45

Object relations—*Continued*
  and transference, 151-155, 164, 171-174, 225, 238-240, 310-315, 337-345
  and working alliance, 206-208
  see also Real relationship
Object representation, 173-175
  change in analysis, 238-240
  loss of, 340
Obscenity, 97, 123, 131, 197; *see also* Word
Obsessional idea, 30-31, 185-188
Obsessive-compulsive neurosis, 52-53, 79, 87, 93, 184, 234-235
  artificial, 351
Oedipus complex, 83, 180, 186, 231, 241, 249, 332, 350, 397, 407
Omnipotence, 94, 243, 397
Oral phase, impulses, 94, 114-116, 120, 186-187, 230, 239-240, 249, 333, 339, 397
Orderliness, 94, 241
Orgasm, 187, 251, 367
Overdetermination, 12, 23, 161

Panic, 147-149, 285, 328
Paranoia, 164, 234, 342, 344-345
Parents
  loss of, 229, 237, 262, 355
  sex life of, 40-44
  sleeping with, 198
  see also Father, Mother
Passivity, 255, 361
  in men, 75, 90
  see also Psychoanalyst
Pathology, assessment of, 53
Patience, 387
Patient
  accidentally meeting psychoanalyst, 331-332
  analyzability of, *see* Analyzability
  chooses subject matter, 12, 145-146
  contribution of, to working alliance, 46, 206-208
  demands on, 51, 53-56, 196, 206-208, 358-364
  does not change, 69, 360
  frequent cheerful hours, 69
  missing hours, 67
  motivation of, 26, 46, 54-55, 98-99, 121, 276, 358-360; *see also* Suffering
  reactions to interruptions of hour, 156, 215
  reactions to interruptions of therapy, *see* Monday hour, Vacations, Weekend

reactions to waiting for psychoanalyst, 153
and reality knowledge about psychoanalyst, 273-275
spontaneous recognition of resistance or transference, 111, 245, 296
Penis envy, 75, 144-145, 187, 240-241, 284, 289
Perception
  of danger, 87
  and reactions to, 218
Personality, assessment of total, 53, 364
Perversion, 52-53, 252
Perversion-psychosis, masked, 342-343, 345
Phallic phase, drives, 83, 90, 93-94, 241, 249
Phobia, 19-20, 24, 52-53, 184
Play therapy, 342
Pleasure and mastery, 178
Pleasure-pain principle, 166, 179, 390
Posture, 63, 88, 107-108, 113, 374
Preconscious, 129, 309, 368, 370, 382
Pregenitality, 83, 86, 180, 230-231, 249, 265, 284, 292, 331, 350, 406-407
Pregnancy fantasy, 22
Preoedipal phase, *see* Pregenitality *and sub* specific phases
Primal scene, 62, 332, 407
Primary process, 21-23, 26, 79, 84, 198, 207, 361-362, 372
Procedures, technical (therapeutic)
  anti-analytic, 37, 50, 136
  changes in, 8-10, 15
  defined, 7
  forces opposing and furthering, 98-100
  nonanalytic, 48-51, 147-149, 269-270
  promoting working alliance, 124-126, 208
  pursuit of transference interpretation, 319-325
  used in therapy, 37-45, 210, 212-214, 268-270, 295-325, 361, 364, 376, 392, 397, 408-410
  see also sub specific procedures
Process, therapeutic, 13, 361
  changes in theory of, 10-15
  defined, 7
  forces opposing and furthering, 98-100
Projection, 77, 86, 93, 154, 164, 169, 173-176, 237, 241-243, 274, 332, 374
  as transference reaction, 175
Promiscuity, 185-188, 258, 331, 348
Protectiveness, 27
Psychiatry, 2, 404

Psychic structures
  change in, and psychoanalytic therapy, 29-32, 190-191
  development of, reflected in transference, 180-181
  influence on each other, 97
  participating in every psychic event, 86
Psychical inertia, 81-82
Psychoanalysis
  fundamental (or basic) rule of, see Free association
  metapsychology of, 20-26, 371-372
  occupational hazards, 336-337, 394, 405
  orthodoxy vs. sectarianism, 2-4
  relation between theory and technique, 15-17, 371-372
  and research, 101
  technique of, see Technique, psychoanalytic
  training in, see Education, psychoanalytic
Psychoanalyst
  absence of reactions to, 157-158
  activity vs. passivity of, 123, 387
  analyzing ego of, 46, 126, 192-193, 369-370, 398, 408
  anonymity (incognito), 165, 216, 274-276, 279-280, 376-379, 388-391, 399, 408, 410
  as auxiliary ego, 333-334, 341
  boredom of, 68
  changing of, 341, 350, 353-355
  choice of, 353
  communication with patient, 100-101, 372-376, 384-388; see also Psychoanalyst, language of
  contradictory demands on, 16, 279-280, 376-379, 388-396
  contribution of, to working alliance, 46-47, 209-216, 221-223, 388-396
  delusional reactions to, 171-172, 344-345
  experienced as: seducer, 244; superego figure, 241-244, 331-332, 334
  explains reasons for rules to patient, 199-201, 214, 218, 222, 278-279, 378, 392
  falling asleep, 157
  how to listen, 100-101, 367, 381
  intense emotional reactions to, 157-158; see also Transference
  interrupting patient, 349
  knowledge of, 370-372, 380, 386
  language of, 108-109, 123-126, 213-215, 297-298, 327, 385-387

  maintaining distance and closeness, 216, 222, 279, 382-383, 388-396
  as mirror, 35, 165, 178, 211-212, 271-275, 279, 389-391
  motivation of, 380, 385, 396-408
  objectionable traits in, 219-220
  orderly work routine, 210, 212-213, 409-410
  passivity of, 149, 199-200, 387, 404, 408
  personal analysis of, 364, 370-371, 380, 394-395
  personality and traits of, 209-216, 221-224, 273-277, 308, 354-355, 380-396
  "presence," 46
  realistic reactions of, 221-224
  realistic reactions to, 217-219, 273, 305, 308, 349-350
  reluctance to expose method, 4-5
  safeguarding patient's rights, 215-216, 222, 278, 378-379, 391-393
  silence of, 123, 149, 199-200, 208, 221, 269-270, 279, 282, 296-297, 349, 386-388, 401, 407, 409
  skills of, 364-380, 396
  splitting of, into good and bad object, 159-160, 266-267
  as target of transference neurosis, 397, 399-402
  therapeutic (physicianly) attitude of, 209-216, 222, 240, 280-281, 378-379, 384, 389-394, 402-408, 410
  transmittor of insight by interpretation, 16, 280, 377-378, 393-395, 397-402
  triggering transference reaction, 308
  unable to work with certain patients, 223-224, 281, 354-355
  unfamiliar with reality situation of patient, 352-353, 392
  utterances of, experienced as food, 230, 240, 249, 306
  see also Counterresistance, Countertransference, Idealization, Patient, Transference, Transference reactions
Psychoanalytic setting, 408-411; see also Psychoanalytic situation
Psychoanalytic situation, 28, 358-411
  always trigger of transference reaction, 308, 354
  contribution of, to working alliance, 46-47, 208-209
  demands on patient, see Patient
  demands on psychoanalyst, see Psychoanalyst

Psychoanalytic situation—*Continued*
  deprivation and gratification in, 209-
    213, 216, 221, 226-227, 376-379,
    388-396, 399-401, 410
  determines course of transference re-
    action, 408-410
  dynamics of, 98-100
  promotes fantasy in patient and psy-
    choanalyst, 401-402
  therapeutic vs. research, 101, 391
  "tilted" (uneven) relationship in, 168,
    214, 278, 360, 409
  transference reactions not created by
    and confined to, 152, 155, 164, 171,
    177, 408
Psychoanalytic technique, *see* Technique,
    psychoanalytic
Psychoanalytic therapy, *see* Therapy, psy-
    choanalytic
Psychological testing, 52
Psychological-mindedness, 84, 339, 362
Psychosis, 36, 52, 76-77, 85-86, 97, 147,
    152, 164, 166, 170-174, 184, 207,
    326, 337
  incipient, 33, 247
  loss of object representation in, 173
  manic-depressive, 52
  neurotic and healthy components, 172
  neurotic façade, 341-343
  regression in, 76, 343
  see also Borderline patient, Schizo-
    phrenia, Transference reactions
Psychosomatic illness, 52-53, 332
Psychotherapy
  analytically oriented, 33
  anti-analytic, 33, 35
  brief, 359
  different approaches to symptom, 29
  gratifying to patient, 341-343
  handling of resistances, 36, 59, 359
  handling of transference, 35, 50-51,
    151
  interpretation in, 39
  preparatory, 359-360
  role-playing of therapist, 50-51
  and secrets, 130
  supportive, 33, 35, 59, 197, 341-344
  symptomatic, 136
Punctuality, 65, 95-96, 175
Punishment, 127, 331
  need for, 85-87, 221

Questions
  asked by psychoanalyst, 282, 303, 307-
    308, 311-315

psychoanalyst's response to patient's,
    175, 200, 215, 222, 228, 273-274,
    279, 292, 375, 392

Rage, 31, 81, 93, 113, 119, 147-148, 193,
    196, 206, 243, 304, 328, 344, 360,
    400
Rapport, 165, 195, 275
Rationalization, 72, 77, 122, 183
Reaction formation, 31, 87, 92-95, 236,
    255, 370-371, 406-407
Real relationship to psychoanalyst, 169,
    171, 216-224
Reality
  factors and resistance, 119-120
  plausible and fantastic, 382
  and transference, 157, 217-219
Reality testing, 175, 181, 244, 333, 361
Reasonableness, 193, 201-203, 232, 253-
    255
Reassurance, 49, 215, 351, 376
Rebelliousness, 180, 255
Recall, *see* Memory, Remembering
Reconstruction, 9, 16, 43, 155, 185, 265,
    268
  upward, 251, 325, 342
  and working through, 319-325
Regression
  and analyzability, 54, 85, 180, 343
  capacity for, 207-208, 288, 361-363
  of ego functions, 84-85, 174-177, 180-
    181, 197-198
  of libido, 73, 83-84, 180-181
  and object relations, 175-176, 182
  optimal for therapy, 85, 288
  and resistance, 82-85, 90, 93-94
  in service of ego, 26, 76, 369, 382-383
  structural, 84
  and transference, 34, 47, 50, 164, 168,
    170-171, 174-177, 180-182, 190, 205,
    207-210, 238, 243, 276, 285-286, 339,
    351, 372, 377-378, 409-410
  types of, 83-85
  and working alliance, 207-208
Remembering, 7, 11-15, 60, 71-75, 115
  of adolescent experiences, 307, 319-320
  of childhood experiences, 319-321
  following interpretation, 41-44
  and repeating, 34, 74, 153, 179, 259-
    260
  see also Memory
Repetition
  and acting out, 68-69, 179
  in action, 179
  and resistance, 36, 74-75, 81-82, 97
  silence as, 61-62

Repetition—*Continued*
and transference, 33-34, 74, 85, 152-156, 166, 171, 177-180, 185, 200, 232, 252, 255, 260, 292-293, 322
see also Remembering
Repetition compulsion, 45, 74, 81-82, 85-86, 153, 166, 179, 184, 259, 411
Repression, 31, 77, 189, 395, 401
and frustration, 83
in hierarchy of defenses, 78
and idealization, 229
and resistance, 73-74, 85-86, 91, 93
return of, 20, 177
Rescue fantasy, 90
Resistance
anal, 88-90, 93, 203-204
analysis of, 1, 26-28, 30-31, 38-39, 74, 96-149, 245, 298-300, 305, 310, 315-319, 373
avoided by Alexander, 135-136, 170
clarification of, 107-111, 122, 204, 374-376
classification of, 85-96
content of, 112, 116-117
and danger situation, 81
and defense, *see* Defense
definition, 59-60
demonstration of, 104-106, 111, 115, 118, 121, 203-204, 374-375
development of concept of, 71-76
and diagnostic categories, 93-94
discovery of, 11-16, 59, 71
of ego, 74-75, 85-88
ego-alien, 36, 78-79, 94-96, 118-119
ego-syntonic, 36, 92, 94-96, 101, 118, 258
explained to patient, 124-126
fear of silence as, 195-197
in first hours, 124-126
hiding of, 126-128
hierarchies, 78-80
identification as, 245-246
ignored by Kleinians, 134-135, 160
increasing, 105-106
interpreted solely in instinctual terms, 134
and loss of ego function, 147-149
minor, 146-147
modes of, 60-71, 104, 107, 110-111, 118-122; *see also sub* specific modes
most stubborn, 239-240, 284
motives of, 80-82, 104, 107, 111-118, 122
multiple function of, 15-16
not only obstacle to treatment, 75-76
oral, 90
into the past, 325
phallic, 93-94
preconscious, 129
premature demonstration, 105
provides information about patient's past, 33, 36, 75, 117
and reality factors, 119-120
recognition of, 60, 101-104, 111, 121
"relative," 79-80
to resistance, 80, 126-128
sarcasm as, 232, 236
self-sufficiency as, 180
silent, 70-71, 92
sources of, 74-75, 85-88; *see also* Resistance, motives of
special problems in analyzing, 124-133, 344-345
theory of, 76-85
and training analysis, 356
transference as source of, 28, 70, 73-74, 91, 117-118, 157-158, 165, 182-183, 227, 231-234, 236-237, 281-284, 288, 344-345
typical manifestation of, 60-71; *see also* Resistance, modes of
uneven, 85, 90
unresolved, 273
weekend a holiday, 330-332
working alliance used as, 193-194, 202-203
and working through, 42-44, 81
see also Id, Superego, Transference resistance
Restitution, 173, 332, 342, 407
Rigidity, 65, 81, 92, 94-96, 161, 177, 210, 214, 229

Sadism, 99, 401, 406-407
Sadomasochism, 90, 342, 405, 407
Sarcasm, 232, 236, 277
Schizophrenia, 52-53, 173, 338
analyzable, 338
see also Psychosis
Scoptophilia, 133, 386
Scotoma, 331
Screen affect, 93
Screen defense, 93-95
Screen identity, 93, 246
Screen memory, 25, 43, 93, 260
Screen resistance, 133
Secondary gain, 85, 99, 359
Secondary process, 21-23, 26, 33, 78, 84, 197, 207, 362, 372
Secret, 68, 128-133
conscious, 129-130, 199

Self
  changing relationship to, 243
  displacement of parts of, to others, 154,
    175, 181
  fusion with object, 173-174
  and object: differentiated, 173; loss of
    distinction between, 172; undifferen-
    tiated, 243
Self representation, 173-175
  and identification, 246
Self-analysis, 245, 394, 398
Self-destructiveness, 82, 216
Self-esteem, 81, 214, 391, 393
Self-image, changes in, 322-323
Self-reproaches, 79, 90, 279
Separation anxiety, 240, 372-373; see also
    Fear
Separation-individuation, 173
Sex, sexuality
  avoidance of, 64-65, 72, 105-106, 112-
    113
  child's conception, 132, 407
  counterphobic, 178
  and dream, 231, 250-251
  infantile, 199
  inhibition, 19-20, 24, 53, 244
  problems, 339-340; see also Frigidity,
    Impotence
  and regression, 83-84
  toiletization of, 30-31
  see also Heterosexuality, Homosexual-
    ity, Libido, Men, Transference,
    Women
Sexualization, 24, 93, 201, 338-341, 400
Shame, 80, 90, 107, 126-127, 133, 142,
    186, 233, 287, 331, 385-387
Sibling
  relations, 365-366, 371
  rivalry, 127, 255, 398, 401
Signal anxiety, 80-81, 87-88
Silence, 61-62, 70, 88-89, 105, 108-109,
    113, 126-127, 133, 199-201, 230, 240
  avoidance of, 351
  for entire hour, 113
  incapacity to bear, 195-197
  psychoanalyst's use of, 123, 373-374,
    386-388; see also Psychoanalyst
  as self-punishment, 127
  supportive, 147
Sleep, 68, 84, 198, 409-410
  disturbances of, 20, 257, 261-263, 339
  during hour, 119
  going to, re-enacted at start of each
    hour, 263-265
"Sleep-talking," 198
Slips, 23, 26, 283, 300

Sloppiness, 92
Smoking, 71, 199-200, 247
Sodium pentothal, 261-262
Somatization, 88, 93, 181
Speech, 100-101, 372-376, 384-388; see
    also Communication, Language, Pa-
    tient, Psychoanalyst, Talking, Verb-
    alization
Stage fright, 176, 385-387, 400
Stimulus hunger, 164
Stinginess, 94
Structural point of view, 21, 25, 138, 145,
    241
Stubbornness, 90, 241
Sublimation, 24, 344, 398, 407; see also
    Neutralization
Suffering
  as motive for seeking therapy, 26, 46,
    54-55, 98-99, 207, 214, 275-276, 356,
    358-360
  need for, 82, 87
  treating of, and mothering, 397, 402-
    407
Suggestion, 7-10, 13, 15, 33, 36, 49-50,
    59, 71-73, 164, 269-270
  dangers in use of, 49-50
Suicide, 113
Sunday neurosis, 330
Superego
  and conflict, 18-20, 29-31
  and fantasy, 167
  formation, 371
  influence on ego, 97
  rational and irrational, 99
  resistance, 74-75, 86-87
  strict, 176, 181
  and technique, 14-15, 26-32
  and transference, 167, 180-181, 241-
    244, 331-332, 334,
Supervision, 146, 219-221, 308, 348-350
Symbolic actions, 107, 186
Symbolism, 293-294
  in dream, 22-23
  of water, 115
Symptom
  and analyzability, 53
  focus on, 8-9, 12
  formation, 18-20, 23-25, 29, 87-88, 97,
    359, 361, 370
  no change in, 69
Symptomatic act, 118, 186, 260-268, 329
Synthetic function, 25, 77, 363

Talking
  incessant, disconnected, 197-198

Talking—*Continued*
  reluctance to, 62, 106-107, 112-113,
    186, 263; *see also* Avoidance
  see also Communication, Language,
    Patient, Psychoanalyst, Verbalization
Task completion, 179
Teasing, 311, 313
Technical procedures, *see* Procedures
Technique, psychoanalytic
  answering of patient's questions, *see*
    Questions
  basic concepts, 15-32
  and cancelled sessions, 215, 304
  components of classical, 32-48, 358
  considerations in determining why and
    when to analyze, 247-295
  deviations, 52, 133-136, 151, 168-171,
    190, 197, 326, 359
  different viewpoints, 1-6
  errors in, 16, 75, 157, 191-192, 221-
    222, 280-281, 335-336, 345-355, 377
  exceptions to rules, 146-149
  extending session, 327
  and faulty theory, 350-351
  modifications, 2, 168, 207, 359
  most important tool, 5, 16, 97-98, 268-
    269, 308-309
  need for open discussion of, 2-5
  questionnaire on, 1, 354, 379
  rules concerning resistance, 136-149
  special problems in analyzing trans-
    ference reactions, 325-356
  steps in analyzing transference, 295-325
  survey of Freud's writings on, 8-15
  theory of, 26-32
Temper tantrum, 81, 103
Termination, 235
Therapeutic alliance, 46, 134, 167-169,
  191-192, 194, 335; *see also* Working
  alliance
Therapeutic procedures, *see* Procedures
Therapeutic process, *see* Process
Therapist, *see* Psychoanalyst
Therapy, psychoanalytic
  aims of, 14-15, 26, 29-30, 59, 378, 391-
    395
  breaking off, 121, 163, 236, 248, 258-
    259, 271, 278, 360, 377
  compact, 99
  compared with other psychotherapies,
    30, 33, 35-36, 39, 48-51, 59, 151,
    308-309, 359, 399
  contract, 99
  definition, 2
  deprivation and gratification in, *see*
    Psychoanalytic situation

duration, 159, 208, 359, 378
early phases of, 184, 223, 238, 241-242,
  270, 278, 285-286, 299, 302, 311,
  388
emergence of impulse-resistance units
  in, 79
and emergency situations, 404
first hours, 124-126, 204-205, 250
forces furthering and opposing, 98-100
frequency of hours, 174, 208, 287, 378
"good hour," 103
historical development of, 7-15
indications and contraindications, 51-
  56, 247, 326, 337-346, 363-364
interminable, 192, 236, 277-278, 341-
  342, 377
interruptions of, *see* Monday hour,
  Vacations, Weekend
limitations of, 167, 359
middle phase, 223, 388
motive for seeking and continuing, *see*
  Patient, Suffering
neglect of past experience by Kleinians,
  175, 190
no changes in life situation during,
  158-159, 363
repeated, 191, 195
requirements of patient, *see* Patient
second, 195-201, 273, 277-279, 392
sitting up in, 202-203, 341
stalemated, 143, 189, 191-192, 233,
  248, 273, 277, 341-342
terminal phase, 217-218, 223, 290
therapeutic action of, 194
Thought processes, regression in, 84
Time, 181
  extending hour, 327-329
  fixation to past or present, 63
Toilet
  anxiety, 65, 185-188; *see also* Anxiety
  fantasy, 88-90, 185-188, 260-261
  habits, 132; details of, 392
  scenes in childhood, 365-366, 370
  training, 121, 186
Topographic point of view, 21-23, 84,
  137, 145
Trial analysis, 55-56, 338
Training, *see* Education
Training analysis, 3, 127, 159, 230, 256,
  265, 274-275, 354-356, 360, 384,
  399; *see also* Transference
Transference
  avoidance of, 64-65, 91, 170, 325
  in child analysis, 179, 188-189
  contamination of, 272-275
  definition, 151-155, 171

Transference—*Continued*
  deprivation, *see* Frustration-gratification, Psychoanalytic situation
  development of concept, 162-171
  discovery of, 12-15, 71, 151, 163
  effective, 46
  and ego functions, 174-177, 287
  eroticized, 252, 338-341, 344
  errors in appraisal of capacity, 337-345
  facilitating, 269, 376-380; *see also* Transference neurosis
  fantasy, 131, 167, 218-219, 274-275, 302-307, 310, 314-315, 331-332, 387; *see also* Fantasy
  gratification, *see* Frustration-gratification, Psychoanalytic situation
  hate, 233-237, 248, 251-252, 283-284
  hostile, 99, 119, 127, 162-163, 174, 182-183, 203, 252, 255, 267-268, 276, 283-284, 287, 346-347
  hunger for, 164, 246
  ignoring of, 191
  improvements, 182
  to institution, 154, 165
  intensification, 282-289
  interpretation of, *see* Interpretation
  Kleinian interpretation of, 190
  and libidinal levels, 230-231, 240-241
  love, 225-236, 248-252, 283-284, 390, 408
  management of, 50-51, 59, 170, 190, 209, 217, 268-269; *see also* Manipulation
  manipulation of, 170-171, 209, 236, 268-269, 351
  masochistic, 234-235
  "matrix" of, 168, 174
  mature, 46, 192
  mishandling of, 259, 271, 346-353
  negative, 34-35, 99, 164-167, 225, 230, 233-239, 267, 276, 284, 290, 299
  nonverbal elements, 168-169
  positive, 34, 99, 162, 164-165, 224-233, 267, 276, 282-285, 287-288, 292, 351-352
  primordial, 194
  rational, 46, 192, 194
  readiness, 168, 177
  and real relationship, 169, 171, 216-224
  and regression, *see* Regression
  reliving in, 325-330
  romantic, 99, 166, 225
  safeguarding against contamination of, 168, 189-190, 211, 271-281

  search for gratification in, 248-252, 283-284, 376, 388
  and secret, 131, 133, 235
  sexual, 99, 161-162, 165, 182-183, 203, 205-206, 231-232, 249-251, 255, 284, 290, 302-303, 339, 346, 351
  and silence, 374
  splitting of, 168, 229-230, 236-237, 267, 283, 344, 346
  technique of analyzing, 203-204, 268-356
  theory of, 171-190
  in training analysis, 3-4, 356
  unresolved, 3-4, 35, 351-352
  and weekend separation, 330-337
  when to analyze, 281-295
Transference cure, 35, 164, 276, 351
Transference neurosis, 14, 34-35, 86, 166-170, 183-191, 224, 238, 258, 276-277, 326, 372, 397, 399-402
  and contamination, 274-275
  facilitating development of, 269, 376-380, 388-396, 399-400, 409-410
  inability to form, 338-346
  and infantile neurosis, 185-189, 287-289, 327-329, 333-334
  and narcissistic neurosis, *see* Narcissistic neurosis
  in training analysis, 356
  and working alliance, 47-48, 191-193, 200-203, 205, 208-209, 216, 281, 338, 346
  see also Transference, Transference reactions
Transference psychosis, 173, 340
Transference reactions, 28-31, 33-35
  absence of, 236, 253-255, 266, 283, 288, 344, 346-347
  and acting out, *see* Acting out
  and affective intensity, 157-159, 162, 184, 269, 282-289, 325-330, 388
  ambivalent, 34, 159-160, 162, 180-181, 183-184, 197, 225, 229-230, 267
  capriciousness, 159-162, 182
  chronic, 283, 344-345, 348
  clarification, 301-310
  classification, 224-247
  compliant, submissive, 167, 195-197, 211, 214, 234-235, 255, 276, 301, 342, 360
  confrontation, 296-301
  defensive, 232, 252-256, 287, 344
  defined, 152-155
  demonstration of, 269, 281, 296-301, 309-310

Transference reactions—*Continued*
  displacement of, 158, 188, 230, 237, 346-347
  ego-alien, 233, 256, 258, 267-268, 284, 312
  ego-syntonic, 233, 256, 258, 267-268, 283, 312, 340, 344
  and error in technique, 347-353
  fear of, 276
  floating, 160, 184
  general characteristics, 155-162
  generalized, 256-258, 283
  hierarchies of, 225
  inappropriateness, 152-153, 155-156, 162, 180-181, 264, 312
  intensity of, 282-292, 296-297, 327-329, 388, 394
  intractable, 274, 337-355, 377
  and libidinal phases, 230-231, 240-241, 248-252
  manifested outside of analysis, 183, 188, 266-268
  of Negro patient, 352-353
  and object relations, *see* Object relations
  origin and nature of, 171-182
  psychotic vs. neurotic, 171-173, 337-346
  pursuit of: affect and impulse, 310-312, 314; intimate detail, 301-305, 392-393; trigger, 305-308
  rigidity of, *see* Rigidity
  sadomasochistic, clinging, 197, 277
  special problems in analyzing, 325-356
  tenacity, 161-162, 177, 183, 229, 334-335
  in terms of structure, 241-244
  tracing antecedents of, 310
  and working alliance, 46-48, 165, 167, 169, 171, 175, 183, 186, 190-216, 271, 281-284, 288, 388-396
  working through, 296, 315-324
  see also Psychoanalyst
Transference resistances, 28, 69-70, 73-74, 85, 91, 112, 120, 133, 143, 145, 149, 157-158, 166-167, 182-183, 200-201, 247-270, 289, 298, 306-307, 319-320, 344-351, 377; *see also* Resistance
Trauma, 75
  in adolescence, 201
  anal, 93
Traumatic experience, 48-49, 91, 93, 107, 178, 260
Traumatic neurosis, 19-20, 130

Traumatic situation, and resistance, 80-83, 87-88, 123, 269, 285, 328

Ulcerative colitis, 252, 263, 272-273
Unconscious
  approached through derivatives, 26
  and conflict, 17-20
  making conscious, 14-15, 101-104, 137, 309, 323
  and primary process, 21-23
  and psychoanalyst's motivation, 396-401
  psychoanalyst's understanding of, 364-372, 380-383
  and transference, 151-155, 159, 171
Undoing, 93

Vacations, 215-217, 287, 311, 373, 388
Vagina, 79, 143-145, 186
Verbalization, 13
  contradictory, 292, 301
  key association, 294-295
  and posture, discrepancies between, 63
  repetitious, 64, 292-293
  of trivia, 64, 106, 126, 282
  see also Communication, Free association, Language, Patient, Psychoanalyst, Talking
Vomiting, 19, 252

Weekend, 287, 330-337, 388
"Wild analyst," 2, 50, 371
Wish
  fulfillment, 153, 260, 265
  gratification and frustration of, 212-213, 220
  passive-feminine, in men, 75
  repressed, 366, 371
  sexual, 142, 366, 371
  to transmit insight, 397-399
  see also Death wish
Wit, 84, 386
Withholding, 90, 231
Women
  primitive love of mother, 284, 340
  seeking cruel men as love objects, 178-179
  special transference problems of, 225-228, 239-240, 338-340, 408
Word, "dirty," 131-132
Work
  inhibition, 263
  pleasure in, 366, 399
Working alliance, 29, 31, 36, 45-48, 78, 99, 115, 118, 120-123, 125-126, 138,

Working alliance—*Continued*
190-216, 240, 244-245, 247, 302, 329, 370
aberrations in development of, 195-203
in classical patient, 203-206
defined, 192-195
development of, 195-206
facilitating development of, 271, 299, 376-380, 388-396, 409-410
factors detrimental to development of, 274-275, 381-382
and identification, *see* Identification
ignored by Kleinians, 134-135
inability to form, 338-346
and infantile neurosis, 193

and negative transference, 234-235, 285, 290
origins of, 206-216
and positive transference, 225-228, 283
rational and irrational components, 207-208
and real relationship, 216-224
and resistance, 94-96, 141, 249, 281-284
and rule of abstinence, 276-278
see also Transference reactions
Working through, 29-32, 37, 42-45, 74, 81, 86, 90, 122-123, 165
and resistance, 47-48
of transference interpretation, 269, 315-324